RISK FACTORS IN DEPRESSION

Risk Factors in Depression

Edited by

Keith S. Dobson and
David J.A. Dozois

AMSTERDAM • BOSTON • HEIDELBERG • LONDON
NEW YORK • OXFORD • PARIS • SAN DIEGO • SAN FRANCISCO
SINGAPORE • SYDNEY • TOKYO
Academic Press is an imprint of Elsevier

Academic Press is an imprint of Elsevier
525 B Street, Suite 1900, San Diego, CA 92101-4495, USA
30 Corporate Drive, Suite 400, Burlington, MA 01803, USA
84 Theobald's Road, London WC1X 8RR, UK
Radarweg 29, PO Box 211, 1000 AE Amsterdam, The Netherlands

First edition 2008

British Library Cataloguing in Publication Data
A catalogue record for this book is available from the British Library

Library of Congress Cataloging-in-Publication Data
A catalog record for this book is available from the Library of Congress

ISBN: 978-0-08-045078-0

For information on all Academic Press publications visit our web site at elsevierdirect.com

Typeset by Charon Tec Ltd., A Macmillan Company (www.macmillansolutions.com)

Printed and bound in the United States of America

08 09 10 10 9 8 7 6 5 4 3 2 1

Contents

PART II

COGNITIVE FACTORS 119

6

COGNITIVE SCHEMAS, BELIEFS AND ASSUMPTIONS 121

DAVID J.A. DOZOIS AND AARON T. BECK

7

INFORMATION PROCESSING: ATTENTION AND MEMORY 145

RICK E. INGRAM, DANA K. STEIDTMANN AND STEVEN L. BISTRICKY

8

OPTIMISM AND PESSIMISM 171

STEPHEN M. SCHUELLER AND MARTIN E.P. SELIGMAN

9

DISPOSITIONAL PESSIMISM ACROSS THE LIFESPAN 195

JOHN R.Z. ABELA, RANDY P. AUERBACH AND MARTIN E.P. SELIGMAN

10

RUMINATIVE RESPONSE STYLE 221

BLAIR E. WISCO AND SUSAN NOLEN-HOEKSEMA

11

NEGATIVE COGNITIVE STYLE 237

LAUREN B. ALLOY, LYN Y. ABRAMSON, JESSICA KEYSER, RACHEL K. GERSTEIN AND LOUISA G. SYLVIA

12

15

PARENTAL PSYCHOPATHOLOGY AND PARENTING STYLE ATTACHMENT AS RISK FACTORS OF DEPRESSION 343

CECILIA A. ESSAU AND SATOKO SASAGAWA

16

MARRIAGE AND RELATIONSHIP ISSUES 363

MARK A. WHISMAN AND ROSELINDE KAISER

17

LOW SOCIAL SUPPORT AND MAJOR DEPRESSION: RESEARCH, THEORY AND METHODOLOGICAL ISSUES 385

BRIAN LAKEY AND ARIKA CRONIN

18

STRESS GENERATION AND DEPRESSION 409

CONSTANCE HAMMEN AND
JOSEPHINE H. SHIH

19

REASSURANCE SEEKING AND NEGATIVE FEEDBACK SEEKING 429

KATHERINE A. TIMMONS AND THOMAS E. JOINER, JR.

20

AVOIDANCE 447

PREFACE

The variable symptoms of Major Depressive Disorder (MDD), or Clinical Depression, indicate that depression is a heterogeneous disorder (Kendler, Gardner, & Prescott, 1999). Individuals who experience depression may suffer from a number of possible symptoms, and the duration of these symptoms may range from a few weeks to years. Increasingly, the chronic and recurrent nature of depression has been recognized, and efforts at treatment and prevention have been emphasized (cf., Dozois & Dobson, 2004).

MDD is a highly debilitating condition, as it affects multiple domains of psychosocial functioning (Judd et al., 2000), including interpersonal relationships, occupational (Broadhead, Blazer, George, & Tse, 1990; McQuaid, Stein, Laffaye, & McCahill, 1999) and academic functioning (Alloy et al., 2001; Ingram, 2001; Dudek et al., 2001; Gotlib, Lewinsohn, & Seeley, 1998), and long-term psychological well-being (Ferguson & Woodward, 2002) . MDD is one of the most common presenting complaints encountered by mental health professionals (Zheng et al., 1997) and is among the most financially costly of disorders. Depression also exacts a heavy toll on society; the direct and indirect annual costs associated with MDD in Canada (Stephens & Joubert, 2001) and the United States (Greenberg et al., 1999) have been estimated at $14.4 billion and $33 billion, respectively. Researchers have predicted that by the year 2020 depression will be second only to ischemic heart disease in terms of cost to society (Keller & Boland, 1998; Lecrubier, 2001). Surprisingly, the economic impact of depression may actually be underestimated, due to the fact that sometimes depression co-occurs with medical problems and so is downplayed or "missed" as a problem, and due to the fact that many depressed people do not seek treatment (Collins, Westra, Dozois & Burns, 2004).

A number of studies have provided international estimates of the incidence and prevalence of depression. Community-based epidemiological studies (e.g., DeMarco, 2000; Murphy, Laird, Monson, Sobol, & Alexander, 2000; Ohayon, Priest, Guilleminault, & Caulet, 1999; Patten, 2000; Regier et al., 1993) suggest some variability in the point prevalence, one-year, and lifetime estimates of this disorder. The average point prevalence rate across the countries represented was 4.75%. The average one-year incidence and lifetime prevalence estimates were 5.18% and

8.75%, respectively. These figures were higher, however, when North American countries were examined (one year prevalence, M = 9.18%; lifetime prevalence, M = 13.98%). As suggested by the above incidence and prevalence rates, MDD is highly recurrent. Between 50% and 85% of individuals with depression experience multiple repeated episodes throughout their lifespan (Coyne, Pepper & Flynn, 1999) and the probability of experiencing subsequent episodes increases with each episode (Kessing, 1998; Solomon et al., 2000). Understanding the factors that increase risk for depression is clearly an important endeavor for both treatment and prevention.

Given the profound and continuing social importance of depression, it is not surprising that it has been examined from a number of theoretical approaches, and has been the subject of a considerable body of literature. There have been significant advances related to neurotransmitter models, stress-generation models of depression, models of relapse prevention, enhancements in the study of information processing problems in depression, and of interpersonal processes such as interpersonal reassurance seeking and rejection. Unfortunately, models in this area have developed in relative isolation from each other, as there is a pronounced tendency for theorists and researchers to highlight a particular model, to the relative diminishment of other constructs and models.

The perspective of the current editors is that it is timely for the various findings related to diverse models of depression to be presented in a single, comprehensive and authoritative textbook. We believe that the virtues of such a source include: (1) the ability to compare and contrast the relative states of development for the different models, and their databases; (2) the ability to examine the predictive power of these models related to various phases of clinical depression, including onset, maintenance and relapse; (3) the opportunity to examine the interface among different theoretical perspectives and variables, to look for the opportunity for more complex, and explanatory models of depression; (4) stimulation of further research into more comprehensive and integrative models of depression; and, (5) examination of the therapeutic implications of comprehensive and integrative models of depression.

The organization of this volume was difficult, given the myriad risk factors that have been implicated in depression. Kaelber, Moul and Farmer (1995), for example, categorized risk factors for depression according to their degree of supportive empirical evidence. Eighteen risk factors were considered highly plausible, 29 plausible and 17 possible. Among the risk factors that were deemed highly plausible were variables such as gender, prior depression, being divorced or separated, low socioeconomic status, psychiatric comorbidity, medical illness, being abused or tortured and major adverse life events. Although many of these topics are covered within the pages of this text, we opted not to allocate an entire chapter to some risk factors (e.g., gender) even though they are clearly associated with increased risk of depression. Our rationale for excluding such variables is that they do not inform researchers about the processes involved in depression onset, maintenance or recurrence. Ingram, Odom, and Mitchusson (2004) argued that knowledge of risk factors informs us about which variables are associated with the increased odds of experiencing a given disorder. Vulnerability, in contrast, elucidates the causal mechanisms involved in the onset or recurrence of depression. To illustrate, research has shown consistently that gender is a risk factor for depression. From early to middle adolescence and throughout adulthood, females are consistently twice as likely to become depressed as males (Garber & Flynn, 2001). Knowledge of gender does not, however, in and of itself, explain the processes or mechanisms that contribute to depression (Ingram et al., 2004). Similarly, while lower socioeconomic status is a known risk factor for depression; knowledge of that risk factor does not elucidate the mechanism whereby risk is conferred.

Consistent with the biopsychosocial approach to psychopathology, we have organized this volume in three main parts. Part I focuses on biological risk factors for depression and includes genetic risk and familial transmission, neural structures, neurobiology and sleep dysregulation. In Part II of this volume, psychological factors related to depression (i.e., cognitive schemas, beliefs, assumptions, information processing, optimism/pessimism, rumination, negative explanatory style and problem-solving) are described. The final section deals with interpersonal risk factors which include attachment, negative life events, parental psychopathology and parenting styles, couple and relationship issues, social support, stress generation, reassurance-seeking and negative feedback-seeking and avoidance. This organization reflects the editors' view that any "ultimate" model of depression will need to incorporate aspects of the biopsychosocial framework towards health status and risk of disorder. The development of this model continues to pose a challenge to the field.

The list of authors chosen to contribute to this book reflects the individuals we consider to be the optimal experts in the field. Each chapter includes a section that summarizes the current evidence that relates each factor to the risk of onset and/ or relapse to depression (i.e. the amount and type of risk), the relative risk of that factor for depression as compared to other related disorders (i.e. the specificity of risk), how that factor potentially operates (i.e. alone, or in concert with other known risk factors), what our knowledge of that risk factor says about resilience to depression (if anything), and directions for future theory and research development. The resulting chapters reveal a wide range of existing knowledge, and yet many opportunities for further theory development and research contributions. We anticipate that this book will be of interest to theoreticians, researchers, practitioners, and students in mental health.

We are pleased that Elsevier was receptive to the way we conceptualized and developed this book. We would like to thank Barbara Makinster (Senior Development Editor) and Nikki Levy (Publisher) for their steady hand which helped to move this book to completion. We were also fortunate to obtain contributions of from active leaders in the area of depression. These authors have done a excellent job of summarizing the latest research and addressing the salient issues in our understanding of risk factors for depression. Of course, we are also grateful for the assistance that we have received from our funding agencies. This includes grants from the Ontario Mental Health Foundation, the Social Sciences and Humanities Research Council of Canada, the Alberta Heritage Foundation for Medical Research, and the Canadian Institutes of Health Research while working on this volume, as well as our regular support from our host universities. We would also like to acknowledge the help of Noah Lazar who provided feedback on one of the chapters, as well as Maegan Sharp and Jessica Daigle who provided administrative support. More personally, we express our thanks to our families (Deborah, Chris and Beth for Keith; Michelle, Rachel and Joshua for David) for their love, support and encouragement.

This book is dedicated to the development of our knowledge about risk factors for depression, which we ultimately believe will inform interventions to help individuals who suffer from depression, and to reduce to the risk of future depression.

REFERENCES

Alloy, L. B., Abramson, L. Y., Tashman, N. A., Berrebbi, D. S., Hogan, M. E., Whitehouse, W. G., Crossfield, A. G., & Morocco, A. (2001). Developmental origins of cognitive vulnerability to depression: Parenting, cognitive, and inferential feedback styles of the parents of individuals at high and low cognitive risk for depression. *Cognitive Therapy and Research, 25*, 397–423.

Broadhead, W. E., Blazer, D. G., George, L. K., & Tse, C. (1990). Depression, disability days, and days lost from work in a prospective epidemiologic survey. *Journal of the American Medical Association, 264*, 2524–2529.

Collins, K. A., Westra, H. A., Dozois, D. J. A., & Burns, D. D. (2004). Gaps in accessing treatment for anxiety and depression: Challenges for the delivery of care. *Clinical Psychology Review, 24*, 583–616.

Coyne, J. C., Pepper, C. M., & Flynn, H. A. (1999). Significance of prior episodes of depression in two patient populations. *Journal of Consulting and Clinical Psychology, 67*, 76–81.

De Marco, R. R. (2000). The epidemiology of major depression: Implications of occurrence, recurrence, and stress in a Canadian community sample. *Canadian Journal of Psychiatry, 45*, 67–74.

Dozois, D. J. A., & Dobson, K. S. (Eds.). (2004). *The Prevention of Anxiety and Depression: Theory, Research, and Practice*. Washington, DC: American Psychological Association.

Dudek, D., Zieba, A., Jawor, M., Szymaczek, M., Opila, J., & Dattilio, F. M. (2001). The impact of depressive illness on spouses of depressed patients. *Journal of Cognitive Psychotherapy: An International Quarterly, 15*, 49–57.

Fergusson, D. M., & Woodward, L. J. (2002). Mental health, educational, and social role outcomes of adolescents with depression. *Archives of General Psychiatry, 59*, 225–231.

Garber, J., & Flynn, C. (2001). Vulnerability to depression in childhood and adolescence. In R. E. Ingram & J. M. Price (Eds.), *Vulnerability to Psychopathology: Risk Across the Lifespan* (pp. 175–225). New York: Guilford Press.

Gotlib, I. H., Lewinsohn, P. M., & Seeley, J. R. (1998). Consequences of depression during adolescence: Marital status and marital functioning in early adulthood. *Journal of Abnormal Psychology, 107*, 686–690.

Greenberg, P. E., Sisitsky, T., Kessler, R. C., Finkelstein, S. N., Berndt, E. R., Davidson, J. R., Ballenger, J. C., & Fyer, A. J. (1999). The economic burden of anxiety disorders in the 1990s. *Journal of Clinical Psychiatry, 60*, 427–435.

Ingram, R. E. (2001). Developing perspectives on the cognitive-developmental origins of depression: Back is the future. *Cognitive Therapy and Research, 25*, 497–504.

Ingram, R. E., Odom, M., & Mitchusson, T. (2004). Secondary prevention of depression: Risk, vulnerability, and intervention. In D. J. A. Dozois & K. S. Dobson (Eds.), *The Prevention of Anxiety and Depression: Theory, Research, and Practice* (pp. 205–231). Washington, DC: American Psychological Association.

Judd, L. L., Akiskal, H. S., Zeller, P. J., Paulus, M., Andrew, C., Maser, J. D., Endicott, J., Coryell, W., Kunovac, J. L., Mueller, T. I., Rice, J. P., & Keller, M. B. (2000). Psychosocial disability during the long-term course of unipolar major depressive disorder. *Archives of General Psychiatry, 57*, 375–380.

Kaelber, C. T., Moul, D. E., & Farmer, M. E. (1995). Epidemiology of depression. In: E. E. Beckham, W. R. Leber (Eds.), *Handbook of Depression* (2nd ed., pp. 3–35). New York: Guilford Press.

Keller, M. B., & Boland, R. J. (1998). Implications of failing to achieve successful long-term maintenance treatment of recurrent unipolar major depression. *Biological Psychiatry, 44*, 348–360.

Kendler, K. S., Gardner, C. O., & Prescott, C. A. (1999). Clinical characteristics of major depression that predict risk of depression in relatives. *Archives of General Psychiatry, 56*, 322–327.

Kessing, L. (1998). Recurrence in affective disorder: II. Effect of age and gender. *British Journal of Psychiatry, 172*, 29–34.

Lecrubier, Y. (2001). The burden of depression and anxiety in general medicine. *Journal of Clinical Psychiatry, 62*, 4–9.

McQuaid, J. R., Stein, M. B., Laffaye, C., & McCahill, M. E. (1999). Depression in a primary care clinic: The prevalence and impact of an unrecognized disorder. *Journal of Affective Disorders, 55*, 1–10.

Murphy, J. M., Laird, N. M., Monson, R. R., Sobol, A. M., & Alexander, H. (2000). A 40-year perspective on the prevalence of depression: The Stirling County Study. *Archives of General Psychiatry, 57*, 209–215.

Ohayon, M. M., Priest, R. G., Guilleminault, C., & Caulet, M. (1999). The prevalence of depressive disorders in the United Kingdom. *Biological Psychiatry, 45*, 300–307.

Patten, S. B. (2000). Major depression prevalence in Calgary. *Canadian Journal of Psychiatry, 45*, 923–926.

Regier, D. A., Narrow, W. E., Rae, D. S., Manderscheid, R. W., Locke, B. Z., & Goodwin, F. K. (1993). The de facto U. *S. mental and addictive disorders service system: Epidemiologic Catchment Area prospective 1-year prevalence rates of disorders and services. Archives of General Psychiatry, 50*, 85–94.

Solomon, D. A., Keller, M. B., Leon, A. C., Mueller, T. I., Lavori, P. W., Shea, M. T., Coryell, W., Warshaw, M., Turvey, C., Maser, J. D., & Endicott, J. (2000). Multiple recurrences of major depressive disorder. *American Journal of Psychiatry, 157*, 229–233.

Stephens, T., & Joubert, N. (2001). The economic burden of mental health problems in Canada. Chronic Diseases in Canada, 22. Retrieved February 19, 2008 from http://www.phac-aspc.gc.ca/publicat/cdic-mcc/22-1/d_e.html

Zheng, D., Macera, C. A., Croft, J. B., Giles, W. H., Davis, D., & Scott, W. K. (1997). Major depression and all-cause mortality among white adults in the United States. *Annals of Epidemiology, 7*, 213–218.

List of Contributors

John R.Z. Abela (195) McGill University, Department of Psychology, Montreal Quebec, Canada.

Lyn Y. Abramson (237) Department of Psychology, University of Wisconsin-Madison, Madison, USA.

Lauren B. Alloy (237) Department of Psychology, Temple University, Philadelphia, PA, USA.

Hymie Anisman (63) Institute of Neuroscience, Life Science Research Centre, Carleton University, Ottawa, Ontario, Canada.

Randy P. Auerbach (195) McGill University, Department of Psychology, Montreal Quebec, Canada.

Heidi Neufeld Bailey (289) Department of Psychology, University of Guelph, Guelph, Ontario, Canada.

Aaron T. Beck (121) Psychopathology Research Unit, University of Pennsylvania, Philadelphia, PA, USA.

Steven L. Bistricky (145) Department of Psychology, University of Kansas, Lawrence, KS, USA.

Melissa A. Clark (263) Department of Psychology, Drexel University, Philadelphia, PA, USA.

Nick Craddock (19) Department of Psychological Medicine, Cardiff University, Heath Park, Cardiff, UK.

Arika Cronin (385) Department of Psychology, George Mason University, Fairfax, VA, USA.

Carey Anne DeOliveira (289) Mental Health Program and Home Visiting Program for Infants, London, Ontario, Canada.

Keith S. Dobson (1, 447) Department of Psychology, University of Calgary, Calgary, Alberta, Canada.

David J.A. Dozois (1, 121) Department of Psychology, University of Western Ontario, London, Ontario, Canada.

Cecilia A. Essau (343) School of Human and Life Sciences, Roehampton University, Whitelands College, London, UK.

Liz Forty (19) Department of Psychological Medicine, Cardiff University, Heath Park, Cardiff, UK.

Anne Germain (91) Western Psychiatric Institute and Clinic, Pittsburgh, PA, USA.

Rachel K. Gerstein (237) Department of Psychology, Temple University, Philadelphia, PA, USA.

Constance Hammen (409) Department of Psychology, University of California, Los Angeles, CA, USA.

Kate L. Harkness (317) Department of Psychology, Queens University, Kingston, Ontario, Canada.

Shawn Hayley (63) Institute of Neuroscince, Life Science Research Centre, Carleton University, Ottawa, Ontario, Canada.

Rick E. Ingram (145) Department of Psychology, University of Kansas, Lawrence, KS, USA.

Thomas E. Joiner, Jr. (429) Department of Psychology, Florida State University, Tallahassee, FL, USA.

Roselinde Kaiser (363) Department of Psychology, University of Colorado, Boulder, CO, USA.

Jessica Keyser (237) Department of Psychology, Temple University, Philadelphia, PA, USA.

Brian Lakey (385) Psychology Department, Grand Valley State University, Allendale, MI, USA.

Glenda MacQueen (37) Mood Disorders Service, Department of Psychiatry and Behavioral Neurosciences, St. Joseph's Healthcare, Hamilton, Ontario, Canada.

Kim Matheson (63) Institute of Neuroscience, Life Science Research Centre, Carleton University, Ottawa, Ontario, Canada.

Greg Moran (289) Department of Psychology, University of Western Ontario, London, Ontario, Canada.

Arthur M. Nezu (263) Department of Psychology, Drexel University, Philadelphia, PA, USA.

Christine Maguth Nezu (263) Department of Psychology, Drexel University, Philadelphia, PA, USA.

Susan Nolen-Hoeksema (221) Department of Psychology, Yale University, New Haven, CT, USA.

Nicole D. Ottenbreit (447) University of Calgary, Child Development Centre, Calgary, Alberta, Canada.

Rajamannar Ramasubbu (37) Department of Psychiatry, University of Calgary, Foothills Medical Centre, Calgary, Alberta, Canada.

Satoko Sasagawa (343) Graduate School of Human Sciences, Waseda University, Mikajima, Tokorozawa, Japan.

Stephen M. Schueller (171) Positive Psychology Center, University of Pennsylvania, Philadelphia, PA, USA

Martin E.P. Seligman (171, 195) Positive Psychology Center, University of Pennsylvania, Philadelphia, PA, USA

Josephine H. Shih (409) Saint Joseph's University, Department of Psychology, Philadelphia, PA, USA.

Dana K. Steidtmann (145) Department of Psychology, University of Kansas, Lawrence, KS, USA.

Michael E. Thase (91) Western Psychiatric Institute and Clinic, Pittsburgh, PA, USA.

Katherine A. Timmons (429) Department of Psychology, Florida State University, Tallahassee, FL, USA.

Mark A. Whisman (363) Department of Psychology, University of Colorado, Boulder, CO, USA.

Blair E. Wisco (221) Department of Psychology, Yale University, New Haven, CT, USA.

Stanley Zammit (19) Department of Psychological Medicine, University Hospital of Wales, Heath Park, Cardiff, UK.

1

INTRODUCTION: ASSESSING RISK AND RESILIENCE FACTORS IN MODELS OF DEPRESSION

KEITH S. DOBSON* AND DAVID J.A. DOZOIS[†]

*Department of Psychology, University of Calgary, Calgary, Alberta, Canada

[†]Department of Psychology, University of Western Ontario, London, Ontario, Canada

This volume provides a comprehensive review of the various literatures that address risk factors for depression. We purposely use the plural term here, since many of these bodies of research and theory have evolved in relative isolation from each other. Thus, many investigators work within a particular paradigm, and do not often look outside of that paradigm for complementary approaches. That said, many of the investigators in this field have adopted consistent research designs and statistical tools to examine the content of their studies. Whereas the remainder of this volume focuses on the content of different models of depression, this introductory chapter emphasizes the research designs and approaches that can be employed to examine the overarching construct of risk itself.

We begin this chapter with a discussion of the nature of depression, and its diagnostic formulation. We then introduce several terms that are employed in the literature which are related to the course of psychopathology; including onset, maintenance, offset, relapse and recurrence. Once these concepts are defined, we discuss the nature of risk and highlight various research designs that can be employed to assess risk for and resilience from psychopathology. Experimental designs are not commonly employed in this field, but correlational designs and statistics are common. Both strengths and limitations of correlational methods are discussed, as is their relative utility for the evaluation of unidimensional and multidimensional risk models. We end with a cautionary note about the need for a comprehensive perspective on risk for depression, and the possibility that the models for risk may actually vary across the course of depression (onset, maintenance, relapse/recurrence). This chapter provides a framework for the chapters that follow, and an overview of methods and tools for the field.

THE NATURE OF MAJOR DEPRESSION

Depression is a human experience that has various forms. In its more subtle form, depression is a momentary feeling of sadness or despondency, most often related to a perceived loss or sense of helplessness about a particular event. Moderately intense experiences of depression often involve biological, psychological and social elements. For example, the affected person may have a strong "blue" or down feeling, coupled with a reduced desire to engage in the world and decreased appetite or an increased desire to withdraw from usual activities. Such a conceptualization of depression can be assessed by a dimensional measure, such as a questionnaire or a rating scale.

In its clinical state, major depression (American Psychiatric Association [APA, 2000]) represents a debilitating syndrome which lasts for a minimum of 2 weeks, although in many instances the length of depression is unfortunately much longer. The symptoms of major depression have been more or less set in the psychiatric literature since the early1970s, when the Research Diagnostic Criteria (Feighner *et al.*, 1972) were originally developed. Although the required pattern of symptoms was modified slightly in the version III-revision of the *Diagnostic and Statistical Manual* (DSM), the symptoms list itself was not. These symptoms are also very similar to those presented in the International Classification of Diseases-10 (World Health Organization, 1992). Indeed, the description of major depression that is used today is not markedly different from descriptions of Melancholia seen in the Enlightenment period (Gruenberg *et al.*, 2005; Jackson, 1986; Radden, 2000).

The current list of symptoms that should be considered for a diagnosis of major depression is presented in Table 1.1. As noted, only five symptoms are required for a diagnosis, yet individuals can experience more than this minimum in increasingly severe cases. Diagnostically, at least one of these symptoms must include pervasive sadness or loss of interest, although this requirement could be refined in future versions of the DSM on the basis of recent and future research (e.g., Zimmerman *et al.*, 2006). Also, the diagnosis requires a minimum of 2 weeks of symptoms, although the length of a given episode of depression can extend over a considerably longer timeframe (years, in some instances).

TABLE 1.1 Diagnostic Criteria for major depression in the DSM-IV

A period of at least 2 weeks, in which at least five of the following symptoms are present most of the day, nearly every day, and of which at least one is the first or second listed symptoms:

1. Sadness (or irritability in children)
2. Loss of interest or pleasure in usual activities
3. Changes in appetite (increased or decreased) or weight change
4. Disturbed sleep (insomnia or hypersomnia)
5. Psychomotor agitation or retardation
6. Fatigue or loss of energy
7. Feelings of guilt, self-blame
8. Decreased ability to concentrate or make decisions
9. Thinking about or planning suicide or suicidal behavior.

Note: Major depression should not be diagnosed if any of the following circumstances exists:
1. There is a medical disorder that can account for the symptoms (e.g., hypothyroidism)
2. There is substance use that can account for the symptoms (e.g., use of a central nervous system depressant such as alcohol).
3. The symptoms are experienced within 8 weeks of the loss of a significant other person (i.e., the person is in grief).

Third, there are several "paradoxical" symptoms, which can present in either increased or decreased forms (appetite, weight, sleep, psychomotor activity). Major depression is typically characterized as an episodic disorder, with a distinct onset and offset. Technically, a first episode is diagnosed as a Major Depressive Episode, but the appropriate diagnosis for recurrent depression is Major Depressive Disorder (MDD).

Given the above flexibility and polythetic nature of the diagnostic criteria, the possible variety of presentations of major depression is immense (Kendler *et al.*, 1999). A person who is chronically sad and also experiences the next four symptoms on the list is diagnosable. Another person who is chronically sad and experiences the last four symptoms on the list is also diagnosable, but note that this individual shares only one symptom with the first person. As another contrast: one person could meet five of the criteria for a period of just 2 weeks, whereas another person might experience all nine for a period of several months. These two people receive the same diagnosis, even though their experiences are decidedly different from each other. With regard to the paradoxical symptoms, two people may suffer "the same" symptom, but have markedly divergent experiences, depending on if the symptom is experienced in one direction or the other. This heterogeneity of numbers, types and chronicity of symptom presentation undoubtedly affects the empirical research and conceptualization of risk and resiliency in depression.

The diagnostic heterogeneity of depression also suggests that it may be difficult to achieve agreement in diagnosis, but the evidence is that clinicians generally agree on this diagnosis (Segal *et al.*, 1994). In part, diagnostic consistency across clinicians may hinge on the two cardinal symptoms of sadness and loss of interest or pleasure; when present inter-rater agreement is relatively high (see Dozois & Dobson, 2002). A second potential implication of the heterogeneity of symptomatology in depression is that there may actually be two or more distinct subtypes of depression embedded within this overall pattern (Kessler, 2002; Thase, 2006). In a previous version of the *DSM* (APA, 1980) a distinction was made between "reactive" and "endogenous" subtypes of depression. According to this distinction, reactive depressions were precipitated by external events to which the person reacted with sadness, loss, despondency, withdrawal and other aspects. In contrast, endogenous depressions were thought to be more biological in nature (literally, "caused from within"), possibly with a greater genetic loading, and better prognosis if treated with medications than psychological interventions. Considerable research was conducted in the 1980s to validate the symptom profiles with these two subtypes, and predictive research was also conducted to demonstrate differential treatment response for these two subtypes of depression. As a summative statement, the evidence to support this subtype was inadequate to sustain it (Beckham *et al.*, 1995; Kessing, 2004, 2007), and in the most recent diagnostic manual this distinction was dropped. What was retained, however, was a distinction between major depression "with or without melancholia," where melancholia is identified by a preponderance of physical symptoms formerly identified with the endogenous subtype of depression (see Thase, 2006). Thus, the current model is of an integrated diagnosis, but with the recognition of possible differences in symptom presentation. It will be interesting to observe the extent to which the organization of MDD changes with the next edition of the nosological system. The revision of DSM-IV will provide an important opportunity to reconsider how depression is conceptualized and classified as well as how risk is understood, and a number of proposals have been advanced (Klein, in press; McGlinchey & Zimmerman, 2007; Watson, 2005). For example, it may be helpful to capture the heterogeneity of depression by formal assessment of the dimensions of severity and chronicity (Klein, in press).

As noted in the preface to this volume, major depression is widely recognized as one of the most common mental disorders (e.g., Blazer *et al.*, 1994; Dozois & Westra, 2004; Kessler *et al.*, 1994; Kessler *et al.*, 2003; Zheng *et al.*, 1997). Lifetime estimates for depression place it as one of the most common forms of mental disorder (Alonso *et al.*, 2004; Eaton *et al.*, 2007). The point prevalence of major depression (i.e., the proportion of the population that is diagnosable with depression today) which is also high, is a function of several factors. These factors include the lifetime risk for depression. A second factor that contributes to high point prevalence is the duration of episodes; it has been estimated that an average episode will last about 4 months (APA, 2000). There is also some evidence that for people who suffer recurrent depression, succeeding episodes tend to be longer in duration than former ones. Third, it is now well-established that the risk of recurrent depression increases with each subsequent episode (Boland &

Keller, 2002; Thase, 2006); the risk of relapse is about 50% within 1 year of recovery after a first episode of depression, increases to 60% after a second episode, and increases yet again up to about 70% after further episodes (Kessing, 1998; Solomon *et al.*, 2000). Thus, any cross-sectional study of the prevalence of depression at a given point in time will reflect the combination of absolute risk, duration of depressive episodes and the chronicity of depression.

THE COURSE OF DEPRESSION

Although it was not so long ago that it was a belief that depression could not happen in children, current theorizing is that depression can occur at any point in a person's lifetime (Hankin & Abela, 2005; Keren & Tyano, 2006). A depressive episode can occur at any point in the lifetime, although adolescence and early adulthood appear to be a stage of life with increased risk for first onset (Hankin *et al.*, 1998; Hankin & Abramson, 2001). Hypothetically, every person has some risk for depression, and everyone experiences depressive symptoms at some points in their lives. Conceptually, a person who has a first onset of major depression will experience an increase in the number and duration of symptoms, until he or she meets diagnostic criteria for a Major Depressive Episode (see Figure 1.1). By definition, this experience must last at least 2 weeks, but its duration will vary from case to case, depending on the course of the depressive episode itself, mitigating life circumstances (e.g., increased social support), or the use of more formal interventions.

As reflected in Figure 1.1, it is expected that as some point, the episode will have an offset. When a person's symptoms transition from being diagnosable to being subthreshold, he or she is said to have *remitted* (Boland & Keller, 2002; Frank *et al.*, 1991). Many remitted individuals, however, continue to have residual symptoms of depression, and the presence of such symptoms is associated with increased risk of a return to depression (e.g., Fergusson *et al.*, 2005).

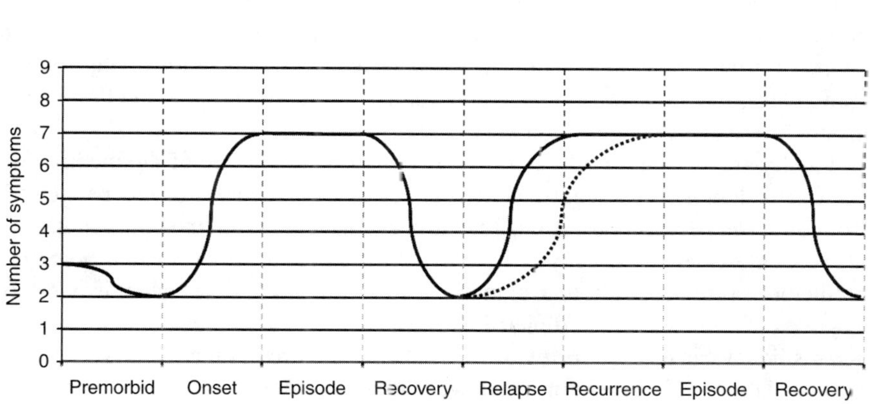

FIGURE 1.1 Phases of major depression.

Moreover, researchers have demonstrated that subclinical depression itself results in substantial impairment, confers a high rate of non-psychiatric health care utilization, and is associated with elevated risk for severe psychiatric conditions (Cuijpers *et al.*, 2007; Fergusson *et al.*, 2005; Gotlib *et al.*, 1995). According to consensus criteria, if individuals can maintain their relapse for a period of at least 2 months, then they have *recovered* from depression.

If the person goes on to have a subsequent episode of depression after a remission, this episode is conceptualized as a *relapse* into the depressive episode just completed. If the person fully recovers and suffers a subsequent episode, this is termed a *recurrence* of depression (Frank *et al.*, 1991). In practice, it is difficult to make the distinction between remission and recovery on the one hand, and relapse and recurrence on the other, but the above criteria have been developed for research purposes (see Boland & Keller, 2002; Frank *et al.*, 1991).

Given the model of the longitudinal course of depression depicted in Figure 1.1, it becomes clear that the study of risk can have different elements. It is possible to study the risk of first onset, relapse or recurrence. Each of these aspects of depression may have different risk and resiliency factors associated with them. Conversely, it is possible to study factors that are associated with the offset of depression, as these may provide indirect evidence of variables that may be associated with risk of depression. Segal *et al.* (1999), for example, found that patients successfully treated with cognitive-behavior therapy showed significantly less activation of dysfunctional attitudes following a negative mood induction than did individuals successfully treated with pharmacotherapy. In a subsequent study, Segal *et al.*, (2006) found that the activation of dysfunctional attitudes, in conjunction with a negative mood state, was predictive of later relapse. Further, factors that either increase the risk of depression (vulnerability factors) or factors that reduce the risk of depression (resilience factors) can be studied. From another perspective, a researcher could investigate factors that provide the distal or early setting conditions from which depression may develop, as opposed to proximal factors that immediately precede the onset of a new episode of depression. As depression can occur at different stages of life, it may be that the risk and resiliency factors vary across the lifespan. Risk factors for depression may vary among different subgroups of the population (e.g., males vs. females; individuals from different cultural or ethnic groups), and these subgroup differences could be studied.

Finally, the evaluation of risk depends in part on the nature of the method for evaluating depression in a given study. As noted above, depression can be viewed from different perspectives. If it is seen as a distinct symptom, then the evaluation of risk and resiliency can only be in terms of the extent to which various potential predictors correlate with that symptom. In contrast, if depression is viewed as a severity score on a dimensional measure, then the evaluation of risk and resiliency can include correlational methods, or more advanced statistics based on correlations. If depression is viewed as a nosological disorder, then other research methods related to psychiatric epidemiology (Oakes & Kaufman, 2006) become possible. As can be seen in the chapters in this volume, much of the extant research uses dimensional assessment models for depression, which has had inevitable consequences for the study of depression risk and resiliency factors.

THE NATURE OF RISK

There is considerable confusion over what constitutes a risk factor and researchers have recently delineated the definitions and methodologies for studying risk (Ingram & Price, 2001; Kazdin *et al.*, 1997; Kraemer *et al.*, 2001). At its most basic level one might think of a risk factor as a variable that is associated with an increased probability of developing a given condition. There are, however, different approaches which may be used to determine risk and which are associated with varying degrees of empirical support. One strategy would simply be to determine that a given variable is a correlate of depression. Once such an association is established, additional evidence is then gathered to ascertain *how* the risk factor operates (e.g., Is it a proxy for another risk factor, does it overlap with other risk factors, is one a moderator or mediator of the other? see Kraemer *et al.*, 2001) and to establish the causal status of the putative risk factor. Although the terms risk and vulnerability are not synonymous (see Ingram & Price, 2001; Ingram *et al.*, 2004), a risk factor that is causally related to depression would be also considered a vulnerability factor. Ingram and Price (2001) suggest that there is support for a vulnerability factor when it is: (1) stable (i.e., an enduring trait, although not necessarily unmodifiable); (2) latent (e.g., present in individuals who show few or no overt signs of the disorder); and (3) endogenous (whether originating within the individual or from learned experiences, the purported vulnerability resides within the individual). Whereas risk in and of itself only provides descriptive information about the relationship to depression, vulnerability (or causal risk factors) provides information about the mechanisms by which a given variable contributes to the onset (or relapse/recurrence) of a given condition. As noted in the preface to this volume, there are myriad risk factors (e.g., gender, low socioeconomic status, medical illness) that could have been included as independent chapters in this book. Yet knowledge of these risk factors in and of themselves does not elucidate the mechanisms by which risk is conferred. We have instead attempted to emphasize those variables for which there is existing support as a risk factor (and some evidentiary claims as a possible causal risk factor).

The literature pertaining to putative risk factors for depression is incredibly large. As illustrated throughout this volume, risk for depression has been studied from numerous perspectives, focusing on biological, cognitive and social aspects of the disorder. There are many important reasons why these models have become as influential as they are in the field (Hayden *et al.*, in press). Cognitive models of depression, for example, have not only characterized the various thinking patterns associated with depression but have also led to highly efficacious empirically supported treatments (e.g., Dobson, 2008). In terms of social variables, robust associations have been found between depression and early attachment, parenting, stress, stress generation and reassurance seeking and social support. Finally, given that all behavior is rooted in biological processes, any comprehensive formulation of depression is incomplete without an account of biological factors implicated in the disorder. Unfortunately, these models are often viewed as competing etiological accounts of the origins of depression rather than as complementary and potentially integrative. Depression may not have a "single cause but a causal chain, or multiple such causal chains" that include biological, psychological, environmental and social risk factors (Kraemer *et al.*, 2001, p. 848).

RESEARCH METHODS FOR STUDYING RISK

There are a number of research designs used in mental health research to evaluate the causal status of various factors in depression (Ingram & Siegle, 2002). These designs largely break down into experimental and correlational methods (Kazdin, 1998). Experimental designs involve the control and manipulation of one or more independent variables, to observe the effect of this manipulation on an outcome or dependent variable. Such designs are commonly employed in psychology, particularly in laboratory-based research where various situations or settings can be created and controlled. Such designs are used in psychopathology research most often to evaluate the response of participant groups to different manipulations, or sets of stimuli. For example, it has been proposed that depressed persons selectively attend and respond to negative information, in preference to positive more neutral information (see Chapter 7). Experimental designs have been created to randomly present material of different valences, to see if this proposal can be substantiated (Clark *et al.*, 1999). Note that even in this case, though, only part of the study is experimental, since the status of the participants for the research (e.g., currently depressed, recovered depressed, never depressed) is not controlled by the experimenter, but simply assessed and observed in the research participants. Such a research design could be said to be quasi-experimental (Campbell & Stanley, 1963).

Correlational research studies take advantage of naturally occurring phenomena or constructs, and evaluate how these constructs covary with other measured variables. For example, people with or without a diagnosis of depression may be obtained, and then compared on socioeconomic status. Alternatively, the attentional biases for negative information of people who are first depressed and later recover from depression might be assessed. In these cases, the variables being observed are found naturally, and are not the result of an experimenter-designed manipulation. Given the nature of the research questions in psychopathology, much of the research is correlational. Indeed, it would be infeasible (e.g., randomly assigning participants to become depressed or not) or unethical (e.g., randomly assigning people to face extreme life stress or not) to do truly experimental research in the study of depression.

Given the primary reliance on correlational and quasi-experimental research in psychopathology, it is not surprising that many of the statistical tools employed also rely on correlational methods. Measures of association for both categorical and continuous variables are replete in the literature. Some studies of association also evaluate higher order constructs through methods such as factor analysis, cluster analysis, latent group analysis and other statistical techniques which examine correlational patterns, to determine underlying or latent patterns among variables. Regression studies, in which one or more independent or predictor variables are used to "predict" another dependent variable (most often depression), are also commonplace. Recently, more complex modeling statistical tools have emerged, in which causal models are developed and evaluated in terms of their fit to the observed data (Byrne, 2001). Fundamentally, though, all of these strategies rely on the natural co-occurrence of the observed variables. In turn, these strategies also rely on the quality of the observations themselves, and on how reliable and valid the assessment of various theoretical constructs is.

Although the statistical tools can accommodate multiple variables, one of the unfortunate truths about correlational methods is that there is a practical limit to the number of constructs that can be conceptualized and evaluated in a given study. In many studies, the investigators evaluate one or a few constructs and their relationship to depression. Rarely are comprehensive and/or competing models tested against each other in the research in depression. Also, researchers often employ correlational methods such a regression analysis within a single time period, but then try to elucidate causal patterns which require longitudinal data collection. Finally, a considerable proportion of the prospective research in depression is conducted in the context of clinical research. While any treatments being evaluated likely perturb associations among variables, it is often impossible to fully disentangle treatment from other influences in the data set.

We note that some investigators use treatment outcome data as a validation of the conceptual underpinnings of the treatment being evaluated. For example, the provision of increased social support may reduce depressive symptomatology, and such a reduction in symptoms may be seen to validate the conceptual link between social support and risk for depression. Such a conclusion may not be warranted, however, since interventions often are complex endeavors that include assessment/evaluation, increased contact with a caregiver, an expectancy of improvement and changes in other variables affected by the intervention. Each of these other factors helps to explain the overall effects of the intervention, so such studies are not simply evaluations of the purported risk factor. Given these considerations, while we agree that treatment studies can provide data that is consistent with conceptual models (or, conversely, provide data that is inconsistent with a conceptual model, which is even more telling), they cannot provide formal evaluations of the model, *per se*.

CONCEPTUAL MODELS FOR STUDYING RISK

While the above discussion considers different methodologies and statistical issues in the evaluation of risk for depression, it does not reflect the broad range of identified factors themselves. Given the ubiquitous nature of depression, and its potentially devastating effects, it is not surprising that many different variables have been examined as potential explanatory factors. Also, given the heterogeneous nature of the disorder, it is also perhaps not surprising that a large number of correlates of depression have been identified, and then examined as possible risk or resilience factors.

While many studies focus on a single or small number of potential risk factors for depression, it is generally understood that any "ultimate" model is likely to be multidimensional and dynamic, possibly changing over the course of the lifespan, or across various individual difference variables. Figure 1.2 is an attempt to demonstrate one way to consider the various factors that might be involved in any final model of depression. This figure suggests that there are fundamental "setting conditions" that are relatively stable individual difference factors which may serve as distal risk and resiliency factors. These factors include gender, age, socioeconomic status, race and culture. We know that some of these factors are clearly related to depression. Beginning in adolescence, and continuing through adulthood, females are at approximately twice the risk of depression as are males (e.g., Angold *et al.*, 1998; Cairney, 1998; Garber & Flynn, 2001; Hankin *et al.*, 1998). Individuals from lower socioeconomic groups are also at

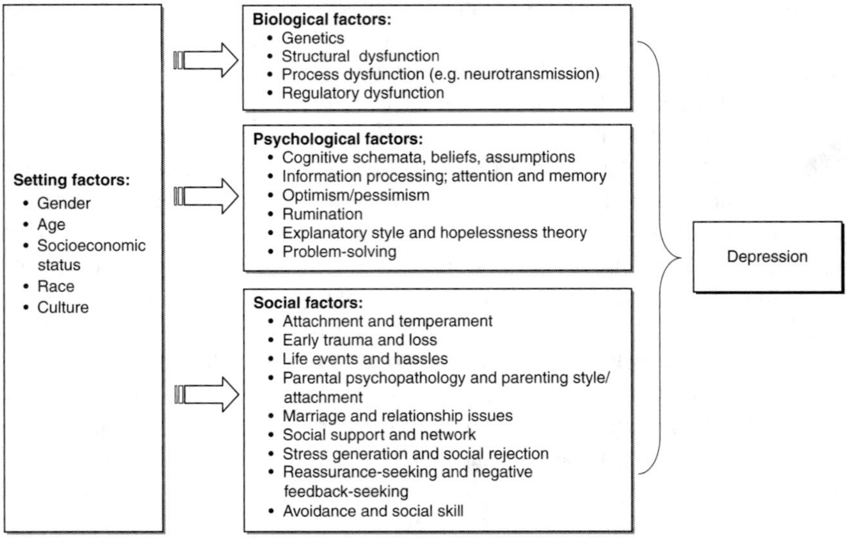

FIGURE 1.2 A conceptual framework of risk factors for depression.

increased risk of depression, relative to those from middle and upper socioeconomic groups (Kaelber *et al.*, 1995). These observations, however, do little to explain why these associations exist. For example, to understand why gender is a risk factor for depression, we need to know more about what biological, psychological or social processes are associated with gender. Rather than the general setting conditions, it is more likely that these more specific processes will figure into the explanatory model for depression. It therefore becomes critical to fully identify and evaluate these processes when exploring risk and resilience.

The approach taken in this volume reflects the views just stated, which are that a multidimensional view of depression is optimal, and that the models should reflect aspects of the biopsychosocial perspective on psychopathology (Moniz & Gorin, 2007), rather than on distal factors. This is not to say that distal factors are unimportant in the genesis of psychopathology, but the view here is that more proximal and ongoing factors will ultimately have greater explanatory power. We do not also intend to suggest that any one risk factor is likely to be both necessary and sufficient for the genesis of depression; in most instances, we would expect that depression is determined by multiple risk factors. We would also note that it is highly likely that these factors do not operate in isolation from each other, but are themselves correlated. For example, problems in childhood attachment may well affect a developing child's sense of self or emerging identity, which later affects his or her ability to engage the social environment and enlist social support in times of stress. Another child may be born with a general predisposition to hyperarousal and reactivity, which leads him or her to develop an avoidant pattern, which ultimately results in social isolation or rejection and inadequate social support. These are but two examples of potential constellation of risk factors that might conspire together to eventuate in elevated risk for depression. Our knowledge about the causal pathways for depression is at a rudimentary level and awaits considerably more longitudinal research.

It is also probable that risk factors do not remain static over the lifespan, but may evolve over time and with experience. The "pernicious nature of depression" (Joiner, 2000) is such that being depressed may increase the strength or magnitude of a particular risk factor (e.g., biochemical pathways; self-schemas; avoidance patterns), or it may increase the potency of other risk factors (e.g., biological dysregulation; lack of social support; social rejection), so that the experience of depression becomes increasingly self-maintaining with recurrent episodes (Post, 1992; Solomon *et al.*, 2000). As such it is possible that validated models for risk of onset will be different than models for risk of relapse or recurrence. It is also possible that the risk factors for onset, relapse or recurrence, will not be the mirror inverse of the factors that are the most effective for intervention. It is highly likely that there are multiple pathways into a state of depression, and myriad and potentially different pathways out. Theorists and researchers need to retain a sense of perspective about the amount of variance that can be associated with any one risk factor.

PREVIEW OF THIS VOLUME

Figure 1.2 previews the risk factors that have been selected for consideration in this volume. They include a series of biological, psychological and social factors, each of which has a substantive literature related to depression. That said, the relative state of these literatures vary. Some of these factors are well-established and have been recognized and evaluated for some time. Others are relatively new factors in the field, and have relatively less well-developed bodies of research associated with them. Each risk factor has been selected, though, because it has at least some initial evidence and has the potential to contribute to our knowledge base regarding variables that are associated with the onset, maintenance, relapse or recurrence of depression.

We recognize that the set of topics covered by the chapters in this volume are not exhaustive. For example, personality features such as perfectionism are not considered here. Also absent are medical disorders that can either simulate or precipitate depressive episodes, such as hypothyroidism or certain forms of cancer, and those chronic health conditions which can exacerbate depression, such as chronic pain. We have also eschewed a discussion here of the various chemicals (notably, central nervous system depressants) which can intensify, prolong, or precipitate depression. These omissions are not the result of manifest ignorance that these constructs also have demonstrated relationships with depression. Rather, they have been omitted as we view these as extraneous variables to the core depressive processes themselves. Whether or not these are sound decisions will await further observation and research.

The volume that we have put together represents what we consider to be the most exciting of research in the area of risk for depression. The text, which is organized in three main sections, begins with a discussion of biological risk factors for depression and includes genetic risk and familial transmission, neural structures, neurobiology and sleep dysregulation. The next section of this volume highlights various cognitive factors that are associated with depression (i.e., schemas, beliefs, assumptions, information processing, optimism, pessimism, negative explanatory style, rumination and problem-solving). The final section emphasizes interpersonal risk for depression and includes the important variables of attachment, negative life events, parental psychopathology and parenting styles, couple and relationship issues, social support, stress generation, reassurance-seeking and negative feedback-seeking and avoidance. We hope that this comprehensive volume will allow readers to compare and contrast different models of risk and their empirical evidence, examine the predictive power of these models as they relate to depression onset, maintenance and relapse/recurrence, stimulate new growth in the development of theory and research on risk factors for depression (and, importantly, more integrative models of depression), advance new and more sophisticated methodological and statistical approaches to the study of risk, and consider the therapeutic implications of this research.

The empirical knowledge base on risk factors for depression is voluminous and continues to grow. There are a number of well-developed and empirically supported models of risk from a wide range of theoretical perspectives. Given the heterogeneity of depression, there are likely multiple causal pathways that interact across the lifespan. In this sense, the effect of one risk factor can only be understood in the context of other risk factors (Kraemer *et al.*, 2001). We hope that this volume will spur further research, understanding and integrating in this important area.

REFERENCES

Alonso, J., Angermeyer, M. C., Bernert, S., Bruffaerts, R., Brugha, T. S., Bryson, H. *et al.* (2004). Prevalence of mental disorders in Europe: Results from the European study of the epidemiology of mental disorders (ESEMeD) project. *Acta Psychiatrica Scandinavica, 109* (Suppl 420), 21–27.

American Psychiatric Association. (1980). *Diagnostic and statistical manual of mental disorders (3rd ed.)*. Washington, DC: American Psychiatric Association.

American Psychiatric Association (2000). *Diagnostic and Statistical Manual of Mental Disorders (4th ed. rev.)*. Washington, DC: American Psychiatric Association.

Angold, A., Costello, E. J., & Worthman, C. M. (1998). Puberty and depression: The roles of age, pubertal status and pubertal timing. *Psychological Medicine, 28*, 51–61.

Beckham, E. E., Leber, W. R., & Youll, L. K. (1995). The diagnostic classification of depression. In E. E. Beckham & W. R. Leber (Eds.), *Handbook of Depression, 2nd ed.* (pp. 36–60). New York: Guilford Press.

Blazer, D. G., Kessler, R. C., McGonagle, K. A., & Swartz, M. S. (1994). The prevalence and distribution of major depression in a national community sample: The National Comorbidity Survey. *American Journal of Psychiatry, 151*, 979–986.

Boland, R. J., & Keller, M. B. (2002). Course and outcome of depression. In I. H. Gotlib & C. L. Hammen (Eds.), *Handbook of Depression* (pp. 43–60). New York: Guilford Press.

Byrne, B. M. (2001). *Structural Equality Modeling with AMOS: Basic Concepts, Applications and Programming*. Mahwah, New Jersey: Lawrence Erlbaum.

Cairney, J. (1998). Gender differences in the prevalence of depression among Canadian adolescents. *Canadian Journal of Public Health, 89*, 181–182.

Campbell, D. T., & Stanley, J. C. (1963). *Experimental and Quasi-experimental Designs for Research*. Chicago: Rand McNally.

Clark, D. A., Beck, A. T., & Alford, B. (1999). *Scientific foundations of cognitive theory and therapy of depression*. New York: Wiley & Sons.

Cuijpers, P., Van Straten, F., & Smit, A. (2007). Psychological treatments of subthreshold depression: A meta-analytic review. *Acta Psychiatrica Scandinavica, 115*, 434–441.

Dobson, K. S. (2008). Cognitive therapy for depression. In M. A. Whisman (Ed.), *Adapting Cognitive Therapy for Depression* (pp. 3–35). New York: Guilford Press.

Dozois, D. J. A., & Dobson, K. S. (2002). Depression. In M. M. Antony & D. H. Barlow (Eds.), *Handbook of Assessment and Treatment Planning for Psychological Disorders* (pp. 259–299). New York: Guilford Press.

Dozois, D. J. A., & Westra, H. A. (2004). The nature of anxiety and depression: Implications for prevention. In D. J. A. Dozois & K. S. Dobson (Eds.), *The Prevention of Anxiety and Depression: Theory, Research, and Practice* (pp. 9–41). Washington, DC: American Psychological Association.

Eaton, W. W., Kalaydjian, A., Scharfstein, D. O., Mezuk, B., & Ding, Y. (2007). Prevalence and incidence of depressive disorder: The Baltimore ECA follow-up, 1981–2004. *Acta Psychiatrica Scandinavica, 116*, 182–188.

Feighner, J. P., Robins, E., Guze, S. B., Woodruff, R. A., Winokur, G., & Munoz, K. (1972). Diagnostic criteria for use in psychiatric research. *Archives of General Psychiatry*, *26*, 57–63.

Fergusson, D. M., Horwood, L., Ridder, E. M., & Beautrais, A. L. (2005). Subthreshold depression in adolescence and mental health outcomes in adulthood. *Archives of General Psychiatry*, *62*, 66–72.

Frank, E., Prien, R. F., Jarrett, R. B., Keller, M. B., Kupfer, D. J., Lavori, P. W., Rush, A. J., & Weissman, M. M. (1991). Conceptualization and rationale for consensus definitions of terms in major depressive disorder: Remission, recovery, relapse, and recurrence. *Archives of General Psychiatry*, *48*, 851–855.

Garber, J., & Flynn, C. (2001). Vulnerability to depression in childhood and adolescence. In R. E. Ingram & J. M. Price (Eds.), *Vulnerability to psychopathology: Risk across the lifespan* (pp. 175–225). New York: Guilford Press.

Gotlib, I. H., Lewinsohn, P. M., & Seeley, J. R. (1995). Symptoms versus a diagnosis of depression: Differences in psychosocial functioning. *Journal of Consulting and Clinical Psychology*, *63*, 90–100.

Gruenberg, A. M., Goldstein, R. D., & Pincus, H. A. (2005). Classification of depression: Research and diagnostic criteria – DSM-IV and ICD-10. In J. Licinio & M. Wong (Eds.), *Biology of Depression: From Novel Insights to Therapeutic Strategies*. Weinheim, Germany: Wiley-VCH.

Hankin, B. L., & Abela, J. R. Z. (2005). Depression from childhood through adolescence and adulthood: A developmental vulnerability and stress perspective. In B. Hankin & J. R. Z. Abela (Eds.), *Development of Psychopathology: A Vulnerability-Stress Perspective* (pp. 245–288). Thousand Oaks, CA: Sage.

Hankin, B. L., & Abramson, L. Y. (2001). Development of gender differences in depression: An elaborated cognitive vulnerability-transactional stress theory. *Psychological Bulletin*, *127*, 773–796.

Hankin, B. L., Abramson, L. Y., Moffitt, T. E., Silva, P. A., McGee, R., & Angell, K. E. (1998). Development of depression from preadolescence to young adulthood: Emerging gender differences in a 10-year longitudinal study. *Journal of Abnormal Psychology*, *107*, 128–140.

Hayden, E., Seeds, P. M., & Dozois, D. J. A. (in press). Risk and vulnerability in adolescent depression. In C. A. Essau (Ed.), *Treatment of Adolescent Depression*. London: Oxford University Press.

Ingram, R. E., & Price, J. M. (2001). The role of vulnerability in understanding psychopathology. In R. E. Ingram & J. M. Price (Eds.), *Vulnerability to Psychopathology: Risk Across the Lifespan* (pp. 3–19). New York: Guilford Press.

Ingram, R. E., & Siegle, G. J. (2002). Contemporary methodological issues in the study of depression: Not your father's Oldsmobile. In I. H. Gotlib & C. L. Hammen (Eds.), *Handbook of Depression* (pp. 86–114). New York: Guilford Press.

Ingram, R. E., Odom, M., & Mitchusson, T. (2004). Secondary prevention of depression: Risk, vulnerability, and intervention. In D. J. A. Dozois & K. S. Dobson (Eds.), *The Prevention of Anxiety and Depression: Theory, Research, and Practice* (pp. 205–231). Washington, DC: American Psychological Association.

Jackson, S. W. (1986). *Melancholia and Depression: From Hippocratic Times to Modern Times*. New Haven, CT: Yale University Press.

Joiner, T. E., Jr (2000). Depression's vicious scree: Self-propagating and erosive processes in depression chronicity. *Clinical Psychology: Science and Practice*, *7*, 203–218.

Kaelber, C. T., Moul, D. E., & Farmer, M. E. (1995). Epidemiology of depression. In E. E. Beckham & W. R. Leber (Eds.), *Handbook of Depression (2nd ed.)* (pp. 3–36). New York: Guilford Press.

Kazdin, A. E. (Ed.) (1998). Methodological issues and Strategies in Clinical Research (2nd ed.), Washington, DC, US: American Psychological Association.

Kazdin, A. E., Kraemer, H. C., Kessler, R. C., Kupfer, D. J., & Offord, D. R. (1997). Contributions of risk-factor research to developmental psychopathology. *Clinical Psychology Review*, *17*, 375–406.

Kendler, K. S., Gardner, C. O., & Prescott, C. A. (1999). Clinical characteristics of major depression that predict risk of depression in relatives. *Archives of General Psychiatry*, *56*, 322–327.

Keren, M., & Tyano, S. (2006). Depression in Infancy. *Child and Adolescent Psychiatric Clinics of North America*, *15*, 883–897.

Kessing, L. (1998). Recurrence in affective disorder. II. Effect of age and gender. *British Journal of Psychiatry*, *172*, 29–34.

Kessing, L. V. (2004). Endogenous, reactive and neurotic depression – Diagnostic stability and long-term outcome. *Psychopathology*, *37*, 124–130.

Kessing, L. V. (2007). Epidemiology of subtypes of depression. *Acta Psychiatrica Scandanavica*, *115* (Suppl 433), 85–89.

Kessler, R. C. (2002). Epidemiology of depression. In I. H. Gotlib & C. L. Hammen (Eds.), *Handbook of Depression* (pp. 23–42). New York: Guilford Press.

Kessler, R. C., McGonagle, K. A., Zhoa, S., Nelson, C. B., Hughes, M., Eshleman, S., Wittchen, H. U., & Kendler, K. S. (1994). Lifetime and 12-month prevalence of DSM-III-R psychiatric disorders in the United States. Results from the National Comorbidity Survey. *Archives of General Psychiatry*, *51*, 8–19.

Kessler, R. C., Berglund, P., Demler, O., Jin, R., Koretz, D., Merikangas, K. R., Rush, A. J., Walters, E. E., & Wang, P. S. (2003). The epidemiology of major depressive disorder: Results from the National Comorbidity Survey Replication (NCS-R). *Journal of the American Medical Association*, *289*, 3095–3105.

Klein, D. N. (in press). Classification of depressive disorders in DSM-V: Proposal for a two-dimension system. *Journal of Abnormal Psychology*.

Kraemer, H. C., Stice, E., Kazdin, A., Offord, D., & Kupfer, D. (2001). How do risk factors work together?: Mediators, moderators, and independent, overlapping, and proxy risk factors. *American Journal of Psychiatry*, *158*, 848–856.

McGlinchey, J. B., & Zimmerman, M. (2007). Examining a dimensional representation of depression and anxiety disorders' comorbidity in psychiatric outpatients with item response modeling. *Journal of Abnormal Psychology*, *116*, 464–474.

Moniz, C., & Gorin, S. (2007). *Health and mental health care policy: A biopsychosocial perspective* (2nd ed.). Boston, MA: Allyn & Bacon.

Oakes, J. M., & Kaufman, J. S. (Eds.) (2006). *Methods in social epidemiology*. San Francisco, CA, US: Jossey-Bass.

Post, R. (1992). Transduction of psychosocial stress into the neurobiology of recurrent affective disorder. *American Journal of Psychiatry*, *149*, 999–1010.

Radden, J. (2000). *The Nature of Melancholy: From Aristole to Kristeva*. Oxford, England: Oxford University Press.

Segal, D. L., Hersen, M., & Van Hasselt, V. B. (1994). Reliability of the structured clinical interview for DSM-III-R: Evaluative review. *Comprehensive Psychiatry*, *35*, 316–327.

Segal, Z. V., Gemar, M., & Williams, S. (1999). Differential cognitive response to a mood challenge following successful cognitive therapy or pharmacotherapy for unipolar depression. *Journal of Abnormal Psychology*, *108*, 3–10.

Segal, Z. V., Kennedy, S., Gemar, M., Hood, K., Pedersen, R., & Buis, T. (2006). Cognitive reactivity to sad mood provocation and the prediction of depressive relapse. *Archives of General Psychiatry*, *63*, 749–755.

Solomon, D. A., Keller, M. B., Leon, A. C., Mueller, T. I., Lavori, P. W., Shea, M. T., Coryell, W., Warshaw, M., Turvey, C., Maser, J. D., & Endicott, J. (2000). Multiple recurrences of major depressive disorder. *American Journal of Psychiatry*, *157*, 229–233.

Thase, M. E. (2006). Major depressive disorder. In M. Hersen, & J. C. Thomas (Series Eds.), F. Andrasik (Vol. Ed.), *Comprehensive Handbook of Personality and Psychopathology: Volume 2. Adult Psychopathology* (pp. 207–230). New York: Wiley.

Watson, D. (2005). Rethinking the mood and anxiety disorders: A quantitative hierarchical model for *DSM–V*. *Journal of Abnormal Psychology*, *114*, 522–536.

World Health Organization (1992). *The ICD-10 classification of mental and behavioural disorders: Clinical descriptions and diagnostic guidelines*. Geneva: World Health Organization.

Zheng, D., Macera, C. A., Croft, J. B., Giles, W. H., Davis, D., & Scott, W. K. (1997). Major depression and all-cause mortality among white adults in the United States. *Annals of Epidemiology*, *7*, 213–218.

Zimmerman, M., McGlinchey, J. B., Young, D., & Chelminski, I. (2006). Diagnosing major depressive disorder IV: Relationship between number of symptoms and the diagnosis of disorder. *Journal of Nervous and Mental Disease*, *194*, 450–453.

PART I

BIOLOGICAL FACTORS

2

Genetic Risk and Familial Transmission of Depression

Liz Forty, Stanley Zammit and Nick Craddock

Department of Psychological Medicine, Cardiff University

It has long been thought that in some cases depression may "run in the family." There are not always clear triggers for an episode of depression, and some individuals appear to be more susceptible than others to suffering with depression. There is now substantial support for the notion that there is an inherited component to most cases of depression, which is the result of susceptibility genes that are passed down from parents to children.

Some rare diseases are caused when major changes or variants occur in genes, including cystic fibrosis and sickle cell anemia. Depression is part of a category of more common, complex disorders where several or many genes are implicated, each of which has only a modest effect on its own but collectively they exert a substantial effect on risk. Other such complex disorders include diabetes, heart disease, asthma and Alzheimer's disease. In order to understand such complex disorders, it is necessary to identify multiple susceptibility genes, environmental causes and the ways in which these factors interact (see Figure 2.1).

This chapter examines depressive episodes that occur in the context of a unipolar affective disorder (also commonly known as major depressive disorder (MDD), or unipolar depression). Depressive episodes are also a prominent feature in bipolar affective disorder (also known as manic depressive illness; Cuellar *et al.*, 2005).

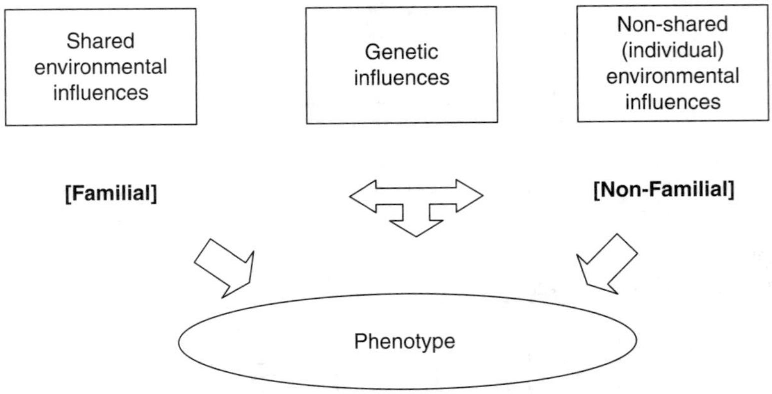

FIGURE 2.1 Genetic and environmental influences on the phenotype.

The diagnosis of bipolar disorder, however, requires that an individual has suffered one or more episodes of mania with or without episodes of depression at other times during the life history, and it is the occurrence of mania which distinguishes bipolar from unipolar disorder, in which individuals suffer one or more episodes of depression without ever experiencing episodes of pathologically elevated mood. There is an extensive literature on familial and genetic risk factors for bipolar disorder (Craddock & Forty, 2006; Craddock & Jones, 1999; Craddock *et al.* 2005).

CLASSIFICATION/DIAGNOSIS OF DEPRESSION

The diagnostic validity of mental disorders remains unclear. Due to a limited understanding of the biological systems involved in MDD, current classification systems aim to identify patients who display signs and symptoms that appear to consistently co-occur and are therefore thought to represent an underlying depressive disorder. Such descriptive, syndromal approaches are based on the best available evidence (Farmer & McGuffin, 1989; Kendell, 1987), but their usefulness is limited by unknown biological validity. There is considerable heterogeneity of symptom patterns among patients who are diagnosed with major depression. Perhaps in part due to this heterogeneity, many patients fail to respond adequately to treatments for depression, and many experience side effects from medication.

The identification of genes that affect susceptibility to depression will lead to an increased understanding of the biological and neuro-chemical pathways involved in depressive disorder. Such findings will introduce new possibilities into classification and diagnosis. It is hoped that this research will result in a classification of disorders that is biologically validated, and may enable the development and use of more targeted and efficient treatments.

MEASURING GENETIC AND ENVIRONMENTAL RISK FACTORS

FAMILY, ADOPTION AND TWIN STUDIES

Family studies compare the prevalence of major depression in biological relatives (usually first-degree relatives) of probands (i.e., individuals with an index case of major depression) to the prevalence of major depression in relatives of suitably matched individuals with no history of major depression. Family studies provide an estimate of familiality (how much a disorder aggregates in families). Family studies cannot, however, establish whether a disorder aggregates in families as a result of genetic factors, environmental risk factors that are also familial, or some other confluence of factors.

Adoption and twin studies are the two main approaches used to disentangle risk factors for disease into three discrete components: genetic influences, shared environmental influences, and unique environmental influences. Adoption studies are based on the offspring of one set of parents, who are reared from early in life by unrelated strangers. Aggregation of depression in the biological parents of affected individuals suggests that a genetic component may influence liability. Aggregation of depression in unrelated parents of adopted affected individuals suggests that environmental factors may play an important role in contributing to disease susceptibility. This study design has become more difficult to conduct as a result of declining adoption rates.

In contrast to adoption studies, twin studies compare genetically identical (monozygotic) twins with fraternal twins who share half their genes on average (dizygotic). Higher concordance rates for depression in monozygotic twin pairs, as compared with dizygotic twin pairs, suggests the involvement of a genetic component in depression susceptibility. Twin studies rely on the equal-environment assumption, which is that monozygotic and dizygotic twins are equally exposed to environmental risk factors for major depression. If this assumption is incorrect, a greater similarity between monozygotic than dizygotic twin pairs could result from environmental and not genetic factors. However, the equal-environment assumption has been examined repeatedly, and there is considerable evidence supporting its validity for major depression (Kendler & Gardner, 1998; Kendler *et al.*, 1994).

MOLECULAR GENETIC STUDIES

Molecular genetic studies can be divided into the positional and candidate gene approaches. The positional approach determines the chromosomal locations of susceptibility genes, usually by linkage studies.

LINKAGE STUDIES

Linkage studies aim to find regions within the genome that are likely to harbor susceptibility genes. Such studies examine genetic marker alleles which covary in members of families with more than one affected member (most commonly comparing an affected person and his/her sibling). Linkage studies require no knowledge of disease pathophysiology and are therefore useful for the study of disorders where pathogenesis is poorly understood. However, the use of linkage analysis in studies of MDD is complicated by an unknown model of inheritance, genetic heterogeneity, and the likely importance of non-genetic factors. It is now recognized that due to the expected small or modest genetic effect sizes in depression, large samples (hundreds to thousands) are required to provide adequate power to detect linkage.

Association studies compare allele frequencies at a marker locus for unrelated cases and appropriate comparison individuals (controls). Differences indicate either that the genetic variant itself is directly involved in the risk of depression susceptibility or that it is very close to a DNA variant that influences susceptibility (called "linkage disequilibrium"). The great advantage of association is that it can detect genes of very small effect that might be overlooked by linkage studies. Association approaches usually focus on variants in a specific gene or genes thought to be candidates for involvement in illness (candidate gene studies).

THE FAMILIALITY/HERITABILITY OF MDD

Family studies have provided strong evidence for the familial aggregation of MDD. A meta-analysis by Sullivan *et al.* (2000) found that all five of the studies that met the inclusion criteria for the meta-analysis supported the familial aggregation of MDD. In contrast, adoption studies have been inconsistent in supporting the role of genetic influences on liability to major depression. Sullivan *et al.* (2000), however, found that two of three studies included in their meta-analysis were consistent with genetic influences on liability to major depression.

Twin studies have consistently shown higher concordance rates in depression for monozygotic twins than for dizygotic twins, consistent with a genetic contribution to the development of major depression. Sullivan *et al.* (2000) concluded from their meta-analysis of five twin studies that familial aggregation was due to additive genetic effects (37%) and individual-specific environmental effects (63%), with a minimal contribution of shared environmental effects.

A focus on clinical samples, or more severe community cases, leads to higher estimates of the heritability of major depression than general population studies. The heritability index in severe samples is only slightly less than the 80% figure usually quoted for schizophrenia or bipolar disorder (McGuffin *et al.*, 2007). However, contrasting with this suggestion, Sullivan *et al.* (2000) found that similar estimates of heritability from community and clinical samples. These studies also demonstrate a graduation in risk of major depression between various classes of relatives, with monozygotic twins showing the highest risk, through first-degree relatives, to unrelated members of the general population showing the lowest risk. The majority of studies suggest the relative risk of affective disorder, to siblings, is in the region of 3 (Jones *et al.*, 2002). However, one study which compared the siblings of unipolar depressives with the siblings of healthy controls found a substantially higher relative risk of over 9 (Farmer *et al.*, 2000).

Heritability estimates (the proportion of variance explained by additive genetic factors) for major depression range from 40% to 70%, depending on the methodology and diagnostic criteria employed (Kendler *et al*, 1993b; McGuffin *et al.*, 1996). All studies to date are consistent with models of inheritance that include multiple genes that interact with each other and environmental factors to confer susceptibility to illness (e.g., Craddock *et al.*, 1995). Table 2.1 describes

TABLE 2.1 Key Features of Family, Adoption and Twin Studies of Major Depression

Feature	Family studies	Adoption studies	Twin studies
What does this study design aim to assess?	The degree of familial clustering of a disorder (in families or sibling pairs)	Resemblance in (a) genetically related individuals who do not share a common family environment (biological parents and adopted-away offspring) and/or (b) individuals who are not genetically related but share the family environment (adoptive parents and adopted offspring)	The similarity of monozygotic (MZ) twin pairs (who are genetically identical) compared to dizygotic (DZ) twin pairs. (who share approximately 50% of their genes)
How is a familial or genetic effect shown?	Familial aggregation is indicated by a significantly higher morbid risk (lifetime expectation) for the disorder in relatives of probands (index cases) than controls	(a) Increased similarity between biological parents and adopted-away offspring suggests a genetic effect (b) Increased similarity between adoptive parents and adopted offspring implicates the contribution of family (shared) environment	If genetic factors are important, MZ twins will be more similar phenotypically than DZ twins. Although it is usually easy to tell if twins pairs are MZ or DZ based on their physical similarities, DNA markers may be used to test the zygosity of twin pairs
Can this design distinguish between genetic and shared environmental effects?	No	Yes	Yes
Do these studies provide evidence for the influence of familial and/or genetic factors in contributing to susceptibility for MDD?	A large number of family studies have demonstrated the familial aggregation of MDD	The few studies of MDD that have been conducted have provided inconsistent support for the influence of familial or genetic factors	Several large-scale studies have provided robust evidence for the involvement of genetic and shared environmental factors in MDD

the key features of family, adoption and twin studies and summarizes findings to date for major depression.

CHILDHOOD DEPRESSION

There is consistent evidence that major depression in childhood and adolescence has a strong familial basis (Rice *et al.*, 2002a) and long-term follow-ups of child and adolescent major depression cases have shown that depression continues into adulthood. However, the familial risk for childhood onset depression does not appear to be substantially greater than for adult depression (Rice *et al.*, 2002a).

Twin studies have shown that depressive symptoms in childhood are heritable, although heritability estimates vary widely according to who rates the symptoms (i.e. parent or child) (Rice *et al.*, 2002a). However, two adoption studies of depressive symptoms in childhood found little evidence for a genetic component (Eley *et al.*, 1998; Van den Oord *et al.*, 1994). It has been suggested that the etiology of depressive symptoms differs by age, with genetic factors becoming more important as the child moves from childhood to adolescence (Rice *et al.*, 2002b).

HERITABILITY, GENDER AND DEPRESSION

Although females are twice as likely to experience major depression relative to males, heritability estimates using a clinical twin sample have been reported to be the same for males and females (McGuffin *et al.*, 1996). However, a recent population-based twin study (Kendler *et al.*, 2006) suggests that the heritability of major depression is higher in females than in males and that some genetic risk factors may be sex-linked in their effect. Some twin studies have also suggested that there may be sex differences in the genes which confer liability to depression (Bierut *et al.*, 1999), though other studies show no such difference (Agrawal *et al.*, 2004). A possible explanation for these findings is that males and females share most but not all genetic influences for depression.

HERITABILITY AND CLINICAL CHARACTERISTICS OF MAJOR DEPRESSION

Some studies have shown that major depression with an earlier age of onset is more familial than later onset depression, although this was not supported by a meta-analysis (Sullivan *et al.*, 2000). A tendency toward recurrent depressive episodes appears to be strongly and consistently associated with increased familiality and heritability (Sullivan *et al.*, 2000). The degree of functional impairment during depression (Kendler *et al.*, 1994, 1999) and duration of the longest depressive episode (Kendler *et al.*, 1999; McGuffin *et al.*, 1996) have also been found to be associated with increased familiality of major depression.

GENE-ENVIRONMENT INTERACTIONS

Kendler (1998c) considered two processes by which genetic and environmental factors might affect risk of depression. First, one theory suggests that genetic factors alter an individual's sensitivity to the negative effects of stressful life events, and therefore affect risk of depression. Although few studies have examined this theory, Kendler *et al.* (1995) found supportive evidence in their study of female twin pairs from the Virginia Twin Registry. They found that given a severe life event, the risk for major depression was about twice as high in those at high genetic risk, as in those at low genetic risk. The second model proposed by Kendler (1998c) involves genetic control of exposure to the environment. According to this model, genes influence the probability that an individual will be exposed to a depressogenic environment. There have been more studies of this theory. McGuffin *et al.* (1988) found not only increased rates of depression among relatives of depressed probands, but also increased reports of life events. Other studies suggest that familial or genetic factors influence risk of exposure to severe life events (Breslau *et al.*, 1991; Kendler *et al.*, 1993a; Lyons *et al.*, 1993; Plomin *et al.*, 1990). A sibling pair study conducted by Farmer *et al.* (2000) found significant correlations for sibling pairs only for life events that were shared by both members of the pair, for example, the death of a parent. It is clear that a complete model of the etiology of MDD will require more understanding of the complex interplay between genetic and environmental factors.

MOLECULAR GENETIC STUDIES AND MDD

LINKAGE STUDIES AND MDD

Compared with other major mental disorders, such as schizophrenia and bipolar disorder, there have been relatively few genome scans with MDD as the main phenotype. Several recent large affected sib-pair and case–control collections of DNA for recurrent major depression have become available for analysis. The results of genome scans have recently been reported (see Table 2.2).

McGuffin *et al.* (2005) conducted a whole genome linkage scan of recurrent depressive disorder with two regions showing genome-wide significant evidence for linkage: 12q23.3–q24.11 and 13q31.1–q31.3. Chromosome 12q22–q23 overlaps with a region previously implicated by linkage studies of unipolar and bipolar disorders (Abkevich *et al.*, 2003) and contains a gene, DAO, that has been associated with both bipolar disorder and schizophrenia. The 13q peak lies within a region previously linked strongly to panic disorder (Hamilton *et al.*, 2003).

TABLE 2.2 Linkage Studies of Major Depression

Study	Number of families	Phenotype	Chromosomal regions showing evidence for linkage
Abkevich *et al.* (2003)	110	MDDR, MDDS, BP I & II.	12q
Camp *et al.* (2005)	87	MDDR (onset before 31) and/or anxiety disorder	3p, 4q, 7p, 15q, 18q,
Holmans *et al.* (2007)	656	MDDR (probands onset before 31, affected relatives onset before 41)	8p, 15q, 17p
McGuffin *et al.* (2005)	417	MDDR (average age at onset early 20s)	12q, 13q, 15q
Nurnberger *et al.* (2001)	262	Depression and/or alcoholism	1p

Note: A study by Zubenko *et al.* (2003) of recurrent early onset depression identified a surprisingly large number of linkage signals but it is difficult to interpret the statistical significance, hence this study was not included in the table above.

A more modest peak was also found at 15q within a region that showed evidence of a locus for recurrent depression in a previous sib-pair study of depression (Holmans *et al.*, 2004). More recently, in the second wave of the study by Holmans *et al.* (2007), evidence for linkage was again observed on chromosome 15q, and also on 17p and 8p when sex was included as a covariate. These results suggest that multiple loci contribute to risk.

A study by Zubenko and colleagues of recurrent early onset depression identified a surprisingly large number of linkage signals; the strongest signal was at 2q close to the gene encoding CREB1 (Zubenko *et al.*, 2003). A theme that seems to be emerging from this and other linkage studies of unipolar disorder is a sex specificity in linkage signals. For example, the 12q signal in the study of Abkevich *et al.* (2003) was present only in males; the 2q signal of Zubenko *et al.* (2003) was present only in females. These findings await replication.

LINKAGE STUDIES, MDD AND COMORBIDITY

Linkage studies have also been undertaken in which the clinical phenotype has included unipolar depression, together with other comorbid (and putatively pathogenetically related) psychiatric phenotypes. In one such study, Nurnberger *et al.* (2001) observed in families multiply affected with alcoholism, a higher prevalence of depression in alcoholic participants than the non-alcoholic ones. Genome-wide sibling-pair linkage analysis suggested that a gene or genes on chromosome 1 may predispose some individuals to alcoholism and others to depression.

The co-occurrence of anxiety and depression is extremely common in clinical practice. Twin studies have suggested that pure anxiety may be genetically distinct from both major depression and major depression with anxiety (Torgersen, 1990). High premorbid neuroticism scores are also a robust predictor of future onset of major depression (Kendler *et al.*, 2004; Kendler *et al.*, 1993c). Kendler estimated that 55% of the genetic risk of MDD was shared with neuroticism. There may be common genetic factors that can predispose one to MDD, neuroticism and anxiety disorders. Camp *et al.* (2005) studied recurrent, early onset MDD and anxiety disorders and found linkage evidence for a novel locus at 3p12.3–q12.3, and at 18q21.33–q22.2, a susceptibility locus previously reported for bipolar disorder. In summary, although there is some evidence for convergence of linkage findings across studies, substantially more data are needed to permit meta-analysis, which will be needed to give appropriate power.

CANDIDATE GENE STUDIES AND MDD

As with linkage studies, less attention has been given to genetic association studies of unipolar disorder than is true for bipolar disorder or schizophrenia. There are no unambiguous positive findings, but the literature is developing rapidly. Given the expected smaller effect sizes and the possibility of greater clinical heterogeneity in unipolar disorder compared with bipolar disorder and schizophrenia, it can be expected that larger samples are likely to be required both for detection and replication of susceptibility loci. Perhaps the most interesting finding to emerge to date is the report of an interaction between a functional variant at the serotonin transporter gene (5-HTTLPR) and the occurrence of stressful life events (Caspi *et al.*, 2003). Individuals with one or more short alleles who were exposed to adult stressful life events were more likely to develop depression than those who were homozygous for the long allele. Caspi *et al.* also found that childhood maltreatment predicted adult diagnosed depression among individuals carrying at least one copy of the short allele.

A substantial number of studies claim to have found evidence of interaction consistent with that reported by Caspi *et al.* However, most of these studies have reported interactions under different statistical models and different genetic models to the original report, or only found evidence of interactions in sample subgroups. Furthermore, the three largest studies to date (Araya *et al.*, personal communication, November 2007; Gillespie *et al.*, 2005; Surtees *et al.*, 2006) find no evidence of interaction between 5-HTTLPR and stressful life events on risk of depression. The average sample size of these three studies is about 10 times greater than the average size of studies reporting evidence of interaction, and as there are apparently no small studies to date that fail to find statistical evidence of interaction, this is highly suggestive of publication bias. Although intriguing, the evidence that the effect of stressful life events on depression is substantially moderated by 5-HTTLPR genotype is therefore far from robust. Studies of interactions need to be approached with caution for a number of reasons (Zammit & Owen, 2006), and in particular as type I errors may be more likely to occur.

It can be expected that the literature for genetic association studies will develop very rapidly with the advent of whole genome association studies in which hundreds of thousands SNP (Single nucleotide polymorphism) can be genotyped in thousands of individuals. Such studies have the potential to identify susceptibility variants in hitherto unsuspected genes.

REFINING THE PHENOTYPE

Some of the difficulties in identifying susceptibility genes for MDD are related to the phenotypic properties of the disorder. For example, high rates of comorbidity and instability of diagnoses throughout the lifespan make for a heterogeneous disorder. It is likely that, rather than reflecting homogeneous disorders, diagnostic categories represent common final pathways of different pathophysiological processes (Charney *et al.*, 2002). Researchers have begun to improve phenotype definition in studies that investigate the etiology of MDD, with the aim of identifying more homogeneous disorders that may be more likely to share some common etiological basis. In the next section, we will consider some of these subtypes and components of MDD.

THE REACTIVE/ENDOGENOUS DIVISION OF MDD

MDD is often divided into reactive (triggered by an event) and endogenous (coming from within) depression. Family studies provide little support for this distinction (Rush & Weissenburger, 1994) with no difference in family history being found for the two types of depression. However, it has been suggested that reactive (neurotic) depression may be less familial than endogenous depression, but only when severe depression in relatives is taken as the relevant phenotype (McGuffin *et al.*, 1987). Twin studies suggest that the genetic contribution to reactive depression is probably small, compared to endogenous depression, at most accounting for about 20% of the variance in liability (McGuffin *et al.*, 1994).

MELANCHOLIC AND ATYPICAL DEPRESSION

Atypical subtypes of major depression have been shown to be at least partially distinct from typical subtypes from a clinical, longitudinal and familial genetic perspective (Kendler *et al.*, 1996). Melancholic depression has been found to identify a subset of individuals with distinct clinical features and a particularly high familial liability to depressive illness (Kendler, 1997). However, from a familial perspective, the differences between melancholic and non-melancholic major depression are quantitative, not qualitative (i.e. melancholic major depression is more severe than, but not etiologically distinct from, non-melancholic major depression). There is no convincing evidence to date of differential genetic risk factors for melancholic or atypical depression, relative to the non-melancholic and typical variants of major depression.

CHILDBIRTH AND MDD

Evidence suggests that, at least in some women, there may be a familial tendency to experience depressive episodes following childbirth (Forty *et al.*, 2006). For these women, the puerperium appears to be a specific period of risk. The findings of Treloar *et al.* (1999) suggest that different genetic factors may play a role in postpartum and non-postpartum depression and suggest modest genetic influences on postpartum major depression.

PSYCHOSIS AND MDD

Although there is evidence for the familiality of psychotic features in bipolar patients (O'Mahony *et al.*, 2002; Potash *et al.*, 2003; Potash *et al.*, 2001), such studies are lacking in unipolar disorder. Winokur *et al.* (1985) found no evidence that psychotic probands were more likely than non-psychotic control participants to have psychotic relatives. This result was supported by another study (Coryell *et al.*, 1985), which found that patterns of familial psychopathology were similar for psychotically depressed inpatients and non-psychotic depressed inpatients. However, Coryell *et al.* (1985) also found increased rates of schizophrenia and decreased rates of depression in the families of depressed patients with mood-incongruent psychosis, as compared to those with mood-congruent psychotic features. Interesting results have emerged recently in relation to phenotypic overlap between bipolar disorder and schizophrenia, which suggest the possibility of common psychosis susceptibility genes (Craddock *et al.*, 2005). Further investigation of the relationship between major depression and psychosis is needed.

SUICIDE AND MDD

Suicide and suicidal behavior are familial, and appear to be heritable, through at least two components: (1) liability to mental disorder in general and (2) liability to impulsive aggression (Brent & Mann, 2005). Kim *et al.* (2005) studied suicidality in the families of adult male suicide completers and community comparison subjects. They found that suicide appears to have a familial component independent of psychopathology, which may be mediated by a combination of factors, including more severe suicidal ideation and aggressive behavior. A recently published genome scan of suicidal behavior in bipolar pedigrees showed linkage on chromosome 2 (Willour *et al.*, 2007), which replicated results from two previous studies of attempted suicide in pedigrees with alcohol dependence (Hesselbrock *et al.*, 2004) and in pedigrees with recurrent early onset depression (Zubenko *et al.*, 2004).

SYMPTOM DIMENSIONS AND MDD

A study by Korszun *et al.* (2004) identified four symptom dimensions within the broad category of recurrent depression. They found evidence for the familiality of these dimensions, suggesting that a dimensional, rather than a categorical approach to depression definition may be useful in studies of the etiology of major depression.

SEASONAL AFFECTIVE DISORDER (SAD)

SAD has been shown to aggregate in families (Allen *et al.*, 1993). Madden *et al.* (1996) found evidence for genetic influence in SAD. The serotonin transporter gene has been implicated in possible susceptibility to SAD (Rosenthal *et al.*, 1998; Sher *et al.*, 1999), as has a gene encoding the serotonin 2A receptor (Sher *et al.*, 1999), although these studies were based on small samples, and statistical significance was modest. Independent replication is required.

TREATMENT RESPONSE

Treatment response may prove to be an important subphenotype of depression, as there is evidence that therapeutic response to certain antidepressant medications runs in families (Tsuang & Faraone, 1990). Despite a lack of twin and adoption studies in this area, research has suggested that genetic factors may play a role in antidepressant response (Malhotra *et al.*, 2004). A number of studies have implicated a polymorphism in the promoter region of the serotonin transporter gene in the therapeutic response to specific serotonin reuptake inhibitors. There are also reports of other candidate genes, particularly in the serotonergic system, but these await replication (Lerer & Macciardi, 2002).

FUTURE DIRECTIONS

The Human Genome Initiative has now produced genetic maps of high density for genetic material across all chromosomes. Alongside this development, there have been significant advances in molecular technology, and also in computing and statistics, which permit efficient handling and analysis of vast amounts of genetic information. For example, whole genome association studies, which involve large-scale genotype analysis of well-characterized samples, aim to identify the associations among specific genomic regions and well-characterized phenotypes. Such studies are beginning to be carried out with MDD as a phenotype.

Due to the heterogeneity of patients with major depression, it will continue to be important to evaluate more refined subgroups or phenotypes of depression. Such phenotyping could involve, for example, assessments of cognitive functioning, personality measures, and measures of cognitive style, as well as improved clinical phenotyping. More specific description will likely facilitate the identification of susceptibility genes for MDD. It will also continue to be important to take account of a broad range of environmental factors, such as poverty, stressful life events and social relationships, in future studies investigating the etiology of MDD.

Promising findings are beginning to emerge from molecular genetic studies of major depression (see Table 2.3). The replication of current findings in large, well-characterized samples are required to determine their robustness and generalizability. The identification of susceptibility genes will facilitate the development of treatments better targeted at the biochemical lesions involved in disease. It may also lead to the development of a classification system based on etiology, which will provide a much better guide to prognosis and treatment than current systems. The detection of susceptibility genes will also facilitate the identification of environmental factors that alter risk. Once these environmental factors are characterized, it may prove possible to provide helpful occupational, social and psychological advice to individuals at genetic risk for affective disorders.

In addition to the undoubted benefits of genetic and lifestyle counseling, it is important to remember that major advances in the genetics of major depression will likely raise ethical issues (Jones & Craddock, 2001). Many of these issues are similar to those that arise in the context of other complex familial disorders, but the combination of genetics and mental illness raises particular concerns and has justifiably received close scrutiny of ethical and psychosocial issues (Nuffield Council on Bioethics, 1998).

In summary, we stand at an exciting time in the history of research in mood disorders. The robust findings from family and twin studies will be translated into improvements in understanding of pathogenesis using genetic methods. In turn, these improvements will lead to improvements in diagnosis and treatment that will benefit those who suffer from major depression.

TABLE 2.3 A Summary of Genetic Risk and Familial Transmission of Depression

1	Family, adoption and twin studies have provided robust evidence for the familiality and heritability of MDD
2	Men and women likely share most, but not all, genetic influences for MDD
3	Recurrence of depressive episodes is the characteristic most strongly associated with increased familiality and heritability for MDD
4	Studies to date are consistent with models of inheritance that include multiple genes that interact with each other and environmental factors to confer susceptibility to depression
5	The literature on genetic studies and MDD is developing rapidly
6	A complete understanding of the etiology of MDD will require an understanding of the complex interplay between genetic and environmental factors
7	Both the improvement of phenotype definition and increased focus on subphenotypes may facilitate the identification of susceptibility genes

REFERENCES

Abkevich, V., Camp, N. J., Hensel, C. H. *et al.* (2003). Predisposition locus for major depression at chromosome 12q22–12q23.2. *American Journal of Human Genetics*, *73*, 1271–1281.

Agrawal, A., Jacobson, K. C., Gardner, C. O. *et al.* (2004). A population based twin study of sex differences in depressive symptoms. *Twin Research*, *7*, 176–181.

Allen, J. M., Lam, R. W., Remick, R. A. *et al.* (1993). Depressive symptoms and family history in seasonal and nonseasonal mood disorders. *American Journal of Psychiatry*, *150*, 443–448.

Bierut, L. J., Heath, A. C., Bucholz, K. K. *et al.* (1999). Major depressive disorder in a community-based twin sample: are there different genetic and environmental contributions for men and women? *Archives of General Psychiatry*, *56*, 557–563.

Brent, D. A., & Mann, J. J. (2005). Family genetic studies, suicide, and suicidal behavior. *American Journal of Medical Genetics Part C: Seminars in Medical Genetics*, *133*, 13–24.

Breslau, N., Davis, G. C., Andreski, P. *et al.* (1991). Traumatic events and posttraumatic stress disorder in an urban population of young adults. *Archives of General Psychiatry*, *48*, 216–222.

Camp, N. J., Lowry, M. R., Richards, R. L. *et al.* (2005). Genome-wide linkage analyses of extended Utah pedigrees identifies loci that influence recurrent, early-onset major depression and anxiety disorders. *American Journal of Medical Genetics Part B: Neuropsychiatric Genetics*, *135*, 85–93.

Caspi, A., Sugden, K., Moffitt, T. E. *et al.* (2003). Influence of life stress on depression: moderation by a polymorphism in the 5-HTT gene. *Science*, *301*, 386–389.

Charney, D. S., Barlow, D. H., Botteron, K. *et al.* (2002). Neuroscience research agenda to guide development of a pathophysiologically based classification system. In D. J. Kupfer, M. B. First, & D. A. Regier (Eds.), *A Research Agenda for DSM-V* (pp. 31–83). Washington, DC: American Psychiatric Association.

Coryell, W., Endicott, J., Keller, M. *et al.* (1985). Phenomenology and family history in DSM-III psychotic depression. *Journal of Affective Disorders*, *9*, 13–18.

Craddock, N., & Forty, L. (2006). Genetics of affective (mood) disorders. *European Journal of Human Genetics*, *14*, 660–668.

Craddock, N., & Jones, I. (1999). Genetics of bipolar disorder. *Journal of Medical Genetics*, *36*, 585–594.

Craddock, N., Khodel, V., Van Eerdewegh, P. *et al.* (1995). Mathematical limits of multilocus models: the genetic transmission of bipolar disorder. *American Journal of Human Genetics*, *57*, 690–702.

Craddock, N., O'Donovan, M. C., & Owen, M. J. (2005). The genetics of schizophrenia and bipolar disorder: dissecting psychosis. *Journal of Medical Genetics*, *42*, 193–204.

Cuellar, A. K., Johnson, S. L., & Winters, R. (2005). Distinctions between bipolar and unipolar depression. *Clinical Psychology Review*, *25*, 307–339.

Eley, T. C., Deater-Deckard, K., Fombonne, E. *et al.* (1998). An adoption study of depressive symptoms in middle childhood. *Journal of Child Psychology and Psychiatry*, *39*, 337–345.

Farmer, A., Harris, T., Redman, K. *et al.* (2000). Cardiff depression study. A sib-pair study of life events and familiality in major depression. *British Journal of Psychiatry*, *176*, 150–155.

Farmer, A., & McGuffin, P. (1989). The classification of the depressions. Contemporary confusion revisited. *British Journal of Psychiatry*, *155*, 437–443.

Forty, L., Jones, L., Macgregor, S. *et al.* (2006). Familiality of postpartum depression in unipolar disorder: results of a family study. *American Journal of Psychiatry*, *163*, 1549–1553.

Gillespie, N. A., Whitfield, J. B., Williams, B. *et al.* (2005). The relationship between stressful life events, the serotonin transporter (5-HTTLPR) genotype and major depression. *Psychological Medicine*, *35*, 101–111.

Hamilton, S. P., Fyer, A. J., Durner, M. *et al.* (2003). Further genetic evidence for a panic disorder syndrome mapping to chromosome. *Proceedings of the National Academy of Sciences USA*, *100*, 2550–2555.

Hesselbrock, V., Dick, D., Hesselbrock, M. *et al.* (2004). The search for genetic risk factors associated with suicidal behavior. *Alcoholism: Clinical and Experimental Research*, *28*, 70S–76S.

Holmans, P., Weissman, M. M., Zubenko, G. S. *et al.* (2007). Genetics of recurrent early-onset major depression (GenRED): final genome scan report. *American Journal of Psychiatry*, *164*, 248–258.

Holmans, P., Zubenko, G. S., Crowe, R. R. *et al.* (2004). Genomewide significant linkage to recurrent, early-onset major depressive disorder on chromosome 15q. *American Journal of Human Genetics*, *74*, 1154–1167.

Jones, I., & Craddock, N. (2001). Familiality of the puerperal trigger in bipolar disorder: results of a family study. *American Journal of Psychiatry*, *158*, 913–917.

Jones, I., Kent, L., & Craddock, N. (2002). Genetics of affective disorders. In P. McGuffin, M. J. Owen, & I. I. Gottesman (Eds.), *Psychiatric Genetics and Genomics* (pp. 211–245). New York: Oxford University Press.

Kendell, R. E. (1987). Diagnosis and classification of functional psychoses. *British Medical Bulletin*, *43*, 499–513.

Kendler, K. S. (1997). The diagnostic validity of melancholic major depression in a population-based sample of female twins. *Archives of General Psychiatry*, *54*, 299–304.

Kendler, K. S. (1998c). Major depression and the environment: a psychiatric genetic perspective. *Pharmacopsychiatry*, *31*, 5–9.

Kendler, K. S., Eaves, L. J., Walters, E. E. *et al.* (1996). The identification and validation of distinct depressive syndromes in a population-based sample of female twins. *Archives of General Psychiatry*, *53*, 391–399.

Kendler, K. S., & Gardner, C. O., Jr. (1998). Twin studies of adult psychiatric and substance dependence disorders: are they biased by differences in the environmental experiences of monozygotic and dizygotic twins in childhood and adolescence? *Psychological Medicine*, *28*, 625–633.

Kendler, K. S., Gardner, C. O., & Prescott, C. A. (1999). Clinical characteristics of major depression that predict risk of depression in relatives. *Archives of General Psychiatry*, *56*, 322–327.

Kendler, K. S., Gatz, M., Gardner, C. O. *et al.* (2006). A Swedish national twin study of lifetime major depression. *American Journal of Psychiatry*, *163*, 109–114.

Kendler, K. S., Kessler, R. C., Walters, E. E. *et al.* (1995). Stressful life events, genetic liability, and onset of an episode of major depression in women. *American Journal of Psychiatry*, *152*, 833–842.

Kendler, K. S., Kuhn, J., & Prescott, C. A. (2004). The interrelationship of neuroticism, sex, and stressful life events in the prediction of episodes of major depression. *American Journal of Psychiatry*, *161*, 631–636.

Kendler, K. S., Neale, M., Kessler, R. *et al.* (1993a). A twin study of recent life events and difficulties. *Archives of General Psychiatry*, *50*, 789–796.

Kendler, K. S., Neale, M. C., Kessler, R. C. *et al.* (1993b). The lifetime history of major depression in women. Reliability of diagnosis and heritability. *Archives of General Psychiatry*, *50*, 863–870.

Kendler, K. S., Neale, M. C., Kessler, R. C. *et al.* (1993c). A longitudinal twin study of personality and major depression in women. *Archives of General Psychiatry*, *50*, 853–862.

Kendler, K. S., Neale, M. C., Kessler, R. C. *et al.* (1994). Parental treatment and the equal environment assumption in twin studies of psychiatric illness. *Psychological Medicine*, *24*, 579–590.

Kim, C. D., Seguin, M., Therrien, N. *et al.* (2005). Familial aggregation of suicidal behavior: a family study of male suicide completers from the general population. *American Journal of Psychiatry*, *162*, 1017–1019.

Korszun, A., Moskvina, V., Brewster, S. *et al.* (2004). Familiality of symptom dimensions in depression. *Archives of General Psychiatry*, *61*, 468–474.

Lerer, B., & Macciardi, F. (2002). Pharmacogenetics of antidepressant and mood-stabilizing drugs: a review of candidate-gene studies and future research directions. *International Journal of Neuropsychopharmacology*, *5*, 255–275.

Lyons, M. J., Goldberg, J., Eisen, S. A. *et al.* (1993). Do genes influence exposure to trauma? A twin study of combat. *American Journal of Medical Genetics*, *48*, 22–27.

Madden, P. A., Heath, A. C., Rosenthal, N. E. *et al.* (1996). Seasonal changes in mood and behavior. The role of genetic factors. *Archives of General Psychiatry*, *53*, 47–55.

Malhotra, A. K., Murphy, G. M., & Kennedy, J. L. (2004). Pharmacogenetics of psychotropic drug response. *American Journal of Psychiatry*, *161*, 780–796.

McGuffin, P., Cohen, S., & Knight, J. (2007). Homing in on depression genes. *American Journal of Psychiatry*, *164*, 195–197.

McGuffin, P., Katz, R., & Bebbington, P. (1987). Hazard, heredity and depression. A family study. *Journal of Psychiatric Research*, *21*, 365–375.

McGuffin, P., Katz, R., & Bebbington, P. (1988). The Camberwell Collaborative Depression Study. III. Depression and adversity in the relatives of depressed probands. *British Journal of Psychiatry*, *152*, 775–782.

McGuffin, P., Katz, R., Watkins, S. *et al.* (1996). A hospital-based twin register of the heritability of DSM-IV unipolar depression. *Archives of General Psychiatry*, *53*, 129–136.

McGuffin, P., Knight, J., Breen, G. *et al.* (2005). Whole genome linkage scan of recurrent depressive disorder from the depression network study. *Human Molecular Genetics*, *14*, 3337–3345.

McGuffin, P., Owen, M., O'Donovan, M. *et al.* (1994). *Seminars in Psychiatric Genetics*. London: Royal College of Psychiatrists.

Nuffield Council on Bioethics (1998). *Mental disorders and genetics: the ethical context*. London: Nuffield Council on Bioethics.

Nurnberger, J. I., Foroud, T., Flury, L. *et al.* (2001). Evidence for a locus on chromosome 1 that influences vulnerability to alcoholism and affective disorder. *American Journal of Psychiatry*, *158*, 718–724.

O'Mahony, E., Corvin, A., O'Connell, R. *et al.* (2002). Sibling pairs with affective disorders: resemblance of demographic and clinical features. *Psychological Medicine*, *32*, 55–61.

Plomin, R., Lichtenstein, P., Pedersen, N. L. *et al.* (1990). Genetic influence on life events during the last half of the life span. *Psychology and Aging*, *5*, 25–30.

Potash, J. B., Chiu, Y. F., MacKinnon, D. F. *et al.* (2003). Familial aggregation of psychotic symptoms in a replication set of 69 bipolar disorder pedigrees. *American Journal of Medical Genetics Part B: Neuropsychiatric Genetics*, *116*, 90–97.

Potash, J. B., Willour, V. L., Chiu, Y. F. *et al.* (2001). The familial aggregation of psychotic symptoms in bipolar disorder pedigrees. *American Journal of Psychiatry*, *158*, 1258–1264.

Rice, F., Harold, G., & Thapar, A. (2002a). The genetic aetiology of childhood depression: a review. *Journal of Child Psychology and Psychiatry*, *43*, 65–79.

Rice, F., Harold, G. T., & Thapar, A. (2002b). Assessing the effects of age, sex and shared environment on the genetic aetiology of depression in childhood and adolescence. *Journal of Child Psychology and Psychiatry*, *43*, 1039–1051.

Rosenthal, N. E., Mazzanti, C. M., Barnett, R. L. *et al.* (1998). Role of serotonin transporter promoter repeat length polymorphism (5-HTTLPR) in seasonality and seasonal affective disorder. *Molecular Psychiatry*, *3*, 175–177.

Rush, A. J., & Weissenburger, J. E. (1994). Melancholic symptom features and DSM-IV. *American Journal of Psychiatry*, *151*, 489–498.

Sher, L., Hardin, T. A., Greenberg, B. D. *et al.* (1999). Seasonality associated with the serotonin transporter promoter repeat length polymorphism. *American Journal of Psychiatry*, *156*, 1837.

Sullivan, P. F., Neale, M. C., & Kendler, K. S. (2000). Genetic epidemiology of major depression: review and meta-analysis. *American Journal of Psychiatry*, *157*, 1552–1562.

Surtees, P. G., Wainwright, N. W., Willis-Owen, S. A. *et al.* (2006). Social adversity, the serotonin transporter (5-HTTLPR) polymorphism and major depressive disorder. *Biological Psychiatry*, *59*, 224–229.

Torgersen, S. (1990). Comorbidity of major depression and anxiety disorders in twin pairs. *American Journal of Psychiatry*, *147*, 1199–1202.

Treloar, S. A., Martin, N. G., Bucholz, K. K. *et al.* (1999). Genetic influences on post-natal depressive symptoms: findings from an Australian twin sample. *Psychological Medicine*, *29*, 645–654.

Tsuang, M. T., & Faraone, S. V. (1990). *The Genetics of Mood Disorders*. Baltimore: The Johns Hopkins University Press.

Van den Oord, E. J., Boomsma, D. I., & Verhulst, F. C. (1994). A study of problem behaviors in 10- to 15-year-old biologically related and unrelated international adoptees. *Behavioral Genetics*, *24*, 193–205.

Willour, V. L., Zandi, P. P., Badner, J. A. *et al.* (2007). Attempted suicide in bipolar disorder pedigrees: evidence for linkage to 2p12. *Biological Psychiatry*, *61*, 725–727.

Winokur, G., Scharfetter, C., & Angst, J. (1985). A family study of psychotic symptomatology in schizophrenia, schizoaffective disorder, unipolar depression, and bipolar disorder. *European Archives of Psychiatry and Neurological Sciences*, *234*, 295–298.

Zammit, S., & Owen, M. J. (2006). Stressful life events, 5-HTT genotype and risk of depression. *British Journal of Psychiatry*, *188*, 199–201.

Zubenko, G. S., Maher, B., Hughes, H. B. 3rd *et al.* (2003). Genome-wide linkage survey for genetic loci that influence the development of depressive disorders in families with recurrent, early-onset, major depression. *American Journal of Medical Genetics Part B: Neuropsychiatric Genetics*, *123*, 1–18.

Zubenko, G. S., Maher, B. S., Hughes, H. B. 3rd *et al.* (2004). Genome-wide linkage survey for genetic loci that affect the risk of suicide attempts in families with recurrent, early-onset, major depression. *American Journal of Medical Genetics Part B: Neuropsychiatric Genetics*, *129*, 47–54.

3

Alterations in Neural Structures as Risk Factors for Depression

Rajamannar Ramasubbu* and Glenda MacQueen†

**Department of Psychiatry, University of Calgary, Foothills Medical Centre, Calgary, Alberta, Canada*

†Mood Disorders Service, Department of Psychiatry and Behavioral Neurosciences, St. Joseph's Healthcare, Hamilton, Ontario, Canada

NEURAL STRUCTURES AS RISK FACTORS

The mechanisms of complex disorders such as depression cannot be defined by simple etiological models. With burgeoning neurobiological information, it is evident that depression is a disorder of multiple neurobiological systems involving molecular, cellular, neuroanatomical, neurochemical, neuroendocrinological, neurophysiological, and neuropsychological domains mediated by multiple etiological factors including genetic vulnerability, developmental insults, and psychosocial stressors. The neuronal network hypothesis has been a focus of depression research in the last two decades within evolving multi-system models of depression. This hypothesis is made possible by the unprecedented opportunities provided by neuroimaging technology to study the *in vivo* characteristics of neural networks. Recent advances in imaging physics and analytic strategies have enabled researchers to identify both individual brain regions and their functional connections to distributed neural networks that mediate depressive disorder.

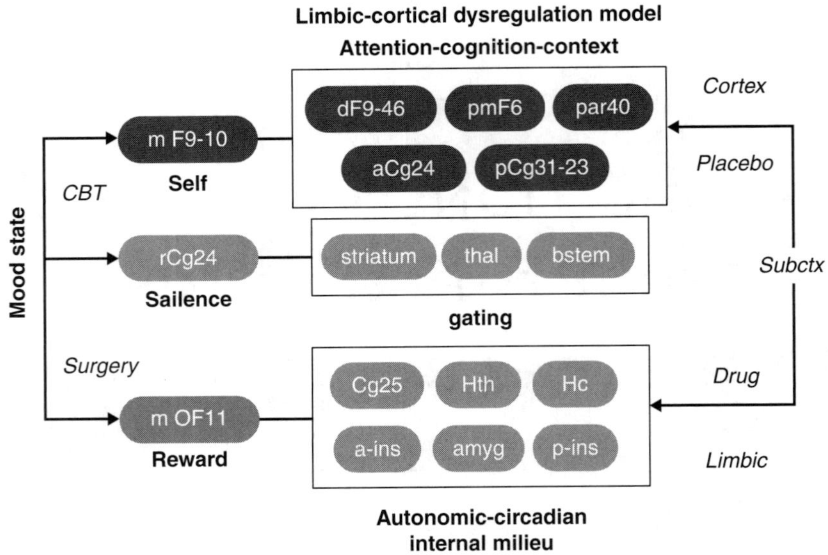

FIGURE 3.1 Limbic – Cortical dysregulation model as proposed by Mayberg (2003). Abbreviations: m F, medial prefrontal; d F, prefrontal; pm; premotor; par, parietal; aCg, dorsal anterior cingulate; pCg, posterior cingulate; rCg, rostral cingulate; thal, thalamus; bstem, brainstem; m OF, medial orbital frontal; CG25, subgenual cingulate, Hth, hypothamus, HC, hippocampus; a-ins, anterior insula; amyg, amygdala; p-ins, posterior insula. Numbers are Brodmann Designations.

The neural network model emphasizes that depression is the manifestation of a failed neural networks that support the capacity of emotional regulation under circumstances of psychosocial or somatic stress (see Figure 3.1; Castren, 2005; Drevets, 2000a; Mayberg 1997; 2003).

This chapter focuses on the brain regions and neural networks relevant to understanding depression. We review the recent brain imaging literature involving clinical and non-clinical subjects, and address the neural mechanisms of the clinical manifestation of depression, vulnerability and resilience related to depression as well as recovery process related to pharmacotherapy and psychotherapy. We will also examine how genetics, environmental stressors, and their interactions affect the neural mechanisms that mediate depression.

NEUROIMAGING APPROACHES

Neuroimaging approaches allow the direct *in vivo* measurement of structure, function, and chemistry of the living human brain. These measurements have significant advantages in the study of the pathophysiology of the neural networks of psychiatric disorders. While postmortem brain studies are useful to study the structures at cellular (size, shape, distribution and physiological state of cells) and molecular (genetic expression) levels, and they complement the data obtained from neuroimaging studies. Magnetic Resonance Imaging (MRI) provides the highest spatial resolution and high contrast signal-to-noise ratios for human neuroanatomy. Diffusion tensor imaging (DTI) methods measure the movement of water and are useful to map fiber pathways non-invasively and to study structural connectivity between brain regions.

Functional imaging refers to the imaging of brain activation. Functional MRI (fMRI) takes advantage of blood flow in active regions of brain, and asseses deoxyhemoglobin in those regions which makes the local magnetic field stronger. Since deoxyhemoglobin has a magnetic influence, it can be used as an endogenous contrast to assess regional brain image intensity during task performance, using what is termed the blood oxygen level dependent (BOLD) effect. The BOLD effect is enhanced with increasing magnetic field strength (Seibyl *et al.*, 2004).

In contrast to MRI and fMRI, functional imaging approaches such as positron emission tomography (PET) and single photon emission computerized tomography (SPECT) involve the administration of radioactively tagged agents that distribute in the brain according to specific kinetic and pharmacological properties. The radioactive substances undergo radioactive decay, which results in photon emission, detected by the camera to produce images. Radiotracer functional imaging studies provide images of brain physiology including blood flow, glucose metabolism, receptor density, monoamine transporters and enzymes. The use of radiotracers makes PET/SPECT procedures more expensive and less safe for studies which require repeated assessments. In addition to these advantages, fMRI has greater temporal and spatial resolution compared to PET and SPECT imaging. Other imaging procedures including magnetoencephalography (MEG), electroencephalography (EEG), and near-infrared (NIR) optical imaging have better temporal resolution in the order of milliseconds but poorer spatial resolution than fMRI. In multimodal imaging, fMRI can be combined with multichannel EEG to have an excellent temporal and spatial resolution.

Evidence from neuroimaging studies reveals that disorders including depression result from the interactions among distributed neural networks and not as a result of any individual brain region (Anand *et al.*, 2005; Seminowicz *et al.*, 2004). Two novel approaches have been developed in to examine and quantify the neural interactions between several brain regions (Friston, 1994). *Functional connectivity analysis* involves the measurement of covariations among neural activations during rest or during task conditions, whereas *effective connectivity analysis* involves the assessment of causal and unidirectional interactions between two brain regions mediated by known anatomical connections. These approaches are used in neuroimaging studies to evaluate neural network models of depression. While cognitive and emotional tasks are used to characterize the specific hypothesis-driven problems in neural interactions, resting state imaging is used to examine functional connectivity among brain regions. Functional imaging during resting state and task conditions in the same experiment allows the examination of abnormalities in interactions among brain regions based on *a priori* hypotheses, as well as model free.

Another major development in explorations functional imaging studies of emotion is the ability to delineate implicit processing from explicit processing, and non-conscious processing from conscious processing which allows a better understanding of the effect of cognitive awareness on neural processing in mood and anxiety disorders. The use of subliminal stimulus presentations, for example, has helped to identify the role of amygdala in non-conscious fear processing and distractors are useful to characterize the role of caudate in implicit learning. (Esteves & Ohman, 1993; Morris *et al.*, 1998; Whelan *et al.*, 1998).

NEURO-ANATOMICAL CORRELATES OF DEPRESSION

Prefrontal Cortex

The prefrontal cortex (PFC) plays a central role in the cognitive regulation of the stress response system and in goal-directed adaptive behavior. The PFC has extensive connections and interactions with limbic and subcortical structures. Alterations in PFC functions result in dysregulation of emotional processing and abnormalities in prefrontal activity are frequently reported in the depression literature. PFC regions that have been implicated in major depressive disorder (MDD) include: (i) the dorsomedial prefrontal cortex (DMPFC), (ii) the dorsolateral prefrontal cortex (DLFPC), (iii) the ventromedial prefrontal cortex, and (iv) the orbitofrontal cortices.

Dorsomedial Prefrontal Cortex

The DMPFC regulates the cognitive ability to modulate emotional responses, through its direct connections to the amygdala (Beauregard *et al.*, 2001; Ochsner *et al.*, 2002, 2004; Phan *et al.*, 2005; Schaefer *et al.*, 2002). The DMPFC also participates in the cognitive regulation of the amygdala mediated by dorsol lateral prefrontal cortex (DLPFC) and dorsal anterior cingulate cortex (ACC) (see Figure 3.2; Ghashghaei & Barbas, 2002). The DMPFC is involved in self-referential processing during positive and negative self-evaluation (Fossati *et al.*, 2003).

Several functional imaging studies have documented decreased activation in the DMPFC in MDD (Drevets, 2000a, b). This reduction in activation may be related to reduction in the density and size of the neurons and glia in the supra- and infragranular layers of the DLPFC in MDD, as observed in postmortem studies (Rajkowska *et al.*, 1999). In contrast, healthy normal subjects show DMPFC increases, especially during the performance of tasks that require emotional evaluations and regulation (Dolan *et al.*, 1996; Matsuo *et al.*, 2007). It has been suggested that decreased activation in DMPFC in MDD may indicate an impairment in the capacity to regulate emotions. Effective treatment with antidepressants seems to normalize or increase in activation in DMPFC

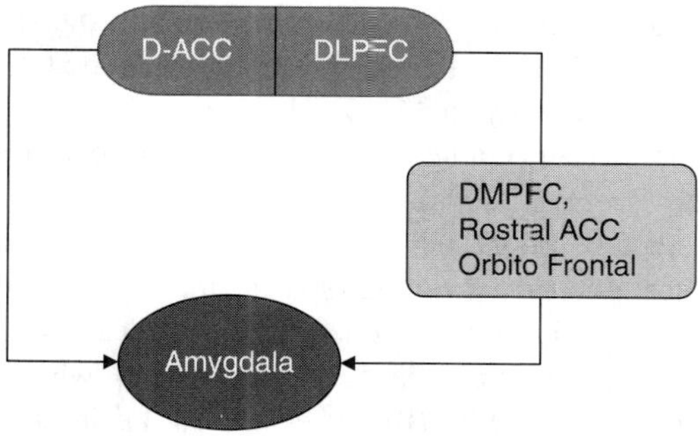

FIGURE 3.2 The Frontal – amygdala circuits.
Note: D-ACC, Dorsal Anterior Cingulate Cortex; DLPFC, Dorsol Lateral Prefrontal Cortex; DMPFC, Dorsomedial Prefrontal Cortex.

(Baxter *et al.*, 1989; Drevets *et al.*, 1999) but treatment response to cognitive behavioral therapy (CBT) has the opposite effect on the same region (Mayberg, 2003).

Dorsolateral Prefrontal Cortex

The DLFPC participates in emotional regulation through its extensive connections to the DMPFC (Beauregard *et al.*, 2001; Ochsner *et al.*, 2002, 2004), and is involved in executive functions and working memory through its connections to the striatum and hippocampus (Cummings, 1995). Disruptions in the DLPFC result in dysfunction in executive control of emotional processing. Consistent with this notion, several PET studies have reported decreased metabolism and cerebral blood flow in the DLPFC in resting state in subjects with MDD compared to healthy controls (Drevets, 2000a). Further, fMRI studies show abnormal activation patterns of the DLPFC in working memory and cognitive control of emotion in depressed patients compared to healthy participants (Johnstone *et al.*, 2007; Matsuo *et al.*, 2007). Postmortem studies of patients with MDD found significant reductions in the density of large and small neurons in the DLPFC, suggesting cell atrophy rather than neuronal loss (Rajkowska, 2000). Activity of the DLPFC seems to increase with antidepressant medication treatment but decrease with CBT improvement (Goldapple *et al.*, 2004; Kennedy *et al.*, 2001). However DLPFC-related executive dysfunction appears to persist despite remission (Clark *et al.*, 2005) suggesting an underlying vulnerability for depressive relapses.

The Orbitoprefrontal Cortex

The orbitoprefrontal cortex (OFC) is crucial for decision-making tasks which involve the evaluation of risk and reward probabilities and perseverative control strategies (Bechara *et al.*, 1998; Rolls, 1995). The OFC has extensive bilateral connections with the amygdala and sends projections to the striatum and hypothalamus (Price, 1999). Contrary to decreased activity in the DLPFC and DMPC, the OFC has increased activity in MDD. The hyper responsive OFC may contribute to failed compensatory attempts to control emotional responses to stressors (see for review Drevets, 2000a).

Postmortem studies of MDD and bipolar depressed participants reveal reductions in gray matter, glia, and neuronal size in the OFC (Bowen *et al.*, 1989; Rajkowska *et al.*, 1997). Successful antidepressant medication treatment seems to inhibit the responses of the OFC (Mayberg *et al.*, 1999), whereas psychotherapy increases metabolism in the OFC (Brody *et al.*, 2001). In summary, functional abnormalities and changes with treatment observed in the OFC are similar to that observed in limbic structures, but these are opposite to that observed in DLPFC and DMPFC. Based on these findings, PFC has been divided into dorsal and ventral compartments (Rauch, 2003). The dorsal compartment including, the dorsal medial and lateral prefrontal cortex are hypoactive, whereas the ventral compartment including the OFC, amygdala, insula and subgenual ACC are hyperactive in a depressed state. These patterns appear to reverse with clinical improvement from antidepressant medication.

Anterior Cingulate Cortex

Another region implicated in MDD is the ACC (Caetano *et al.*, 2006). The ACC has two subdivisions, and is crucial for emotional processing and the integration of emotional, cognitive, and physiological stimuli (Bush *et al.*, 2000; Devinsky *et al.*, 1995). The affective subdivision encompasses rostral and ventral areas of the ACC, whereas the cognitive subdivision involves the dorsal regions of the ACC. The affective subdivision has extensive connections with limbic regions and is involved in the regulation of visceral and autonomic responses to stressful emotional events, whereas the cognitive subdivision is closely connected with DLPFC and plays an important role in discriminative attention, conflict monitoring, and response selection for action.

Imaging studies consistently reported structural and functional abnormalities of the ACC in depression, including small volumes on the left in men with MDD compared to controls (Hastings *et al.*, 2004), and a reduction in the network of processes, dendrites, proximal axons, and glial cells surrounding the neuronal cell body. Changes in neuronal size, including significant decreases in cortical layer 5, but increases in neuronal soma in layer 1, have been observed in tissue from patients with MDD (Chana *et al.*, 2003). Further, recent studies have reported white matter volume decreases in the left ACC and right middle frontal gyrus (Bell-McGinty *et al.*, 2002), as well as loss to the interhemispheric and major longitudinal tracts (McDonald *et al.*, 2005). This loss may result in a decrease in corpus colossal volume, although the middle genus area of the corpus callosum in patients with familial MDD has been reported to be enlarged compared to both healthy controls and to patients with non-familial depression (Lacerda *et al.*, 2005).

Functional imaging studies show decreased activity in the dorsal ACC in the left and right in the depressed state (Bench *et al.*, 1992; Drevets *et al.*, 1997; Mayberg *et al.*, 1994) and increased activity in the same region with remission (Bench *et al.*, 1995; Mayberg *et al.*, 1999). Increased activity in subgenual or rostral cingulate cortex predicts clinical response to antidepressant treatments including pharmacotherapy, cognitive behavioral therapy, electroconvulsive treatment, sleep deprivation, and neurosurgical techniques (see Mayberg, 2006). Based on these findings, it has been hypothesized that dysfunctional neural interactions between the dorsal ACC, PFC regions, and limbic regions may result in depression and modulation of the ACC is critical for remission (Mayberg *et al.*, 2005). In summary, hyperactivation of the subgenual ACC and the connected limbic areas (orbito frontal cortex, amygdala, insula, hypothalamus) might reflect an increased sensitivity to affective conflict and affective symptoms of depression whereas the hypoactive dorsal ACC and connected lateral and medial prefrontal cortices might reflect failed attempts to resolve this conflict or to control the affective responses related to hyperactivation. The successful treatment of depression appears to reverse these abnormalities.

Amygdala

The amygdala plays a crucial role in conscious and non-conscious perceptual processing of threat and ambiguous stimuli, as well as in emotional learning (Davis & Whalen, 2001; Whelan *et al.*, 1998). Emotional processing functions of the amygdale are congruent with its anatomical connections with brain regions involved the ACC, DMPFC, hippocampus, and hypothalamus.

Structural and functional abnormalities of the amygdale are reported in MDD. Recent studies of the amygdala in patients with MDD have included reports of right unilateral small amygdala (Hastings *et al.*, 2004), but bilaterally enlarged amygdalae in women but not men are also reported (Lange & Irle, 2004). Volumetric studies of the amygdala in patients with mood disorders have provided inconsistent results, perhaps due to of the multiple discrete nuclei with anatomic borders in the amygdale, that are difficult to identify. Histological changes have also been reported in amygdala of patients with mood disorders. Reduced density of oligodendrocytes was observed in the left amygdala of MDD patients (Bowley *et al.*, 2002; Hamidi *et al.*, 2004) along with a decreased neuronal size in the lateral amygdala subnucleus (Bezchlibnyk *et al.*, 2005) compared to healthy controls.

Functional studies show increased activity in the amygdala in major depression (Drevets, 1999) and bipolar depression (Ketter *et al.*, 2001). This activation correlates with depression severity and dispositional negative affect in depressed patients (Abercrombie *et al.*, 1998; Drevets & Raichle, 1992). Pharmacologically induced remission is associated with decreases in amygdala activity (Drevets, 1999; Fu *et al.*, 2004, 2007), although increased amygdalar activation may also represent increased vulnerability to depressive disorders. Drevets and Raichle (1992) reported persistence of amygdala activation in remitted familial depression and Bremner *et al.* (1997) showed increases in amygdalar activation in patients who relapsed with tryptophan depletion. Recent studies also suggest an association between increased amygdalar responses and genetic and personality risk factors for MDD. Hariri *et al.* (2002) demonstrated that participants with single or two copies of a short allele of the serotonin transporter region polymorphism, showed increased amygdala responses to aversive stimuli compared to participants with long alleles (LL) and this finding has been replicated in five independent studies (Hariri *et al.*, 2006). The s allele confers risk for MDD associated with stress (Caspi *et al.*, 2003) and therefore the increased amygdale responses could represent an endophenotype of genetic risk for MDD.

If hyper responsive amygdale is both a state and trait marker in MDD, increased amygdalar activation might bias the cognitive systems and responses toward aversive and emotionally arousing information. Such a bias might favor the emergence of rumination of emotionally negative memories and thus relate to depression onset, severity, and the susceptibility to relapse (Drevets, 2000a). Hyperactive amygdale could also contribute to elevated corticotrophic-releasing hormone (CRH) secretion, and the sympathetic autonomic arousal observed in depression (Herman & Cullinan, 1997; Veith *et al.*, 1994). Increased CRH is reported to induce decreased appetite, sexual behavior sleep disturbances, and anxiety (Nemeroff, 2004). Taking into account the findings that amygdalar hyperactivation persists during sleep in MDD (Nofzinger *et al.*, 2004) and also during non-conscious processing of fearful faces (Whelan *et al.*, 1998), it is possible that the hyper responsivity of the amygdala may be an intrinsic problem that cannot be fully modulated by voluntary control. Antidepressant drug treatment seems to modulate the amygdale responses to non-conscious threat cues (Harmer *et al.*, 2006) but the effect of psychotherapies on amygdale responses to non-conscious processing needs evaluation.

Hippocampus

Several lines of evidence implicate the hippocampus and its interactions with frontal regions, amygdala and the hypothalamus in the pathophysiology of MDD. First, as discussed below, the hypothalamus and the hippocampus are key central nervous system integrators of neuroendocrine and autonomic responses to psychological and physiological stressors. Second, meta-analytic studies suggest that the cognitive processes that are most impaired when depressed people are compared with healthy people are the learning and memory processes that rely on intact integration between hippocampal and frontal regions (Zakzanis *et al.*, 1998). Hippocampal-dependent verbal learning and memory deficits also appear to persist into euthymia (MacQueen *et al.*, 2003; Westheide, 2007). Third, MRI volumetric studies in patients with MDD have reported alterations in frontal and temporal regions (see Campbell & MacQueen, 2006).

Two meta-analytic studies have concluded that the hippocampus is smaller bilaterally in people with MDD than in age- and sex-matched comparison subjects (Campbell & MacQueen, 2004; Videbech & Ravnkilde, 2004). Videbech and Ravnkilde (2004) further reported evidence of an association between total number of depressive episodes and right HC volume. Smaller hippocampal volumes in MDD have been linked to depression severity (Saylam *et al.*, 2006; Vakili *et al.*, 2000), age at onset (Hickie *et al.*, 2005; Lloyd *et al.*, 2004; Taylor *et al.*, 2005), non-responsiveness to treatment (Frodl *et al.*, 2004; Vakili *et al.*, 2000), untreated days of illness (Sheline *et al.*, 2003), illness burden (MacQueen *et al.*, 2003; Sheline *et al.*, 1999), history of childhood abuse (Vythilingam *et al.*, 2002), and level of anxiety (Rusch *et al.*, 2001; MacMillan *et al.*, 2003). Postmortem studies report increased pyramidal neuron density (35%), decreased soma size (22%) in the cornu ammonis, and increased density of granule cells in the dentate gyrus and glial cells in cornu ammonis in depressed patients compared to controls (Stockmeier *et al.*, 2004). Thus, despite stable cell numbers, MDD may be associated with cellular volume loss and decreased neuropil.

HPA Axis Hippocampus Interactions

Neuroendocrine neurons of the paraventricular nucleus of the hypothalamus (PVN) secrete CRH into the pituitary portal circulation in response to stress. This process leads to increases in circulating adrenocorticotrophic hormone (ACTH) and consequent synthesis and secretion of glucocorticoids from the adrenal gland (Nemeroff, 2004; Sapolsky *et al.*, 1987). Glucocorticoids inhibit hypothalamic-pituitary-adrenal (HPA) axis activity by negative feedback via direct and indirect pathways. The hippocampus indirectly regulates the release of hypothalamic CRH, as hippocampal neurons have glucocorticoid receptors resulting in a regulatory feedback loop with the hippocampus suppressing hypothalamic release of CRH.

Hyperactivity of the HPA axis is the most prominent neuroendocrine abnormality in MDD (Barden, 2004), which is a highly stress sensitive disorder (Kessler, 1997). There are increased levels of basal cortisol, lack of suppression of cortisol levels by dexamethasone and abnormal responses of the HPA to various physical and psychological stressors in people with mood and anxiety disorders (Yehuda, 1997). Successful resolution of depression normalizes the HPA axis (Heuser *et al.*, 1996; Nickel *et al.*, 2003). Since the hippocampus is involved in negative feedback regulation of the HPA axis and hippocampal atrophy or dysfunction is associated with MDD, early-life stress may result in a reduction of inhibitory control over the HPA axis, which then may lead to a hyperactive HPA axis (Jacobson & Saplosky, 1991). Given the evidence of close association between hippocampal atrophy with lifetime duration of depression, early-onset depression and childhood abuse, chronic stress and long-term exposure to high cortisol levels may lead to hippocampal atrophy (Sheline *et al.*, 1999).

The Hippocampus and Neurogenesis

Several studies emphasize the crucial role of the brain-derived neurotropic factor (BDNF) and its contribution to neurogenesis in mood disorders. Postmortem work has demonstrated increased BDNF immunoreactivity in the hippocampus of antidepressant-treated patients compared with untreated patients (Chen *et al.*, 2001). Depressed patients have reduced serum BDNF levels (Aydemir *et al.*, 2006; Karege *et al.*, 2002a; Karege *et al.*, 2005) and BDNF levels may return to normal following successful antidepressant treatment (Aydemir *et al.*, 2006).

Animal studies have confirmed that chronic stress leads to decreased transcription of BDNF and decreased neurogenesis. In contrast, treatment with antidepressant medications and ECT increases transcription of BDNF and neurogenesis (Altar *et al.*, 2003; Chen *et al.*, 2001 Li *et al.*, 2007; Pham *et al.*, 2003; Xu *et al.*, 2004), as do transcranial magnetic stimulation and exercise (Levkovitz *et al.*, 2001; Adlard & Cotman, 2004). There is also evidence that the damaging effects of stress may be mediated by decreased expression of nerve growth factor and neurotrophin-3 (Faure, 2007; Ueyama *et al.*, 1997). Stress may also decrease the expression of another class of growth factor, vascular endothelial growth factor (VEGF). Decreased expression of VEGF and its receptor may contribute to the down regulation of adult neurogenesis by stress (Hoshaw, 2005; Malberg, 2007).

Chronic stress and chronic treatment therefore appear to have opposing effects on two types of hippocampal plasticity. *Structural* plasticity of the hippocampus refers to reorganization of synapses and changes in dendritic arborization. *Cellular* plasticity involves neurogenesis, new cell formation, in the subgranular zone of the dentate gyrus of the hippocampus. Neurogenesis has been convincingly documented only in the hippocampus, although it may occur in the subventricular zone and possibly other regions. Given that the normal function of adult neurogenesis must reflect the function of the brain structures in which those cells emerge, there is speculation that new cells have a role in the creation of new memories, and perhaps in the modulation of the stress response.

Neural progenitor cells are localized to the subgranular zone of the hippocampus and divide and give rise to new cells that differentiate and migrate into the granule cell layer. These new neurons extend dendrites to other key regions of the hippocampus and have morphological and physiological characteristics of adult granule cells. The rate of proliferation and survival of new neurons in the hippocampus is regulated by several factors, with stress being one of the most robust negative regulators. Malberg and Duman (2003) found that recurrent exposure of rats to inescapable shock decreased neurogenesis, and that chronic treatment with selective serotonin reuptake inhibitors (SSRIs), tricyclic antidepressants, monoamine oxidase inhibitors, and electroconvulsive shock increase neurogenesis in rodents. Thus, stress is likely associated with reduced neurogenesis, while interventions that increase monoamine levels in the hippocampus increase rates of neurogenesis. Finally, exercise and enriched environments result in the same behavioral changes as antidepressants in animals and also stimulate hippocampal neurogenesis.

Striatum and Other Brain Areas

There is a high incidence of depression in patients with basal ganglia disease (Parkinson's disease, Huntington's disease) and stroke patients with basal ganglia lesions. Structural imaging studies show reduced volume of caudate head and ventral striatum in depression (Baumann *et al.*, 1999; Krishnan *et al.*, 1992). The functional abnormalities related to caudate dysfunction in MDD include executive dysfunction and psychomotor retardation, especially in elderly patients. Further, reductions in caudate blood flow following tryptophan depletion are associated with depressive relapse (Smith *et al.*, 1999). The basal ganglia have extensive connections with the prefrontal cortex and such disturbances have been implicated in defective reward processing (anhedonia), amotivational behavior (apathy), and executive dysfunction (slowing and deficits in implicit learning) (see Rogers *et al.*, 1998). Further, consistent with the role of dysfunctional reward system and motivational circuits in mediating depression, there is growing interest in elucidating the effectiveness of deep brain stimulation of the ventral striatum and nucleus accumbens in the treatment of resistant depression (Aquizerate *et al.*, 2005). The other brain structures that have been implicated in MDD include the insula, thalamus, PCC, medial cerebellum and lateral temporal and parietal areas (Drevets, 2000a). As these regions are well connected with PFC, ACC and other limbic regions, dysfunction in these regions may produce component specific or network specific abnormalities in mood disorder.

BRAIN MARKERS OF VULNERABILITY TO DEPRESSION

Depression Trait Markers

Neuroimaging studies that measure neural markers of vulnerability to depression use one of four methodological approaches: (i) differences in neural responses to mood or other challenges between remitted euthymic depressives and healthy normal subjects; (ii) similarities in neural responses to challenge conditions between remitted depressives and acutely depressed patients; (iii) differences in neural responses between presyndromal subjects with established high personality risk factors (e.g., high neuroticism) or genetic risk factors (e.g., presence of the low functioning short allele of serotonin transporter polymorphism) or unaffected sibling and healthy subjects with no or low risk factors; and (iv) abnormalities in morphology in neural structures in remitted compared to depressed state or healthy subjects. Although neuroimaging studies of twins would help to identify the functional neural markers of genetic and environmental vulnerability factors and their interactions, this approach has seldom been used in studies of depression.

Mayberg and colleagues examined the neural markers of depression vulnerability in bipolar and unipolar depression in a series of PET – mood provocation studies. They showed decreases in medial prefrontal regions to sad mood induction in both remitted bipolar patients and in depressed bipolar patients relative to healthy subjects (Kruger *et al.*, 2003). In another study, similar changes were observed in medial prefrontal activity in remitted bipolar patients and in their unaffected siblings (Kruger *et al.*, 2006). In unipolar depression, mood provocation revealed decreases in medial prefrontal cortices in both remitted and acutely depressed subjects (Liotti *et al.*, 2002). Further subjects with high neuroticism scores showed unique decreases in ventromedial frontal activity compared to a low group (Keightley *et al.*, 2003). These results suggest that the medial frontal region may be an important brain region mediating vulnerability and resilience to unipolar and bipolar depression. Besides the medial frontal region, decreased activity in the dorsal ACC to transient mood changes has emerged as a neural marker of vulnerability for relapse.

Genetic Effects

Several studies have investigated the role of monoamine candidate genes in mediating vulnerability to depression. Most of these studies have reported an association between a low active s allele and stress related major depression (Caspi *et al.*, 2003, Kendler *et al.*, 2005). Neuroimaging studies have also reported a relation between the 5-HTTLPR short allele and hyper responsive amygdala in a cohort of healthy volunteers (Hariri *et al.*, 2002). Further, s allele carriers showed lower structural and functional correlation between amygdala and ACC than LL individuals (Heinz *et al.*, 2005; Pezawas *et al.*, 2005). It appears that since the short allele affects the structural and functional connectivity of the ACC and amygdale, and these circuits are involved in depression, it is possible to link genetic vulnerability to impaired interactions of neural networks for stress-related depression. Besides its effect on amygdala and ACC, the short allele is linked to volume reduction of hippocampus and caudate (Hickie *et al.*, 2007; Taylor *et al.*, 2005). The gene that encodes catechol-*O*-methyltransferase (COMT) is another candidate gene that influences amygdala and prefrontal activity, as it determines the availability of dopamine in prefrontal executive function. Met alleles of COMT seem to mediate increased amygdala activity by biasing prefrontal ability to regulate amygdala responses during changing affective demands (Smolka *et al.*, 2005, 2007; Darbant *et al.*, 2006). There is also evidence of an association between small hippocampal volume and common polymorphisms of the BDNF gene (Frodl *et al.*, 2007). Based on the evidence supporting the role of BDNF in neurogenesis in hippocampus and hippocampal atrophy in stress related depression, studies have examined the effect of BDNF polymorphisms as a risk factor for hippocampal atrophy and depression.

Additional studies are needed to examine the effects of this polymorphism on hippocampal functions in the regulation of emotion in mood disorder.

Early-life Stress and Gene Interactions

Early-life stress (abuse and neglect) and subsequent stressors may increase the risk for major depression and other disorders in adulthood (Francis & Meaney, 1999; Heim *et al.*, 2002; Kendler *et al.*, 2001; Kendler *et al.*, 2005; Kessler, 1997; Nemeroff, 2004). Early-life stress alters the organization and functions of brain regions, monoamine neurotransmitter systems and the HPA axis, all of which are implicated in MDD (Heim *et al.*, 2002; Kaufman *et al.*, 2000; Nemeroff, 2004). Further, these long-term effects of early-life stress can be moderated by genetic factors. Neuroimaging methods provide an opportunity to identify the neural mechanisms which underlie the complex interaction of genetic and environmental factors.

Given the evidence of small hippocampal volume among adults exposed to severe childhood adverse events (Bremner, 2003) and the role of BDNF polymorphism in hippocampal neurogenesis (Frodl *et al.*, 2007), the hippocampus could be an important region for gene and early-life stress interactions in depression. Similarly, the findings of reduced volumes in the ACC among subjects who experienced adverse childhood events (Cohen *et al.*, 2006) and the role of the ACC in maternal care and bonding (Devinsky *et al.*, 1995; Lorberbaum *et al.*, 2002; Ramasubbu *et al.*, 2007) suggest that early-life parental care may be crucial for the development of the ACC. As discussed in the previous sections, the ACC participates in emotional regulation by modulating amygdala responses and variations in 5-HTTLPR polymorphism. A COMT polymorphism also influences the functionality of the ACC and amygdala responses (Smolka *et al.*, 2005, 2007). The ACC-amygdala connection could therefore constitute another neural pathway for the mediation of genetic and early-life insults in the pathogenesis of major depression. Further, there is evidence of volume reduction in caudate and volumetric changes in amygdala among subjects with early-life stress (Bremner, 2003; Cohen *et al.*, 2006) suggesting that the structural abnormalities in these subcortical regions may also represent early-life stress-related vulnerability to depression.

A central question in depression research is why exposure to chronic stress leads to depression in some individuals, but not in others. At the neural level, it can be postulated that the defective functioning of neural systems (the ACC, PFC, amygdala, caudate, hippocampus) that support emotional regulation may lead to depression. Early life trauma and chronic life stress in concert with specific polymorphism (e.g., the 5-HTTLPR, COMT, and BDNF genes) may adversely affect the development or repair and regeneration of the neural system. Castren (2005) has suggested that both antidepressant treatment and psychotherapy may improve the structural and functional neuroplasticity in the damaged neural systems that are needed for recovery and remission from depression.

Neural Mechanisms underlying Pharmacotherapy and Psychotherapy

The systematic assessment of neural markers that correlate with treatment effects in depression enhance our understanding of treatment mechanisms specific to treatment modalities (pharmacotherapy/psychotherapy), prediction of treatment response and non-response. The identification of neural markers of treatment response may help to target drug treatment, and develop brain-based algorithms to optimize treatment selection. As non-response is closely linked to chronicity and increased risk of relapse, the characterization of neural networks of treatment non-response is also crucial for understanding treatment resistance and illness progression.

Several studies have examined the brain changes associated with various treatments used for depression. In double-blind placebo-controlled pharmacological PET studies, clinical improvement after 6–8 weeks treatment of SSRIs (fluoxetine, paroxetine) has showed metabolic decreases in limbic-paralimbic and striatal structures and metabolic increases in prefrontal cortical regions (prefrontal, ACC), parietal and brain stem regions (Brody *et al.*, 2001; Kennedy *et al.*, 2001; Mayberg *et al.*, 2000), whereas failed treatment showed increases in the hippocampal and striatal region and an absence of prefrontal changes. In fMRI studies, 8 weeks of SSRI treatment showed reduction in baseline amygdala responses to fearful or negative stimuli corresponding to symptom improvement (Fu *et al.*, 2004; Sheline *et al.*, 2001). It has been suggested that limbic and subcortical structures may be the primary sites of drug action and cortical change may be secondary to its effects on limbic-subcortical structures (Mayberg, 2003).

In contrast to the neural effects pharmacological treatment, cognitive behavioral therapy (CBT) and interpersonal psychotherapy (IPT) consistently decrease the activity in dorsal prefrontal regions and increase activity in ventral frontal and hippocampal, parahippocampal regions. Based on this differential effect, Goldapple *et al.* (2004) and her colleagues have proposed a modality specific model of treatment response in MDD. Pharmacotherapy has been proposed to induce a bottom-up cascade of response patterns with limbic-subcortical deactivation and cortical activation, whereas psychotherapy may exert top-down changes, with decreases in cortical processing in favor of ventral and limbic processing of emotion. However, in healthy normal subjects voluntary cognitive control of negative emotion seem to increase the DLPFC and ACC activation and decrease amygdale activity (Ochsner *et al.*, 2002, 2004). The differential activation and deactivation pattern of PFC-limbic regions seen in healthy and depressed subjects with cognitive regulation strategies require further evaluation (see review Roffman *et al.*, 2005).

A Neural Circuitry Model of Stress Related Mood Disorder

The neural circuitry model of stress related mood disorder hypothesizes that MDD is a brain disorder, which results from maladaptive functional interactions among the cortico-limbic neural networks that are responsible for maintaining emotional control in response to stress. This model is based on the premise that difficulties in emotional regulation are due to a combined process of increased responsivity to stress and decreased cognitive capacity to regulate stress responses. There are three major fronto-limbic circuits involved in the top-down cognitive control over limbic responses to stress that include fronto-amygdala, fronto-striatal, and fronto-hippocampal circuits. Early life experience and genetic factors influence the development and functioning of these neural circuits. Taking into account the functionality of these circuits, the pathogenesis of mood disorder can be conceptualized as an abnormality in emotional regulation due to a combination of pathogenic processes involving hyper responsive limbic structures to stress, and deficient fronto-limbic circuits that mediate the inhibitory control over limbic responses. Early life stress and vulnerability genes and their interactions may contribute to the development of hyper responsive amygdala and other associated limbic structures or inadequate fronto-limbic cognitive control systems.

Prefontal – Amygdala Circuits (Cognitive Reappraisal Circuitry)

The prefrontal amygdala neural circuit supports the capacity to regulate negative emotions by using cognitive reappraisal strategies to normalize an increased amygdala activation in response to emotional stimulus. The DMPFC and ACC have extensive interconnections with the amygdala and this network seems to be involved in the cognitive process of reformulating the salience of an emotional situation by a self-distancing technique. This region contributes to emotional down-regulation of amygdala responses mediated through its connections with the DMPFC (see Figure 3.2, Ghashghaei & Barbas, 2002). In support of this idea, several studies have showed functional decoupling between prefrontal and amygdala activations during cognitive reappraisal performance in healthy normal subjects (Beauregard *et al.*, 2001; Ochsner *et al.*, 2002, 2004). Clinical fMRI studies showed that patients with major depression experienced more task difficulty and had dysfunctional top-down control mechanisms during cognitive modulation of negative emotions than healthy subjects (Beauregard *et al.* 2006, Johnstone *et al.*, 2007).

Prefrontal-Striatal Circuits (Resiliency–Motivational–Adaptive Circuitry)

Alexander *et al.* (1990) proposed five striato-frontal circuits, of which two are for motor functions, and the other three are involved in mediating cognitive motivational and affective behaviors (see Figure 3.3). The dorsolateral prefrontal circuit between the DLPFC and the dorsolateral caudate mediates executive functions and the two circuits between the ACC and ventral striatum and the lateral orbito-frontal cortex and the ventro-medial caudate play a role in the mediation of motivational and affective behavior, respectively. The DLPFC circuit dysfunction is associated with impairment in executive functions, ACC circuit dysfunction with apathy and lack of spontaneous activity and OFC circuit dysfunction with dyscontrol syndrome (Cummings, 1995). Thus fronto-striatal circuit insult

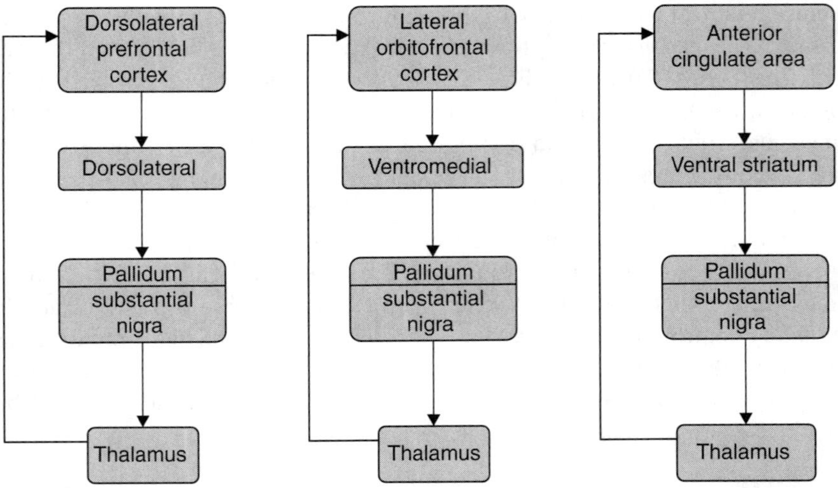

FIGURE 3.3 Three frontal-striatal circuits based on original scheme by Alexander *et al.* (1986).

may affect the executive and motivational functions, leading to deficits in coping strategies and depression.

The ventral striatum (also called the nucleus accumbens) and its inputs from the ventral tegmental area (VTA) are important for the processing of natural rewards such as food, sex, and social interaction (Koob & Le Moal, 2001). Further, ventral striatum dopamine release is related to euphoric responses and the formation of associations between stimuli and reward processing (Drevets *et al.*, 2001; Zink *et al.*, 2006). Hence the core features of MDD, including blunted responses to incentives and amotivation (loss of interest in sex, food, work, money, and socialization) are thought to be the manifestation of a defective brain reward pathways (Nestler, 2002; Nestler & Carlezon, 2006). An intact and well-functioning reward pathway is crucial for effective coping against stress and mediating resilience against stress and depression. Although stress and aversive stimuli potentially activate dopaminergic neurotransmission in the nucleus accumbens, stress-induced activation of brain reward pathways may represent a positive coping mechanism to increase the motivation to cope effectively with the stress.

Prefrontal-hippocampal Circuits (Context Regulation Circuitry)

Hippocampal connections with the prefrontal cortex and amygdala are involved in context regulation of affect. Impairment in hippocampal circuits may result in defective context coding of stress responses, and lead to generalized stress responses to inappropriate contexts. Context inappropriate emotional responding may lead to a hyper responsive stress system. Although the context regulation model of affect has not been well studied in depressed subjects,

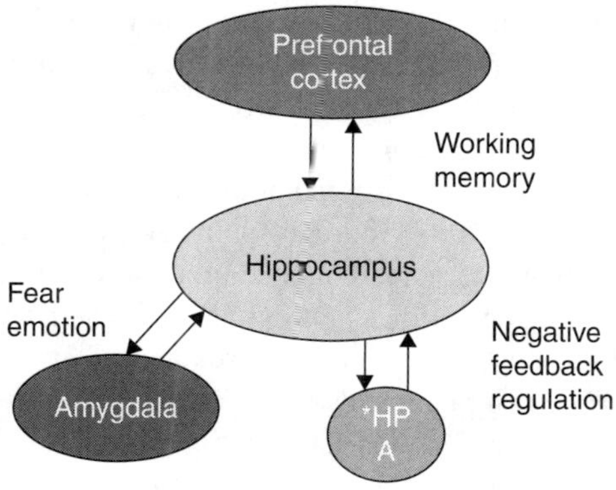

FIGURE 3.4 The Frontal-Hippocampal circuits in depression.
Note: HPA axis – Hypothalamopituitary adrenal axis.

it provides a model of how sad affect persists beyond the relevant situations, and over time may lead to depression (Davidson *et al.*, 2002). As discussed in the previous sections, clinical studies have shown that hippocampal dysfunction may disrupt the negative feedback regulation of the HPA axis (Jacobson & Saplosky, 1991; see Figure 3.4) and adversely affect executive functioning. The persistence of deficits in executive functioning in remitted depressives have been related to abnormalities in hippocampal prefrontal circuits which may represent underlying cognitive vulnerability for depressive relapses (Clarke *et al.* 2005).

CONCLUSIONS AND FUTURE PERSPECTIVES

The conceptualization of mood disorders as disturbances in neural regulation of emotion has several important implications. Neural network models of depression provide opportunities to guide treatments for resistant depressions (see Giacobbe & Kennedy, 2006). As the understanding of genetic determinants of neural networks improves, these approaches might help to define brain endophenotypes that predict vulnerability and resilience. The neuroplasticity model of depression recovery strongly implies that full recovery from depression will not be possible with drug treatment alone. Psychosocial therapies are crucial for full recovery as they are important to select or maintain appropriate network connections. Learning cognitive control of emotions will improve or strengthen the top-down control influences of the PFC on limbic responses. Neuroimaging studies of psychotherapy will enhance our understanding of how psychotherapy affects the brain function and mediates the recovery process and this knowledge would further validate psychotherapy in the eyes of patients and clinicians.

Neuroimaging plays an important role in new drug discoveries as this approach allows validation of brain targets in mental disorders. Animal models of depression cannot identify brain targets for drug discovery and development. Also, brain markers may be more sensitive than clinical measures of change with medication. Hence small test populations will be sufficient to screen candidate drugs (Agid *et al.*, 2007). Further, neuroimaging methods allow for the screening of drugs that promote reorganization of decompensated functional networks of emotional regulation. Neuroimaging methods permit personalized treatment plans based on brain markers of treatment responsiveness and recovery (Mayberg, 2007). Such plans may allow for the selection of pharmacological treatment and psychotherapies for an individual patients. In conclusion, the neural network model of depression offers the promise to provide an empirical framework to validate effective individualized treatments for depression, and to achieve the ultimate goal of full recovery and possibly a cure for depression.

REFERENCES

Abercrombie, H. C., Schaefer, S. M., Larson, C. L., Oakes, T. R., Lindgren, K. A., Holden, J. E., Perlman, S. B., Turski, P. A., Krahn, D. D., Benca, R. M., & Davidson, R. J. (1998). Metabolic rate in the right amygdala predicts negative affect in depressed patients. *Neuroreport, 9*(14), 3301–3307.

Adlard, P. A., & Cotman, C. W. (2004). Voluntary exercise protects against stress-induced decreases in brain-derived neurotrophic factor protein expression. *Neuroscience, 124*, 985–992.

Agid, Y., Buzsaki, G., Diamond, D. M., Frackowiak, R., Giedd, J., Girault, J. A., Grace, A., Lambert, J. J., Manji, H., Mayberg, H., Popoli, M., Prochiantz, A., Richter-Levin, G., Somogyi, P., Spedding, M., Svenningsson, P., & Weinberger, D. (2007). How can drug discovery for psychiatric disorders be improved? *Nature Reviews Drug Discovery, 6*, 189–201.

Alexander, G. E., DeLong, M. R., Strick, P. L., (1986). Parallel organization of functionally segregated circuits linking basal ganglia and cortex. *Annual Review of Neuroscience, 9*, 357–381.

Altar, C. A., Whitehead, R. E., & Chen, R. (2003). Effects of electroconvulsive seizures and antidepressant drugs on brain-derived neurotrophic factor protein in rat brain. *Biological Psychiatry, 54*, 703–709.

Anand, A., Li, Y., Wang, Y., Wu, J., Gao, S., Bukhari, L., Mathews, V. P., Kalnin, A., & Lowe, M. J. (2005). Activity and connectivity of brain mood regulating circuit in depression: A functional magnetic resonance study. *Biological Psychiatry, 57*, 1079–1088.

Aquizerate, B., Martin-Guehl, C., & Cuny, E. (2005). Deep brain stimulation for OCD and major depression. *American Journal of Psychiatry, 162*, 2192.

Aydemir, C., Yalcin, E. S., & Aksaray, S. (2006). Brain-derived neurotrophic factor (BDNF) changes in the serum of depressed women. *Progress in Neuropsychopharmacology Biological Psychiatry, 30*, 1256–1260.

Barden, N. (2004). Implication of the hypothalamic-pituitary-adrenal axis in the physiopathology of depression. *Journal of Psychiatry Neuroscience, 29*, 185–193.

Baumann, B., Dano, P., Krell, D., Diekmann, S., Leschinger, A., & Stauch, R. (1999). Reduced volume of limbic systems-affiliated basal ganglia in mood disorders: Preliminary data from a postmorten study. *Journal of Neuropsychiatry Clinical Neuroscience, 11*, 71–78.

Beauregard, M., Levesque, J., & Bourgouin, P. (2001). Neural correlates of conscious regulation of negative emotion. *Journal of neuroscience, 21*, RC165.

Beauregard, M., Paquette, V., & Levesque, J. (2006). Dysfunction in the neural circuitry of emotional self regulation in major depressive disorder. *Neuroreport*, *17*, 843–846.

Bechara, A., Damasio, H., Tranel, D., & Anderson, S. W. (1998). Dissociation of working memory from decision making within the human prefrontal cortex. *Journal of Neuroscience*, *18*, 428–437.

Bell-McGinty, S., Butters, M. A., & Meltzer, C. C. (2002). Brain morphometric abnormalities in geriatric depression: Long-term neurobiological effects of illness duration. *American Journal of Psychiatry*, *159*, 1424–1427.

Baxter, L. R., Schwartz, J. M., Phelps, M. E., Mazziota, J. C., Guze, B. H., & Selin, C. E. (1989). Reduction of prefrontal cortex glucose metabolism common to three types of depression. *Archives of General Psychiatry*, *46*, 243–250.

Bench, C. J., Friston, K. J., Brown, R. G., Scott, L. C., Frackowiak, R. S. J., & Dolan, R. J. (1992). The anatomy of melancholia-focal abnormalities of cerebral blood flow in Major depression. *Psychological Medicine*, *22*, 607–615.

Bench, C. J., Frackowiak, R. S. J., & Dolan, D. J. (1995). Changes in cerebral blood flow on recovery from depression. *Psychological Medicine*, *25*, 247–251.

Bezchlibnyk, Y. B., Sun, X., Wang J. F., Macqueen, G., McEwen, B. S., & Young, L. T. (2007). Neuron somal size is decreased in the lateral amygdalar nucleus of subjects with bipolar disorder. *Journal of Psychiatry and Neuroscience*, *32*, 203–210.

Bowen, D. M., Najlerahim, A., Procter, A. W. Francis, P. T., & Murphy, E. (1989). Circumscribed changes of the cerebral cortex in neuropsychiatric disorders of later life. *Proceedings of the National Academy of Science USA*, *86*, 9504–9508.

Bowley, M. P., Drevets, W. C., Ongur, D., & Price, J. L. (2002). Low glial numbers in the amygdala in major depressive disorder. *Biological Psychiatry*, *52*, 404–412.

Bremner, J. D. (2003). Longterm effects of childhood abuse on brain and neurobiology. *Child and Adolescent Psychiatric Clinics*, *12*, 271–292.

Bremner, J. D., Innis, R. B., Salomon, R. M., Staib, L. H., Ng, C. K., & Miller, H. L. (1997). Positron emission tomography measurement of cerebral metabolic correlates of tryptophan depletion-induced depressive relapse. *Archives of General Psychiatry*, *54*, 346–374.

Brody, A. L., Saxena, S., & Stoessel, P. (2001). Regional brain metabolic changes in patients with major depression treated with either paroxetine or interpersonal therapy. *Archives of General Psychiatry*, *58*, 631–640.

Bush, G., Lu, R., & Posner, M. I. (2000). Cognitive and emotional influences in anterior cingulate cortex. *Trends in Cognitive Sciences*, *4*, 215–222.

Caetano, S. C., Kaur, S., & Brambilla, P. (2006). Smaller cingulate volumes in unipolar depressed patients. *Biological Psychiatry*, *59*, 702–706.

Campbell, S., & MacQueen, G. (2004). The role of the hippocampus in the pathophysiology of major depression. *Journal of Psychiatry Neuroscience*, *29*, 417–426.

Campbell, S., & MacQueen, G. (2006). An update on regional brain volume differences associated with mood disorders. *Current Opinion in Psychiatry*, *19*, 25–33.

Caspi, A., Sugden, K., & Moffitt, T. E. (2003). Influence of life stress on depression: Moderation by a polymorphism in the 5-HTT gene. *Science*, *301*, 386–389.

Castren, E. (2005). Is mood chemistry?. *Nature Reviews Neuroscience*, *6*, 244–245.

Chana, G., Landau, S., Beasley, C., Everall, I. P., & Cotter, D. (2003). Two-dimensional assessment of cytoarchitecture in the anterior cingulate cortex in major depressive disorder, bipolar disorder, and schizophrenia: evidence for decreased neuronal somal size and increased neuronal density. *Biological Psychiatry*, *53*, 1086–1098.

Chen, B., Dowlatshahi, D., & MacQueen, G. M. (2001). Increased hippocampal BDNF immunoreactivity in subjects treated with antidepressant medication. *Biological Psychiatry*, *50*, 260–265.

Clark, L., Sarna, A., & Goodwin, G. M. (2005). Impairment of executive function but not memory in first-degree relatives of patients with bipolar disorder and in euthymic patients with unipolar depression. *American Journal of Psychiatry*, *162*, 1980–1982.

Cohen, R. A., Grieve, S., Hoth, K. F., Paul, R. H., Sweet, L., Tate, D., Gunstad, J., Stroud, L., McCaffery, J., Hitsman, B., Niaura, R., Clark, C. R., MacFarlane, A., Bryant, R., Gordon, E., & Williams, L. M. (2006). Early life stress and morphometry of the adult anterior cingulate cortex and caudate nuclei. *Biological Psychiatry*, *59*(10), 975–982.

Cummings, J. L. (1995). Anatomic and behavioral aspects of frontal-subcortical circuits. *Annals of New York Academy of Science*, *769*, 1–13.

Darbant, E. M., Hariri, A. R., & Meyer-Lindenberg, A. (2006). Catechol *O*-methyltransferase Val 158 Met genotype and neural mechanisms related to affective arousal and regulation. *Archives of General Psychiatry*, *63*, 1396–1406.

Davidson, R. J., Pizzagalli, D., Nitschke, J. B., & Putnam, K. (2002). Depression: Perspectives from affective neuroscience. *Annual Review of Psychology*, *53*, 545–574.

Davis, M., & Whalen, P. J. (2001). The amygdala: Vigilance and emotion. *Molecular psychiatry*, *6*, 13–34.

Devinsky, O., Morrell, M. J., & Vogt, B. A. (1995). Contributions of anterior cingulate cortex to behaviour. *Brain*, *118*, 279–306.

Dolan, R. J., Fletcher, P., Morris, J., Kapur, N., Deakin, J. F., & Frith, C. D. (1996). Neural activation during covert processing of positive emotional expressions. *Neuroimage*, *4*, 194–200.

Drevets, W. C. (1999). Prefrontal cortical-amygdalar metabolism in major depression. *Annals of the New York Academy of Sciences*, *877*, 614–637.

Drevets, W. C. (2000a). Functional anatomical abnormalities in limbic and prefronal cortical structures in major depression. *Progress in Brain Research*, *126*, 413–431.

Drevets, W. C. (2000b). Neuroimaging studies of mood disorders. *Biological Psychiatry*, *48*, 813–829.

Drevets, W. C., & Raichle, M. E. (1992). Neuroanatomical circuits in depression: Implication for treatment mechanism. *Psychopharmacological Bulletin*, *28*, 261–274.

Drevets, W. C., Price, J. L., Simpson, J. R., Jr., Todd, R. D., Reich, T., Vannier, M., & Raichle, M. E. (1997). Subgenual prefrontal cortex abnormalities in mood disorders. *Nature*, *386*, 824–827.

Drevets, W. C., Gadde, K., & Krishnan, R. (1999). Neuroimaging studies of depression. In D. S. Charney, E. J. Nestler, & B. J. Bunney (Eds.), *Neurobiology of Mental Illness* (pp. 394–418). New York: Oxford University Press.

Drevets, W. C., Gautier, C., Price, J. C., Kupfer, D. J., Kinahan, P. E., Grace, A. A., Price, J. L., & Mathis, C. A. (2001). Amphetamine-induced dopamine release in human ventral striatum correlates with euphoria. *Biological Psychiatry*, *49*, 81–96.

Esteves, F., & Ohman, A. (1993). Masking the face: Recognition of emotional facial expressions as a function of the parameters of backward masking. *Scandinavian Journal of Psychology*, *34*, 1–18.

Faure, J. (2007). Early maternal separation alters the response to traumatization: Resulting in increased levels of hippocampal neurotrophic factors. *Metabolic Brain Disease*, *22*, 183–195.

Fossati, P., Hevenor, S. J., Graham, S. J., Grady, C., Keightley, M. L., Craik, F., & Mayberg, H. (2003). In search of the emotional self: An FMRI study using positive and negative emotional words. *American Journal of Psychiatry*, *160*, 1938E–1945E.

Francis, D. D., & Meaney, M. J. (1999). Maternal care and development of stress responses. *Current Opinion in Neurobiology*, *9*, 128–134.

Friston, K. J. (1994). Functional and effective connectivity in neuroimaging: A synthesis. *Human Brain Mapping*, *2*, 56–78.

Frodl, T., Meisenzahl, E. M., & Zetzsche, T. (2004). Hippocampal and amygdala changes in patients with major depressive disorder and healthy controls during a 1-year follow-up. *Journal of Clinical Psychiatry*, *65*, 492–499.

Frodl, T., Schule, C., & Schmitt, G. (2007). Association of the brain-derived neurotrophic factor Val66Met polymorphism with reduced hippocampal volumes in major depression. *Archives of General Psychiatry*, *64*, 410–416.

Fu, C. H., Williams, S. C., Cleare, A. J., Brammer, M. J., Walsh, N. D., & Kim, J. (2004). Attenuation of the neural response to sad faces in major depression by antidepressant treatment: A prospective, event-related functional magnetic resonance imaging study. *Archives of General Psychiatry*, *61*, 877–889.

Ghashghaei, H. T., & Barbas, H. (2002). Pathways for emotion: Interactions of prefrontal and anterior temporal pathways in the amygdala of the rhesus monkey. *Neuroscience, 115*, 1261–1279.

Giacobbe, P., & Kennedy, S. H. (2006). Deep brain stimulation for treatment-resistant depression: A psychiatric perspective. *Current Psychiatry Reports, 8*, 437–444.

Goldapple, K., Segal, Z., Garson, C., Lau, M., Bieling, P., Kennedy, S., & Mayberg, H. (2004). Modulation of cortical-limbic pathways in major depression. *Archives in General Psychiatry, 61*, 34–41.

Hamidi, M., Drevets, W. C., & Price, J. L. (2004). Glial reduction in amygdala in major depressive disorder is due to oligodendrocytes. *Biological Psychiatry, 55*, 563–569.

Hariri, A. R., Mattay, V. S., Tessitore, A., Frea, F., & Goldman, D. (2002). Serotonin transporter genetic variation and the response of the human amygdala. *Science, 297*, 400–403.

Hariri, A. R., Drabant, E. M., & Weinberger, D. R. (2006). Imaging genetics: perspectives from studies of genetically driven variation in serotonin function and corticolimbic affective processing. *Biological Psychiatry, 59*(10), 888–897.

Harmer, C. J., Mackay, C. E., & Reid, C. B. (2006) Antidepressant drug treatment modifies the neural processing of nonconscious threat cues. *Biological Psychiatry, 59*, 816–820.

Hastings, R. S., Parsey, R. V., Oquendo, M. A., Arango, V., & Mann, J. J. (2004). Volumetric analysis of the prefrontal cortex, amygdala, and hippocampus in major depression. *Neuropsychopharmacology, 29*, 952–959.

Heim, C., Newport, D. J., Heit, S., Graham, Y. P., Wilcox, M., Bonsall, R., Miller, A. H., & Nemeroff, C. B. (2002). Pituitary-adrenal and autonomic responses to stress in women after sexual and physical abuse in childhood. *JAMA: The Journal of the American Medical Association, 284*(5), 592–597.

Heinz, A., Braus, D. F., Smolka, M. N., Wrase, J , Puls, I., Hermann, D., Klein, S., Grusser, S. M., Flor, H., Schumann, G., Mann, K., & Buchel, C. (2005). Amygdala-prefrontal coupling depends on a genetic variation of the serotonin transporter. *Nature Neuroscience, 8*, 20–21.

Herman, J. P., & Cullinan, W. E. (1997). Neurocircuitry of stress: Central control of the hypothalamo-pituitary-adrenocortical axis. *Trends in Neuroscience, 20*, 78–84.

Heuser, I. J., Schweiger, U., & Gotthardt, U. (1995). Pituitary-adrenal-system regulation and psychopathology during amitriptyline treatment in elderly depressed patients and normal comparison subjects. *American Journal of Psychiatry, 15?*, 93–99.

Hickie, I., Naismith, S., & Ward, P. B. (2005). Reduced hippocampal volumes and memory loss in patients with early- and late-onset depression *British Journal of Psychiatry, 186*, 197–202.

Hickie, I. B., Naismith, S. L., & Ward, P. B. (2007). Serotonin transporter gene status predicts caudate nucleus but not amygdala or hippocampal volumes in older persons with major depression. *Journal of Affective Disorders, 98*, 137–142.

Hoshaw, B. A. (2005). Central administration of IGF-I and BDNF leads to long-lasting antidepressant-like effects. *Brain Research, 1037*, 204–208.

Jacobson, L., & Saplosky, R. M. (1991). The role of the hippocampus in feed back regulation of the hypothalamic-pituitary-adrenocortical axis. *Endocrine Review, 12*, 118–134.

Johnstone, T., Van Reekum, C. M., Urry, H. L., Kalin, N. H., & Davidson, R. J. (2007). Failure to regulate: Counterproductive recruitment of top-down prefrontal-subcortical circuitary in major depression. *Journal of Neuroscience, 27*, 8877–8884.

Karege, F., Perret, G., & Bondolfi, G. (2002). Decreased serum brain-derived neurotrophic factor levels in major depressed patients. *Psychiatry Research, 109*, 143–148.

Karege, F., Bondolfi, G., & Gervasoni, N. (2005). Low brain-derived neurotrophic factor (BDNF) levels in serum of depressed patients probably results from lowered platelet BDNF release unrelated to platelet reactivity. *Biological Psychiatry, 57*, 1068–1072.

Kaufman, J., Plotsky, P. M., Nemeroff, C. B., & Charney, D. S. (2000). Effects of early adverse experiences on brain structure and function: Clinical implications. *Biological Psychiatry, 48*, 778–790.

Keightley, M. L., Seminowicz, D. A., Bagby, A. M., Costa, P. T., Fossati, P., & Mayberg, H. S (2003). Personality influences limbic-cortical interactions during sad mood induction. *NeuroImage, 20*, 2031–2039.

Kendler, K. S., Thornton, L. M., & Gardner, C. O. (2001). Stressful life events and previous episodes and stressful life events in predicting onset of depression. *American Journal of Psychiatry, 158*, 582–586.

Kendler, K. S., Khun, J. W., Vittum, J., Prescott, C. A., & Riley, B. (2005). The interaction of stressful life events and serotonin transporter polymorphism in the prediction of episodes of major depression: A replication. *Archives of General Psychiatry, 62*, 529–535.

Kennedy, S. H., Evans, R., Kruger, S., Mayberg, H. S., Meyer, J. H., McCam, S., Arifuzzman, A. L., Houle, S., & Vaccarino, F. J. (2001). Changes in regional brain glucose metabolism measured with position emission tomography after paroxetine treatment of major depression. *American Journal of Psychiatry, 158*, 889–905.

Kessler, R. C. (1997). The effects of stressful life events on depression. *Annual Review of Psychology, 48*, 191–214.

Ketter, T. A., Kimbrell, T. A., George, M. S., Dunn, R. T., Speer, A. M., Benson, B. E., Willis, M. W., Danielson, A., Frye, M. A., Herscovitch, P., & Post, R. M. (2001). Effects of mood and subtype on cerebral glucose metabolism in treatment-resistant bipolar disorder. *Biological Psychiatry, 49*, 97–109.

Koob, G. F., & Le Moal, M. (2001). Drug addiction, dysregulation of reward, and allostasis. *Neuropsychopharmacology, 24*, 97–129.

Krishnan, K. R. R., McDonald, W. M., Escalona, P. R., Doraiswamy, P. M., Na, C., & Husain, M. M. (1992). Magnetic resonance imaging of the caudate nuclei in depression: Preliminary observations. *Archives of General Psychiatry, 49*, 553–557.

Kruger, S., Seminowicz, D., Goldapple, K., Kennedy, S. H., & Mayberg, H. (2003). State and trait influences on mood regulation in bipolar disorder: Blood flow differences with an acute mood challenge. *Biological Psychiatry, 54*, 1274–1283.

Kruger, S., Alda, M., Young, T. L., Goldapple, K., Parikh, S., & Mayberg, H. S. (2006). Risk and resilience markers in bi polar disorder: brain responses to emotional challenge in bipolar patients and their healthy siblings. *American Journal of Psychiatry, 163*, 224–257.

Lacerda, A. L., Brambilla, P., Sassi, R. B., Nicoletti, M. A., Mallinger, A. G., Frank, E., Kupfer, D. J., Keshavan, M. S., & Soares, J. C. (2005). Anatomical MRI study of corpus callosum in unipolar depression. *Journal of Psychiatric Research, 39*, 347–354.

Lange, C., & Irle, E. (2004). Enlarged amygdala volume and reduced hippocampal volume in young women with major depression. *Psychological Medicine, 34*, 1059–1064.

Levkovitz, Y., Grisaru, N., & Segal, M. (2001). Transcranial magnetic stimulation and antidepressive drugs share similar cellular effects in rat hippocampus. *Neuropsychopharmacology, 24*, 608–616.

Li, B., Suemaru, K., Cui, R., & Araki, H. (2007). Repeated electroconvulsive stimuli have long-lasting effects on hippocampal BDNF and decrease immobility time in the rat forced swim test. *Life Science, 80*, 201–10.

Liotti, M., Mayberg, H. S., McGinnis, S., Brannan, S., & Jerabek, P. (2002). Unmasking disease-specific cerebral blood flow abnormalities: Mood challenge in patients with remitted unipolar depression. *American Journal of Psychiatry, 159*, 1830–1840.

Lloyd, A. J., Ferrier, I. N., & Barber, R. (2004). Hippocampal volume change in depression: Late- and early-onset illness compared. *British Journal of Psychiatry, 184*, 488–495.

Lorberbaum, J. P., Newman, J. D., Horwitz, A. R., Dubno, J. R., Lydiard, R. B., Hammer, M. B., Bohning, D. E., & George, M. S. (2002). A potential role for thalamocingulate circuitry in human maternal behavior. *Biological Psychiatry, 51*, 431–445.

MacMillan, S., Szeszko, P. R., & Moore, G. J. (2003). Increased amygdala: Hippocampal volume ratios associated with severity of anxiety in pediatric major depression. *Journal of Child Adolescent Psychopharmacology, 13*, 65–73.

MacQueen, G. M., Campbell, S., & McEwen, B. S. (2003). Course of illness, hippocampal function, and hippocampal volume in major depression. *Proceedings of National Academy of Sciences USA, 100*, 1387–1392.

Malberg, J. E., Platt, B., Rizzo, S. J., Ring, S. H., Lucki, I., Schechter, L. E., & Rosenzweig-Lipson, S. (2007). Increasing the levels of insulin-like growth factor-I by an IGF binding protein inhibitor produces anxiolytic and antidepressant-like effects. *Neuropsychopharmacology, 32*, 2360–2368.

Malberg, J. E., & Duman, R. S. (2003). Cell proliferation in adult hippocampus is decreased by inescapable stress: Reversal by fluoxetine treatment. *Neuropsychopharmacology, 28*, 1562–1571.

Matsuo, K., Glahn, D. C., Peluso, M. A. M., Hatch, J. P., Monkul, E. S., Najt, P., Sanches, M., Zamarripa, F., Li, J., Lancaster, J. L., Fox, P. T., Gao, J.-H., & Soares, J. C. (2007). Prefrontal hyperactivation during working memory task in untreated individuals with major depressive disorder. *Molecular Psychiatry, 12*, 158–166.

Mayberg, H. S. (1994). Frontal lobe dysfunction in secondary depression. *Journal of Neuropsychiatry & Clinical Neurosciences, 6*(4), 428–442.

Mayberg, H. S. (1997). Limbic-cortical dysregulation: A proposed model of depression. *Journal of Neuropsychiatry & Clinical Neurosciences, 9*, 471–481.

Mayberg, H. S. (2003). Modulating dysfunctional limbic-cortical circuits in depression: Towards development of brain-based algorithms for diagnosis and optimized treatment. *British Medical Bulletin, 65*, 193–207.

Mayberg, H. S. (2006). Defining neurocircuits in depression: Strategies toward treatment selection based on the neuroimaging phenotypes. *Psychiatric Annals, 36*, 259–268.

Mayberg, H. S. (2007). Defining the neural circuitry of depression: Toward a new nosology with therapeutic implications. *Biological Psychiatry, 61*(6), 729–730.

Mayberg, H. S., Lewis, P. J., Regenold, W., & Wagner, H. N., Jr. (1994). Paralimbic hypoperfusion in unipolar depression. *Journal of Nuclear Medicine, 35*(6), 929–934.

Mayberg, H. S., Brannan, S. K., Mahurin, R. K., Jerabek, P. A., & Brickman, J. S. (1997). Cingulate function in depression: A potential predictor of treatment response. *NeuroReport, 8*, 1057–1061.

Mayberg, H. S., Liotti, M., Brannan, S. K., McGinnis, S., & Mahurin, R. K. (1999). Reciprocal limbic-cortical function and negative mood: Converging PET findings in depression and normal sadness. *American Journal of Psychiatry, 156*, 675–682.

Mayberg, H. S., Brannan, S. K., & Mahurin, R. K. (2000). Regional metabolic effects of fluoxetine in major depression: Serial changes and relationship to clinical response. *Biological Psychiatry, 48*, 830–843.

Mayberg, H. S., Lozano, A. M., & Voon, V. (2005). Deep brain stimulation for treatment-resistant depression. *Neuron, 45*, 651–660.

McDonald, C., Bullmore, E., Sham, P., Chitnis, X., Suckling, J., MacCabe, J., Walshe, M., & Murray, R. M. (2005). Regional volume deviations of brain structure in schizophrenia and psychotic bipolar disorder: Computational morphometry study. *British Journal of Psychiatry, 186*, 369–377.

Morris, J. S., Ohman, A., & Dolan, R. J. (1998). Conscious and unconscious emotional learning in the human amygdala. *Nature, 393*, 467–470.

Nickel, T., Sonntag, A., & Schill, J. (2003). Clinical and neurobiological effects of tianeptine and paroxetine in major depression. *Journal of Clinical Psychopharmacology, 23*, 155–168.

Nemeroff, C. C. (2004). Early-life adversity, CRF dysregulation, and vulnerability to mood and anxiety disorders. *Psychopharmacology Bulletin, 38*, 14–20.

Nestler, E. J. (2002). Neurobiology of depression. *Neuron, 34*, 13–25.

Nestler, E. J., & Carlezon, W. A., Jr. (2006). The mesolimbic dopamine reward circuit in depression. *Biological Psychiatry, 59*, 1151–1159.

Nofzinger, E. A., Buysse, D. J., Germain, A., Carter, C., Luna, B., Price, J. C., Meltzer, C. C., & Miewald, J. M. (2004). In: C. F. 3rd Reynolds, & D. J. Kupfer. Increased activation of anterior paralimbic and executive cortex from waking to rapid eye movement sleep in depression. *Archives of General Psychiatry, 61*, 695–702.

Ochsner, K. N., Bunge, S. A., Gross, J. J., & Gabrieli, J. D. (2002). Rethinking feelings: An FMRI study of the cognitive regulation of emotions. *Journal of Cognitive Neuroscience, 14*, 1215–1229.

Ochsner, K. N., Ray, R. D., Cooper, J. C., Robertson, E. R., Chopra, S., Gabrielli, J. D., & Gross, J. J. (2004). For better or worse: Neural systems supporting the cognitive down- and up-regulation of negative emotion. *Neuroimage*, *23*, 483–499.

Pezawas, L., Meyer-Lindenberg, A., Drabant, E. M., Verchinski, B. A., Munoz, K. E., Kolachana, B. S., Egan, M. F., Mattay, V. S., Hariri, A. R., & Weinberger, D. R. (2005). 5-HTTLPR polymorphism impacts human cingulated-amygdala regulatory interactions: A genetic susceptibility mechanism for depression. *Nature Neuroscience*, *8*, 828–834.

Pham, K., Nacher, J., & Hof, P. R. (2003). Repeated restraint stress suppresses neurogenesis and induces biphasic PSA-NCAM expression in the adult rat dentate gyrus. *European Journal of Neuroscience*, *17*, 879–886.

Phan, K. L., Fitzgerald, D. A., Nathan, P. J., Moore, G. J., Uhde, T. W., & Tancer, M. E. (2005). Neural substrates for voluntary suppression of negative affect: A functional magnetic resonance imaging study. *Biological Psychiatry*, *57*, 210–219.

Price, J. L. (1999). Networks within the orbital and medial prefrontal cortex. *Neurocase*, *5*, 231–241.

Rajkowska, G. (2000). Postmortem studies in mood disorders indicated altered numbers of neurons and glial cells. *Biological Psychiatry*, *48*, 766–777.

Rajkowska, G., Selemon, L. D., & Goldman-Rakic, P. S. (1997). Marked glial neuropathology in prefrontal cortex distinguishes bipolar disorder from schizophrenia. *Schizophrenia Research*, *24*, 41.

Rajkowska, G., Miguel-Hidalgo, J. J., Wei, J., Dilley, G., Pittman, S. D., Meltzer, H. Y., Overholser, J. C., & Stockmeier, C. A. (1999). Morphometric evidence for neuronal and glial prefrontal cell pathology in major depression. *Biological Psychiatry*, *45*, 1085–1098.

Ramasubbu, R., Maslovitch, S., Peltier, S., Holtzheimer, P., Heim, C., & Mayberg, H. (2007). Neural representation of maternal face processing: A functional magnetic resonance imaging study. *Canadian Journal of Psychiatry*, *52*, 726–734.

Rauch, S. L. (2003). Neuroimaging and neurocircuitry models pertaining to the neurosurg. *Clinics of North America*, *14*, 213–223.

Roffman, J., Marci, C. D., Glick, D. M., Dougherty, D. D., & Rauch, S. L. (2005). Neuroimaging and the functional neuroanatomy of psychotherapy. *Psychological Medicine*, *35*, 1385–1398.

Rogers, M. A., Bradshaw, J. L., Pantelis, C., & Philips, J. G. (1998). Frontostriatal deficits in unipolar major depression. *Brain Research Bulletin*, *47*, 297–310.

Rolls, E. T. (1995). A theory of emotion and consciousness, and its application to understanding the neural basis of emotion. In M. S. Gazzaniga (Ed.), *The Cognitive Neurosciences* (pp. 1091–1106). Cambridge MA: MIT Press.

Rusch, B. D., Abercrombie, H. C., & Oakes, T. R. (2001). Hippocampal morphometry in depressed patients and control subjects: Relations to anxiety symptoms. *Biological Psychiatry*, *50*, 960–964.

Sapolsky, R., Rivier, C., & Yamamoto, G. (1987). Interleukin-1 stimulates the secretion of hypothalamic corticotropin-releasing factor. *Science*, *238*, 522–524.

Saylam, C., Ucerler, H., & Kitis, O. (2006). Reduced hippocampal volume in drug-free depressed patients. *Surgical and Radiological Anatomy*, *28*, 82–87.

Schaefer, S. M., Jackson, D. C., Davidson, R. J., Aguirre, G. K., Kimberg, D. Y., & Thompson-Schill, S. L. (2002). Modulation of amygdala activity by the conscious regulation of negative emotion. *Journal of Cognitive Neuroscience*, *14*, 913–921.

Seibyl, J. P., Scanley, B. E., Krystal, J. H., & Innis, R. B. (2004). Neuroimaging methodologies: Utilizing radiotracers or nuclear magnetic resonance. In D. S. Charney & E. J. Nestler (Eds.), *Neurobiology of Mental Illness* (pp. 190–209). Oxford University Press: New York.

Seminowicz, D. A., Mayberg, H. S., Mcintosh, A. R., Goldapple, K. K., Kennedy, S. H., Segal, Z., & Rafi-Tari, S. (2004). Limbic-frontal circuitry in major depression: A path modeling meta analysis. *Neuroimage*, *22*, 409–418.

Sheline, Y. I., Sanghavi, M., & Mintun, M. A. (1999). Depression duration but not age predicts hippocampal volume loss in medically healthy women with recurrent major depression. *Journal of Neuroscience*, *19*, 5034–5043.

Sheline, Y. I., Barch, D. M., Donnelly, J. M., Ollinger, J. M., Snyder, A. Z., & Mintun, M. A. (2001). Increased amygdala response to masked emotional faces in depressed subjects resolves with antidepressant treatment. *An fMRI Study Biological Psychiatry*, *50*, 551–658.

Sheline, Y. I., Gado, M. H., & Kraemer, H. C. (2003). Untreated depression and hippocampal volume loss. *American Journal of Psychiatry*, *160*, 1515–1518.

Smith, K. A., Morris, J. S., Friston, K. J., Cowen, P. J., & Dolan, R. J. (1999). Brain mechanisms associated with depressive relapse and associated cognitive impairment following tryptophan depletion. *British Journal of Psychiatry*, *174*, 525–529.

Smolka, M. N., Shumann, G., Wrase, J., Grusser, S. M., Flor, H., Mann, K., Braus, D. F., Goldman, D., Buchel, C., & Heinz, A. (2005). Catechol-*O*-Methyltransferase val158 met genotype affects processing of emotional stimuli in the amygdala and prefrontal cortex. *Journal of Neuroscience*, *12*(4), 836–842.

Smolka, M. N., Buhler, M., Schumann, G., Klein, S., Hu, X.-Z., Moayer, M., Zimmer, A., Wrase, J., Flor, H., Mann, K., Braus, D. F., Goldman, D., & Heinz, A. (2007). Gene-gene effects on central processing of aversive stimuli. *Molecular Psychiatry*, *12*, 307–317.

Stockmeier, C. A., Mahajan, G. J., Konick, L. C., Overholser, J. C., Jurjus, G. J., Meltzer, H. Y., Uylings, H. B., Friedman, L., & Rajkowska, G. (2004). Cellular changes in the postmortem hippocampus in major depression. *Biological Psychiatry*, *56*, 640–650.

Taylor, W. D., Steffens, D. C., & Payne, M. E. (2005). Influence of serotonin transporter promoter region polymorphisms on hippocampal volumes in late-life depression. *Archives of General Psychiatry*, *62*, 537–544.

Ueyama, T., Kawai, Y., & Nemoto, K. (1997) Immobilization stress reduced the expression of neurotrophins and their receptors in the rat brain. *Neuroscience Research*, *28*, 103–110.

Vakili, K., Pillay, S. S., & Lafer, B. (2000). Hippocampal volume in primary unipolar major depression: A magnetic resonance imaging study. *Biological Psychiatry*, *47*, 1087–1090.

Veith, R. C., Lewis, N., Linares, O. A., Barnes, R. F., Raskind, M. A., & Villacres, E. C. (1994). Sympathetic nervous system activity in major depression. *Archives of General Psychiatry*, *51*, 411–422.

Videbech, P., & Ravnkilde, B. (2004). Hippocampal volume and depression: A meta-analysis of MRI studies. *American Journal of Psychiatry*, *161*, 1957–1966.

Vythilingam, M., Heim, C., & Newport, J. (2002). Childhood trauma associated with smaller hippocampal volume in women with major depression. *American Journal of Psychiatry*, *159*, 2072–2080.

Westheide, J. (2007). Neuropsychological performance in partly remitted unipolar depressive patients: focus on executive functioning. *European Archives of Psychiatry and Clinical Neuroscience*, *257*, 389–395.

Whelan, P. J., Rauch, S. L., Etcoff, N. L. McInerney, S. C., Lee, M. B., & Jenike, M. A. (1998). Masked presentations of emotional facial expressions modulate amygdala activity without explicit knowledge. *Journal of Neuroscience*, *18*, 411–418.

Xu, H., Luo, C., & Richardson, J. S. (2004). Recovery of hippocampal cell proliferation and BDNF levels, both of which are reduced by repeated restraint stress, is accelerated by chronic venlafaxine. *Pharmacogenomics Journal*, *4*, 322–331.

Yehuda, R. (1997). Stress and glucocorticoid. *Science*, *275*, 1662–1663.

Zakzanis, K. K., Leach, L., & Kaplan, E. (1998). On the nature and pattern of neurocognitive function in major depressive disorder. *Neuropsychiatry Neuropsychology & Behavioural Neurology*, *11*, 111–119.

Zink, C. F., Pagnoni, G., & Chappelow, J. (2006). Human striatal activation reflects degree of stimulus saliency. *Neurimage*, *29*(3), 977–983.

4

NEUROCHEMICAL AND TRANSMITTER MODELS OF DEPRESSION

HYMIE ANISMAN, KIM MATHESON
AND SHAWN HAYLEY

Institute of Neuroscience, Life Science Research Centre, Carleton University, Ottawa, Ontario, Canada

The processes related to major depressive disorder (MDD) have been explored from multiple perspectives, and it is clear that several organismic variables (genetic, age, and sex) and experiential factors (ongoing stressors, previous stressful experiences) contribute to the provocation and the maintenance of this illness, as well as relapse/recurrence that frequently occurs following successful treatment. Just as the symptoms of depression, as well as the etiological processes associated with MDD vary across individuals, the disorder appears to be biochemically heterogeneous (Hasler *et al.*, 2004; Millan, 2006). Multiple neurochemical processes may additively or interactively subserve MDD, and the constellation of factors that are related to depression in one individual may differ from those associated with depression in a second. The present review is meant to provide a broad overview of some of the neurochemical processes that have been implicated in MDD, including the classical neurotransmitters, as well as more recent conceptualizations concerning mechanisms that might underlie this illness.

The data regarding the biochemical processes subserving MDD have come from several different approaches. These have included (1) biochemical and pharmacological analyses using animal models of the disorder, (2) pharmacological studies assessing the effectiveness of antidepressants, and other agents, in modifying depressive illness, (3) analyses of hormones and neurochemical factors in blood and cerebrospinal fluid, (4) imaging studies (e.g., PET, fMRI) that evaluated neuroanatomical and functional changes in specific brain regions, (5) analyses of neurochemical factors in postmortem tissues, mainly from brain samples of depressed individuals that had died by suicide, and (6) genetic analyses (polymorphisms) related to depression. Although, each research avenue has considerable merit, the data that have been derived both within and between these approaches have not always provided a uniform portrayal of the processes governing the illness.

Inasmuch as the symptoms of depression, the hormonal/neurochemical responses elicited by stressful events, and the efficacy of pharmacological treatments differ across individuals, it comes as no surprise that the biological correlates of depression also vary widely. This variability, coupled with inconsistencies of findings regarding the mechanisms subserving depression, has lead investigators to question the viability of assessing depressive illness as a unitary syndrome. In fact, such findings provided the impetus for a paradigm shift, wherein greater attention has focused on evaluating endophenotypes that comprise the disorder (e.g., genetic and biological components that link to specific characteristics of the illness; Cryan & Slattery, 2007). This approach may be particularly effective, as it allows for analysis of linkages between specific genes, intermediate factors, and features (phenotypes) of the illness. As well, the approach may facilitate the identification of risk factors, or premorbid conditions, responsible for the wide variability evident concerning the features of depression and the variability that exists regarding the impact of experiential factors (e.g., stressors) on the provocation of MDD. As will be seen, several risk factors for MDD have, in fact, been shown to moderate the effects of stressors (or other experiences) on neurochemical functioning, and might thereby influence the emergence of depression.

The ensuing sections provide brief synopses regarding animal and human experimentation that entailed different approaches to uncovering the processes associated with or leading to depression. It is suggested that, although altered serotonin (5-HT) functioning may play an important role in mediating depressive disorder (Millan, 2006), there has been considerable support for the proposition that corticotropin releasing hormone (CRH) (Reul & Holsboer, 2002) together with arginine vasopressin (AVP) (Hayley *et al.*, 2005) contribute to MDD. It was suggested that CRH and 5-HT processes may reciprocally influence one another's activity, and that $GABA_A$ functioning may be integral in coordinating these effects (Hayley *et al.*, 2005). In addition to these processes, increasingly greater focus has been placed on the potential contribution of growth factors (e.g., brain-derived neurotrophic factor; BDNF) (Duman & Monteggia, 2006; Manji *et al.*, 2001), and there is reason to suspect that activation of the inflammatory immune system, and the resulting neurotransmitter changes and processes related to neurogenesis, might contribute to depressive disorders.

MONOAMINE VARIATIONS ASSOCIATED WITH STRESSORS

Many of the neurochemical changes that occur in response to stressors appear to serve in an adaptive capacity in that they facilitate appropriate responses being adopted, and limit physiological outcomes that might engender adverse effects. However, if the stressor persists, especially when the stressor is uncontrollable or unpredictable, adaptive biological processes may become excessively taxed (allostatic overload), rendering the individual more vulnerable to pathology (McEwen, 2000).

Although several monoamines and their receptors have been implicated in depression, particular attention has been devoted to the contribution of 5-HT functioning, likely owing to the treatment efficacy of selective serotonin reuptake inhibitors (SSRIs) (Millan, 2006). Studies in animals indicated that stressors (including social disturbances) that led to depressive-like behaviors also influenced 5-HT utilization and levels, just as they affected norepinephrine (NE) and dopamine (DA) functioning, and were prominent in brain regions often associated with depression (e.g., hippocampus and prefrontal cortex). In general, the monoamine variations elicited by stressors were robust, and the behavioral disturbances elicited stressors could be antagonized by treatments that increased 5-HT functioning (Anisman & Matheson, 2005).

To a significant degree, the effects of stressors on monoamine functioning are determined by a constellation of factors related to experiential and organismic variables, as well as the characteristics of the stressor itself (Anisman & Matheson, 2005). In the latter regard, it seems that in response to uncontrollable stressors amine utilization exceeds its synthesis, thus engendering reduced NE and 5-HT levels (Hayley *et al.*, 2005). Moreover, stressors that were uncontrollable were particularly effective in provoking 5-HT release at the basolateral amygdala, medial prefrontal cortex (PFC), ventral hippocampus, and nucleus accumbens (Maier *et al.*, 2006). In addition, the functioning of specific 5-HT receptors is thought to be fundamental in determining pathology. In this regard, stressors altered the density of several 5-HT receptor subtypes, such as 5-HT_{1A} (auto)receptors in the dorsal raphe nucleus (the site of 5-HT cell bodies) and hippocampus (Briones-Aranda *et al.*, 2005), and it appeared that an uncontrollable stressor regimen that engendered behavioral impairments (in a learned helplessness paradigm) also increased mRNA expression of 5-HT_{1B} receptors within the DRN (Neumaier *et al.*, 1997). Clearly, aversive events may have pronounced effects on multiple aspects of central monoamine functioning, and these effects are aligned with the controllability of the stressor.

As indicated earlier, several neurochemical changes elicited by stressors may be adaptively significant, but when biological systems are overly taxed, the organism may be at increased risk for pathology (McEwen, 2000). In the case of monoamine alterations, the sustained amine synthesis and utilization provoked by chronic stressor experiences could lead to adverse outcomes, but further compensatory changes occur that might temper the otherwise excessive neuronal activation. For instance, sustained activation of NE and 5-HT functioning may result in down regulation of β-NE receptor activity and the NE sensitive cAMP response, reduced 5-HT_{1B} receptor expression, and elevated frontal cortex 5-HT_{2A} mRNA expression (Hayley *et al.*, 2005). Although these regulatory-like effects may have positive effects, they may also contribute to behavioral disturbances associated with aversive events. For instance, altered hippocampal and hypothalamic 5-HT_{2A} mRNA expression was most pronounced among those rats that displayed behavioral impairments in a learned helplessness test (Dwivedi *et al.*, 2005), but it is equally possible that these receptor changes are not causally related to the behavioral impairments.

SENSITIZATION

The monoamine variations engendered by acute stressors persist for a relatively brief period (typically within the realm of minutes or hours), depending on the nature and severity of the stressor as well as several organismic factors (age, genetics). It is of considerable clinical significance, however, that stressful experiences may proactively influence the response to later aversive events. In particular, among previously stressed animals, re-exposure to a mild stressor (even one that differed from the initial challenge) resulted in elevated mesocortical NE, DA and 5-HT utilization (Anisman *et al.*, 2003), and influenced both 5-HT_{1A} and 5-HT_{2A} receptor density and affinity (Harvey *et al.*, 2003). Given the proactive effects of stressor experiences, it was suggested that the sensitization of neuronal processes might be a key factor that increases vulnerability to later stressor-provoked pathology, as well as the very high rate of illness recurrence that is characteristic of depression (Post, 1992).

No doubt, multiple processes could lead to sensitized neurochemical and behavioral responses, and the processes responsible for the sensitization of a given neurotransmitter (or its receptors) may differ from those associated with a second transmitter process. For instance, a ligand related to CRH_2 receptors might be essential for the sensitization of dorsal raphe 5-HT neuronal activity (Maier & Watkins, 2005), whereas sensitized hypothalamic–pituitary–adrenal (HPA) responses may involve CRH and AVP co-expression within the median eminence (Anisman *et al.*, 2003). Likewise, basic fibroblast growth factor (bFGF), a neurotrophic factor produced by astrocytes, may contribute to the neuronal plasticity and protracted effects elicited by other types of challenges that could be viewed as stressors, such as catecholamine stimulants (Flores & Stewart, 2000). Whatever the case, it seems that stressor (and drug) experiences result in several neurochemical systems becoming sensitized, so that later stressor experiences result in exaggerated neurobiological changes that favor the development of depressive characteristics.

GENETIC ENGINEERING AND BEHAVIORAL IMPAIRMENTS

To a considerable extent, neurochemical accounts of depression suggest that stressful events are most likely to lead to pathology in the presence of particular genetic backgrounds. As such, animal models have increasingly focused on the effects of stressors on behavioral outputs given the deletion (knockout) or insertion (transgenic) of genes that have been implicated as vulnerability factors for depression. It has been shown, for instance, that mice deficient of the 5-HT transporter (5-HTT) exhibited anxiety and depression in several behavioral paradigms (Lira *et al.*, 2003). Moreover, these effects could be antagonized by repeated antidepressant (fluoxetine) treatment (Holmes *et al.*, 2002) as well as by the 5-HT_{1A} antagonist, WAY 100635, suggesting the involvement of 5-HT_{1A} receptors in these outcomes (Holmes *et al.*, 2003). These findings are somewhat paradoxical, as it might have been expected that deletion of the transporter would increase 5-HT availability, and hence diminish depressive symptoms. There are several potential explanations for this outcome, including the possibility that knocking out the gene for 5-HTT from birth may have promoted compensatory changes involving other systems. In fact, treatment over 2 weeks by short interfering RNA (siRNA) mediated knockdown of 5-HTT within the raphe nucleus was associated with attenuated immobility in a forced swim test, just as the antidepressant, citalopram, provoked this outcome (Thakker *et al.*, 2005).

It is of particular interest that although 5-HTT knockout mice displayed hypoactivity, there was no evidence of anhedonia (a key feature of depression) (Kalueff *et al.*, 2006). It may be that 5-HTT influences one component of the depressive profile, whereas 5-HT_{1A} receptor variations that occur secondary to the 5-HTT deletion influences a second component (e.g., anxiety). In line with the perspective that multiple changes are associated with the depressive profile, it was shown that among double knockout mice deficient of both 5-HTT and BDNF, the elevation of ACTH in response to a stressor was especially marked, and the presence of dendrites on hypothalamic and hippocampal neurons was diminished (Ren-Patterson *et al.*, 2005). It may be significant, as well, that studies in 5-HT receptor knockout mice have also indicated that anxiety responses and depression-like characteristics varied between males and females (Jones & Lucki, 2005; Ren-Patterson *et al*, 2006). In this regard, it was suggested that, in females, estrogen may afford protection against the BDNF changes that contribute to depression (Ren-Patterson *et al.*, 2005). Likewise, sex-linked disinhibition of 5-HT release might account for the stressor-elicited 5-HT depletion and the ensuing behavioral impairments (Jones & Lucki, 2005).

STUDIES IN HUMANS: IMAGING, BINDING AND POSTMORTEM ANALYSES

The impact of neurotransmitters is dependent on the functional effectiveness of various types of receptors, including those that appear postsynaptically as well presynaptic autoreceptors that govern transmitter synthesis. There have been numerous reports demonstrating 5-HT receptor changes associated with depression, but frequent inconsistencies across studies exist (Stockmeier, 2003), so that conclusions regarding 5-HT receptor involvement in depression ought to be considered highly provisional.

As 5-HT_{1A} (auto)receptors in the DRN influence 5-HT availability within the forebrain, these receptors have received considerable attention. It was, indeed, reported that 5-HT_{1A} receptors were reduced in the DRN (Drevets *et al.*, 2000; Stockmeier *et al.*, 1998), particularly in the caudal portion of this nucleus (Boldrini *et al.*, 2007). The fact that the rostral DRN was associated with elevated 5-HT_{1A} receptors might account for earlier reports suggesting that this receptor subtype did not differ between controls and depressed suicides (Arango *et al.*, 2001). In addition to the DRN variations, in some studies elevated 5-HT_{1A} receptor binding (Arango *et al.*, 1995) and mRNA expression (Anisman *et al.*, 2008b) were detected in aspects of the PFC and in the CA1 of the hippocampus, but in other studies 5-HT_{1A} binding was reduced. Still other studies revealed that when factors such as age, postmortem interval (between death and tissue extraction), and the time of tissue storage, were controlled for, the 5-HT_{1A} differences between controls and depressed persons that had died by suicide were not evident (Stockmeier, 2003). In light of these findings it seems unlikely that 5-HT_{1A} alterations alone accounted for the appearance of depression, although Positron Emission Tomography (PET) analyses indicated that 5-HT_{1A} binding predicted treatment response (Parsey *et al.*, 2006a,b). Moreover, it appeared that the presence of elevated 5-HT_{1A} binding potential itself was not necessarily evident in depressed patients, but receptor binding differed as a function of whether patients had previously received antidepressant treatment (Parsey *et al.*, 2006b). Thus, diminished 5-HT_{1A} binding in PFC and hippocampus might be related to prior depressive episodes or the individual's drug history.

In addition to 5-HT_{1A} variations, the expression of 5-HT_{1B} protein was diminished in cortical regions of depressed individuals (Svenningsson *et al.*, 2006). This was accompanied by the reduction of mRNA expression for p11 (also known as calpactin I and S100A10), a protein involved in the functional expression of 5-HT_{1B} receptors. We likewise observed that 5-HT_{1B} and p11 mRNA expression were diminished in several brain regions of depressed suicides, including the frontopolar and orbital frontal cortex, as well as the hippocampus and amygdala, and the appearance of p11 was highly correlated with 5-HT_{1B} mRNA expression (Anisman *et al.*, 2008a).

It was reported that 5-HT_{2A} receptors were increased in the PFC of suicides (Lemonde *et al.*, 2003; Turecki *et al.*, 1999), as was mRNA expression of these receptors (Pandey *et al.*, 2002). Interestingly, inositol triphosphate (IP_3), a second messenger of 5-HT, was elevated in the hippocampus of depressed suicides, suggesting that depression (or suicide) was related to hypersensitivity of 5-HT_{2A} receptors (Rosel *et al.*, 2004a, b). As well, PET analysis confirmed that the elevated density of 5-HT_{2A} receptors in the frontal cortex normalized with symptom remission associated with paroxetine treatment (Zanardi *et al.*, 2001). In contrast, other investigators failed to detect differences of 5-HT_{2A} receptors between controls and depressed individuals that died by suicide, and likewise imaging studies of suicide attempters did not show 5-HT_{2A} differences from that of nondepressed individuals (see review in Stockmeier, 2003). Supporting these findings, DNA microarray analyses did not reveal molecular genetic differences within the dorsolateral and ventral PFC of suicides and controls (Sibille *et al.*, 2004). However, increased 5-HT_{2A} binding was reported in the dorsolateral PFC among those patients who scored highly on the Dysfunctional Attitudes Scale, particularly with respect to elevated feelings of pessimism and hopelessness (Meyer *et al.*, 2003). Thus, 5-HT receptor variations might not be a reflection of depression/suicide *per se*, but instead may be aligned with a particular aspect comprising the depressive syndrome.

There have been several reports implicating 5-HT_{2C} receptor variations in depressive illness. In particular, among depressed suicides, RNA editing (which affects second messenger signaling disturbances) was found at specific sites of the 5-HT_{2C} receptor (reviewed in Schmauss, 2003). It is interesting that the altered 5-HT_{2C} editing was also evident in highly stress-reactive mice (BALB/c) that had been exposed to a stressor (Alfonso *et al.*, 2005). However, raising mice in an enriched environment (following weaning) attenuated the behavioral disturbances without affecting 5-HT_{2C} editing (Bhansali *et al.*, 2007). Evidently, the altered 5-HT_{2C} editing and behavioral outcomes could be dissociated from one another, suggesting that the receptor changes were not causally related to behavioral disturbances or that enrichment influences other adaptive processes that affect depressive-like behaviors, despite the presence of disturbed 5-HT_{2C} editing.

As most antidepressants act on uptake processes, it might be expected that MDD would be associated with 5-HTT disturbances, but inconsistent findings have been reported in this regard (Stockmeier, 2003). However, using effective ligands (e.g., ^{3}H-paroxetine and ^{3}H-citalopram), 5-HTT binding was reduced in the PFC of depressed individuals that had died by suicide (Arango *et al.*, 1995). As well, 5-HTT binding was diminished in the amygdala, midbrain and brainstem during a major depressive episode (Malison *et al.*, 1998). Yet, Meyer *et al.* (2004) reported that during a major depressive episode, 5-HTT binding potential was elevated in the PFC, particularly among individuals with exceptionally negative dysfunctional attitudes. Thus, it is possible that the differential effects reported concerning 5-HTT functioning in depression might be related to individual differences regarding depressive symptoms.

Summarizing, although imaging and postmortem analyses revealed several 5-HT receptor and 5-HTT variations associated with depression/suicide, there have been frequent inconsistent findings. In a review of this literature, Stockmeier (2003) accommodated some of the contradictory findings on the basis of factors such as presence of antidepressants (or duration of washout periods), life-time episodes of depression, and the specific aspects of the brain regions examined (e.g., different portions of the PFC, and particularly the importance of the dorsolateral

PFC in association with suicide). One can add to this that particular features of depression may be associated with certain 5-HT receptor changes. Indeed, as patients present with varied symptoms, and are differentially influenced by diverse drug treatments, it would seem likely that different processes are involved in depression across individuals.

GENETIC LINKS BETWEEN SEROTONIN FUNCTIONING AND DEPRESSION

Heritability studies have made it clear that a family history of depression represents a risk factor for the illness, and numerous efforts have been made to determine the gene(s) associated with this disorder (Arango *et al.*, 2003). Several 5-HT-related candidate genes have been identified as potentially being linked to MDD, including 5-HT_{2A} receptor and tryptophan hydroxylase gene polymorphisms, increased frequency of the long (L) allele of the 5-HTT gene (reviewed in Millan, 2006), and a gene polymorphism was detected of a repressor of the 5-HT_{1A} receptor gene promoter (Lemonde *et al.*, 2003). In addition, a polymorphism was discovered regarding the gene controlling tryptophan hydroxylase-2, which translates into reduced 5-HT synthesis. This gene was found to be present at high frequencies among depressed patients and was also predictive of diminished SSRI responsiveness (Zill *et al.*, 2004).

Consistent with postmortem analyses showing that depression/suicide was associated with 5-HTT disturbances, a 5-HTT gene promotor polymorphism (5-HTTLPR) was reported in relation to depression (Arango *et al.*, 2003). Subsequent studies indicated that depression and suicidality were more frequent among individuals with one or two copies of the short allele of the 5-HTT promoter than among individuals that were homozygous for the long allele (Caspi *et al.*, 2003). As well, individuals homozygous for the long allele displayed better SSRI responsivity than did individuals with the short allele (Serretti *et al.*, 2007). Consistent with earlier reports suggesting interplay between 5-HTT and 5-HT_{1A}, it appeared that those individuals homozygous for the short allele also displayed reduced postsynaptic 5-HT_{1A} receptors (David *et al.*, 2005). As these receptors may be fundamental for the effects of SSRIs, this aspect of the 5-HTT promoter polymorphism may account for the blunted response to SSRI treatment.

Of particular interest, however, was the finding that depression was most common among individuals with the short alleles if they had also encountered major life stressors or early life trauma (Caspi *et al.*, 2003). In a related fashion, it was reported that among carriers of the short allele, amygdala and hippocampal functioning was tonically activated and the response to negative events was altered (Canli *et al.*, 2006). In a sense, the tonic activation would have effects like those associated with a chronic state of distress that might be linked to hypervigilance, threat, and rumination. As a result, the response to potent stressors might be augmented, and might thus encourage MDD. These findings suggest that genetic constitution disposes individuals to depression (or increased reactivity to stressors), but the depressive phenotype only emerges upon exposure to particular life challenges.

PHARMACOLOGICAL STUDIES

It will be recalled that pharmacological studies have been used to support a role for 5-HT in subserving MDD. As indicated by Millan (2006), adverse effects associated with older antidepressants were less pronounced using SSRIs, although a good number of side effects still persist. Moreover, it is questionable whether SSRIs have a therapeutic advantage over the earlier generation of antidepressants. Positive therapeutic outcomes of SSRIs are still only at 50–60%, the therapeutic lag is usually 2–4 weeks, residual symptoms persist, and relapse/recurrence is fairly high. This hardly speaks well for this class of antidepressants, and has prompted the endorsement of multi-targeted approaches in the treatment of MDD, as well as the search for biomarkers informative of the most effective treatment strategies.

The effectiveness of SSRIs may be derived, in part from effects on reuptake, but activation of certain 5-HT receptor subtypes, particularly 5-HT_{1A}, 5-HT_{1B}, 5-HT_{2A} and 5-HT_{2C}, likely contribute to the actions of these compounds. As well, there is reason to believe that NE and DA changes contribute to the antidepressant effects of SSRIs (Millan, 2006). Together, these findings, coupled with the beneficial effects of drugs that affect both 5-HT and NE reuptake (serotonin and norepinephrine reuptake inhibitors, SNRIs) speak to the importance of targeting multiple sites to augment the beneficial effects of antidepressants, and concurrently diminish the adverse side effects of the treatments. At the same time, these findings also highlight the likelihood that multiple risk factors, possibly through different neurochemical processes, contribute to the emergence of MDD.

CORTICOTROPIN RELEASING HORMONE

CRH is a primary regulator of the HPA system, and upon stressor exposure it is readily released from the terminal regions of paraventricular (PVN) neurons, acting to promote ACTH secretion from the anterior pituitary, and hence cortisol (corticosterone in rodents) release from the adrenal cortex. Once corticosterone is released, it enters the bloodstream and eventually, through actions on the hippocampus or hypothalamus, causes termination of the CRH response.

In contrast to monoamine variations, the influence of stressor controllability on HPA functioning is limited. The HPA response occurs rapidly, too quickly, in fact, for animals to appraise or learn whether a stressor will be brief or prolonged, controllable or uncontrollable, and predictable or unpredictable. Thus, these factors have limited effects, if any, on circulating HPA hormones. Indeed, the animal's well-being would be best served by a rapid HPA response being mounted, and as information is acquired about the stressor (e.g., its controllability), neuroendocrine responses could be adjusted to meet the demands placed on the organism.

The CRH changes elicited by stressors are not limited to the hypothalamus, being pronounced at mesolimbic sites, including the PFC and various amygdala nuclei. In this regard, stressors were shown to increase CRH mRNA expression and *in vivo* CRH release at the central amygdala (Lee & Davis, 1997; Merali *et al.*, 1998). Moreover, fear-eliciting stimuli increased CRH expression within the central and the basolateral amygdala (LeDoux, 2000), whereas diffuse stimuli that are more closely aligned with general anxiety, promoted greater CRH variations at the bed nucleus of the stria terminalis (Lee & Davis, 1997). Similarly, whereas systemic stressors (e.g., immune challenge) markedly influenced central amygdala activity, psychogenic stressors had more potent effects on the medial amygdala (Dayas *et al.*, 2001).

Consistent with a role for CRH in mediating emotional responses, elevated levels of anxiety were apparent in genetically engineered mice that overproduce CRH (van Gaalen *et al.*, 2002). Conversely, CRH antagonism attenuated the behavioral disturbance associated with uncontrollable shock in a learned helplessness paradigm (Mansbach *et al.*, 1997). Moreover, CRH antagonists attenuated the effects of neurogenic stressors or learned fear cues (e.g., predators). However, antagonists were less effective in attenuating the anxiety associated with naturalistic stressors that were proposed to involve pre-wired neural circuits (Merali *et al.*, 2004b). Thus, although CRH is fundamental in mediating anxiety, other processes may also contribute to emotional responses to particular adverse situations.

CRH RECEPTORS

Two types of CRH receptors, CRH_1 and CRH_2, have been implicated as being involved in stressor-provoked anxiety/depression. Data stemming from animal studies have supported CRH_1 involvement in depression/anxiety, but there is increasing evidence supporting a role for CRH_2 as well. In this regard, anxiety was relatively high in genetically engineered mice in which CRH_1 receptors were elevated (Muller *et al.*, 2003), and conversely, anxiety levels were diminished in CRH_1 receptor knockout mice (Smith *et al.*, 1998). Such effects likely did not involve HPA functioning, as anxiety-like behaviors were reduced among conditional knockout mice in which CRH_1 receptors were selectively inactivated in the anterior forebrain and in limbic brain regions, but leaving pituitary receptors unaffected.

Among mice in which CRH_2 receptors were knocked out, elevated anxiety-like behaviors were apparent (Bale *et al.*, 2000; Kishimoto *et al.*, 2000); however, this effect was most notable among males (Bale *et al.*, 2000). It was proposed that CRH_2 promotes a central anxiolytic response that acts to antagonize the anxiogenic actions stemming from CRH_1 activation (Kishimoto *et al.*, 2000). Using single and double knockouts of the CRH_1 and CRH_2 genes, it was shown that anxiety and HPA neuroendocrine responses to stressors were most closely aligned with CRH_1 functioning (Preil *et al.*, 2001). Interestingly, in the double knockouts there were clear differences in the responses of male and female mice, with males showing an anxiogenic response, whereas females displayed an anxiolytic reaction. Significantly, the effects evident in the double knockouts were moderated by maternal factors (Bale *et al.*, 2002), supporting the critical role of early experiences in determining the actions of genetic contributions. In effect, it seems that both early experiences and gender, well-known risk factors for depression, might have their effects through actions involving specific CRH receptor subtypes.

CRH IN DEPRESSION/SUICIDE

It has long been known that MDD is associated with disturbed HPA functioning, including elevated cortisol levels, early escape from dexamethasone-induced cortisol suppression, and a blunted ACTH response to CRH or dexamethasone/CRH challenge (Nemeroff & Vale, 2005). These endocrine disturbances are not simply correlates or markers of depression, but may play a provocative role in eliciting depression, as glucocorticoid antagonists diminished the symptoms of depression (Belanoff *et al.*, 2001; Murphy, 1997). As well, HPA abnormalities were present prior to the presentation of clinical symptoms among probands of patients with major depression (Holsboer, 2003), raising the possibility that basal cortisol levels could serve as a biomarker for increased risk of illness.

In line with the position that CRH might be involved in depression, elevated concentrations of this hormone were reported in cerebrospinal fluid of depressed patients and CRH mRNA expression and/or CRH immunoreactivity was increased in hypothalamic nuclei, locus coeruleus, PFC, and raphe nuclei of depressed suicides (Bissette *et al.*, 2003; Merali *et al.*, 2004a). Although there have been inconsistent reports regarding variations of central CRH receptor binding in association with depression, it was reported that CRH levels were elevated in the frontopolar and the dorsomedial PFC of depressed individuals who had died by suicide, and this was accompanied by reduced mRNA expression of CRH_1, possibly reflecting a down regulation associated with sustained CRH elevation (Merali *et al.*, 2004a). Although CRH_2 mRNA expression was not affected, supporting a primary role for the CRH_1 receptor in depression, a role for CRH_2 in some capacity should probably not be dismissed (Reul & Holsboer, 2002). This is particularly the case, given the data suggesting sex-dependent involvement of this receptor subtype in anxiety-related behaviors.

As alluded to earlier, CRH may regulate a subpopulation of raphe neurons, and hence alterations of CRH at the raphe may come to influence 5-HT activity in forebrain regions (Price & Lucki, 2001). In this regard, manipulations of both CRH_1 (Oshima *et al.*, 2003) and CRH_2 receptors (Hammack *et al.*, 2003) may affect 5-HT functioning and behavioral disturbances associated with stressors, and CRH may interact with 5-HT functioning at other brain regions associated with depression, such as the hippocampus (Linthorst *et al.*, 2002). Likewise, paralleling the effects of stressors, CRH infusion increased locus coeruleus NE neuronal activity, and conversely, CRH antagonists attenuated such effects (Li *et al.*, 1998), and also reduced *in vivo* hippocampal 5-HT release (Linthorst *et al.*, 2002).

HPA POLYMORPHISMS RELATED TO MDD

Several glucocorticoid receptor (GR)-related polymorphisms have been described that are relevant to depressive disorders. These polymorphisms were associated with hypersensitivity to glucocorticoids, and individuals carrying a polymorphism related to glucocorticoid resistance were at increased risk of developing MDD and exhibited an altered clinical response to antidepressant medication (van Rossum *et al.*, 2006). In addition to GR polymorphisms, several single-nucleotide polymorphisms (SNPs) were identified involving the CRH_1 gene that appeared to be relevant to MDD, and one of these was related to the therapeutic response to fluoxetine among anxious-depressed patients (Liu *et al.*, 2007). In effect, just as risk factors for depression may be linked to 5-HT gene polymorphisms, it seems that CRH and GR gene polymorphisms might act in a similar fashion. It is uncertain whether the effects of these polymorphisms, like the 5-HTT polymorphism described earlier, are moderated by stressful life experiences or with other gene mutations.

CRH–AVP INTERACTIONS

The data concerning AVP involvement in depression has been limited, although there have been indications that the levels of this hormone are elevated in MDD, particularly in melancholic illness (van Londen *et al.*, 1997) and anxious-retarded depression (where motivational inhibition is pronounced) (Goekoop *et al.*, 2006). As well, a challenge with desmopressin (an analog of vasopressin that stimulates the V3 receptor), provoked greater ACTH and cortisol responses in MDD patients than in controls (Dinan *et al.*, 2004). Centrally, immunoreactive AVP and oxytocin were elevated in the PVN of major depressive and bipolar individuals (Purba *et al.*, 1996) and immunoreactive AVP was elevated in the PVN, locus coeruleus and dorsomedial PFC (but not frontopolar cortex) of depressed persons that had committed suicide, whereas in the dorsal vagal complex, AVP immunoreactivity was reduced (Merali *et al.*, 2006).

Just as stressor exposure results in the sensitization of processes related to monoamine functioning, it seems that stressors enhanced the HPA response to subsequent insults. It has been suggested that AVP may be particularly important in augmenting the proactive effects associated with CRH release. In particular, it seems that PVN neurosecretory neurons have the capacity for phenotypic plasticity (Tilders & Schmidt, 1999). Following a chronic stressor regimen, or with the passage of time following an acute stressor (or challenge with immune signaling molecules, such as interleukin-1β or tumor necrosis factor-α), increased co-storage of CRH and AVP occurs within CRH terminals (Hayley *et al.*, 1999; Tilders & Schmidt, 1999). Upon subsequent stressor exposure, the co-release of CRH and AVP synergistically stimulate pituitary ACTH and adrenal corticosterone secretion. As the CRH–AVP changes were persistent, it was suggested that the synergistic effects of these peptides might have long-term behavioral ramifications (Tilders & Schmidt, 1999). Essentially, this view is in line with that advanced by Post (1992) suggesting that with successive stressor experiences (or with successive episodes of depression), the increased CRH–AVP co-expression would augment vulnerability to depression, and would result in milder stressors being capable of eliciting such episodes.

PHARMACOLOGICAL STUDIES

Although there has been considerable interest in CRH as a target for depression (e.g., Holsboer, 2003), progress on this front has been relatively limited. It had been reported that a CRH_1 antagonist, R121919, reduced the symptoms of depression in a study of 24 MDD patients (Zobel *et al.*, 1999), and altered the depressive Electroencephalography (EEG) sleep profile, with few side effects or disturbances of neuroendocrine functioning (Holsboer, 2003). Although there have been few subsequent reports with this compound, there has been continued interest in the development of treatment strategies that target CRH receptors (Hemley *et al.*, 2007). It will be recalled that multi-targeted approaches might be advantageous in treating depressive illness (Millan, 2006), and targeting CRH may be a component of such a treatment strategy.

MORPHOLOGICAL CORRELATES OF MAJOR DEPRESSIVE ILLNESS

Major depressive illness has been associated with both structural and functional changes within discrete brain regions (Drevets, 2000; Videbech & Ravnkilde, 2004). Most notably, hippocampal volume was reduced in association with MDD, and this was related to illness duration (see meta-analysis in Campbell *et al.*, 2004) and was particularly marked after repeated depressive episodes (MacQueen *et al.*, 2003). Moreover, hippocampal volume was lower in nonremitted patients than among those in remission (Frodl *et al.*, 2004). The source for the hippocampal disturbances are not fully known, but genetic factors, previous distressing events, or corticoid variations in response to chronic strain (MacQueen *et al.*, 2003; McEwen, 2005) may contribute to this outcome. However, the possibility cannot be dismissed that pre-existing hippocampal disturbances acted as a risk factor for depression. Furthermore, diminished hippocampal volume was not unique to depression, having been observed in schizophrenia

(Boos *et al.*, 2007) and posttraumatic stress disorder (Gilbertson *et al.*, 2002), and morphological disturbances in other brain regions were apparent in association with anxiety, obsessive-compulsive disorder, and paranoia (Starkman *et al.*, 2007). In effect, morphological disturbances might dispose individuals to particular pathological states, and it is also possible that hippocampal abnormalities act as a general risk factor for a constellation of psychological disturbances.

NEUROGENESIS AND DEPRESSION

Disturbances of hippocampal neurogenesis elicited by stressors have been implicated in the emergence of depressive symptoms (Duman & Monteggia, 2006), and it is possible that the variations of neurogenesis were related to stressor controllability (Bland *et al.*, 2006). It is significant, as well, that stressors likely influenced specific stages of the cell cycle, as chronic mild stressor exposure did not influence the proliferation or differentiation of new-born cells, but diminished their survival (Lee *et al.*, 2006).

Pharmacological studies have supported a role for neurogenesis in relation to depression. By example, the positive effects of several antidepressants (and electroconvulsive shock) were accompanied by increased hippocampal neurogenesis (Perera *et al.*, 2007; Warner-Schmidt & Duman, 2006). Moreover, paralleling the effects of antidepressants on growth factor expression and on behavioral disturbances, antidepressants blocked the down regulation of hippocampal cell proliferation ordinarily induced by stressors (Malberg & Duman, 2003; Xu *et al.*, 2006). Similarly, the diminished BDNF and hippocampal progenitor cell proliferation observed in chronically stressed mice, were attenuated by repeated antidepressant administration (Lee *et al.*, 2006). Conversely, irradiation of the hippocampus, which inhibited neurogenesis, precluded the antidepressant effects of fluoxetine and imiprimine (Santarelli *et al.*, 2003). Thus, it seems that neurogenesis may be essential for functional consequences of antidepressant treatment, and likely involves activation of growth factor signaling, although enhanced 5-HT neurotransmission may also support such processes (Djavadian, 2004). To be sure, the role of 5-HT in supporting neurogenesis is uncertain given that co-depletion of both 5-HT and NE, but not 5-HT depletion alone, effectively reduced neurogenesis (Jha *et al.*, 2006). As well, although neurogenesis can be inhibited by stressor-induced glucocorticoid elevations (Manji *et al.*, 2003), it does not seem that corticoids are essential in mediating the altered neurogenesis associated with depression (Malberg & Duman 2003).

GROWTH FACTORS IN RELATION TO STRESSORS AND DEPRESSION

Increasing attention has focused on the possibility that neurotrophic growth factors, particularly BDNF, might be involved in the provocation of depression

(Duman & Monteggia, 2006; Manji & Duman, 2001). In this regard, stressors were found to reduce the expression of BDNF in limbic regions (Duman & Monteggia, 2006; Manji *et al.*, 2001) and BDNF disturbances may contribute to the hippocampal atrophy that has been associated with depression (MacQueen *et al.*, 2003). Such effects were not only provoked by neurogenic insults, but could also be elicited by explicit or contextual cues that had been associated with previously encountered stressor (Rasmusson *et al.*, 2002).

Consistent with the view that BDNF was involved in depressive illness, in animals the infusion of this growth factor into the DRN or the hippocampus elicited antidepressant-like behavioral effects (Shirayama *et al.*, 2002). Predictably, clinically beneficial antidepressant treatments (e.g.. SSRIs, tricyclics, and electroconvulsive therapy), increased hippocampal BDNF expression (Manji *et al.*, 2003; Shirayama *et al.*, 2002), and antagonized the BDNF inhibition associated with a stressor (Duman *et al.*, 1999). Conversely, the antidepressant actions of desipramine were diminished among mice with targeted deletion of genes for BDNF (Monteggia *et al.*, 2007).

Consistent with studies in animals, it was reported that BDNF expression and protein levels and that of its receptor (tyrosine kinase B) were lower within the PFC and hippocampus of depressed persons that died by suicide than in age- and sex-matched controls (Dwivedi *et al.*, 2003). As well, it was reported that BDNF concentrations were reduced in the serum of depressed patients, and were inversely related to the degree of clinical impairment, and directly related to hippocampal volume (Shimizu *et al.*, 2003). As expected, with clinical improvement following antidepressant treatment, serum BDNF levels increased (Piccinni *et al.*, 2007), although it was also reported that reduced serum BDNF levels, and the positive effects of antidepressants on this growth factor, were only evident in females (Huang *et al.*, 2007).

Variations of BDNF associated with aging have been associated with changes of 5-HT activity (Mattson *et al.*, 2004). As well, BDNF expression varied with estrus cycle, being relatively low when estradiol levels were high, and were reduced by exogenous estradiol treatment. Moreover, administration of estradiol attenuated the BDNF up regulation ordinarily elicited by a 5-HT_{2A} agonist (Cavus & Duman, 2003). Thus, it is possible that the sex differences that have frequently been reported in depression involve complex interactions involving BDNF levels, sex hormones as well as alterations of 5-HT receptors.

INFLAMMATORY PROCESSES ASSOCIATED WITH MDD

The function of the immune system is that of protecting the organism from bacterial and viral insults. Ordinarily, immune cells (T and B lymphocytes, macrophages as well as endothelial cells) synthesize signaling molecules, referred to as cytokines, which elicit growth and differentiation of lymphocytes, and are essential for an effective immune response to be mounted. Several signaling molecules (i.e., cytokines) are involved in regulating the immune response, including those that promote inflammatory responses, such as interleukin-1β, (IL-1β), IL-6, tumor necrosis factor-α (TNF-α) and interferon-α (IFN-α), as well as several anti-inflammatory cytokines (e.g., IL-4, IL-10, and the endogenous IL-1 receptor antagonist, IL-1ra).

In addition to their role in immunological functioning, cytokines may also contribute to the evolution of depressive illness, as well as varied neurological conditions. It is of particular relevance that cytokines and their receptors are endogenously expressed in the brain, being synthesized by microglia and possibly by neurons (Simard & Rivest, 2005). Further, brain cytokine levels or mRNA expression are markedly increased by neurotoxins and are elevated in neurological conditions, such as traumatic head injury, stroke and seizure, (Kamm *et al.*, 2006), as well as in response to bacterial endotoxins and by neurogenic and psychogenic stressors (Anisman *et al.*, 2008b; Nguyen *et al.*, 1998).

In addition to a role for centrally derived cytokine variations, elevations of peripheral cytokines that accompany an immune response may influence central processes. Although cytokines do not readily gain access to the brain, they may enter where the blood–brain barrier (BBB) is relatively permeable (i.e., at circumventricular organs). Moreover, saturable transport mechanisms serve to move IL-1β and TNF-α into the brain (Banks, 1999), and cytokines may also indirectly influence brain processes through stimulation of vagal afferent fibers projecting from the periphery to the CNS (Maier & Watkins, 1998). As well, infectious and traumatic insults may compromise the integrity of the BBB, thereby permitting greater cytokine passage into the brain. Once cytokines enter the brain parenchyma, they may interact with endogenous cytokine receptors (Rivest *et al.*, 2000) and affect neuronal functioning within brain regions associated with MDD (Nadeau & Rivest, 1999).

There are several processes by which pro-inflammatory cytokines may come to affect 5-HT functioning. As already alluded to, cytokines may activate CRH release, which may give rise to 5-HT alterations, thus leading to MDD (Hayley *et al.*, 2005). Alternatively, inflammatory factors may stimulate processes (indoleamine-2,3-dioxygenase) that either foster degradation of the 5-HT precursor, tryptophan, thereby reducing 5-HT functioning or by promoting neurotoxic actions (e.g., increasing oxidative metabolites, 3-hydroxy-kynurenine, and quinolinic acid) that favor the development of depression (Wichers & Maes, 2002, 2004).

In many respects, the neurochemical and neuroendocrine alterations engendered by cytokines resemble those that are associated with neurogenic and psychogenic stressors. Among other things, pro-inflammatory cytokines increase hypothalamic CRH release (as well as CRH activity at the central amygdala), leading to elevated ACTH and corticosterone secretion (Anisman & Merali, 1999) and growth factors that have been associated with depression (e.g., BDNF) (Duman & Monteggia, 2006). As well, cytokines promote monoamine and CRH alterations (e.g., NE, 5-HT) in several limbic brain regions in rodents (Anisman & Merali, 1999;

Anisman *et al.*, 2007b), and cytokine treatments (such as acute IFN-α) modestly increased cortisol and circulating IL-6 in humans (Anisman *et al.*, 2008b).

In parallel with the neurochemical variations, animals treated with pro-inflammatory cytokines or immune activating agents (e.g., lipopolysaccharide; LPS) present with a depressive-like behavioral profile, including anhedonia (Borowski *et al.*, 1998; Merali *et al.*, 2002), and disrupted social interaction (Konsman *et al.*, 2002). The anhedonia is coupled with a characteristic profile of sickness behaviors (e.g., anorexia, fatigue, reduced motor activity, curled body posture, and ptosis) mediated, at least in part, by central mechanisms (Konsman *et al.*, 2002). These behaviors, which are reminiscent of some of the neuro-vegetative features of depression, were attenuated by chronic antidepressant treatments (Merali *et al.*, 2002; Yirmiya *et al.*, 2001), supporting the perspective that cytokines elicit a depressive syndrome. Furthermore, consistent with the perspective that inflammatory factors are involved in depression, the effects of IFN-α were attenuated by pretreatment with an anti-inflammatory agent (NSAID) (Asnis & De La Garza, 2006).

Given that systemic cytokines engender several stressor-like neurochemical alterations that can be antagonized by antidepressants, and some of the effects of stressors can be attenuated by an IL-1β antagonist (IL-1ra), it was suggested that the brain interprets inflammatory immune activation as if it were a stressor (Anisman & Merali, 1999). Of course, the effects of psychological and systemic stressors are not identical (Anisman *et al.*, 2008b), and it is unlikely that inflammatory immune activation involves appraisal or information processing in the same way as psychogenic stressors. In fact, as different types of psychological stressors lead to excitation of diverse neuronal pathways (Merali *et al.*, 2004b), it is not surprising that cytokines and psychogenic stressors would not involve all of the same neural circuits (Herman & Cullinan, 1997).

PROACTIVE EFFECTS OF CYTOKINES

As indicated earlier, cytokine administration increased the response to later challenge with either a stressor or the cytokine treatment (Anisman *et al.*, 2003). Likewise, exposure to a psychogenic or neurogenic stressor augmented the neuroendocrine response elicited by later LPS administration (Johnson *et al.*, 2003). It will be recalled that the proactive effects of stressors have been attributed to increased co-expression of CRH and AVP at the external zone of the median eminence, leading to augmented HPA activation upon later challenges. It likewise appears that cytokines may engender comparable changes of hypothalamic CRH and AVP, which grow with the passage of time, and might thus promote MDD (Tilders & Schmidt, 1999). However, the proactive effects of cytokines are not restricted to HPA hormones, as cytokines also increased CRH immunoreactivity at the central amygdala, although the time course for this outcome differed from the hypothalamic variations (Hayley, 2001). Nevertheless, the increased CRH reactivity could potentially contribute to the emergence of depressive symptoms upon later re-exposure to a cytokine or with stressor exposure (Anisman *et al.*, 2008b).

There is an appreciable body of literature attesting to the effects of early life experiences in increasing vulnerability to stressors encountered during adulthood. In this regard, even impoverished dam–pup interactions, increased the subsequent stress response (Meaney *et al.*, 2007). In a similar fashion, early life exposure to a bacterial endotoxin increased subsequent adult stressor-elicited corticosterone reactivity, promoted lymphocyte sensitivity to suppression by stressors, and augmented protection against adjuvant-induced arthritis (Shanks *et al.*, 2000). Although it is uncertain whether the effects of early life stressors and inflammatory activation involve similar processes, both treatments seem to influence stressor reactivity and might represent risk factors for adult depression.

CYTOKINES IN RELATION TO DEPRESSION IN HUMANS

MDD was accompanied by several indices of an inflammatory response being mounted, such as elevated acute phase proteins, such as C-reactive protein (Maes, 1999). As well, circulating and mitogen-provoked cytokine concentrations were elevated in severely depressed patients (Maes, 1999). Although there have been reports that the elevated levels of IL-1β, IL-6, TNF-α, and IFN-γ normalized with antidepressant medication (reviewed in Hayley *et al.*, 2005), other investigators did not find this to occur (Anisman *et al.*, 1999; Maes, 1999). It is thus possible that cytokine disturbances represent a trait marker of the illness, possibly being a harbinger for illness recurrence. Alternatively, cytokine activation might contribute selectively to some of the symptoms that comprise the depressive profile (e.g., IL-1β contributes to impaired appetite associated with depression; Andreasson *et al.*, 2007). Finally, it is possible that factors secondary to MDD (e.g., recent stressful experiences, stressors encountered early in life, and altered appraisal and coping with ongoing stressors, drug use, institutionalization, sleep disturbances, altered circadian rhythms) could have been responsible for the cytokine alterations (Irwin, 1999). As well, depression is highly comorbid with anxiety, heart disease, diabetes and Parkinson's disease (Anisman *et al.*, 2008b), and cytokine alterations might have been related to any of these illnesses rather than depression *per se*.

Beyond the correlational data indicating a relationship between inflammatory factors and depression, immune activating agents (e.g., endotoxin treatment) administered to healthy adults elicited depressive-like behaviors (Reichenberg *et al.*, 2001). Conversely, nonsteroidal, anti-inflammatory agents (i.e., COX-2 antagonists) enhanced the effectiveness of antidepressant medication in treating depression (Muller *et al.*, 2006). Furthermore, IFN- α immunotherapy in the treatment of some forms of cancer and hepatitis C, frequently elicited depressive-like states (see review in Raison *et al.*, 2006). Inasmuch as patients treated with IFN-α also presented with cognitive disturbances, impaired concentration and memory, as well as numerous nonspecific features (confusional state characterized by disorientation, psychotic-like features, irritability, anxiety, disturbed vigilance, alertness, and some memory problems) (Raison *et al.*, 2006), it is possible that the effects of IFN-α might actually reflect general malaise or toxicity engendered by the treatment.

Contrary to this perspective, major depressive symptoms in response to IFN-α were particularly pronounced among individuals with subsyndromal levels of depression prior to immunotherapy or those with poor social support (Capuron *et al.*, 2004) as well as among women with a history of depression (Capuron *et al.*, 2003a). Likewise, the cytokine-induced depression was prominent in individuals with low levels of tryptophan (Capuron *et al.*, 2003a), in those with elevated baseline levels of IL-6 and IL-10 (Wichers *et al.*, 2006), or ACTH and cortisol elevations following IFN-α administration (Capuron *et al.*, 2003b). Finally, SSRIs, such as sertraline, paroxetine and citalopram, reduced the depressive symptoms provoked by IFN-α (Raison *et al.*, 2006), and when administered prophylactically, limited the emergence of depressive symptoms (Kraus *et al.*, 2005).

In considering the cytokine involvement in MDD there is a fundamental issue that needs to be discussed. Specifically, although about 50% of patients treated with interferon-α develop marked symptoms of depression and accompanying neuroendocrine alterations (Raison *et al.*, 2006), among rodents treated with this cytokine, only modest behavioral changes and HPA activation are evident (Anisman *et al.*, 2007b; De La Garza & Asnis, 2003). It has been suggested that this apparent paradox stems from the fact that patients undergoing immunotherapy are typically experiencing considerable distress, and that the marked depression may reflect the synergistic actions of the cytokine when superimposed on a stressful backdrop (Hayley *et al.*, 2005). Indeed, there have been several reports documenting such synergies, including effects on *in vivo* hippocampal 5-HT release (Anisman & Merali, 1999), plasma corticosterone elevations, and behavioral functioning (Anisman *et al.*, 2007b). Clearly, the effects of cytokines are not independent of environmental influences, and their actions are contextually dependent.

CONCLUDING COMMENTS

Although 5-HT processes appear to be related to depression, this neurotransmitter represents only one of several that contribute to the features of MDD. In this regard, depressive symptoms may also be subserved by CRH and other neuropeptides (e.g., AVP, substance P, neuromedin-B) as well as by growth factors supporting neurogenesis, such as BDNF and fibroblast growth factor (FGF), and by inflammatory processes. These substrates are inter-related, and it has been shown, for example, that overexpression of IL-6 or administration of LPS inhibited hippocampal neurogenesis, whereas anti-inflammatory treatments, such as minocycline and indomethacin, prevented this inhibitory outcome (Monje *et al.*, 2003).

In this review we have focused on MDD, but it may be heuristically and practically important to underscore that a high degree of comorbidity exists between depression and a constellation of other illnesses. Indeed, the comorbidity between MDD and several neurodegenerative disorders (e.g., Parkinson's, Alzheimer's Disease), the aftermath of stroke, and heart disease, might involve several common mechanisms (Anisman *et al.*, 2008b). Although there are multiple molecular pathways through which cytokines could influence these pathologies, accumulating evidence has suggested the importance of the nuclear factor kappa B (NFκB) signaling in mediating some of the central effects of cytokines (Mattson *et al.*, 2004). It is possible that NFκB signaling may result in the synthesis of inflammatory factors, reactive oxygen species, and excitotoxins that contribute to neurodegeneration (Mattson *et al.*, 2004). As well, NFκB may be an important down-stream signaling factor provoked by cytokines that contribute to major depressive illness (Pace *et al.*, 2007). Ultimately, however, given the range of symptoms and neurochemical processes implicated in MDD, and the fact that appreciable interindividual differences are apparent with respect to the features presented, it may be advantageous to tie specific symptoms of depression to individual (or combinations of several) neurotransmitter and hormonal processes. Likewise, a potential useful strategy might be one of identifying risk factors for specific endophenotypes, and relating these to specific features of the depressive profile.

ACKNOWLEDGMENTS

Supported by the Canadian Health Research Institutes. HA and SH hold Canada Research Chairs in Neuroscience.

REFERENCES

Alfonso, J., Frasch, A. C., & Flugge, G. (2005). Chronic stress, depression and antidepressants: Effects on gene transcription in the hippocampus. *Review in Neuroscience*, *16*, 43–56.

Andreasson, A., Arborelius, L., Erlanson-Albertsson, C., & Lekander, M. A. (2007). Putative role for cytokines in the impaired appetite in depression. *Brain Behavior and Immunity*, *21*, 147–152.

Anisman, H., & Matheson, K. (2005). Stress, anhedonia and depression: Caveats concerning animal models. *Neuroscience and Biobehavioral Reviews*, *29*, 525–546.

Anisman, H., & Merali, Z. (1999). Anhedonic and anxiogenic effects of cytokine exposure. *Advances in Experimental Medicine and Biology*, *461*, 199–233.

Anisman, H., Ravindran, A. V., Griffiths, J., & Merali, Z. (1999). Interleukin-1 beta production in dysthymia before and after pharmacotherapy. *Biological Psychiatry*, *46*, 1649–1655.

Anisman, H., Hayley, S., & Merali, Z. (2003). Cytokines and stress: Sensitization and cross-sensitization. *Brain Behavior and Immunity*, *17*, 86–93.

Anisman, H., Poulter, M. O., Gandhi, R., Merali, Z., & Hayley, S. (2007). Interferon-alpha effects are exaggerated when administered on a psychosocial stressor backdrop: Cytokine, corticosterone and brain monoamine variations. *Journal of Neuroimmunology*, *186*, 45–53.

Anisman, H., Du, L., Palkovits, M., Faludi, G., Kovacs, G. G., Szontagh-Kishazi, P., *et al.* (2008a). Serotonin receptor subtype and p11 mRNA expression in stress-relevant brain regions of suicides and controls. *Journal of Psychiatry and Neuroscience*, *33*, 131–141.

Anisman, H., Merali, Z., & Hayley, S. (2008b). Neurotransmitter, peptide and cytokine processes in relation to depressive disorder: Comorbidity of depression with neurodegenerative disorders. *Progress in Neurobiology*, *85*, 1–74.

Arango, V., Underwood, M. D., Gubbi, A. V., & Mann, J. J. (1995). Localized alterations in pre- and postsynaptic serotonin binding sites in the ventrolateral prefrontal cortex of suicide victims. *Brain Research*, *688*, 121–133.

Arango, V., Underwood, M. D., Boldrini, M., Tamir, H., Kassir, S. A., Hsiung, S. *et al.* (2001). Serotonin 1λA receptors, serotonin transporter binding and serotonin transporter mRNA expression in the brainstem of depressed suicide victims. *Neuropsychopharmacology*, *25*, 892–903.

Arango, V., Huang, Y. Y., Underwood, M. D., & Mann, J. J. (2003). Genetics of the serotonergic system in suicidal behavior. *Journal of Psychiatric Research*, *37*, 375–386.

Asnis, G. M., & De La Garza, R. (2006). Interferon-induced depression in chronic hepatitis c: A review of its prevalence, risk factors, biology, and treatment approaches. *Journal of Clinical Gastroenterology*, *40*, 322–335.

Bale, T. L., Contarino, A. B., Smith, G. W., Chan, R., Gold, L. H., Sawchenko, P. E. *et al.* (2000). Mice deficient for corticotropin-releasing hormone receptor-2 display anxiety-like behaviour and are hypersensitive to stress. *Nature Genetics*, *24*, 410–414.

Bale, T. L., Picetti, R., Contarino, A., Koob, G. F., Vale, W. W., & Lee, K. F. (2002). Mice deficient for both corticotropin-releasing factor receptor 1 (CRFR1) and CRFR2 have an impaired stress response and display sexually dichotomous anxiety-like behavior. *Journal of Neuroscience*, *22*, 193–199.

Banks, W. A. (1999). Physiology and pathology of the blood-brain barrier: Implications for microbial pathogenesis, drug delivery and neurodegenerative disorders. *Journal of Neurovirology*, *5*, 538–555.

Belanoff, J. K., Flores, B. H., Kalezhan, M., Sund, B., & Schatzberg, A. F. (2001). Rapid reversal of psychotic depression using mifepristone. *Journal of Clinical Psychopharmacology*, *21*, 516–521.

Bhansali, P., Dunning, J., Singer, S. E., David, L., & Schmauss, C. (2007). Early life stress alters adult serotonin 2C receptor pre-mRNA editing and expression of the alpha subunit of the heterotrimeric G-protein G q. *Journal of Neuroscience*, *27*, 1467–1473.

Bissette, G., Klimek, V., Pan, J., Stockmeier, C., & Ordway, G. (2003). Elevated concentrations of CRF in the locus coeruleus of depressed subjects. *Neuropsychopharmacology*, *28*, 1328–1335.

Bland, S. T., Schmid, M. J., Greenwood, B. N., Watkins, L. R., & Maier, S. F. (2006). Behavioral control of the stressor modulates stress-induced changes in neurogenesis and fibroblast growth factor-2. *Neuroreport*, *17*, 593–597.

Boldrini, M., Underwood, M. D., Mann, J. J., & Arango, V. (2007). Serotonin-1 A autoreceptor binding in the dorsal raphe nucleus of depressed suicides. *Journal of Psychiatric Research,* 14, (Epub ahead of print) *42*, 433–442.

Boos, H. B., Aleman, A., Cahn, W., Pol, H. H., & Kahn, R. S. (2007). Brain volumes in relatives of patients with schizophrenia: A meta-analysis. *Archives of General Psychiatry*, *64*, 297–304.

Borowski, T., Kokkinidis, L., Merali, Z., & Anisman, H. (1998). Lipopolysaccharide, central *in vivo* biogenic amine variations, and anhedonia. *NeuroReport*, *9*, 3797–3802.

Briones-Aranda, A., Rocha, L., & Picazo, O. (2005). Influence of forced swimming stress on 5-HT1A receptors and serotonin levels in mouse brain. *Progress in Neuropsychopharmacology and Biological Psychiatry*, *29*, 275–281

Campbell, S., Marriott, M., Nahmias, C., & MacQueen, G. M. (2004). Lower hippocampal volume in patients suffering from depression: A meta-analysis. *American Journal of Psychiatry*, *161*, 598–607.

Canli, T., Qiu, M., Omura, K., Congdon, E., Haas, B. W., Amin, Z. *et al.* (2006). Neural correlates of epigenesist. *Proceedings of the National Academy of Sciences*, *103*, 16033–16038.

Capuron, L., Neurauter, G., Musselman, D. L., Lawson, D. H., Nemeroff, C. B., Fuchs, D. *et al.* (2003a). Interferon-alpha-induced changes in tryptophan metabolism relationship to depression and paroxetine treatment. *Biological Psychiatry*, *54*, 906–914.

Capuron, L., Raison, C. L., Musselman, D. L., Lawson, D. H., Nemeroff, C. B., & Miller, A. H. (2003b). Association of exaggerated HPA axis response to the initial injection of interferon-alpha with development of depression during interferon-alpha therapy. *American Journal of Psychiatry*, *160*, 1342–1345.

Capuron, L., Ravaud, A., Miller, A. H., & Dantzer, R. (2004). Baseline mood and psychosocial characteristics of patients developing depressive symptoms during interleukin-2 and/or interferon-alpha cancer therapy. *Brain, Behavior and Immunity*, *18*, 205–213.

Caspi, A., Sugden, K., Moffitt, T. E., Taylor, A., Craig, I. W., Harrington, H. *et al.* (2003). Influence of life stress on depression: Moderation by a polymorphism in the 5-HTT gene. *Science*, *301*, 386–389.

Cavus, I., & Duman, R. S. (2003). Influence of estradiol, stress, and 5-HT2A agonist treatment on brain-derived neurotrophic factor expression in female rats. *Biological Psychiatry*, *54*, 59–69.

Cryan, J. F., & Slattery, D. A. (2007). Animal models of mood disorders: Recent developments. *Current Opinion in Psychiatry*, *20*, 1–7.

David, S. P., Murthy, N. V., Rabiner, E. A., Munafo, M. R., Johnstone, E. C., Jacob, R. *et al.* (2005). A functional genetic variation of the serotonin (5-HT) transporter affects 5-HT1A receptor binding in humans. *Journal of Neuroscience*, *25*, 2586–2590.

Dayas, C. V., Buller, K. M., Crane, J. W., Xu, Y., & Day, T. A. (2001). Stressor categorization: Acute physical and psychological stressors elicit distinctive recruitment patterns in the amygdala and in medullary noradrenergic cell groups. *European Journal of Neuroscience*, *14*, 1143–1152.

De La Garza, R., & Asnis, G. M. (2003). The non-steroidal anti-inflammatory drug diclofenac sodium attenuates IFN-alpha induced alterations to monoamine turnover in prefrontal cortex and hippocampus. *Brain Research*, *977*, 70–79.

Dinan, T. G., O'Brien, S., Lavelle, E., & Scott, L. V. (2004). Further neuroendocrine evidence of enhanced vasopressin V3 receptor responses in melancholic depression. *Psychological Medicine*, *34*, 169–172.

Djavadian, R. L. (2004). Serotonin and neurogenesis in the hippocampal dentate gyrus of adult mammals. *Acta Neurobiologiae Experimentalis*, *64*, 189–200.

Drevets, W. C. (2000). Functional anatomical abnormalities in limbic and prefrontal cortical structures in major depression. *Progress in Brain Research*, *126*, 413–431.

Drevets, W. C., Frank, E., Price, J. C., Kupfer, D. J., Greer, P. J., & Mathis, C. (2000). Serotonin type-1 A receptor imaging in depression. *Nuclear Medicine and Biology*, *27*, 499–507.

Duman, R. S., & Monteggia, L. M. (2006). A neurotrophic model for stress-related mood disorders. *Biological Psychiatry*, *59*, 1116–1127.

Duman, R. S., Malberg, J., & Thome, J. (1999). Neural plasticity to stress and antidepressant treatment. *Biological Psychiatry*, *46*, 1181–1191.

Dwivedi, Y., Rizavi, H. S., Conley, R. R., Roberts, R. C., Tamminga, C. A., & Pandey, G. N. (2003). Altered gene expression of brain-derived neurotrophic factor and receptor tyrosine kinase B in postmortem brain of suicide subjects. *Archives General Psychiatry*, *60*, 804–815.

Dwivedi, Y., Mondal, A. C., Payappagoudar, G. V., & Rizavi, H. S. (2005). Differential regulation of serotonin (5HT)2 A receptor mRNA and protein levels after single and repeated stress in rat brain: Role in learned helplessness behavior. *Neuropsychopharmacology*, *48*, 204–214.

Flores, C., & Stewart, J. (2000). Basic fibroblast growth factor as a mediator of the effects of glutamate in the development of long-lasting sensitization to stimulant drugs: Studies in the rat. *Psychopharmacology*, *151*, 152–165.

Frodl, T., Meisenzahl, E. M., Zetzsche, T., Höhne, T., Banac, S., Schorr, C. *et al.* (2004). Hippocampal and amygdala changes in patients with major depressive disorder and healthy controls during a 1-year follow-up. *Journal of Clinical Psychiatry*, *65*, 492–499.

Gilbertson, M. W., Shenton, M. E., Ciszewski, A., Kasai, K., Lasko, N. B., Orr, S. P. *et al.* (2002). Smaller hippocampal volume predicts pathologic vulnerability to psychological trauma. *Nature Neuroscience*, *5*, 1242–1247.

Goekoop, J. G., de Winter, R. P., de Rijk, R., Zwinderman, K. H., Frankhuijzen-Sierevogel, A., & Wiegant, V. M. (2006). Depression with above-normal plasma vasopressin: Validation by relations with family history of depression and mixed anxiety and retardation. *Psychiatry Research, 141*, 201–211.

Hammack, S. E., Schmid, M. J., LoPresti, M. L., Der-Avakian, A., Pellymounter, M. A., Foster, A. C. *et al.* (2003). Corticotropin releasing hormone type 2 receptors in the dorsal raphe nucleus mediate the behavioral consequences of uncontrollable stress. *Journal of Neuroscience, 23*, 1019–1025.

Harvey, B. H., Naciti, C., Brand, L., & Stein, D. J. (2003). Endocrine, cognitive and hippocampal/cortical 5HT 1A/2A receptor changes evoked by a time-dependent sensitisation (TDS) stress model in rats. *Brain Research, 983*, 97–107.

Hasler, G., Drevets, W. C., Manji, H. K., & Charney, D. S. (2004). Discovering endophenotypes for major depression. *Neuropsychopharmacology 29*, 1765–1781.

Hayley, S., Brebner, K., Lacosta, S., Merali, Z., & Anisman, H. (1999). Sensitization to the effects of tumor necrosis factor-a; neuroendocrine, central monoamine and behavioral variations. *Journal of Neuroscience, 19*, 5654–5665.

Hayley, S., Staines, W. M., & Merali Z., Anisman, H. (2001). Time-dependent sensitization of corticotropin-releasing hormone, arginine vasopressin and c-fos immunoreactivity within the mouse brain in response to tumor necrosis factor-alpha. *Neuroscience, 106*, 137–148.

Hayley, S., Poulter, M., Merali, Z., & Anisman, H. (2005). The pathogenesis of clinical depression: Stressor- and cytokine-induced alterations of neuroplasticity. *Neuroscience, 135*, 659–678.

Hemley, C. F., McCluskey, A., & Keller, P. A. (2007). Corticotropin releasing hormone – A GPCR drug target. *Current Drug Targets, 8*, 105–115.

Herman, J. P., & Cullinan, W. E. (1997). Neurocircuitry of stress: Central control of hypothalamo-pituitary-adrenocortical axis. *Trends in Neuroscience, 20*, 78–84.

Holmes, A., Yang, R. J., Murphy, D. L., & Crawley, J. N. (2002). Evaluation of antidepressant-related behavioral responses in mice lacking the serotonin transporter. *Neuropsychopharmacology, 27*, 914–923.

Holmes, A., Yang, R. J., Lesch, K. P., Crawley, J. N., & Murphy, D. L. (2003). Mice lacking the serotonin transporter exhibit 5-HT(1A) receptor-mediated abnormalities in tests for anxiety-like behavior. *Neuropsychopharmacology, 28*, 2077–2088.

Holsboer, F. (2003). Corticotropin-releasing hormone modulators and depression. *Current Opinion in Investigational Drugs, 4*, 46–50.

Huang, T. L., Lee, C. T., & Liu, Y. L. (2007). Serum brain-derived neurotrophic factor levels in patients with major depression: Effects of antidepressants. *Journal of Psychiatric Research*, (Epub ahead of print) *42*, 521–523.

Irwin, M. (1999). Immune correlates of depression. *Advances in Experimental Medical Biology, 461*, 1–24.

Jha, S., Rajendran, R., Davda, J., & Vaidya, V. A. (2006). Selective serotonin depletion does not regulate hippocampal neurogenesis in the adult rat brain: Differential effects of p-chlorophenylalanine and 5,7-dihydroxytryptamine. *Brain Research, 1075*, 48–59.

Johnson, J. D., O'Connor, K. A., Hansen, M. K., Watkins, L. R., & Maier, S. F. (2003). Effects of prior stress on LPS-induced cytokine and sickness responses. *American Journal of Physiology: Regulatory, Integrative, and Comparative Physiology, 284*, 422–432.

Jones, M. D., & Lucki, I. (2005). Sex differences in the regulation of serotonergic transmission and behavior in 5-HT receptor knockout mice. *Neuropsychopharmacology, 30*, 1039–1047.

Kalueff, A. V., Gallagher, P. S., & Murphy, D. L. (2006). Are serotonin transporter knockout mice "depressed"?: Hypoactivity but no anhedonia. *Neuroreport, 17*, 1347–1351.

Kamm, K., Vanderkolk, W., Lawrence, C., Jonker, M., & Davis, A. T. (2006). . *The effect of traumatic brain injury upon the concentration and expression of interleukin-1beta and interleukin-10 in the rat, Journal of Trauma, 60*, 152–157.

Kishimoto, T., Radulovic, J., Radulovic, M., Lin, C. R., Schrick, C., Hooshman, F. *et al.* (2000). Deletion of crhr2 reveals an anxiolytic role for corticotropin-releasing hormone receptor-2. *Nature Genetics, 24*, 415–419.

Konsman, J. P., Parnet, P., & Dantzer, R. (2002). Cytokine-induced sickness behaviour: Mechanisms and implications. *Trends in Neurosciences*, *25*, 154–159.

Kraus, M. R., Schafer, A., Csef, H., & Scheurlen, M. (2005). Psychiatric side effects of pegylated interferon alfa-2b as compared to conventional interferon alfa-2b in patients with chronic hepatitis C. *World Journal of Gastroenterology*, *11*, 1769–1774.

LeDoux, J. E. (2000). Emotion circuits in the brain. *Annual Reviews of Neuroscience*, *23*,155–184.

Lee, K. J., Kim, S. J., Kim, S. W., Choi, S. H., Shin, Y. C., Park, S. H. *et al.* (2006). Chronic mild stress decreases survival, but not proliferation, of new-born cells in adult rat hippocampus. *Experimental and Molecular Medicine*, *38*, 44–54.

Lee, Y., & Davis, M. (1997). Role of the hippocampus, bed nucleus of the stria terminalis, and the amygdala in the excitatory effect of corticotropin-releasing hormone on the acoustic startle reflex. *Journal of Neuroscience*, *17*, 6434–6446.

Lemonde, S., Turecki, G., Bakish, D., Du, L., Hrdina, P. D., Bown, C. D. *et al.* (2003). Impaired repression at a 5-hydroxytryptamine 1A receptor gene polymorphism associated with major depression and suicide. *Journal of Neuroscience*, *23*, 8788–8799.

Li, J., Takeda, H., Tsuji, M., Liu, L., & Matsumiya, T. (1998). Antagonism of central CRF systems mediates stress-induced changes in noradrenaline and serotonin turnover in rat brain regions. *Methods and Findings in Experimental and Clinical Pharmacology*, *20*, 409–417.

Linthorst, A. C., Penalva, R. G., Flachskamm, C., Holsboer, F., & Reul, J. M. (2002). Forced swim stress activates rat hippocampal serotonergic neurotransmission involving a corticotropin-releasing hormone receptor-dependent mechanism. *European Journal of Neuroscience*, *16*, 2441–2452.

Lira, A., Zhou, M., Castanon, N., Ansorge, M. S., Gordon, J. A., Francis, J. H. *et al.* (2003). Altered depression-related behaviors and functional changes in the dorsal raphe nucleus of serotonin transporter-deficient mice. *Biological Psychiatry*, *54*, 960–971.

Liu, Z., Zhu, F., Wang, G., Xiao, Z., Tang, J., Liu, W. *et al.* (2007). Association study of corticotropin-releasing hormone receptor1 gene polymorphisms and antidepressant response in major depressive disorders. *Neuroscience Letters*, *414*, 155–158.

MacQueen, G. M., Campbell, S., McEwen, B. S., Macdonald, K., Amano, S., Joffe, R. T. *et al.* (2003). Course of illness, hippocampal function, and hippocampal volume in major depression. *Proceedings of the National Academy of Sciences*, *100*, 1387–1392.

Maes, M. (1999). Major depression and activation of the inflammatory response system. *Advances in Experimental Medicine and Biology*, *461*, 25–45.

Maier, S. F., & Watkins, L. R. (1998). Cytokines for psychologists: Implications of bidirectional immune-to-brain communication for understanding behavior, mood, and cognition. *Psychological Review*, *105*, 83–107.

Maier, S. F., & Watkins, L. R. (2005). Stressor controllability and learned helplessness: The roles of the dorsal raphe nucleus, serotonin, and corticotropin-releasing factor. *Neuroscience and Biobehavioral Reviews*, *29*, 829–841.

Maier, S. F., Amat, J., Baratta, M. V., Paul, E., & Watkins, L. R. (2006). Behavioral control, the medial prefrontal cortex, and resilience. *Dialogues in Clinical Neuroscience*, *8*, 397–406.

Malberg, J. E., & Duman, R. S. (2003). Cell proliferation in adult hippocampus is decreased by inescapable stress: Reversal by fluoxetine treatment. *Neuropsychopharmacology*, *28*, 1562–1671.

Malison, R. T., Price, L. H., Berman, R., van Dyck, C. H., Pelton, G. H., Carpenter, L. *et al.* (1998). Reduced brain serotonin transporter availability in major depression as measured by [123I]-2 beta-carbomethoxy-3 beta-(4-iodophenyl)tropane and single photon emission computed tomography. *Biological Psychiatry*, *44*, 1090–1098.

Manji, H. K., & Duman, R. S. (2001). Impairments of neuroplasticity and cellular resilience in severe mood disorders: Implications for the development of novel therapeutics. *Psychopharmacology Bulletin*, *35*, 5–49.

Manji, H. K., Drevets, W. C., & Charney, D. S. (2001). The cellular neurobiology of depression. *Nature Medicine*, *7*, 541–547.

Manji, H. K., Quiroz, J. A., Sporn, J., Payne, J. L., Denicoff, K. A., Gray, N. *et al.* (2003). Enhancing neuronal plasticity and cellular resilience to develop novel, improved therapeutics for difficult-to-treat depression. *Biological Psychiatry*, *53*, 707–742.

Mansbach, R. S., Brooks, E. N., & Chen, Y. L. (1997). Antidepressant-like effects of CP-154,526, a selective CRF1 receptor antagonist. *European Journal of Pharmacology*, *323*, 21–26.

Mattson, M. P., Maudsley, S., & Martin, B. (2004). BDNF and 5-HT: A dynamic duo in age-related neuronal plasticity and neurodegenerative disorders. *Trends in Neurosciences*, *27*, 589–594.

McEwen, B. S. (2000). Allostasis and allostatic load: Implications for neuropsychopharmacology. *Neuropsychopharmacology*, *22*, 108–124.

McEwen, B. S. (2005). Glucocorticoids, depression, and mood disorders: structural remodeling in the brain. *Metabolism*, *54*, 20–23.

Meaney, M. J., Szyf, M., & Seckl, J. R. (2007). Epigenetic mechanisms of perinatal programming of hypothalamic-pituitary-adrenal function and health. *Trends in Molecular Medicine*, *13*, 269–277.

Merali, Z., McIntosh, J., Kent, P., Michaud, D., & Anisman, H. (1998). Aversive as well as appetitive events evoke the release of corticotropin releasing hormone and bombesin-like peptides at the central nucleus of the amygdala. *Journal of Neuroscience*, *18*, 4758–4766.

Merali, Z., Brennan, K., Brau, P., & Anisman, H. (2002). Dissociating anorexia and anhedonia elicited by interleukin-1β: Antidepressant and gender effects on responding for "free chow" and "earned" sucrose intake. *Psychopharmacology*, *165*, 413–418.

Merali, Z., Du, L., Hrdina, P., Palkovits, M., Faludi, G., Poulter, M. O. *et al.* (2004a). Dysregulation in the suicide brain: mRNA expression of corticotropin-releasing hormone receptors and GABA(A) receptor subunits in frontal cortical brain region. *Journal of Neuroscience*, *24*, 1478–1485.

Merali, Z., Khan, S., Michaud, D. S., Shippy, S. A., & Anisman, H. (2004b). Does amygdaloid corticotropin-releasing hormone (CRH) mediate anxiety-like behaviors? Dissociation of anxiogenic effects and CRH release. *European Journal of Neuroscience*, *20*, 229–239.

Merali, Z., Kent, P., Du, L., Hrdina, P., Palkovits, M., Faludi, G. *et al.* (2006). Corticotropin-releasing hormone, arginine vasopressin, gastrin-releasing peptide, and neuromedin B alterations in stress-relevant brain regions of suicides and control subjects. *Biological Psychiatry*, *59*, 594–602.

Meyer, J. H., McMain, S., Kennedy, S. H., Korman, L., Brown, G. M., DaSilva, J. N. *et al.* (2003). Dysfunctional attitudes and 5-HT2 receptors during depression and self-harm. *American Journal of Psychiatry*, *160*, 90–99.

Meyer, J. H., Houle, S., Sagrati, S., Carella, A., Hussey, D. F., Ginovart, N. *et al.* (2004). Brain serotonin transporter binding potential measured with carbon 11-labeled DASB positron emission tomography: Effects of major depressive episodes and severity of dysfunctional attitudes. *Archives of General Psychiatry*, *61*, 1271–1279.

Meynen, G., Unmehopa, U. A., van Heerikhuize, J. J., Hofman, M. A., Swaab, D. F., & Hoogendijk, W. J. (2006). Increased arginine vasopressin mRNA expression in the human hypothalamus in depression: A preliminary report. *Biological Psychiatry*, *60*, 892–895.

Millan, M. J. (2006). Multi-target strategies for the improved treatment of depressive states: Conceptual foundations and neuronal substrates, drug discovery and therapeutic application. *Pharmacology and Therapeutics*, *110*, 135–370.

Monje, M. L., Toda, H., & Palmer, T. D. (2003). Inflammatory blockade restores adult hippocampal neurogenesis. *Science*, *302*, 1760–1765.

Monteggia, L. M., Luikart, B., Barrot, M., Theobold, D., Malkovska, I., Nef, S. *et al.* (2007). Brain-derived neurotrophic factor conditional knockouts show gender differences in depression-related behaviors. *Biological Psychiatry*, *61*, 187–197.

Muller, M. B., Zimmermann, S., Sillaber, I., Hagemeyer, T. P., Deussing, J. M., Timpl, P. *et al.* (2003). Limbic corticotropin-releasing hormone receptor 1 mediates anxiety-related behavior and hormonal adaptation to stress. *Nature Neuroscience*, *6*, 1100–1107.

Muller, N., Schwarz, M. J., Dehning, S., Douhe, A., Cerovecki, A., Goldstein-Muller, B. *et al.* (2006). The cyclooxygenase-2 inhibitor celecoxib has therapeutic effects in major depression:

Results of a double-blind, randomized, placebo controlled, add-on pilot study to reboxetine. *Molecular Psychiatry*, *11*, 680–684.

Murphy, B. E. (1997). Antiglucocorticoid therapies in major depression: A review. *Psychoneuroendo crinology*, *22*, 125–132.

Nadeau, S., & Rivest, S. (1999). Effects of circulating tumor necrosis factor on the neuronal activity and expression of the genes encoding the tumor necrosis factor receptors in the rat brain: A view from the blood-brain barrier. *Neuroscience*, *93*, 1449–1464.

Nemeroff, C. B., & Vale, W. (2005). The neurobiology of depression: Inroads to treatment and new drug discovery. *Journal of Clinical Psychiatry*, *66*, 5–13.

Neumaier, J. F., Petty, F., Kramer, G. L., Szot, P., & Hamblin, M. W. (1997). Learned helplessness increases 5-hydroxytryptamine1B receptor mRNA levels in the rat dorsal raphe nucleus. *Biological Psychiatry*, *41*, 668–674.

Nguyen, K. T., Deak, T., Owens, S. M., Kohno, T., Fleshner, M., Watkins, L. R. *et al.* (1998). Exposure to acute stress induces brain interleukin-1β protein in the rat. *Journal of Neuroscience*, *19*, 2799–2805.

Oshima, A., Flachskamm, C., Reul, J. M., Holsboer, F., & Linthorst, A. C. (2003). Altered serotonergic neurotransmission but normal hypothalamic-pituitary-adrenocortical axis activity in mice chronically treated with the corticotropin-releasing hormone receptor type 1 antagonist NBI 30775. *Neuropsychopharmacology*, *28*, 2148–2159.

Pace, T. W., Hu, F., & Miller, A. H. (2007). Cytokine-effects on glucocorticoid receptor function: Relevance to glucocorticoid resistance and the pathophysiology and treatment of major depression. *Brain Behavior and Immunity*, *21*, 9–19.

Pandey, G. N., Dwivedi, Y., Rizavi, H. S., Ren, X., Pandey, S. C., Pesold, C. *et al.* (2002). Higher expression of serotonin 5-HT(2 A) receptors in the postmortem brains of teenage suicide victims. *American Journal of Psychiatry*, *159*, 419–429.

Parsey, R. V., Olvet, D. M., Oquendo, M. A., Huang, Y. Y., Ogden, R. T., & Mann, J. J. (2006a). Higher 5-HT1A receptor binding potential during a major depressive episode predicts poor treatment response: Preliminary data from a naturalistic study. *Neuropsychopharmacology*, *31*, 1745–1749.

Parsey, R. V., Oquendo, M. A., Ogden, R. T., Olvet, D. M., Simpson, N., & Huang, Y. Y. (2006b). Altered serotonin 1 A binding in major depression: A [carbonyl-C-11]WAY100635 positron emission tomography study. *Biological Psychiatry*, *59*, 106–113.

Perera, T. D., Coplan, J. D., Lisanby, S. H., Lipira, C. M., Arif, M., Carpio, C. *et al.* (2007). Antidepressant-induced neurogenesis in the hippocampus of adult nonhuman primates. *Journal of Neuroscience*, *27*, 4894–4901.

Piccinni, A., Marazziti, D., Catena, M., Domenici, L., Del Debbio, A., Bianchi, C., *et al.* (2007). Plasma and serum brain-derived neurotrophic factor (BDNF) in depressed patients during 1 year of antidepressant treatments. *Journal of Affective Disorders*, (Epub ahead of print) *105*, 279–283.

Post, R. M. (1992). Transduction of psychosocial stress into the neurobiology of recurrent affective disorder. *American Journal of Psychiatry*, *149*, 999–1010.

Preil, J., Muller, M. B., Gesing, A., Reul, J. M., Sillaber, I., van Gaalen, M. M. *et al.* (2001). Regulation of the hypothalamic-pituitary-adrenocortical system in mice deficient for CRH receptors 1 and 2. *Endocrinology*, *42*, 4946–4955.

Price, M. L., & Lucki, I. (2001). Regulation of serotonin release in the lateral septum and striatum by corticotropin-releasing factor. *Journal of Neuroscience*, *21*, 2833–2841.

Purba, J. S., Hoogendijk, W. J., Hofman, M. A., & Swaab, D. F. (1996). Increased number of vasopressin- and oxytocin-expressing neurons in the paraventricular nucleus of the hypothalamus in depression. *Archives of General Psychiatry*, *53*, 137–143.

Raison, C. L., Capuron, L., & Miller, A. H. (2006). Cytokines sing the blues: inflammation and the pathogenesis of depression. *Trends in Immunology*, *27*, 24–31.

Rasmusson, A. M., Shi, L., & Duman, R. (2002). Downregulation of BDNF mRNA in the hippocampal dentate gyrus after re-exposure to cues previously associated with footshock. *Neuropsychopharmacology*, *27*, 133–142.

Reichenberg, A., Yirmiya, R., Schuld, A., Kraus, T., Haack, M., Morag, A. *et al.* (2001). Cytokine-associated emotional and cognitive disturbances in humans. *Archives of General Psychiatry, 58*, 445–452.

Ren-Patterson, R. F., Cochran, L. W., Holmes, A., Sherrill, S., Huang, S. J., Tolliver, T. *et al.* (2005). Loss of brain-derived neurotrophic factor gene allele exacerbates brain monoamine deficiencies and increases stress abnormalities of serotonin transporter knockout mice. *Journal of Neuroscience Research, 79*, 756–771.

Ren-Patterson, R. F., Cochrane, L. W., Holmes, A., Lesch, K. P., Lu, B., & Murphy, D. L. (2006). Gender-dependent modulation of brain monoamines and anxiety-like behaviors in mice with genetic serotonin transporter and BDNF deficiencies. *Cellular and Molecular Neurobiology, 26*, 755–780.

Reul, M. H. M., & Holsboer, F. (2002). Corticotropin-releasing factor receptors 1 and 2 in anxiety and depression. *Current Opinion in Pharmacology, 2*, 23–33.

Rivest, S., Lacroix, S., Vallieres, L., Nadeau, S , Zhang, J., & Laflamme, N. (2000). How the blood talks to the brain parenchyma and the paraventricular nucleus of the hypothalamus during systemic inflammatory and infectious stimuli. *Proceedings of Society of Experimental Biology and Medicine, 223*, 22–38.

Rosel, P., Arranz, B., Urretavizcaya, M., Oros, M., San, L., & Navarro, M. A. (2004a). Altered 5-HT2A and 5-HT4 postsynaptic receptors and their intracellular signalling systems IP3 and cAMP in brains from depressed violent suicide victims. *Neuropsychobiology, 49*, 189–195.

Rosel, P., Arranz, B., Urretavizcaya, M., Oros, M., San, L., & Navarro, M. A. (2004b). Altered 5-HT2A and 5-HT4 postsynaptic receptors and their intracellular signalling systems IP3 and cAMP in brains from depressed violent suicide victims. *Neuropsychobiology, 49*, 189–195.

Santarelli, L., Saxe, M., Gross, C., Surget, A., Battaglia, F., Dulawa, S. *et al.* (2003). Requirement of hippocampal neurogenesis for the behavioral effects of antidepressants. *Science, 301*, 805–809.

Schmauss, C. (2003). Serotonin 2C receptors: Suicide, serotonin, and runaway RNA editing. *Neuroscientist, 9*, 237–242.

Serretti, A., Kato, M., De Ronchi, D., & Kinoshita, T. (2007). Meta-analysis of serotonin transporter gene promoter polymorphism (5-HTTLPR) association with selective serotonin reuptake inhibitor efficacy in depressed patients. *Molecular Psychiatry, 12*, 247–257.

Shanks, N., Windle, R. J., Perks, P. A., Harbuz, M. S., Jessop, D. S., Ingram, C. D. *et al.* (2000). Early-life exposure to endotoxin alters hypothalamic-pituitary-adrenal function and predisposition to inflammation. *Proceedings of the National Academy of Sciences, 97*, 5645–5650.

Shimizu, E., Hashimoto, K., Okamura, N., Koike, K., Komatsu, N., Kumakiri, C. *et al.* (2003). Alterations of serum levels of brain-derived neurotrophic factor (BDNF) in depressed patients with or without antidepressants. *Biological Psychiatry, 54*, 70–75.

Shirayama, Y., Chen, A. C., Nakagawa, S., Russell, D. S., & Duman, R. S. (2002). Brain-derived neurotrophic factor produces antidepressant effects in behavioral models of depression. *Journal of Neuroscience, 22*, 3251–3261.

Sibille, E., Arango, V., Galfalvy, H. C., Pavlicis, P., Erraji-Benchekroun, L., Ellis, S. P. *et al.* (2004). Gene expression profiling of depression and suicide in human prefrontal cortex. *Neuropsychopharmacology, 29*, 351–361.

Simard, A. R., & Rivest, S. (2005). Do pathogen exposure and innate immunity cause brain diseases? *Neurological Research, 27*, 717–725.

Smith, G. W., Aubry, J. M., Dellu, F., Contarino, A., Bilezikjian, L. M., Gold, L. H. *et al.* (1998). Corticotropin releasing factor receptor 1-deficient mice display decreased anxiety, impaired stress response, and aberrant neuroendocrine development. *Neuron, 20*, 1093–1102.

Starkman, M. N., Giordani, B., Gebarski, S. S., & Schteingart, D. E. (2007). Improvement in mood and ideation associated with increase in right caudate volume. *Journal of Affective Disorders, 101*, 139–147.

Stockmeier, C. A. (2003). Involvement of serotonin in depression: Evidence from postmortem and imaging studies of serotonin receptors and the serotonin transporter. *Journal of Psychiatric Research, 37*, 357–373.

Stockmeier, C. A., Shapiro, L. A., Dilley, G. E., Kolli, T. N., Friedman, L., & Rajkowska, G. (1998). Increase in serotonin-1 A autoreceptors in the midbrain of suicide victims with major depression-postmortem evidence for decreased serotonin activity. *Journal of Neuroscience*, *18*, 7394–7401.

Svenningsson, P., Chergui, K., Rachleff, I., Flajolet, M., Zhang, X., El Yacoubi, M. *et al.* (2006). Alterations in 5-HT1B receptor function by p11 in depression-like states. *Science*, *311*, 77–80.

Thakker, D. R., Natt, F., Husken, D., van der Putten, H., Maier, R., Hoyer, D. *et al.* (2005). siRNA-mediated knockdown of the serotonin transporter in the adult mouse brain. *Molecular Psychiatry*, *10*, 782–789.

Tilders, F. J. H., & Schmidt, E. D. (1999). Cross-sensitization between immune and non-immune stressors, A role in the etiology of depression?. *Advances in Experimental Medicine and Biology*, *461*, 179–197.

Turecki, G., Briere, R., Dewar, K., Antonetti, T., Lesage, A. D., Seguin, M. *et al.* (1999). Prediction of level of serotonin 2 A receptor binding by serotonin receptor 2 A genetic variation in post-mortem brain samples from subjects who did or did not commit suicide. *American Journal of Psychiatry*, *156*, 1456–1458.

van Gaalen, M. M., Reul, J. M., Gesing, A., Stenzel-Poore, M. P., Holsboer, F., & Steckler, T. (2002). Mice overexpressing CRH show reduced responsiveness in plasma corticosterone after a5-HT1A receptor challenge. *Genes, Brain and Behavior*, *1*, 174–177.

van Londen, L., Goekoop, J. G., van Kempen, G. M., Frankhuijzen-Sierevogel, A. C., Wiegant, V. M., van der Velde, E. A. *et al.* (1997). Plasma levels of arginine vasopressin elevated in patients with major depression. *Neuropsychopharmacology*, *17*, 284–292.

van Rossum, E. F., Binder, E. B., Majer, M., Koper, J. W., Ising, M., Modell, S. *et al.* (2006). Polymorphisms of the glucocorticoid receptor gene and major depression. *Biological Psychiatry*, *59*, 681–688.

Videbech, P., & Ravnkilde, B. (2004). Hippocampal volume and depression: A meta-analysis of MRI studies. *American Journal of Psychiatry*, *161*, 1957–1966.

Warner-Schmidt, J. L., & Duman, R. S. (2006). Hippocampal neurogenesis: Opposing effects of stress and antidepressant treatment. *Hippocampus*, *16*, 239–249.

Wichers, M., & Maes, M. (2002). The psychoneuroimmuno-pathophysiology of cytokine-induced depression in humans. *International Journal of Neuropsychopharmacology*, *5*, 375–388.

Wichers, M. C., & Maes, M. (2004). The role of indoleamine 2,3-dioxygenase (IDO) in the pathophysiology of interferon-alpha-induced depression. *Journal of Psychiatry and Neuroscience*, *29*, 11–17.

Wichers, M. C., Kenis, G., Leue, C., Koek, G., Robaeys, G., & Maes, M. (2006). Baseline immune activation as a risk factor for the onset of depression during interferon-alpha treatment. *Biological Psychiatry*, *60*, 77–79.

Xu, H., Chen, Z., He, J., Haimanot, S., Li, X., Dyck, L. *et al.* (2006). Synergetic effects of quetiapine and venlafaxine in preventing the chronic restraint stress-induced decrease in cell proliferation and BDNF expression in rat hippocampus. *Hippocampus*, *16*, 551–559.

Yirmiya, R., Pollak, Y., Barak, O., Avitsur, R., Ovadia, H., Bette, M. *et al.* (2001). Effects of anti-depressant drugs on the behavioral and physiological responses to lipopolysaccharide (LPS) in rodents. *Neuropsychopharmacology*, *24*, 531–544.

Zanardi, R., Artigas, F., Moresco, R., Colombo, C., Messa, C., Gobbo, C. *et al.* (2001). Increased 5-hydroxytryptamine-2 receptor binding in the frontal cortex of depressed patients responding to paroxetine treatment: A positron emission tomography scan study. *Journal of Clinical Psychopharmacology*, *21*, 53–58.

Zill, P., Buttner, A., Eisenmenger, W., Moller, H. J., Bondy, B., & Ackenheil, M. (2004). Single nucleotide polymorphism and haplotype analysis of a novel tryptophan hydroxylase isoform (TPH2) gene in suicide victims. *Biological Psychiatry*, *56*, 581–586.

Zobel, A. W., Yassouridis, A., Frieboes, R. M., & Holsboer, F. (1999). Prediction of medium-term outcome by cortisol response to the combined dexamethasone-CRH test in patients with remitted depression. *American Journal of Psychiatry*, *156*, 949–951.

5

Sleep Dysregulation and Related Regulatory Models

Anne Germain* and Michael E. Thase*,†

*Department of Psychiatry, University of Pittsburgh Medical Center, Western Psychiatric Institute and Clinic, Pittsburgh, PA, USA

†Departments of Psychiatry, University of Pennsylvania School of Medicine and the Philadelphia Veterans Affairs Medical Center, Western Psychiatric Institute and Clinic, Pittsburgh, PA, USA

There is increasing recognition that consolidated and restorative sleep is a critical component of mental health. Sleep disruption affects mood regulation in healthy individuals, and people with more longstanding sleep difficulties are at increased risk to develop clinical forms of depression. Insomnia, hypersomnia, and fatigue are frequently reported by depressed patients, and objective indices of sleep disruption and of neurobiological alterations during sleep are consistently observed in depressed patients. In fact, sleep disturbance often precedes relapse or recurrence of depression. The sleep disturbances associated with depression can persist despite otherwise successful antidepressant therapies, and such residual symptoms can increase the risk for depression recurrence. The close, bidirectional relationship between sleep and mood likely arises from their common neurobiological and physiological underpinnings. Monitoring the potentially disruptive effects of antidepressants on sleep, and the effective and timely use of adjunctive treatments that specifically target sleep disturbances in depressed patients, are thus important considerations in the clinically management.

This chapter focuses on sleep in Major Depressive Disorder (MDD) and dysthymia, which are the so-called unipolar depressions. We first describe the physiology, neurobiological, and architecture of normal sleep. We then review the nature of sleep disturbances in depression, and the physiological and neurobiologcal alterations that characterize depression during sleep. Sleep-based and circadian models of depression are then presented. Evidence that sleep disturbances constitute a risk factor for depression and for poor clinical and treatment outcomes is discussed. The effects of antidepressants on sleep are briefly summarized, and we conclude with recommendations for adjunctive pharmacological and non-pharmacological treatments that specifically target sleep disturbances in depressed patients.

OVERVIEW OF NORMAL SLEEP

CONTROL MECHANISMS OF NORMAL SLEEP

Sleep is an active physiological state that is regulated by a circadian component (which is sometimes referred to as process C) which determines the timing of sleep; and a non-circadian, homeostatic process (also called process S) which determines the propensity for sleep based on the duration of prior wakefulness. The circadian process subsumes the endogenous cyclic variations in biological, psychological, and behavioral processes occurring over the 24-hour dark–light cycle (Figure 5.1a). The orchestration of these multiple oscillator systems is managed by pacemakers in the brainstem, including the suprachiasmatic nucleus. While endogenously generated, pacemakers can be trained directly or indirectly by external time givers, or *zeitgebers*, such as light, hormone secretion, and regular social activities such as meal time or bedtime. Circadian variations promote or inhibit the propensity to remain alert and/or fall and stay asleep throughout the 24-hour cycle. Human sleep is promoted during darkness and is coincident with the peak of melatonin release from the pineal gland, the nadir of core body temperature and cortisol secretion. When individuals must sleep at a suboptimal circadian time, such as is the case with delayed sleep phase syndrome or shift work, sleep is both perceived to be of poorer quality and, by more objective measures, lighter and more disrupted. Even 1 day of suboptimal sleep is accompanied by mood dysregulation and cognitive impairments and more sustained periods of disrupted sleep are associated with deleterious – and oft underappreciated – consequences.

The homeostatic process of sleep regulation refers to the increase in sleep propensity as a function of prior wakefulness (see Figure 5.1b; Borbely & Wirz-Justice, 1982a). Slow-wave sleep (SWS) and slow-wave activity (SWA) are objective indices of the homeostatic sleep process. SWS and SWA are derived

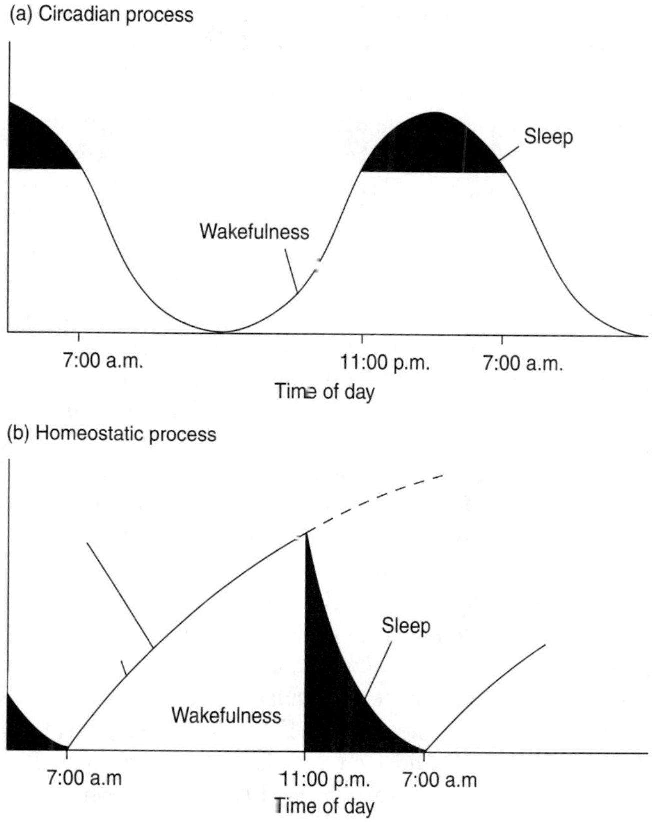

FIGURE 5.1 Two-process model of sleep regulation (from Achermann & Borbely, 2003). The circadian process (process C) enhances the maintenance of wakefulness during the circadian day, and the maintenance of sleep at night. The homeostatic process (process S) increases with increasing duration of prior wakefulness.

from quantitative electroencephalographic (EEG) power spectral analysis. They are amplified during sleep following sleep deprivation, are more prominent in the first half of the night, and gradually decrease across each successive 90-minute cycle of rapid eye movement (REM) and non-REM sleep (described below). SWS and SWA are also considered markers of the restorative function of sleep (Borbely & Achermann, 1992).

Sleep quality and consolidation are optimized when sleep occurs at the optimal circadian time (night, around the nadir of core body temperature and cortisol secretion, and peak melatonin secretion) and after enough awake time has elapsed so that sleep propensity reaches a sufficient threshold to permit a rapid sleep onset and consolidation-yielding restorative sleep.

NORMAL SLEEP ARCHITECTURE AND SLEEP NEUROBIOLOGY

The circadian and homeostatic processes of sleep regulation are the fundamental templates in which multiple neurophysiological changes occur in arousal- and sleep-promoting brain networks. These changes have been measured in humans by polysomnography (PSG) since the 1960s. PSG refers to the ensemble of electroencephalographic (EEG), electromyographic (EMG), and electooculographic (EOG) measures collected during wakefulness and sleep. PSG provided the measurement tool by which the two distinct neurobiological states of rapid eye movement (REM) sleep and non-REM (NREM) sleep were identified. PSG characteristics of wakefulness, REM sleep and NREM sleep are described below (see Figure 5.2). PSG sleep measurements reflect summative integration of electrical signals arising from cortical and subcortical areas, and the brainstem. Animal models of wake–sleep regulation and, more recently, sleep neuroimaging methods have identified activation/deactivation patterns in different brain regions across the sleep–wake cycle. Sleep is not a process of uniform, brain-wide neuronal deactivation, since not all brain regions are equally deactivated or activated during sleep relative to wakefulness.

Wakefulness is characterized by high-frequency, low-amplitude EEG activity, REMs, and elevated muscle tone (Figure 5.2a). Cortical arousal and wakefulness are maintained via sustained activity of cholinergic and monoaminergic brainstem arousal centers of the brainstem reticular formation, including the pedunculopontine and dorsolateral tegmenta (PPT/LDT), locus coeruleus (LC), and raphe nucleus via a dorsal pathway through the thalamus and to the cortex, and via a ventral pathway, from the brainstem through the basal forebrain and the cortex (Jones, 2005). Activity of these systems also is mediated by orexin/hypocretin (Mignot *et al.*, 2002; Moore *et al.*, 2001; Zeitzer *et al.*, 2003), a neuromodulator produced by the lateral hypothalamus. Orexin/hypocretin neurons have efferents to the areas of the brainstem and basal forebrain that promote arousal.

Saper *et al.* (2001) proposed that the reciprocally inhibitory system formed by the lateral hypothalamus and ventrolateral preoptic area (VLPOA) constitutes a "flip-flop" sleep switch by which the transitions between sleep and wakefulness are regulated. Neurons of the VLPOA are one group of the few brain cells dedicated to generating and maintaining sleep (Sherin *et al.*, 1996), via two pathways: a direct pathway via inhibition of the thalamus, and an indirect pathway via inhibition of the brainstem monoaminergic system and orexin/hypocretin system. The VLPOA shares reciprocal inhibitory connections with the orexin neurons of the lateral hypothalamus, and with the aminergic ascending arousal system. The "on" switch position triggers and maintains sleep, while the "off" position triggers and maintains wakefulness. Activation of the solitary tract nucleus and VLPOA inhibits all wake-promoting areas such as the brainstem reticular formation, lateral hypothalamus, and basal forebrain, and enables NREM sleep. NREM sleep includes both lighter (stages 1 and 2) and deeper (SWS; stages 3 and 4) stages of sleep. NREM sleep is characterized by rhythmic thalamocortical oscillations

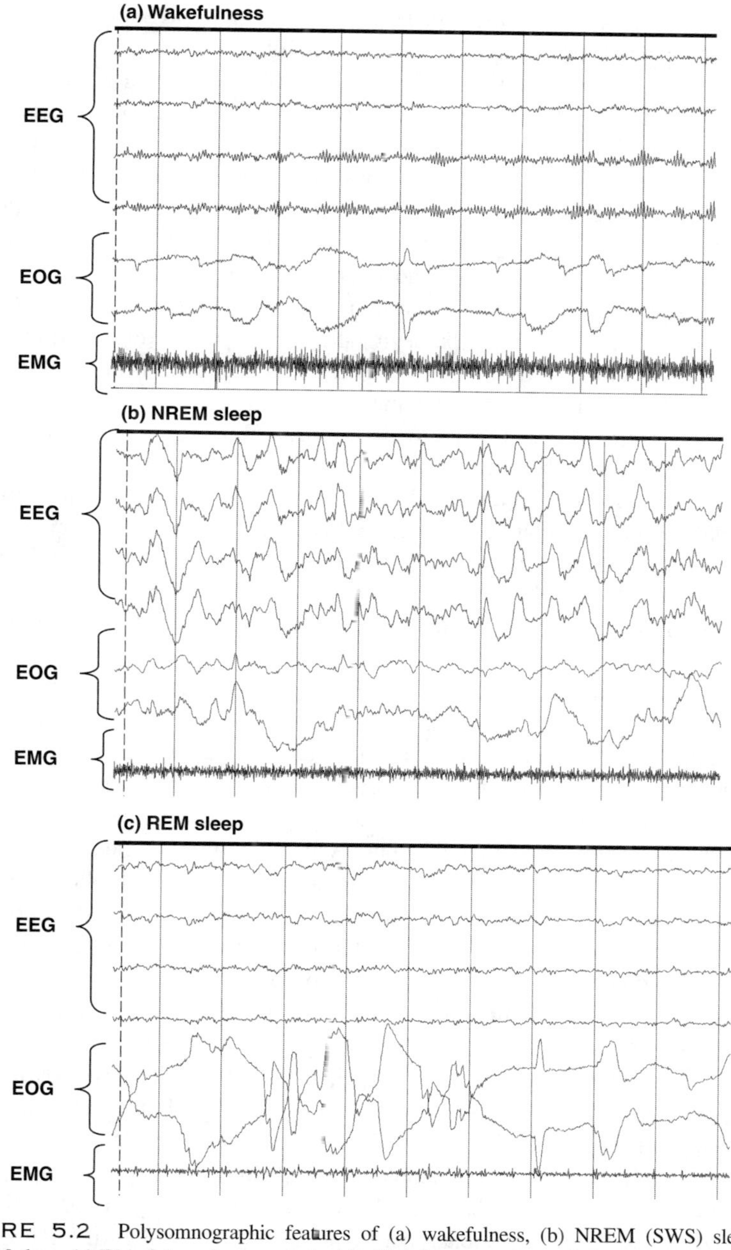

FIGURE 5.2 Polysomnographic features of (a) wakefulness, (b) NREM (SWS) sleep, and (c) REM sleep. (a) Wakefulness is characterized by high-frequency, low-amplitude EEG activity, rapid eye movements, and elevated muscle. (b) Slow-wave sleep is characterized by low-frequency, high-amplitude EEG waves, absence of eye movements, and a slight decrease in muscle tone compared to wakefulness. (c) REM is characterized by fast-frequency low-amplitude EEG signal, rapid eye movements, and muscle atonia. EEG: electroencephalogram; EOG: electrooculogram; EMG: electromyogram.

most marked during SWS, rolling or no eye movements, and a slight decrease in muscle tone compared to wakefulness (Figure 5.2b).

Stages 1 and 2 sleep account for the majority of a night's sleep. Stage 1 sleep is characterized by slowing of the EEG, the onset of slow, rolling eye movements, and slightly decreased muscle tone. Sleep spindles and the K-complex identify the onset of stage 2 sleep. SWS is characterized by low-frequency, high-amplitude EEG signals. Stages 3 and 4 only differ in the proportion of slow waves within a determined period of recording. SWS is more prominent during the first half of the night, and decreases progressively over the course of the sleep period. Autonomic activation is greatly attenuated during NREM sleep, as indicated by increased parasympathetic tone and reduced sympathovagal tone (Pagani *et al.*, 1986). Neuroimaging sleep studies in healthy individuals have shown that whole-brain glucose metabolism and blood flow are reduced by 30–40% during NREM sleep relative to wakefulness (Nofzinger *et al.*, 2002). NREM sleep is associated with reduced metabolic and blood flow in the wake-promoting areas including the pontine and midbrain reticular formation and thalamus, and in associative cortices relative to wakefulness (Braun *et al.*, 1997; Jones, 1994; Jones, 2000; Pace-Schott & Hobson, 2002; Saper *et al.*, 2001). Blunted activity of these regions during NREM sleep indicates that NREM is induced by attenuated brainstem input to the thalamus, and thalamocortical oscillations. In healthy subjects, NREM sleep is also characterized by reduced activity of paralimbic cortical regions, including the anterior cingulate gyrus and parahippocampal gyrus relative to wakefulness (Braun *et al.*, 1997; Nofzinger *et al.*, 2002). Braun *et al.* (1997) suggested that this disengagement of paralimbic structures and isolation of limbic structures (e.g., amygdala, hippocampus) from other heteromodal cortical regions may facilitate the restorative function of NREM sleep.

REM sleep occurs on average 90 minutes after the onset of sleep, and is characterized by fast-frequency low-amplitude EEG signals similar to those observed during wakefulness, REMs, and muscle atonia (Figure 5.2c). REM sleep arises from increased cholinergic activity from the LDT and PPT nuclei following the release of noradrenergic and serotonergic inhibition by the LC and raphe nucleus, respectively. Increased cholinergic activity, in turn, facilitates disinhibition of the thalamus and cortex, and produces EEG desynchrony (Hobson & Pace-Schott, 2002; Pace-Schott & Hobson, 2002; Siegel, 2000). REM sleep periods increase in duration as the night progresses. Awakenings from REM sleep are more often associated with dream recalls than awakenings from light or deep sleep. At the autonomic level, REM sleep is characterized by heightened sympathovagal and lower parasympathetic tones than NREM sleep in healthy subjects (Berlad *et al.*, 1993). Whole-brain glucose metabolism is increased by 16% during REM sleep relative to NREM sleep; in fact, whole-brain glucose metabolism during REM sleep does not differ significantly from wakefulness levels (Braun *et al.*, 1997). Neuroimaging studies in healthy subjects have reliably shown that REM sleep is characterized by increased regional cerebral metabolic activity and blood flow in the amygdala and anterior paralimbic areas, and increased activity in the medial pons and thalamus, relative to wakefulness. Lateral prefrontal, parietal regions, and primary sensory cortices are further deactivated relative to wakefulness during REM sleep. These selective activation and deactivation patterns during REM sleep have yielded the hypothesis that dreams reflect the mental representations of high limbic activations in conjunction with deactivation of high-order cortical regions (Maquet *et al.*, 1996). Together, the heightened activity of brainstem cholinergic nuclei, thalamus, and limbic regions as well as increased autonomic activity observed indicate that REM sleep is an endogenous state of heightened central and autonomic arousal.

In summary, findings derived from animal models and PSG and functional neuroimaging studies of sleep in humans indicate that NREM sleep is a state of lower arousal that may contribute to the restorative function of sleep, whereas REM is a state of heightened limbic and physiological arousal. As the neurophysiological processes of NREM and REM sleep overlap considerably with central brain and peripheral physiological mechanisms that are involved in mood regulation, which have been shown to be altered during in depression, it is not surprising that sleep disturbances are one of the hallmarks of depression and related affective disorders.

SLEEP AND CIRCADIAN DISTURBANCES IN DEPRESSION

Insomnia is the difficulty to fall or stay asleep despite adequate opportunity for sleep, and is reported by as many as 90% of depressed patients (e.g., Tsuno *et al.*, 2005). Hypersomnia, which is prolonged sleep duration extended by more than 1 hour over habitual total sleep time, is reported from between 6% and 36% of depressed persons, but more commonly endorsed by younger depressed people and in patients with seasonal, bipolar, and atypical depressive disorders (Posternak & Zimmerman, 2001; Roberts *et al.*, 2000). Of note, fatigue and low energy are endorsed by the vast majority of depressed patients, regardless of whether they experience insomnia or hypersomnia (e.g., Maurice-Tison *et al.*, 1994; Tylee *et al.*, 1999). Depressed people often report other sleep disturbances, including nightmares, nocturnal panic attacks, and excessive daytime sleepiness (Ohayon *et al.*, 1997).

Objective, polysomnographic measures of sleep support the subjective complaints of sleep disruption in depression, although the strength of these correlations usually is relatively weak (see Riemann *et al.*, 2001 for review). In addition to sleep fragmentation, alterations in the timing, duration, and intensity of REM sleep, as well as decreases in both the timing and quantitative indices of non-REM (NREM) sleep, have been consistently observed in depressed people. Sleep fragmentation is evidenced by an increased latency to sleep, an increased number and duration of nocturnal awakenings, and sustained awakening before the desired "good morning" time. Difficulty falling or staying asleep results in reduced total sleep time and poor sleep efficiency (ratio of total sleep time/total time spent in bed). Reduced sleep efficiency in depression is affected by age (i.e., older people are more likely to suffer from this than younger people) as well as depression severity. Thus, younger people with relatively mild depressions may manifest no objective signs of sleep fragmentation in the sleep lab.

REM disturbances, such as reduced latency to the first episode of REM sleep episode and increased density of REMs are recurrent findings in depression when compared to healthy subjects (Argyropoulos & Wilson, 2005a; Benca *et al.*, 1992b). Kupfer initially proposed that reduced REM latency may be a biomarker for depressive disease, which could even distinguish primary from secondary depression (Kupfer, 1976), although latter studies challenged this hypothesis (Thase *et al.*, 1984). Subsequent work has documented that reduced REM latency is observed a relatively broad range of psychiatric disorders (Benca *et al.*, 1992).

The several sleep disturbances associated with depression evince different patterns of expression across time and may therefore represent both correlates of the disorder and/ or correlates of vulnerability to the disorder. Some objective sleep disturbances observed in depressed patients are more trait-like, such as decreased SWS and reduced REM latency. Other disturbances, such as increased REM density and reduced sleep efficiency, are more state-dependent, and tend to normalize during remission (Buysse *et al.*, 2001). The more consistent sleep characteristics are observed in non-depressed relatives of depressed patients, and thus, may be considered to be correlates of genetic phenotypes of depression.

Functional sleep neuroimaging studies provide further evidence that the neurobiological underpinnings of sleep differ significantly in depression and healthy subjects. Using positron emission tomography (PET), Ho *et al.* (1996) reported that depressed patients showed increased cerebral glucose metabolism in the amygdala and hippocampus, posterior cingulate, occipital and temporal cortices, and the pons during NREM sleep compared to healthy subjects. They also found that depressed patients were relatively hypofrontal during NREM sleep. Together, these observations were taken as indicative of a hyperarousal state during sleep in depression.

The results which suggest central hyperarousal and hypofrontality during NREM sleep in depressed patients were replicated and further investigated by Nofzinger *et al.* (2005). Based on the observation that SWS and SWA are reduced in depressed patients, and that increases in SWS following sleep deprivation is predominantly increased in frontal cortical regions, it was hypothesized that NREM sleep changes in depression would be associated with deficits in frontal executive function. Because NREM sleep involves the reduction of activity in brainstem and forebrain arousal-promoting regions, it was also hypothesized that sleep disturbances in depression may arise from the persistence of neuronal activity in arousal-promoting regions during NREM sleep. Results showed that relative regional glucose metabolism in broad prefrontal cortical regions remained elevated during NREM sleep relative to wakefulness in depressed patients compared to healthy subjects. Further analyses indicated that this pattern was attributable to a "floor effect" in depressed patients, as hypometabolism in prefrontal cortical regions during wakefulness limited further deactivation during NREM sleep, in contrast to marked decline in regional brain glucose metabolism in healthy subjects.

Hypometabolism in frontal regions and decreased SWS/SWA during NREM in depression may directly interfere with the restorative role of sleep for executive functions. Both NREM sleep and wakefulness were associated with hypermetabolism in an extended area including the brainstem and basal forebrain, amygdala, pregenual and subgenual anterior cingulate cortices, parahippocampal and fusiform gyrus, and occipital cortex in depressed patients. Thalamic metabolic activity remained elevated during NREM sleep relative to wakefulness in patients compared to healthy subjects. Since these regions are components of the ventral emotional neural network that subserves production of affect (Phillips *et al.*, 2003a, b), it was suggested that heightened metabolic activity during NREM sleep contributes to sleep disruption in depression by maintaining elevated levels of central, affect-related arousal during sleep.

The neurobiological correlates of REM sleep in depressed patients also differ from those observed in healthy subjects. Depressed patients show greater and broader activation of limbic and paralimbic regions, compared to healthy subjects during REM sleep. They also show greater activation of the midbrain reticular formation, dorsolateral prefrontal cortex bilaterally, and left primary sensorimotor, premotor, and parietal cortices compared to healthy subjects. These regional brain patterns' hypermetabolism in depression may relate to the affect dysregulation in depression and to cognitive deficits (Nofzinger *et al.*, 2005).

Attenuation of hyperarousal may underlie the mood-lifting effects of sleep deprivation (see below). Sleep deprivation is associated with rapid improvements in mood in depressed patients, which is reversed following recovery sleep. Several studies reveal elevated metabolism and cerebral blood flow in the anterior paralimbic and ventral frontal regions predict positive response to sleep deprivation, and that elevated neuronal activity in these regions are normalized in responders to sleep deprivation (Ebert *et al.*, 1991; Smith *et al.*, 2002a, Volk *et al.*, 1992, 1997; Wu *et al.*, 1992, 1999). It remains to be seen if these alterations in central arousal pertain to all depressions or only those in which insomnia is a prominent feature; it is not clear if people who oversleep during depressive episodes evince a characteristic pattern of cerebral metabolism. PSG studies can characterize sleep in patients who meet criteria for clinical subtypes such as atypical depression (McGrath *et al.*, 2006), seasonal affective disorder (Rosenthal *et al.*, 1984), and anergic bipolar depression (Thase *et al.*, 1989), in which hypersomnolence is more common than insomnia. These subtypes have increased REM indices which may reflect increased cerebral metabolism in the paralimbic regions, but relatively normal SWS and sleep continuity.

Other neurobiological disturbances that suggest dysregulation of circadian rhythms have been observed in depressed patients. For instance, increased mean core body temperature and decreased period amplitude are relatively robust findings in depression (e.g., Souetre *et al.*, 1989a). Alterations of patterns of secretion for other indices of the endogenous circadian period such as melatonin, growth hormone, and cortisol have also been reported in depressed patients in some (e.g., Claustrat *et al.*, 1984; Koenigsberg *et al.*, 2004a; Peeters *et al.*, 2004) but not all (e.g., Posener *et al.*, 2000; Thompson *et al.*, 1988) studies. There is some evidence that circadian rhythms are less affected by social *zeitgebers* in depression (Stetler *et al.*, 2004). Diurnal mood variations also differ in healthy and depressed subjects. Many patients with non-seasonal depression show more severe symptoms in the morning (Joyce *et al.*, 2005), whereas healthy subjects typically report a worsening of mood in the evening compared to the morning (e.g., Gordijn *et al.*, 1994; Tolle & Goetze, 1987). Evening improvements in mood in depressed patients are associated with increased activation in brain regions that are part of the dorsal cortical neural network that is involved in mood regulation (Germain *et al.*, 2007). Increased activation in the dorsal cortical network involved in affect regulation in the evening may reflect a delayed compensatory mechanism to normalize the hypermetabolic activity of the ventral cortical network previously described during wakefulness and NREM sleep in depressed patients (Germain *et al.*, 2004; Nofzinger *et al.*, 2005).

Advances in molecular biology have provided indications that genetic polymorphisms involved in the regulation of circadian processes, called clock genes, may constitute a critical mechanism by which circadian and sleep disturbances predispose individuals to mood disorders (Bunney & Bunney, 2000a). Clock gene polymorphisms have been associated with disease chronicity in patients with bipolar disorder (Benedetti *et al.*, 2003b), and propensity to relapse in recurrent major depression (Serretti *et al.*, 2004). More research is clearly needed, and advances in genetics will offer new insights into the molecular underpinnings of sleep- and circadian-specific mechanisms that may contribute to the vulnerability to depression.

In summary, fatigue is a prominent clinical feature of depression and virtually all people who seek treatment for depression report either insomnia or hypersomnia. Objective PSG measurements corroborate patients' subjective complaints of sleep disruption in depression, and sleep neuroimaging studies show that arousal-promoting brain regions and networks involved in affect regulation are hypermetabolic during sleep in depression, at least among those experiencing insomnia. In addition to directly contributing to sleep disruption, these anomalies may directly contribute to daytime symptoms by interfering with the role of sleep in mood regulation and cognitive functions. Together, these findings raise the possibility that improving clinical outcomes in depression may require the normalization of the pathophysiological and abnormal neurobiological underpinnings of depression throughout the sleep–wake cycle.

SLEEP-FOCUSED MODELS OF DEPRESSION

Based on the observations that sleep and circadian disturbances characterize depression, models that emphasize the role of these disturbances in the pathogenesis of depression have been proposed. Of note, these models are not mutually exclusive. Heterogeneous symptom clusters in depression may arise from disturbances in multiple sleep and circadian processes.

A group of phase-advance models of depression hypothesize that depression arises from a mismatch between the circadian rhythm that regulates temperature, cortisol, and REM sleep and the sleep–wake rhythm. These hypotheses are derived from observations that depressed patients show shorter circadian periods, early morning awakenings, and reduced REM sleep latency compared to healthy subjects. The internal phase coincidence model postulates that depression arises when awakening from sleep occurs at a sensitive phase of the circadian period (Koenigsberg *et al.*, 2004a). However, controlled studies of the phase-advance hypothesis have failed to show consistent alterations of the circadian period in depressed subjects (Avery *et al.*, 1982; Borbely & Wirz-Justice, 1982b; Lund *et al.*, 1983). A variant of the phase-advance hypothesis proposes weakened coupling between endogenous circadian pacemakers and entrainment stimuli in depression, which underlie circadian and sleep disturbances (Buysse *et al.*, 1990). Such vulnerability in turn increases the risk of depression after life events that disrupt social *zeitgebers* such as regular times for meals, exercise, or bedtime. Recent advances in molecular biology support the latter hypothesis, as polymorphisms in clock gene alleles may mediate the association between the endogenous pacemakers and entrainment cues in depression (Bunney & Bunney, 2000a; Souetre *et al.*, 1989a).

A second sleep model of depression posits that increased REM sleep is depressogenic. This model is based on the observation that depression is associated with an increased "pressure" to REM sleep, as revealed by the reduced latency to REM sleep, increased duration and proportion of REM sleep during sleep, increased number of REMs, and the observation that REM sleep suppression (whether pharmacologically or by selective REM sleep deprivation) is associated with decreased symptom severity (Vogel *et al.*, 1980; Wirz-Justice, 2006). Support for this model has diminished, however, as recent studies found total sleep deprivation more rapidly induces improvements in mood symptoms than selective REM deprivation (Vogel *et al.*, 1990), and that REM sleep suppression is neither a necessary nor a sufficient characteristic of effective antidepressant medications (Wirz-Justice & Van den Hoofdakker, 1999a).

Another model suggests that the apparent increased pressure for REM sleep in depression is in fact a consequence of a primary deficiency of the homeostatic sleep process (Process S), which permits the early occurrence of REM sleep (Borbély & Wirz-Justice, 1982b). According to this hypothesis, the antidepressant effects of sleep deprivation are attributable to a transient enhancement of Process S. Conversely, the relapse of depression following recovery sleep is attributed to Process S returning to its weak, baseline level (Borbely & Wirz-Justice, 1982a). However, effective antidepressants do not typically enhance SWS or SWA, and may even further reduce both parameters, depending on the particular type of medication employed (Argyropoulos & Wilson, 2005a).

Finally, the social rhythms hypothesis suggests that depression arises at least in part from the disrupted social rhythms that entrain the circadian pacemaker and regulate sleep in the etiology of depression. This approach suggests that changes in social rhythms directly affect physiological rhythms (Ehlers *et al.*, 1988; Sharpley & Cowen, 1995; Ehlers *et al.*, 1993). It is proposed that individuals are at higher risk for depression when social rhythms are disrupted or become less regular with the occurrence of life events that affect daily routines (e.g., retirement and bereavement, birth of a child, jet lag). There is evidence that social rhythms are less regular in depressed patients compared to non-depressed subjects (Ehlers *et al.*, 1988; Sharpley & Cowen, 1995), and that enhancing the regularity of daily routines improves both sleep and depressive symptoms (Brown *et al.*, 1996; Monk *et al.*, 1994; Shear *et al.*, 1994; Frank *et al.*, 1995, 1997). A definitive test of this hypothesis has yet to be undertaken.

CIRCADIAN AND SLEEP DISTURBANCES AS RISK FACTORS FOR DEPRESSION

There is a close bidirectional relationship between sleep and mood disturbances. Mood disturbances are a reliable consequence of sleep deprivation in healthy individuals (Banks & Dinges, 2007; Durmer & Dinges, 2005), and people with primary sleep disorders have high rates of depression (Buysse *et al.*, 2006). Insomnia, sleep apnea, narcolepsy, and circadian disorders such as advanced or delayed sleep phase syndrome and shift work disorders are often associated with symptoms of depression, including depressed affect, fatigue, apathy, and impaired attention and concentration, and memory deficits (American Academy of Sleep Medicine, 2005) (Greenberg *et al.*, 1987; Moul *et al.*, 2002; Regestein & Monk, 1995; Vandeputte & de Weerd, 2003). Depression is a common comorbid psychiatric condition in sleep-disordered populations (Buysse *et al.*, 2006; Ohayon, 2007; Ohayon & Roth, 2003).

Sleep disturbances, and especially insomnia, are risk factors for depression onset and recurrence. As many as 40% of depressed patients report that insomnia preceded the onset of a first depressive episode, and 56% of depressed patients report that insomnia preceded the recurrence of depression (Ohayon & Roth, 2003). Longitudinal studies have also consistently found that individuals who report insomnia are at increased risk to develop new or recurrent depressive episodes during prospective follow-up (Breslau *et al.*, 1996; Breslau *et al.*, 1998; Chang *et al.*, 1997; Dryman & Eaton, 1991; Eaton *et al.*, 1995; Foley *et al.*, 1999a, b; Ford & Kamerow, 1989; Gillin, 1998; Livingston *et al.*, 1993; Mallon *et al.*, 2000; Szuba *et al.*, 1992; Weissman *et al.*, 1997). This heightened risk, which ranges between 2- and 39-fold across studies, is evident from adolescence to late life. Insomnia is also associated with increased risk of developing an anxiety disorder or a drug use disorder (Ohayon & Roth, 2003). However, most people with an anxiety or drug use disorder report that insomnia occurred concurrently with or after the onset of these disorders, and not as a prodromal feature as is typical in depression. The latter findings suggest that insomnia may arise from a mechanism that is disturbed early in the progression of mood disorders, whereas the sleep mechanism may be disrupted later in the development of an anxiety and/or drug use disorder. Idiopathic hypersomnia and fatigue have also been found to increase the risk for new onset depression (Ford & Cooper-Patrick, 2001; Roberts *et al.*, 2000).

Subjective sleep disturbances in depression are associated with poor clinical outcomes, and predict treatment response. Depressed patients who experience significant insomnia, hypersomnia, and nightmares are at increased severity of suicidality (Agargun *et al.*, 1997; Nowell & Buysse, 2001; Perlis *et al.*, 2006). Reports of poor sleep quality prior to psychotherapy for depression predicts poorer response to treatment (Buysse *et al.*, 1999; Dew *et al.*, 1996), whereas reports of improved sleep quality post-treatment are associated with lower rates of recurrence of depression (Buysse *et al.*, 1997). Nevertheless, between 20% and 50% of depressed patients who show clinically meaningful improvements in depression with cognitive-behavioral or pharmacological treatments of depression continue to experience significant sleep disturbances (Carney *et al.*, 2007; Dombrovski *et al.*, 2007; Manber *et al.*, 2003; Nierenberg *et al.*, 1999; Thase *et al.*, 1998). Residual insomnia and variability in symptoms of insomnia following antidepressant treatment, increase the risks of recurrence and relapse (Dombrovski *et al.*, 2007; Karp *et al.*, 2004; Paykel *et al.*, 1995). Hypersomnia and fatigue are also often persistent, despite treatment, and are also associated with an increased risk of relapse (Nierenberg *et al.*, 1999).

Objective indices of sleep disruption predict clinical outcomes in depression. Sleep latency, sleep duration, sleep maintenance, and some REM sleep parameters such as the density of REMs sometimes normalize in depressed patients during periods of recovery (Buysse *et al.* 1992; Reynolds *et al.*, 1997). However, the persistence of REM sleep anomalies and of fragmented sleep post-psychotherapy treatment for depression is associated with non-response (Buysse *et al.* 1999; Thase *et al.*, 1998) and increased risks of the recurrence (Buysse *et al.* 1997; Thase *et al.*, 1998). Of note, persistently increased REM density post-treatment in alcoholics has predicted relapse at follow-up (Clark *et al.*, 1998), which suggests that increased REM sleep intensity may be a correlate of altered brainstem arousal mechanisms during sleep that increases the risk for relapse in vulnerable populations.

SPECIFICITY OF SLEEP DISTURBANCES AS RISK FACTORS FOR DEPRESSION

The determination of which sleep disturbances are risk factors for depression requires longitudinal epidemiological studies, which are not yet available. Such studies must include concomitant thorough assessments of sleep disturbances and various psychiatric disorders. However, there are indications that insomnia is a more robust predictor of the onset or recurrence of depression than are anxiety or substance use disorders. Some evidence suggests that the occurrence of insomnia early after exposure to a trauma event increases the risk for developing post-traumatic stress disorder, but definitive longitudinal population studies are not yet available.

Growing evidence indicates that a sufficient amount of consolidated sleep is a critical component of physical and mental health. This evidence highlights the need for effective treatment of sleep disturbances, and implies the inclusion of sleep-specific assessment measures, as well as consideration of adjunctive sleep interventions for psychiatric patients who experience clinically significant sleep disturbances. Sleep disturbance should be thought of as a risk factor that can be modified through the use of effective, targeted treatments.

TREATMENT IMPLICATIONS

Given that sleep disturbances predict the onset or recurrence of a depressive episode and that they often persist despite treatment, close attention to the effects of antidepressants on sleep should be a primary component of depression treatment strategies. In a significant minority of patients, adjunctive treatments that target sleep disturbances may be needed to reduce insomnia, hypersomnia and/or daytime fatigue. Improvements in sleep disturbances, in turn, may directly contribute to improve the daytime mood dysregulation and cognitive deficits of depression.

Effects of antidepressants on sleep

A significant minority of depressed patients continue to report insomnia, fatigue, and hypersomnia following remission of depression. Sleep may be differentially affected by diverse antidepressant medications (see Table 5.1; Thase *et al.*, 2006). Tricyclic antidepressants (TCA) suppress REM sleep and may have limited benefit for initiating or maintaining sleep. Monoamine oxidase inhibitors are

TABLE 5.1 Effects of Antidepressants on Objective Sleep Measures

Antidepressant category	Sleep continuity	Slow-wave sleep	REM sleep
Tricyclic antidepressants	↓ to ↑	↔	↓ *
Monoamine oxidase inhibitors	↔ to ↓	↔ to ↓	↓
SSRI	↔ to ↓	↔ to ↓	↓
Venlaflaxine	↔ to ↓	↔	↓
SNRI	↔ to ↓	↔ to ↓	↓
Trazodone	↑	↔ to ↑	↔ to ↑
Bupropion	↓	↔ to ↓	↔
Mirtazepine	↑	↔	↔

Note: ↓ Sleep parameter is decreased post-treatment compared to pre-treatment baseline;
↑ Sleep parameter is increased post-treatment compared to pre-treatment baseline;
↔ Sleep parameter is not affected post-treatment compared to pre-treatment baseline.

*May increase eye movement density.

likewise potent REM suppressors and generally do not improve, or may actually worsen sleep continuity. Selective serotonin reuptake inhibitors (SSRIs) generally decrease total sleep time, sleep efficiency, and increase the number and duration of nocturnal arousal and movement time (Jindal *et al.*, 2003; Kapur *et al.*, 2005). The serotonin and norepinephrine reuptake inhibitor (SNRI) venlafaxine has likewise been found to suppress REM sleep, reduce stage 2/3 sleep, and increase wakefulness and light sleep in healthy subjects and depressed patients. In depressed subjects, SSRIs and SNRIs have minimal benefits for improving sleep consolidation or enhancing SWS (Thase *et al.*, 2006).

Only a few antidepressant drugs reliably improve sleep continuity disturbances: trazodone, nefazodone, and mirtazapine, as well as the investigational compound agomelatine (see Thase *et al.*, 2006). Although three of these medications are structurally distinct (nefazodone and trazodone are related), they all share two common properties: none of them are potent monoamine reuptake inhibitors and all block 5HT-2 receptors. None of these medications are widely used as antidepressants in the United States, although trazodone is widely prescribed "off label" as a sedative-hypnotic because it has no liability for development of tolerance or abuse. The advantage of nefazodone over the SSRI fluoxetine for improvement of insomnia was clearly demonstrated in the study of Rush *et al.* (1998), though the drug is rarely used today because of rare but potentially fatal liver failure. Mirtazapine is more widely prescribed, both alone and in combination with SSRIs or SNRIs. Mirtazapine is also a potent antihistamine, however, and is associated with relatively high rates of daytime sedation, increased appetite, and weight gain over time. Agomelatine is distinguished by blocking melatonin receptors (see Zupancic & Guilleminault, 2006), but its use in treating sleep disturbance is still being explored.

While insomnia and sedation can be side effects of antidepressant medications, residual insomnia and fatigue symptoms are often present prior to treatment in individuals who endorse these residual symptoms (Nierenberg *et al.*, 1999). In light of findings that residual symptoms increase the risk of relapse and recurrence of depression, as well as poor social functioning and reduced quality of life, adjunctive treatments that target sleep disturbances in depressed patients may reasonably contribute to improving clinical outcomes.

Adjunctive pharmacological treatments for sleep disturbances in depression

A number of clinical trials indicate that residual sleep disturbances in depression can be effectively reduced by adjunctive sleep treatments. Benzodiazepines (e.g., temazepam, lorazepam) and γ-aminobutyric acid (GABA) type A receptor agonists also called non-benzodiazepines hypnotics (e.g., zolpidem, eszopiclone) have been used to treat insomnia in depressed patients (Asnis *et al.*, 1999; Dolberg *et al.*, 1998; Fava *et al.*, 2006; Nowell and Buysse, 2001). GABA-A receptor agonists are also effective, safe, have limited abuse potential, and are approved for long-term use in the treatment of insomnia (Mendez-Sanchez & Uscanga, 1991; Roth *et al.*, 2005; Walsh *et al.*, 2007). Objective improvements in sleep latency and sleep consolidation have been reported. Benzodiazepines remain the most widely prescribed hypnotics, but the evidence is limited that objective sleep improvements are maintained over time (Perlis *et al.*, 2006). Consensus recommendations suggest that they should be used with caution for 3 weeks or less given their potential for abuse and increased risks of falls in elderly patients. Table 5.2 presents recommended pharmacological treatments of insomnia in depression. For instance, combination of an SSRI with trazodone yields improvements in 65–92% of patients, but as many as one-third of patients may also experience excessive daytime sedation. Close monitoring may avoid a potential "serotonin syndrome" with SSRI-trazodone combination (Metz and Shader, 1990; Nierenberg *et al.*, 1994).

Evidence does not support the belief that adjunctive hypnotic treatment may interfere with the response to antidepressant treatment. Rather, two studies have shown treatment augmentation with zolpidem or eszopiclone, which can improve sleep symptoms and enhance therapeutic gains in daytime symptom severity (Asnis *et al.*, 1999; Fava *et al.*, 2006). In the first study, depressed patients on an SSRI and who received zolpidem (10 mg) for 4 weeks showed significant increases in total sleep time and reduced duration of nocturnal awakenings compared to patients on a SSRI who were randomized to the placebo condition (Asnis *et al.*, 1999). In the second study, the combination of fluoxetine and eszopiclone (3 mg) administered over an 8-week trial was associated with significantly greater improvement in total sleep time compared to patients who received fluoxetine and placebo (Fava *et al.*, 2006). Greater reductions in daytime symptoms of depression were also observed in the combined group, suggesting that sleep improvements can directly contribute to daytime mood. However, neither of these two studies evaluated the durability of the therapeutic gains reported in the combined therapy groups.

Other adjunctive treatments for persistent hypersomnia and fatigue in depressed patients are also available (Baldwin & Papakostas, 2006). One recommendation is to preferentially prescribe antidepressants that are unlikely to be associated with hypersomnia and fatigue as a side effect (e.g., bupropion,

TABLE 5.2 Pharmacological Treatments of Insomnia in Depression

Medication (generic name)	Suggested dosage
Lorazepam	0.5–2 mg qhs
Tamazepam	7.5–30 mg qhs
Trazodone	50–200 mg qhs
Mirtrazapine	15–30 mg qhs
Gabapentin	300–1200 mg qhs
Eszopiclone	3 mg qhs
Zolpidem	5–10 mg (12.5 mg CR) qhs
Melatonin	5–10 mg qhs
Amitriptyline, Doxepin	25–150 mg qhs

fluoxetine, and venlafaxine). The second recommendation is to use non-stimulant adjunctive agents to reduce fatigue and hypersomnia. Modafinil may reduce symptoms in patients who have persistent fatigue and sleepiness despite antidepressant therapy (DeBattista *et al.*, 2003; Fava *et al.*, 2005; Fava *et al.*, 2007). Although longer-term studies of modafinil augmentation have not been undertaken, results of one 12-week open-label extension study did suggest that the benefits were sustained (Thase *et al.*, 2006). Case series are available for the use of bupropion as an adjunctive treatment for fatigue and hypersomnia (e.g., Masand *et al.*, 1998) but controlled studies on such combinations have not been conducted to ascertain efficacy and safety of these agents as adjunct treatments for depression. Finally, atomoxetine has shown some potential to alleviate hypersomnia and fatigue in an open-label trial with depressed patients (Papakostas *et al.*, 2006). When severe fatigue and hypersomnolence persist, one might also consider adding psychostimulants, although the potential benefits of adjunctive therapy must be weighed against the uncertain risks of protracted "off-label" treatment with controlled substances.

Adjunctive non-pharmacological treatments for sleep disturbances in depression

Cognitive-behavioral strategies to treat insomnia, such as stimulus control and sleep restriction, have been shown to effectively reduce sleep latency and wake time after sleep onset, and to improve sleep efficiency in patients with primary insomnia, as well as in patients with insomnia comorbid with other psychiatric and medical conditions (Edinger *et al.*, 2005; Montgomery & Dennis, 2003; Morin *et al.*, 1994; Murtagh & Greenwood, 1995; Smith *et al.*, 2002b). Stimulus control limits the use of the sleep environment (bed, bedroom) to sleep (and sexual activity), and may directly address sleep avoidance and compensatory behaviors that disrupt circadian sleep–wake regulation mechanisms (Bootzin & Nicassio, 1978). Sleep restriction involves a routine sleep–wake schedule, which limits the time spent in bed while awake and favors sleep consolidation (Spielman *et al.*, 1987). Stimulus control (limiting the use of sleep environment to sleep), and sleep restriction allow for the normalization of the two processes that control sleep by aligning the timing and duration of sleep. Of note, sleep hygiene is not equivalent to stimulus control and sleep restriction. Sleep hygiene refers to an ensemble recommendations aimed at increasing the frequency of sleep-promoting habits (e.g., early light exposure) and at decreasing the frequency of habits and factors that may interfere with sleep quality (e.g., caffeine use, uncomfortable sleep environment). Sleep hygiene does not include specific, patient-tailored recommendations for sleep restriction or stimulus control. Meta-analysis and clinical trials have repeatedly shown that sleep hygiene is much less effective for alleviating insomnia than stimulus control and sleep restriction (Morin *et al.*, 1994; Montgomery and Dennis, 2003).

Cognitive-behavioral interventions for insomnia (CBI-I) have been successfully used in depressed patients in two published studies. Morawetz (2003) reported that a 6-week self-help insomnia treatment administered to patients with comorbid depression and insomnia was associated with significant improvements in sleep quality, as defined by one or more of the following: reduction of at least 2 hours in the time taken to fall asleep; an increase of at least 2 hours in total sleep time during the night; a reduction of at least eight in the number of awakenings during the night; elimination of usage of sleeping medication, with no deterioration in key sleep parameters. Clinically meaningful reductions in depressive symptoms on the Beck Depression Inventory (BDI) were observed. Taylor *et al.* (2007a, b) also reported that a cognitive-behavioral treatment for insomnia delivered over six face-to-face individual visits was associated with clinically significant changes in sleep latency, wake time after sleep onset, total sleep time, and sleep efficiency. Therapy gains were maintained at the 3-month follow-up. Furthermore, treatment completers showed normalized sleep patterns post treatment, and 87.5% showed depression scores on the BDI within normal range. While randomized control trials will ascertain the efficacy and durability of CBT-I in depressed patients, these preliminary findings support the hypothesis that improvements in sleep contribute to improving depression symptoms.

Other non-pharmacological interventions may also accelerate and augment the effects of first-line antidepressant treatments on circadian and sleep disturbances (Wirz-Justice *et al.*, 2005). These include bright light exposure and sleep deprivation (wake therapy). Bright light therapy has been mainly used for seasonal affective disorder. However, there is some evidence that bright light therapy can also be associated with rapid and clinically significant improvements in non-seasonal depression. Benedetti *et al.* (2003a) have used light therapy as an adjunct to antidepressant medication in depressed patients, and have shown more rapid and enhanced treatment response rate compared to medications only. A recent meta-analysis on the efficacy of phototherapy for non-seasonal depression indicated that the therapeutic benefits associated with bright light therapy are modest, and best when administered in the morning as an adjunctive treatment to sleep deprivation responders (Benedetti *et al.*, 2003b). Bright light therapy is typically delivered with light boxes, but visors are also available. Effective doses and times of exposure for bright light exposure range >2500 lux for 2 hours per day (in the morning), to 10 000 lux for 30 minutes per day (Terman & Terman, 2005a; Tuunainen *et al.*, 2004). Morning light exposure has more pronounced effects. Common side effects of light therapy include eyestrain, headache, nausea, agitation, and insomnia. Hypomania can also occur as potential adverse effect. Bright light therapy is a viable option for depressed patients who prefer non-pharmacological treatments, who do not respond or do not tolerate other pharmacological options, for antepartum and postpartum depression, and in depressed patients for whom pharmacological antidepressants may be contraindicated.

The antidepressants effects of sleep deprivation have been recognized for over 30 years (see Tuunainen *et al.*, 2004) More than half of depressed patients show rapid and considerable improvements in mood with sleep deprivation. Total sleep deprivation, partial sleep in the second half of the night, and REM sleep deprivation have all been associated with mood improvements in depressed patients.

The main limitation of sleep deprivation is the rapid reversal of therapeutic effects following recovery sleep or naps. A variety of strategies have been used to prevent or delay depression relapse following sleep deprivation. Some strategies consist of advancing the timing of sleep by several hours abruptly and returning it progressively to the habitual schedule (Wirz-Justice & Van den Hoofdakker, 1999b) or administering bright light therapy immediately after the sleep deprivation. A short sleep phase advance following a single night of wake therapy can also prevent relapse following sleep deprivation (Riemann *et al.*, 1996). Combining sleep deprivation with pharmacological treatments hastens the antidepressant effects of medication, and extends the beneficial effects of sleep deprivation (Benedetti *et al.*, 1997, 2003b; Lam & Kennedy, 2004). The major problem with sleep deprivation strategies is implementation, as very few patients and even fewer clinicians seem willing to persevere with sleep deprivation schedules in real-world settings, despite a wealth of empirical data to support its therapeutic promise.

DIRECTIONS FOR FUTURE THEORY AND RESEARCH DEVELOPMENT

A large body of evidence has accumulated in the past 30 years to support a bidirectional relationship between sleep disturbances and depression. Objective measures of sleep and sleep neuroimaging point to functionally significant overlaps between the physiological and neurobiological mechanisms that are hypothesized to underlie depression and those involved in sleep–wake regulation. However, the molecular, physiological, neurobiological, behavioral, and psychosocial pathways that underlie and modulate the relationship between mood disorders and sleep disturbances remain scarcely investigated. Carefully designed longitudinal and clinical studies are necessary to elucidate the nature and mechanism that underlie the relationship between sleep disturbances and depression, to identify environmental risk factors that stimulate genetic vulnerability to sleep disturbances and depression and to identify potential protective factors to reduce the risk of mood disorders in individuals who experience sleep disruption. Studies that combine state-of-the science sleep measurement methods and thorough depression assessment in combination with the use of treatment probes are required for developing integrative models of the mechanisms underlying and affected by depression across the sleep–wake cycle.

There is an urgent need for the development and testing of innovative, empirically based treatments that target and normalize the substrate(s) of sleep disturbances in depression. There is also a clear need for development of rational, evidence-based guidelines for the treatment of sleep disturbances in depressed patients. While there is some evidence that combination treatments confer additional therapeutic benefits during the acute treatment phase, controlled clinical studies with long-term follow-ups are required to assess the durability of adjunctive pharmacological and non-pharmacological sleep-focused treatments. Long-term follow-ups will also permit the evaluation of the role of consolidated sleep in the relationship between depression and poor physical health outcomes. Studies that compare the efficacy of various sequential treatments in patients who show treatment-resistant sleep disturbances, as well as studies that compare the effects of sequential and/or combination treatments are required to determine the clinical usefulness and safety of these approaches. Comparative studies are needed to assess the acceptability, efficacy, and durability of sleep-focused pharmacological and non-pharmacological treatments. Finally, the investigation of the predictors and correlates of sleep resistance to antidepressant treatments, and of response to sleep-focused interventions, will help to identify new venues for the development of more specific treatment options.

REFERENCES

Achermann, P., & Borbely, A. A. (2003). Mathematical models of sleep regulation. *Frontiers in Bioscience, 8*, S683–S693.

Agargun, M. Y., Kara, H., & Solmaz, M. (1997). Sleep disturbances and suicidal behavior in patients with major depression. *Journal of Clinical Psychiatry, 58*, 249–251.

American Academy of Sleep Medicine. The International Classification of Sleep Disorders, Second Edition (ICSD-2): Diagnostic and Coding Manual. Second Edition ed. 2005.

Argyropoulos, S. V., & Wilson, S. J. (2005a). Sleep disturbances in depression and the effects of antidepressants, 1. *International Review of Psychiatry, 17*, 237–245.

Asnis, G. M., Chakraburtty, A., DuBoff, E. A., Krystal, A., Londborg, P. D., Rosenberg, R. *et al.* (1999). Zolpidem for persistent insomnia in SSRI-treated depressed patients. *Journal of Clinical Psychiatry, 60*, 668–676.

Avery, D. H., Wildschiodtz, G., & Rafaelsen, O. J. (1982). Nocturnal temperature in affective disorder. *Journal of Affective Disorder*, 4, *61*–71.

Baldwin, D. S., & Papakostas, G. I. (2006). Symptoms of fatigue and sleepiness in major depressive disorder. *Journal of Clinical Psychiatry, 67*(Suppl. 6), 9–15.

Banks, S., & Dinges, D. F. (2007). Behavioral and physiological consequences of sleep restriction. *Journal of Clinical and Sleep Medicine, 3*, 519–528.

Benca, R. M., Obermeyer, W. H., Thisted, R. A., & Gillin, J. C. (1992). Sleep and psychiatric disorders: A meta-analysis. *Archives of General Psychiatry, 49*, 651–668.

Benedetti, F., Barbini, B., Lucca, A., Campori, E., Colombo, C., & Smeraldi, E. (1997). Sleep deprivation hastens the antidepressant action of fluoxetine. *European Archives of Psychiatry and Clinical Neuroscience, 247*, 100–103.

Benedetti, F., Colombo, C., Pontiggia, A., Bernasconi, A., Florita, M., & Smeraldi, E. (2003a). Morning light treatment hastens the antidepressant effect of citalopram: A placebo-controlled trial. *Journal of Clinical Psychiatry, 64*, 648–653.

Benedetti, F., Colombo, C., Serretti, A., Lorenzi, C., Pontiggia, A., Barbini, B. *et al.* (2003b). Antidepressant effects of light therapy combined with sleep deprivation are influenced by a functional polymorphism within the promoter of the serotonin transporter gene. *Biological Psychiatry, 54*, 687–692.

Berlad, I., Shlitner, A., Ben Haim, S., & Lavie, P. (1993). Power spectrum analysis and heart rate variability in Stage 4 and REM sleep: Evidence for state-specific changes in autonomic dominance. *Journal of Sleep Research, 2*, 88–90.

Bootzin, R. R., & Nicassio, P. M. (1978). Behavioral treatments of insomnia. In M. Hersen, R. E. Eisler, & P. M. Miller (Eds.), *Progress in Behavior Modification* (vol. 6, pp. 1–45). New York: Academic Press.

Borbely, A. A., & Achermann, P. (1992). Concepts and models of sleep regulation: An overview. *Journal of Sleep Research, 1*, 63–79.

Borbely, A. A., & Wirz-Justice, A. (1982a). A two-process model of sleep regulation. II. Implications for depression. *Human Neurobiology*, *1*, 205–210.

Borbely, A. A., & Wirz-Justice, A. (1982b). Sleep, sleep deprivation and depression. A hypothesis derived from a model of sleep regulation. *Human Neurobiology*, *1*, 205–210.

Braun, A. R., Balkin, T. J., Wesenten, N. J., Carson, R. E., Varga, M., Baldwin, P. *et al.* (1997). Regional cerebral blood flow throughout the sleep–wake cycle. An H2(15)O PET study. *Brain*, *120*, 1173–1197.

Breslau, N., Roth, T., Rosenthal, L., & Andreski, P. (1996). Sleep disturbance and psychiatric disorders: A longitudinal epidemiological study of young adults. *Biological Psychiatry*, 39, 411–418.

Breslau, N., Chilcoat, H., & Schultz, L. R. (1998). Anxiety disorders and the emergence of sex differences in major depression. *Journal of Gender Specific Medicine*, *1*, 33–39.

Brown, L. F., Reynolds, C. F., Monk, T. H., Prigerson, H. G., Dew, M. A., Houck, P. R. *et al.* (1996). Social rhythm stability following late-life spousal bereavement: Associations with depression and sleep impairment. *Psychiatry Research*, *62*, 161–169.

Bunney, W. E., & Bunney, B. G. (2000a). Molecular clock genes in man and lower animals: Possible implications for circadian abnormalities in depression. *Neuropsychopharmacology*, *22*, 335–345.

Buysse, D. J., Jarrett, D. B., Miewald, J. M., Kupfer, D. J., & Greenhouse, J. (1990). Minute-by-minute analysis of REM sleep timing in major depression. *Biological Psychiatry*, *28*, 911–925.

Buysse, D. J., Kupfer, D. J., Frank, E., Monk, T. H., & Ritenour, A. (1992). Electroencephalographic sleep studies in depressed outpatients treated with interpersonal psychotherapy. II. Longitudinal studies at baseline and recovery. *Psychiatry Research*, *40*, 27–40.

Buysse, D. J., Frank, E., Lowe, K. K., Cherry, C. R., & Kupfer, D. J. (1997). Electroencephalographic sleep correlates of episode and vulnerability to recurrence in depression. *Biological Psychiatry*, *41*, 406–418.

Buysse, D. J., Tu, X. M., Cherry, C. R., Begley, A. E., Kowalski, J., Kupfer, D. J. *et al.* (1999). Pretreatment REM sleep and subjective sleep quality distinguish depressed psychotherapy remitters and nonremitters. *Biological Psychiatry*, *45*, 205–213.

Buysse, D. J., Hall, M., Begley, A., Cherry, C. R., Houck, P. R., Land, S. *et al.* (2001). Sleep and treatment response in depression: New findings using power spectral analysis. *Psychiatry Research*, *103*, 51–67.

Buysse, D. J., Germain, A., Nofzinger, E. A., & Kupfer, D. J. (2006). Mood disorders and sleep. In D. J. Stein, D. J. Kupfer, & A. F. Schatzberg (Eds.), *American Psychiatric Publishing Textbook of Mood Disorders* (pp. 717–737). Arlington Virginia: American Psychiatric Publishing, Inc.

Carney, C. E., Segal, Z. V., Edinger, J. D., & Krystal, A. D. (2007). A comparison of rates of residual insomnia symptoms following pharmacotherapy or cognitive-behavioral therapy for major depressive disorder. *Journal of Clinical Psychiatry*, *68*, 254–260.

Chang, P. P., Ford, D. E., Mead, L. A., Cooper-Patrick, L., & Klag, M. J. (1997). Insomnia in young men and subsequent depression. The Johns Hopkins Precursors Study. *American Journal of Epidemiology*, *146*, 105–114.

Clark, C. P., Gillin, J. C., Golshan, S., Demodena, A., Smith, T. L., Danowski, S. *et al.* (1998). Increased REM sleep density at admission predicts relapse by three months in primary alcoholics with a lifetime diagnosis of secondary depression. *Biological Psychiatry*, *43*, 601–607.

Claustrat, B., Chazot, G., Brun, J., Jordan, D., & Sassolas, G. (1984). A chronobiological study of melatonin and cortisol secretion in depressed subjects: Plasma melatonin, a biochemical marker in major depression. *Biological Psychiatry*, *19*, 1215–1228.

DeBattista, C., Doghramji, K., Menza, M. A., Rosenthal, M. H., & Fieve, R. R. (2003). Adjunct modafinil for the short-term treatment of fatigue and sleepiness in patients with major depressive disorder: A preliminary double-blind, placebo-controlled study. *Journal of Clinical Psychiatry*, *64*, 1057–1064.

Dew, M. A., Reynolds, C. F., Buysse, D. J., Houck, P. R., Hoch, C. C., Monk, T. H. *et al.* (1996). EEG sleep profiles during depression: Effects of episode duration and other clinical and psychosocial factors in older adults. *Archives of General Psychiatry*, *53*, 148–156.

Dolberg, O. T., Hirschmann, S., & Grunhaus, L. (1998). Melatonin for the treatment of sleep disturbances in major depressive disorder. *American Journal of Psychiatry*, *155*, 1119–1121.

Dombrovski, A. Y., Mulsant, B. H., Houck, P. R., Mazumdar, S., Lenze, E. J., Andreescu, C. *et al.* (2007). Residual symptoms and recurrence during maintenance treatment of late-life depression. *Journal of Affective Disorders*, *103*, 77–82.

Dryman, A., & Eaton, W. W. (1991). Affective symptoms associated with the onset of major depression in the community: Findings from the U.S. National Institute of Mental Health Epidemiologic Catchment Area Program. *Acta Psychiatrica Scandinavica*, *84*(1), 1–5.

Durmer, J. S., & Dinges, D. F. (2005). Neurocognitive consequences of sleep deprivation. *Seminars in Neurology*, *25*, 117–129.

Eaton, W. W., Badawi, M., & Melton, B. (1995). Prodromes and precursors: Epidemiologic data for primary prevention of disorders with slow onset. *American Journal of Psychiatry*, *152*, 967–972.

Ebert, D., Feistel, H., & Barocka, A. (1991). Effects of sleep deprivation on the limbic system and the frontal lobes in affective disorders: A study with Tc-99m-HMPAO SPECT. *Psychiatry Research*, *40*, 247–251.

Edinger, J. D., Wohlgemuth, W. K., Krystal, A. D., & Rice, J. R. (2005). Behavioral insomnia therapy for fibromyalgia patients: A randomized clinical trial. *Archives of Internal Medicine*, *165*, 2527–2535.

Ehlers, C. L., Frank, E., & Kupfer, D. J. (1988). Social zeitgebers and biological rhythms: A unified approach to understanding the etiology of depression. *Archives of General Psychiatry*, *45*, 948–952.

Ehlers, C. L., Kupfer, D. J., Frank, E., & Monk, T. H. (1993). Biological rhythms and depression: The role of zeitgebers and zeitstoreres. *Depression*, *1*, 285–293.

Fava, M., Thase, M. E., & DeBattista, C. (2005). A multicenter, placebo-controlled study of modafinil augmentation in partial responders to selective serotonin reuptake inhibitors with persistent fatigue and sleepiness. *Journal of Clinical Psychiatry*, *66*, 85–93.

Fava, M., McCall, W. V., Krystal, A., Wessel, T., Rubens, R., Caron, J., *et al.* (2006). Eszopiclone co-administered with fluoxetine in patients with insomnia coexisting with major depressive disorder. *Biological Psychiatry, 59*, 1052–1060.

Fava, M., Thase, M. E., DeBattista, C., Doghramji, K., Arora, S., & Hughes, R. J. (2007). Modafinil augmentation of selective serotonin reuptake inhibitor therapy in MDD partial responders with persistent fatigue and sleepiness. *Annals of Clinical Psychiatry*, *19*, 153–159.

Foley, D. J., Monjan, A., Simonsick, E. M., Wallace, R. B., & Blazer, D. G. (1999a). Incidence and remission of insomnia among elderly adults: An epidemiologic study of 6,800 persons over three years. *Sleep*, *22*, S366–S372.

Foley, D. J., Monjan, A. A., Izmirlian, G., Hays, J. C., & Blazer, D. G. (1999b). Incidence and remission of insomnia among elderly adults in a biracial cohort. *Sleep*, *22*, S373–S378.

Ford, D. E., & Kamerow, D. B. (1989). Epidemiologic study of sleep disturbances and psychiatric disorders. An opportunity for prevention? *JAMA*, *262*, 1479–1484.

Ford, D. E., & Cooper-Patrick, L. (2001). Sleep disturbances and mood disorders: An epidemiologic perspective. *Depression and Anxiety*, *14*, 3–6.

Frank, E., Kupfer, D. J., Ehlers, C. L., Monk, T. H., Cornes, C., Carter, S. *et al.* (1995). Interpersonal and social rhythm therapy for bipolar disorder: Integrating interpersonal and behavioral approaches. *The Behavioral Therapist*, *17*, 144–149.

Frank, E., Hlastala, S., Ritenour, A., Houck, P., Tu, X. M., Monk, T. H. *et al.* (1997). Inducing lifestyle regularity in recovering bipolar disorder patients: Results from the maintenance therapies in bipolar disorder protocol. *Biological Psychiatry*, *41*, 1165–1173.

Germain, A., Nofzinger, E. A., Kupfer, D. J., & Buysse, D. J. (2004). Neurobiology of non-REM sleep in depression: Further evidence for hypofrontality and thalamic dysregulation. *American Journal of Psychiatry*, *161*, 1856–1863.

Germain, A., Nofzinger, E. A., Meltzer, C. C., Wood, A., Kupfer, D. J., Moore, R. Y. *et al.* (2007). Diurnal variation in regional brain glucose metabolism in depression. *Biological Psychiatry*, *62*, 438–445.

Gillin, J. C. (1998). Are sleep disturbances risk factors for anxiety, depressive and addictive disorders? *Acta Psychiatrica Scandinavica – Supplement*, *393*, 39–43.

Gordijn, M. C., Beersma, D. G., Bouhuys, A. L., Reinink, E., & Van den Hoofdakker, R. H. (1994). A longitudinal study of diurnal mood variation in depression; characteristics and significance. *Journal of Affective Disorders*, *31*, 261–273.

Greenberg, G. D., Watson, R. K., & Deptula, D. (1987). Neuropsychological dysfunction in sleep apnea. *Sleep, 10*, 254–262.

Ho, A. P., Gillin, J. C., Buchsbaum, M. S., Wu, J. C., Abel, L., & Bunney, W. E. (1996). Brain glucose metabolism during non-rapid eye movement sleep in major depression: A positron emission tomography study. *Archives of General Psychiatry, 53*, 645–652.

Hobson, J. A., & Pace-Schott, E. F. (2002). The cognitive neuroscience of sleep: Neuronal systems, consciousness and learning. *Nature Reviews of Neuroscience, 3*, 679–693.

Jindal, R. D., Friedman, E. S., Berman, S. R., Fasiczka, A. L., Howland, R. H., & Thase, M. E. (2003). Effects of sertraline on sleep architecture in patients with depression. *Journal of Clinical Psychopharmacology, 23*, 540–548.

Jones, B. E. (1994). Basic mechanisms of sleep–wake states. In M. H. Kryger, T. Roth, & W. C. Dement (Eds.), *Principles and Practice of Sleep Medicine, 2nd ed.* (pp. 145–162). Philadelphia: W. B. Saunders Company.

Jones, B. E. (2000). Basic mechanisms of sleep–wake states. In M. H. Kryger, T. Roth, & W. E. Dement (Eds.), *Principles and Practice of Sleep Medicine, 3rd ed.* (pp. 134–154). Philadelphia, PA: W. B. Saunders Company.

Jones, B. E. (2005). Basic mechanisms of sleep–wake states. In M. H. Kryger, T. Roth, & W. C. Dement (Eds.), *Principles and Practice of Sleep Medicine, 4th ed.*, (pp. 136–153).

Joyce, P. R., Porter, R. J., Mulder, R. T., Luty, S. E., McKenzie, J. M., Miller, A. L. *et al.* (2005). Reversed diurnal variation in depression: associations with a differential antidepressant response, tryptophan: large neutral amino acid ratio and serotonin transporter polymorphisms. *Psychological Medicine, 35*, 511–517.

Kapur, V. K., Baldwin, C. M., Resnick, H. E., Gottlieb, D. J., & Nieto, F. J. (2005). Sleepiness in patients with moderate to severe sleep-disordered breathing. *Sleep, 28*, 472–477.

Karp, J. F., Buysse, D. J., Houck, P. R., Cherry, C., Kupfer, D. J., & Frank, E. (2004). Relationship of variability in residual symptoms with recurrence of major depressive disorder during maintenance treatment. *American Journal of Psychiatry, 161*, 1877–1884.

Koenigsberg, H. W., Teicher, M. H., Mitropoulou, V., Navalta, C., New, A. S., Trestman, R. *et al.* (2004a). 24-h Monitoring of plasma norepinephrine, MHPG, cortisol, growth hormone and prolactin in depression. *Journal of Psychiatric Research, 38*, 503–511.

Kupfer, D. J. (1976). REM latency: a psychobiologic marker for primary depressive disease. *Biological Psychiatry, 11*, 159–174.

Lam, R. W., & Kennedy, S. H. (2004). Evidence-based strategies for achieving and sustaining full remission in depression: Focus on metaanalyses. *Canadian Journal of Psychiatry, 49*, 17S–26S.

Livingston, G., Blizard, B., & Mann, A. (1993). Does sleep disturbance predict depression in elderly people? A study in inner London. *British Journal of General Practice, 43*, 445–448.

Lund, R., Kammerloher, A., & Dirlich, G. (1983). Body temperature in endogenously depressed patients during depression and remission. In T. A. Wehr & F. K. Goodwin (Eds.), *Circadian Rhythms in Psychiatry* (pp. 77–88). Pacific Grove, CA: The Boxwood Press.

Mallon, L., Broman, J. E., & Hetta, J. (2000). Relationship between insomnia, depression, and mortality: A 12-year follow-up of older adults in the community. *International Psychogeriatrics*, 12, 295–306.

Manber, R., Rush, A. J., Thase, M. E., Arnow, B., Klein, D., Trivedi, M. H. *et al.* (2003). The effects of psychotherapy, nefazodone, and their combination on subjective assessment of disturbed sleep in chronic depression. *Sleep, 26*, 130–136.

Maquet, P., Peters, J., Aerts, J., Delfiore, G., Degueldre, C., Luxen, A. *et al.* (1996). Functional neuroanatomy of human rapid-eye-movement sleep and dreaming. *Nature, 383*, 163–166.

Masand, P. S., Anand, V. S., & Tanquary, J. F. (1998). Psychostimulant augmentation of second generation antidepressants: a case series. *Depression and Anxiety, 7*, 89–91.

Maurice-Tison, S., Bourgeois, M., Perez, P., & Salamon, R. (1994). [Fatigue and signs of depressive symptoms in general practice in Aquitaine]. *Encephale, 20*(3), 611–614.

McGrath, P. J., Stewart, J. W., Quitkin, F. M., Chen, Y., Alpert, J. E., Nierenberg, A. A. *et al.* (2006). Predictors of relapse in a prospective study of fluoxetine treatment of major depression. *American Journal of Psychiatry, 163*, 1542–1548.

Mendez-Sanchez, N., & Uscanga, L. (1991). Physiopathology of cholesterol biliary calculi. *Review of Gastroenterology Mex*, *56*, 137–143.

Metz, A., & Shader, R. I. (1990). Adverse interactions encountered when using trazodone to treat insomnia associated with fluoxetine. *International Clinical Psychopharmacology*, *5*, 191–194.

Mignot, E., Taheri, S., & Nishino, S. (2002). Sleeping with the hypothalamus: Emerging therapeutic targets for sleep disorders. *Nature Neuroscience*, *5*(Suppl), 1071–1075.

Monk, T. H., Petrie, S. R., Hayes, A. J., & Kupfer, D. J. (1994). Regularity of daily life in relation to personality, age, gender, sleep quality and circadian rhythms. *Journal of Sleep Research*, *3*, 196–205.

Montgomery, P. & Dennis, J. (2003). Cognitive behavioural interventions for sleep problems in adults aged 60+. *The Cochrane Database of Systematic Reviews, CD003161.*

Moore, R. Y., Abrahamson, E. A., & Van Den Pol, A. (2001). The hypocretin neuron system: An arousal system in the human brain. *Archives Italiennes de Biologie*, *139*, 195–205.

Morawetz, D. (2003). Insomnia and depression: Which comes first? *Sleep Research Online*, *5*, 77–81.

Morin, C. M., Culbert, J. P., & Schwartz, S. M. (1994). Nonpharmacological interventions for insomnia: A meta-analysis of treatment efficacy. *American Journal of Psychiatry*, *151*, 1172–1180.

Moul, D. E., Nofzinger, E. A., Pilkonis, P. A., Houck, P. R., Miewald, J. M., & Buysse, D. J. (2002). Symptom reports in severe chronic insomnia. *Sleep*, *25*, 553–563.

Murtagh, D. R., & Greenwood, K. M. (1995). Identifying effective psychological treatments for insomnia: A meta-analysis. *Journal of Consulting and Clinical Psychology*, *63*, 79–89.

Nierenberg, A. A., Adler, L. A., Peselow, E., Zornberg, G., & Rosenthal, M. (1994). Trazodone for antidepressant-associated insomnia. *American Journal of Psychiatry*, *151*, 1069–1072.

Nierenberg, A. A., Keefe, B. R., Leslie, V. C., Alpert, J. E., Pava, J. A., Worthington, J. J. *et al.* (1999). Residual symptoms in depressed patients who respond acutely to fluoxetine. *Journal of Clinical Psychiatry*, *60*, 221–225.

Nofzinger, E. A., Buysse, D. J., Miewald, J. M., Meltzer, C. C., Price, J. C., Sembrat, R. C. *et al.* (2002). Human regional cerebral glucose metabolism during non-rapid eye movement sleep in relation to waking. *Brain*, *125*, 1105–1115.

Nofzinger, E. A., Buysse, D. J., Germain, A., Price, J. C., Meltzer, C. C., Miewald, J. M. *et al.* (2005). Alterations in regional cerebral glucose metabolism across waking and non-rapid eye movement sleep in depression. *Archives of General Psychiatry*, *62*, 387–396.

Nowell, P. D., & Buysse, D. J. (2001). Treatment of insomnia in patients with mood disorders. *Depression and Anxiety*, *14*, 7–18.

Ohayon, M. M. (2007). Insomnia: A ticking clock for depression? *Journal of Psychiatric Research*, *41*, 893–894.

Ohayon, M. M., & Roth, T. (2003). Place of chronic insomnia in the course of depressive and anxiety disorders. *Journal of Psychiatric Research*, *37*, 9–15.

Ohayon, M. M., Morselli, P. L., & Guilleminault, C. (1997). Prevalence of nightmares and their relationship to psychopathology and daytime functioning in insomnia subjects. *Sleep*, *20*, 340–348.

Pace-Schott, E. F., & Hobson, J. A. (2002). The neurobiology of sleep: genetics, cellular physiology and subcortical networks. *Nature Reviews Neuroscience*, *3*, 591–605.

Pagani, M., Lombardi, F., Guzzetti, S., Rimoldi, O., Furlan, R., Pizzinelli, P. *et al.* (1986). Power spectral analysis of heart rate and arterial pressure variabilities as a marker of sympatho-vagal interaction in man and conscious dog. *Circulation Research*, *59*, 178–193.

Papakostas, G. I., Petersen, T. J., Burns, A. M., & Fava, M. (2006). Adjunctive atomoxetine for residual fatigue in major depressive disorder. *Journal of Psychiatric Research*, *40*, 370–373.

Paykel, E. S., Ramana, R., Cooper, Z., Hayhurst, H., Kerr, J., & Barocka, A. (1995). Residual symptoms after partial remission: an important outcome in depression. *Psychological Medicine*, *25*, 1171–1180.

Perlis, M. L., Smith, L. J., Lyness, J. M., Matteson, S. R., Pigeon, W. R., Jungquist, C. R. *et al.* (2006). Insomnia as a risk factor for onset of depression in the elderly. *Behavioral Sleep Medicine*, *4*, 104–113.

Phillips, M. L., Drevets, W. C., Rauch, S. L., & Lane, R. (2003a). Neurobiology of emotion perception I: The neural basis of normal emotion perception. *Biological Psychiatry*, *54*, 504–514.

Phillips, M. L., Drevets, W. C., Rauch, S. L., & Lane, R. (2003b). Neurobiology of emotion perception II: Implications for major psychiatric disorders. *Biological Psychiatry, 54*, 515–528.

Posener, J. A., DeBattista, C., Williams, G. H., Chmura, K. H., Kalehzan, B. M., & Schatzberg, A. F. (2000). 24-Hour monitoring of cortisol and corticotropin secretion in psychotic and nonpsychotic major depression. *Archives of General Psychiatry, 57*, 755–760.

Posternak, M. A., & Zimmerman, M. (2001). Symptoms of atypical depression. *Psychiatry Research, 104*, 175–181.

Regestein, Q. R., & Monk, T. H. (1995). Delayed sleep phase syndrome: A review of its clinical aspects. *American Journal of Psychiatry, 152*, 602–608.

Reynolds, C. F., Frank, E., Houck, P. R., Mazumdar, S., Dew, M. A., Cornes, C. *et al.* (1997). Which elderly patients with remitted depression remain well with continued interpersonal psychotherapy after discontinuation of antidepressant medication? *American Journal of Psychiatry, 154*, 958–962.

Riemann, D., Hohagen, F., Konig, A., Schwarz, B., Gomille, J., Voderholzer, U. *et al.* (1996). Advanced vs. normal sleep timing: Effects on depressed mood after response to sleep deprivation in patients with a major depressive disorder. *Journal of Affective Disorders, 37*, 121–128.

Riemann, D., Berger, M., & Voderholzer, U. (2001). Sleep and depression-results from psychobiological studies: An overview. *Biological Psychiatry, 57*, 67–103.

Roberts, R. E., Shema, S. J., Kaplan, G. A., & Strawbridge, W. J. (2000). Sleep complaints and depression in an aging cohort: A prospective perspective. *American Journal of Psychiatry, 157*, 81–88.

Rosenthal, N. E., Sack, D. A., Gillin, J. C., Lewy, A. J., Goodwin, F. K., Davenport, Y. *et al.* (1984). Seasonal affective disorder: A description of the syndrome and preliminary findings with light therapy. *Archives of General Psychiatry, 41*, 72–80.

Roth, T., Walsh, J. K., Krystal, A., Wessel, T., & Roehrs, T. A. (2005). An evaluation of the efficacy and safety of eszopiclone over 12 months in patients with chronic primary insomnia. *Sleep Medicine, 6*, 487–495.

Rush, A. J., Armitage, R., Gillin, J. C., Yonkers, K. A., Winokur, A., Moldofsky, H. *et al.* (1998). Comparative effects of nefazodone and fluoxetine on sleep in outpatients with major depressive disorder. *Biological Psychiatry, 44*, 3–14.

Saper, C. B., Chou, T. C., & Scammell, T. E. (2001). The sleep switch: hypothalamic control of sleep and wakefulness. *Trends in Neurosciences, 24*, 726–731.

Serretti, A., Artioli, P., Lorenzi, C., Pirovano, A., Tubazio, V., & Zanardi, R. (2004). The C(-1019)G polymorphism of the 5-HT1A gene promoter and antidepressant response in mood disorders: preliminary findings. *International Journal of Neuropsychopharmacology, 7*, 453–460.

Sharpley, A. L., & Cowen, P. J. (1995). Effect of pharmacologic treatments on the sleep of depressed patients. *Biological Psychiatry, 37*, 85–98.

Shear, M. K., Randall, J., Monk, T. H., Ritenour, A., Tu, X., Frank, E. *et al.* (1994). Social rhythm in anxiety disorder patients. *Anxiety, 1*, 90–95.

Sherin, J. E., Shiromani, P. J., McCarley, R. W., & Saper, C. B. (1996). Activation of ventrolateral preoptic neurons during sleep. *Science, 271*, 216–219.

Siegel, J. M. (2000). Brainstem mechanisms generating REM sleep. In M. H. Kryger, T. Roth, & W. C. Dement (Eds.), *Principles and Practice of Sleep Medicine, 3rd ed.* (pp. 112–133). Philadelphia: W. B. Saunders Company.

Smith, G. S., Reynolds, C. F., Houck, P. R., Dew, M. A., Ma, Y., Mulsant, B. H. *et al.* (2002a). Glucose metabolic response to total sleep deprivation, recovery sleep, and acute antidepressant treatment as functional neuroanatomic correlates of treatment outcome in geriatric depression. *American Journal of Geriatric Psychiatry, 10*, 561–567.

Smith, M. T., Perlis, M. L., Park, A., Smith, M. S., Pennington, J., Giles, D. E. *et al.* (2002b). Comparative meta-analysis of pharmacotherapy and behavior therapy for persistent insomnia. *American Journal of Psychiatry, 159*, 5–11.

Souetre, E., Salvata, E., Belugou, J., Fringuey, D., Candito, M., Krebs, B. *et al.* (1989a). Circadian rhythms in depression and recovery: Evidence for blunted amplitude as the main chronobiological abnormality. *Psychiatry Research, 28*, 263–278.

Spielman, A. J., Saskin, P., & Thorpy, M. J. (1987). Treatment of chronic insomnia by restriction of time in bed. *Sleep, 10*, 45–56.

Stetler, C., Dickerson, S. S., & Miller, G. E. (2004). Uncoupling of social zeitgebers and diurnal cortisol secretion in clinical depression. *Psychoneuroendocrinology, 29*, 1250–1259.

Szuba, M., Yager, A., Guze, B. H., Allen, E. M., & Baxter, J. R. (1992). Disruption of social circadian rhythms in major depression: A preliminary report. *Psychiatry Research, 42*, 221–230.

Taylor, D. J., Lichstein, K. L., Weinstock, J., Sanford, S., & Temple, J. R. (2007a). A pilot study of cognitive-behavioral therapy of insomnia in people with mild depression. *Behavior Therapy, 38*, 49–57.

Taylor, D. J., Mallory, L. J., Lichstein, K. L., Durrence, H. H., Riedel, B. W., & Bush, A. J. (2007b). Comorbidity of chronic insomnia with medical problems. *Sleep, 30*, 213–218.

Terman, M., & Terman, J. S. (2005a). Light therapy for seasonal and nonseasonal depression: Efficacy, protocol, safety, and side effects. *CNS Spectrometry, 10*, 647–663.

Thase, M. E., Kupfer, D. J., & Spiker, D. G. (1984). Electroencephalographic sleep in secondary depression: A revisit. *Biological Psychiatry, 19*, 805–815.

Thase, M. E., Himmelhoch, J. M., Mallinger, A. G., Jarrett, D. B., & Kupfer, D. J. (1989). Sleep EEG and DST findings in anergic bipolar depression. *American Journal of Psychiatry, 146*, 329–333.

Thase, M. E., Fasiczka, A. L., Berman, S. R., Simons, A. D., & Reynolds, C. F. (1998). Electroencephalographic sleep profiles before and after cognitive behavior therapy of depression. *Archives of General Psychiatry, 55*, 138–144.

Thase, M. E., Fava, M., DeBattista, C., Arora, S., & Hughes, R. J. (2006). Modafinil augmentation of SSRI therapy in patients with major depressive disorder and excessive sleepiness and fatigue: A 12-week, open-label, extension study. *CNS Spectrometry, 11*, 93–102.

Thompson, C., Franey, C., Arendt, J., & Checkley, S. A. (1988). A comparison of melatonin secretion in depressed patients and normal subjects. *British Journal of Psychiatry, 152*, 260–265.

Tolle, R., & Goetze, U. (1987). On the daily rhythm of depression symptomatology. *Psychopathology, 20*, 237–249.

Tsuno, N., Besset, A., & Ritchie, K. (2005). Sleep and depression. *Journal of Clinical Psychiatry, 66*, 1254–1269.

Tuunainen, A., Kripke, D. F., & Endo, T. (2004). Light therapy for non-seasonal depression. *Cochrane Database Syst Rev, CD004050.*

Tylee, A., Gastpar, M., Lepine, J. P., & Mendlewicz, J. (1999). DEPRES II (Depression Research in European Society II): A patient survey of the symptoms, disability and current management of depression in the community. DEPRES Steering Committee. *International Clinical Psychopharmacology, 14*, 139–151.

Vandeputte, M., & de Weerd, A. (2003). Sleep disorders and depressive feelings: A global survey with the Beck depression scale. *Sleep Medicine, 4*, 343–345.

Vogel, G. W., Vogel, F., McAbee, R. S., & Thurmond, A. J. (1980). Improvement of depression by REM sleep deprivation. *Archives of General Psychiatry, 37*, 247–253.

Vogel, G. W., Buffenstein, A., Minter, K., & Hennessey, A. (1990). Drug effects on REM sleep and on endogenous depression. *Neuroscience and Biobehavioral Reviews, 14*, 49–63.

Volk, S., Kaendler, S. H., Weber, R., Georgi, K., Maul, F., Hertel, A. *et al.* (1992). Evaluation of the effects of total sleep deprivation on cerebral blood flow using single photo emission computerized tomography. *Acta Psychiatrica Scandinavica, 86*, 478–483.

Volk, S. A., Kaendler, S. H., Hertel, A., Maul, F. D., Manoocheri, R., Weber, R. *et al.* (1997). Can response to partial sleep deprivation in depressed patients be predicted by regional changes of cerebral blood flow? *Psychiatry Research, 75*, 67–74.

Walsh, J. K., Krystal, A. D., Amato, D. A., Rubens, R., Caron, J., Wessel, T. C. *et al.* (2007). Nightly treatment of primary insomnia with eszopiclone for six months: Effect on sleep, quality of life, and work limitations. *Sleep, 30*, 959–968.

Weissman, M. M., Greenwald, S., Nino-Murcia, G., & Dement, W. C. (1997). The morbidity of insomnia uncomplicated by psychiatric disorders. *General Hospital Psychiatry*, 19, 245–250.

Wirz-Justice, A. (2006). Biological rhythm disturbances in mood disorders. *International Clinical Psychopharmacology, 21*(Suppl 1), S11–S15.

Wirz-Justice, A., & Van den Hoofdakker, R. H. (1999). Sleep deprivation in depression: What do we know, where do we go? *Biological Psychiatry*, *46*, 445–453.

Wirz-Justice, A., Benedetti, F., Berger, M., Lam, R. W., Martiny, K., Terman, M. *et al.* (2005). Chronotherapeutics (light and wake therapy) in affective disorders. *Psychological Medicine*, *35*, 939–944.

Wu, J., Buchsbaum, M. S., Gillin, J. C., Tang, C., Cadwell, S., Wiegand, M. *et al.* (1999). Prediction of antidepressant effects of sleep deprivation by metabolic rates in the ventral anterior cingulate and medial prefrontal cortex. *American Journal of Psychiatry*, *156*, 1149–1158.

Wu, J. C., Gillin, J. C., Buchsbaum, M. S., Hershey, T., Johnson J. C., & Bunney, W. E. (1992). Effect of sleep deprivation on brain metabolism of depressed patients. *American Journal of Psychiatry*, *149*, 538–543.

Zeitzer, J. M., Buckmaster, C. L., Parker, K. J., Hauck, C. M., Lyons, D. M., & Mignot, E. (2003). Circadian and homeostatic regulation of hypocretin in a primate model: Implications for the consolidation of wakefulness. *The Journal of Neuroscience*, *23*, 3555–3560.

Zupancic, M., & Guilleminault, C. (2006). Agomelatine: A preliminary review of a new antidepressant. *CNS Drugs*, *20*, 981–992.

PART II

Cognitive Factors

6

Cognitive Schemas, Beliefs and Assumptions

David J. A. Dozois* and Aaron T. Beck[†]

*Department of Psychology, University of Western Ontario, London, Ontario, Canada
[†]Psychopathology Research Unit, University of Pennsylvania, Philadelphia, PA, USA

Cognitive models of depression share the premise that maladaptive thinking and negative appraisals of life circumstances contribute to the development of this debilitating condition (Abramson *et al.*, 2002; Beck, 1967; Beck *et al.*, 1979; Beevers, 2005; Hankin & Abramson, 2001; Ingram, 1984; Ingram *et al.*, 1998, 2006; Teasdale, 1997; Teasdale & Barnard, 1993). These theories are effectively diathesis–stress models because maladaptive cognition is believed to contribute to the onset of depression in the context of stressful life circumstances. Beck's (1967; Beck *et al.*, 1979) original theory has served as the catalyst for a veritable explosion of research in the area of cognitive vulnerability to depression. Indeed, most contemporary cognitive models of depression have involved refinements and expansions of this basic diathesis–stress framework.

This chapter reviews the evidence pertaining to Beck's theory, highlighting research related to schemas, beliefs and assumptions. After describing Beck's theory, we examine schemas, beliefs and assumptions as vulnerability factors for depression, reviewing evidence pertaining to their sensitivity, specificity and stability. Empirical studies that bear on the theoretical assumption that schemas develop early in life are also discussed and factors that impinge on the development of negative beliefs and schemas are highlighted briefly. We conclude by providing some suggestions for future research.

BECK'S COGNITIVE MODEL

Beck (1967) contended that there are three main levels of thinking involved in the onset, maintenance and exacerbation of depression: depressive self-schemas, maladaptive beliefs/assumptions and negative automatic thoughts. Schemas are central to Beck's cognitive model. Although schemas have been defined in a variety of ways, most definitions incorporate the idea that they consist of both structural (i.e., organizational) properties and propositional (i.e., content) elements (Ingram *et al.*, 1998). Schmidt *et al.* (1999), for example, referred to schemas as "the basic structural components of cognitive organization through which humans come to identify, interpret, categorize, and evaluate their experiences" (p. 129; also see Clark *et al.*, 1999; James *et al.*, 2007). This organized structure is often adaptive insofar as it facilitates the speed with which humans process information, requiring fewer controlled cognitive resources. However, well-organized internal representations of information are sometimes associated with a cost in that information may be selectively attended to, encoded and retrieved in a manner that is colored by one's internal representation (e.g., when individuals are stereotyped based on preconceived ideas of an outgroup; Linville, 1982). In the case of depression, this efficiency entails a bias toward attending to, encoding and retrieving schema-consistent (i.e., negative) information at the expense of positive or neutral information. In other words, previous experience and knowledge structures influence the processing of new information. The self-schemas of individuals who are vulnerable to depression "are considered dysfunctional in that they embody a constellation of dysfunctional attitudes that lead to negative perspectives about oneself, the world, and the future" (Scher *et al.*, 2005, p. 489).

Depressive self-schemas are presumed to develop during early childhood but remain latent until activated later in life by adverse circumstances (see Beck *et al.*, 1979; James *et al.*, 2007; Young *et al.*, 2003). An individual who is vulnerable to depression, for instance, may have dormant core beliefs that he or she fundamentally inept or unlovable. This person may not succumb to depression, however, as long as this belief system is not activated. Once this schema is kindled by life stress (e.g., a failure or rejection experience), however, the individual may engage in information processing biases (see Chapter 7; Scher *et al.*, 2005) and experience negative thoughts that center on themes of loss, failure, worthlessness, defectiveness, incompetence and inadequacy (Beck, 1995; Beck *et al.*, 1979; Clark *et al.*, 1999).

Core beliefs that are organized within the self-schema influence the development of another level of thinking, which is that of dysfunctional beliefs, rules and assumptions (Beck, 1995; Beck *et al.*, 1979; Clark *et al.*, 1999). These beliefs often pertain to maladaptive themes of contingent self-worth (Kuiper & Olinger, 1986). For example, an individual may believe that his or her self-worth or happiness depends on the approval of others, or that failing partially is equivalent to complete failure. Such dysfunctional attitudes are often represented as "if-then" statements (e.g., "*If* I am not approved by everyone, *then* I am not worthwhile"). As long as such individuals believe that they are meeting their personal criteria for self-worth, they may not experience depression. For instance, the rule "*If* I am not approved by everyone, *then* I am not worthwhile," although dysfunctional in and of itself, nevertheless is not assumed to result in feelings of worthlessness as long as the individual continues to feel accepted. As a result, vulnerable individuals often generate personal rules and compensatory strategies (see Young *et al.*, 2003) for coping with negative core beliefs (e.g., "I must succeed in everything I do"). Once this conditional requirement is not fulfilled, however, depression will possibly follow (Burwell & Shirk, 2006; Kuiper & Olinger, 1986).

When depressotypic self-schemas are activated by negative life experiences, cognitive errors and negative automatic thoughts ensue (see Table 6.1 for a list of possible cognitive errors). Automatic thoughts refer to the stream of cognitions that arise in our day-to-day lives and are not accompanied by direct deliberation or volition; instead, they arise associatively as different aspects of one's core belief system are activated via external environmental cues, or reactions to internal states and emotions. These thoughts usually take the form of a negative view of oneself, the world and the future, what Beck *et al.* (1979) coined the "cognitive triad." Automatic thoughts are more superficial and proximal to a given stimulus than are other levels of cognition but are functionally related to one's deeper beliefs and schemas. As such, automatic thoughts are considered the cognitive by-products of activated schemas. Figure 6.1 presents an illustration of the relationships among core beliefs, intermediate beliefs and automatic thoughts.

Beck (1983) later refined his theory to highlight two personality dimensions that have specific content represented within the self-schema. The first is described as sociotropy and refers to defining self-worth on the basis of interpersonal approval and acceptance. The second theme is concerned with achievement, independence, mobility and control, and is referred to as autonomy. Individuals with sociotropic concerns are believed to be especially prone to depression when they experience negative life events in a relevant interpersonal domain. In contrast, autonomous individuals are predicted to be more vulnerable to depression following congruent experiences of failure or threats to their independency and personal control. These personality dimensions are quite consistent with the broad categories of core beliefs identified by researchers and clinicians. Beck (1995) argued, for instance, that an individual's core beliefs typically fall into one of two categories: helplessness (e.g., "I am inadequate"; "I am incompetent") and unlovability ("I am unworthy"; "I am undesirable"). Although the research supporting the "congruency hypothesis" has been equivocal

TABLE 6.1 Examples of Cognitive Errors

Label	Description
Dichotomous thinking	Things are seen in terms of two mutually exclusive categories with no "shades of gray" in between. For example, believing that one is *either* a success *or* a failure and that anything short of a perfect performance is a total failure.
Overgeneralization	A specific event is seen as being characteristic of life in general rather than as being one event among many. For example, concluding that an inconsiderate response from one's spouse shows that she doesn't care despite her having showed consideration on other occasion.
Selective abstraction	One aspect of a complex situation is the focus of attention, and other relevant aspects of the situation are ignored. For example, focusing on the one negative comment in a performance evaluation received at work and overlooking a number of positive comments.
Disqualifying the positive	Positive experiences that would conflict with the individual's negative views are discounted by declaring that they "don't count." For example, disbelieving positive feedback from friends and colleagues and thinking "they're only saying that to be nice."
Mind reading	The individual assumes that others are reacting negatively without evidence that this is the case. For example, thinking, "I just *know* he thought I was an idiot!", despite the other person's having behaved politely.
Fortune-telling	The individual reacts as though his or her negative expectations about future events are established facts. For example, thinking, "He's leaving me, I just know it!", and acting as though this is definitely true.
Catastrophizing	Negative events that might occur are treated as intolerable catastrophes rather than being seen in perspective. For example, thinking "Oh my God, what if I faint!" without considering that, whereas fainting may be unpleasant and embarrassing, it is not terribly dangerous.
Minimization	Positive characteristics or experiences are treated as real but insignificant. For example, thinking, "Sure, I'm good at my job, but so what, my parents don't respect me."
Emotional reasoning	Assuming that emotional reactions necessarily reflect the true situation. For example, deciding that because one feels hopeless, the situation must really be hopeless.
"Should" statements	The use of *should* and *have-to* statements to provide motivation or control behavior. For example, thinking, "I shouldn't feel aggravated. She's my mother, I *have* to listen to her."
Labeling	Attaching a global label to oneself rather than referring to specific events or actions. For example, thinking, "I'm a failure!", rather than "Boy, I blew that one!"
Personalization	Assuming that one is the cause of a particular external event when, in fact, other factors are responsible. For example, assuming that a supervisor's lack of friendliness is a reflection of her feelings about the client rather than realizing that she is upset over a death in the family.

Note: Freeman, A., Pretzer, J., Fleming, B. and Simon, K. M. ©1990. *Clinical Applications of Cognitive Therapy.* Reprinted with permission from Springer Science and Business Media.

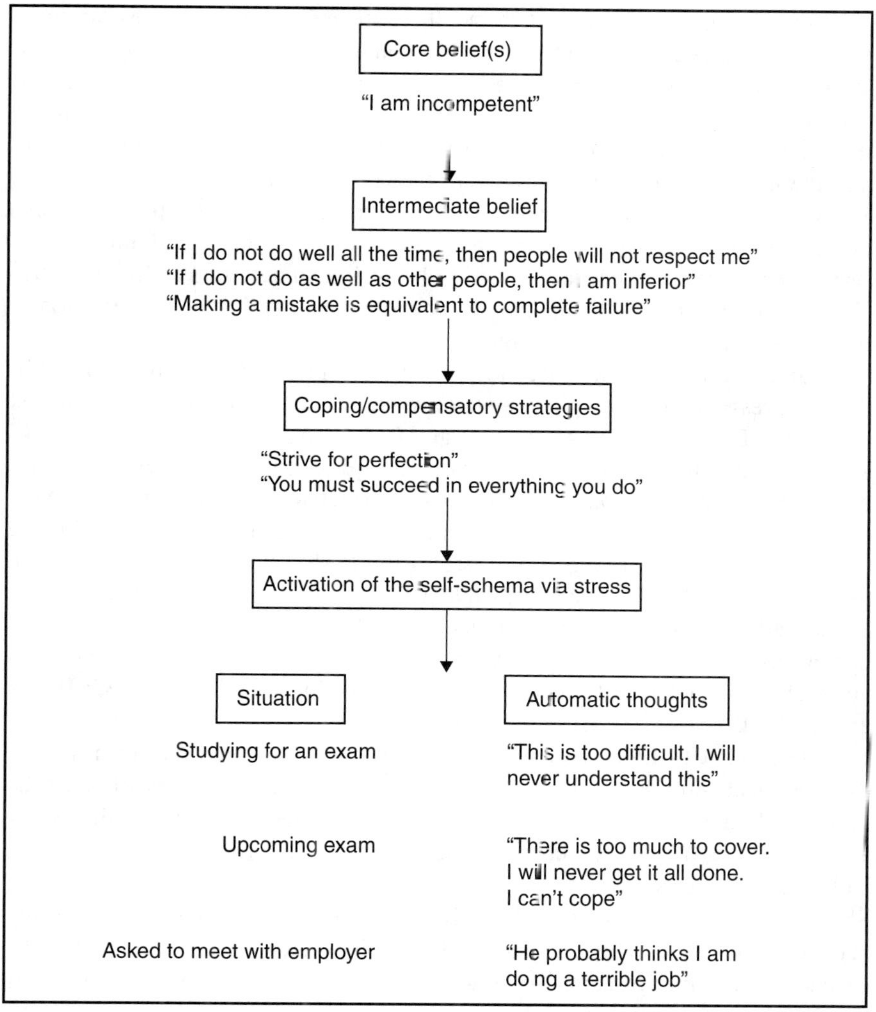

FIGURE 6.1 An illustration of the cognitive model.

(Coyne & Whiffen, 1995), it appears that negative thinking related to interpersonal themes confers a particular risk factor for depression (Cogswell *et al.*, 2006; Dozois, 2007).

THE MEASUREMENT OF BELIEFS AND SCHEMAS

Although the literature has typically discussed the constructs of depressive schemas (i.e., structure and content), core beliefs and assumptions (e.g., dysfunctional attitudes) as though they are interchangeable, they are quite distinct conceptually. Ingram (Ingram & Kendall, 1986; Ingram *et al.*, 1998) proposed a cognitive taxonomy so that researchers could more consistently operationalize and evaluate different constructs of cognition related to depression. The four main components of the cognitive taxonomy that were advanced are cognitive structures, propositions, operations and products. Cognitive structure refers to the internal representation and organization of information in memory which together with cognitive propositions (e.g., core beliefs) make up the schema. Cognitive operations are defined as the processes of the schema and include such variables as attention, encoding, retrieval and interpretation. Finally, cognitive products are the accessible thoughts and beliefs that arise from the interaction of schemas and information processing.

Cognitive product indices are most ubiquitous in tests of cognitive vulnerability to depression. For example, maladaptive beliefs are most commonly assessed using the Dysfunctional Attitude Scale (DAS; Weissman & Beck, 1978). Research with this instrument has supported the descriptive hypotheses of cognitive theory that depression is *associated* with negative thinking. However, many of the early studies of cognitive vulnerability have demonstrated that negative thinking, as assessed by measures such as the DAS, improves once depression remits (e.g., Dobson & Shaw, 1987; Dohr *et al.*, 1989; Lewinsohn *et al.*, 1981). These findings have led to suggestions that maladaptive thinking might perhaps operate as a state marker or "epiphenomenon" of depression rather than as a vulnerability factor (see Barnett & Gotlib, 1988; Coyne & Gotlib, 1983; Haaga *et al.*, 1991).

Consistent with Ingram's cognitive taxonomy, we contend that measures of dysfunctional attitudes and accessible beliefs are merely proxies of the self-schema. Although some investigators have attempted to examine the structural properties of the self-schema in depression (e.g., Dozois, 2007; Dozois & Dobson, 2001a, b; Segal & Gemar, 1997; Segal *et al.*, 1988; Segal & Vella, 1990; Showers *et al.*, 1998; Showers *et al.*, 2004), other innovative methodologies are needed to assess this construct as a vulnerability factor in depression. With the caveat in mind that research has normally examined cognitive products rather than schemas *per se*, we turn now to the empirical evidence pertaining to cognitive vulnerability.

REQUIREMENT FOR A VULNERABILITY FACTOR

For a variable to be considered a vulnerability factor, it should demonstrate *sensitivity* (be present in depressed individuals), *specificity* (be shown more frequently in depressed individuals than in other psychiatric samples) and *stability* (be present and accessible, although not always accessed). We review evidence that supports each of these criteria with respect to negative cognition. It is important to note, however, that meeting each criterion does not guarantee that a variable represents a vulnerability factor for depression (Just *et al.*,

2001). Demonstration that negative cognition is present in individuals who have remitted from an episode of depression, for example, does not rule out the possibility that it represents a "scar" of the disorder (e.g., Oei *et al.*, 2006) rather than a cause. Therefore, the strongest evidence in support of the causal status of maladaptive cognition is to demonstrate that it is present in individuals who have never experienced depression and that it predicts the initial onset of a depressive episode. Although there is a dearth of research that provides this type of evidence, some studies have addressed the temporal antecedence of negative thinking in depression (e.g., Alloy *et al.*, 2006; see Chapter 11).

CONTENT SENSITIVITY

Countless studies have demonstrated that depressed individuals filter information and respond to stimuli in a negative way that is consistent with their idiosyncratic beliefs and assumptions (Beck, 2005; Clark *et al.*, 1999). Depression is consistently associated with dysfunctional attitudes, negative automatic thoughts, pessimism, hopelessness, low perceived self-worth, negative explanatory styles and irrational beliefs. Studies that have assessed negative cognition through information processing measures also tend to support the tenet that depression is associated with biases of memory, attention and interpretation (see Chapter 7). Notwithstanding support for the relationship between negative thinking and depression, studies on the causal aspects of these theories have, until recently, yielded equivocal results.

Recent factor analytic and experimental research has also suggested that purported cognitive vulnerability factors are not synonymous (Gotlib *et al.*, 2004; Hankin *et al.*, 2007; Spangler & Burns, 1999); yet, we do not presently know which is most predictive of depression. For example, Haeffel *et al.* (2003) found that negative explanatory style was predictive of depression, whereas dysfunctional attitudes were not. In contrast, other researchers have found that dysfunctional attitudes are better predictors of major depression than are attributional biases (e.g., Lewinsohn *et al.*, 2001; Spangler & Burns, 1999). Using structural equation modeling, Spangler and Burns (1999) found that attributional style was no longer correlated with depression after dysfunctional attitudes were controlled statistically. On the other hand, dysfunctional attitudes remained strongly associated with depression after controlling for attributional style. Clarifying the contribution of different cognitive vulnerability markers represents an important direction for future research.

CONTENT-SPECIFICITY

Another important axiom of Beck's model is that of content-specificity (Alford & Beck, 1997; Clark *et al.*, 1999). According to the content-specificity hypothesis, each emotional state and psychological disorder has a specific cognitive profile (Beck, 1976; Clark *et al.*, 1999). At its most basic level, an individual's appraisal of an event determines the kind of emotion(s) he or she experiences.

Most of the research pertaining to cognitive specificity has focused on depression and anxiety (Clark *et al.*, 1999). Beck proposed that these emotions are governed by similar cognitive processes, but may be distinguished by the specific content of their dysfunctional attitudes and beliefs. Anxiety is related to a future orientation with a focus on threat cognitions of harm or danger (Beck & Emery, 1985). In depression, the emphasis is more on the past with the content of cognition relating to themes of loss, deprivation, self-deprecation and hopelessness (Beck, 1967; Beck *et al.*, 1979).

Research in experimental psychopathology has generally supported the content-specificity hypothesis (Beck *et al.*, 1987, 2006; Beck, R. *et al.*, 2003; Clark *et al.*, 1990; Hankin *et al.*, 2004; Joiner *et al.*, 1999; McDermut & Haaga, 1994; Ohrt *et al.*, 1999; Schniering & Rapee, 2004; Westra & Kuiper, 1997; Woody *et al.*, 1998). Westra and Kuiper (1997), for instance, conducted a study in which undergraduates made self-descriptive ratings on several adjectives sampled from the depression, anxiety, eating disorders and personality literature. Dysphoria was uniquely related to adjectives pertaining to loss, failure and hopelessness, whereas the themes in anxiety centered on threat and stigmatization. Schniering and Rapee (2004) tested the content-specificity hypothesis in community and clinical samples of youth (ages 7–16 years) with anxiety, depression or behavioral disorders. Thoughts related to personal failure or loss were the strongest predictors of depressive symptoms, thoughts pertaining to social threat were the optimal predictors of anxiety and thoughts regarding hostility or revenge best predicted aggression.

The idea that anxiety and depression are related to similar information processing mechanisms has also been found, although less consistently. Anxiety and depression both involve similar cognitive processes, but anxiety seems to relate more to automatic processing and attention biases whereas depression is more strongly associated with elaborative processing and memory biases. As such, individuals with anxiety are said to be in an *orienting* mode, whereas those with depression operate more consistently in an *oriented* mode (Clark *et al.*, 1990; Mineka *et al.*, 1998).

Recent longitudinal work has also supported the content-specificity hypothesis. Joiner *et al.* (1999) found evidence of content-specificity using a "mid-term methodology." Undergraduate students were assessed a couple of weeks before their midterm examination and again after receiving their mid-term grade. Consistent with the diathesis–stress model, students who were high in dysfunctional attitudes showed increases in depressive symptoms but only if this coexisted with low mid-term examination grades. Moreover, this relationship was mediated specifically by depressive (not anxious) cognitions. In three longitudinal studies (5 week follow-up, 2 year follow-up and using a midterm methodology), Hankin *et al.* (2004) tested the hypothesis that cognitive vulnerability would interact with negative life events to predict depression specifically. The results indicated that negative life events functioned as a nonspecific risk factor for anxiety and depression. As predicted, cognitive vulnerability interacted with negative life events to predict future depression specifically.

Other studies have found only partial support for the content-specificity hypothesis. For example, there appears to be less support for the content-specificity of anxious (e.g., danger, threat) than depressive (e.g., loss, failure, hopelessness) cognitions (e.g., Greenberg & Beck, 1989; McDermut & Haaga, 1994). In their meta-analysis of self-report measures, Beck and Perkins (2001) found mixed support for the content-specificity hypothesis in depression and anxiety. There was some support for the specificity of cognitive content in depression depending on how specificity was defined. Support was obtained, for example, when the criterion was that the measure should be more highly related to the construct of interest than to the other construct (rather than exhibiting an exclusive relationship).

Depressive and anxious cognitive content do appear to share significant variance with both depression and anxiety symptoms and syndromes. This relationship is likely due, in part, to the genuine overlap between these two disorders. It is widely acknowledged that anxiety and depression are highly co-occurring conditions (Mineka *et al.*, 1998). This co-occurrence manifests itself in the high correlation observed among measures of depression and anxiety, and in the comorbidity between these disorders (see Dozois & Westra, 2004 for review). This relationship is perhaps best understood by the concept of negative affect. General distress or negative affect seems to be a common denominator of depression and anxiety disorders. What appears to be specific to depression is low positive affect (e.g., Brown *et al.*, 1998). Research that has evaluated the interconnectedness of positive and negative self-referent content in depression and anxiety has also demonstrated both shared (e.g., interconnected negative content) and specific (the lack of an interconnected positive self-structure) features (Dozois & Dobson, 2001b; Dozois & Frewen, 2006).

Factor analytic studies have also demonstrated that negative affect accounts for a considerable proportion of the variance on depression and anxiety symptom scores. When the variance associated with negative affect is controlled statistically, or the unique symptom features of each disorder are examined, cognitive factors specific to each disorder appear to emerge (Clark *et al.*, 1994; Steer *et al.*, 1995). Beck, R. *et al.* (2003), for instance, used an instrument (the Mood and Anxiety Symptom Questionnaire) designed to distinguish depression- and anxiety-specific symptoms from general distress. The results indicated that depression- and anxiety-specific symptoms were uniquely related to their respective cognitions. Worry (e.g., cognitive rumination) was identified as a problem common to both anxiety and depression. Depression was distinguished from anxiety, however, with respect to anhedonic states related to being self-critical and hopeless (also see Beck *et al.*, 2006).

In sum, the cognitive content-specificity of depression and anxiety is well supported but not robust. Both syndromes share cognitive features and symptoms which may reflect genuine covariance associated with a common underlying pathogenesis. Negative affectivity accounts for a considerable proportion of this shared variance. Yet the content-specificity hypothesis is supported when the relationship of specific cognitions are examined in the context of specific symptoms.

COGNITIVE STABILITY

The use of remitted depressed participants is a common strategy used to test stability of cognitions related to depression. The rationale underlying this approach is that if negative cognitions represent a stable aspect of depressive vulnerability, then individuals who have improved from an episode of depression should continue to demonstrate cognitive vulnerability even in their remitted or recovered state (unless treatment has modified these structures) (but see Just *et al.*, 2001 and Haeffel *et al.*, 2005 for a critique). A number of studies have followed up depressed individuals into remission to assess the stability of negative beliefs and assumptions or compared individuals who have experienced depression in the past, but are no longer depressed, to individuals who have never experienced depression. In contrast to the stability hypothesis, these studies have generally found that negative cognition improves significantly when individuals are retested in remission and have typically failed to find reliable differences between individuals with remitted depression and those without a psychiatric history (see Ingram *et al.*, 1998 for review).

Some studies have found stability of negative cognition in previously depressed adults (e.g., Dozois, 2007; Dozois & Dobson, 2001a). Dozois and Dobson (2001a) argued that stability of cognition may be found if the structure of the schema (rather than simply its products) is assessed. In their research, the structure of the self-schema was evaluated using a computerized task in which participants rated self-referential adjectives on a grid based on perceived self-descriptiveness and valence. It was assumed that the manner in which individuals organize adjective content is reflective of the degree of schema consolidation or interconnectedness. A sample of depressed females was assessed on this task and was also administered information processing tasks measuring attention to and recall of positive and negative interpersonal information. Participants were retested 6 months later when half of the sample had remained depressed and the other half was remitted. Negative information processing was evident only during episodes and shifted significantly once depression improved, suggesting that this variable operates more as a state than trait marker. In contrast, negative cognitive organization remained stable across time in those individuals who no longer met diagnostic criteria for major depression. This finding was replicated in a subsequent study which also found that the stability of negative cognitive organization was specific to interpersonal self-referent content (Dozois, 2007). These results suggest that negative interpersonal self-structures may be vulnerability factors for depression and its recurrence (*cf.* Joorman & Gotlib, 2007).

In contrast to the above research, most studies have shown that negatively biased thinking improves once depression subsides. Some researchers have reasoned that previously depressed individuals do not show negative cognition as a defensive strategy, in which they suppress negative thoughts to repair their negative mood state and maintain a positive mind set (Beevers, 2005; Sheppard & Teasdale, 2004; Wang *et al.*, 2005). Wenzlaff and Bates (1998) examined depressed, at-risk and nondepressed participants on a scrambled sentences task whereby unscrambling the sentence could produce either a positive or negative statement. Half of participants received a cognitive load (intended to undermine their efforts to suppress negative thoughts) while completing this task. Without a cognitive load, at-risk participants showed little evidence of negative thinking; those individuals under a cognitive load, however, demonstrated an increase in the production of negative statements.

The fact that negative cognitive products may operate more as concomitants than causes of depression is not entirely inconsistent with Beck's cognitive model. As mentioned previously, this diathesis–stress model proposes that vulnerable individuals will experience depression when their negative self-system is activated by certain stressors (Ingram *et al.*, 2006). As Scher *et al.* (2005) pointed out, the very notion that depressive schemas are theoretically latent until activated has unfortunately laid dormant in many investigations of cognitive vulnerability. Indeed, most of the early studies of cognitive vulnerability did not examine vulnerability by stress interactions or attempt to activate the self-schema prior to assessment.

Empirical data have shown that, following a mood challenge or prime (i.e., an experimental or naturalistic induction of negative mood), individuals with a history of depression do show an increase in dysfunctional attitudes, irrational beliefs or information processing biases that is not present in never-depressed but primed controls (e.g., Hedlund & Rude, 1995; Ingram & Ritter, 2000; Ingram *et al.*, 1994; Miranda & Persons, 1988; Miranda *et al.*, 1990, 1998; Persons & Miranda, 1992; Segal *et al.*, 1999; Solomon *et al.*, 1998; Teasdale & Dent, 1987; for a review see Scher *et al.*, 2005).

Segal *et al.* (1999) provided direct evidence that schema activation is related to vulnerability to depression. These investigators compared patients who were successfully treated with either cognitive therapy or antidepressant medication. Following treatment, participants were administered the DAS, a self-report measure of negative beliefs and attitudes concerning self. They were subsequently induced into a dysphoric mood state and then administered a parallel form of the DAS. Individuals who were treated pharmacologically showed elevated DAS scores. This increase in negative thinking was not present in individuals who received cognitive therapy. Segal *et al.* (2006) also found that such mood-linked changes in dysfunctional attitudes were predictive of relapse 18 months later.

Although research with previously depressed individuals may attest to psychological scarring rather than cognitive vulnerability *per se*, these results are not inconsistent with the predictive role of cognition in depression and lend credence to the idea that negative cognitive structures are present but latent until activated by sad mood (see Lau *et al.*, 2004).

STUDIES OF "VULNERABLE" POPULATIONS

Studies of remitted samples cannot elucidate mechanisms related to the onset of depression, which may be quite different from those related to its relapse or recurrence. To address this issue, cognitive vulnerability has also been studied in individuals who are considered vulnerable but not currently depressed. One common strategy has been to assess children of depressed mothers (see Garber & Martin, 2002) who present with a greater risk for developing depression themselves than do the offspring of nonpsychiatric controls (e.g., Halligan *et al.*, 2007; Hammen, 2002).

Although the precise mechanism(s) of transmission is not entirely clear, children of depressed mothers exhibit depressive information processing, negative explanatory styles, greater hopelessness and lower perceived self-worth than do children of nonpsychiatric mothers (Garber & Flynn, 2001; Garber & Robinson, 1997; Goodman *et al.*, 1994; Joorman *et al.*, 2007; Stark *et al.*, 1996; Taylor & Ingram, 1999). The precise age at which such vulnerability develops is not presently known, as some research has found evidence of cognitive vulnerability in children as young as 5 years of age (Murray *et al.*, 2001). However, other research has demonstrated that the predictive utility of the cognitive vulnerability by stress interaction is stronger in adolescence than in childhood, possibly due to the ability of older youth to engage in abstract reasoning about the self (e.g., Cole *et al.*, 2008; Lakdawalla *et al.*, 2007).

LONGITUDINAL STUDIES OF COGNITIVE VULNERABILITY

Recent longitudinal studies have also supported Beck's theory, in that the interaction of cognitive vulnerability (e.g., dysfunctional attitudes) and life stress has predicted depression (e.g., Abela & D'Alessandro, 2002; Alloy *et al.*, 2006; Dykman & Johll, 1998; Hankin *et al.*, 2004, 2005; Joiner *et al.*, 1999; Kwon & Oei, 1992; Lewinsohn *et al.*, 2001; but see Otto *et al.*, 2007). Kwon and Oei (1992, Study 2), for example, found that the interaction of dysfunctional attitudes and negative life events in undergraduate students predicted depressive symptoms over a period of 3 months. Yet, these researchers found that negative thinking was also a consequence of depression. Abela and D'Alessandro (2002) found that scores on a youth measure of dysfunctional attitudes interacted with negative information about university admissions to predict increases in depressed mood.

Fewer studies have examined the relationship of cognitive vulnerability to the onset of depressive disorder. These studies have provided compelling data that the interaction of cognitive vulnerability and stressful life events predicts depression onset prospectively (Alloy *et al.*, 2006; Evans *et al.*, 2005; Lewinsohn *et al.*, 2001). Lewinsohn *et al.* (2001) followed up a large sample of adolescents over a period of 1 year to predict depression onset. A statistical trend was found supporting the predictive utility of the dysfunctional attitudes by stress interaction. These researchers also found that the incidence of depression was highest when dysfunctional attitudes and life stress both reached a high level of intensity. Evans *et al.* (2005) examined the onset of depression in a large sample of 12 003 pregnant women. Women who scored in the upper third on a measure of schematic content (a measure of interpersonal sensitivity) were three times more likely to score in the depressed range on the Edinburgh Postnatal Depression Scale 14 weeks later than were women who scored in the bottom third. This relationship remained significant after controlling for baseline depression scores. Moreover, this relationship was stable as it predicted the onset of depression 3 years later. Using a behavioral high risk design (see Chapter 11), Alloy *et al.* (2006) found that cognitively high risk participants (i.e., those individuals who scored in the upper quartile on a composite index of the Dysfunctional Attitudes Scale and the Cognitive Style Questionnaire) were 3.5–6.8 times more likely to experience major, minor and hopelessness depression than were low risk participants over a period of two and a half years. Together, these findings provide convincing evidence for Beck's cognitive model of vulnerability to depression.

MECHANISMS RELATED TO THE DEVELOPMENT OF CORE BELIEFS/SCHEMAS

Beck's model (e.g., Beck *et al.*, 1979) suggests that the initial development of maladaptive schemas, beliefs and assumptions occurs in early childhood yet this idea has not been clearly articulated or studied until recently (e.g., Ingram, 2001; Rose & Abramson, 1992). In contrast to the proliferation of research on maladaptive cognition and schematic processing, few studies have examined how core beliefs related to depression develop in the first place. According to attachment theory, children form cognitive representations of the meaning, function and value of social relationships (i.e., internal working models) based on previous interactions with caregivers (see Chapter 13). Children who are securely attached develop positive beliefs about themselves and view subsequent relationships favorably (Bowlby, 1988). In contrast, children with insecure attachments perceive insufficient emotional support from their caregivers, perceive the world as unsupportive and view themselves as isolated, vulnerable or unworthy. Thus, internal working models (aka, schemas) formed via attachment relationships presumably serve as the cognitive scaffolding of adult core beliefs related to self and others (Ingram, 2003).

Young and his colleagues (Young, 1999; Young *et al.*, 2003) have shifted attention toward developmental factors in cognitive theory of depression. Young theorizes that the unique circumstances an individual experiences in childhood contribute to the development of a distinctive set of core beliefs, which he has labeled "Early Maladaptive Schemas" (EMS). Although termed schemas, EMS are really more closely aligned with core beliefs as they do not provide information about the organization of this cognitive content. The five sets of EMS and their constituents are described in Table 6.2. The research literature has generally supported the temporal stability of EMS as assessed by means of the Young Schema Questionnaire (Riso *et al.*, 2006; Stallard, 2007). What remains unclear is the extent to which particular EMS are associated with distinctive parenting styles and practices.

A related body of research has demonstrated links between early parent–child interactions and the development of negative thinking in adulthood. McCranie and Bass (1984), for instance, demonstrated that parental over-control during childhood was associated with core beliefs related to dependency and self-criticism in adulthood. Other researchers have found that perceived insecurity in one's

TABLE 6.2 Early Maladaptive Schemas

1. Disconnection and rejection
   (a) Abandonment/instability
   (b) Mistrust abuse
   (c) Emotional deprivation
   (d) Defectiveness/shame
   (e) Social isolation/alienation
2. Impaired autonomy and performance
   (a) Dependence/incompetence
   (b) Vulnerability to harm or illness
   (c) Enmeshment/underdeveloped self
   (d) Failure
3. Impaired limits
   (a) Entitlement/grandiosity
   (b) Insufficient self-control/self-discipline
4. Other directedness
   (a) Subjugation
   (b) Self-sacrifice
   (c) Approval seeking/recognition seeking
5. Overvigilance and inhibition
   (a) Negativity/pessimism
   (b) Emotional inhibition
   (c) Unrelenting standards/hypercriticalness
   (d) Punitiveness

Source: Young *et al.* (2003).

parental attachment as an adult is associated with endorsement of dysfunctional attitudes related to dependency and performance evaluation (e.g., Roberts *et al.*, 1996).

Early maltreatment and negative parental feedback have also been shown to set the stage for cognitive vulnerability (Bruce *et al.*, 2006; Gibb *et al.*, 2006; Lumley & Harkness, 2007; Mezulis *et al*, 2006; Rose & Abramson, 1992). Not only do distal risk factors (adverse childhood experiences) appear to precede the development of negative cognitive styles, they may also mediate the relationship between early maltreatment and depression (e.g., Oliver *et al.*, 2007; Whisman & Kwon, 1992). It may not simply be familial relationships during childhood that contribute to cognitive vulnerability to depression later in life. Gibb *et al.* (2004) found that peer victimization during childhood contributed to cognitive vulnerability even after controlling for parenting variables (also see Williams *et al.*, 2001). Thus, although there is debate regarding the age at which children can develop cognitive vulnerability, emerging evidence supports the idea that early experiences lay the foundation for later cognitive functioning.

CONCLUSIONS AND FUTURE DIRECTIONS

This chapter has documented the evidence related to schemas, beliefs and assumptions as risk factors for depression. Although the early research on cognitive vulnerability demonstrated that maladaptive thinking waxes and wanes with depression, studies that have tested the diathesis–stress components of Beck's model using naturalistic or experimental mood manipulations have provided empirical support that schemas, beliefs and assumptions predict depressive symptoms when they are activated by life stress. Longitudinal research that has examined vulnerability by stress interactions has provided further support for this model. Arguably, the most exciting research of late has been the demonstration that maladaptive thinking in at-risk but nondepressed populations is predictive of the incidence of depression.

The research on cognitive vulnerability has come a long way since Beck's model (1967; Beck *et al.*, 1979) was initially proposed over 40 years ago. Although there is now fairly consistent support for causal status of schemas, beliefs and assumptions in depression, there are also many unanswered questions and important directions for future research. Given space constraints, we highlight just a few areas for future research that we believe are particularly salient: (1) levels of cognition; (2) the development of core beliefs and schemas; (3) the neurobiological correlates of cognition; and (4) the methodologies needed to examine cognitive vulnerability to depression.

As mentioned earlier in this chapter, research has focused heavily on cognitive products of depression in tests of vulnerability. Numerous intriguing findings have emerged from this literature and have advanced our understanding of cognitive vulnerability. Notwithstanding these encouraging data, there continues to be a lack of understanding regarding the relationships among various cognitive factors involved in depression (Gotlib *et al.*, 2004; Hankin *et al.*, 2007). Research is needed to better understand the relationships among various cognitive vulnerability factors. Further research is also needed to examine the structure of the self-schema in depression, and how this organization affects cognitive processing and products.

Beevers (2005) argued that cognitive vulnerability occurs when negatively biased associative processing is uncorrected by reflective processing. This dual process model, derived from cognitive psychology, has important implications for how cognitive vulnerability develops. It is possible that cognitive vulnerability has as much to do with what an individual does behaviorally and cognitively when his or her schema becomes activated as the activation itself. Whereas activation may occur automatically through an associated network, the extent to which negative mood is maintained, improved or exacerbated may be contingent on reflective processing (*cf.* Haeffel *et al.*, 2007).

Another fruitful line of inquiry is to further explore how it is that people come to develop core beliefs and organize negative self-representations in the first place. Although this question has historically received less theoretical emphasis in the writings of Beck, his model does assume that core beliefs and maladaptive thoughts develop primarily as a result of prior experiential learning, especially learning that takes place during early childhood. We are now beginning to witness research on the development of depressive schemas and information processing biases, and we encourage further exploration in this area.

An understanding of the relationships between psychological constructs (e.g., dysfunctional attitudes and maladaptive core beliefs) and neurobiological processes is increasingly possible with progress in the cognitive and affective neurosciences. For example, Goldapple *et al.* (2004) examined the neural effects of cognitive therapy of depression using positron emission tomography (PET). This type of research is now being conducted in other disorders as well (for a review see Frewen *et al.*, in press). Similarly, researchers are beginning to show that negative cognitive processing is associated with the short version of the serotonin transporter gene (Beevers *et al.*, 2007; Canli & Lesch, 2007; Hayden *et al.*, 2008). Hayden and her colleagues, for example, found that children who were homozygous for the short allele of the 5-HTTLPR gene (see Chapter 4) showed greater negative processing on a self-referent encoding task following a negative mood manipulation than did children with other genotypes. Understanding the neurobiological correlates of cognitive variables will undoubtedly advance our knowledge base in the area of cognitive vulnerability.

Research on cognitive vulnerability would also benefit from more refined tests of diathesis–stress models. Abela and Sarin (2002), for example, found that it was an adolescent's "weakest link" (i.e., the most depressogenic inferential style rather than his or her overall negative inferential style) that interacted with subsequent negative events to predict depressive symptomatology. Researchers have also begun to test diathesis–stress interactions in more proximal ways to understand the predictive utility of cognitive vulnerability. Employing multiple assessments periods (e.g., using daily diary methodologies) or more sophisticated data analytic techniques may better capture the dynamic nature of cognitive vulnerability–stress interactions as they unfold over time (*cf.* Abela & Skitch, 2007; Hankin *et al.*, 2005).

In summary, Beck's theory has been refined and elaborated over time; however, the fundamental assumptions of cognitive theory of depression have, for the most part, been well supported. We have highlighted data that has supported the sensitivity, specificity and stability of negative cognition in depression. We anticipate that future research will further elucidate the mechanisms related to cognitive vulnerability.

REFERENCES

Abela, J. R., & D'Alessandro, D. U. (2002). Beck's cognitive theory of depression: A test of the diathesis–stress and causal mediation components. *British Journal of Clinical Psychology, 41*, 111–128.

Abela, J. R., & Sarin, S. (2002). Cognitive vulnerability to hopelessness depression: A chain is only as strong as its weakest link. *Cognitive Therapy and Research, 26*, 811–829.

Abela, J. R. Z., & Skitch, S. A. (2007). Dysfunctional attitudes, self-esteem, and hassles: Cognitive vulnerability to depression in children of affectively ill parents. *Behaviour Research and Therapy, 45*, 1127–1140.

Abramson, L. Y., Alloy, L. B., Hankin, B. L., Haeffel, G. J., MacCoon, D. G., & Gibb, B. E. (2002). Cognitive vulnerability–stress models of depression in a self-regulatory and psychobiological context. In I. H. Gotlib & C. L. Hammen (Eds.), *Handbook of Depression* (pp. 268–294). New York: Guilford.

Alford, B. A., & Beck, A. T. (1997). *The Integrative Power of Cognitive Therapy*. New York: Guilford.

Alloy, L. B., Abramson, L. Y., Whitehouse, W. G., Hogan, M. E., Panzarella, C., & Rose, D. T. (2006). Prospective incidence of first onsets and recurrences of depression in individuals at high and low cognitive risk for depression. *Journal of Abnormal Psychology, 115*, 145–156.

Barnett, P. A., & Gotlib, I. H. (1988). Psychosocial functioning and depression: Distinguishing among antecedents, concomitants, and consequences. *Psychological Bulletin, 104*, 97–126.

Beck, A. T. (1967). *Depression: Causes and Treatment*. Philadelphia, PA: University of Pennsylvania Press.

Beck, A. T. (1976). *Cognitive Therapy and the Emotional Disorders*. New York: Basic Books.

Beck, A. T. (1983). Cognitive therapy of depression: New perspectives. In P. J. Clayton & J. E. Barrett (Eds.), *Treatment of Depression: Old Controversies and New Approaches* (pp. 265–290). New York: Raven.

Beck, A. T. (2005). The current state of cognitive therapy: A 40-year retrospective. *Archives of General Psychiatry, 62*, 953–959.

Beck, A. T., Rush, A. J., Shaw, B. F., & Emery, G. (1979). *Cognitive Therapy of Depression*. New York: Guilford.

Beck, A. T., Brown, G., Steer, R. A., Eidelson, J. I., & Riskind, J. H. (1987). Differentiating anxiety and depression: A test of the cognitive content-specificity hypothesis. *Journal of Abnormal Psychology, 96*, 179–183.

Beck, A. T., Benedict, B., & Winkler, A. (2003). Depression and anxiety: Integrating the tripartite and cognitive content-specificity assessment models. *Journal of Psychopathology and Behavioral Assessment, 25*, 251–256.

Beck, A. T., Wenzel, A., Riskind, J. H., Brown, G., & Steer, R. A. (2006). Specificity of hopelessness about resolving life problems: Another test of the cognitive model of depression. *Cognitive Therapy and Research*, *30*, 773–781.

Beck, J. S. (1995). *Cognitive Therapy: Basics and Beyond*. New York: Guilford.

Beck, A. T., & Emery, G. (with Greenberg, R. L.). (1985). *Anxiety disorders and phobias: A cognitive perspective*. New York: Basic Books.

Beck, R., & Perkins, T. S. (2001). Cognitive content-specificity for anxiety and depression: A meta-analysis. *Cognitive Therapy and Research*, *25*, 651–663.

Beck, R., Benedict, B., & Winkler, A. (2003). Depression and anxiety: Integrating tripartite and cognitive content-specificity assessment models. *Journal of Psychopathology and Behavioral Assessment*, *25*, 251–256.

Beevers, C. G. (2005). Cognitive vulnerability to depression: A dual process model. *Clinical Psychology Review*, *25*, 975–1002.

Beevers, C. G., Gibb, B. E., McGeary, J. E., & Miller, I. W. (2007). Serotonin transporter genetic variation and biased attention for emotional word stimuli among psychiatric inpatients. *Journal of Abnormal Psychology*, *116*, 208–212.

Bowlby, J. (1988). *A Secure Base: Parent–Child Attachment and Healthy Human Development*. New York: Basic books.

Brown, T. A., Chorpita, B. F., & Barlow, D. H. (1998). Structural relationships among dimensions of the DSM-IV anxiety and mood disorders and dimensions of negative affect, positive affect, and autonomic arousal. *Journal of Abnormal Psychology*, *107*, 179–192.

Bruce, A. E., Cole, D. A., Dallaire, D. H., Jacquez, F. M., Pineda, A. Q., & LaGrange, B. (2006). Relations of parenting and negative life events to cognitive diatheses for depression in children. *Journal of Abnormal Child Psychology*, *34*, 321–333.

Burwell, R. A., & Shirk, S. R. (2006). Self processes in adolescent depression: The role of self-worth contingencies. *Journal of Research on Adolescence*, *16*, 479–490.

Canli, T., & Lesch, K. (2007). Long story short: The serotonin transporter in emotion regulation and social cognition. *Nature Neuroscience*, *10*, 1103–1109.

Clark, D. A., Beck, A. T., & Stewart, B. (1990). Cognitive specificity and positive–negative affectivity: Complementary or contradictory views on anxiety and depression?. *Journal of Abnormal Psychology*, *99*, 148–155.

Clark, D. A., Steer, R. A., & Beck, A. T. (1994). Common and specific dimensions of self-reported anxiety and depression: Implications for the cognitive and tripartite models. *Journal of Abnormal Psychology*, *103*, 645–654.

Clark, D. A., Beck, A. T., & Alford, B. A. (1999). *Scientific Foundations of Cognitive Theory and Therapy of Depression*. Philadelphia, PA: Wiley.

Cogswell, A., Alloy, L. B., & Spasojevic, J. (2006). Neediness and interpersonal life stress: Does congruency predict depression?. *Cognitive Therapy and Research*, *30*, 427–443.

Cole, D. A., Ciesla, J. A., Dallaire, D. H., Jacquez, F. M., Pineda, A. Q., LaGrange, B., Truss, A. E., Folmer, A. S., Tilghman-Osbourne, C., & Felton, J. W. (2008). Emergence of attributional style and its relation to depressive symptoms. *Journal of Abnormal Psychology*, *117*, 16–31.

Coyne, J. C., & Gotlib, I. H. (1983). The role of cognition in depression: A critical reappraisal. *Psychological Bulletin*, *94*, 472–505.

Coyne, J. C., & Whiffen, V. E. (1995). Issues in personality as diathesis for depression: The case of sociotropy-dependency and autonomy-self-criticism. *Psychological Bulletin*, *118*, 358–378.

Dobson, K. S., & Shaw, B. F. (1987). Specificity and stability of self-referent encoding in clinical depression. *Journal of Abnormal Psychology*, *96*, 34–40.

Dohr, K. B., Rush, A. J., & Bernstein, I. H. (1989). Cognitive biases and depression. *Journal of Abnormal Psychology*, *98*, 263–267.

Dozois, D. J. A. (2007). Stability of negative self-structures: A longitudinal comparison of depressed, remitted, and nonpsychiatric controls. *Journal of Clinical Psychology*, *63*, 319–338.

Dozois, D. J. A., & Dobson, K. S. (2001a). A longitudinal investigation of information processing and cognitive organization in clinical depression: Stability of schematic interconnectedness. *Journal of Consulting and Clinical Psychology*, *69*, 914–925.

Dozois, D. J. A., & Dobson, K. S. (2001b). Information processing and cognitive organization in unipolar depression: Specificity and comorbidity issues. *Journal of Abnormal Psychology*, *110*, 236–246.

Dozois, D. J. A., & Frewen, P. A. (2006). Specificity of cognitive structure in depression and social phobia: A comparison of interpersonal and achievement content. *Journal of Affective Disorders*, *90*, 101–109.

Dozois, D. J. A., & Westra, H. A. (2004). The nature of anxiety and depression: Implications for prevention. In D. J. A. Dozois & K. S. Dobson (Eds.), *The Prevention of Anxiety and Depression: Theory, Research, and Practice* (pp. 9–41). Washington, DC: American Psychological Association.

Dykman, B. M., & Johll, M. (1998). Dysfunctional attitudes and vulnerability to depressive symptoms: A 14-week longitudinal study. *Cognitive Therapy and Research*, *22*, 337–352.

Evans, J., Heron, J., Lewis, G., Araya, R., & Wolke, D. (2005). Negative self-schemas and the onset of depression in women: A longitudinal study. *British Journal of Psychiatry*, *186*, 302–307.

Frewen, P. A., Dozois, D. J. A., & Lanius, R. A. (2008). Neuroimaging studies of psychological interventions for mood and anxiety disorders: Empirical and methodological review. *Clinical Psychology Review*, *28*, 228–246.

Garber, J., & Flynn, C. (2001). Predictors of depressive cognitions in young adolescents. *Cognitive Therapy and Research*, *25*, 353–376.

Garber, J., & Martin, N. C. (2002). Negative cognitions in offspring of depressed parents: Mechanisms of risk. In S. H. Goodman & I. H. Gotlib (Eds.), *Children of Depressed Parents: Mechanisms of Risk and Implications for Treatment* (pp. 121–153). Washington, DC: American Psychological Association.

Garber, J., & Robinson, N. S. (1997). Cognitive vulnerability in children at risk for depression. *Cognition and Emotion*, *11*, 619–635.

Gibb, B. E., Abramson, L. Y., & Alloy, L. B. (2004). Emotional maltreatment from parents, verbal victimization, and cognitive vulnerability to depression. *Cognitive Therapy and Research*, *28*, 1–21.

Gibb, B. E., Alloy, L. B., Walshaw, P. D., Comer, J. S., Shen, G. H. C., & Villari, A. G. (2006). Predictors of attributional style change in children. *Journal of Abnormal Child Psychology*, *34*, 425–439.

Goodman, S. H., Adamson, L. B., Riniti, J., & Cole, S. (1994). Mothers' expressed attitudes: Associations with maternal depression and children's self-esteem and psychopathology. *Journal of the American Academy of Child and Adolescent Psychiatry*, *33*, 1265–1274.

Goldapple, K., Segal, Z., Garson, C., Lau, M., Bieling, P., Kennedy, S., *et al.* (2004). Modulation of cortical-limbic pathways in major depression: Treatment-specific effects of cognitive behavior therapy. *Archives of General Psychiatry*, *61*, 34–41.

Gotlib, I. H., Kasch, K. L., Saskia, T., Joorman, J., Arnow, B. A., & Johnson, S. L. (2004). Coherence and specificity of information-processing biases in depression and social phobia. *Journal of Abnormal Psychology*, *113*, 386–398.

Greenberg, M. S., & Beck, A. T. (1989). Depression versus anxiety: A test of the content-specificity hypothesis. *Journal of Abnormal Psychology*, *98*, 9–13.

Haaga, D. A. F., Dyck, M. J., & Ernst, D. (1991). Empirical status of the cognitive theory of depression. *Psychological Bulletin*, *110*, 215–236.

Haeffel, G. J., Abramson, L. Y., Voelz, Z. R., Metalsky, G. I., Halberstadt, L., Dykman, B. M., Donovan, P., Hogan, M. E., Hankin, B. L., & Alloy, L. B. (2003). Cognitive vulnerability to depression and lifetime history of Axis I psychopathology: A comparison of negative cognitive styles (CSQ) and dysfunctional attitudes (DAS). *Journal of Cognitive Psychotherapy*, *17*, 3–22.

Haeffel, G. J., Abramson, L. Y., Voelz, Z. R., Metalsky, G. I., Halberstadt, L., Dykman, B. M., Donovan, P., Hogan, M. E., Hankin, B. L., & Alloy, L. B. (2005). Negative cognitive styles, dysfunctional attitudes, and the remitted depression paradigm: A search for the elusive cognitive vulnerability to depression factor among remitted depressives. *Emotion, 5*, 343–348.

Haeffel, G. J., Abramson, L. Y., Brazy, P., Shah, J., Teachman, B., & Nosek, B. (2007). Explicit and implicit cognition: A preliminary test of a dual-process theory of cognitive vulnerability. *Behaviour Research and Therapy, 45*, 1155–1167.

Halligan, S. L., Murray, L., Martins, C., & Cooper, P. J. (2007). Maternal depression and psychiatric outcomes in adolescent offspring: A 13-year longitudinal study. *Journal of Affective Disorders, 97*, 145–154.

Hammen, C. (2002). Context of stress in families of children with depressed parents. In S. H. Goodman & I. H. Gotlib (Eds.), *Children of Depressed Parents: Mechanisms of Risk and Implications for Treatment* (pp. 175–199). Washington, DC: American Psychological Association.

Hankin, B. L., & Abramson, L. Y. (2001). Development of gender differences in depression: An elaborated cognitive vulnerability-transactional stress theory. *Psychological Bulletin, 127*, 773–796.

Hankin, B. L., Abramson, L. Y., Miller, N., & Haeffel, G. J. (2004). Cognitive vulnerability–stress theories of depression: Examining affective specificity in the prediction of depression versus anxiety in three prospective studies. *Cognitive Therapy and Research, 28*, 309–345.

Hankin, B. L., Fraley, C., & Abela, J. R. Z. (2005). Daily depression and cognitions about stress: Evidence for a trait-like depressogenic cognitive style and the prediction of depressive symptoms in a prospective daily diary study. *Journal of Personality and Social Psychology, 88*, 673–685.

Hankin, B. L., Lakdawalla, Z., Carter, I., Abela, J. R. Z., & Adams, P. (2007). Are neuroticism, cognitive vulnerabilities and self-esteem overlapping or distinct risks for depression? Evidence from exploratory and confirmatory factor analyses. *Journal of Social and Clinical Psychology, 26*, 29–63.

Hayden, E. P., Dougherty, L. R., Maloney, B., Olino, T. M., Sheikh, H., Durbin, E., Nurnberger Jr., J. I., Lahiri, D. K., & Klein, D. N. (2008). Early-emerging cognitive vulnerability to depression and the serotonin transporter promoter region polymorphism. *Journal of Affective Disorders, 107*, 227–230.

Hedlund, S., & Rude, S. S. (1995). Evidence of latent depressive schemas in formerly depressed individuals. *Journal of Abnormal Psychology, 104*, 517–525.

Ingram, R. E. (1984). Toward an information-processing analysis of depression. *Cognitive Therapy and Research, 8*, 443–447.

Ingram, R. E. (2001). Developing perspectives on the cognitive-developmental origins of depression: Back is the future. *Cognitive Therapy and Research, 25*, 497–504.

Ingram, R. E. (2003). Origins of cognitive vulnerability to depression. *Cognitive Therapy and Research, 27*, 77–88.

Ingram, R. E., & Kendall, P. C. (1986). Cognitive clinical psychology: Implications of an information processing perspective. In R. E. Ingram (Ed.), *Information Processing Approaches to Clinical Psychology* (pp. 3–21). London: Academic Press.

Ingram, R. E., & Ritter, J. (2000). Vulnerability to depression: Cognitive reactivity and parental bonding in high-risk individuals. *Journal of Abnormal Psychology, 109*, 588–596.

Ingram, R. E., Bernet, C. Z., & McLaughlin, S. C. (1994). Attentional allocation processes in individuals at risk for depression. *Cognitive Therapy and Research, 18*, 317–332.

Ingram, R. E., Miranda, J., & Segal, Z. V. (1998). *Cognitive Vulnerability to Depression*. New York: Guilford.

Ingram, R. E., Miranda, J., & Segal, Z. (2006). Cognitive vulnerability to depression. In L. B. Alloy & J. H. Riskind (Eds.), *Cognitive Vulnerability to Emotional Disorders* (pp. 63–91). Mahwah, NJ: Erlbaum.

James, I. A., Reichelt, F. K., Freeston, M. H., & Barton, S. B. (2007). Schemas as memories: Implications for treatment. *Journal of Cognitive Psychotherapy: An International Quarterly, 21*, 51–57.

Joiner, T. E., Jr, Metalsky, G. I., Lew, A., & Klocek, J. (1999). Testing the causal mediation component of Beck's theory of depression: Evidence for specific mediation. *Cognitive Therapy and Research, 23*, 401–412.

Joorman, J., & Gotlib, I. H. (2007). Selective attention to emotional faces following recovery from depression. *Journal of Abnormal Psychology, 116*, 80–85.

Joorman, J., Talbot, L., & Gotlib, I. H. (2007). Biased processing of emotional information in girls at risk for depression. *Journal of Abnormal Psychology, 116*, 1135–1143.

Just, N., Abramson, L. Y., & Alloy, L. B. (2001). Remitted depression studies as tests of the cognitive vulnerability hypotheses of depression onset: A critique and conceptual analysis. *Clinical Psychology Review, 21*, 63–83.

Kuiper, N. A., & Olinger, L. J. (1986). Dysfunctional attitudes and a self-worth contingency model of depression. In P. C. Kendall (Ed.), *Advances in Cognitive-Behavioral Research and Therapy* (Vol. 5, pp. 115–142). New York: Academic Press.

Kwon, S.-M., & Oei, T. P. S. (1992). Differential causal roles of dysfunctional attitudes and automatic thoughts in depression. *Cognitive Therapy and Research, 16*, 309–328.

Lakdawalla, Z., Hankin, B. L., & Mermelstein, R. (2007). Cognitive theories of depression in children and adolescents: A conceptual and quantitative review. *Clinical Child and Family Psychology, 10*, 1–24.

Lau, M. A., Segal, Z. V., & Williams, M. G. (2004). Teasdale's differential activation hypothesis: Implications for mechanisms of depressive relapse and suicidal behaviour. *Behaviour Research and Therapy, 42*, 1001–1007.

Lewinsohn, P. M., Steinmetz, J. L., Larson, D. W., & Franklin, J. (1981). Depression-related cognitions: Antecedent or consequence?. *Journal of Abnormal Psychology, 90*, 213–219.

Lewinsohn, P. M., Joiner, T. E., & Rohde, P. (2001). Evaluation of cognitive diathesis–stress models in predicting major depressive disorder in adolescents. *Journal of Abnormal Psychology, 110*, 203–215.

Linville, P. W. (1982). The complexity-extremity effect and age-based stereotyping. *Journal of Personality and Social Psychology, 42*, 193–211.

Lumley, M. N., & Harkness, K. L. (2007). Specificity in the relations among childhood adversity, early maladaptive schemas, and symptom profiles in adolescent depression. *Cognitive Therapy and Research, 31*, 639–657.

McCranie, E. W., & Bass, J. D. (1984). Childhood family antecedents of dependency and self-criticism: Implications for depression. *Journal of Abnormal Psychology, 93*, 3–8.

McDermut, W., & Haaga, D. A. F. (1994). Cognitive balance and specificity in anxiety and depression. *Cognitive Therapy and Research, 18*, 333–352.

Mezulis, A. H., Shibley Hyde, J., & Abramson, L. Y. (2006). The developmental origins of cognitive vulnerability to depression: Temperament, parenting, and negative life events in childhood as contributors to negative cognitive style. *Developmental Psychology, 42*, 1012–1025.

Mineka, S., Watson, D., & Clark, L. A. (1998). Comorbidity of anxiety and unipolar mood disorders. *Annual Review of Psychology, 49*, 377–412.

Miranda, J., & Persons, J. B. (1988). Dysfunctional attitudes are mood-state dependent. *Journal of Abnormal Psychology, 97*, 76–79.

Miranda, J., Persons, J. B., & Byers, C. N. (1990). Endorsement of dysfunctional beliefs depends on current mood state. *Journal of Abnormal Psychology, 99*, 237–241.

Miranda, J., Gross, J. J., Persons, J. B., & Hahn, J. (1998). Mood matters: Negative mood induction activates dysfunctional attitudes in women vulnerable to depression. *Cognitive Therapy and Research, 22*, 363–376.

Murray, L., Woolgar, M., Cooper, P., & Hipwell, A. (2001). Cognitive vulnerability to depression in 5-year-old children of depressed mothers. *Journal of Child Psychology and Psychiatry, 42*, 891–899.

Oei, T. P. S., Bullbeck, K., & Campbell, J. (2006). Cognitive change processes in group cognitive behavior therapy with mood disorders. *Journal of Affective Disorders, 92*, 231–241.

Ohrt, T., Sjödin, I., & Thorell, L. (1999). Cognitive distortions in panic disorder and major depression: Specificity for depressed mood. *Nordic Journal of Psychiatry, 53*, 459–464.

Oliver, J. M., Murphy, S. L., Ferland, D. R., & Ross, M. J. (2007). Contributions of the Cognitive Style Questionnaire and the Dysfunctional Attitudes Scale to measuring cognitive vulnerability to depression. *Cognitive Therapy and Research, 31*, 51–69.

Otto, M. W., Teachman, B. A., Cohen, L. S., Soares, C. N., Vitonis, A. F., & Harlow, B. L. (2007). Dysfunctional attitudes and episodes of major depression: Predictive validity and temporal stability in never-depressed, depressed, and recovered women. *Journal of Abnormal Psychology, 116*, 475–483.

Persons, J. B., & Miranda, J. (1992). Cognitive theories of vulnerability to depression: Reconciling negative evidence. *Cognitive Therapy and Research, 16*, 485–502.

Riso, L. P., Froman, S. E., Raouf, M., Gable, P., Maddux, R. E., Turini-Santorelli, N., Penna, S., Blandino, J. A., Jacobs, C. H., & Cherry, M. (2006). The long-term stability of early maladaptive schemas. *Cognitive Therapy and Research, 30*, 515–529.

Roberts, J. E., Gotlib, I. H., & Kassel, J. D. (1996). Adult attachment security and symptoms of depression: The mediating roles of dysfunctional attitudes and low self-esteem. *Journal of Personality and Social Psychology, 70*, 310–320.

Rose, D. T., & Abramson, L. Y. (1992). Developmental predictors of depressive cognitive style: Research and theory. In D. Cicchetti & S. L. Toth (Eds.), *Rochester Symposium on Developmental Psychopathology* (Vol. 4, pp. 323–349). Hillsdale, NJ: Erlbaum.

Scher, C. D., Ingram, R. E., & Segal, Z. V. (2005). Cognitive reactivity and vulnerability: Empirical evaluation of construct activation and cognitive diatheses in unipolar depression. *Clinical Psychology Review, 25*, 487–510.

Schmidt, N. B., Schmidt, K. L., & Young, J. E. (1999). Schematic and interpersonal conceptualizations of depression: An integration. In T. Joiner & J. C. Coyne (Eds.), *The Interactional Nature of Depression* (pp. 127–148). Washington, DC: American Psychological Association.

Schniering, C. A., & Rapee, R. M. (2004). The relationship between automatic thoughts and negative emotions in children and adolescents: A test of the content-specificity hypothesis. *Journal of Abnormal Psychology, 113*, 464–470.

Segal, Z. V., & Gemar, M. (1997). Changes in cognitive organization for negative self-referent material following cognitive behavior therapy for depression: A primed Stroop study. *Cognition and Emotion, 11*, 501–516.

Segal, Z. V., & Vella, D. D. (1990). Self-schema in major depression: Replication and extension of a priming methodology. *Cognitive Therapy and Research, 14*, 161–176.

Segal, Z. V., Hood, J. E., Shaw, B. F., & Higgins, E. T. (1988). A structural analysis of the self-schema construct in major depression. *Cognitive Therapy and Research, 12*, 471–485.

Segal, Z. V., Gemar, M., & Williams, S. (1999). Differential cognitive response to a mood challenge following successful cognitive therapy or pharmacotherapy for unipolar depression. *Journal of Abnormal Psychology, 108*, 3–10.

Segal, Z. V., Kennedy, S., Gemar, M., Hood, K., Pedersen, R., & Buis, T. (2006). Cognitive reactivity to sad mood provocation and the prediction of depressive relapse. *Archives of General Psychiatry, 63*, 749–755.

Sheppard, L. C., & Teasdale, J. D. (2004). How does dysfunctional thinking decrease during recovery from major depression?. *Journal of Abnormal Psychology, 113*, 64–71.

Showers, C. J., Abramson, L. Y., & Hogan, M. E. (1998). The dynamic self: How the content and structure of the self-concept change with mood. *Journal of Personality and Social Psychology, 75*, 478–493.

Showers, C. J., Limke, A., & Zeigler-Hill, V. (2004). Self-structure and self-change: Applications to psychological treatment. *Behavior Therapy, 35*, 167–184.

Solomon, A., Haaga, D. A. F., Brody, C., Kirk, L., & Friedman, D. G. (1998). Priming irrational beliefs in recovered-depressed people. *Journal of Abnormal Psychology, 107*, 440–449.

Spangler, D. L., & Burns, D. D. (1999). Are dysfunctional attitudes and attributional style the same or different? *Behavior Therapy, 30*, 239–252.

Stallard, P. (2007). Early maladaptive schemas in children: Stability and differences between a community and a clinic referred sample. *Clinical Psychology and Psychotherapy, 14*, 10–18.

Stark, K. D., Schimidt, K. L., & Joiner, T. E., Jr (1996). Cognitive triad: Relationship to depressive symptoms, parents' cognitive triad, and perceived parental messages. *Journal of Abnormal Child Psychology, 24*, 615–631.

Steer, R. A., Clark, D. A., Beck, A. T., & Ranieri, W. F. (1995). Common and specific dimensions of self-reported anxiety and depression: A replication. *Journal of Abnormal Psychology, 104*, 542–545.

Taylor, L., & Ingram, R. E. (1999). Cognitive reactivity and depressotypic information processing in children of depressed mothers. *Journal of Abnormal Psychology, 108*, 202–210.

Teasdale, J. D. (1997). The relationship between cognition and emotion: The mind-in-place in mood disorders. In D. M. Clark & C. G. Fairburn (Eds.), *Science and Practice of Cognitive Behaviour Therapy* (pp. 67–93). Oxford: Oxford Medical Publications.

Teasdale, J. D., & Barnard, P. J. (1993). *Affect, Cognition and Change: Re-modelling Depressive Thought*. Hillsdale, NJ: Erlbaum.

Teasdale, J. D., & Dent, J. (1987). Cognitive vulnerability to depression: An investigation of two hypotheses. *British Journal of Clinical Psychology, 26*, 113–126.

Wang, C. E., Brennen, T., & Holte, A. (2005). Mechanisms of recurrent depression: A cognitive battle model and some preliminary results. *Clinical Psychology and Psychotherapy, 12*, 427–442.

Weissman, A. N., & Beck, A. T. (1978). *Development and validation of the Dysfunctional Attitude Scale*. Paper presented at the annual meeting of the Association for Advancement of Behavior Therapy, Chicago, Illinois.

Wenzlaff, R. M., & Bates, D. E. (1998). Unmasking a cognitive vulnerability to depression: How lapses in mental control reveal depressive thinking. *Journal of Personality and Social Psychology, 75*, 1559–1571.

Westra, H. A., & Kuiper, N. A. (1997). Cognitive content specificity in selective attention across four domains of maladjustment. *Behavior Research and Therapy, 35*, 349–365.

Whisman, M. A., & Kwon, P. (1992). Parental representation, cognitive distortions and mild depression. *Cognitive Therapy and Research, 16*, 557–568.

Williams, S., Connolly, J., & Segal, Z. V. (2001). Intimacy in relationships and cognitive vulnerability to depression in adolescent girls. *Cognitive Therapy and Research, 25*, 477–496.

Woody, S. R., Taylor, S., McLean, P. D., & Koch, W. J. (1998). Cognitive specificity in panic and depression: Implications for comorbidity. *Cognitive Therapy and Research, 22*, 427–443.

Young, J. E. (1999). *Cognitive Therapy for Personality Disorders: A Schema-Focused Approach* (3rd ed.). Sarasota, FL: Professional Resource Press.

Young, J. E., Klosko, J. S., & Weishaar, M. E. (2003). *Schema Therapy: A Practitioner's Guide*. New York: Guilford.

7

Information Processing: Attention and Memory

Rick E. Ingram, Dana K. Steidtmann and Steven L. Bistricky

Department of Psychology, University of Kansas, Lawrence, KS, USA

Attention and memory are among numerous cognitive factors that may play a role in the risk process. Attention and memory can also be thought of as the basic building blocks of cognition, and arguably as such, lay the foundation for all cognitive approaches to depression. For example, schemas, which feature prominently in cognitive models of depression (e.g., Beck, 1967; 1976; see Chapter 6) function by relying heavily on attention and memory processes (Ingram *et al.*, 1998). One function of a negative schema in depression is to direct attention toward negative and self-reinforcing information (Segal, 1988). Another function of schemas is to organize memories of similar types, so that one negative memory provides access to others. Further, processes linked to schemas like rumination rely on attention and memory, and have been proposed to do so for some time now. For instance, Ingram (1984) argued that rumination reflects the "recycling" of depressive memories, and requires attention to those memories.

Clearly attention and memory represent core constructs in cognitive theories of depression. Yet, these variables are not featured prominently in these models. That is, variables such as schemas, beliefs, dysfunctional attitudes, and automatic thoughts/rumination receive the majority of theoretical interest; and deservedly so, as these variables are unarguably important components of the depressive state. Yet, what about the underlying foundation of these cognitive variables? There is reason to believe that a focus on information processing in the form of attention and memory can help elucidate important variables in the risk process. Such elucidation is hampered, however, by a fundamental problem; little direct research has examined these variables in the specific context of risk. Risk research can take many forms, but at its most basic level it requires examining presumed risk variables in the absence of the active depressive state. For example, comparing nondepressed individuals who are characterized by some specific attention or memory variable and then assessing the incidence of past depressive states in such individuals would be one way to examine these variables in the context of risk. Another strategy would be to determine if these attention or memory variables predict future depression.

We are unaware of studies that have taken this approach, partly because negative attention and memories are depressive state linked. That is, theoretical models and empirical research suggest that the emergence of schemas (and the attention and memory processes that are associated with them) occurs with the emergence of the depressive state or in lab settings, in the context of evocative events (Ingram *et al.*, 1998). Given this evidence, it is difficult to determine what, for example, a memory risk factor looks like and how to measure it.

There is, thus, little direct research bearing on these processes, at least in the sense of these variables being associated with the fundamental elements of risk. Given that the purpose of this chapter is to examine information processing as a risk variable, is this then to be the shortest chapter ever? Fortunately the answer is no. Although there is little in the way of direct evidence, inferences can be drawn from more indirect research, and, as the foundation of arguably all cognitive processes in depression, they would appear to warrant this scrutiny. In particular, we argue that examining these processes in people at risk for depression is relevant to understanding the role of these variables in risk.

Risk can be defined in a variety of ways.[1] For example, given high relapse and recurrence rates in depression (Kessler, 2002), individuals who have previously experienced a depressive episode are thought to be at high risk for a subsequent episode. Individuals who experience subclinical levels of depression are also at high risk for the onset of major depression, as are the offspring of depressed mothers. Although there are other operational definitions of risk (e.g., Alloy & Abramson, 1999), most of the available literature on information processing employs one of these samples. We therefore examine possible risk mechanisms

[1] Risk reflects any variable that is correlated with, in the present context, the onset of depression (Ingram *et al.*, 1998). Vulnerability, on the other hand, reflects variables pertaining to the mechanisms of onset. Although this distinction is important, in the present chapter we use these terms interchangeably.

in the realm of information processing in general, and memory and attention more specifically, within these samples.

MEMORY AND RISK

Although it has long been recognized that memory deficits are a symptom of current major depression, some research suggests that abnormalities in memory may actually place people at risk for initial onset and/or relapse of the disorder. Memory deficits and biases associated with depression are frequently subdivided into problems with encoding vs. problems with retrieval. Because encoding seems to fall mainly under the realm of attentional processes, the literature relevant to memory encoding is reviewed in the attention section of this chapter. Thus, this section focuses primarily on research relevant to memory retrieval processes.

RECALL BIAS

A common way that memory retrieval has been examined within the context of depression is to present participants with a list of emotional words during a lab task such as the emotional Stroop (Williams *et al.*, 1996), emotional dot-probe (MacLeod *et al.*, 1986), or a self-referent encoding task (SRET; Derry & Kuiper, 1981) and then ask them to recall as many of the words as possible after some delay period. Sometimes participants are told ahead of time that they will be asked to recall the words at a later time (i.e., intentional recall). However, more commonly, participants are asked to perform an incidental recall task in which they are unaware that they will be asked to recall the words involved in the task. It has been suggested that the incidental recall paradigm reflects a more automatic form of processing whereas intentional recall reflects more conscious, effortful processing (Ingram *et al.*, 1995). Use of the recall paradigms with currently depressed people has revealed a "negative recall bias." Although currently there is variation within the literature in terms of how this bias is manifested, evidence is accumulating that depressed people, and people at risk for depression, tend to recall a greater amount of negative information or recall less positive information when compared to relatively lower-risk groups. For example, depressed people tend to recall more negative emotional words via intentional recall (Ingram *et al.*, 1995) and fewer positive emotional words via incidental recall (Taylor & John, 2004) than nondepressed people. In addition, a currently depressed group recalled more negative than positive words overall while a nondepressed group recalled more positive than negative words (Denny & Hunt, 1992). In an undiagnosed sample of college students, recall of positive self-descriptive words was negatively related to scores on the Dysfunctional Attitude Scale (DAS; Weissman & Beck, 1978) and the Beck Depression Inventory (BDI; Beck *et al.*, 1988; Moilanen, 1993).

However, the more compelling evidence of negative recall biases as a risk factor for depression comes from longitudinal studies. In one study, for example, nondepressed pregnant women were administered an incidental recall task. Those women who recalled more negative than positive words were classified as "susceptible" to depression. After classification, the women completed the BDI and 3 months later the women were assessed for stressful life events and were re-administered the BDI. For those women who were classified as susceptible and had stressful life events in the interim, BDI scores increased significantly. However, for nonsusceptible women, and susceptible women without stressful life events, BDI scores decreased (Bellew & Hill, 1991). In a similar paradigm, college students were assessed via incidental recall, the DAS and the Cognitive Style Questionnaire (CSQ; Alloy *et al.*, 2000), followed up for 2½ years and reassessed for stressful life events and depression level. Individuals who were initially classified as "at-risk" based on DAS and CSQ scores, and who recalled more negative than positive information on the incidental recall task, were significantly more likely than low-risk individuals to have had a first-onset major depressive episode during the follow-up period. In addition, a composite score based on a variety of assessments and tasks including an incidental recall task significantly predicted depression during the subsequent 2½ year period (Steinberg *et al.*, 2003). These studies suggest that memory recall by itself may not be predictive of subsequent depression. However, in combination with other assessments, especially an assessment of stressful life events, it does offer predictive information.

Some negative recall biases have been found in formerly depressed individuals. For example, Hedlund and Rude (1995) found that, following a self-focus manipulation, previously depressed adults recalled significantly more negative words than never depressed adults, and did not differ significantly in recall of negative words from a currently depressed group. In addition, following a negative mood induction, and employing a Stroop task, previously dysphoric individuals have been found to recall significantly more negative emotional words than never dysphoric participants (Gilboa & Gotlib, 1997). Likewise, in an fMRI (functional MRI) study, formerly depressed participants were compared to never depressed participants during an SRET and then performed an incidental recall task. Amygdala activation during the SRET significantly predicted incidental recall of negative words in the formerly depressed group but only after a negative priming procedure (Ramel *et al.*, 2007).

Some important associations have been observed in children. For example, in a study reported by Timbremont and Braet (2004), never depressed children recalled significantly more positive words than negative words, but currently and formerly depressed children did not differ significantly on the number of positive and negative words recalled, suggesting that children at risk for depression may lack a positive processing bias. In a different type of paradigm, Taylor and Ingram (1999) assessed incidental recall in children of depressed mothers. In this study, half of each group underwent a negative priming procedure, with results indicating that high-risk children who were primed were significantly more likely to recall negative self-descriptive words than high-risk children who were not primed. Hence, memory biases may be evident in groups at risk, but only in the context of a life stressor or a priming procedure. These findings again suggest that a failure or difficulty in retrieving positive information during times of stress is an important manifestation of memory biases as a risk factor.

MEMORY SPECIFICITY

Another memory phenomenon that has been empirically examined with regard to risk for depression is specificity of memory, most frequently assessed using the Autobiographical Memory Test (AMT; Williams & Broadbent, 1986). In this task, people are asked to recall a specific life memory in response to various positive and negative cue words. Research using the AMT or similar tasks has indicated that people at risk for depression are more likely to provide general categories of memories in response to AMT cues when compared to people who are at less risk (see Williams *et al.*, 2007 for a review). This has frequently been termed categoric or overgeneral memory in the research literature. Consistent with the idea that overgeneral memory places people at risk for emotional distress, McBride and Cappaliez (2004) demonstrated that the induction of a depressed mood in an unselected sample of nondepressed individuals increased overgeneral memory. In addition, inducing overgeneral memory of an emotional event appears to lead to greater emotional distress than does inducing specific retrieval of an emotional event (Raes *et al.*, 2006). Raes *et al.* (2005) proposed that the lack of memory specificity functions as a risk factor for depression by way of inhibiting effective problem solving. These researchers presented data showing that reduced memory specificity significantly mediates the relationship between rumination and reduced problem solving in currently depressed people.

A number of longitudinal studies have examined overgeneral memory in the context of depression or people at risk for depression. In one study, the AMT was administered to currently depressed participants who were followed up prospectively. Although AMT specificity scores did not change significantly from initial assessment to follow up, difficulty in recalling specific positive memories at the initial AMT was highly associated with failure to recover from depression in the subsequent 7 months. In fact, categoric recall to positive cues accounted for 33% of the variability in Hamilton Rating Scale for Depression scores (HRSD; Hamilton, 1960) at follow up (Brittlebank *et al.*, 1993). This finding suggests that overgeneral memory may be a stable trait that predicts the course of depression. Similarly, in a sample of men admitted for alcohol treatment, specificity in response to positive cue words on the AMT at intake significantly predicted a decrease in depressive symptoms at discharge 3 weeks later. This finding was still evident after controlling for initial depression severity and level of alcohol dependence (Mackinger *et al.*, 2004). However, it should be noted that several other studies have found that initial specificity on the AMT did not predict depression course (Brewin *et al.*, 1999; Kremers *et al.*, 2006; Spinhoven *et al.*, 2006) and did not remain stable during treatment (Kremers *et al.*, 2006). The findings of Kremers *et al.* (2006) were obtained on a sample of participants with comorbid depression and borderline personality disorder, which may account for the conflicting findings.

Other longitudinal studies on special populations have suggested that memory specificity may be predictive of subsequent mood or depressive symptom level. In a sample of people with a seasonal onset pattern of major depression, decreased specificity in response to positive cues during winter depression significantly predicted HRSD scores in the summer despite the fact that no participants met full criteria for depression during the summer assessment. This predictive finding remained even after controlling for initial symptom severity during the winter months (Dalgleish *et al.*, 2001). In another study, pregnant women who were not selected based on their depression status were administered the AMT and given a self-report measure of negative affect between their 25th and 40th week of gestation. Three months after delivery, they completed the same self-report measure of negative affect. Results showed that the more categoric a woman was in response to negative cues on the AMT, the more likely she was to have increased negative affect during the follow-up period (Mackinger *et al.*, 2000a).

Very few studies have examined formerly depressed samples on the AMT. However, it has been found that previously depressed women showed less specificity in response to negative cues on the AMT than did never depressed women (Mackinger *et al.*, 2000b). In addition, adolescents with major depression in full remission had more categoric responses to positive AMT cue words than never depressed adolescents (Park *et al.*, 2002). One study found that a remitted depression diagnosis did not significantly predict degree of memory specificity (Wessel *et al.*, 2001).

There have been few empirical attempts to integrate the findings from the memory recall and categoric memory literatures. Based on the recall literature, it appears that people at risk for depression may be prone to recall negative information at a greater rate than positive information. In addition, when considering the overgeneral memory literature, it is possible that once people at risk for depression retrieve and attend to negative information, they are particularly likely to think about it in a ruminative and global way rather than to confine it to specific instances or to use effective interpersonal problem solving strategies to stop ruminating about the negative information. There has been one study in which aspects of both autobiographical memory and incidental memory recall were assessed. In a sample of nondepressed college students, depression risk was assigned as "high" or "low" based on responses to the CSQ and a modified version of the Attributional Style Questionnaire (ASQ; Peterson & Villanova, 1988). Students completed an SRET were asked to provide past personal stories illustrating why certain self-relevant words were characteristic or not characteristic of the self, and then performed an incidental recall task for the

SRET words. Those students identified as high risk for depression recalled significantly fewer positive self-descriptive words than those labeled as low risk for depression. In addition, participants labeled as high risk provided significantly more past behavioral examples of why negative words applied and significantly fewer past behavioral examples of why positive words applied than low-risk participants (Alloy *et al.*, 1997). Although seemingly at odds with the findings that people are risk for depression recalled fewer specific negative memories, recalling behavioral examples of negative traits is a related but distinct measure from recalling specific memories. The discrepancy between this study and the overgeneral memory literature indicates a need for further study of diverse aspects of memory in depression.

ATTENTION AND RISK

Cognitive theorists argue that, when depressive affect is experienced, biased attentional processes could serve to prolong these mood states (Ingram *et al.*, 1998). An abundance of evidence has shown that attentional biases exist in individuals who are experiencing clinical depression, but evidence has been less plentiful and more contentious as to whether such attentional biases exist prior to the development of depressive episodes, and thus whether these biases can be regarded as mechanisms of vulnerability. As accumulated evidence for particular information processing biases in depressed individuals has neared conclusive thresholds, vulnerability researchers have sought to discern whether similar information processing biases play a causal role in the development of depression.

ATTENTIONAL AFFECTIVE BIAS

Among information processing tasks that have been employed to examine potential cognitive biases in depressed and depression vulnerable groups, the Stroop task is one of the oldest and most commonly used. The original Stroop task tapped general inhibition of an automatic primary response in favor of a rule-based secondary response (Stroop, 1935). Specifically, the respondent is usually instructed to name the color of ink of words, inhibiting the primary response to read the words. Interference effects are identified by the extent to which reaction times (RTs) are slowed by the presence of the task irrelevant information (i.e., semantic processing of the word). Attentional capacity deficits have been found consistently in depressed individuals' ability to inhibit an automatic primary response in general, but affective biases have been of greater interest to vulnerability researchers. A particular modified version called the emotional Stroop task consists of words associated with elation or depression, and thus attentional bias is revealed by the interference effect of the affective words. Several studies have provided evidence that individuals with clinical depression perform differently than nondepressed individuals on the emotional Stroop (e.g., Segal & Vella, 1990), although some studies have failed to find significant differences (e.g., Bradley *et al.*, 1995; see Williams *et al.*, 1996 for review).

Investigators have also found some evidence that groups who are considered to be at risk, as defined by the presence of dysphoria, perform differently on the Stroop than low-risk groups. For instance, Gotlib and McCann (1984) compared the performance of dysphoric to nondysphoric individuals, and found that dysphoric participants had significantly greater response times for depressive words. Additionally, they found that nondysphoric individuals who were primed with sad mood did not exhibit differences in interference for positive or negative words, and concluded that sad mood could not sufficiently explain the interference effect for negative words in dysphoric individuals. Klieger and Cordner (1990) replicated Gotlib and McCann (1984), finding that response times were greater for dysphoric compared to nondysphoric participants for negative words than positive ones.

Other studies have failed to support the existence of biased interference effects specific to depression vulnerable populations. In one study, individuals who had recently remitted from a depressive episode performed no differently than a control group on the modified Stroop, whereas those same formerly depressed individuals had shown biased interference effects for negative information when they were depressed. Hedlund and Rude (1995) compared the emotional Stroop performance of never depressed, formerly depressed, and currently depressed individuals, and found that when participants responded both verbally and manually (e.g., key press), no interference differences due to negative words were found. It is possible that the multiple response format introduced greater random error and thus may have diminished power to detect differences. In a study that examined the effects of cognitive reactivity in formerly depressed as compared to never depressed individuals, both groups underwent a negative mood induction procedure and then completed the emotional Stroop; but performance of the groups did not differ significantly (Gilboa & Gotlib, 1997).

Taken as a whole, evidence from studies that have assessed for early attentional biases in depression vulnerable groups, as measured by the Stroop task, has been mixed. Results of some studies appear to suggest that the interference effects evoked by negative content reflect stable biases in depression vulnerable individuals rather than state-based mood fluctuations, while other studies have either failed to show any differences or have suggested that attentional biases that may exist within a depressive episode dissipate after remission. These varied results may be due to differing stimulus presentation durations, response formats, and sample sizes. Further, it is necessary to consider critiques of the Stroop task. Chiefly, results from the emotional Stroop task are open to attentional and nonattentional interpretations because the Stroop outcome measure of response time is composed of encoding and response production (Gotlib *et al.*, 2005), which cannot be disentangled. Thus, it could be argued that group differences ascribed to interference could be due to biases in response.

ATTENTIONAL CAPACITY AND ALLOCATION

Dichotic listening tasks have also been used to assess attentional processing allocation in depressed and depression vulnerable individuals. In this task, participants are presented with competing auditory messages and are asked to track a target message in one ear while attempting to ignore distracting verbal content (e.g., emotionally valenced words) presented to the other ear. The extent to which the distracter content interrupts the participants' ability to repeat the target message is thought to reflect their existing cognitive structures and corresponding attentional allocation. That is, tracking errors indicate that a significant portion of the individual's limited attention has been diverted toward schematically pertinent distracter information. It is thought that dichotic listening assesses very early stages of information processing, and thus, this information is screened prior to higher-order processing (Lachman *et al.*, 1979).

Evidence suggests that people who are clinically depressed or who are vulnerable to depression may show greater attentional interference to emotionally toned distracting information as operationalized by the dichotic listening task. For example, Ingram *et al.* (1994) compared the performance of a high-risk group (formerly depressed individuals) to a low-risk group (never depressed individuals) who were primed with neutral or sad mood. Significant differences were not found between the number of dichotic listening errors that the high- and low-risk groups committed in a neutral mood, but the high-risk group made significantly more errors related to both negative and positive distractors in the sad mood condition than the low-risk group. In a related study, Ingram and Ritter (2000) found no significant differences between the low- and high-risk groups in normative moods; however, high-risk individuals committed significantly more tracking errors following negative distracter words when primed with a sad mood. Furthermore, results indicated that the group differences were moderated by self-reported low maternal care, itself a contributor to risk for developing depression. Therefore, individuals who were at most risk for developing future depression – those who reported experiencing low maternal care and a past depressive episode – showed the greatest impairment in performance in the midst of negatively toned distracting information.

Although results from the several studies using the dichotic listening task with depression vulnerable individuals have not been identical, the evidence suggests that an early attentional sensitivity to emotional information, possibly more pronounced for negative information, may distinguish vulnerable from nonvulnerable individuals. If this is true, biased early detection of *any* emotional information in vulnerable individuals could indicate an activated dysfunctional schema, a theoretical mediator of vulnerability. In later processing stages, discriminatory filtering may lead to the elaborative processing of salient negative information and relatively decreased processing of positive information (Ingram *et al.*, 1994).

Another task used to assess attentional allocation in depressed and depression vulnerable individuals has been the *dot-probe task*. In these studies, individuals are first presented with a pair of valenced stimuli (e.g., faces or affective words). The pair of stimuli is immediately replaced by a single dot, which is located in the former position of one of the two stimuli. The participant responds as quickly and accurately as possible by pushing one of two buttons representing the correct position of the dot. To the degree that attentional allocation is greater toward the stimulus replaced by the dot, response speed for identifying the dot's position is facilitated. On the contrary, if attentional allocation is greater toward the stimulus opposite to the position where the dot ultimately appears, response times are slowed. Thus, investigators can assess whether pathological or at-risk groups allocate greater attentional resources toward positive, negative, or neutral words than healthy control groups.

Studies using the dot-probe task with depressed samples have often used valenced word stimuli as initial probes and have reported biases that distinguish depressed from healthy control groups. Some studies have suggested that depressed individuals shift attention toward negative or socially threatening words, unlike nondepressed individuals (Mathews *et al.*, 1996; Mogg *et al.*, 1995), whereas other studies have suggested that depressed individuals lack a protective bias that would shift attention away from threat words (MacLeod *et al.*, 1986), which is exhibited by nondepressed individuals.

Dot-probe studies with depression vulnerable samples have also indicated that biases distinguish these individuals from healthy, low-risk individuals. Bradley *et al.* (1997) conducted two studies comparing dysphoric and nondysphoric individuals, one with naturally occurring dysphoria, and the other with induced dysphoria. The investigators manipulated stimulus exposure duration of word stimuli (e.g., 14 ms, 500 ms, 1000 ms), and found that the naturally dysphoric group showed significantly greater attentional vigilance for depression-related words than the nondysphoric group only when words were presented for 1000 ms, suggesting that these later biases were in elaborative (effortful) but not automatic processing. The dysphoric-mood-primed group evinced significantly greater vigilance for depression-related words presented for 500 ms, with a trend for 1000 ms presentations. Biases evoked by longer presentation durations could reflect difficulties disengaging attention from negative information, whereas earlier biases (500 ms) may reflect initial orienting (Bradley *et al.*, 2000) or facilitated attentional engagement with negative information.

Using a prospective study design, Beevers and Carver (2003) examined the possible interaction between selective attention to negative information (in this case representing a high level of cognitive vulnerability at initial assessment) and subsequent life stress in predicting levels of dysphoria approximately 7 weeks later. Although all participants (i.e., vulnerable and nonvulnerable) were primed with a sad mood, those who both exhibited a bias for shifting their attention toward negative information and who experienced higher levels of life stress in the interim period reported the highest levels of dysphoria in the follow-up assessment. The results of this study suggest that individuals who show attentional biases to negative information may be at greater risk of dysphoria and depression. Despite a converse angle of approach, these results are congruent with findings in which alternate operationalizations of vulnerability (e.g., dysphoria) are associated with negative information processing biases.

Several investigators have studied attentional processing of depressed and depression vulnerable individuals using facial stimuli on the dot-probe task, often reporting biases that distinguish these individuals from healthy control groups. In these studies, rather than two words being presented before the dot presentation, two valenced faces are presented as the stimulus (e.g., positive–neutral, positive–negative, or negative–neutral of the same poser). In one such investigation Gotlib *et al.* (2004) found that depressed individuals selectively attended to sad, but not angry or happy faces on a dot-probe task, a pattern not found in the study's anxious or nonpsychiatric control groups. These results suggest that in the time course of attentional processing, depressed individuals maintain and perhaps have difficulty disengaging their attention from sad faces. Findings have also supported a *content-specificity hypothesis*, meaning that general sensitivity to emotional expressions or to nonspecific negative affect do not drive the observed bias (Gotlib *et al.*, 2004; Karparova *et al.*, 2005).

As for dot-probe studies that have examined depression vulnerable individuals, Joormann *et al.* (2007) compared the performance of daughters of mothers with a history of recurrent depression with an age-matched control group on the dot-probe task following a sad mood prime. Sad–neutral or happy–neutral facial expressions were presented preceding the dot-probe, with results showing that daughters of recurrently depressed mothers showed biased selective attention toward negative facial expressions, which was not observed in the control group. On the other hand, daughters without this elevated risk for depression selectively attended to positive facial expressions. In a young adult sample, Bradley *et al.* (1998) found that dysphoria was associated with a tendency to shift attention away from happy faces relative to neutral faces. These biases were apparent when facial stimuli were presented for 500 ms, but not for 1250 ms, implicating attention-orienting processes. Similarly, Bradley *et al.* (2000) found that the group who scored highest on the BDI exhibited reduced attentiveness to happy faces, but no biases for sad faces. These results fit with the idea that high risk as defined by dysphoria is not characterized by a bias for orienting attention toward sad information, but by a failure to adaptively orient attention to positive stimuli.

A similar task, the *deployment of attention task* (DOAT) has been used to examine whether depressed or depression vulnerable individuals exhibit attentional processing that differentiates them from individuals with no history and low risk of depression. In this task, word pairs (e.g., negative–neutral, positive–neutral, positive–negative) are presented to participants simultaneously. However, participants are misinformed that one word will appear slightly before the other, and they are instructed to indicate this word. When participants answer that a particular word appeared first, this hypothetically indicates a greater attentional allocation toward that word, as it became consciously identifiable earlier than its counterpart word.

In a study examining attentional allocation and current depression, the DOAT was administered to moderately depressed patients and nondepressed controls twice, preceding and following a 6-week interval. Patients with depression attended more to negative words than did nondepressed participants, who exhibited a positivistic bias (Karparova *et al.*, 2007). With respect to vulnerability to depression, McCabe *et al.* (2000) compared never depressed and formerly depressed women, with half of each group completing the DOAT after a sad mood prime and the other half in a neutral mood. Both state and trait adjectives were used as stimuli. McCabe *et al.* (2000) found that in a neutral mood, both groups showed a protective bias (i.e., significant difference from 50% probability of choosing either word in pair), shifting attention away from negative trait-like adjectives. Of the participants primed with a sad mood, however, formerly depressed women lacked a protective bias for negative trait-like adjectives, unlike never depressed women. Meanwhile, the never depressed women lacked a protective bias for state-like adjectives, unlike the formerly depressed women. The authors reasoned that, compared to state-like adjectives, negative trait-like adjectives are more likely to pose a threat to the core conception of self, evoking the protective bias seen in nonvulnerable but not sad-mood-primed formerly depressed women, who may possess latent negative self-schemas. In contrast, state-like negative words are less stable, more prone to fluctuation, and thus less threatening to both never depressed and formerly depressed groups. Unbiased attention to this kind of negative information, as seen in the nonvulnerable women, may adaptively alert an individual to alter an unsatisfactory state of affairs. Conversely, a bias away from a negative but mutable state might allow the unsatisfactory situation to persist. In addition to underscoring the importance of the nature of the stimuli (e.g., trait vs. state), McCabe *et al.* (2000) articulate how the absence of a protective bias to negative information would lead to greater vulnerability to depression. Specifically, greater access to negative trait-like (global, stable) information could serve to increase the frequency and duration of sad moods as well as further strengthening negative cognitive structures.

Although the DOAT has been critiqued as a "coarse measure" of attentional bias (Koster *et al.*, 2005), it has nonetheless identified attentional processing differences between depressed and nondepressed individuals and between vulnerable and nonvulnerable groups. The limited studies available suggest that, while depressed individuals direct their attention more toward negative information than nondepressed individuals, depression vulnerable individuals lack protective biases that would shift their attention away from negative and toward positive trait-like descriptive information, perhaps making them more susceptible to extended depressive moods or even episodes.

INHIBITION OF ATTENTION

Investigators have also employed information processing paradigms to examine inhibition processes (e.g., Joormann 2004) and the concurrent, related interference processes (e.g., Gotlib *et al.*, 2005) in depressed and depression vulnerable individuals. Selective attention has been commonly studied as if it were a single excitatory process, but cognitive science has come to view attention as being composed of both excitatory and inhibitory processes (Houghton & Tipper, 1994; Neumann & DeSchepper, 1992). Inhibition dampens the intrusion of irrelevant information into working memory (Neill *et al.*, 1995). Thus, efficient selection of information occurs through facilitating the activation of selected, relevant information and dampening unselected, nonrelevant information. Inhibition is thought to be reactive to attentional interference in that the more interference a distracter causes, the more it must be inhibited (Beech *et al.*, 1989; Milliken *et al.*, 1994; Neill *et al.*, 1995). As such, previous research has supported the positive correlation between measures of interference and inhibition.

Joormann (2004) compared the inhibitory processing of dysphoric and nondysphoric individuals via a negative affective priming paradigm. The negative priming effect represented the delay in a target response when affective content from a previous distracter trial became the target (e.g., distracter on prime trial = "sad," target on test trial = "depressed"). To the extent that the valence of the distracter word in the prime trial is still being inhibited on the subsequent test trial, it should result in slower response times for targets of matching emotional valence. Thus, the lack of a negative affective priming effect signifies a lack of inhibitory processing. In this study, participants were asked to identify the valence of a target word, a task that focuses attention on emotional aspects of information. Joormann (2004) found that dysphoric individuals showed inhibitory dysfunction in the immediate attentional processing of negative information on the task. In another experiment, Joormann (2004) found that, of a group of participants who had previously completed a self-reference task, *formerly depressed* individuals exhibited significantly less inhibition to negative words than never depressed individuals.

Affective interference is a proposed phenomenon where the performance of dysphoric or depressed individuals on a nonaffective information processing task is hindered by the presence (i.e., interference) of negatively valenced affective information, despite its irrelevance to the task. For example, Siegle *et al.* (2002a) found that dysphoric individuals, unlike nondysphoric individuals, exhibited slowed performance when identifying the nonemotional aspects of negative words, despite being quicker to identify the *emotional valence* of negative words. Using a similar paradigm, Gotlib *et al.* (2005) found that depression-susceptible participants exhibited increased interference for negative distracter words, but not for positive distracter words, unlike the nonsusceptible participants who did not exhibit interference effects for either positive or negative distractors. Susceptible participants also exhibited elevated inhibition of negative, but not positive, distracter words. Thus, when susceptible participants encountered a negative distracter in the prime display, their response time to a negative target word in the subsequent probe display was slowed. Nondysphoric participants did not show elevated inhibition of negative or positive distractors. Interference findings from this study are consistent with previous results that showed that depressed participants exhibit interference from negative but not positive distractors (McCabe & Gotlib, 1993).

These findings suggest that dysphoric and formerly depressed individuals may exhibit inhibitory deficits for negative content when they must focus on and respond to emotional aspects of information (e.g., Joormann, 2004). It may be that such an inhibitory deficit for negative information could lead to greater contamination of irrelevant negative information in working memory, which could lead to greater elaboration. Greater elaboration could strengthen associations among negative cognitive structures, increase rumination, and maintain depressive mood (Ingram, 1984; Nolen-Hoeksema *et al.*, 1993). Additionally, cluttered working memory could decrease performance in complex problem solving required in daily life. Collectively, this could indicate greater vulnerability to developing major depression.

The *emotional modification of the endogenous cueing task* (Posner, 1980) has also been employed with depression vulnerable groups to examine potential attentional processing differences from nonvulnerable individuals. The task begins with a fixation cross, followed by the presentation of two white rectangles. Cues (e.g., negative, positive, or neutral words) and targets (single black squares) are presented in the middle of the rectangles. The sequence is for a cue word to appear in one of the two rectangles briefly, and soon thereafter a target square appears in either the same rectangle or the opposite rectangle. The participant responds to which of the two positions the target square appears. The *cue validity effect* and the *inhibition of return effect* are of interest to investigators. The cue validity effect represents the degree to which participants respond faster when the cue is a valid indicator for the subsequent location of the target square, rather than in the invalid opposite rectangle. The inhibition of return effect (Posner & Cohen, 1984) occurs when, as stimulus onset asynchronies increase, the cue validity effect disappears and then reverses so that the previous cue location is inhibited; the cue begins to be regarded as arbitrary information to be inhibited, and thus response times to valid trials are slowed. The emotional modification aspect of the endogenous cueing task introduces the assessment of an *enhanced* cue validity effect, the idea that the cue validity effect could be augmented by particular emotionally relevant stimuli (i.e., valenced words). This could lead to enhanced attentional engagement to an emotional cue compared to a neutral cue for valid trials. For example, a person might respond more quickly to a box that replaces the word "lonely" than for "bland," if predisposed in some way to negative information. Also, the enhanced cue validity effect could lead to a delay of disengagement of attention from the emotional cue to the target on invalid trials, causing the participant to take longer to respond when the box appears opposite the salient emotional word. A key benefit of this task is that it can assess interrelated components of attention: initial orienting to stimuli, engagement of attention with stimuli, and attentional disengagement from stimuli (Posner *et al.*, 1987).

Koster *et al.* (2005) conducted two experiments using the endogenous cueing task comparing dysphoric and nondysphoric groups. Although no group differences were found in orienting to negative words, investigators found that dysphoric individuals consistently engaged their attention with negative words significantly more than to neutral words (i.e., enhanced cue validity effect), which was not characteristic of nondysphoric individuals. Also, dysphoric individuals lacked attentional engagement with positive words (i.e., no enhanced cue validity effect), compared to nondysphoric individuals who did engage their attention with positive words. In addition, Koster *et al.* (2005) found that dysphoric individuals exhibited impaired attentional disengagement from negative words, whereas nondysphoric individuals did not show this impairment. This effect was consistent for longer intervals, which likely tapped attentional engagement and maintenance processes. This again suggests that in dysphoria attentional biases for negative information occur in later stages of information processing, but not the earliest stage. These results also support the idea that depressed and depression vulnerable individuals may lack the adaptive engagement with positive information in the environment that healthy individuals show. Difficulty shifting attention away from negative information and insufficient engagement with positive information in the environment could lead to proportionally negativistic perception and interpretation of events (Ellenbogen *et al.*, 2002), rumination, and prolonged periods of depressed mood, making the dysphoric individuals more vulnerable to developing a depressive episode. Overall, it appears that dysphoric individuals may show difficulty disengaging attention from negative information when they are not under acute stress, but that under duress, they exhibit reduced disengagement to all affective stimuli, which may be mediated by diminished motivational influence.

EYE MOVEMENT INDICATORS OF ATTENTION

Another paradigm, the *naturalistic visual scanning approach* attempts to track continuous attentional processing, with its fluctuating engagement, shifts, and re-engagements across a longer timescale (Eizenman *et al.*, 2003). Proponents of this approach tout the recording of eye movements as participants view pictures or text as being a more ecologically valid measure of attention than studies of response latencies, as in the dot-probe and Stroop tasks. Bower (1981) had hypothesized that studies of eye fixations might reveal that a negative or positive mood would direct a person's gaze toward mood-congruent information, and shifts in attention are known to precede and guide shifts in gaze location (Kowler *et al.*, 1995). The naturalistic visual scanning protocol presents participants with more than two complex visual stimuli that compete for their attention. The person has sufficient time (10.5 s) to scan and re-scan each of the images, and thus, eye movements provide a continuous indicator of attentional deployment. The duration of time a person fixates on each image and his or her ability to shift attention from image to image is assessed.

The frequency and duration of eye fixations on affective stimuli have been assessed in studies to ascertain whether depressed and depression vulnerable individuals show differences compared to healthy and nonvulnerable individuals. For example, Eizenman *et al.* (2003) found that clinically depressed individuals focused their attention on dysphoric themes for significantly longer than nondepressed controls, but did not vary in how long they focused on neutral, threatening, or social themes. The depressed group also exhibited difficulty with disengaging attention specifically from dysphoric stimuli as compared to nondepressed. Therefore, the fixation and inability to shift attention was specific to dysphoric content.

Several information processing tasks that incorporate, but less exclusively target, attentional processing have also been used to assess possible differences that distinguish depressed and depression vulnerable individuals from healthy nonvulnerable individuals. For example, Siegle *et al.* (2004) attempted to link behavioral, self-report, and physiological data (i.e., sustained pupil dilation via pupillometry, changes in blood flow captured by fMRI) during performance of emotional or nonemotional information processing tasks. Following the presentation of stimuli, sustained pupil dilation, an index of cognitive and emotional processing load is measured. Longer sustained dilation is thought to represent deeper processing, and greater spreading neural activation. Semantic (nonemotional) and emotional aspects of information are thought to be processed in parallel, and attentional resources can be differentially allocated to either aspect (Kitayama, 1990; Matthews & Harley, 1996). To assess emotional information processing, an *emotional valence identification task* (i.e., immediately responding to whether presented words are positive, negative, or neutral) has been used.

Studies that have tracked the pupil dilation of participants as they complete information processing tasks have provided behavioral RT and physiological data, which suggest altered processing in depressed and depression vulnerable individuals. Behaviorally, depressed individuals have shown slower RTs when naming the emotion of positive words (Siegle *et al.*, 2001; Siegle *et al.*, 2002a) which, given similar results from studies using other tasks, may reflect lesser attentional engagement with positive information. Also, depressed individuals have identified negatively valenced words significantly faster than positively valenced words, an effect that has not been observed in nondepressed individuals (Siegle *et al.*, 2001; Siegle *et al.*, 2002a). Comparing across tasks, depressed individuals have shown greater sustained pupil dilation when performing emotional rather than nonemotional information processing tasks (Siegle *et al.*, 2001). This tendency may be particularly marked when depressed individuals process negatively valenced or personally relevant information (Siegle *et al.*, 2003).

The sustained processing explanation of sustained pupil dilation was further corroborated by evidence that depressed individuals exhibited substantially longer amygdala activation (implicated in coding emotional features) than non-depressed individuals concurrent with emotional processing of negative words (Siegle *et al.*, 2004). Greater elaborative processing of negative information has also been associated with self-reported rumination (Siegle *et al.*, 2002b; Siegle *et al.*, 2003), which itself has been implicated as a vulnerability factor for depression (Just & Alloy, 1997; Nolen-Hoeksema *et al.*, 1993; Spasojevic & Alloy, 2001; see Chapter 10). Thus, it has been concluded that sustained dilation and processing of negative information may form essential building blocks of the rumination process (Siegle *et al.*, 2002b; Siegle *et al.*, 2003), which may extend and intensify periods of depressed mood.

Steidtmann *et al.* (2008) used pupillometry and a valence identification task to examine potential information processing differences in a vulnerability paradigm. Prior to a sad mood induction, formerly depressed individuals showed greater sustained pupil dilation to negative words than never depressed individuals. However, following the sad mood induction, formerly depressed individuals showed a decrease in sustained pupil dilation to negative words and overall reactivity. Similar to an interpretation by Ellenbogen *et al.* (2002), Steidtmann and colleagues concluded that a small amount of negative information could be especially salient to vulnerable individuals, but that large amounts could be overwhelming, leading to a cognitive blunting or diminished motivation.

THOUGHT SUPPRESSION

Information processing tasks have also been used to examine the potential relationship of thought suppression to vulnerability and worsening of depression. Thought suppression involves intentional efforts to stifle unwanted thoughts when they intrude into consciousness. Thought suppression can be effective under ordinary circumstances, but can also paradoxically increase the frequency of intrusive, unwanted thoughts when cognitive resources are overwhelmed. In this vein, Wegner (1994) articulated *ironic processes theory* as an explanation of thought suppression effects. According to Wegner, an effortful information processing system redirects attention toward mental content conducive to a desired state, while an automatic ironic processing component searches for content in conflict with achieving that state.

Several investigators have examined thought suppression as it relates to vulnerability to depression. Rude *et al.* (2002) and Wenzlaff and Bates (1998) examined thought suppression and cognitive load in the context of a scrambled sentences task (SST; Wenzlaff, 1993). In this task participants are presented with scrambled words that can be unscrambled in either a positive or negative way, and they must unscramble the words into a sentence as quickly as possible. Inasmuch as depression vulnerable individuals use effortful information processing capacity to redirect attention toward more desirable information, these authors hypothesized that occupying effortful processing capacity with an alternate cognitive load would incapacitate thought suppression, unmasking negative cognitive biases in depression vulnerable individuals. Thus, instituting cognitive load represents an alternative to mood priming, which theoretically *activates* "latent" negative schemas. Findings from these two studies support the hypothesis that a distracting cognitive load can usurp some of the attentional capacity that is required to suppress negative cognitions effectively. In addition, these findings supported the idea that individuals who habitually use thought suppression to cope paradoxically strengthen connections with the kind of negative cognitive content they seek to bar from their attention. A related study found that the tendency to unscramble words into negative sentences under cognitive load accounted for 14% of the variation in depressive symptoms 4–6 weeks later (Rude *et al.*, 2002). These studies suggest that under conditions of cognitive stress the emergence of negative biases indicates potential risk for depression.

SUMMARY OF ATTENTION AND RISK

It is likely that vulnerable populations are characterized by biases in some but not all components of attention. Whereas studies that have presented stimuli for shorter durations have generally failed to find biases differentiating depressed from nondepressed individuals (MacLeod *et al.*, 1986; Mathews *et al.*, 1996; Mogg *et al.*, 1993; Mogg *et al.*, 1995) or vulnerable from nonvulnerable populations (Bradley *et al.*, 1997), studies using longer stimulus presentations have fairly consistently found attentional biases in depressed and depression vulnerable individuals (Bradley *et al.*, 1997; Gotlib & Cane, 1987; Mogg *et al.*, 1995). Bradley *et al.* (1997) have suggested that biases in depression occur later in attentional processing, and perhaps in post-attentional elaborative processes.

Given attentional findings for individuals at risk for depression, similar biases may also occur in stable subthreshold dysphoria, or in formerly depressed individuals after being administered a sad mood prime or a cognitive load. Current evidence suggests that vulnerable individuals may not initially orient their attention preferentially to negative information, but that they engage their attention less with positive than negative information. When present in the environment, vulnerable individuals may even direct attention *away* from positive content. After engaging with negative information, vulnerable individuals may tend to maintain or fixate their attention for longer periods of time than nonvulnerable individuals. Further, vulnerable individuals may have difficulty disengaging from negative content, impairing their ability to shift attention to other potentially important information processing. When vulnerable individuals focus on emotional content, they appear to show less inhibition to negative information than positive information, allowing for proportionally greater processing of negative than positive content. When vulnerable individuals focus on nonemotional content in the midst of other emotional content, they may show greater interference of negative emotional content, requiring greater inhibitory processing capacity to quell the interference.

TREATMENT AND FUTURE DIRECTIONS

Our review of the information processing literature as defined by memory and attention offers little in the way of new treatment insights, but reinforces the underlying rationale for current treatment approaches for depression. As we noted at the outset of this chapter, memory and attention underlie the more "glamorous" constructs that are featured in cognitive models (e.g., schemas). Likewise, treatments that target the modification of constructs such as schemas must by necessity alter the information processing that is associated with schemas. Given that memory is organized around schematic constructs, how does a treatment like cognitive therapy alter memory? We suppose it is theoretically possible that therapy could modify memories, but we are unaware of any theory or research that would suggest this. Rather, treatments that alter schemas alter beliefs, and to the extent that beliefs are tied to depressotypic memories, such memories may become more difficult to access. To the extent that negative or sad memories reinforce depressive thinking and the onset of symptoms, diminished accessibility of these memories may aid in resolving acute episodes of depression but may also play a role in preventing, damping, or delaying future onsets or, when depression does occur, shorten its duration. Arguably the foremost reason to understand risk factors is so that future, or first, onsets can be prevented, or their impact diminished.

Like memory, attention modification may also reflect important treatment goals. In that maladaptive attentional processing likely occurs in later stages of attention, these processes are potentially malleable to more adaptive intentional processing. Empirical efforts to defuse negative attentional biases and diminish vulnerability to recurrent depression have shown promise. Mindfulness-based cognitive therapy (MBCT), a form of attentional control, has been shown to reduce significantly the risk of relapse among patients who have experienced three or more episodes of depression (Teasdale *et al.*, 1995). However, MBCT appears to be less effective with previously depressed individuals who have experienced fewer than three depressive episodes (Ma & Teasdale, 2004; Teasdale *et al.*, 2000), suggesting that the attentional contribution to depression vulnerability is dynamic. For individuals with a history of one or two depressive episodes, inducing benign modes of information processing or distraction may offer alternative ways to disengage attention from negative emotional content and reduce the intensity of negative moods, reducing vulnerability (Mathews & MacLeod, 2002; Singer & Dobson, 2007).

As we have noted, we are unaware of prospective studies of information processing as a risk factor, at least from the perspective of identifying an information processing constructs and then determining the relation to future onsets of depression, or perhaps to past depression. As noted, the lack of this research may be due to the fact that information processing biases cannot be easily identified outside of the active depressed state, or at least outside of laboratory-based stress simulations (e.g., mood inductions). This reality, however, does not preclude the study of information processing in the context of risk. Two recent studies by Segal and colleagues (Segal *et al.*, 1999; Segal *et al.*, 2006) illustrate these points. These studies examined depressed individuals who had been treated into a nondepressed state, following which a mood prime was used and the endorsement of dysfunctional attitudes assessed; the endorsement of these attitudes predicted depressive relapse over a year later.

These studies offer information that serves to validate important aspects of cognitive models, but also offer promise for helping to identify risk variables that might be targeted in prevention efforts. From a methodological standpoint, this line of research suggests a prototype of how studies of information processing variables as potential risk indicators could be conducted. That is, even if information processing constructs are state dependent, as appears to be the case with other constructs (e.g., dysfunctional attitudes), the Segal studies show how these constructs could be assessed in a true risk paradigm, rather than on relying on more indirect risk indicators (e.g., the assessment of memory or attentional variables in people known or suspected to be at risk). The methodologies are available and, to the extent that vulnerability researchers are willing to adopt them, much can be understood about the mechanisms underlying schemas and how these mechanisms function in the onset, course, treatment, and prevention of depression.

REFERENCES

Alloy, L. B., & Abramson, L. Y. (1999). The Temple–Wisconsin cognitive vulnerability to depression (CVD) project: Conceptual background, design, and methods. *Journal of Cognitive Psychotherapy: An International Quarterly*, *13*, 227–262.

Alloy, L. B., Abramson, L. Y., Murray, L. A., Whitehouse, W. G., & Hogan, M. E. (1997). Self-referent information processing in individuals at high and low cognitive risk for depression. *Cognition and Emotion*, *11*, 539–568.

Alloy, L. B., Abramson, L. Y., Hogan, M. E., Whitehouse, W. G., Rose, D. T., Robinson, M. S., Kim, R. S., & Lapkin, J. B. (2000). The Temple–Wisconsin cognitive vulnerability to depression project: Lifetime history of Axis I psychopathology in individuals at high and low cognitive risk for depression. *Journal of Abnormal Psychology*, *109*, 403–418.

Beck, A. T. (1967). *Depression: Causes and Treatment*. Philadelphia, PA: University of Philadelphia Press.

Beck, A. T. (1976). *Cognitive Therapy and the Emotional Disorders*. New York: International Universities Press.

Beck, A. T., Steer, R. A., & Garbin, M. G. (1988). Psychometric properties of the Beck Depression Inventory: Twenty-five years of evaluation. *Clinical Psychology Review*, *8*, 77–100.

Beech, A., Powell, T., McWilliam, J., & Claridge, G. (1989). Evidence of reduced "cognitive inhibition" in schizophrenia. *British Journal of Clinical Psychology*, *28*(Pt 2), 109–116.

Beevers, C. G., & Carver, C. S. (2003). Attentional bias and mood persistence as prospective predictors of dysphoria. *Cognitive Therapy and Research*, *27*(6), 619–637.

Bellew, M., & Hill, A. B. (1991). Schematic processing and the prediction of depression following childbirth. *Personality and Individual Differences*, *12*, 942–949.

Bower, G. H. (1981). Mood and memory. *American Psychologist*, *36*(2), 129–148.

Bradley, B. P., Mogg, K., Millar, N., & White, J. (1995). Selective processing of negative information: Effects of clinical anxiety, concurrent depression, and awareness. *Journal of Abnormal Psychology*, *104*(3), 532–536.

Bradley, B. P., Mogg, K., & Lee, S. C. (1997). Attentional biases for negative information in induced and naturally occurring dysphoria. *Behaviour Research and Therapy*, *35*, 911–927.

Bradley, B. P., Mogg, K., Falla, S. J., & Hamilton, L. R. (1998). Attentional bias for threatening facial expressions in anxiety: Manipulation of stimulus duration. *Cognition and Emotion*, *12*, 737–753.

Bradley, B. P., Mogg, K., & Millar, N. H. (2000). Covert and overt orienting of attention to emotional faces in anxiety. *Cognition and Emotion*, *14*(6), 789–808.

Brewin, C. R., Reynolds, M., & Tata, P. (1999). Autobiographical memory processes and the course of depression. *Journal of Abnormal Psychology*, *108*, 511–517.

Brittlebank, A. D., Scott, J., Williams, J. M. G., & Ferrier, I. N. (1993). Autobiographical memory in depression: State of trait marker? *British Journal of Psychiatry*, *162*, 118–121.

Dalgleish, T., Spinks, H., Yiend, J., & Kuyken, W. (2001). Autobiographical memory style in seasonal affective disorder and its relationship to future symptom remission. *Journal of Abnormal Psychology*, *110*, 335–340.

Denny, E. B., & Hunt, R. R. (1992). Affective valence and memory in depression: Dissociation of recall and fragment completion. *Journal of Abnormal Psychology*, *101*, 575–580.

Derry, P. A., & Kuiper, N. A. (1981). Schematic processing and self-reference in clinical depression. *Journal of Abnormal Psychology*, *96*, 34–40.

Eizenman, M., Yu, L. H., Grupp, L., Eizenman, E., Ellenbogen, M., Gemar, M. et al. (2003). A naturalistic visual scanning approach to assess selective attention in major depressive disorder. *Psychiatry Research*, *118*, 117–128.

Ellenbogen, M. A., Schwartzman, A. E., Stewart, J., & Walker, C. D. (2002). Stress and selective attention: the interplay of mood, cortisol levels, and emotional information processing. *Psychophysiology*, *39*(6), 723–732.

Gilboa, E., & Gotlib, I. H. (1997). Cognitive biases and affect persistence in previously dysphoric and never-dysphoric individuals. *Cognition and Emotion*, *11*, 517–538.

Gotlib, I. H., & Cane, D. B. (1987). Construct accessibility and clinical depression: A longitudinal investigation. *Journal of Abnormal Psychology*, *96*(3), 199–204.

Gotlib, I. H., & McCann, C. D. (1984). Construct accessibility and depression: An examination of cognitive and affective factors. *Journal of Personality and Social Psychology*, *47*(2), 427–439.

Gotlib, I. H., Krasnoperova, E., Yue, D. N., & Joormann, J. (2004). Attentional biases for negative interpersonal stimuli in clinical depression. *Journal of Abnormal Psychology*, *113*(1), 121–135.

Gotlib, I. H., Yue, D. N., & Joormann, J. (2005). Selective attention in dysphoric individuals: The role of affective interference and inhibition. *Cognitive Therapy and Research*, *29*, 417–432.

Hamilton, M. (1960). A rating scale for depression. *Journal of Neurology, Neurosurgery and Psychiatry*, *23*, 56–62.

Hedlund, S., & Rude, S. S. (1995). Evidence of latent depressive schemas in formerly depressed individuals. *Journal of Abnormal Psychology*, *104*(3), 517–525.

Houghton, G., & Tipper, S. P. (1994). A model of inhibitory mechanisms in selective attention. In D. Dagenbach & T. Carr (Eds.), *Inhibitory Mechanisms in Attention Memory and Language*. San Diego, CA: Academic Press.

Ingram, R. E. (1984). Toward an information-processing analysis of depression. *Cognitive Therapy and Research*, *8*(5), 443–478.

Ingram, R. E., & Ritter, J. (2000). Vulnerability to depression: Cognitive reactivity and parental bonding in high-risk individuals. *Journal of Abnormal Psychology, 109*(4), 588–596.

Ingram, R. E., Bernet, C. Z., & McLaughlin, S. C. (1994). Attentional allocation processes in individuals at risk for depression. *Cognitive Therapy and Research, 18*, 317–332.

Ingram, R. E., Fidaleo, R. A., Friedberg, R., Shenk, J. L., & Bernet, C. Z. (1995). Content and mode of information processing in Major Depressive Disorder. *Cognitive Therapy and Research, 19*(3), 281–293.

Ingram, R. E., Miranda, J., & Segal, Z. (1998). *Cognitive Vulnerability to Depression*. New York: Guilford Press.

Joormann, J. (2004). Attention bias in dysphoria: The role of inhibitory processes. *Cognition and Emotion, 18*(1), 125–147.

Joormann, J., Talbot, L., & Gotlib, I. H. (2007). Biased processing of emotional information in girls at risk for depression. *Journal of Abnormal Psychology, 116*(1), 135–143.

Just, N., & Alloy, L. B. (1997). The response styles theory of depression: Tests and an extension of the theory. *Journal of Abnormal Psychology, 106*(2), 221–229.

Karparova, S. P., Kersting, A., & Suslow, T. (2005). Disengagement of attention from facial emotion in unipolar depression. *Psychiatry and Clinical Neurosciences, 59*(6), 723–729.

Karparova, S. P., Kersting, A., & Suslow, T. (2007). Deployment of attention in clinical depression during symptom remission. *Scandinavian Journal of Psychology, 48*(1), 1–5.

Kessler, R. C. (2002). Epidemiology of depression. In I. Gotlib & C. Hammen (Eds.), *Handbook of Depression* (pp. 23–42). New York: Guilford Press.

Kitayama, S. (1990). Interaction between affect and cognition in word perception. *Journal of Personality and Social Psychology, 58*(2), 209–217.

Klieger, D. M., & Cordner, M. D. (1990). The Stroop task as a measure of construct accessibility in depression. *Personality and Individual Differences, 11*, 19–27.

Koster, E. H., De Raedt, R., Goeleven, E., Franck, E., & Crombez, G. (2005). Mood-congruent attentional bias in dysphoria: Maintained attention to and impaired disengagement from negative information. *Emotion, 5*(4), 446–455.

Kowler, E., Anderson, E., Dosher, B., & Blaser, E. (1995). The role of attention in the programming of saccades. *Vision Research, 35*(13), 1897–1916.

Kremers, I. P., Spinhoven, P., Van der Does, A. J. W. & Van Dyck, R. (2006). Autobiographical memory in depressed and nondepressed patients with borderline personality disorder after long-term psychotherapy. *Cognition and Emotion*, 20, 448–465.

Lachman, R., Lachman, J. L., & Butterfield, E. (1979). *Cognition: Human Information Processing*. Hillsdale, NJ: Lawrence Erlbaum Associates.

Ma, S. H., & Teasdale, J. D. (2004). Mindfulness-based cognitive therapy for depression: Replication and exploration of differential relapse prevention effects. *Journal of Consulting and Clinical Psychology, 72*(1), 31–40.

MacLeod, C. M., Mathews, A., & Tata, P. (1986). Attentional bias in emotional disorders. *Journal of Abnormal Psychology, 95*(1), 15–20.

Mackinger, H. F., Loschin, G. G., & Leibetseder, M. M. (2000a). Prediction of postnatal affective changes by autobiographical memories. *European Psychologist, 5*, 52–61.

Mackinger, H. F., Pachinger, M. M., Leibetseder, M. M., & Fartacek, R. R. (2000b). Autobiographical memories in women recovered from major depression. *Journal of Abnormal Psychology, 109*, 331–334.

Mackinger, H. F., Leibetseder, M. F., Kunz-Dorfer, A. A., Fartacek, R. R., Whitworth, A. B. & Feldinger, F. F. (2004). Autobiographical memory predicts the course of depression during detoxification therapy in alcohol dependent men. *Journal of Affective Disorders, 78*, 61–65.

Mathews, A., & MacLeod, C. (2002). Induced processing biases have causal effects on anxiety. *Cognition and Emotion, 16*(3), 331–354.

Mathews, A., Ridgeway, V., & Williamson, D. A. (1996). Evidence for attention to threatening stimuli in depression. *Behaviour Research and Therapy, 34*(9), 695–705.

Matthews, G., & Harley, T. A. (1996). Connectionist models of emotional distress and attentional bias. *Cognition and Emotion, 10*(6), 561–600.

McBride, C., & Cappaliez, P. (2004). Effects of manipulating valence and arousal components of mood on specificity of autobiographical memory. *Psychological Reports, 95*, 615–630.

McCabe, S. B., & Gotlib, I. H. (1993). Attentional processing in clinically depressed subjects: A longitudinal investigation. *Cognitive Therapy and Research, 17*(4), 359–377.

McCabe, S. B., Gotlib, I. H., & Martin, R. A. (2000). Cognitive vulnerability for depression: Deployment of attention as a function of history of depression and current mood state. *Cognitive Therapy and Research, 24*(4), 427–444.

Milliken, B., Tipper, S. P., & Weaver, B. (1994). Negative priming in a spatial localization task: Feature mismatching and distracter inhibition. *Journal of Experimental Psychology: Human Perception and Performance, 20*(3), 624–646.

Mogg, K., Bradley, B. P., Williams, R., & Mathews, A. (1993). Subliminal processing of emotional information in anxiety and depression. *Journal of Abnormal Psychology, 102*(2), 304–311.

Mogg, K., Bradley, B. P., & Williams, R. (1995). Attentional bias in anxiety and depression: The role of awareness. *British Journal of Clinical Psychology, 34*(Pt 1), 17–36.

Moilanen, D. L. (1993). Depressive information processing among nonclinic, nonreferred college students. *Journal of Counseling Psychology, 40*, 340–347.

Neill, W. T., Valdes, L. A., & Terry, K. M. (1995). Selective attention and the inhibitory control of cognition. In F. N. Dempster & C. J. Brainerd (Eds.), *Interference and Inhibition in Cognition* (pp. 207–261). New York: Academic Press.

Neumann, E., & DeSchepper, B. G. (1992). An inhibition-based fan effect: Evidence for an active suppression mechanism in selective attention. *Canadian Journal of Psychology, 46*, 1–40.

Nolen-Hoeksema, S., Morrow, J., & Fredrickson, B. L. (1993). Response styles and the duration of episodes of depressed mood. *Journal of Abnormal Psychology, 102*(1), 20–28.

Park, R. J., Goodyer, I. M. & Teasdale, J. D. (2002). Categoric overgeneral autobiographical memory in adolescents with major depressive disorder. *Psychological Medicine, 32*, 267–276.

Peterson, C., & Villanova, P. (1988). An expanded attributional style questionnaire. *Journal of Abnormal Psychology, 97*, 87–89.

Posner, M. I. (1980). Orienting of attention. *Quarterly Journal of Experimental Psychology, 32*(1), 3–25.

Posner, M. I., & Cohen, Y. (1984). Components of visual orienting. In H. Bouma & D. Bouwhuis (Eds.), *Attention and Performance* (Vol. X, pp. 531–556). Hove, England: Erlbaum.

Posner, M. I., Inhoff, A. W., Friedrich, F. J., & Cohen, A. (1987). Isolating attentional systems: A cognitive-anatomical analysis. *Psychobiology, 15*, 107–121.

Raes, F., Hermans, D., Williams, J. M. G., Demyttenaere, K., Sabbe, B., Pieters, G. & Eelen, P. (2005). Reduced specificity of autobiographical memory: A mediator between rumination and ineffective social problem-solving in major depression? *Journal of Affective Disorders, 87*, 331–335.

Raes, F., Hermans, D., Williams, J. M. G., Geypen, L. & Eelen, P. (2006). The effect of overgeneral autobiographical memory retrieval on rumination. *Psychological Belgica, 46*, 131–141.

Ramel, W., Goldin, P. R., Eyler, L. T., Brown, G. G., Gotlib, I. H., & McQuaid, J. R. (2007). Amygdale reactivity and mood congruent memory in individuals at risk for depressive relapse. *Biological Psychiatry, 61*, 231–239.

Rude, S. S., Wenzlaff, R. M., Gibbs, B., Vane, J., & Whitney, T. (2002). Negative processing biases predict subsequent depressive symptoms. *Cognition and Emotion, 16*(3), 423–440.

Segal, Z. V. (1988). Appraisal of the self-schema construct in cognitive models of depression. *Psychological Bulletin, 103*, 147–162.

Segal, Z. V., & Vella, D. D. (1990). Self-schema in major depression: Replication and extension of a priming methodology. *Cognitive Therapy and Research, 14*, 161–176.

Segal, Z. V., Gemar, M., & Williams, S. (1999). Differential cognitive response to a mood challenge following successful cognitive therapy or pharmacotherapy for unipolar depression. *Journal of Abnormal Psychology, 108*, 3–10.

Segal, Z. V., Kennedy, M. D., Gemar, M., Hood, K., Pedersen, R., & Buis, T. (2006). Cognitive reactivity to sad mood provocation and the prediction of depressive relapse. *Archives of General Psychiatry*, *63*, 749–755.

Siegle, G. J., Granholm, E., Ingram, R. E., & Matt, G. E. (2001). Pupillary and reaction time measures of sustained processing of negative information in depression. *Biological Psychiatry*, *49*(7), 624–636.

Siegle, G. J., Ingram, R. E., & Matt, G. E. (2002a). Affective interference: An explanation for negative attention biases in Dysphoria? *Cognitive Therapy and Research*, *26*(1), 73–87.

Siegle, G. J., Steinhauer, S. R., Thase, M. E., Stenger, V. A., & Carter, C. S. (2002b). Can't shake that feeling: Event-related fMRI assessment of sustained amygdala activity in response to emotional information in depressed individuals. *Biological Psychiatry*, *51*(9), 693–707.

Siegle, G. J., Steinhauer, S. R., Carter, C. S., Ramel, W., & Thase, M. E. (2003). Do the seconds turn into hours? Relationships between sustained pupil dilation in response to emotional information and self-reported rumination. *Cognitive Therapy and Research*, *27*(3), 365–382.

Siegle, G. J., Steinhauer, S. R., & Thase, M. E. (2004). Pupillary assessment and computational modeling of the Stroop task in depression. *International Journal of Psychophysiology*, *52*(1), 63–76.

Singer, A. R., & Dobson, K. S. (2007). An experimental investigation of the cognitive vulnerability to depression. *Behaviour Research and Therapy*, *45*(3), 563–575.

Spasojevic, J., & Alloy, L. B. (2001). Rumination as a common mechanism relating depressive risk factors to depression. *Emotion*, *1*(1), 25–37.

Spinhoven, P., Bockting, C. L. H., Schene, A. H., Koeter Maarten, W. J., Wekking, E. M. & Williams, J. M. G. (2006). Autobiographical memory in the euthymic phase of recurrent depression. *Journal of Abnormal Psychology*, *115*, 590–600.

Steidtmann, D., Ingram, R. E., & Siegle, G. (2008). Sustained pupil dilation in response to emotional information in depression susceptible individuals. Manuscript submitted for publication.

Steinberg, J. A., Gibb, B. E., Alloy, L. B., & Abramson, L. Y. (2003). Childhood emotional maltreatment, cognitive vulnerability to depression and self-referent information processing in adulthood: Reciprocal relations. *Journal of Cognitive Psychotherapy: An International Quarterly*, *17*, 347–358.

Stroop, J. R. (1935). Studies of interference in serial verbal reactions. *Journal of Experimental Psychology*, *18*, 643–662.

Taylor, J. L., & John, C. H. (2004). Attentional and memory bias in persecutory delusions and depression. *Psychopathology*, *37*, 233–241.

Taylor, L., & Ingram, R. E. (1999). Cognitive reactivity and depressotypic information processing in children of depressed mothers. *Journal of Abnormal Psychology*, *108*(2), 202–210.

Teasdale, J. D., Segal, Z., & Williams, J. M. (1995). How does cognitive therapy prevent depressive relapse and why should attentional control (mindfulness) training help? *Behaviour Research and Therapy*, *33*(1), 25–39.

Teasdale, J. D., Segal, Z. V., Williams, J. M., Ridgeway, V. A., Soulsby, J. M., & Lau, M. A. (2000). Prevention of relapse/recurrence in major depression by mindfulness-based cognitive therapy. *Journal of Consulting and Clinical Psychology*, *68*(4), 615–623.

Timbremont, B., & Braet, C. (2004). Cognitive vulnerability to depression in remitted depressed children and adolescents. *Behaviour Research and Therapy*, *42*, 423–437.

Weissman, A., & Beck, A. T. (1978). *Development and validation of the Dysfunctional Attitudes Scale: A preliminary investigation*. Paper presented at the meeting of the American Education Research Association, Toronto, Canada.

Wegner, D. M. (1994). Ironic processes of mental control. *Psychological Review*, *101*(1), 34–52.

Wenzlaff, R. M. (1993). The mental control of depression: Psychological obstacles to emotional well-being. In D. M. Wegner & J. W. Pennebaker (Eds.), *Handbook of Mental Control* (pp. 239–257). Englewood Cliffs, NJ: Prentice-Hall.

Wenzlaff, R. M., & Bates, D. E. (1998). Unmasking a cognitive vulnerability to depression: How lapses in mental control reveal depressive thinking. *Journal of Personality and Social Psychology*, *75*(6), 1559–1571.

Wessel, I., Meeren, M., Peeters, F., Arntz, A. & Merckelbach, H. (2001). Correlates of autobiographical memory specificity: The role of depression, anxiety, and childhood trauma. *Behaviour Research and Therapy*, *39*, 409–421.

Williams, J. M. G. & Broadbent, K. (1986). Autobiographical memory in attempted suicide patients. *Journal of Abnormal Psychology*, *95*, 144–149.

Williams, J. M. G., Matthews, A., & MacLeod, C. (1996). The emotional Stroop task and psychopathology. *Psychological Bulletin*, *120*, 3–24.

Williams, J. M. G., Barnhofer, T., Crane, C., Hermans, D., Raes, D., Watkins, E., & Dalgleish, T. (2007). Autobiographical memory specificity and emotional disorder. *Psychological Bulletin*, *133*, 122–148.

8

OPTIMISM AND PESSIMISM

STEPHEN M. SCHUELLER
AND MARTIN E.P. SELIGMAN

Positive Psychology Center, University of Pennsylvania, Philadelphia, PA, USA

INTRODUCTION

The beliefs we hold about the future have a powerful impact on how we approach the present. As we set goals, our beliefs in their attainability influences our actions to achieve them. Classifying individual differences in beliefs about the future and examining the consequences of these differences is an important research endeavor. Optimists – in common parlance – look on the bright side of life and retain hope in the face of significant challenges because they believe that things will turn out well. Optimists see a future of opportunities, whereas pessimists fear that current struggles will lead to additional failures. Optimistic individuals tend to be happier, more successful, and more resistant to a variety of mental disorders, including depression. Pessimists, on the other hand, worry about the future, doubt they will reach their goals, and expect the worst. Not surprisingly, pessimists are more likely to experience depression and the most pessimistic individuals experience the most severe episodes. Indeed, hopelessness, a closely related construct, is one of the best predictors of the worst outcome for depressed individuals, suicide.

Optimism is related to the onset of depression, the characteristics of depressive episodes, and the occurrence of subsequent episodes. The link between optimism and depression is best understood within the framework of cognitive theories of depression. Cognitive theories of depression posit that onset is caused by a maladaptive cognitive style (Abramson, Metalsky, & Alloy, 1989; Beck, 1967; see Chapter 6). Depressogenic cognitions are a risk factor for depression in just the same way that smoking is a risk factor for lung cancer. One such depressogenic cognition is pessimism. In this chapter, we will discuss the link between pessimism and optimism and the onset and recurrence of depression. We close by discussing different optimism interventions that have been successful in preventing depression.

Although optimism is commonly defined as expecting the best and looking to the positive side of life, in the research literature there are two dominant modes of measurement: dispositional optimism and attributional style. We will now turn to a discussion of each of these modes.

EXPECTING THE BEST: "DISPOSITIONAL OPTIMISM" MORE ACCURATELY CALLED "EXPECTATIONAL OPTIMISM"

One way to define optimists and pessimists is based on the expectations of these groups. Optimists expect the best and believe that in the future, their goals will be achieved. Pessimists, on the other hand, expect the worst; they believe that they will not reach their goals and that their hopes and dreams will not be realized. These expectations are pervasive and enduring patterns of thoughts, hence traits. This trait is called "dispositional optimism" and is assessed most frequently with the Life Orientation Test (LOT; Scheier & Carver, 1985). This label, however, is misleading. Other measures of optimism, such as attributional style are dispositions as well. The difference between the LOT and other measures of optimism is that it emphasizes expectations about the future. In order to better define what is unique about this measure of optimism we have used the term "expectational optimism" throughout this discussion and hope the future literature will conform to this nomenclature. The LOT is a brief self-report measure of expectational optimism that assesses the degree to which an individual believes that things will turn out well and projects the best outcomes for the future. Typical questions on the LOT are "In uncertain times, I usually expect the best" and "Overall, I expect more good things to happen to me than bad." The LOT is a reliable and valid measure of optimism. LOT scores are stable over time and across situations even during life catastrophes such as experiencing or caring for a person with a stroke (Scheier & Carver, 1985; Schulz *et al.*, 1988).

Scheier and Carver (2001) conceptualize optimism using an expectancy-value model. The first component of this model is how valuable the goal is based on its importance. Some goals are quite important, such as getting a promotion, finding the love of our life, or establishing a warm and caring family. Others are relatively minor like remembering to buy groceries for dinner or picking a movie to watch tonight. The more important the goal, and the greater the value we assign to it, the greater potential it has to motivate us. The second component of this model is expectancy – how much confidence we have in the attainability of the goal. Expectancies differentiate optimists from pessimists. Optimists are confident that their goals are attainable and will therefore work to obtain their goals; pessimists believe that their goals are unachievable and therefore do not work toward them or do so with less perseverance, creating a self-fulfilling prophecy of failure. Viewing optimism and pessimism in this way provides an initial explanation for how pessimistic thinking might be related to depression.

Psychological distress (and elation) stems from goal pursuit. We strive to achieve things we desire (a goal) or to avoid things that are undesirable (an anti-goal). Working toward our goals and thinking we are doing well will lead to elation and joy whereas failing to progress toward our goals will lead to depression. Furthermore, avoiding our anti-goals and preventing what we fear will lead to relief whereas believing we are approaching these undesired events causes anxiety.

EXPLAINING EVENTS: EXPLANATORY STYLE

The other way to conceptualize optimism and pessimism concerns our explanations for past or current events, rather than our expectations for the future. Explanatory style measures three distinct dimensions of causal inferences for past, current, or hypothetical events: internal vs. external, stable vs. unstable, and global vs. specific. Consider the explanations one might generate when encountering a negative event (i.e., failure to get accepted into college). A stable attribution is an explanation that does not change over time, such as being stupid, vs. an unstable attribution that is changeable, such as exhaustion at the time of writing the application. A specific attribution applies in limited circumstances, such as explaining one's failure to get accepted based on that particular colleges' quota for applicants vs. a global explanation that applies to college in general, such as not having a good enough high school record. Lastly, an internal attribution blames the self; whereas an external attribution puts the blame on other circumstances, such as the school. Individuals with a pessimistic explanatory style use a pattern of stable, global, and internal explanations for setbacks whereas those with optimistic explanatory styles use unstable, specific, and external attributions.

What are the consequences – theoretically – of an optimistic vs. a pessimistic explanatory style? The optimist, believing the cause is temporary and local, will be less debilitated over time and across situations than the pessimist who will be passive, experience cognitive deficits, emotional disturbance, and (if he or she internalizes the failure) reduced self-esteem. Since this debilitation corresponds to many of the symptoms of depression, the pessimist will experience depression more often than the optimist (Seligman, 1975).

The debilitating explanatory style for positive events is the opposite of that for negative events. When faced with a positive situation, the optimist will explain his or her success with internal, stable, and global causes whereas the pessimist will explain it with external, unstable, and specific causes. Optimists will, in theory, get on a roll after a victory, whereas pessimists will remain passive even when success occurs and fail to use victories to boost self-esteem. For pessimists, positive events are not expected to reduce depressive symptoms; therefore emotional reactions to negative events will endure despite future victories.

There are two ways to measure explanatory style. The most widely used is the Attributional Style Questionnaire (ASQ; Peterson *et al.*, 1982; Peterson, Bettes, & Seligman, 1985; Seligman *et al.*, 1979) that poses 12 hypothetical events (half good and half bad) to individuals and asks them to provide the major causes of each event if it happened to them. Validity studies of the ASQ show that explanatory style for negative events has better predictive validity than explanatory style for positive events (Metalsky *et al.*, 1987; Peterson & Villanova, 1988). Other self-report measures combine other maladaptive cognitive styles with explanatory style. The Cognitive Style Questionnaire (CSQ), for example, measures the tendency to infer stable and global causes, negative consequences, and negative characteristics about the self (Alloy *et al.*, 2000).

A second method of assessment analyzes verbatim spoken and written material for causal language. The Content Analysis of Verbatim Explanations (CAVE) codes written and spoken materials such as campaign speeches, diary entries, and biographies (Peterson *et al.*, 1982; Peterson, Bettes, & Seligman, 1985). From these written materials, causal explanations for both positive and negative events are extracted and scored on a 1–7 scale for internality, stability, and globality. The observed correlations between assessing explanatory style using these two methods are often significant, but modest (Peterson, Bettes, & Seligman, 1985 found correlations of $r = 0.41$ for internality, 0.19 for stability, 0.23 for globality, and 0.30 for the composite; see Peterson, 1991; Peterson & Seligman, 1984).

Most studies examine explanatory style for negative events more closely than the style for positive events. The styles for positive and negative events do not correlate strongly and a pessimistic explanatory style for negative events is a stronger predictor of important outcomes than style for positive events (Peterson, 1991). Explanatory style also does not show a consistent relationship with expectational optimism. Scheier and Carver (1992) reported that correlations between explanatory style and expectational optimism range from the high teens to low twenties. Other studies have found much larger correlations ranging from 0.41 (Hjelle *et al.*, 1996) to as high as 0.77 when corrected for attenuation (Gillham *et al.*, 1998). Explanatory style and expectational optimism are not necessarily the same underlying construct and need not be strongly correlated. Inferred consequences need not be isomorphically related to the inferred causes of the events (Brickman *et al.*, 1975). So if one is disfigured facially in an auto accident, the cause of which is a drunken stranger (unstable and specific), the consequences – being looked on with horror by all future acquaintances – are stable and global. Even though these constructs do not demonstrate perfect correspondence both are measures of different aspects of optimism. Attributional measures focus on how our interpretations of past events shape our inferences for the future. Therefore both constructs include predictions for future events with pessimists tending to believe bad things will come and their troubles will persist (stable and global causes in attributional terms). Given that these terms have conceptual overlap, researchers use the terms pessimist and optimist to refer to individuals who score in the extremes on both measures.

RELATED CONSTRUCTS: SELF-EFFICACY AND HOPE

Optimism used colloquially means the belief that good things will happen and is often used interchangeably with 'positive thinking" or being hopeful. It is important to point out the theoretical distinctions between optimism and two other closely related constructs: self-efficacy and hope

Bandura's theory of self-efficacy makes an important distinction between expectations of personal agency or control (efficacy expectations) and the expectation that things will turn out well (outcome expectations) (Bandura, 1977). Self-efficacy refers to a sense that one has the competencies required to achieve one's goals. Therefore, whether or not one takes the actions necessary to reach a goal will depend on the evaluation of one's own ability to produce change. Outcome expectancies, on the other hand, refer to the belief that a particular action will lead to a particular consequence and can include forces outside the individual (e.g., circumstances, other people, and religious faith). Therefore, an individual could have high self-efficacy and believe very strongly in his or her own abilities, but fail to pursue goals because he or she believes the environment will be unresponsive. Expectational optimism does not distinguish between expectations based on oneself or the environment. Furthermore, Bandura's conception of self-efficacy focuses on domain-specific competencies; one can develop self-efficacy with regards to schoolwork yet still lack a feeling of self-efficacy when it comes to performance on the softball team. Expectational optimism, on the other hand, refers to a generalized sense that things will turn out well and is more general and pervasive than domain or action specific self-efficacy beliefs. An individual with high self-efficacy tends to make internal attributions for positive events. Self-efficacy, however, is more strongly related to perceived control beliefs which overlap with explanatory style, but refer more to beliefs about the future (i.e., my actions will be efficacious) than inferences about the past (e.g., I was responsible for that event).

A final concept that is closely related to the construct of optimism is hope. Hope, like optimism, connotes a view that the future is promising. In explanatory style theory, hope refers to the stable and global components of attributions: the belief that bad events are caused by temporary and local causes, means that the bad events will not persist into the future and across situations. The belief that good events are stable and global means that good events will recur in the future and in new situations.

In hope theory, hope is a motivating factor that links us to our goals through two components: agency and pathways (Snyder, 1994). Agency is similar to Bandura's concept of self-efficacy and refers to the belief that one can make progress toward one's goals. The pathway component includes the ability to generate strategies and move toward that goal. Although this model incorporates general expectations about the future, it also contains elements that are not included in the definition of optimism. The expectancy portion of hope theory puts an emphasis on efficacy beliefs, which is absent in explanatory and expectational definitions of optimism. Hope theory also states explicitly that the ability to generate pathways to achieve one's goals is an important aspect of being hopeful. Although optimists engage in more planning, this component is left out of definitions of optimism. The pathways component, however, incorporates learning about causality, which is strongly related to forming causal inferences, a key aspect of explanatory style. Furthermore, agentic thinking is closely related to the internal dimension of explanatory style. Therefore, although hope overlaps with the construct of optimism it includes other aspects that are left out of optimism. The remainder of the chapter will focus on optimism as measured by expectational optimism and explanatory style.

COGNITIVE MODELS OF DEPRESSION

To understand the role of pessimism as a risk factor for depression, an overview of cognitive theories of depression is important. Evidence linking pessimism to depression supports the hypothesis that the causes we infer for events and the way we think about the future can either predispose or prevent depression. In Beck's (1967) cognitive formulation, depression develops due to negative views of the self, world, and future. Reformulated helplessness and hopelessness theories are specific versions of Beck's theory and implicate pessimistic explanatory style as a risk factor for depression; we now examine them in more detail.

FROM HELPLESSNESS TO HOPELESSNESS: THE ROLE OF EXPLANATORY STYLE IN DEPRESSION

Learned helplessness was originally observed in dogs subjected to inescapable shock. Over repeated exposure, they became passive and would no longer attempt to escape even when escape was possible (Overmier & Seligman, 1967; Seligman & Maier, 1967). Helplessness in these animals was marked by cognitive, emotional, and motivational deficits. These deficits are similar to the symptoms of a diagnosis of clinical depression in humans. Both naturally occurring depression and laboratory induced helplessness reduce initiation of voluntary responses, promote a negative cognitive set, create loss of appetite, and induce physiological differences in neurotransmitters (Seligman, 1975). This substantial overlap in symptoms between the helpless reactions of both humans and animals in well-controlled experiments and depressed humans in their natural settings supports the notion that helplessness models clinical depression. In fact, of the nine symptoms of major depressive disorder listed in the fourth edition of the *Diagnostic and Statistical Manual* (DSM-IV-TR; American Psychiatric Association, 2000), eight are induced by learned helplessness in the laboratory, with only thoughts of death and suicide not induced (Seligman, 1975).

One appeal of a laboratory model of a disorder is it can shed light on the etiology, prevention, and treatment of naturally occurring depression. This model had an important caveat. An uncontrollable event did not always cause helplessness. In most studies, a sizeable minority of participants did not develop helplessness. In order to address individual differences, the theory was reformulated to include a cognitive component. Specifically, a person's explanations of the event were incorporated as a critical determinant of the development of helplessness and depression, rather than simply the objective uncontrollable nature of the event (Abramson *et al.*, 1978). Individual differences in explanatory style emerged as an important risk factor that predisposes an individual to become depressed.

The Hopelessness theory of depression is a variant on the Reformulated Helplessness theory of depression (Abramson *et al.*, 1978; Chapter 11). Hopelessness theory is a specific diathesis–stress model of depression that links a pessimistic or depressogenic explanatory style to the development of a specific form of depression dubbed "hopelessness depression." Although, there are differences between these two models, an examination of these differences is beyond the scope of this chapter. Most important for a discussion of optimism and pessimism is that both theories make the same prediction: that a pessimistic explanatory style will lead to depression.

EVIDENCE FOR PESSIMISM AS A RISK FACTOR FOR DEPRESSION

Both the Reformulated Helplessness theory and Hopelessness theory claim that a pessimistic explanatory style should be correlated with depressive symptoms at a given time point, should be predictive of depressive symptoms over time, and should mediate the relationship between negative events and depressive symptoms. We will first review cross-sectional studies that support the relationship between pessimism and depression and then discuss the longitudinal research suggesting that pessimism predicts depression. Lastly, we review the diathesis–stress hypothesis, examining the evidence that pessimism is causally related to the occurrence of depression.

Research indicates that both expectational optimism and explanatory style are related to depressive symptoms. As previously discussed, these two ways of operationalizing optimism have different foci, the former on expectations for the future and the latter on inferred causes for the past. Most of the research conducted has tested the predictions of Helplessness and Hopelessness theories and investigated explanatory style. One implication of these theories is that pessimism should be related to depressive symptoms and that individuals with depression should make global and stable causal inferences. Indeed, this relationship is robust and consistent. A meta-analysis of 104 studies found that the average effect sizes between pessimistic attributions for negative outcomes and depression were small to moderate (Sweeney *et al.*, 1986). There were smaller, but still significant, relationships between pessimistic attributions for positive events and depressive symptoms. A smaller relationship is not surprising given that both theories predict that pessimism mediates the relationship between negative events and depression. In the absence of negative events, there is no stressor to allow the cognitive diathesis to lead to depressive symptoms. A more recent meta-analysis of 28 published studies in children found similar results with effect sizes for the relationship between explanatory style and depression approximately the same as those found in adults (Gladstone & Kaslow, 1995).

Individuals with depression are more likely to attribute negative events to global, stable, and internal causes than individuals with other clinical diagnoses. For example, male patients with depression are more likely to have a pessimistic explanatory style than are non-depressed individuals with schizophrenia and non-depressed medical patients (Raps *et al.*, 1982). A further study replicated these findings. Individuals with unipolar depression showed a significantly more pessimistic explanatory style than individuals with schizophrenia who did not differ in their attributions from a non-psychiatric comparison group (Silverman & Peterson, 1993). This finding supports the idea that explanatory style is not related to depressive symptoms alone, but marks clinical levels of depression as well. Additionally, these measures have specificity to depression; a pessimistic explanatory style is not characteristic of all psychopathology.

Expectational optimism is also associated with depressive symptoms. This relationship is likely explained by the overlap between expectational optimism and negative explanatory style: When controlling for one, the other makes no further contribution to the prediction of depressive symptoms (Morris, 2007). These findings suggest that expectational optimism and negative explanatory style do not represent unique pathways to depression. One study assessed expectational optimism by having participants predict the likelihood of events and compared this prediction to their actual occurrence. An individual was considered pessimistic if he or she overestimated the likelihood of negative events and underestimated the likelihood of positive events. Those who scored high on pessimism reported higher levels of depressive symptoms, with the most depressed individuals showing the greatest pessimistic bias (Strunk *et al.*, 2006). In studies that assess expectational optimism through the use of the LOT, strong relationships are reported between pessimism, levels of depressive symptoms, and hopelessness. Expectational optimism is negatively correlated with depressive symptoms as measured by the Beck Depression Inventory (BDI) whereas correlations between LOT and the Beck Hopelessness Scale are moderate. One study also found that expectational optimism, as assessed by both the LOT-R and actual predictions of the occurrence of both good and bad events, mediated the relationship between depressive symptoms and explanatory style in college students (Peterson & Vaidya, 2001).

The fact that pessimism correlates reliably with depression does not demonstrate that pessimism is a risk factor for depression. Depression could cause pessimistic attributions or a third variable could account for both. Longitudinal research designs provide evidence for pessimism as a risk factor for depression by demonstrating that pessimism predicts subsequent depressive symptoms. An early study of college students found that global and stable causal inferences for negative events were predictive of depressive symptoms 1 month later even after controlling for initial scores on the BDI (Golin *et al.*, 1981). Isaacowitz and Seligman (2001) recruited community-dwelling adults over age 65 to investigate whether pessimism continues to be a risk factor later in life. Consistent with other findings, pessimistic expectations predicted depressive symptoms 1 year later.

In addition to preceding depressive symptoms, a pessimistic explanatory style predicts severity, number of episodes, recurrence, and recovery from depressive disorders (Alloy *et al.*, 1992; Alloy *et al.*, 2006; Iacoviello *et al.*, 2006; Seligman *et al.*, 1988). Changing individuals' pessimistic attributions may also be an important mechanism of change in cognitive therapy for depression. To test this hypothesis, 39 individuals diagnosed with unipolar depression were given the ASQ and BDI at the beginning and end of therapy and 1 year following termination (Seligman *et al.*, 1988). Explanatory style changes from intake to termination marginally predicted depressive symptoms at follow-up with a more optimistic explanatory style at termination related to lower depressive symptoms at 1-year follow-up. Explanatory style and depressive symptoms change together and changing an individual's thinking to be more optimistic may be an important causal mechanism of cognitive therapy. The design of this study, however, did not rule out the possibility that changes in explanatory style were a result of improvements in depression or that a third variable accounted for both symptom relief and the more optimistic explanatory style.

We will now review studies that go beyond correlation and prediction and test the strongest implication of helplessness and hopelessness theories: that pessimism is a cognitive diathesis of depression – both for depressive symptoms and depressive disorder.

The proposed link between pessimism and depression is a diathesis–stress model of depression. When faced with a negative event, individuals with a pessimistic explanatory style make attributions that lead them to see the future as hopeless and make it likely they will develop depressive symptoms. Research designs, therefore, need to use a method that examines the interaction of pessimistic explanatory style with life stressors. In the first study to use such a methodology, participants were recruited from an undergraduate psychology course to examine reactions to poor exam performance (Metalsky *et al.*, 1982). At the beginning of the term, participants took the ASQ and stated their desired grades for the midterm. Researchers also measured depressive symptoms 5 days prior to the midterm and immediately after students received their grades. A pessimistic explanatory style for negative events predicted increases in depressive symptoms but only for students who received a lower grade than they expected (see Peterson & Seligman, 1984, for a review of related studies).

A similar study found that students' scores on an exam predicted initial depressive reactions; however, a combination of pessimistic explanatory style and low self-esteem with low exam performance predicted depressive symptoms over the next 5 days (Metalsky *et al.*, 1993). Whereas initial reactions to failure may be related to the negative event itself, the enduring psychological effects may be more strongly associated with specific personality characteristics of the individual (e.g., pessimism). These enduring emotional consequences of poor performance may also be due to divergent coping strategies used by optimists and pessimists. Pessimists tend to use poor coping strategies following failure, such as ruminating on negative emotions (Scheier *et al.*, 1989). Continuing to ruminate on the negative emotions and the consequences of receiving a disappointing grade, as opposed to engaging in more problem-focused coping strategies, such as going to the professor to discuss the midterm or studying harder for the next exam, may exacerbate the normal emotional reaction to poor exam performance. This is consistent with the helplessness view, which implicates lack of response as an important precursor to depression and with Hankin and Abramson's (2001) cognitive vulnerability-transactional stress model that posits that increases in depression lead to more negative events which in turn lead to more negative affect. Pessimistic thinking, therefore, sets off a cycle of increasing levels of depression and increasing occurrence of negative events.

Further evidence of pessimism as a risk factor of depression comes from studies of the benefits of expectational optimism in the face of health-related stressors. This literature typically focuses on well-being, quality of life, and post-event adjustment as measures of outcome (see Scheier & Carver, 1992, for a review of the effects of optimism on psychological well-being). In one study, participants were recruited from a childbirth education class and later assessed between 21 and 30 days postpartum (Carver & Gaines, 1987). Controlling for initial levels of depression, pessimistic individuals were more likely to report depressive symptoms postpartum. There was a stronger benefit of optimism in those individuals with initial BDI scores 5 or below, suggesting that optimism acts as a protective factor by preventing against new depressive symptoms.

In several other studies, pessimistic attributions for negative events predicted higher levels of depressive symptoms. Gibb *et al.* (2006), for example, asked college undergraduates about the occurrence of negative life events and their depressive symptoms every other week for a 6-week period. These researchers used Hierarchical Linear Modeling to model the relationship between negative life events and depressive symptoms on one level and the moderating effect of explanatory style on another. For pessimistic individuals, experiencing negative events led to increases in depressive symptoms. Even among these individuals, however, no changes were obtained in depressive symptoms in the absence of significant stressors.

Pessimism may also represent a significant causal risk factor for depressive symptoms in adolescents. Researchers recruited 270 high school students to complete measures of explanatory style, negative life events, and depressive symptoms and re-assessed students 5 weeks later to examine occurrence of negative events as well as changes in depressive symptoms (Hankin *et al.*, 2001). Students who had a depressogenic explanatory style (global and stable responses to negative hypothetical events) in the presence of negative events showed an increase in depressive symptoms. This was not the case for pessimistic students who did not experience negative events. For those individuals without the pessimistic style, there was no relationship between changes in depressive symptoms and the occurrence of negative events. Thus, studies with both adults and adolescents suggest that negative events and negative attributions interact to influence emotional reactions.

Furthermore, in the presence of positive events, an optimistic explanatory style appears to improve depressive symptoms. In one study, 58 students with BDI scores greater than 16 were followed for 6 weeks and assessed for occurrence of positive and negative events, explanatory style, and depressive symptoms (Needles & Abramson, 1990). Individuals with an optimistic explanatory style who experienced positive events had a reduction in depressive symptoms over the 6 weeks. Therefore, an element of recovery from depression is not only having positive experiences but also making optimistic attributions and gaining hope from those events. Optimism seems to prevent and alleviate depression and may be a useful target for preventative interventions.

This diathesis–stress model holds not only for the development of depressive symptoms but for depressive disorder as well. A series of studies have assessed the effects of having a negative cognitive style on depressive episodes. A negative cognitive style refers to a pessimistic explanatory style for negative events as well as negative self-schemas, which include being overly concerned with others' approval and being perfectionistic (Alloy *et al.*, 2006). One study found that those with negative cognitive styles were 3.5 times more likely to develop a minor depressive episode (BDI $\geq$ 10 as well as relevant DSM criteria) and 6.7 times more likely to develop a major depressive episode (BDI $\geq$ 16 as well as relevant DSM criteria) than individuals who had a more optimistic cognitive style (Alloy *et al.*, 2006). Even after individuals develop clinical depression, negative cognitive style predicts the characteristics of the episode. One study identified individuals who were non-depressed, but later experienced a clinical depressive episode

(Iacoviello *et al.*, 2006). Individuals with a negative cognitive style experienced more depressive episodes with increased severity and longer duration than those without this cognitive style. Pessimism may, therefore, predispose individuals to develop depression and also impact its severity.

INTERVENTIONS THAT INCREASE OPTIMISM AND LOWER DEPRESSION

The evidence presented in this chapter supports the notion that a pessimistic style puts a person at risk for depression. But can an optimistic outlook prevent depression? We have developed and tested two separate prevention programs for different age groups. Both are aimed at increasing optimism by using cognitive behavior therapy (CBT)-style exercises delivered in a group format. The Penn Resilience Program (PRP) is a 12-session school-based workshop program that is based on the exercises from Learned Optimism (Seligman, 1991) which are similar to CBT programs used in adults. CBT techniques, such as cognitive restructuring and disputing, along with social skills training are applied to middle school students (ages 10–14 years) in accessible and engaging ways. Students are presented with age appropriate examples and worksheets that mirror the style of schoolwork. For example, common cognitive errors are presented as thinking traps and framed in terms for adolescents. Mind reading is compared to a psychic fortune-teller and overgeneralizations are referred to as character assassination. Disputing is taught with an example of two fictional detectives, one, who is a bad detective because he comes up with only one suspect and overlooks the evidence (similar to accepting an automatic thought and failing to evaluate it). The other, Sherlock Holmes, generates a list of suspects and carefully collects evidence to support his case (generating alternatives and collecting evidence). The APEX program, also a Learned Optimism workshop is designed for college undergraduates who are deemed at risk for depression due to mild-to-moderate levels of depressive symptoms as measured by the BDI, also uses CBT techniques (Seligman *et al.*, 1999; Seligman *et al.*, 2007).

Research on PRP has demonstrated its effectiveness at preventing depressive symptoms in students during this particularly difficult time of transition. There are 14 replications of the PRP in diverse samples (incarcerated adolescents, Australian adolescents, inner city students, Chinese students, and primary care) and different modifications (all girls vs. co-ed groups, an additional parent component, and randomizing based on schools) to test the intervention and a variety of moderators (see Gillham Brunwasser & Freres, 2007, for a review). These studies have mixed findings: seven studies report overall reductions in depressive symptoms, three studies had mixed results (reductions in subgroups but not overall), and four studies found no effects on depression. In the first test of PRP, 69 children at risk for depression were compared to a matched no-treatment control group. Workshop participants developed a more optimistic explanatory style and reported fewer depressive symptoms (Jaycox *et al.*, 1994). These effects remained when assessing participants 2 years after the end of the intervention (Gillham *et al.*, 1995). Participants receiving the PRP intervention were half as likely as the control group to report moderate-to-severe depressive symptoms. Furthermore, changes in explanatory style partially mediated the improvement in depressive symptoms. Additional studies have looked at modifications of the initial program in attempts to increase its efficacy and discover its limitations.

A complete review of the replications of PRP is beyond the scope of this chapter. Overall, however, there is more support for the effectiveness of PRP than studies finding null or mixed results. A recent meta-analysis of the effectiveness of PRP found the average effect sizes of these studies were small yet significant (Brunwasser, 2007). PRP is more effective when delivered in a manualized format either from the primary research team or from individuals highly trained by the primary research team. Additional studies should address aspects of adherence that are most important to the effectiveness of the intervention and how to improve the results of attempts to disseminate the program.

The APEX program is an 8-week group targeted prevention workshop aimed to promote optimistic explanatory styles in undergraduates at risk for depression. The workshop contains lessons on the following topics: (1) the cognitive theory of change (the relationship between thoughts, feelings, and behaviors); (2) Identifying automatic negative thoughts and underlying beliefs; (3) marshaling evidence to question and dispute automatic negative thoughts and irrational beliefs (empirical hypothesis testing); (4) replacing automatic negative thoughts with more constructive interpretations, beliefs, and behaviors (generating alternatives, distraction techniques); (5) behavioral activation strategies (graded task breakdown, time management, anti-procrastination techniques, creative problem solving, assertiveness training); (6) interpersonal skills (active listening, taking each other's perspectives, controlling emotions, passive vs. assertive vs. aggressive behaviors); (7) stress management (relaxation training); and (8) generalizing these coping skills to new and relevant situations.

The APEX program was first tested by recruiting University of Pennsylvania undergraduates deemed at risk for depression because they scored in the lowest quartile on the ASQ (Seligman *et al.*, 1999). Researchers mailed all incoming undergraduates ASQs in May preceding their freshman year. Participants who were signed up to participate were randomly assigned to the workshop or an assessment-only control. Participants in the control group were 1.4 times more likely to have a depressive episode and 1.6 times more likely to have an anxiety episode than those participants who received the APEX workshop. Furthermore, the workshop group had significant lower levels of symptoms of both depression and anxiety. Explanatory style, hopelessness, and dysfunctional attitudes were all significant mediators of depressive symptoms, post-intervention and at follow-up, but only dysfunctional attitudes mediated anxiety symptoms.

A further study bolstered the initial APEX program by adding web-based material and e-mail coaching to boost long-term effects of the program. This study found a significant change in depression and anxiety symptoms 6 months post-intervention but no significant differences in the number of episodes of depression and anxiety were obtained (Seligman *et al.*, 2007). Furthermore, APEX led to significant changes in explanatory style with participants having a more optimistic explanatory style following the workshop. This improvement in optimism was a partial mediator of the reduction in depressive symptoms.

Both the PRP and APEX results support that targeted prevention measures aimed at increasing optimism significantly reduce depressive symptoms. The random assignment intervention design unravels causality, as well as suggesting therapeutics. The intervention does not just correlate with improvement it causes improvement. So we can safely infer that teaching optimism reduces depression. But why exactly are optimistic people less likely to become depressed than pessimists?

BENEFITS OF OPTIMISM

There are several reasons why optimism leads to well-being (see Peterson, 2000; Scheier *et al.*, 2001, for a review). First, optimism is related to positive goal pursuit. Second, optimists' coping strategies are more adaptive than those of pessimists. Third, the positive expectations of optimism can motivate action and prevent catastrophic thinking. Fourth, optimism is related to increased control beliefs such as self-esteem and self-mastery.

Optimists are more likely to pursue and therefore achieve their goals (Segerstrom, 2001; Snyder *et al.*, 1991). Goal pursuit is an important predictor of happiness and achieving one's goals gives a sense of accomplishment (Lyubomirsky *et al.*, 2005; Sheldon & Elliot, 1999).

Optimists also appear to use better problem-focused coping strategies, than pessimists, such as acceptance and resignation, positive reinterpretation, seeking social support and suppressing activities (Aspinwall & Taylor, 1992; Scheier & Carver, 1992; Scheier *et al.*, 1986). Problem-focused coping refers to tackling a problem directly by making a plan to deal with the situation and acting before things get out of control. Acceptance and resignation refers to accepting the situation for what it is and resigning to the fact that some events are out of our control, which is an adaptive coping strategy in uncontrollable situations where nothing can be done. Positive reinterpretation of the negative event refers to focusing on what the meaning of the event is – what can be learned and gained.

A third way optimism may act to fight depression is through positive expectations that motivate individuals and prevent catastrophic thinking. Optimists may try harder because they expect that they will be successful. Pessimists avoid and ignore their problems, believe their actions will be ineffective, and are unlikely to reach resolution. Consistent with this, optimists do not disengage and focus on emotions as much as pessimists (Scheier *et al.*, 1986).

Consistent with the findings linking optimism to more adaptive coping strategies, several studies demonstrated that optimism is related to better emotional adjustment and less distress after childbirth (Carver & Gaines, 1987), coronary artery bypass graft surgery (Scheier *et al.*, 1989), and being diagnosed and treated for cancer (Carver *et al.*, 1993). Attacking the problem head on and engaging in proactive coping strategies help an optimistic outlook become a self-fulfilling prophecy, with optimistic predictions reinforced by positive outcomes. Furthermore, positive expectations reduce catastrophic thinking and allow individuals to focus on the present.

Fourth, optimism is also strongly related to two constructs that are associated with better psychological adjustment, functioning, and other measures of success-self-mastery and self-esteem. Although optimism overlaps with self-mastery and self-esteem, there are distinctions among these different concepts. Self-mastery refers to the belief that one has control over the events in one's life (Pearlin & Schooler, 1978). Optimism does not necessarily indicate a belief of control or mastery over situations, rather optimism only implies that we expect positive outcomes or that we attribute bad outcomes to unstable and specific causes (and good outcomes to stable and global causes), whether or not they are controllable. Optimism is distinguishable from self-esteem because self-esteem refers to our own evaluation of worth. In terms of explanatory style, self-esteem is closely related to the internal dimension, which is one of the weakest predictors of other outcomes. Therefore, optimistic individuals do not necessarily make external attributions for failure or internal attributions for success.

Although related, these constructs are both theoretically and empirically distinct. A study attempting to distinguish optimism from mastery, self-esteem, anxiety, and neuroticism found that these constructs have high zero-order correlations (the correlations between optimism and these measures ranged from $r = 0.50$ to 0.59). These constructs, however, were all unique predictors of other outcomes of interest. Most importantly, optimism continues to predict depressive symptoms controlling for mastery, self-esteem, anxiety, and neuroticism (Scheier *et al.*, 1994). Optimism, therefore, is connected to a host of benefits, each of which may have some role in helping to prevent depressive symptoms.

BUILDING THE POSITIVE: POSITIVE PSYCHOLOGY AND OPTIMISM

Increasing a person's level of optimism may protect him or her from future depressive episodes. Optimism is only one of a class of variables, which does not entail the relief of a negative state, but the building of a positive state (see Seligman, 2002, for a discussion of this distinction). These variables constitute the raw material of the field of positive psychology. In the remainder of this chapter, we discuss the field of positive psychology and its explicit focus on building positive emotion, engagement, strengths, and meaning in order to promote well-being and prevent mental disorders.

One of the major goals of positive psychology is the promotion of individual characteristics that allow individuals to flourish and prevent mental disorders

(Seligman & Csikszentmihalyi, 2000). Psychology has long been dominated by a medical model, which focuses on moving people from illness to being illness free. In the case of pessimism, this would mean treating severe pessimism but not necessarily promoting a highly optimistic outlook. The goal of positive psychology is not just to move people toward the absence of disorder but also the promotion of health and well-being (Seligman, 2001).

Positive psychology is not the first movement in psychology to raise doubts about the medical model and to advocate for the promotion of human strengths. Positive psychology focuses on what people do well and capitalizes on this capacity to treat and prevent disorders. This is a viable model of combating mental disorders. A meta-analysis of programs that prevent social and behavioral problems in children and adolescents found that interventions that increase competencies are just as effective as ones that reduce deficits (Durlak & Wells, 1997). Researchers have developed several more interventions aimed to promote human strengths and well-being.

Some of the positive interventions focus on cultivating an optimistic outlook on life, in ways similar to the studies just reviewed. Focusing on a future that holds positive possibilities – successes, growth, new opportunities – is an important way to be happier and healthier (Lyubomirsky, 2007; Seligman, 1991).

One such exercise involves visualizing a best future. Researchers adapted an expressive writing task that typically asks participants to write about a trauma. The benefits of writing about traumatic experiences have been well documented (see Frattaroli, 2006, for a review); however, writing about something positive, might be beneficial without the same emotional cost of recalling a trauma. In a study by King (2001), participants who wrote about a traumatic life event were compared to participants who wrote about their best possible self. These participants received the following instructions:

Think about your life in the future. Imagine that everything has gone as well as it possibly could. You have worked hard and succeeded at accomplishing all of your life goals. Think of this as the realization of all of your life dreams. Now, write about what you imagined.

Participants wrote on this topic 20 minutes each day for 4 consecutive days, and increased happiness, fewer negative emotions, and better physical health ensued. Furthermore, this exercise outperformed the trauma condition. So a short-term intervention that increased optimism had benefits on both psychological and physical well-being.

Sheldon and Lyubomirsky (2006) assessed the benefits of optimism over a longer period of time. They introduced the "Best Possible Self" exercise to participants and followed these participants for 4 weeks. Participants who completed the exercise had increases in positive emotions and decreases in negative emotions throughout the follow-up. A further investigation found that participants who engaged in a regular practice of optimism once a week for 8 weeks had increases in well-being and decreases in depressive symptoms for up to 9 months after the end of the intervention (Dickerhoof *et al.*, 2007). The main focus of these studies was to increase happiness in a non-depressed sample. The exercises did lead to decreases in depressive symptoms, however, the question remains as to whether these same exercises would work for individuals with depression.

Our lab has investigated similar exercises (Seligman *et al.*, 2005). In one test we designed five happiness exercises and one placebo exercise and delivered these exercises via the Internet. One of these exercises focused on building gratitude, two focused on increasing awareness of what is most positive about oneself, and two focused on identifying strengths of character. Table 8.1 displays a description of each exercise. In a randomized, placebo-controlled study, we compared the effects of these exercises with a plausible placebo control: journaling for 1 week about early memories. We recruited a convenience sample from visitors to the website created for Seligman's (2002) book *Authentic Happiness* by creating a link called "Happiness Exercises." Through this website we recruited 577 adult participants who were randomly assigned to one of the six conditions. We followed our participants for six months, periodically measuring symptoms of both depression and happiness.

TABLE 8.1 Description of Positive Psychology Exercises (From Seligman, Steen, Park, & Peterson, 2005)

Exercise	Description
Placebo control exercise: Early memories	Participants were asked to write about their early memories every night for one week.
Gratitude Visit	Participants were given one week to write and then deliver a letter of gratitude in person to someone who had been especially kind to them but had never been properly thanked.
Three good things in life	Participants were asked to write down three things that went well each day and their causes every night for one week. In addition, they were asked to provide a causal explanation for each good thing.
You at your best	Participants were asked to write about a time when they were at their best and then to reflect on the personal strengths displayed in the story. They were told to review their story once every day for a week and to reflect on the strengths they had identified.
Using signature strengths in a new way	Participants were asked to take our inventory of character strengths online at www.authentichappines.org and to received individualized feedback about their top five ("signature") strengths (Peterson et al., 2005). They were then asked to use one of these top strengths in a new and different way every day for one week.
Identifying signature strengths	This exercise was a truncated version of the one just described, without the instruction to use the signature strengths in new ways. Participants were asked to take the survey, to note their five highest strengths, and to use them more often during the next week.

Two of the exercises – using signature strengths in a new way and three good things – increased happiness and decreased depressive symptoms for 6 months. Participants performing the gratitude visit experienced large increases in happiness and decreases in depression, however, these benefits were shorter lived, lasting only 1 month. The other exercises and the placebo control created positive but transient effects on happiness and depressive symptoms. Not surprisingly, the degree to which participants continued the assigned exercise on their own and beyond the prescribed 1-week period mediated the long-term benefits.

Thus, positive psychology exercises presented briefly, with little instruction, presented online with no human interaction or therapeutic relationship led to lasting changes in happiness and decreases in depressive symptoms. This made us eager to investigate further uses of these exercises. Could these exercises be integrated into traditional forms of therapy or could new forms of therapy based along these principles be created?

Psychotherapy, as defined now, is where one goes to talk about troubles and shortcomings. Mental "health" in the hands of talk therapy is all too often seen as the relief of troubles, the nullification of shortcomings, and the mere absence of symptoms of illness. Although notions such as individuation, self-realization, and peak experiences (Maslow, 1971), full functioning (Rogers, 1961), maturity (Allport, 1961), and positive mental health (Jahoda, 1958) dot the literature, these are mostly viewed as the by-products of symptom relief or as clinical luxuries that, in this rushed age of managed care, clinicians cannot afford to address head on. We suggest that therapies focused explicitly on increasing well-being may be equally important in alleviating depression as therapies that focus on troubles and weakness.

We define this approach to treatment as "Positive Psychotherapy" (PPT) (Seligman *et al.*, 2006). PPT rests on the hypothesis that depression can be treated effectively not only by directly reducing its negative symptoms but also by directly building positive emotions, character strengths, and meaning in life. It is possible that directly building these positive resources will counteract negative symptoms and may also buffer against their future recurrence (Fredrickson & Losada, 2005; Haidt, 2006; Joseph & Lindley, 2005; Seligman, 2002; Seligman *et al.*, 2005). To this end, we evaluated both group and individual versions of PPT as a treatment for individuals suffering from mild-to-moderate depressive symptoms and for patients diagnosed with unipolar depression.

In the group form of PPT, mild-to-moderately depressed undergraduate students (as defined by a score on the BDI ranging from 10 to 24) participated in a 6-week group treatment. Participants were randomly assigned to either group PPT or a no-treatment control group. The group PPT used exercises that had previously been validated to increase happiness and reduce depressive symptoms. The exercises included: using signature strengths, writing three good things nightly, writing a positive obituary, conducting a gratitude visit, practicing active-constructive responding, and savoring experiences. Each session was evenly split between a group discussion of the previous week's exercise and a lecture-style introduction of the current week's exercise that included explicit instructions for how to do the exercise. Overall, group PPT worked significantly better than no treatment. Participants receiving PPT had a significant BDI score reduction compared to those in the control group. Substantial symptom relief lasted through 1 year of follow-up. The PPT participants, on average, scored in the non-depressed range on depressive symptoms, whereas controls remained in the mild-to-moderate range.

In a study examining individual PPT, 46 clients were recruited from the university counseling center. All participants met diagnostic criteria for major depressive disorder, without current Axis I comorbidity, and were not receiving current treatment. They were then randomly assigned to either individual PPT (n = 13) or treatment as usual (n = 15). PPT clients were also compared with a non-randomized matched group receiving TAU and antidepressant medications during the same time period (TAUMED; n = 17). (We do not think it ethical to randomly assign people to medication and so matched them for diagnosis, time of start of treatment, and level of symptom severity.)

Participants in the individual PPT condition received at most 14 sessions of a manualized protocol (Rashid & Seligman, in press) that included exercises based on the same principles as the group PPT. These sessions were all related to themes of building engagement, pleasure, and meaning.

We assessed four kinds of outcomes: Depressive symptoms, overall functioning, happiness, and remission. Overall, PPT did best. On self-report measures, PPT significantly exceeded TAUMED, with large effect sizes (d = 1.22 for depressive symptoms and 1.13 for overall functioning). On clinician-rated measures (the HRSD and GAF), PPT did significantly better than TAU, with large effect sizes (d = 1.41 and 1.16, respectively). Results for measures of well-being were mixed: the three groups did not differ significantly in life satisfaction, but PPT differed significantly from both TAU and TAUMED on a measure of happiness). On fourfold remission criteria, 7 of 11 (64%) clients in PPT, 1 of 9 (11%) in TAU, and 1 of 12 (8%) in TAUMED remitted by the end of treatment, $\chi^2(2, N = 32)$ $p < 0.005$. Overall, these results indicate that PPT did better than two active treatments with large effect sizes. Thus, systematically enhancing positive emotions, engagement, and meaning was quite efficacious in treating unipolar depression.

PPT is much different in focus from other traditional treatments for depression such as CBT. At the very onset of CBT, the therapist asks clients to record their pessimistic, self-critical, and globally negative thoughts and then helps them to identify how such thinking causes and maintains depression. By contrast, PPT builds a congenial positive relationship from the outset by asking clients to introduce themselves through telling a real-life story that shows them at their best. This is followed by asking clients to identify signature strengths and coaching them to find practical ways of using these strengths more often in work, love, play, friendship, and parenting. Clients set goals of using and enhancing their signature strengths through real-life exercises. Substantial time is spent coaching clients to reorient their attention and memory to what is good in their lives, with the goal of providing them with a more balanced context in which to place their problems. Although some problem-solving and discussion of troubles does take place in PPT, the goal is to keep the positive aspects of the clients' lives in the forefront of their minds, to teach behaviors that bring positive feedback from others, and to strengthen already existing positive aspects, rather than teaching the reinterpretation of negative aspects.

We are encouraged by the efficacy of positive psychology exercises, both those reviewed here tested in laboratory settings and those delivered on the Web. Although the evidence is preliminary, we speculate that future therapy for depression may combine talking about troubles with building positive emotion, engagement, and meaning.

THE FUTURE OF OPTIMISM/PESSIMISM

The current state of the research strongly suggests that a pessimistic outlook on life is a risk factor for depression. Expecting the worst becomes a self-fulfilling prophecy that may lead to hopelessness and despair. The value of future research on optimism as a risk factor for depression rests largely on the success of preventive interventions designed to promote optimistic thinking to protect against future depressive episodes. Depression is such a widespread problem that it remains one of the largest concerns for the mental health profession. Unipolar depression is one of the most common psychological disorders in adulthood and adolescence, affecting approximately 11 million individuals each year in the United States alone. When depressive symptoms at a sub-clinical level are taken into account, these numbers do not even begin to total up the amount of human suffering. Yet there are not enough therapists or financial resources to treat all of the serious depressions – either by medications or psychotherapy – that are projected in the near future. Optimism, in particular, and positive psychology in general may be a key component in implementing low-cost yet effective interventions to help counter depression.

The link between our thoughts and depression as emphasized by cognitive theories is the most revolutionary development in informing modern psychological treatment of depression. Pessimism seems to be close to the essence of the depressogenic thoughts and the study of optimism has given us some insight into how to prevent the disorder. Optimism is but a special case of positive psychology and the empirical test of exercises, built on positive psychology principles has shown initial promise for cost-effective and engaging ways of treating and preventing depression. Furthermore, these programs are easily disseminated online and, in the hands of skilled clinicians, will likely work even better. We believe that the future of the treatment and prevention of depression will join our current methods of combating troubles and weakness with new methods of building positive emotion, strength, and meaning.

REFERENCES

Abramson, L. Y., Seligman, M. E. P., & Teasdale, J. D. (1978). Learned helplessness in humans: Critique and reformulation. *Journal of Abnormal Psychology, 87*, 49–74.

Abramsom, L. Y., Metalsky, G. I., & Alloy, L. B. (1989). Hopelessness depression: A theory-based subtype of depression. *Psychological Review, 96*, 358–372.

Alloy, L. B., Abramson, L. Y., Hogan, M. F., Whitehouse, W. G., Rose D. T., Robinson, M. S., Kim, R. S., & Lapkin, J. B. (2000). The Temple-Wisconsin Cognitive Vulnerability to Depression Project: Lifetime history of Axis I psychopathology in individuals at high and low cognitive risk for depression. *Journal of Abnormal Psychology, 109*, 403–418.

Alloy, L. B., Abramson, L. Y., Whitehouse, W. G., Hogan, M. F., Panzarella, C., & Rose, D. T. (2006). Prospective incidence of first onsets and recurrences of depression in individuals at high and low cognitive risk for depression. *Journal of Abnormal Psychology, 115*, 145–156.

Alloy, L. B., Lipman, A. J., & Abramson, L. Y. (1992). Attributional style as a vulnerability factor for depression: Validation by past history of mood disorders. *Cognitive Therapy and Research, 16*, 391–407.

Allport, G. (1961). *Patterns and Growth in Personality*. New York: Holt, Rinehart, & Winston.

American Psychiatric Association. (2000). *Diagnostic and Statistical Manual of Mental Disorders DSM-IV-TR (Text revision)*. Washington, DC: Author.

Aspinwall, L. G., & Taylor, S. E. (1992). Modeling cognitive adaptation: A longitudinal investigation of the impact of individual differences and coping on college adjustment and performance. *Journal of Personality and Social Psychology, 63*, 989–1003.

Bandura, A. (1977). Self-efficacy: Towards a unifying theory of behavioral change. *Psychological Review, 84*, 191–215.

Beck, A. T. (1967). *Depression: Clinical, experimental, and theoretical aspects*. New York: Harper & Row.

Brickman, P., Ryan, K., & Wortman, C. B. (1975). Causal chains: Attribution of responsibility as a function of immediate and prior causes. *Journal of Personality and Social Psychology, 32*, 1060–1067.

Brunwasser, S. (2007). A meta-analytic review of the penn resiliency project. Manuscript in preparation.

Carver, C. S., & Gaines, J. G. (1987). Optimism, pessimism, and postpartum depression. *Cognitive Therapy and Research, 11*, 449–462.

Carver, C. S., Pozo, C., Harris, S. D., Noriega, V., Scheier, M. F., Robinson, D. S., Ketcham, A. S., Moffat, F. L., Jr, & Clark, K. C. (1993). How coping mediates the effect of optimism on distress: A study of women with early stage breast cancer. *Journal of Personality and Social Psychology, 65*, 375–390.

Dickerhoof, R., Lyubomirsky, S., & Sheldon, K. M. (2007). How and why do positive activities work to boost well-being? A longitudinal investigation of regularly practicing optimism and gratitude. Manuscript submitted for publication.

Durlak, J. A., & Wells, A. M. (1997). Primary prevention mental health programs for children and adolescents: A meta-analytic review. *American Journal of Community Psychology, 25*, 115–152.

Frattaroli, J. (2006). Experimental disclosure and its moderators: A meta-analysis. *Psychological Bulletin, 132*, 823–865.

Fredrickson, B. L., & Losada, M. (2005). Positive affect and the complex dynamics of human flourishing. *American Psychologist, 60*, 678–686.

Gibb, B. E., Beevers, C. G., Andover, M. S., & Holleran, K. (2006). The hopelessness theory of depression: A prospective multi-wave test of the vulnerability-stress hypothesis. *Cognitive Therapy and Research, 30*, 763–772.

Gillham, J. E., Reivich, K., Jaycox, L., & Seligman, M. E. P. (1995). Prevention of depressive symptoms in school children: Two-year follow up. *Psychological Science, 6*, 343–351.

Gillham, J. E., Tassoni, R. J., Engel, R. A., DeRubeis, R. J., & Seligman, M. E. P. (1998). *The Relationship of Explanatory Style to Other Depression Relevant Constructs*. Philadelphia, PA: University of Pennsylvania. Unpublished manuscript

Gillham, J. E., Brunwasser, S. M., & Freres, D. R. (2007). Preventing depression early in adolescents: The Penn Resilience Program (Chapter to be published). In J. R. Z. Abela & B. L. Hankin (Eds.), *Handbook of Depression in Children and Adolescents*. New York: Guilford Press.

Gladstone, T. R., & Kaslow, N. J. (1995). Depression and attributions in children and adolescents: A meta-analytic review. *Journal of Abnormal Child Psychology*, *23*, 597–606.

Golin, S., Sweeney, P. D., & Shaeffer, D. E. (1981). The causality of causal attributions in depression: A cross-lagged panel correlational analysis. *Journal of Abnormal Psychology*, *90*, 14–22.

Haidt, J. (2006). *The happiness hypothesis: Finding modern truth in ancient wisdom*. New York: Basic Books.

Hankin, B. L., & Abramson, L. Y. (2001). Development of gender differences in depression: An elaborated cognitive vulnerability-transactional stress theory. *Psychological Bulletin*, *127*, 773–796.

Hankin, B. L., Abramson, L. Y., & Siler, M. (2001). A prospective test of the hopelessness theory of depression in adolescence. *Cognitive Therapy and Research*, *25*, 607–632.

Hjelle, L., Belongia, C., & Nesser, J. (1996). Psychometric properties of the life orientation test and the attributional style questionnaire. *Psychological Reports*, *78*, 507–515.

Iacoviello, B. M., Alloy, L. B., Abramson, L. Y., Whitehouse, W. G., & Hogan, M. E. (2006). The course of depression in individuals at high and low cognitive risk for depression: A prospective study. *Journal of Affective Disorders*, *93*, 61–69.

Isaacowitz, D. M., & Seligman, M. E. P. (2001). Is pessimism a risk factor for depressive mood among community-dwelling older adults?. *Behaviour Research and Therapy*, *39*, 255–272.

Jahoda, M. (1958). *Current Concepts of Positive Mental Health*. New York: Basic Books.

Jaycox, L., Reivich, K., Gillham, J. E., & Seligman, M. E. P. (1994). Prevention of depressive symptoms in school children. *Behaviour Research and Therapy*, *32*, 801–816.

Joseph, S., & Lindley, A. P. (2005). Positive psychological approaches to therapy. *Counseling and Psychotherapy Research*, *5*, 5–10.

King, L. A. (2001). The health benefits of writing about life goals. *Personality and Social Psychology Bulletin*, *27*, 798–807.

Lyubomirsky, S. (2007). *The How of Happiness*. New York: Penguin Press.

Lyubomirsky, S., Sheldon, K. M., & Schkade, D. (2005). Pursuing happiness: The architecture of sustainable change. *Review of General Psychology*, *9*, 111–131.

Maslow, A. H. (1971). *The Farther Reaches of Human Nature*. New York: Penguin.

Metalsky, G. I., Abramson, L. Y., Seligman, M. E. P., Semmel, A., & Peterson, C. (1982). Attributional styles and life events in the classroom: Vulnerability and invulnerability to depressive mood reactions. *Journal of Personality and Social Psychology*, *43*, 612–617.

Metalsky, G. I., Halberstadt, L. J., & Abramson, L. Y. (1987). Vulnerability to depressive mood reactions: Toward a more powerful test of the diathesis–stress and causal mediation components of the reformulated theory of depression. *Journal of Personality and Social Psychology*, *52*, 386–393.

Metalsky, G. I., Joiner, T. E., Hardin, T. S., & Abramson, L. Y. (1993). Depressive reactions to failure in a naturalistic setting: A testing of the hopelessness and self-esteem theories of depression. *Journal of Abnormal Psychology*, *102*, 101–109.

Morris, S. J. (2007). Attributional biases in subclinical depression: A schema-based account. *Clinical Psychology and Psychotherapy*, *14*, 32–47.

Needles, D. J., & Abramson, L. Y. (1990). Positive life events, attributional style, and hopefulness: Testing a model of recovery from depression. *Journal of Abnormal Psychology*, *99*, 156–165.

Overmier, J. B., & Seligman, M. E. P. (1967). Effects of inescapable shock upon subsequent escape and avoidance behavior. *Journal of Comparative and Physiological Psychology*, *63*, 23–33.

Pearlin, L. I., & Schooler, C. (1978). The structure of coping. *Journal of Health and Social Behavior*, *19*, 2–21.

Peterson, C. (1991). Meaning and measurement of explanatory style. *Psychological Inquiry*, 2, 1–10.

Peterson, C. (2000). The future of optimism. *American Psychologist*, *55*, 44–55.

Peterson, C., & Seligman, M. E. P. (1984). Causal explanations as a risk factor for depression: Theory and evidence. *Psychological Review*, *91*, 347–374.

Peterson, C., & Villanova, P. (1988). An expanded attributional style questionnaire. *Journal of Abnormal Psychology, 97*, 87–89.

Peterson, C., & Vaidya, R. S. (2001). Explanatory style, expectations, and depressive symptoms. *Personality and Individual Differences, 31*, 1217–1223.

Peterson, C., Bettes, B. A., & Seligman, M. E. P. (1985). Depressive symptoms and unprompted causal attribution: Content analysis. *Behaviour Research and Therapy, 23*, 379–382.

Peterson, C., Semmel, A., von Baeyer, C., Abramson, L. Y., Metalsky, G. I., & Seligman, M. E. P. (1982). The attributional style questionnaire. *Cognitive Therapy and Research, 6*, 287–299.

Raps, C. S., Peterson, C., Reinhard, K. E., Abramson, L. Y., & Seligman, M. E. P. (1982). Attributional styles among depressed patients. *Journal of Abnormal Psychology, 91*, 102–103.

Rashid, T. & Seligman, M. E. P. (in press). *Positive Psychotherapy: A Treatment Manual*. New York: Oxford University Press.

Rogers, C. R. (1961). *On Becoming a Person: A Therapist's View of Psychotherapy*. Boston: Houghton Mifflin.

Scheier, M. F., & Carver, C. S. (1985). Optimism coping, and health: Assessment and implications of generalized outcome expectancies. *Health Psychology, 4*, 219–247.

Scheier, M. F., & Carver, C. S. (1992). Effects of optimism on psychological and physical well-being: Theoretical overview and empirical update. *Cognitive Therapy and Research, 16*, 201–228.

Scheier, M. F., & Carver, C. S. (2001). Optimism, pessimism, and self-regulation. In E. C. Chang (Ed.), *Optimism and Pessimism: Implication for Theory, Research, and Practice* (pp. 31–51). Washington, DC: American Psychological Association.

Scheier, M. F., Weintraub, J. K., & Carver, C. S (1986). Coping with stress: Divergent strategies of optimists and pessimists. *Journal of Personality and Social Psychology, 51*, 1257–1264.

Scheier, M. F., Matthews, K. A., Owens, J. F., Magovern, G. J., Lefebvre, R. C., Abbott, R. A., & Carver, C. S. (1989). Dispositional optimism and recovery from coronary artery bypass surgery: The beneficial effects on physical and psychological well-being. *Journal of Personality and Social Psychology, 57*, 1024–1040.

Scheier, M. F., Carver, C. S., & Bridges, M. W. (1994). Distinguishing optimism from neuroticism (and trait anxiety, self-mastery, and self-esteem): A reevaluation of the life orientation test. *Journal of Personality and Social Psychology, 67*, 1063–1078.

Scheier, M. F., Carver, C. S., & Bridges, M. W. (2001). Optimism, pessimism, and self-regulation. In E. C. Chang (Ed.), *Optimism and Pessimism: Implication for Theory, Research, and Practice* (pp. 189–216). Washington, DC: American Psychological Association.

Schulz, R., Tompkins, C. A., & Rau, M. T. (1988). A longitudinal study of the psychological impact of stroke on primary support persons. *Psychology and Aging, 3*, 131–141.

Segerstrom, S. C. (2001). Optimism, goal conflict, and stressor-related immune change. *Journal of Behavioral Medicine, 24*, 441–467.

Seligman, M. E. P. (1975). *Helplessness: On Development, Depression, and Death*. New York: W. H. Freeman and Company.

Seligman, M. E. P. (1991). *Learned Optimism*. New York: Knopf.

Seligman, M. E. P. (2001). Positive psychology, positive prevention, and positive therapy. In C. R. Snyder & S. J. Lopez (Eds.), *The Handbook of Positive Psychology*. New York: Oxford University Press.

Seligman, M. E. P. (2002). *Authentic Happiness*. New York: Free Press.

Seligman, M. E. P., & Maier, S. F. (1967). Failure to escape traumatic shock. *Journal of Experimental Psychology, 74*, 1–9.

Seligman, M. E. P., & Csikszentmihalyi, M. (2000). Positive psychology: An introduction. *American Psychologist, 55*, 5–14.

Seligman, M. E. P., Abramson, L. Y., Semmel, A., & von Baeyer, C. (1979). Depressive attributional style. *Journal of Abnormal Psychology, 88*, 242–247.

Seligman, M. E. P., Castellon, C., Cacciola, J., Schulman, P., Luborsky, L., Ollove, M., & Downing, R. (1988). Explanatory style change during cognitive therapy for unipolar depression. *Journal of Abnormal Psychology, 97*, 13–18.

Seligman, M. E. P., Schulman, P., DeRubeis, R. J., & Hollon, S. D. (1999). The prevention of depression and anxiety. *Prevention & Treatment*, 2, np.

Seligman, M. E. P., Steen, T. A., Park, N., & Peterson, C. (2005). Positive psychology progress: An empirical validation of interventions. *American Psychologist*, *60*, 410–421.

Seligman, M. E. P., Rashid, T., & Parks, A. C. (2006). Positive psychotherapy. *American Psychologist*, *61*, 774–788.

Seligman, M. E. P., Schulman, P., & Tryon, A. (2007). Group prevention of depression and anxiety symptoms. *Behaviour Research and Therapy*, *45*, 1111–1126.

Sheldon, K. M., & Elliot, A. J. (1999). Goal striving, need satisfaction, and longitudinal well-being: The self-concordance model. *Journal of Personality and Social Psychology*, *76*, 482–497.

Sheldon, K. M., & Lyubomirsky, S. (2006). How to increase and sustain positive emotion: The effects of expressing gratitude and visualizing best possible selves. *Journal of Positive Psychology*, *1*, 73–82.

Silverman, R. J., & Peterson, C. (1993). Explanatory style of schizophrenic and depressed outpatients. *Cognitive Therapy and Research*, *17*, 457–470.

Snyder, C. R. (1994). *The Psychology of Hope: You Can Get There From Here*. New York: Free Press.

Snyder, C. R., Harris, C., Anderson, J. R., Holleran, S. A., Irving, L. M., Sigman, S. T., Yoshinobu, L., Gibb, J., Langelle, C., & Harney, P. (1991). The will and the ways: Development and validation of an individual-differences measure of hope. *Journal of Personality and Social Psychology*, *60*, 570–585.

Strunk, D. R., Lopez, H., & DuRubeis, R. J. (2006). Depressive symptoms are associated with unrealistic negative predictions of future life events. *Behaviour Research and Therapy*, *44*, 861–882.

Sweeney, P. D., Anderson, K., & Bailey, S. (1986). Attributional style in depression: A meta-analytic review. *Journal of Personality and Social Psychology*, *50*, 974–991.

9

Dispositional Pessimism Across the Lifespan

John R.Z. Abela*, Randy P. Auerbach*
and Martin E.P. Seligman†

*McGill University, Montreal, Quebec
†University of Pennsylvania, Philadelphia, Pennsylvania

"Is the glass half empty or half full?" research suggests that the way in which one answers such a question has implications for physical and mental health outcomes including depression (for reviews see Gillham *et al.*, 2002; Scheier *et al.*, 2002). Optimists are expected to reply *half full* whereas pessimists are expected to reply *half empty*. Most definitions of optimism and pessimism focus on one of two related interpretations of these constructs. The first interpretation emphasizes the manner in which individuals tend to perceive events and circumstances in their lives. Whereas optimists exhibit "a tendency to expect the best possible outcome or to dwell on the most hopeful aspects of a situation" pessimists emphasize "the negative or unfavorable or to take the gloomiest possible view" (The American Heritage Dictionary of the English Language, 2000). The second interpretation concerns general beliefs about the relation between goodness and evil in the world. Whereas optimists ascribe to the doctrine that "this world is the best of all possible worlds" and that "good must ultimately prevail over evil in the universe," pessimists are hypothesized to ascribe to the doctrine that our world "is the worst of all possible worlds and that all things ultimately tend toward evil" (Oxford Pocket Dictionary of Current English, 2007).

There are two approaches to the operationalization and assessment of the constructs of optimism and pessimism in the field of psychology, both of which are consistent with the above definitions of optimism and pessimism. Some theorists and researchers have operationalized and assessed these constructs in a direct manner – they ask individuals to report their generalized expectations about the future (i.e., dispositional optimism and pessimism). Other theorists and researchers, however, operationalize and assess these constructs indirectly, by asking people to explain the causal patterns for events that occur in their lives (i.e., explanatory style). We will examine theoretical models pertaining to each of these two approaches to optimism and pessimism and related assessment tools. We will present research that examines the prospective association between these approaches and changes in depressive symptoms over time. We will conclude by highlighting the similarity and difference between the dispositional optimism and the explanatory style literatures and provide directions for future research.

DISPOSITIONAL OPTIMISM

Scheier and Carver (1992) posit that optimism and pessimism play a significant role in the development and maintenance of psychological and physical well-being. Optimism and pessimism are posited to be individual difference variables that are stable over time and across environments (Scheier & Carver, 1992; Scheier *et al.*, 1994a). Scheier and Carver's model is primarily based on behavioral self-regulation theory in that it posits that individuals' actions are governed by their expectation of the consequences of their actions (e.g., Carver & Scheier, 1990; Scheier & Carver, 1988). Specifically, individuals who view outcomes as "attainable" are posited to continue to "strive" toward such goals even when obstacles emerge. In contrast, individuals who view outcomes as "unattainable" are posited to "withdraw their effort and disengage themselves from the goals" (Scheier & Carver, 1992, p. 202). These differences parallel affective experiences in that optimists tend to report lower levels of depressive symptoms whereas pessimists tend to exhibit higher levels of such symptoms.

ASSESSING DISPOSITIONAL OPTIMISM

Scheier and Carver (1985) measure expectancies directly. They ask individuals to report whether they believe their generalized future outcomes. Such expectancies have typically been assessed utilizing either the Life Orientation Test (LOT; Scheier & Carver, 1985) or the briefer Life Orientation Test-Revised (LOT-R; Scheier *et al.*, 1994a). The LOT and LOT-R include an equal number of positive (e.g., "In uncertain times, I usually expect the best" or "I always look on the bright side of things") and negative (e.g., "If something can go wrong for me, it will" or "Things never work out the way I want them to") Likert-type items. Research that has examined the factor structure of the LOT-R has yielded only one factor (Scheier *et al.*, 1994a). In contrast, research examining the factor analytic structure of the LOT has shown that it consists of two factors, optimism and pessimism, which correspond to the positively and negatively worded items, respectively. The two factors are highly and positively associated with each other ($r = 0.64$) indicating significant redundancy between the subscales. As a result, Scheier and Carver (1985) suggest treating the LOT as a unidimensional scale, in which higher scores represent more optimistic tendencies and lower scores suggest lower optimism (Scheier & Carver, 1985; Scheier *et al.*, 1994a). The LOT and LOT-R are viewed as dispositional and unidimensional measures of optimism, operationalized as the tendency to expect that good outcomes will occur. Scheier *et al.* (1994a) caution that low-optimism scores are not equivalent to pessimism, and that optimism (i.e., positively worded items) and pessimism (i.e., negatively worded items) should not be viewed as bipolar dimensions.

EXAMINING THE PROSPECTIVE ASSOCIATION BETWEEN DISPOSITIONAL OPTIMISM AND DEPRESSION

A large body of research has examined the hypothesis that dispositional optimism plays a significant role in the development and maintenance of psychological (e.g., Chang, 1998a, b; Schuller, 1995) and physical (e.g., Curbow *et al.*, 1993; Given *et al.*, 1993; Long & Sangster, 1993) well-being. The vast majority of research has been cross-sectional and indicates that higher levels of optimism are associated with lower levels of distress (Scheier *et al.*, 2002). As optimism and distress, however, have been assessed contemporaneously in such studies, it cannot be ascertained with any degree of certainty whether higher levels of optimism result in lower levels of distress or vice versa. Given this interpretational ambiguity, longitudinal research is needed to examine this relationship.

To date, few studies have examined the prospective relationship between dispositional optimism and depressive symptoms. Results from preliminary research suggest that dispositional optimism positively impacts individuals' mood states in the face of hardship and misfortune. The following review of the empirical literature focuses on prospective studies which examined the association between optimism and change in depressive symptoms over time. Studies will be presented according to the type of sample they employed.

ADOLESCENTS AND UNIVERSITY STUDENTS

Higher levels of dispositional optimism have been associated with fewer depressive symptoms in early adolescents (i.e., sixth and seventh graders) and better adjustment over the course of a 1-year follow-up interval, irrespective of whether youth were experiencing low or high levels of adversity (Herman-Stahl & Petersen,

1996). Similar results have been obtained for older adolescents, university students, and graduate students (e.g., law and medical students), which suggests that dispositional optimism protects individuals from painful, negative affect even in the absence of negative events (Aspinwall & Taylor, 1992; Cohen, 1990; Jackson *et al.*, 2005; Segerstrom *et al.*, 1998; Stewart *et al.*, 1997). In contrast, in a sample of 121 university students followed over a 12-week period, O'Connor and Cassidy (2007) found that positive future thinking did not moderate the relationship between optimism and dysphoria, and that the only significant predictor of dysphoria was the occurrence of negative life events.

OLDER ADULTS

Few studies have prospectively examined the association between optimism and depressive symptoms over time in older, adult samples. Bromberger and Matthews (1996) followed 460 premenopausal women over the course of 3 years. After controlling for initial levels of depressive symptoms, lower scores of dispositional optimism were associated with more depressive symptoms following the occurrence of recent or chronic stressful life events. Similarly, in research examining a community sample of 464 elderly men between the ages of 64 and 84 over the course of 15 years, results indicated that higher levels of dispositional optimism, as compared to lower levels, were associated with lower levels of depressive symptoms at each of the follow-ups which occurred every 5 years (Giltay *et al.*, 2007).

PREGNANCY AND CHILDBIRTH

Optimism and pessimism may play a significant role in the development of depression in pregnant women following childbirth (e.g., Carver & Gaines, 1987). In a study of 179 adult women, higher levels of dispositional optimism, as assessed during the middle trimester of pregnancy, predicted lower levels of depressive symptoms at 6 and 12 months postpartum even after controlling for initial levels of such symptoms (Grote & Bledsoe, 2007). Furthermore, expectant mothers who reported higher levels of optimism were at lower risk for the development of significant levels of symptomatology following high levels of financial, spousal, and physical stress than expectant mothers who reported lower levels of optimism. Similarly, Carver and Gaines (1987) found that mothers who reported higher levels of dispositional optimism exhibited lower levels of depressive symptoms 3 weeks following childbirth, as compared to individuals who reported lower levels of optimism. In contrast, whereas higher levels of optimism predicted lower levels of depressive symptoms 6 weeks prior to childbirth, the effect was no longer significant after controlling for the effect of self-esteem (Fontaine & Jones, 1997). Consequently, the results of Fontaine and Jones

(1997) suggest that previous results may be accounted for by differing levels of self-esteem.

ABORTION

Dispositional optimism buffers women from distress following the negative life event of abortion. In a sample of 527 women obtaining a first-trimester abortion, women who reported higher levels of optimism appraised their abortion as less stressful and reported lower levels of distress at the 1-month follow-up (Major *et al.*, 1998). Similarly, in a sample of 336 women, Cozzarelli (1993) found that higher levels of optimism were associated with fewer depressive symptoms both 30 minutes and 3 weeks after the abortion, suggesting that optimism may help to shield women having an abortion from negative affect.

CANCER

Preliminary research has examined the relationship between dispositional optimism and well-being among cancer patients (e.g., Carver *et al.*, 1993). In a sample of 274 adult cancer patients, higher levels of initial dispositional optimism were associated with lower levels of depressive symptoms and higher levels of physical functioning 3 years following patients' bone marrow transplants, even after controlling for initial levels of such variables. For individuals who found meaning from their struggle with cancer, such a belief mediated the relationship between higher levels of optimism and lower depressive symptom scores 1 year after treatment (Tallman *et al.*, 2007). Research related to the effect of optimism on well-being in breast cancer patients has found that the prevalence of depressive and anxiety disorders was lower among individuals who reported higher levels of optimism, as compared to those with lower levels of optimism (Schou *et al.*, 2004). Similarly, Johnson (1996) found that higher levels of optimism predicted lower levels of negative affect, both during treatment and 3 months after radiation treatment for prostate cancer was completed.

PATIENT–CAREGIVER DYADS

Few studies have examined the psychosocial impact of personality traits on the psychological health and well-being of the caregiver in a patient–caregiver dyad. In a 10-year, multi-wave study examining spouse–caregivers whose partners suffered from early stage Parkinson's disease, caregivers who reported higher levels of pessimism experienced higher levels of depressive symptoms, poorer caregiver health, and a faster decline in health for their partner (Lyons *et al.*, 2004). While levels of pessimism were not associated with the rate of change in depressive symptoms, symptom scores for pessimistic individuals increased by an average of 4 points at the 10-year follow-up. Similarly, in a 30-day diary study of spouse–caregivers of persons with a confirmed diagnosis of Alzheimer's or dementia, caregivers with higher levels of dispositional optimism experienced lower levels of negative affect. The results did not exhibit a lead–lag relationship with fluctuations in optimism predicting later fluctuations in affect, which suggests that optimism's impact on future affect may have temporal limitations. The well-being of caregivers of stroke patients found that lower levels of dispositional optimism at Time 1 (approximately 7 weeks following the patients' stroke) were associated with higher levels of depressive symptoms at the 1-year follow-up. Further, caregivers with lower levels optimism were also more likely to have lower household incomes and fewer people in their social networks.

SURGICAL OUTCOMES

Optimism and pessimism play a role in post-transplant affective recovery. In a sample of 76 individuals undergoing lung, liver, and bone marrow transplants, patients who reported higher levels of optimism pre-transplant were more likely to report a higher quality of life as well as fewer depressive symptoms 12 months following the transplant (Goetzmann *et al.*, 2007). Similar results have been found with individuals undergoing coronary surgery (e.g., Fitzgerald *et al.*, 1993; King *et al.*, 1998; Ruiz *et al.*, 2006; Scheier *et al.*, 1989). For example, lower levels of pre-surgical optimism were associated with higher levels of depressive symptoms in a multi-wave, prospective study of 111 adult patients who received coronary artery bypass grafts (Ruiz *et al.*, 2006). Furthermore, low optimism was associated with a greater amount of caregiver burden. In contrast, research examining elective surgeries has not yielded similar findings. For example, while higher levels of optimism predicted greater improvement in 57 individuals who underwent elective joint replacement surgery recovery, optimism was not associated with a reduced level of distress throughout the follow-up period (Chamberlain *et al.*, 1992).

HIV AND AIDS

Taylor *et al.* (1992) have found that higher levels of dispositional optimism were associated with lower levels of distress in both seropositive and seronegative men. In a related study, Ironson *et al.* (2005) conducted a 2-year study with a sample of 177 individuals living with HIV, and the results indicated that higher levels of dispositional optimism were associated with slower disease progression as well as lower levels of depressive symptoms.

MEDIATING PATHWAYS THROUGH WHICH DISPOSITIONAL OPTIMISM PREDICTS DEPRESSION

The above research generally indicates that individuals who report higher levels of dispositional optimism experience less distress, as compared to those who report lower levels. While few studies have examined the mechanisms through which optimism exerts its benefits, the bulk of research to date has focused on coping (Scheier *et al.*, 1986, 2002). Scheier *et al.* (2002) posit that optimists are more likely to utilize coping strategies that directly address the problem, which in turn attenuates stress and negative affect. In contrast, pessimists tend to engage in avoidance-based coping strategies in an effort to escape such states.

Brissette *et al.* (2002) found that higher levels of dispositional coping were associated with more use of active coping, planning, and positive reinterpretation and growth in university students. Optimistic participants were also less likely to utilize maladaptive coping strategies, including denial and behavioral disengagement. Results of the 3-month prospective analyses indicated that higher levels of adaptive coping (i.e., positive reinterpretation and growth) mediated the relationship among higher levels of dispositional optimism, and lower levels of both stress and depressive symptoms. In other research related to how undergraduates cope with stressful life events, students who reported higher levels of optimism were more likely to utilize problem-focused coping and positive reframing. In contrast, individuals with higher levels of optimism were less likely to use maladaptive coping strategies such as denial and distancing oneself from the problem (Scheier *et al.*, 1986). Puskar *et al.* (1999) have also found that adolescents with higher levels of dispositional optimism utilize more problem-focused coping strategies such as logical analysis, seeking guidance or support, and positive reappraisal as compared to pessimists. Furthermore, when problem-focused coping is not an option, individuals who report high levels of optimism tend to utilize more adaptive emotion-focused strategies (Taylor *et al.*, 1992). Shen *et al.* (2004) explored the independent and mediated contributions of optimism and coping among 142 patients who received 6 weeks of cardiac rehabilitation following surgery. The results indicated that higher levels of dispositional optimism were associated with both better health outcomes and lower levels of depressive symptoms. Greater endorsement of positive coping strategies such as planning, positive reframing, acceptance, and seeking emotional support also mediated the relationship between higher levels of dispositional optimism and lower levels of depressive symptomology.

In sum, research suggests that an optimistic orientation increases the likelihood of using adaptive coping strategies. Future research should explore whether optimism can be increased, and if higher levels of optimism are associated with subsequent changes in one's use of approach- vs. avoidant-based strategies. Further, research should continue to explore mechanisms through which optimism may exert its effect on distress. For example, as positive interpersonal relationships are an important component of well-being, levels of optimism may contribute to the quality and nature of relationships, which may in turn impact affect. Similarly, dispositional optimism may contribute to underlying cognitive processes and/or core beliefs which consequently influence distress.

EXPLANATORY STYLE

According to both the reformulated learned helplessness theory (Abramson *et al.*, 1978) and the hopelessness theory (Abramson *et al.*, 1989) of depression, individuals possess explanatory styles or habitual ways of perceiving the causes of negative events, which are associated with increased risk of depression.

REFORMULATED LEARNED HELPLESSNESS THEORY

The reformulated learned helplessness theory (Abramson *et al.*, 1978) operationalizes a pessimistic explanatory style as the tendency to attribute the causes of negative events to internal, global, and stable factors. In contrast, the theory views an optimistic explanatory style as the tendency to attribute the causes of negative events to external, specific, and unstable factors. A pessimistic explanatory style poses risk for the development of depressive symptoms after negative events, because this style leads individuals to make depressogenic attributions for such events. Making depressogenic attributions increases the likelihood of developing helplessness expectancies – the belief that one has no control over the occurrence of future events. Once helplessness expectancies develop, depression is inevitable as helplessness expectancies are posited to be proximal and sufficient causes of depression.

HOPELESSNESS THEORY

According to the hopelessness theory of depression (Abramson *et al.*, 1989), individuals with a pessimistic explanatory style tend to attribute the causes of negative events to global and stable factors, whereas individuals with an optimistic explanatory style exhibit the tendency to attribute such causes to specific and unstable factors. Individuals with a pessimistic explanatory style are also more likely to make depressogenic inferences about the causes of negative events than individuals without such style. Such inferences increase the likelihood of hopelessness, and once hopelessness develops, depression is inevitable, since hopelessness is viewed as a proximal and sufficient cause of depression. The hopelessness theory elaborates on the reformulated learned helplessness theory by delineating two additional cognitive styles that play a role in the etiology of depression. Individuals with pessimistic cognitive styles about consequences and the self tend to view negative events as having many disastrous consequences and view the self as flawed and deficient following negative events. In contrast, individuals with optimistic cognitive styles tend to infer that negative consequences will not follow from negative events and believe that negative events in their life do not mean that they are flawed in any way.

ASSESSING EXPLANATORY STYLE

Most researchers who have examined the attributional vulnerability hypothesis of the reformulated learned helplessness and hopelessness theories of depression have used some variation of the Attributional Style Questionnaire (ASQ; Peterson *et al.*, 1982) to assess explanatory style. The ASQ is a self-report questionnaire that consists of six negative and six positive hypothetical life events. Participants imagine that each event happened to them and then write down a cause for each event. Participants subsequently rate each cause on a 1–7 scale along three separate dimensions: internal vs. external, global vs. specific, and stable vs. unstable. Separate composite scores are computed for explanatory style for negative and positive events, and higher scores represent more internal, global, and stable explanatory styles. Since both theories of depression operationalize vulnerability to depression as the manner in which individuals perceive the causes of negative events, the remainder of this chapter will focus on explanatory style for negative events. It is important to note that although explanatory style for positive events has not been implicated in the initial development of depression, subsequent research and theory have suggested that it plays a role in the recovery from depression (Needles & Abramson, 1990). In order to increase its reliability, expanded versions of the ASQ with 12 (Metalsky *et al.*, 1987) or 24 (Peterson & Villanova, 1988) hypothetical negative events have been developed. Similarly, to assess cognitive styles about consequences and the self, Abramson *et al.* (1988a) developed the Cognitive Style Questionnaire.

The majority of research examining the attributional vulnerability hypothesis in youth has utilized the Children's Attributional Style Questionnaire (CASQ; Seligman *et al.*, 1984). The CASQ is a 48-item forced-choice questionnaire. Each item consists of a hypothetical positive or negative event and two possible causes of the event. Children choose the option that best describes the way they would think if that event happened to them. The two choices for each item hold constant two dimensions of attributional style while varying the third. Recently researchers have also developed the Children's Attributional Style Interview (CASI; Conley *et al.*, 2001). Similar to the ASQ, the CASI allows youth to generate their own causal attributions and then rate each attribution on dimensions of internality, stability, and globality. Unlike the ASQ, events are illustrated pictorially and children rate their attributions using a sliding pointer on large, colorful scales with icons representing the concepts of internality, stability, and globality.

PROSPECTIVE STUDIES OF THE ASSOCIATION BETWEEN EXPLANATORY STYLE AND DEPRESSION

Early research focused on the cross-sectional association between explanatory style and depressive symptoms and the prospective relationship between explanatory style and change in depressive symptoms. Critical reviews of the literature, however, argued that such early studies provided an inadequate examination of the theories, as they failed to examine the idea that individuals with a pessimistic explanatory style are only more likely than other individuals to experience increases in depressive symptoms in the face of negative events. In the absence of such events, individuals with a pessimistic explanatory style are no more likely than others to exhibit depression (Abramson *et al.*, 1988b; Alloy *et al.*, 1988). In response to such critiques, the field saw a shift in methodology, as prospective diathesis–stress designs became standard. Our review below will focus on such studies.

UNIVERSITY STUDENTS

The majority of research that has examined pessimistic explanatory style and depression has been conducted using university student samples. Several early studies tested whether explanatory style is a predictor of depressive mood reactions following the receipt of a negative outcome on mid-term examinations. Consistent with the attributional vulnerability hypothesis, in a study of 94 undergraduate students, Metalsky *et al.* (1987) reported that a pessimistic explanatory style for achievement, but not interpersonal, events was associated with depressive mood reactions 4 days following, but not immediately following, receipt of an unsatisfactory mid-term examinations grade. In contrast, Follette and Jacobson (1987) reported that explanatory style was not associated with depressive mood reactions immediately following receipt of mid-term examination grades in a study of 129 university students. Similarly, in a study of 131 university students, Hunsley (1989) reported that a pessimistic explanatory style was associated with depressive mood reactions immediately following the completion of a mid-term examination, but not immediately following the receipt of mid-term examination grades.

Abela and Seligman (2000) examined whether explanatory style is a predictor of depressive mood reactions following the receipt of a negative university admissions outcome or a negative fraternity/sorority rush outcome. Providing partial support for the attributional vulnerability hypothesis, but inconsistent with the pattern of findings obtained by Metalsky *et al.* (1987), they reported that pessimistic explanatory styles for both negative achievement and negative interpersonal events predicted depressive mood reactions immediately following, but not 4 days following, receipt of a negative admissions outcome in a sample of 149 university applicants. Similarly, in a study of 77 university freshmen rushing fraternities or sororities, Abela and Seligman reported that pessimistic explanatory styles for both negative achievement and negative interpersonal events predicted depressive mood reactions immediately following, but not 4 days following, receipt of a negative rush outcome.

Other studies have examined whether a pessimistic explanatory style is associated with increases in depressive symptoms following the occurrence of negative life events, as assessed by life event questionnaires. Consistent with the attributional vulnerability hypothesis, in a 5-week longitudinal study of 152 university students, Metalsky and Joiner (1992) reported that a pessimistic explanatory style was associated with increases in depressive symptoms following the experience of a high number of negative events. Similar results were reported in other samples (Fresco *et al.*, 2006; Kwon & Laurenceau, 2002), although in a 1-week, multi-wave longitudinal study of 44 university students using experience sampling methodology, Swendsen (1997) reported that explanatory style failed to interact with the number of negative events to predict level of depressed mood. Similarly, in a 4-week prospective study of 100 university students, Johnson (1992) reported that explanatory style failed to interact with the occurrence of negative events to predict change in depressive symptoms.

Metalksy *et al.* (1993) proposed that an integration of the hopelessness and self-esteem theories may lead to a more precise test of both theories. Their integrative theory hypothesizes that a pessimistic explanatory style interacts with the occurrence of negative events to predict increases in depression in individuals with low self-esteem, but not in individuals with high self-esteem. Consistent with the integrative model, in a longitudinal study of 114 university students, Metalksy *et al.* (1993) reported that among participants with low levels of self-esteem, a pessimistic explanatory style for negative achievement, but not interpersonal, events was associated with depressive mood reactions in the 4 days following (but not the day of) receipt of an unsatisfactory mid-term examination grade. Further, in a study of 136 university applicants, Abela (2002) reported that for participants with low levels of self-esteem, a pessimistic explanatory style for negative achievement, but not interpersonal events, was associated with depressive mood reactions 4 days following, but not immediately following, receipt of a negative admissions outcome. However, in a short-term longitudinal study of 141 university students, Ralph and Mineka (1998) reported that a pessimistic explanatory style failed to predict increases in depressive symptoms or nonspecific distress following a negative examination outcome irrespective of levels of self-esteem. Unexpectedly, the interaction between a pessimistic explanatory style and low-self esteem was associated with increases in distress and anxious arousal after receipt of a positive examination outcome.

Abela and colleagues (Abela & Brozina, 2004; Abela *et al.*, 2004) proposed that the integration of the hopelessness theory and Persons and Miranda's (1992) activation hypothesis may lead to a more precise test of both theories. According to the activation hypothesis, cognitive vulnerability factors, including pessimistic explanatory style, must be activated in order to be accurately assessed. Therefore, studies that do not activate or prime explanatory styles before assessing them may not assess the true propensity of participants' pessimistic thinking. Such studies are therefore less likely to yield results that support the hopelessness theory. In a 5-week study of 165 university students, Abela *et al.* (2004) had participants' complete measures of explanatory style before and after completing a cognitive priming questionnaire. Unprimed explanatory style failed to interact with negative events occurring during the subsequent 5 weeks to predict increases in depressive symptoms. In line with the activation hypotheses, however, primed pessimistic explanatory style interacted with negative events during the follow-up interval to predict increases in depressive symptoms, even after controlling for the variance in depressive symptoms accounted for by the unprimed explanatory style–stress interaction. Abela and Brozina (2004) reported similar findings in a short-term study of 93 university students. Although unprimed explanatory style failed to interact with a negative mid-term examination outcome to predict increases in depressed mood, primed pessimistic explanatory style for achievement events predicted depressive moods in negative outcome students both right after receipt of the mid-term examination grade and 4 days later.

Several researchers have proposed that a pessimistic explanatory style confers vulnerability to the development of a specific subtype of depression characterized by a unique symptom profile. It has been further hypothesized that more consistent support is likely to be obtained for the attributional vulnerability hypothesis if researchers assess the symptoms of this depressive subtype rather than depressive symptoms in general. Consistent with this hypothesis, in a 10-week longitudinal study of 174 university students, Metalsky and Joiner (1997) reported that a pessimistic explanatory style interacted with the occurrence of negative events to predict specific increases in hopelessness depression symptoms. Similarly, in a 1-month study of 100 university students, Alloy and Clements (1998) reported that a pessimistic explanatory style interacted with the occurrence of negative events to predict changes in hopelessness depression specifically. Finally, in a study of 108 nondepressed university students classified as at high or low risk for depression based on their explanatory style, Alloy *et al.* (1997) had participants provide daily reports for 28 days of life events as well as daily ratings of their highest, lowest, and average levels of symptoms of depression. High-risk participants exhibited higher levels, greater within-day variability, and greater across-days variability of hopelessness depression symptoms, but not other depression symptoms, than did low-risk participants. Further, the interaction of a pessimistic explanatory style and negative events predicted greater across-day variability in hopelessness depression symptoms but not other depression symptoms.

DEPRESSED ADULT PATIENTS

Although several studies have examined the effect of explanatory style on depressive symptoms in samples of adults suffering from clinically significant depression (Barber *et al.*, 2005; Dalgleish *et al.*, 2004; Ilardi *et al.*, 1997; Jacobson *et al.*, 1996), to our knowledge, only one study has examined this association in such a sample from within a vulnerability–stress perspective. In a 12-month multi-wave study of two samples, 36 adults diagnosed with a current major depressive episode and 66 adults diagnosed with a past major depressive episodes, Abela *et al.* (2006) reported that a more pessimistic explanatory style was associated with greater increases in depressive symptoms following the occurrence of negative events in both samples.

CHILDREN AND ADOLESCENTS

A large body of research has examined whether youth who possess a pessimistic explanatory style are more likely than other youth to experience increases in depressive symptoms following negative events. Several studies have provided full support for this hypothesis. In a 1-year longitudinal study of 521 third- through fifth-grade schoolchildren, Panak and Garber (1992) reported that a pessimistic explanatory style was associated with increases in depressive symptoms following the experience of peer rejection. In another longitudinal study of 439 fifth-and sixth-grade children, Hilsman and Garber (1995) reported that a pessimistic explanatory style predicted increases in depressed mood 5 days following, but not immediately after, receipt of an unsatisfactory report card. In a 1-month prospective study of 84 nine- to twelve-year olds referred to summer camp for academic, behavioral, or interpersonal problems, Dixon and Ahrens (1992) reported that a pessimistic explanatory style interacted with negative events to predict increases in depressive symptoms. In a 6-week prospective study of 319 ninth-grade students, Abela *et al.* (in press) reported that a pessimistic explanatory style interacted with negative events during the follow-up interval to predict increases in depressive symptoms. In a 2-month prospective study of 60 youth psychiatric inpatients, Joiner (2000) reported that a pessimistic explanatory style at the time of hospital admission was associated with increases in depressive symptoms 2 months after discharge among youth experiencing high, but not low levels of negative events.

Other studies using youth samples have provided only partial support for the attributional vulnerability hypothesis. Three studies comparing children at different stages of development have found support for the attributional vulnerability hypothesis in older but not younger children. (Abela, 2001; Gibb & Alloy, 2006; Nolen-Hoeksema *et al.*, 1986, 1992). Other studies have found the effect of explanatory style on depression in youth to vary as a function of initial level of depressive symptoms. For example, in a 6-week prospective study of 480 grade schoolchildren, Brozina and Abela (2006) reported that a pessimistic explanatory style was associated with increases in depressive symptoms following the occurrence of negative events in children possessing low, but not high, initial levels of symptoms.

As with university student samples, some studies have found the effect of explanatory style on depression in youth to vary as a function of youth's levels of self-esteem or self-competence. In a 5-month study of 239 sixth-grade children, Robinson *et al.* (1995) found that a pessimistic explanatory style in interaction with stressors that occurred during the transition from elementary to middle school predicted increases in depressive symptoms for youth possessing low, but not high, levels of self-perceived competence. In a 14-week study of grade students, Southall and Roberts (2002) reported that a pessimistic explanatory style and low self-esteem interacted to predict increases in depressive symptoms following negative events among adolescents possessing low, but not high, initial levels of symptoms. In a 1-month prospective study of 147 five- to ten-year old children, Conley *et al.* (2001) reported that a pessimistic attributional style was associated with increases in depressive symptoms among children aged 5–7 years, but not aged 8–10 years, with low but not high self-esteem.

Some studies have found the effect of explanatory style on depression in youth to vary as a function of gender. In a 17-month study of 158 adolescents, Prinstein and Aikens (2004) reported that a pessimistic explanatory style interacted with peer rejection to predict increases in depressive symptoms among girls, but not boys. In contrast, in a 5-week study of 270 ninth- through twelfth-grade students, Hankin *et al.* (2001) reported that a pessimistic explanatory style interacted with negative events occurring during the 5-week follow-up interval to predict increases in general depressive symptoms in boys, but not girls. At the same time, a pessimistic explanatory style was associated with increases in hopelessness depression symptoms following negative events in both boys and girls.

In contrast to the above results, three prospective studies using samples of 79 seventh-grade students (10 weeks; Abela & Sarin, 2002), 95 eleven- to thirteen-year olds (6 months; Bennett & Bates, 1995), and 773 eleven- to thirteen-year olds (12 months; Spence *et al.*, 2002) have reported that the interaction between a pessimistic explanatory style and negative events failed to predict change in depressive symptoms over time. Similarly, in a 6-month study of 79 eight- to sixteen-year olds with affectively ill, medically ill, or control parents, Hammen *et al.* (1988) reported that the interaction between a pessimistic explanatory style and negative events failed to predict the onset of depressive disorders in the 6-month follow-up interval. In a 1-year study of 1507 ninth- through twelfth-grade students, Lewinsohn *et al.* (2001) reported that a pessimistic explanatory style was associated with increased likelihood of experiencing the onset of a clinically significant depressive episode in the absence, but not the presence of, negative events.

MEDIATING PATHWAYS THROUGH WHICH EXPLANATORY STYLE PREDICTS DEPRESSION

Most of the studies that examined the pathways through which explanatory style predicts depression following the occurrence of negative events have focused on specific causal inferences and/or negative outcome/helplessness expectancies as mediators of this association. Individuals who exhibit a pessimistic explanatory style have been found to be more likely than other individuals to make internal, global, and stable causal attributions for the negative life events they encounter, and this attributional pattern has in turn been found to predict increases in depressive symptoms over time (Follette & Jacobson, 1987; Metalsky *et al.*, 1987; Swendsen, 1997). Finally, after controlling for the effect of specific causal attributions made for real life stressors on depressive symptoms, the effect of explanatory style on depression has been found to be significantly reduced (Metalsky *et al.*, 1987; for an exception see Swendsen, 1997).

A pessimistic explanatory style has been associated with increases in negative outcome and helplessness expectancies (i.e., hopelessness) following the occurrence of negative events (Abela, 2002; Alloy & Clements, 1998; Metalsky & Joiner, 1992; Metalksy *et al.*, 1993; for exceptions see Abela, 2001; Ralph & Mineka, 1998). Increases in hopelessness have also been associated with increases in depressive symptoms over time (Abela, 2001, 2002; Alloy & Clements, 1998; Metalsky & Joiner, 1992; Metalksy *et al.*, 1993). Finally, after controlling for the effect of hopelessness on depressive symptoms, the effect of explanatory style has been found to be significantly reduced (Abela, 2002; Alloy & Clements, 1998; Metalsky & Joiner, 1992; Metalksy *et al.*, 1993; for exceptions see Abela, 2001; Ralph & Mineka, 1998).

A small handful of studies have examined whether explanatory style impacts the manner in which individuals cope with the stressors that they experience in their lives as well as the emotions triggered by such stressors. Results have been contrary to theoretical predictions. For example, Follette and Jacobson (1987) reported that university students with a pessimistic explanatory style reported they would spend more time preparing for subsequent examinations than did university students with an optimistic explanatory style, following unsatisfactory performance on a mid-term examination. In contrast, other studies have reported that maladaptive coping strategies mediate the association between explanatory style and increases in depressive symptoms following the occurrence of stressors. For example, Spasojevic and Alloy (2001) reported that rumination mediated the association between a pessimistic explanatory style and subsequent of major depressive episodes.

RELATIONSHIP BETWEEN DISPOSITIONAL OPTIMISM AND EXPLANATORY STYLE

Although the bulk of research that has examined the association between dispositional optimism and depressive symptoms has been conducted independently of research examining the association between explanatory style and depressive symptoms, on a theoretical level, there are several reasons to expect that dispositional optimism and explanatory style are related. An examination of the studies that have assessed both predictor variables confirms that moderate-to-strong associations between these two variables have been observed (e.g., Gillham *et al.*, 2002; Hjelle *et al.*, 1996; Scheier & Carver, 1992).

THEORETICAL PERSPECTIVES

The theoretical work of both Scheier and colleagues (Scheier & Carver, 1985, 1992; Scheier *et al.*, 2002) and Abramson *et al.* (1978, 1989) identifies expectations about the future as critical in the development of depressive symptoms, although the hypothesized content of such expectations differs across these theories. Whereas Scheier and colleagues focus on negative outcome expectancies, Abramson and colleagues focus on the fusion of negative outcome expectancies and helplessness expectancies. In addition, although both theories posit that expectancies play a role in the etiology of depression, they assign different types of causal status to such expectations. Within the context of Scheier and colleagues' model, pessimistic expectations about the future represent a distal, contributory cause of depression as they are conceptualized as a relatively enduring, stable, individual difference variable. Abramson and colleagues' model views negative outcome and helplessness expectancies as a proximal sufficient cause of depression. In other words, such expectancies are viewed to play a role in triggering the onset of depressive symptoms in the "here and now" and are hypothesized to be the cognitive product of more stable, enduring cognitive vulnerabilities.

Within the context of the reformulated learned helplessness and hopelessness theories, explanatory style is hypothesized to play a contributory role in the development of expectations about the future. Individuals who possess a pessimistic style are hypothesized to be more likely than other individuals to develop negative outcome and helplessness expectancies. At the same time, the reformulated learned helplessness and hopelessness theories hypothesize that explanatory style is one of many pathways that lead to the development of negative outcome and helplessness expectancies. For example, the reformulated learned helplessness theory highlights how contextual factors (e.g., consensus and consistency information) may promote the development of such expectancies. The hopelessness theory proposes that negative cognitive styles about consequences and the self also predict the development of depression through the mediating role of negative outcome and helplessness expectancies. Finally, the hopelessness theories acknowledge that other cognitive-interpersonal models, such as Brown and Harris' (1978) self-esteem theory, propose psychosocial vulnerabilities other than explanatory style which predict depression through the mediating role of hopelessness. Since the development of expectations is multi-factorial, we would expect the association between explanatory style and expectancies about the future to only be modest to moderate in magnitude.

EMPIRICAL OBSERVATIONS

Few studies have examined the strength of the association between dispositional optimism and explanatory style. In a review of their prior work on dispositional optimism, Scheier and Carver (1992) reported that the correlation between the LOT and ASQ ranged from the high teens to the low twenties. At the same time, they provide no citations for these studies; nor do they provide characteristics of the samples in which such correlations were observed. In a sample of university students, Hjelle *et al.* (1996) reported the correlation between LOT and ASQ scores to be 0.41. Similarly, in a two-time point study of university students, Gillham *et al.* (2002) reported the correlation between these two measures to be 0.63 and 0.41 at the initial and follow-up assessments, respectively. At the same time, after correcting for attenuation, these correlations rose to 0.77 and 0.49, respectively.

Although moderate-to-high correlations have been observed in most studies of the association between dispositional optimism and explanatory style, there are exceptions. In a study of community dwelling older adults, Isaacowitz and Seligman (2001) found LOT and ASQ scores to be uncorrelated. Similarly, in a series of three studies examining the convergent and predictive validity of measures of optimism and pessimism, Reilley *et al.* (2005) reported the strength of the association between the LOT and the ASQ to be only modest. Further research is needed to examine the factors that influence the degree of inter-relatedness among these two constructs.

DIRECTIONS FOR FUTURE RESEARCH

As this chapter illustrates, although inconsistencies in the findings of studies clearly exist, there is convincing evidence that both dispositional optimism and explanatory style play a role in the development of depression across the lifespan. Although more research is needed in order to understand the parameters of these relations in explaining the onset, maintenance, remission, and recurrence of depression, it seems safe to conclude that both dispositional optimism and explanatory style, particularly in interaction with negative events, play an important role in the development of depression. At the same time, much additional research is needed to develop a more comprehensive understanding of the role of optimism/pessimism in the development of depression – particularly research addressing the following issues.

First, research is needed to identify both the common and the unique components of the constructs of *optimism* and *pessimism*. Optimism and pessimism are viewed as opposite poles of the same dispositional continuum. Researchers and theorists have argued, however, that this perspective results in a lack of attention to important distinctions between these constructs (Chang, 1998c; Chang *et al.*, 1994). For example, an individual who expects that good outcomes will occur does not necessarily expect that bad outcomes will not occur. Chang *et al.*,

(1994) recommend the term "optimism" to refer to expectations about positive outcomes and "pessimism" to refer to expectations about negative outcomes. Such an approach treats optimism and pessimism as relatively independent constructs. Consistent with such an approach, as noted earlier, research examining the factor analytic structure of the LOT has shown that it consists of two factors, which correspond to the positively and negatively worded items respectively (Chang, 1998c; Chang *et al.*, 1994). At the same time, contrary to such an approach, positive and negative factors are strongly correlated with one another.

Similarly, in the literature examining explanatory style, optimism and pessimism are viewed as opposite poles of the same continuum. Although it is not possible for an individual to exhibit both an optimistic and a pessimistic explanatory style for negative events, it is possible for an individual to exhibit a pessimistic explanatory style for negative events (i.e., attribute negative events to internal, global, and stable causes) and an optimistic explanatory style for positive events (i.e., attribute positive events to internal, global, and stable causes). Consistent with this possibility, explanatory style for negative and positive events has been found to be either uncorrelated or only modestly correlated (see review by Peterson, 1991). Research also suggests that explanatory styles for negative and positive events have different correlates and predict different outcomes. For example, explanatory style for negative events predicts the development of depression whereas explanatory style for positive events has been found to predict recovery from depression (e.g., Needles & Abramson, 1990).

Second, explanatory style has been posited to be a multi-dimensional construct. The dimensions of internality–externality, globality–specificity, and stability–instability have been the most commonly examined dimensions. In the prediction of depression, however, it has become common practice to collapse data across these three dimensions. Such an approach has been questioned given the relatively low correlations typically observed among the different dimensions and research that suggests that the different dimensions may be related to different types of outcomes (Peterson, 1991). For example, it has been suggested that the globality and stability dimensions carry greater weight in the development of the syndrome of depression (Abramson *et al.*, 1989), whereas the internality dimension may carry greater weight in the prediction of specific symptoms of depression such as worthlessness or increased dependency. More research is needed to identify both the central dimensions of explanatory style and their relative degrees of importance in the prediction of different physical and mental health outcomes. In contrast, research examining dispositional optimism has treated it as a unidimensional construct. At the same time, different dimensions of optimism may exist, which are differentially related to different outcomes. Research is needed to examine whether a multi-dimensional approach to dispositional optimism increases the explanatory power of the construct.

Third, the literature at times confuses both the constructs of dispositional optimism and the explanatory style as indices of optimism/pessimism. Although Peterson (1991) has presented arguments for researchers to use the terms "optimism" and "pessimism" when investigating explanatory style, others have questioned the use of the terms "optimism" and "pessimism" in conjunction with causal attributions because there are intuitive notions for these variables about expectations (Abramson *et al.*, 1991; Gillham *et al.*, 2002). These theorists and researchers have argued that, while optimism and pessimism are useful modifiers of the term "explanatory style," these terms used in isolation should be reserved for future expectancies.

Fourth, little research has examined the developmental changes between optimism/pessimism and depression over time, and the mechanisms underlying such associations. Although the current review suggests that both dispositional optimism and explanatory style confer vulnerability to depression across the lifespan, meaningful differences likely exist in the mechanisms through which these constructs predict depression at various stages of development, and how these constructs interact with environmental influences and other risk, vulnerability, and protective processes (see Abela & Hankin, 2008).

Research is also needed to examine the developmental processes that play a role in the development of dispositional optimism and explanatory style. There is support for at least five such pathways: (1) the experience of elevated levels of depressive symptoms (e.g., the scar hypothesis, Gibb *et al.*, 2006; Nolen-Hoeksema *et al.*, 1986, 1992), (2) repeated exposure to negative events occurring in multiple and likely interacting domains (i.e., family conflict, divorce, poverty; Garber & Flynn, 1998; Rudolph *et al.*, 2001), (3) childhood emotional maltreatment (Gibb & Alloy, 2006; Gibb *et al.*, 2006; Hankin, 2005), (4) maladaptive parenting practices (e.g., high levels of parental criticism, indifference, and control, low levels of parental acceptance and care; Bruce *et al.*, 2006), and (5) modeling of feedback provided to the child by the parent (Alloy *et al.*, 2001; Garber & Flynn, 2001, Turk & Bry, 1992; for exception, see Gibb *et al.*, 2006). Such pathways are likely influenced by even more distal risk factors for depression, including the presence of parental psychopathology, genetic inheritance, socio-cultural factors, and/or child temperament (Hankin & Abramson, 2001). Research that examines the impact of developmental processes on the associations between dispositional optimism, explanatory style, and prospective changes in depression should aim not only to uncover developmental differences early in life but also through later stages of development, including later in adulthood and in old age (e.g., Isaacowitz & Seligman, 2001).

Finally, although a large body of research links dispositional optimism and explanatory style with prospective change in depressive symptoms over time, research has yet to uncover the mechanisms underlying these associations. It is clear that negative events serve as powerful moderators of such associations – particularly with respect to the construct of explanatory style. It also appears that coping represents a potent mediator of such associations – particularly with respect to the construct of dispositional optimism. Future research aimed at the identification of additional moderators, and mediators of these associations will enrich our understanding of the pathways leading to the development of depression across the lifespan. Such research will benefit from more sophisticated research methodologies than the typical two-time point design, as such designs will likely enrich the questions that can be examined (i.e., idiographic vs. nomothetic approaches to analysis; Abela *et al.*, 2006) as well as increase the ecological validity of the data (i.e., experience sampling methodology; Abela *et al.* 2007; Abela & Scheffler, in press). Such research will also benefit from the integration of the constructs of optimism/pessimism with other vulnerability, risk, and protective factors. As the literature that examines these and other related questions accumulates, a stronger perspective on the etiology, maintenance, and recurrence of depression will emerge. This understanding will contribute to the development of empirically supported treatment approaches for use both in the treatment of acute episodes of depression and with prevention programs for those at risk.

REFERENCES

Abela, J. R. Z. (2001). The hopelessness theory of depression: A test of the diathesis-stress and causal mediation components in third and seventh grade children. *Journal of Abnormal Child Psychology*, *29*, 241–254.

Abela, J. R. Z. (2002). Depressive mood reactions to failure in the achievement domain: A test of the integration of the hopelessness and self-esteem theories of depression. *Cognitive Therapy and Research*, *26*, 531–552.

Abela, J. R. Z., & Brozina, K. (2004). The use of negative events to prime cognitive vulnerabilities to depression. *Cognitive Therapy and Research*, *28*, 209–227.

Abela, J. R. Z., & Hankin, B. L. (2008). Cognitive vulnerability to depression in children and adolescents: A developmental psychopathology perspective. In J. Abela, & B. L. Hankin (Eds.), *Handbook of Child and Adolescent Depression* (pp. 35–78). NY: Guilford Press.

Abela, J. R. Z., & Sarin, S. (2002). Cognitive vulnerability to hopelessness depression: A chain is only as strong as its weakest link. *Cognitive Therapy and Research*, *26*, 811–829.

Abela, J. R. Z. & Scheffler, P. (in press). Conceptualizing cognitive and interpersonal vulnerability to depression in youth: A comparison of the weakest link and additive approaches. *Journal of Cognitive Psychotherapy*.

Abela, J. R. Z., & Seligman, M. E. P. (2000). The hopelessness theory of depression: A test of the diathesis-stress component in the interpersonal and achievement domains. *Cognitive Therapy and Research*, *24*, 361–378.

Abela, J. R. Z., Brozina, K., & Seligman, M. E. P. (2004). A test of the integration of the activation hypothesis and the diathesis-stress component of the hopelessness theory of depression. *British Journal of Clinical Psychology*, *43*, 111–128.

Abela, J. R. Z., Aydin, C., & Auerbach, R. P. (2006). Operationalizing the "vulnerability" and "stress" components of the hopelessness theory of depression: A multi-wave longitudinal study. *Behavior Research and Therapy*, *44*, 1565–1583.

Abela, J. R. Z., Morrison, E. J. P., & Starrs, C. (2007). Excessive reassurance seeking, self-esteem, and depressive symptoms in children of affectively-ill parents: An experience sampling analysis. *Journal of Social and Clinical Psychology*, *26*, 837–857.

Abela, J. R Z., Parkinson, C., Stolow, D., & Starrs, C. (in press). A test of the integration of the hopelessness and response styles theories of depression in middle adolescence. *Journal of Clinical Child and Adolescent Psychology*.

Abramson, L. Y., Seligman, M. E. P., & Teasdale, J. (1978). Learned helplessness in humans: Critique and reformulation. *Journal of Abnormal Psychology*, *87*, 49–74.

Abramson, L. Y., Alloy, L. B., Metalsky, G. I. (1988a). The cognitive style questionnaire: A measure of the vulnerability featured in the hopelessness theory of depression. Unpublished manuscript, University of Wisconsin-Madison.

Abramson, L. Y., Alloy, L. B., & Metalsky, G. I. (1988b). The cognitive diathesis-stress theories of depression: Toward an adequate evaluation of the theories' validities. In L. B. Alloy (Ed.), *Cognitive Processes in Depression* (pp. 3–30). New York: Guilford.

Abramson, L. Y., Metalsky, G. I., & Alloy, L. B. (1989). Hopelessness depression: A theory-based subtype of depression. *Psychological Review*, *96*, 358–372.

Abramson, L. Y., Dykman, B. N., & Needles, D. J. (1991). Attributional style and theory: Let no one tear them asunder. *Psychological Inquiry*, *2*, 11–49.

Alloy, L. B., & Clements, C. M. (1998). Hopelessness theory of depression: Tests of the symptom component. *Cognitive Therapy and Research*, *22*, 303–335.

Alloy, L. B., Hartlage, S., & Abramson, L. Y. (1988). Testing the cognitive diathesis-stress theories of depression: Issues of research design, conceptualization, and assessment. In L. B. Alloy (Ed.), *Cognitive Processes in Depression* (pp. 31–73). New York: Guilford.

Alloy, L. B., Just, N., & Panzarella, C. (1997). Attributional style, daily life events, and hopelessness depression: Subtype validation by prospective variability and specificity of symptoms. *Cognitive Therapy and Research*, *21*, 221–244.

Alloy, L. B., Abramson, L. Y., Tashman, N. A., Berrebbi, D. S., Hogan, M. E., Whitehouse, W. G., Crossfield, A. G., & Morocco, A. (2001). Developmental origins of cognitive vulnerability to depression: Parenting, cognitive, and inferential feedback styles of the parents of individuals at high and low cognitive risk for depression. *Cognitive Therapy and Research*, *25*, 397–423.

Aspinwall, L. G., & Taylor, S. E. (1992). Modeling cognitive adaptation: A longitudinal investigation of the impact of individual differences and coping on college adjustment and performance. *Journal of Personality and Social Psychology*, *63*, 989–1003.

Barber, J. P., Abrams, M. J., Connolly-Gibbons, M. B., Crits-Christoph, P., Barrett, M. S., Rynn, M., & Siqueland, L. (1995). Contrib Title: Explanatory style change in supportive-expressive dynamic therapy. *Journal of Clinical Psychology*, *61*, 257–268.

Bennett, D. S., & Bates, J. E. (1995). Prospective models of depressive symptoms in early adolescence: Attributional style, stress, and support. *Journal of Early Adolescence*, *15*, 299–315.

Brissette, I., Scheier, M. F., & Carver, C. S. (2002). The role of optimism in social network development, coping, and psychological adjustment during a life transition. *Journal of Personality and Social Psychology*, *82*, 102–111.

Bromberger, J. T., & Matthews, K. A. (1996). A longitudinal study of the effects of pessimism, trait anxiety, and life stress on depressive symptoms in middle-aged women. *Psychology and Aging*, *11*, 207–213.

Brown, G. W., & Harris, T. (1978). *Social Origins of Depression*. London: Tavistock.

Brozina, K., & Abela, J. R. Z. (2006). Symptoms of hopelessness depression and anxiety in children: Specificity of the hopelessness theory. *Journal of Clinical Child and Adolescent Psychology*, *35*, 515–527.

Bruce, A. E., Cole, D. A., Dallaire, D. H., Jacquez, F. M., Pineda, A. Q., & LaGrange, B. (2006). Relation of parenting and negative life events to cognitive diatheses for depression in children. *Journal of Abnormal Child Psychology*, *34*, 321–333.

Carver, C. S., & Gaines, J. G. (1987). Optimism, pessimism, and postpartum depression. *Cognitive Therapy and Research*, *11*, 449–462.

Carver, C. S., & Scheier, M. F. (1990). Origins and functions of positive and negative affect: A control-process view. *Psychological Review*, *97*, 19–35.

Carver, C. S., Pozo, C., Harris, S. D., Noriega, V., Scheier, M. F., Robinson, D. S., Ketcham, A. S., Moffat, F. L., & Clark, K. C. (1993). How coping mediates the effect of optimism on distress: A study of women with early stage breast cancer. *Journal of Personality and Social Psychology*, *65*, 375–390.

Chamberlain, K., Petrie, K., & Azariah, R. (1992). The role of optimism and sense of coherence in predicting recovery following surgery. *Psychology and Health*, *7*, 301–310.

Chang, E. C. (1998a). Dispositional optimism and primary and secondary appraisal of a stressor: Controlling for confounding influences and relations to coping and psychological and physical adjustment. *Journal of Personality and Social Psychology*, *74*, 1109–1120.

Chang, E. C. (1998b). Does dispositional optimism moderate the relations between perceived stress and psychological well-being? A preliminary investigation. *Personality and Individual Differences, 25*, 233–240.

Chang, E. C. (1998c). Distinguishing between optimism and pessimism: A second look at the "optimism-neuroticism hypothesis". In R. R. Hoffman, M. F. Sherrik, & J. S. Warm (Eds.), *Viewing Psychology as a Whole: The Integrative Science of William N. Dember* (pp. 415–432). Washington, DC: American Psychological Association Press.

Chang, E. C., D'Zurilla, T. J., & Maydeau-Olivares, A. (1994). Assessing the dimensionality of optimism and pessimism using a multi-measure approach. *Cognitive Therapy and Research, 18*, 143–160.

Cohen, J. H. (1990). Community nurse executives' psychologic well-being: Relationships among stressors, social support, coping, and optimism. *Public Health Nursing, 7*, 194–203.

Conley, C. S., Haines, B. A., Hilt, L. M., & Metalsky, G. I. (2001). The children's attributional style interview: Developmental tests of cognitive diathesis-stress theories of depression. *Journal of Abnormal Child Psychology, 29*, 445–463.

Cozzarelli, C. (1993). Personality and self-efficacy as predictors of coping with abortion. *Journal of Personality and Social Psychology, 65*, 1224–1236.

Curbow, B., Somerfield, M. R., Baker, F., Wingard, J. R., & Legro, M. W. (1993). Personal changes, dispositional optimism, and psychological adjustment to bone marrow transplantation. *Journal of Behavioral Medicine, 16*, 423–443.

Dalgleish, T., Spinks, H., Golden, A., & du Toit, P. (2004). Processing of emotional information in seasonal depression across different cognitive measures. *Journal of Abnormal Psychology, 113*, 116–126.

Dixon, J. F., & Ahrens, A. H. (1992). Stress and attributional styles as predictors of self-reported depression in children. *Cognitive Therapy and Research, 16*, 623–634.

Fitzgerald, T. E., Tennen, H., Affleck, G., & Pransky, G. S. (1993). The relative importance of dispositional optimism and control appraisals in quality of life after coronary artery bypass surgery. *Journal of Behavioral Medicine, 16*, 25–43.

Follette, V. M., & Jacobson, N. S. (1987). Importance of attributions as a predictor of how people cope with failure. *Journal of Personality and Social Psychology, 52*, 1205–1211.

Fontaine, K. R., & Jones, L. C. (1997). Self-esteem, optimism, and postpartum depression. *Journal of Clinical Psychology, 53*, 59–63.

Fresco, D. M., Alloy, L. B., & Reilly-Harrington, N. (2006). Association of attributional style for negative and positive events and the occurrence of life events with depression and anxiety. *Journal of Social and Clinical Psychology, 25*, 1140–1159.

Garber, J., & Flynn, C. (1998). Origins of the depressive cognitive style. In D. Routh, & R. J. DeRebeis (Eds.), *The Science of Clinical Psychology: Evidence of a Century's Progress* (pp. 53–93). Washington, DC: American Psychological Association.

Garber, J., & Flynn, C. (2001). Predictors of depressive cognitions in young adolescents. *Cognitive Therapy and Research, 25*, 353–376.

Gibb, B. E., & Alloy, L. B. (2006). A prospective test of the hopelessness theory of depression in children. *Journal of Clinical Child and Adolescent Psychology, 35*, 264–274.

Gibb, B. E., Alloy, L. B., Walshaw, P. D., Comer, J. S., Shen, G. H. C., & Villari, A. G. (2006). Predictors of attributional style change in children. *Journal of Abnormal Child Psychology, 34*, 425–439.

Gillham, J. E., Shatté, A. J., Reivich, K. J., & Seligman, M. E. P. (2002). Optimism, pessimism, and explanatory style. In E. C. Chang (Ed.), *Optimism and Pessimism: Implications for Theory, Research, and Practice* (pp. 53–74). Washington, DC: APA Press.

Giltay, E. J., Zitman, F. G., & Kromhout, D. (2007). Dispositional optimism and the risk of depressive symptoms during 15 years of follow-up: The Zutphen elderly study. *Journal of Affective Disorders, 91*, 45–52.

Given, C. W., Stommel, M., Given, B., Osuch, J., Kurtz, M. E., & Kurtz, J. C. (1993). The influence of cancer patients' symptoms and functional states on patients' depression and family caregivers' reaction and depression. *Health Psychology, 12*, 277–285.

Goetzmann, L., Klaghofer, R., Wagner-Huber, R., Halter, J., Boehler, A., Muellhaupt, B., Schanz, U., Buddeberg, C. (2007). *Journal of Psychosomatic Research, 62*, 93–100.

Grote, N. K., & Bledsoe, S. E. (2007). Predicting postpartum depressive symptoms in new mothers: The role of optimism and stress frequency during pregnancy. *Health & Social Work, 32*, 107–118.

Hammen, C. L., Adrian, C., & Hiroto, D. (1988). A longitudinal test of the attributional vulnerability model of depression in children at risk for depression. *British Journal of Clinical Psychology, 27*, 37–46.

Hankin, B. L. (2005). Childhood maltreatment and psychopathology: Prospective tests of attachment, cognitive vulnerability, and stress as mediating processes. *Cognitive Therapy and Research, 29*, 645–671.

Hankin, B. L., & Abramson, L. Y. (2001). Development of sex differences in depression: An elaborated cognitive vulnerability-transactional stress theory. *Psychological Bulletin, 127*, 773–796.

Hankin, B. L., Abramson, L. Y., & Siler, M. (2001). A prospective test of the hopelessness theory of depression in adolescence. *Cognitive Therapy and Research, 25*, 607–632.

Herman-Stahl, M., & Petersen, A. C. (1996). The protective role of coping and social resources for depressive symptoms among young adolescents. *Journal of Youth and Adolescence, 25*, 733–753.

Hilsman, R., & Garber, J. (1995). A test of the cognitive diathesis-stress model of depression in children: Academic stressors, attributional style, perceived competence, and control. *Journal of Personality and Social Psychology, 69*, 370–380.

Hjelle, L., Belongia, C., & Nesser, J. (1996). Psychometric properties of the life orientation test and attributional style questionnaire. *Psychological Reports, 78*, 507–515.

Hunsley, J. (1989). Vulnerability to depressed mood: An examination of the temporal consistency of the reformulated learned helplessness model. *Cognitive Therapy and Research, 13*, 599–608.

Ilardi, S. S., Craighead, W. E., & Evans, D. D. (1997). Modeling relapse in unipolar depression: The effects of dysfunctional cognitions and personality disorders. *Journal of Consulting and Clinical Psychology, 65*, 381–391.

Ironson, G., Balbin, E., Stuetzle, R., Fletcher, M. A., O'Cleirigh, C., Laurenceau, J. P., Schneiderman, N., & Solomon, G. (2005) Dispositional optimism and the mechanisms by which it predicts slower disease progression in HIV: Proactive behavior, avoidant coping, and depression. *International Journal of Behavioral Medicine, 12*, 86–97.

Isaacowitz, D. M., & Seligman, M. E. P. (2001). Is pessimistic explanatory style a risk factor for depressive mood among community-dwelling older adults? *Behaviour Research and Therapy, 39*, 255–272.

Jackson, L. M., Pratt, M. W., Hunsberger, B , & Pancer, S. M. (2005). Optimism as a mediator of the relation between perceived parental authoritativeness and adjustment among adolescents: Finding the sunny side of the street. *Social Development, 14*, 273–304.

Jacobson, N. S., Dobson, K. S., Truax, P. A., Addis, M. E., Koerner, K., Gollan, J. K., Grtner, E., & Prince, S. E. (1996). A component analysis of cognitive-behavioral treatment for depression. *Journal of Consulting and Clinical Psychology, 64*, 295–304.

Johnson, J. E. (1992). Gender and mood as mediators of the relationship between attributional style, daily life events, depressive symptoms, and hopelessness. *Cognitive Therapy and Research, 16*, 623–634.

Johnson, J. E. (1996). Coping with radiation therapy: Optimism and the effect of preparatory interventions. *Research in Nursing and Health, 19*, 3–12.

Joiner, T. E., Jr (2000). A test of the hopelessness theory of depression in youth psychiatric inpatients. *Journal of Clinical Child Psychology, 29*, 167–176.

King, K. B., Rowe, M. A., Kimble, L. P., & Zerwic, J. J. (1998). Optimism, coping, and long-term recovery from coronary artery surgery in women. *Research in Nursing & Health, 21*, 15–26.

Kwon, P., & Laurenceau, J. (2002). A longitudinal study of the hopelessness theory of depression: Testing the diathesis-stress model within a differential reactivity and exposure framework. *Journal of Clinical Psychology*, *58*, 1305–1321.

Lewinsohn, P. M., Joiner, T. E., & Rohde, P. (2001). Evaluation of cognitive diathesis-stress models in predicting major depressive disorder in adolescents. *Journal of Abnormal Psychology*, *110*, 203–215.

Long, B. C., & Sangster, J. I. (1993). Dispositional optimism/pessimism and coping strategies: Predictors of psychosocial adjustment of rheumatoid and osteoarthritis patients. *Journal of Applied Social Psychology*, *23*, 1069–1091.

Lyons, K. S., Stewart, B. J., Archbold, P. G., Carter, J. H., & Perrin, N. A. (2004). Pessimism and optimism as early warning signs for compromised health for caregivers of patients with Parkinson's Disease. *Nursing Research*, *53*, 354–362.

Major, B., Richards, C., Cooper, M. L., Cozzarelli, C., & Zubeck, J. (1998). Personal resilience, cognitive appraisals, and coping: An integrative model of adjustment to abortion. *Journal of Personality and Social Psychology*, *74*, 735–752.

Metalsky, G. I., & Joiner, T. E., Jr (1992). Vulnerability to depressive symptomatology: A prospective test of the diathesis-stress and causal mediation components of the hopelessness theory of depression. *Journal of Personality and Social Psychology*, *63*, 667–675.

Metalsky, G. I., & Joiner, T. E., Jr (1997). The hopelessness depression symptom questionnaire. *Cognitive Therapy and Research*, *21*, 359–384.

Metalsky, G. I., Halberstadt, L. J., & Abramson, L. Y. (1987). Vulnerability to depressive mood reactions: Toward a more powerful test of the diathesis-stress and causal mediation components of the reformulated theory of depression. *Journal of Personality and Social Psychology*, *52*, 386–393.

Metalksy, G. I., Joiner, T. E., Jr, Hardin, T. S., & Abramson, L. Y. (1993). Depressive reactions to failure in a naturalistic setting: A test of the hopelessness and self-esteem theories of depression. *Journal of Abnormal Psychology*, *102*, 101–109.

Needles, D. J., & Abramson, L. Y. (1990). Positive life events, attributional style, and hopefulness: Testing a model of recovery from depression. *Journal of Abnormal Psychology*, *99*, 156–165.

Nolen-Hoeksema, S., Girgus, J. S., & Seligman, M. E. P. (1986). Learned helplessness in children: A longitudinal study of depression, achievement, and attributional style. *Journal of Personality and Social Psychology*, *51*, 435–442.

Nolen-Hoeksema, S., Girgus, J. S., & Seligman, M. E. P. (1992). Predictors and consequences of childhood depressive symptoms: A five-year longitudinal study. *Journal of Abnormal Psychology*, *101*, 405–422.

O'Connor, R. C., & Cassidy, C. (2007). Predicting hopelessness: The interaction between optimism/pessimism and specific future expectancies. *Cognition and Emotion*, *21*, 596–613.

Oxford Pocket American Dictionary of Current English (2007). Oxford: Oxford University Press.

Panak, W. F., & Garber, J. (1992). Role of aggression, rejection, and attributions in the prediction of depression in children. *Development and Psychopathology*, *4*, 145–165.

Persons, J. B., & Miranda, J. (1992). Cognitive theories of vulnerability to depression: Reconciling negative evidence. *Cognitive Therapy and Research*, *16*, 485–502.

Peterson, C. (1991). The meaning and measurement of explanatory style. *Psychological Inquiry*, 2, 1–10.

Peterson, C., & Villanova, P. (1988). An expanded attributional style questionnaire. *Journal of Abnormal Psychology*, *97*, 87–89.

Peterson, C., Semmel, A., von Baeyer, C., Abramson, L. Y., Metalsky, G., & Seligman, M. E. P. (1982). The attributional style questionnaire. *Cognitive Therapy and Research*, *6*, 287–300.

Prinstein, M. J., & Aikens, J. W. (2004). Cognitive moderators of the longitudinal association between peer rejection and adolescent depressive symptoms. *Journal of Abnormal Child Psychology*, *32*, 147–158.

Puskar, K. R., Sereika, S. M., Lamb, J., Tusaie-Mumford, K., & McGuinness, T. (1999). Optimism and its relationship to depression, coping, anger, and life events in rural adolescents. *Issues in Mental Health Nursing*, *20*, 115–130.

Ralph, J. A., & Mineka, S. (1998). Attributional style and self-esteem: The prediction of emotional distress following a midterm exam. *Journal of Abnormal Psychology*, *107*, 203–215.

Reilley, S. P., Geers, A. L., Lindsay, D. L., Deronde, L., & Dember, W. M. (2005). Convergence and predictive validity in measures of optimism and pessimism: Sequential studies. *Current Psychology, 24*, 43–59.

Robinson, N. S., Garber, J., & Hilsman, R. (1995). Cognitions and stress: Direct and moderating effects on depressive versus externalizing symptoms during the junior high school transition. *Journal of Abnormal Psychology, 104*, 453–463.

Rudolph, K. D., Kurlakowsky, K. D., & Conley, C. S. (2001). Developmental and social-contextual origins of depressive control-related beliefs and behavior. *Cognitive Therapy and Research, 25*, 447–475.

Ruiz, J. M., Matthews, K. A., Scheier, M. F., & Schulz, R. (2006). Does who you marry matter for your health? Influence of patients' and spouses' personality on their partners' psychological well-being following coronary artery bypass surgery. *Journal of Personality and Social Psychology, 91*, 255–267.

Scheier, M. F., & Carver, C. S. (1985). Optimism, coping, and health: Assessment and implications of generalized outcome expectancies. *Health Psychology, 4*, 219–247.

Scheier, M. F., & Carver, C. S. (1988). A model of behavioral self-regulation: Translating intention into action. In L. Berkowitz (Ed.), *Advances in Experimental Social Psychology* (pp. 303–346). San Diego: Academic Press.

Scheier, M. F., & Carver, C. S. (1992). Effects of optimism on psychological and physical well-being: Theoretical overview and empirical update. *Cognitive Therapy and Research, 16*, 201–228.

Scheier, M. F., Weintraub, J. K., & Carver, C. S. (1986). Coping with stress: Divergent strategies of optimists and pessimists. *Journal of Personality and Social Psychology, 51*, 1257–1264.

Scheier, M. F., Matthews, K. A., Owens, J. F., Magovern, G. J., Lefebvre, R. C., Abbot, R. A., & Carver, C. S. (1989). Dispositional optimism and recovery from coronary artery bypass surgery: The beneficial effects on physical and psychological well-being. *Journal of Personality and Social Psychology, 57*, 1024–1040.

Scheier, M. F., Carver, C. S., & Bridge, M. W. (1994). Distinguishing optimism from neuroticism (and trait anxiety, self-mastery, and self-esteem): A reevaluation of the life orientation test. *Journal of Personality and Social Psychology, 67*, 1063–1078.

Scheier, M. F., Carver, C. S., & Bridge, M. W. (2002). Optimism, pessimism, and psychological well-being. In E. C. Chang (Ed.), *Optimism and Pessimism: Implications for Theory, Research, and Practice* (pp. 189–216). Washington, DC: American Psychological Association Press.

Schou, I., Ekeberg, O., Rulan, C. M., Sandvik, L., & Karesen, R. (2004). Pessimism as a predictor of emotional morbidity one year following breast cancer surgery. *Psycho-Oncology, 13*, 309–320.

Schuller, I. S. (1995). Cognitive style categorization width and anxiety. *Studia Psycholgica, 37*, 142–145.

Segerstrom, S. C., Taylor, S. E., Kemeny, M. E., & Fahey, J. L. (1998). Optimism is associated with mood, coping, and immune change in response to stress. *Journal of Personality and Social Psychology, 74*, 1646–1655.

Seligman, M. E. P., Peterson, C., Kaslow, N. J., Tenenbaum, R. L., Alloy, L. B., & Abramson, L. Y. (1984). Attributional style and depressive symptoms among children. *Journal of Abnormal Psychology, 93*, 235–241.

Shen, B. J., McCreary, C., & Myers, H. F. (2004). Independent and mediated contributions of personality, coping, social support, and depressive symptoms to physical functioning outcome among patients in cardiac rehabilitation. *Journal of Behavioral Medicine, 27*, 39–62.

Southall, D., & Roberts, J. E. (2002). Attributional style and self-esteem in vulnerability to adolescent depressive symptoms following life stress: A 14-week prospective study. *Cognitive Therapy and Research, 26*, 563–579.

Spasojevic, J., & Alloy, L. B. (2001). Rumination as a common mechanism relating depressive risk factors to depression. *Emotion, 1*, 25–37.

Spence, S. H., Sheffield, J., & Donovan, C. (2002). Problem-solving orientation and attributional style: Moderators of the impact of negative life events on the development of depressives in adolescence? *Journal of Clinical Child Psychology, 31*, 219–229.

Stewart, S. M., Betson, C., Lam, T. H., Marshall, I. B., Lee, P. W. H., & Wong, C. M. (1997). Predicting stress in first year medical students: A longitudinal study. *Medical Education*, 31, 163–168.

Swendsen, J. D. (1997). Anxiety, depression, and their comorbidity: An experience sampling test of the hopelessness theory. *Cognitive Therapy and Research, 21*, 97–114.

Tallman, B. A., Altmaier, E., & Garcia, C. (2007). Finding benefit from cancer. *Journal of Counseling Psychology, 54*, 481–487.

Taylor, S. E., Kemeny, M., Aspinwall, L., Scheider, S., Rodriquez, R., & Herbert, M. (1992). Optimism, coping, psychological distress, and high-risk sexual behavior among men at risk for AIDS. *Journal of Personality and Social Psychology, 63*, 460–473.

The American Heritage Dictionary of the English Language (4th ed.). (2000). Boston: Houghton Mifflin Company.

Turk, E., & Bry, B. (1992). Adolescents' and parents' explanatory styles and parents' causal explanations about their adolescents. *Cognitive Therapy and Research, 16*, 349–357.

10

Ruminative Response Style

Blair E. Wisco and
Susan Nolen-Hoeksema

Department of Psychology, Yale University, New Haven, CT

Rumination has been defined as a mode of responding to distress by passively focusing on the possible causes and consequences of one's distress without moving into active problem-solving (Nolen-Hoeksema, 1991). Content analyses show that when ruminating, distressed people think about how badly they feel and the problems they face in a repetitive fashion (Lyubomirsky *et al.*, 1999). The content of ruminative thought is typically negative in valence, and rumination is associated with a number of other maladaptive cognitive styles, including dysfunctional attitudes, neuroticism, and pessimism (see Nolen-Hoeksema *et al.*, in press). However, rumination continues to be related to depression even after statistically controlling for these other cognitive styles (e.g., Nolen-Hoeksema *et al.*, 1994). Moreover, we define rumination as characterized by its style rather than its content. Rumination is conceptualized as a pattern of thought and is distinguished from other forms of depressive cognition by its perseverative nature.

Much of the research investigating depressive rumination is based on the *response styles theory* (Nolen-Hoeksema, 1991), which proposes that, while almost everyone ruminates at one time or another, a subset of individuals tend to respond to distress often with rumination and can be described as having a ruminative response style. As we review below, the ruminative response style is correlated with depressive symptoms and predicts the development of future depressive episodes. Gender is also related to rumination, with more women than men reporting a tendency to ruminate in response to distress. Indeed, the response styles theory was proposed in part to explain the greater prevalence of depression in women than in men, and the gender difference in rumination has been shown to mediate the gender difference in depression (e.g., Nolen-Hoeksema *et al.*, 1999).

A ruminative response style is thought to increase risk for depression through a variety of mechanisms (Nolen-Hoeksema, 1991). As reviewed below, rumination leads to several depressogenic cognitive, motivational, and interpersonal outcomes, including more negative thinking and memory, impaired concentration and overgeneral memory recall, inhibition of instrumental behavior, impaired interpersonal problem-solving, and reduced social support. Recent evidence also suggests that in addition to depression, rumination increases risk for anxiety and for escapist behaviors including binge eating and alcohol abuse (Nolen-Hoeksema *et al.*, 2007).

In the following chapter, we review the evidence that a ruminative response style increases risk for depression, describe the proposed mechanisms by which rumination increases this risk, argue that the increased risk is not specific to depression but generalizes to other forms of psychopathology, and discuss possible treatment implications.

EVIDENCE OF RISK FOR DEPRESSION

A body of longitudinal research indicates that a tendency to respond to distress with rumination, or a ruminative response style, increases the risk of developing depressive symptoms in the future. Ruminative response style is typically assessed using the 22-item Ruminative Response Scale of the Response Styles Questionnaire (RSQ; Nolen-Hoeksema & Morrow, 1991). Respondents are asked to indicate how often they engage in different ruminative thoughts or behaviors when they feel down, sad, or depressed. The ruminative thoughts include responses to sad mood that are self-focused (e.g., I think "Why do I react this way?"), symptom-focused (e.g., I think about how hard it is to concentrate), and focused on the possible consequences and causes of one's mood (e.g., I think "I won't be able to do my job if I don't snap out of this"). As assessed by this scale, ruminative response style is a relatively stable individual difference across time, even among individuals who experience significant decreases in depressive symptoms (Bagby *et al.*, 2004; Just & Alloy, 1997; Kuehner & Weber, 1999; Nolen-Hoeksema & Davis, 1999; Nolen-Hoeksema *et al.*, 1993; Nolen-Hoeksema *et al.*, 1994). Prospective, longitudinal research, mostly in community samples, indicates that individuals with ruminative response styles are more likely to develop depressive disorders in the future and to experience more severe depressive symptoms (Abela *et al.*, 2002; Just & Alloy, 1997; Kuehner & Weber, 1999; Nolan *et al.*, 1998; Nolen-Hoeksema, 2000; Nolen-Hoeksema *et al.*, 1993, 1994, 1999, 2007; Sarin *et al.*, 2005; Schwartz & Koenig, 1996; Segerstrom *et al.*, 2000; Spasojevic & Alloy, 2001; Wood *et al.*, 1990).

Because rumination is conceptualized as a repetitive focus on one's distress, the Ruminative Response Scale of the RSQ includes several items assessing thoughts about depressive symptoms (e.g., "Think about how sad you feel," "Think about your feelings of fatigue and achiness"). Measures of depressive symptoms, such as the Beck Depression Inventory, assess the presence of these symptoms, whereas the RSQ measures repetitive thinking about these symptoms. The similarity of these constructs creates considerable overlap in the item content of measures of depressive symptoms and the RSQ (e.g., Cox *et al.*, 2001; Roberts *et al.*, 1998; Segerstrom *et al.*, 2000; Treynor *et al.*, 2003). The observed relationship between rumination and depressive symptoms could be an artifact of this item content overlap, rather than a true relationship between the experiences of rumination and depression. To address this possibility, Treynor *et al.* (2003) modified the Ruminative Response Scale of the RSQ by removing all items containing overlap with measures of depressive symptoms, and conducted a factor analysis of the remaining items. They found two factors, reflection and brooding. Reflection contained items corresponding to a more neutral contemplation (e.g., "Go someplace alone to analyze your feelings"), whereas brooding refers to a more "moody," passive form of contemplation (e.g., Think "Why do I have problems other people don't have?"). Both factors significantly predicted concurrent and future depressive symptoms, with brooding emerging as the stronger predictor. A similar approach was taken by Roberts *et al.* (1998), who conducted a factor analysis on the Ruminative Response Scale and found a three factor solution, with one factor corresponding to thoughts of depressive symptoms, and two other factors which they named Introspection/Self-isolation and Self-blame. Because they found that depressed individuals scored significantly higher than nondepressed individuals on all three factors, they concluded that the relationship between depression and rumination is not due to item overlap. Segerstrom *et al.* (2000) also removed potentially confounding items from the Ruminative Response Scale, and found a significant relationship between the remaining rumination items and concurrent depressive symptoms. Therefore, the relationship between rumination and depression risk does not appear to be driven by item content overlap, because the relationship between rumination and depressive symptoms persists even after removing potentially problematic items.

Most of the studies investigating ruminative response style as a risk factor for depression have utilized change scores in continuous measures of depressive symptoms, which cannot distinguish between new onsets and prolonged duration of depressive episodes. A few studies have differentiated the increased risk of depression onset vs. maintenance resulting from a ruminative response style. Some of these studies find that rumination predicts onsets, but not maintenance, of major depression. For example, Nolen-Hoeksema (2000) found that over a period of 1 year, rumination predicted new onsets of major depressive episodes, as assessed by the Structured Clinical Interview for the DSM-IV, but did not predict episode duration for those already experiencing major depression at the initial assessment. Just and Alloy (1997) found that rumination predicted new onsets, but not duration, of depressive episodes over a period of 18 months. Lara *et al.* (2000) also found that rumination did not predict episode duration over a 6-month period in college students currently experiencing a major depressive episode.

The effect of baseline rumination on episode duration in patients receiving treatment for major depression has also been investigated extensively (Arnow *et al.*, 2004; Bagby & Parker, 2001; Park *et al.*, 2004; Schmaling *et al.*, 2002). Although these studies also found that rumination did not predict episode duration, the results of such research must be interpreted with caution. Because antidepressant medications and psychotherapy likely reduce ruminative thoughts directly, pre-treatment rumination levels might not be expected to predict episode duration in this situation. Future research examining the effects of different pharmacological and psychosocial treatments on rumination, depressive symptoms, and the interaction between rumination and depressive symptoms would be beneficial.

Other studies *have* found that rumination predicts the duration of depressive episodes. Kuehner and Weber (1999) assessed rumination in patients at the end of their treatment for depression, and found that those with higher rumination scores were more likely to still be in an episode of major depression 3 months later, and to have higher levels of depression at 3 months post-discharge. Roberts *et al.* (1998) found that rumination retrospectively predicted duration of depressive symptoms. Individuals with histories of major depressive episodes, with symptoms lasting 2 weeks or longer, reported greater current rumination than individuals with histories of depressive symptoms lasting less than 2 weeks. Finally, two studies found that people who were both high on rumination and had negative cognitive styles had longer episodes of diagnosed depression (Ciesla & Roberts, 2002; Robinson & Alloy, 2003). These findings suggest that the combination of negatively biased, irrational thoughts with a passive and repetitive focus on such thoughts can maintain depressive symptoms.

Rumination may not consistently predict the duration of depression in people already meeting criteria for major depression because seriously depressed people may be relatively homogeneous for rumination, reducing variance in scores and thus reducing the statistical power for rumination to predict duration of depression. In addition, because rumination is likely to be correlated with initial levels of depression in already depressed participants, the typical procedure of statistically controlling for initial levels of depression in predicting duration of episodes further reduces the power of rumination to predict the duration of depressive symptoms.

Alternatively, the effects of rumination could truly be more pronounced for episode onset than duration. Rumination might cause moderate depressive symptoms to develop into a full blown major depressive episode. But once individuals are already experiencing an episode, self-perpetuating processes other than rumination emerge that determine the episode's duration. These processes could be cognitive, as in the activation of negative schemas (Beck, 1967). Interpersonal consequences of depression could also play a strong role in its maintenance (Joiner, 2002). Another possibility is that neurobiological functioning, such as the functioning of neurotransmitter systems or circadian rhythms, could change as individuals "cross the line" into major depression in ways that perpetuate episodes (Thase *et al.*, 2002).

Rumination has also been examined in the context of gender differences in depression. Women are about twice as likely as men to suffer depression (Kessler *et al.*, 1993). Nolen-Hoeksema (1991) suggested that one of many contributors to women's greater vulnerability to depression compared to men is that women are more likely than men to fall into a ruminative cycle. Self-report studies of rumination in adults have found that women are more likely to report ruminating (e.g., Butler & Nolen-Hoeksema, 1994; Nolen-Hoeksema *et al.*, 1994, 1999). These self-report studies are open to gendered response biases; however, Butler and Nolen-Hoeksema (1994) attempted to observe gender differences in responses to depressed mood in the laboratory. They induced a sad mood or a neutral mood in otherwise healthy college students, then gave them the option of focusing on and analyzing their mood or doing a non-emotion-focused task. Women overwhelmingly chose to focus on their moods, even when they were in a sad mood, whereas men chose the emotion-focused and non-emotion-focused tasks equally often. When Rusting and Nolen-Hoeksema (1998) induced an angry mood in participants, however, the majority of women chose to do the non-emotion-focused task, while more of the men chose to emotion-focus than to divert their attention away from their emotions. Thus, these studies suggest that women do choose to focus on their emotions when sad more than men do, but that when they are angry, women are less likely than men to focus on their emotions.

Women could have higher prevalence of depression compared to men because they have more first onsets, longer depressive episodes, or a greater recurrence of depression, or all of these. Data from several studies of adults (Eaton *et al.*, 1997; Keller & Shapiro, 1981; Kessler *et al.*, 1993) and children or adolescents (Hankin *et al.*, 1998; Kovacs, 2001) suggest that the gender difference is primarily due to a greater number of first onsets of depression, and not to gender differences in the duration or recurrence of depression. Interestingly, this parallels the findings that rumination predicts onsets of depression more consistently than the duration of depression. Thus, the original hypothesis in the response styles theory that women's greater tendency to ruminate compared to men leads them to have longer episodes of depression, and that this accounts for the gender difference in depression, has not been supported. But the findings that rumination predicts onsets more than the duration of depression, and that gender differences occur in onsets but not in duration of depression, suggest that rumination may play a role, albeit a different one than originally hypothesized, in the gender differences in depression.

In sum, rumination has consistently emerged as a risk factor for the development of depression. Prospective, longitudinal research, mostly in community samples, has shown that individuals with ruminative response styles are more likely to develop depressive disorders and to experience more severe depressive symptoms. Ruminative response style does not always predict the duration of depressive episodes, but does predict the onset of new episodes. The combination of negative cognitive styles and rumination may increase risk for prolonged depressive episodes. Women appear to have a greater tendency to ruminate compared to men, and this may contribute to the higher rate of depression in women compared to men.

PROPOSED MECHANISMS OF RISK

Rumination is proposed to lead to depression through several mechanisms: by exacerbating negative mood directly and through its depressogenic cognitive, motivational, and interpersonal consequences. Much of the experimental work investigating these consequences of rumination has been conducted using inductions developed by Nolen-Hoeksema and Morrow (1993). Participants are given prompts to focus their attention on their current feelings and life circumstances for 8 min (e.g., "Think about the level of motivation you feel right now," "Think about the long-term goals you have set"). Because the prompts themselves are emotionally neutral, they do not affect the mood of nondysphoric individuals. Given that individuals who are dysphoric or clinically depressed have more negative feelings and more negative associations with the self, they are expected to experience more negative mood following this induction. The rumination induction is commonly compared to a distraction induction, which includes emotionally neutral, nonself-relevant prompts (e.g., "Think about a fan slowly rotating back and forth," "Think about the layout of your local shopping center"). The distraction induction is expected to temporarily lift the moods of dysphoric individuals by directing their attention away from themselves and their problems, but to have no effect on the moods of nondysphoric individuals. Dysphoric and clinically depressed individuals consistently report significantly sadder mood following the rumination induction and significantly improved mood following the distraction induction (e.g., Donaldson & Lam, 2004; Lyubomirsky & Nolen-Hoeksema, 1993, 1995; Nolen-Hoeksema & Morrow, 1993; Watkins & Teasdale, 2001). In all of these studies, the moods of nondysphoric individuals were not affected by either induction. When nondysphoric individuals are given a negative mood induction prior to ruminating, however, they also exhibit prolonged negative mood (Morrow & Nolen-Hoeksema, 1990).

In addition to increased negative mood, rumination leads to several cognitive consequences in dysphoric individuals that may exacerbate their depressive symptoms. Dysphoric individuals induced to ruminate display more negative thinking about their past, present, and future than do those induced to distract. Regarding memories of the past, dysphoric individuals induced to ruminate rate negative events as having happened more frequently in their past than dysphoric individuals induced to distract, or nondysphoric individuals who ruminate or distract (Lyubomirsky *et al.*, 1998). Similarly, dysphoric participants who have ruminated freely recall more negative memories (as rated by judges; Lyubomirsky *et al.*, 1998), and are slower to recall positive memories when asked to do so (Joormann & Siemer, 2004), compared to dysphoric participants who have been distracted or nondysphoric participants.

Regarding thoughts about the present, dysphoric participants induced to ruminate talk about more negative situations that they are currently facing (Lyubomirsky *et al.*, 1999), and interpret hypothetical life events in a negatively biased way (Lyubomirsky *et al.*, 1999) compared to dysphoric participants who have been distracted or nondysphoric groups. Dysphoric participants in the rumination conditions also report more pessimistic expectations for the future, predicting a lower likelihood of positive events occurring to them (Lyubomirsky & Nolen-Hoeksema, 1995), less confidence in their ability to solve future problems (Lyubomirsky *et al.*, 1999, Studies 1 and 3), and a reduced likelihood of engaging in pleasant activities in the future (Lyubomirsky & Nolen-Hoeksema, 1993, Study 1), compared to dysphoric participants in the distraction condition or nondysphoric participants. Such negatively biased thinking is a hallmark feature of major depression, and negatively biased or pessimistic thinking is theorized to lead to the development of depression (e.g., Abramson *et al.*, 1989; Beck, 1967; see Chapter 6). Although much of our own work has been conducted with dysphoric college students, parallel studies with community participants meeting criteria for major depressive disorder have also found that those induced to ruminate subsequently show more negative thinking about themselves and the future than those in comparison induction conditions (Lavender & Watkins, 2004; Rimes & Watkins, 2005).

As well as negatively biasing thinking, rumination interferes with adaptive cognitive processing. Dysphoric individuals induced to ruminate display impaired concentration on academic tasks, including reading passages from the Graduate Record Examination, watching videotaped lectures, and proofreading written texts (Lyubomirsky *et al.*, 2003), compared to dysphoric participants distracted from ruminations or nondysphoric participants. Depressed patients induced to ruminate (Watkins & Brown, 2002) and individuals who score highly on the Ruminative Response Scale, or ruminators, (Davis & Nolen-Hoeksema, 2000) demonstrate a tendency to perseverate on cognitive tasks. Therefore, rumination appears to exacerbate another symptom of depression in addition to sad mood, namely, difficulty concentrating. Dysphoric patients induced to ruminate also demonstrate reduced specificity of autobiographical memory recall (e.g., Watkins & Teasdale, 2001). Finally, ruminators have more difficulty inhibiting negative, irrelevant words on a cognitive task than nonruminators, even after levels of depressive symptoms are statistically controlled (Joormann, 2006). Both overgeneral memory recall and difficulty inhibiting negative words have been associated with depression in a number of experimental studies (Joormann, 2005; Williams *et al.*, 2007), although it is unclear whether depression is a cause or consequence of such cognitive processes. Thus, rumination leads to cognitive consequences that exacerbate depressive symptoms including negative mood and difficulty concentrating, and leads to cognitive processing difficulties that have been consistently associated with the experience of depression.

In addition to these effects on cognition, rumination has the motivational consequence of inhibiting instrumental behavior. Dysphoric individuals induced to ruminate indicate a reduced willingness to engage in pleasant, distracting activities, despite predicting that such activities would likely improve their mood (Lyubomirsky & Nolen-Hoeksema, 1993) compared to dysphoric individuals who have been distracted or nondysphoric groups. Thus, rumination may contribute to depression by preventing individuals from engaging in positively reinforcing, mood-elevating activities.

Even when inaction is potentially life-threatening, there is evidence that rumination inhibits instrumental behavior. When asked to predict their response to discovering a breast lump, women with ruminative response styles are less likely to report that they will seek a medical diagnosis (Lyubomirsky *et al.*, 2006). Among breast cancer survivors, ruminators reported having delayed the presentation of their initial cancer symptoms to a physician more than 2 months longer than nonruminators (Lyubomirsky *et al.*, 2006). Given these relationships of rumination with impaired instrumental behaviors, rumination might be expected to interfere with treatment-seeking behavior in depressed individuals. Although the relationship between rumination and treatment seeking has not been examined directly in this population, ruminating might make it more difficult for depressed individuals to seek appropriate treatment.

Rumination may also increase the risk for depression by interfering with interpersonal relationships. Interpersonal theories of depression propose that difficulties in interpersonal relationships can lead to the development of depression (e.g., Hammen, 2005; Joiner, 2002). Rumination has also been associated with undesirable personality characteristics that may interfere with relationships. Ruminators are more likely than nonruminators to display dependency and neediness (Spasojevic & Alloy, 2001), sociotropy (Gorski & Young, 2002), and "unmitigated communion," or the tendency to assume undue responsibility for the well-being of others (Nolen-Hoeksema & Jackson, 2001). Ruminators are also more likely than nonruminators to report aggressive tendencies in the face of interpersonal stressors (e.g., Collins & Bell, 1997; McCullough *et al.*, 1998; McCullough *et al.*, 2001).

A number of experimental studies have demonstrated that rumination impairs interpersonal problem-solving in dysphoric and clinically depressed individuals (e.g., Donaldson & Lam, 2004; Lyubomirsky & Nolen-Hoeksema, 1995; Watkins & Moulds, 2005). Lyubomirsky & Nolen-Hoeksema (1995) induced dysphoric and nondysphoric participants either to ruminate or to distract themselves before completing a measure of interpersonal effectiveness. This measure presents participants with a hypothetical interpersonal problem (e.g., you notice that one of your friends is avoiding you), and the participants generate stories explaining how they would solve the problem. Independent raters blind to dysphoria status and induction condition found that dysphoric participants induced to ruminate generated less effective solutions than dysphorics who distracted themselves and nondysphoric participants. These effects have been replicated in clinically depressed samples using a similar measure of interpersonal problem-solving (Donaldson & Lam, 2004; Watkins & Moulds, 2005).

The impaired social problem-solving associated with rumination may lead to depression through the deterioration of relationships. Nolen-Hoeksema & Davis (1999) found that although bereaved ruminators were more likely to reach out for social support than bereaved nonruminators, they were less likely to receive such support. This is detrimental because the ruminators who were able to elicit social support effectively benefited from lower levels of depressive symptoms. Therefore, the impaired social problem-solving and lack of social support caused by rumination may both increase the risk for depression.

Thus, rumination increases risk for depression both through its direct effect on mood and through cognitive, motivational, and interpersonal consequences that in turn increase risk for depression. In these ways, rumination may exacerbate existing depressive symptoms, either converting subclinical depressive symptoms into a major depressive episode, or increasing the severity of an existing depressive episode.

SPECIFICITY OF RISK

While rumination was originally conceptualized as a risk factor for depression, recent evidence suggests that rumination also increases risk of other forms of psychopathology. Several longitudinal studies, most conducted with community samples, have found that individuals prone to ruminate also have higher levels of general anxiety and post-traumatic stress (Fritz, 1999; Nolen-Hoeksema, 2000; Nolen-Hoeksema & Morrow, 1991; Schwartz & Koenig, 1996; Segerstrom *et al.*, 2000; for cross-sectional evidence see Abbott & Rapee, 2004; Fresco *et al.*, 2002; Harrington & Blankenship, 2002; Kocovski *et al.*, 2005; Muris *et al.*, 2005). Given the high levels of comorbidity between depression and anxiety, it is unsurprising that these disorders would share common risk factors. Rumination is a particularly likely candidate given its similarity to worry, which is common among individuals with anxiety disorders and is a necessary symptom for a diagnosis of generalized anxiety disorder (American Psychiatric Association, 2000; Borkovec *et al.*, 1991). As forms of repetitive thought, rumination and worry share many common features, including a perseverative nature, seeming uncontrollability, and a tendency to increase negative affect (e.g., Segerstrom *et al.*, 2000). When assessed by self-report, rumination and worry tend to be correlated but statistically distinguishable (Fresco *et al.*, 2002; Muris *et al.*, 2004; Segerstrom *et al.*, 2003; Watkins *et al.*, 2005). Nolen-Hoeksema (2000) found that rumination predicted symptoms of both anxiety and depression, and was especially predictive of a mixed anxiety–depression syndrome. Content analyses of ruminative thought have found that it contains both uncertainty about the future (e.g., "What if I can't pull myself together?"), which may be more closely related to anxiety, and rehashing of past events ("How could I have been so stupid to say that?"; Lyubomirsky *et al.*, 1999), which may be more closely related to the hopelessness and negative evaluations of the self that are central to depression (Abramson *et al.*, 1989; Beck, 1967). Ruminators may move between anxiety and depression as their thoughts vacillate between uncertainty and hopelessness (see Nolen-Hoeksema *et al.*, in press).

In addition to depression and anxiety, rumination has been associated with increased risk for escapist behaviors including binge eating and binge drinking. According to self-regulation theories of binge eating and alcohol abuse, these behaviors constitute motivated attempts to escape aversive self-awareness (e.g., Baumeister, 1991; Heatherton & Baumeister, 1991). As a form of negative self-directed thought, rumination might be expected to lead to such escapist behaviors, and prospective studies indicate that rumination is associated with binge drinking and alcohol abuse (Nolen-Hoeksema & Harrell, 2002; Nolen-Hoeksema & Larson, 1999; Nolen-Hoeksema *et al.*, 2007) as well as bulimia nervosa symptoms, particularly binge eating (Nolen-Hoeksema *et al.*, 2007). Rumination does not appear, however, to predict changes in externalizing symptoms other than alcohol abuse (e.g., delinquency), suggesting that rumination is specific to escapist behaviors and internalizing symptoms (Nolen-Hoeksema *et al.*, 2007). Although a paucity of research has investigated the interrelationships between rumination, internalizing symptoms, and escapist behaviors, one possibility is that rumination leads to increases in negative affect, which can be expressed as either anxiety or sadness, and that desire to avoid this negative affect leads to escapist behaviors such as binge eating and alcohol abuse.

Given the increased risk of both depression and impulsive, escapist behaviors associated with rumination, individuals with ruminative response styles might be expected to be at especially high risk for suicidal behavior. Ruminative response style has been found to predict suicidal ideation (Miranda & Nolen-Hoeksema, 2007; Smith *et al.*, 2006; see also Eshun, 2000) and suicide attempts (Miranda & Nolen-Hoeksema, 2007) prospectively. In addition, Hilt *et al.* (2008) found that rumination predicted nonsuicidal self-injury (e.g., self-cutting) in adolescent girls. The increased risk for self-injury and suicidality associated with rumination, as a consequence of depression or independent of major depression, should be addressed in future work.

TREATMENT IMPLICATIONS

Reducing the frequency of rumination is a worthy treatment goal in and of itself, given the negative effects of rumination on mood in the absence of any known benefits. Additionally, the cognitive and motivational consequences of rumination may interfere with some of the strategies commonly used in psychosocial interventions for depression, suggesting that reducing rumination might facilitate treatment engagement. Because rumination is known to decrease willingness to engage in pleasant, mood-lifting activities, rumination may interfere with behavioral activation strategies commonly used in cognitive behavioral therapy. The impaired concentration, negative thinking, and negative memory recall resulting from rumination might make it difficult to challenge negative automatic thoughts as required by cognitive therapy. Because rumination is associated with impaired interpersonal problem-solving, rumination might impede progress in interpersonal psychotherapy. Thus, reducing rumination at the start of depression treatment might facilitate therapy both by improving mood directly and by aiding engagement in these therapeutic techniques. These potential benefits, however, remain speculative until further research is completed examining the effects of targeting rumination in treatment.

Given the potential utility of reducing the frequency of rumination, how might clinicians help their clients quell ruminative thoughts? Although little research has been done on which treatment strategies might be most effective in overcoming rumination (although see Watkins *et al.*, 2007), we consider the possible treatment implications of the research to date on rumination. Much experimental research indicates that using pleasant distractions temporarily improves mood and reduces ruminative thinking. Directing dysphoric or clinically depressed participants to attend to externally focused, emotionally neutral activity for just 8 min results in significantly improved mood and reductions in negative, ruminative thinking (see above, and Lyubomirsky & Tkach, 2004). Clinicians might instruct depressed clients to engage in pleasant, distracting activities when they notice themselves becoming caught up in ruminative thought. Because rumination may reduce the willingness to engage in such distracting activities, practice of such strategies in session, or scheduling of such activities may be necessary. Behavioral activation interventions include similar strategies for interrupting negative ruminations through the incorporation of positively reinforcing activities and training in attention to experience (Jacobson *et al.*, 2001). Mindfulness exercises, such as those used in mindfulness-based cognitive therapy (Segal *et al.*, 2002), might also be used to help depressed individuals disengage from rumination. Theoretically, mindfulness exercises allow depressed individuals to distance themselves from their thoughts, thus allowing them to break out of seemingly uncontrollable ruminative thought patterns. While the effect of mindfulness interventions on the process of rumination has not been examined directly, mindfulness-based cognitive therapy has been found to prevent depression relapse (Teasdale *et al.*, 2000).

The evidence that rumination is a risk factor for depression, as well as anxiety, binge eating, and binge drinking, suggests that rumination may be an important target in preventative interventions. In particular, we see a need for prevention programs aimed at young adolescent girls, a group who shows substantial increases in depression, anxiety, and eating disorders over the adolescent period (Nolen-Hoeksema, 2002). Moreover, rumination is more prevalent in girls or women than in boys or men, and accounts partially for gender differences in depression (Grant *et al.*, 2004; Nolen-Hoeksema *et al.*, 1999; Roberts *et al.*, 1998).

Prevention programs could aim to teach girls to cope adaptively with the stresses of early adolescence, by engaging in active problem-solving rather than in rumination in response to problems. For example, girls could be taught assertiveness techniques for handling conflicts with peers, rather than only ruminating over these conflicts. Because some girls fall into "co-rumination" with girlfriends (Rose, 2002), prevention programs could encourage girls to foster friendships with peers who do not feed worries about popularity, appearance, self-worth, and so on. Self-regulation theories (e.g., Carver & Scheier, 1998; Martin & Tesser, 1996) suggest that rumination develops when individuals perseverate on goals they cannot attain. This suggests that prevention programs should help girls recognize unhealthy goals they have (e.g., being thin) and help them develop healthier goals and activities. Finally, prevention programs could use cognitive-restructuring techniques to help girls question negative messages they receive about themselves from their social environment.

DIRECTIONS FOR FUTURE RESEARCH

Rumination exacerbates depressed mood directly and leads to cognitive, motivational, and interpersonal consequences that in turn increase risk for depression. All of these mechanisms likely play some role in the development of depression, but some of these factors may be more central to depression risk. There is evidence that rumination increases risk not only for depression, but also for other internalizing disorders and for binge eating and alcohol abuse. Rumination may lead to these different outcomes through similar pathways, or the particular consequences of rumination may determine the mental health outcome of ruminative thought. The interrelationships between rumination, its cognitive, motivational, and interpersonal consequences, and different forms of psychopathology constitute an important topic for future research.

REFERENCES

Abbott, M. J., & Rapee, R. M. (2004). Post-event rumination and negative self-appraisal in social phobia before and after treatment. *Journal of Abnormal Psychology*, 113, 136–144.

Abela, J. R. Z., Brozina, K., & Haigh, E. P. (2002). An examination of the response styles theory of depression in third- and seventh-grade children: A short-term longitudinal study. *Journal of Abnormal Child Psychology*, 30, 515–527.

Abramson, L. Y., Metalsky, G. L., & Alloy, L. B. (1989). Hopelessness depression: A theory based subtype of depression. *Psychological Review*, 96, 358–372.

American Psychiatric Association (2000). *Diagnostic and statistical manual of mental disorders* (4th ed., Test Revision). Washington, DC: American Psychiatric Association.

Arnow, B. A., Spangler, D., Klein, D. N., & Burns, D. D. (2004). Rumination and distraction among chronic depressives in treatment: A structural equation analysis. *Cognitive Therapy and Research*, 28, 67–83.

Bagby, R. M., & Parker, J. D. A. (2001). Relation of rumination and distraction with neuroticism and extraversion in a sample of patients with major depression. *Cognitive Therapy and Research*, 25, 91–102.

Bagby, R. M., Rector, N. A., Bacchiochi, J. R., & McBride, C. (2004). The stability of the response styles questionnaire rumination scale in a sample of patients with major depression. *Cognitive Therapy and Research*, 28, 527–538.

Baumeister, R. F. (1991). *Escaping the self: Alcoholism, spirituality, masochism, and other flights from the burden of selfhood*. New York: Basic Books.

Beck, A. T. (1967). *Depression: Clinical, experimental and theoretical aspects*. New York: Harper & Row.

Borkovec, T. D., Shadick, R. N., & Hopkins, M. (1991). The nature of normal and pathological worry. In R. M. Rapee & D. H. Barlow (Eds.), *Chronic anxiety: Generalized anxiety disorder and mixed anxiety-depression* (pp. 29–51). New York, NY: Guilford Press.

Butler, L. D., & Nolen-Hoeksema, S. (1994). Gender differences in response to depressed mood in a college sample. *Sex Roles*, 30, 331–346.

Carver, C. S., & Scheier, M. F. (1998). *On the self-regulation of behavior*. New York, NY: Cambridge University Press.

Ciesla, J. A., & Roberts, J. E. (2002). Self-directed thought and response to treatment for depression: A preliminary investigation. *Journal of Cognitive Psychotherapy*, 16, 435–453.

Collins, K., & Bell, R. (1997). Personality and aggression: The Dissipation-Rumination Scale. *Personality and Individual Differences*, 22, 751–755.

Cox, B. J., Enns, M. W., & Taylor, S. (2001). The effect of rumination as a mediator of elevated anxiety sensitivity in major depression. *Cognitive Therapy and Research*, 25, 525–534.

Davis, R. N., & Nolen-Hoeksema, S. (2000). Cognitive inflexibility among ruminators and nonruminators. *Cognitive Therapy and Research*, 24, 699–711.

Donaldson, C., & Lam, D. (2004). Rumination, mood and social problem-solving in major depression. *Psychological Medicine*, 34, 1309–1318.

Eaton, W., Anthony, J., Gallo, J., Cai, G., Tien, A., Romanoski, A., Lyketsos, C., & Chen, L. (1997). Natural history of Diagnostic Interview Schedule/DSM-IV Major Depression. *Archives of General Psychiatry*, 54, 993–999.

Eshun, S. (2000). Role of gender and rumination in suicide ideation: A comparison of college samples from Ghana and the United States *Cross-Cultural Research: The Journal of Comparative Social Science*, 34, 250–263.

Fresco, D. M., Frankel, A. N., Mennin, D. S., Turk, C. L., & Heimberg, R. G. (2002). Distinct and overlapping features of rumination and worry: The relationship of cognitive production to negative affective states. *Cognitive Therapy and Research*, 26, 179–188.

Fritz, H. L. (1999). The role of rumination in adjustment to a first coronary event. *Dissertation Abstracts International: Section B: The Sciences and Engineering*, 60(1-B), 0410.

Gorski, J., & Young, M. A. (2002). Sociotropy/autonomy, self-construal, response style, and gender in adolescents. *Personality and Individual Differences*, 32, 463–478.

Grant, K. E., Lyons, A. L., Finkelstein, J. S., Conway, K. M. Reynolds, L. K., O'Koon, J. H. et al. (2004). Gender differences in rates of depressive symptoms among low-income, urban, African American youth: A test of two mediational hypotheses. *Journal of Youth and Adolescence*, 33, 523–533.

Hammen, C. (2005). Stress and depression. *Annual Review of Clinical Psychology*, 1, 293–319

Hankin, B. L., Abramson, L. Y., Moffitt, T. E., McGee, R., Silva, P., & Angell, K. E. (1998). Development of depression from preadolescence to young adulthood: Emerging gender differences in a 10-year longitudinal study. *Journal of Abnormal Psychology*, 107, 128–140.

Harrington, J. A., & Blankenship, V. (2002). Ruminative thoughts and their relation to depression and anxiety. *Journal of Applied Social Psychology*, 32, 465–485.

Heatherton, T. F., & Baumeister, R. F. (1991). Binge eating as escape from self-awareness. *Psychological Bulletin*, 110, 86–108.

Hilt, L. M., Cha, C. B., & Nolen-Hoeksema, S. (2008). Nonsuicidal self-injury in young adolescent girls: Moderators of the distress-function relationship. *Journal of Consulting and Clinical Psychology*, 76, 63–71.

Jacobson, N. S., Martell, C. R., & Dimidjian, S. (2001). Behavioral activation treatment for depression: Returning to contextual roots. *Clinical Psychology: Science and Practice*, 8, 255–270.

Joiner, T. E., Jr. (2002). Depression in its interpersonal context. In I. H. Gotlib & C. L. Hammen (Eds.), *Handbook of depression* (pp. 295–313). New York: Guilford Press.

Joormann, J. (2005). Inhibition, rumination, and mood regulation in depression. In R. W. Engle, G. Sedek, U. von Hecker, & D. N. McIntosh (Eds.), *Cognitive Limitations in Aging and Psychopathology: Attention, Working Memory, and Executive Functions* (pp. 275–312). New York: Cambridge University Press.

Joormann, J. (2006). Differential effects of rumination and dysphoria on the inhibition of irrelevant emotional material: Evidence from a negative priming task. *Cognitive Therapy and Research*, 30, 149–160.

Joormann, J., & Siemer, M. (2004). Memory accessibility, mood regulation, and dysphoria: Difficulties in repairing sad mood with happy memories?. *Journal of Abnormal Psychology*, 113, 179–188.

Just, N., & Alloy, L. B. (1997). The response styles theory of depression: Tests and an extension of the theory. *Journal of Abnormal Psychology*, 106, 221–229.

Keller, M., & Shapiro, R. (1981). Major depressive disorder: Initial results from a one-year prospective naturalistic follow-up study. *Journal of Nervous Mental Disorders*, 169, 761–768.

Kessler, R. C., McGonagle, K. A., Swartz, M., Blazer, D. G., & Nelson, C. B. (1993). Sex and depression in the National Comorbidity Survey I: Lifetime prevalence, chronicity, and recurrence. *Journal of Affective Disorders*, 29, 85–96.

Kocovski, N. L., Endler, N. S., Rector, N. A., & Flett, G. L. (2005). Ruminative coping and post-event processing in social anxiety. *Behaviour Research and Therapy*, 43, 971–984.

Kovacs, M. (2001). Gender and the course of major depressive disorder through adolescence in clinically referred youngsters. *Journal of the American Academy of Child and Adolescent Psychiatry*, 40, 1079–1085.

Kuehner, C., & Weber, I. (1999). Responses to depression in unipolar depressed patients: An investigation of Nolen-Hoeksema's response styles theory. *Psychological Medicine*, 29, 1323–1333.

Lara, M. E., Klein, D. N., & Kasch, K. L. (2000). Psychosocial predictors of the short-term course and outcome of major depression: A longitudinal study of a non clinical sample with recent-onset episodes. *Journal of Abnormal Psychology*, 109, 644–650.

Lavender, A., & Watkins, E. (2004). Rumination and future thinking in depression. *British Journal of Clinical Psychology*, 43, 129–142.

Lyubomirsky, S., & Nolen-Hoeksema, S. (1993). Self-perpetuating properties of dysphoric rumination. *Journal of Personality and Social Psychology*, 65, 339–349.

Lyubomirsky, S., & Nolen-Hoeksema, S. (1995). Effects of self-focused rumination on negative thinking and interpersonal problem solving. *Journal of Personality and Social Psychology*, 69, 176–190.

Lyubomirsky, S., & Tkach, C. (2004). The consequences of dysphoric rumination. In C. Papageorgiou & A. Wells (Eds.), *Depressive Rumination: Nature, Theory, and Treatment* (pp. 21–42). New York: Wiley.

Lyubomirsky, S., Caldwell, N. D., & Nolen-Hoeksema, S. (1998). Effects of ruminative and distracting responses to depressed mood on retrieval of autobiographical memories. *Journal of Personality and Social Psychology*, 75, 166–177.

Lyubomirsky, S., Tucker, K. L., Caldwell, N. D., & Berg, K. (1999). Why ruminators are poor problem solvers: Clues from the phenomenology of dysphoric rumination. *Journal of Personality and Social Psychology*, 77, 1041–1060.

Lyubomirsky, S., Kasri, F., & Zehm, K. (2003). Dysphoric rumination impairs concentration on academic tasks. *Cognitive Therapy and Research*, 27, 309–330.

Lyubomirsky, S., Kasri, F., Chang, O., & Chung, I. (2006). Ruminative response styles and delay of seeking diagnosis for breast cancer symptoms. *Journal of Social and Clinical Psychology*, 25, 276–304.

Martin, L. L., & Tesser, A. (1996). Some ruminative thoughts. In R. S. Wyer, Jr. (Ed.), *Ruminative Thoughts* (pp. 1–47). Mahwah, NJ: Lawrence Erlbaum.

McCullough, M. E., Rachal, K. C., Sandage, S. J., Worthington, E. L., Jr., Brown, S. W., & Hight, T. L. (1998). Interpersonal forgiving in close relationships: II. Theoretical elaboration and measurement. *Journal of Personality and Social Psychology*, 75, 1586–1603.

McCullough, M. E., Bellah, C. G., Kilpatrick, S. D., & Johnson, J. L. (2001). Vengefulness: Relationships with forgiveness, rumination, well-being, and the Big Five. *Personality and Social Psychology Bulletin*, 27, 601–610.

Miranda, R., & Nolen-Hoeksema, S. (2007). Brooding and reflection: Rumination predicts suicidal ideation at 1-year follow-up in a community sample. *Behaviour Research and Therapy, 45*, 3088–3095.

Morrow, J., & Nolen-Hoeksema, S. (1990). Effects of responses to depression on the remediation of depressive affect. *Journal of Personality and Social Psychology*, 58, 519–527.

Muris, P., Roelofs, J., Meesters, C., & Boomsma, P. (2004). Rumination and worry in nonclinical adolescents. *Cognitive Therapy and Research*, 28, 539–554.

Muris, P., Roelofs, J., Rassin, E., Franken, I., & Mayer, B. (2005) Mediating effects of rumination and worry on the links between neuroticism, anxiety, and depression. *Personality and Individual Differences*, 39, 1105–1111.

Nolan, S. A., Roberts, J. E., & Gotlib, I. H. (1998). Neuroticism and ruminative response style as predictors of change in depressive symptomatology. *Cognitive Therapy and Research*, 22, 445–455.

Nolen-Hoeksema, S. (1991). Responses to depression and their effects on the duration of depressive episodes. *Journal of Abnormal Psychology*, 100, 569–582.

Nolen-Hoeksema, S. (2000). The role of rumination in depressive disorders and mixed anxiety/depressive symptoms. *Journal of Abnormal Psychology*, 109, 504–511.

Nolen-Hoeksema, S. (2002). Gender differences in depression. In I. H. Gotlib & C. L. Hammen (Eds.), *Handbook of Depression* (pp. 492–509). New York: Guilford Press.

Nolen-Hoeksema, S., & Davis, C. G. (1999). "Thanks for sharing that": Ruminators and their social support networks. *Journal of Personality and Social Psychology*, 77, 801–814.

Nolen-Hoeksema, S., & Harrell, Z. A. (2002). Rumination, depression, and alcohol use: Tests of gender differences. *Journal of Cognitive Psychotherapy*, 16, 391–403.

Nolen-Hoeksema, S., & Jackson, B. (2001). Mediators of the gender difference in rumination. *Psychology of Women Quarterly*, 25, 37–47.

Nolen-Hoeksema, S., & Larson, J. (1999). *Coping with Loss*. Mahwah, NJ: Lawrence Erlbaum.

Nolen-Hoeksema, S., Larson, J., & Grayson, C. (1999). Explaining the gender difference in depressive symptoms. *Journal of Personality and Social Psychology*, 77, 1061–1072.

Nolen-Hoeksema, S., & Morrow, J. (1991). A prospective study of depression and posttraumatic stress symptoms after a natural disaster: The 1989 Loma Prieta earthquake. *Journal of Personality and Social Psychology*, 61, 115–121.

Nolen-Hoeksema, S., & Morrow, J. (1993). Effects of rumination and distraction on naturally occurring depressed mood. *Cognition and Emotion*, 7, 561–570.

Nolen-Hoeksema, S., Morrow, J., & Fredrickson, B. L. (1993). Response styles and the duration of episodes of depressed mood. *Journal of Abnormal Psychology*, 102, 20–28.

Nolen-Hoeksema, S., Parker, L., & Larson, J. (1994). Ruminative coping with depressed mood following loss. *Journal of Personality and Social Psychology*, 67, 92–104.

Nolen-Hoeksema, S., Stice, E., Wade, E., & Bohon, C. (2007). Reciprocal relations between rumination and depressive, bulimic, and substance abuse symptoms. *Journal of Abnormal Psychology*, 116, 198–207.

Nolen-Hoeksema, S., Wisco, B. E., & Lyubomirsky, S. (in press). Rethinking rumination. *Perspectives in Psychological Science*.

Park, R. J., Goodyer, I. M., & Teasdale, J. D. (2004). Effects of induced rumination and distraction on mood and overgeneral autobiographical memory in adolescent Major Depressive Disorder and controls. *Journal of Child Psychology and Psychiatry*, 45, 996–1006.

Rimes, K. A., & Watkins, E. (2005). The effects of self-focused rumination on global negative self-judgements in depression. *Behaviour Research and Therapy*, 43, 1673–1681.

Roberts, J. E., Gilboa, E., & Gotlib, I. H. (1998). Ruminative response style and vulnerability to episodes of dysphoria: Gender, neuroticism, and episode duration. *Cognitive Therapy and Research*, 22, 401–423.

Robinson, L. A., & Alloy, L. B. (2003). Negative cognitive styles and stress-reactive rumination interact to predict depression: A prospective study. *Cognitive Therapy and Research*, 27, 275–292.

Rose, A. J. (2002). Co-rumination in the friendships of girls and boys. *Child Development*, 73, 1830–1843.

Rusting, C., & Nolen-Hoeksema, S. (1998). Regulating responses to anger: Effects of rumination and distraction on angry mood. *Journal of Personality and Social Psychology*, 74, 790–803.

Sarin, S., Abela, J. R. Z., & Auerbach, R. P. (2005). The response styles theory of depression: A test of specificity and causal mediation. *Cognition and Emotion*, 19, 751–761.

Schmaling, K. B., Dimidjian, S., Katon, W., & Sullivan, M. (2002). Response styles among patients with minor depression and dysthymia in primary care. *Journal of Abnormal Psychology*, 111, 350–356.

Schwartz, J. A. J., & Koenig, L. J. (1996). Response styles and negative affect among adolescents. *Cognitive Therapy and Research*, 20, 13–36.

Segal, A., Williams, J. M. G., & Teasdale, J. D. (2002). *Mindfulness-based cognitive therapy for depression: A new approach to preventing relapse*. New York: Guilford.

Segerstrom, S. C., Tsao, J. C. I., Alden, L. E., & Craske, M. G. (2000). Worry and rumination: Repetitive thought as a concomitant and predictor of negative mood. *Cognitive Therapy and Research*, 24, 671–688.

Segerstrom, S. C., Stanton, A. L., Alden, L. E., & Shortridge, B. E. (2003). A multidimensional structure for repetitive thought: What's on your mind, and how much? *Journal of Personality and Social Psychology*, 85, 909–921.

Smith, J. M., Alloy, L. B., & Abramson, L. Y. (2006). Cognitive vulnerability to depression, rumination, hopelessness, and suicidal ideation: Multiple pathways to self-injurious thinking. *Suicide and Life-Threatening Behavior*, 36, 443–454.

Spasojevic, J., & Alloy, L. B. (2001). Rumination as a common mechanism relating depressive risk to depression. *Emotion*, 1, 25–37.

Teasdale, J. D., Segal, Z., Williams, J. M. G., Ridgeway, J. A., Sousby, J. M., & Lau, M. A. (2000). Prevention of relapse/recurrence in major depression by mindfulness-based cognitive therapy. *Journal of Consulting and Clinical Psychology*, 68, 615–623.

Thase, M. E., Jindal, R., & Howland, R. H. (2002). Biological aspects of depression. In I. H. Gotlib & C. L. Hammen (Eds.), *Handbook of Depression* (pp. 192–218). New York: Guilford Press.

Treynor, W., Gonzalez, R., & Nolen-Hoeksema, S. (2003). Rumination reconsidered: A psychometric analysis. *Cognitive Therapy and Research*, 27, 247–259.

Watkins, E., & Brown, R. G. (2002). Rumination and executive function in depression: An experimental study. *Journal of Neurology, Neurosurgery, and Psychiatry*, 72, 400–402.

Watkins, E., & Moulds, M. (2005). Distinct modes of ruminative self-focus: Impact of abstract versus concrete rumination on problem solving in depression. *Emotion*, 5, 319–328.

Watkins, E., & Teasdale, J. D. (2001). Rumination and overgeneral memory in depression: Effects of self-focus and analytic thinking. *Journal of Abnormal Psychology*, 110, 353–357.

Watkins, E., Moulds, M., & Mackintosh, B. (2005). Comparisons between rumination and worry in a non-clinical population. *Behaviour Research and Therapy*, 43, 1577–1585.

Watkins, E., Scott, J., Wingrove, J., Rimes, K., Bathurst, N., Steiner, H., Kennell-Webb, S., Moulds, M., & Malliaris, Y. (2007). Rumination-focused cognitive behaviour therapy for residual depression: A case series. *Behaviour Research and Therapy*, 45, 2144–2154.

Williams, J. M. G., Barnhofer, T., Crane, C., Herman, D., Raes, F., Watkins, E., & Dalgeish, T. (2007). Autobiographical memory specificity and emotional disorder. *Psychological Bulletin*, 133, 122–148.

Wood, J. V., Saltzberg, J. A., Neale, J. M., Stone, A. A., & Rachmiel, T. B. (1990). Self-focused attention, coping responses, and distressed mood in everyday life. *Journal of Personality and Social Psychology*, 58, 1027–1036.

11

Negative Cognitive Style

Lauren B. Alloy*, Lyn Y. Abramson†, Jessica Keyser*, Rachel K. Gerstein* and Louisa G. Sylvia¶

**Department of Psychology, Temple University, Philadelphia, PA, USA*
†Department of Psychology, University of Wisconsin-Madison, Madison WI, USA
¶Massachussetts General Hospital, Boston, MA, USA

The World Health Organization's Global Burden of Disease Study ranked depression as the most burdensome disease worldwide (Murray & Lopez, 1996). Moreover, depression has been hailed as one of the most common forms of psychopathology (Kessler, 2002). Depression is also highly recurrent, associated with significant impairment, has high lifetime prevalence, and onsets at an early age with a typically chronic and persistent course (Judd, 1997; Kessler, 2000). Thus, perhaps it is not surprising that depression has been heavily researched for decades. An outcome of some of this research is that negative cognitive style has been found to be a robust risk factor for depression. In this chapter, we will discuss this risk factor as well as how negative cognitive style affects the onset, course, and treatment of depression. We will conclude by discussing areas of future research needed in understanding cognitive vulnerability to depression.

DESCRIPTION OF NEGATIVE COGNITIVE STYLE

Beck's cognitive theory of depression (1967, 1987) was the first to propose that an individual's cognitive style may be a risk factor for developing depression.

Specifically, Beck (1967, 1987) hypothesized that individuals who have negative self-schemata, particularly involving themes of inadequacy, failure, loss, and worthlessness, may be more vulnerable to depression. Such negative self-schemata are often represented as a set of dysfunctional attitudes, such as "I am nothing if I do not succeed at this job," in which the person believes that his or her self-worth is dependent on being perfect or on others' approval. Further, when confronted with a negative life event, individuals with this type of cognitive style are hypothesized to develop negatively biased perceptions of themselves (low self-esteem), their personal world, and their future (hopelessness).

In the hopelessness theory of depression, Abramson *et al.* (1989) also proposed a cognitive risk factor for depression, but they hypothesized that the relevant depressogenic style is the tendency to make negative inferences regarding stressful life events (see Figure 11.1). A negative inferential style has three

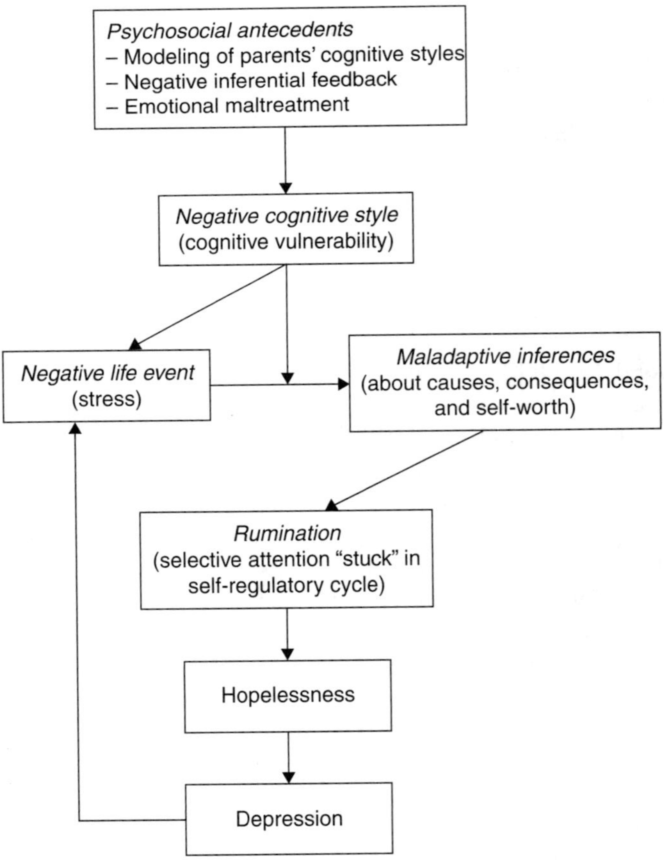

FIGURE 11.1 A cognitive vulnerability–stress model of hopelessness depression. Relations between the various components of the model are explained throughout the chapter.

components: (1) a general tendency to attribute negative events to stable (enduring) and global (widespread) causes (e.g., "It will persist and it will impact everything"); (2) a tendency to infer that further negative consequences will follow from a current negative event (e.g., "By failing this test, I will never get into college"); and (3) a tendency to infer that the occurrence of a negative event in one's life means that one is deficient, flawed, or unworthy (e.g., "I was fired from my job, so I must be worthless"). Thus, an individual with a negative inferential style is likely to make negative inferences about the causes, consequences, and self-implications of any particular negative event he or she experiences, thereby increasing the likelihood that he or she will develop hopelessness. In the theory, hopelessness is a proximal cause of the symptoms of depression, particularly the subtype of "hopelessness depression," and is defined by two expectations: that negative events will occur or desired events will not occur (negative outcome expectancy) and that there is nothing that one can do to change the situation (helplessness expectancy).

Although both hopelessness and Beck's theories hypothesize that negative cognitive styles increase risk for depression when individuals experience negative life events, studies have suggested that the negative attributional style component of cognitive vulnerability, as defined by the hopelessness theory, and the dysfunctional attitude component of Beck's theory, do represent distinct constructs (e.g., Gotlib *et al.*, 1993; Haeffel *et al.*, 2003; Joiner & Rudd, 1996; Spangler *et al.*, 1997). Throughout this chapter, we will use the term "negative cognitive style" to encompass the cognitive vulnerabilities featured in both of these theories of depression: that is, dysfunctional attitudes as well as negative inferential styles, unless otherwise specified (see Figure 11.1). Further, "cognitive risk" also represents the vulnerability constructs from both theories. Specifically, individuals determined to be at "low or high cognitive risk" are categorized based on their scores on the Dysfunctional Attitudes Scale (DAS; Weissman & Beck, 1978), assessing the main risk construct of Beck's cognitive theory, as well as the Cognitive Style Questionnaire (CSQ; Alloy *et al.*, 2000), measuring the vulnerability concept associated with the hopelessness theory of depression. The next section discusses how these two theories specify the mechanisms underlying depression.

MECHANISMS BY WHICH NEGATIVE COGNITIVE STYLE INCREASES RISK FOR DEPRESSION

Both hopelessness and Beck's theories hypothesize that negative cognitive styles operate to increase risk for depression through their effects on processing or appraisals of personally relevant negative life experiences. That is, these theories propose that individuals who possess "depressogenic" cognitive styles are vulnerable to depression because they tend to generate interpretations of their stressful experiences that have negative implications for themselves and their futures (hopelessness).

In addition, depressed individuals often create life events that, in turn, worsen their illness. This "stress generation" effect indicates that depressed individuals experience an increased rate of life events that are dependent on their behavior, particularly interpersonal events (e.g., Daley *et al.*, 1997; Hammen, 1991; Simons *et al.*, 1993). Despite much evidence for stress generation, it is unclear whether depression itself or vulnerabilities associated with depression are responsible for the effect (Daley *et al.*, 1997; Joiner *et al.*, 2005a, b; Nelson *et al.*, 2001; Shih, 2006; Simons *et al.*, 1993). Indeed, Safford *et al.* (2007) found that never depressed individuals with negative cognitive styles generated more dependent, interpersonal negative events than those with positive cognitive styles. That is, the stress generation effect was attributable to negative cognitive styles, rather than to depression itself. An expanded, transactional cognitive vulnerability theory (Safford *et al.*, 2007) suggests a "two-hit model" in which cognitively vulnerable individuals not only interpret stressful events more negatively (i.e., are more "reactive" to stressors), but also generate such events more frequently which, in turn, contributes to precipitating depression.

In the cognitive vulnerability models of depression, hopelessness mediates the link between the cognitive vulnerability-stress component and onset of depression (see Figure 11.1). Research has indicated that the interaction of life events and negative cognitive style predicts increases in depressive symptoms through its effects on increasing hopelessness (e.g., Alloy & Clements, 1998; Alloy *et al.*, 1997a; Metalsky *et al.*, 1993). These results highlight the importance of hopelessness in triggering depressive episodes, in addition to cognitive vulnerability and life events.

Abramson *et al.* (2002; Alloy & Abramson, 2007) also elaborated the cognitive vulnerability–stress model of depression to emphasize the role of rumination in the causal chain leading to depression. Self-regulation theorists (Carver & Scheier, 1998) emphasize that when faced with a negative event, it is adaptive to switch attention to this event, find a resolution, and then continue goal-directed behavior (i.e., the self-regulatory cycle). Selective attention often remains focused on the negative event until it is resolved or reduced. Abramson *et al.* (2002; Alloy & Abramson, 2007) highlighted three ways to exit this self-regulatory cycle: generate a solution to the problem, decrease the importance of the event, or distract attention away from it. However, individuals with negative cognitive styles should have difficulty with all three exits due to their negative inferences. For example, if a cognitively vulnerable adolescent attributes not getting a date to "ugliness," no solution is readily available. Instead, such individuals become "stuck" in the self-regulatory cycle with their attention focused on negative cognitive content because the inferences they generate in response to negative events only lead to further perceived problems (e.g., "no one will marry me because I am so ugly") rather than to resolutions. Such self-regulatory perseveration (Pyszczynski & Greenberg, 1987) constitutes rumination because selective attention remains focused on negative content, which, in turn, should result in the spiral into clinically significant depression. This self-regulatory perspective, then, highlights rumination as mediating the effects of negative cognitive styles on depression (see Figure 11.1).

EMPIRICAL SUPPORT FOR NEGATIVE COGNITIVE STYLE AS A RISK FACTOR FOR DEPRESSION

In this section, we review empirical support for the role of negative cognitive style as a vulnerability to depression. Because an extensive evaluation of the research in this area is beyond the scope of this chapter, we focus on the results from research studies that have utilized prospective research designs. We begin by providing an overview of the prospective design and results of studies that have utilized this design. Following this, we provide an overview of a specific type of prospective research design called the behavioral high-risk study, and summarize the results from studies that have utilized this design. Finally, we review the design and results from a landmark behavioral high-risk study, the Temple–Wisconsin Cognitive Vulnerability to Depression (CVD) Project (Alloy & Abramson, 1999).

PROSPECTIVE RESEARCH ON COGNITIVE VULNERABILITY TO DEPRESSION

Overview of the Prospective Design

Prospective studies utilize a baseline assessment of a hypothesized vulnerability factor to predict the future manifestation of a particular set of symptoms and/or episodes of a disorder. Using this design affords researchers many potential benefits, including the ability to establish both the temporal precedence of the vulnerability factor and its independence from symptoms (Alloy *et al.*, 1999a), the ability to control for potentially confounding effects of the previous presence of the disorder (e.g., of medication, hospitalization), the ability to decrease experimenter bias because the researcher does not know who will eventually develop the symptoms or disorder, and the ability to establish if the hypothesized cognitive vulnerability specifically relates to the clinical disorder of interest and not other disorders (i.e., discriminant validity).

Summary of Results from Prospective Studies

Over the past few decades, several prospective studies have investigated the relation between negative cognitive style and depression. A number of these studies have provided empirical support for negative cognitive style as a predictor of depressive symptoms in children (Abela, 2001; Abela & Payne, 2003; Abela & Sarin, 2002; Conley *et al.*, 2001; Dixon & Ahrens, 1992; Gibb & Alloy, 2006; Hilsman & Garber, 1995; Nolen-Hoeksema *et al.*, 1992; Robinson *et al.*, 1995), adolescents (Hankin *et al.*, 2001; Spence *et al.*, 2002), and adults (Abela *et al.*, 2006; Alloy *et al.*, 1999b; Brown *et al.*, 1995; Chaney *et al.*, 2004;

Dykman & Johll, 1998; Hankin *et al.*, 2004; Hong *et al.*, 2006; Joiner *et al.*, 1999; Klocek *et al.*, 1997; Kwon & Oei, 1992; Kwon & Laurenceau, 2002; Lewinsohn *et al.*, 2001; Metalsky & Joiner, 1997; Mongrain & Blackburn, 2005; Olinger *et al.*, 1987; Reilly-Harrington *et al.*, 1999; see Ingram *et al.*, 1998, for a review of non-supportive studies as well). However, despite the preponderance of supportive prospective studies, few prospective studies have examined whether negative cognitive style actually lends vulnerability to full-blown, clinically significant depressive disorders. In adult samples, the two studies that have examined this have found a link between negative cognitive style and clinical depressive disorders (Hankin *et al.*, 2004, Study 2; Lewinsohn *et al.*, 2001).

Overview of the Behavioral High-risk Design

Among prospective designs, the *behavioral high-risk design* is particularly potent for testing vulnerability hypotheses (Alloy & Abramson, 1999; Alloy *et al.*, 1999a). In this type of design, participants are selected who are currently non-disordered, but who possess behavioral or psychological characteristics theoretically linked to a greater vulnerability to developing a particular disorder. These "high-risk" participants, along with a comparison group of participants who score low on the hypothesized risk factor, are then followed prospectively over several time points. One of the greatest advantages associated with this type of study is its ability to allow researchers to establish the precedence and stability of the hypothesized vulnerability factor in individuals who do not initially have the disorder of interest. Specifically, this provides researchers with better control of the potential effects of current dysfunction on future symptom presentation. Additionally, it allows researchers the ability to examine the role of other factors (e.g., stress, protective factors) that may moderate or influence which high risk participants later develop the disorder under investigation.

Summary of Results from Behavioral High-risk Studies

Consistent with other prospective studies, the results from several studies approximating a prospective behavioral high-risk design have shown that individuals who evince negative cognitive styles are more likely to develop depressive moods or symptoms when they experience negative life events than are individuals without such negative styles (e.g., Alloy & Clements, 1998; Alloy *et al.*, 1997a; Metalsky & Joiner, 1992; Metalsky *et al.*, 1987; Metalsky *et al.*, 1993; Nolen-Hoeksema *et al.*, 1986, 1992).

The CVD Project: Design and Key Findings

A particularly important study using the behavioral high-risk design, the CVD Project, is a collaborative, two-site study designed to examine cognitive, psychosocial, and developmental risk factors and mechanisms in unipolar depression (Alloy & Abramson, 1999). Results from this study provide strong support for negative cognitive style as a risk factor for the onset of clinically significant depressive disorders, a more negative course of depression, and suicidal behaviors, as well as the moderating influence of negative life events and the mediating role of rumination and hopelessness. Here, we discuss the CVD Project's design and key findings.

Design of the CVD Project

In the CVD Project, university freshmen who had no current Axis I psychiatric disorders at the outset of the study, but who were hypothesized to be at high risk (HR) or low risk (LR) for depression based on the presence vs. absence of negative cognitive styles, were followed prospectively every 6 weeks for 2.5 years and then every 16 weeks for an additional 3 years. At each assessment point, participants' stressful life events, cognitions, symptoms, and diagnosable episodes of psychopathology were assessed using both self-report inventories and structured interviews.

Participants and Procedures

Participants were selected for the CVD Project using a two-phase screening procedure. In phase 1, we administered the DAS (Weissman & Beck, 1978) and CSQ (Alloy *et al.*, 2000), which assess inferential styles regarding the causes, consequences, and self-implications of negative life events, to 5378 freshmen at Temple University and the University of Wisconsin. Participants who scored in the highest, or most negative, quartile on both the DAS and the CSQ composite for negative events were considered potential HR participants. Similarly, participants who scored in the lowest, or most positive, quartile on both instruments were considered potential LR participants. In phase 2, we interviewed a random subset of participants who met phase 1 criteria using the Schedule for Affective Disorders and Schizophrenia–Lifetime Version (SADS-L; Endicott & Spitzer, 1978), which was expanded to permit Research Diagnostic Criteria (RDC; Spitzer *et al.*, 1978), DSM-III-R (American Psychiatric Association, 1987), and DSM-IV (American Psychiatric Association, 1994) diagnoses. We excluded participants who met RDC or DSM criteria for any current Axis I disorder at the time of the phase 1 screening. In order to avoid creating an unrepresentative sample of HR participants, we included participants with a past unipolar mood disorder, providing it had remitted for a minimum of 2 months (for rationale, see Alloy & Abramson, 1999; Alloy *et al.*, 2000). The final CVD Project sample consisted of 173 high-risk and 176 low-risk ethnically and socioeconomically diverse participants across the two sites (for sample demographic characteristics and representativeness, see Alloy *et al.*, 2000).

At Time 1 of the CVD Project, participants completed the Personality Disorders Examination (PDE; Loranger, 1988), an interview that assesses Axis II disorders and dimensions, a set of tasks designed to assess self-referent information processing (SRIP Task Battery; Alloy *et al*, 1997b), as well as further measures of cognitive style (sociotropy-autonomy, self-consciousness), coping styles (rumination vs. distraction), and social support. During the initial 2.5 years of follow-up, we assessed participants every 6 weeks for the onset of depressive symptoms and episodes, other disorders, stressful life events, and hypothesized mediating cognitions (inferences for actual events experienced, and negative views of self, world, and future). In order to obtain information regarding new onsets of depression and other disorders, we interviewed participants using the SADS–Change (SADS-C; Spitzer & Endicott, 1978). We used DSM-IV and RDC criteria to diagnose depression, as well as explicit criteria for diagnosing hopelessness depression (HD; see Alloy *et al.*, 2000, 2006b). Inter-rater reliability for diagnoses was excellent, with kappas > 0.90 for all project diagnoses. In addition to interviewing the participants with the SADS-C, we used the Life Events Scale (LES; Alloy & Clements, 1992; Needles & Abramson, 1990) and a Stress Interview (SI; Alloy & Abramson, 1999; Safford *et al.*, 2007) to assess stressful life events experienced by participants. The SI contained explicit criteria for defining what experiences qualified as an instance of each event type; thus, we disqualified events reported on the LES that did not meet the event definition criteria on the SI. We also dated and rated the objective severity of each event (for SI reliability and validity data, see Safford *et al.*, 2007). Throughout the project, both the SADS-C interviewers and the SI interviewers were blind to participants' cognitive risk status. Additionally, the SADS-C interviewer differed from the SI interviewer, and the SI interviewers were kept blind to participants' diagnostic information.

Further, during the first 2.5 years of follow-up, participants and their parents completed a number of measures assessing parental history of psychopathology, as well as parental cognitive styles, inferential feedback, and parenting styles. Participants' childhood life events and reports of childhood maltreatment were also assessed. For further details about the rationale, design, and methodology of the CVD project, see Alloy and Abramson (1999). The results presented below focus primarily on findings from the first 2.5 years of follow-up.

CVD PROJECT RESULTS

A primary hypothesis of the cognitive theories of depression is that certain negative cognitive styles confer vulnerability to symptoms and diagnoses of depression. Although cognitive styles are not immutable (e.g., Just *et al.*, 2001) and are open to modification (e.g., through cognitive therapy; see DeRubeis & Hollon, 1995), these styles are typically viewed as relatively stable risk factors. Findings from the CVD project have supported the relative stability of cognitive styles. Specifically, the cognitive styles of the participants remained relatively stable over up to 7 years of follow-up (Romens *et al.*, 2008). In addition, participants' attributions and inferences for particular negative life events remained stable over a 5-year follow-up (Raniere, 2000). Thus, cognitive styles appear to be relatively trait-like; but do they increase risk for clinically significant depression as hypothesized?

Does Negative Cognitive Style Predict First Onset and Recurrence of Depression?

Most participants in the CVD Project entered college with no prior history of clinically significant depression. Within this group of never-depressed participants, HR individuals were significantly more likely than LR individuals to experience a first lifetime onset of major depression (16.2% vs. 2.7%, odds ratio [OR] = 7.4), minor depression (45.9% vs. 14.4%, OR = 5.6), and HD (35.1% vs. 3.6%, OR = 11.6) during the first 2.5 years of follow-up, after controlling for initial depressive symptoms (Alloy *et al.*, 2006b). Based on a truly prospective test and uncontaminated by prior history of depression, these results provide particularly strong support for negative cognitive style as a vulnerability to initial development of depression. We also examined whether negative cognitive style confers risk for recurrences of depression. Among participants with a history of prior depression, HR individuals were significantly more likely than LR individuals to experience a recurrence of major depression (28.6% vs. 9.4%, OR = 3.8), minor depression (56.1% vs. 32.8%, OR = 3.1), and HD (50.0% vs. 18.8%, OR = 4.1) during the first 2.5 years of follow-up, after controlling for initial depressive symptoms (Alloy *et al.*, 2006b). Taken together, these results provide strong empirical support for negative cognitive styles as risk factors for both the development of first onset of depression as well as recurrence of depression.

Does Negative Cognitive Style Predict the Course of Depression?

Individuals who have a negative cognitive style are also hypothesized to experience a worse course of depression. To test this hypothesis, Iacoviello *et al.* (2006) examined the relation between cognitive style and the number of major or minor depressive episodes experienced by CVD participants, as well as the severity, duration, and chronicity associated with these episodes. After controlling for participants' past history of depression and baseline levels of depressive symptoms, Iacoviello *et al.* (2006) found that HR participants not only experienced more episodes of depression they also experienced more severe episodes, and a more chronic course of depression relative to the LR participants. However, HR participants did not experience longer duration episodes than LR participants. One of the first prospective tests of the relation between negative cognitive style and the course of depression, this study suggests that cognitive vulnerability also helps to determine the maintenance and severity of depressive symptoms over time.

Does Negative Cognitive Style Predict Suicidal Behaviors?

In addition to conferring vulnerability to depression, the cognitive theories hypothesize that negative cognitive styles should increase the risk of suicidal ideation and attempts, and that levels of hopelessness should mediate this relation. Findings from the CVD project provide support for this hypothesis (Abramson *et al.*, 1998). Abramson *et al.* (1998) found that HR participants were more likely than LR participants to evince suicidal thinking and attempts over the first 2.5 years of prospective follow-up, and this relation was mediated by participants' mean levels of hopelessness across the 2.5-year period. Furthermore, the relation between negative cognitive style and future suicidal behaviors persisted even after participants' prior history of suicidal behavior and other known risk factors for suicide (i.e., prior history of major and minor depression, borderline and antisocial personality dysfunction, and parental history of depression) were controlled.

Does Negative Cognitive Style Confer Specific Risk to Depression vs. Other Disorders?

Negative cognitive style is hypothesized to confer specific risk to depressive disorders vs. a more general vulnerability to disorders of negative affect. Moreover, negative cognitive style is hypothesized to relate more specifically to symptoms of HD vs. non-HD. Given the high comorbidity of anxiety disorders and depression (Alloy *et al.*, 1990; Mineka *et al.*, 1998), researchers have examined the link between negative cognitive style and depression vs. anxiety. The results from several retrospective and cross-sectional studies support the specific relation of negative cognitive style to depressive vs. anxiety symptoms (see Alloy *et al.*, 2006b, for a review), albeit, this specific relation was not supported in all studies (Haeffel *et al.*, 2003; Luten *et al.*, 1997). Additionally, the results from some prospective studies that have examined the interaction between negative cognitive style and stressful life events also support the specificity of negative cognitive style to depressive symptoms vs. anxiety symptoms or symptoms of other disorders (Alloy & Clements, 1998; Hankin *et al.*, 2004; Robinson *et al.*, 1995). Still, the results of other prospective studies did not support this specificity (Cole & Turner, 1993; Hammen *et al.*, 1988; Luten *et al.*, 1997; Ralph & Mineka, 1998).

In the CVD Project, Alloy *et al.* (2006b) found that in addition to being more likely to develop a depressive disorder over the prospective period, HR participants were significantly more likely to develop an anxiety disorder than were LR participants (HR = 8.7%; LR = 2.3%; OR = 5.7). However, a closer analysis of our data revealed that this relation was due entirely to the co-occurrence between depression and anxiety. After dividing participants with anxiety disorders into one of two groups: those with and without comorbid depression, we found that negative cognitive style significantly predicted the onset of an anxiety disorder comorbid with depression (HR = 5.7%; LR = 0.6%; OR = 19.6), but not the onset of an anxiety disorder alone (HR = 2.9%; LR = 1.7%; OR = 1.4, $p < 0.80$). Furthermore, negative cognitive style did not predict the onset of any other Axis I disorders. In sum, these results lend considerable support to the specificity of negative cognitive style to depressive disorders, given there were no differences between HR and LR participants' likelihood of developing anxiety or other disorders, unless they co-occurred with depression.

Does Negative Cognitive Style Confer Specific Risk to HD?

In addition to the hypothesized specificity between negative cognitive style and depression, negative cognitive style is hypothesized to relate more specifically to symptoms of HD vs. non-HD. Consistent with this hypothesis, the results of several prospective studies suggest that negative cognitive style, alone and in interaction with negative life events, is more strongly predictive of increases in symptoms of HD vs. symptoms of non-HD or symptoms of other types of psychopathology (Alloy & Clements, 1998; Alloy *et al.*, 1997a; Hankin *et al.*, 2001; Joiner *et al.*, 2001; Metalsky & Joiner, 1997). Preliminary results from the CVD Project also support this relation. Based on the first 2.5 years of the prospective follow-up period, negative cognitive style predicted first onsets and recurrences of HD, but not *DSM* melancholic depression.

Does Negative Cognitive Style Interact with Stressful Life Events to Predict Depression?

Inasmuch as the cognitive theories of depression are vulnerability–stress models in which maladaptive cognitive styles are hypothesized to increase individuals' risk for depression when they experience negative life events, it is important to examine the interaction between cognitive style and the occurrence of negative life events in predicting onset of depression. Many studies have found that the cognitive vulnerability–stress combination predicts depressive symptoms (see Alloy *et al.*, 2006b, for a review). However, there have also been some published studies that have failed to find support for this hypothesis (e.g., Cole & Turner, 1993; Joiner & Wagner, 1995; Tiggemann *et al.*, 1991).

To date, the cognitive vulnerability–stress hypothesis has received relatively little evaluation with data from the CVD Project. Preliminary analyses of the CVD data from the Temple University site have provided support for this hypothesized relation. Specifically, cognitive risk status interacted with the number of negative life events participants experienced in the prior 6 weeks to predict onset of major or minor depressive episodes and of HD episodes. When compared to HR participants who experienced low levels of recent stress, or to LR participants regardless of their recent stress levels, HR participants who experienced high levels of recent negative life events were significantly more likely to develop major or minor depression and HD. Thus, preliminary evidence supports the cognitive vulnerability hypothesis that individuals with a negative cognitive style are more likely to become depressed after experiencing negative life events than are individuals without this vulnerability. However, more definitive analyses of the CVD Project remain to be conducted based on both sites.

Does Negative Cognitive Style Predict Processing or Appraisals of Personally Relevant Negative Life Experiences?

According to the cognitive theories of depression, individuals with negative cognitive styles are vulnerable to depression because they tend to make negative inferences following the occurrence of stressful events and perceive, interpret, and remember information about themselves in a negative manner. Consistent with this hypothesis, using CVD Project data, Panzarella *et al.* (2006) found that participants' cognitive styles prospectively predicted the inferences they made for negative life events they experienced. HR individuals made more negative inferences regarding the causes, consequences, and self-worth implications of negative events they experienced than did LR individuals.

This hypothesis was also tested using data from the Self-referent Information Processing (SRIP) Task Battery, administered at the Time 1 assessment of the CVD Project. Given Beck's hypothesis that individuals with a negative self-schema should demonstrate biased information processing only for depression-relevant stimuli (i.e., stimuli related to themes of incompetence, worthlessness, and low motivation), Alloy *et al.* (1997b) predicted that HR participants would exhibit information processing biases for depression-relevant, but not depression-irrelevant, self-referent adjectives. As predicted, when compared to LR participants, HR participants showed preferential self-referent processing for negative depression-relevant material (e.g., words such as "failure," "passive," and "useless") as evidenced by relatively greater endorsement, faster processing, greater accessibility, better recall, and higher predictive certainty of this material. Additionally, HR participants were less likely than LR participants to process positive depression-relevant stimuli (e.g., words such as "resourceful," "energetic," and "important"). Importantly, all of the risk group differences were maintained even after statistically controlling for participants' levels of depressive symptoms. These findings are unique in demonstrating that the information processing biases previously found in depressed individuals (see Ingram *et al.*, 1998; Segal, 1988) also extend to non-depressed individuals at high cognitive risk for depression.

Does Hopelessness Mediate the Effects of Negative Cognitive Style on Depression?

Another tenet of the hopelessness theory (Abramson *et al.*, 1989) is that the interaction between negative cognitive styles and stress predicts onset of depression precisely because it increases the probability that an at-risk individual will become hopeless. Alloy and Clements (1998) examined whether, as hypothesized, hopelessness plays a mediational role in the association between the vulnerability–stress interaction and manifestation of symptoms related to HD. Consistent with underlying theory, with previous research (e.g., Lynd-Stevenson, 1997; Metalsky & Joiner, 1992), and more specifically with hopelessness as the proximal cause of HD symptoms, the results supported the role of hopelessness as a mediator in this association. Subsequent research has replicated these results (e.g., Abela, 2002), although not all studies have reported results consistent with the role of hopelessness as a mediator in the relationship between the vulnerability–stress interaction and depressive symptoms (e.g., Kapçi & Cramer, 2000). Of note, although hopelessness theory predicts only that this mediational relationship will hold in HD, much of the research conducted in this regard since the Alloy and Clements (1998) study has examined depressive symptomatology in a broad sense, and has not focused strictly on HD.

Does Rumination Mediate the Effects of Negative Cognitive Style on Hopelessness, Depression, and Suicidal Behavior?

According to the response styles theory of depression (Nolen-Hoeksema, 1991), individuals who tend to ruminate in response to dysphoria will be at increased risk for experiencing more severe and prolonged depression than will individuals who tend to distract themselves from their dysphoria. Rumination refers to "behaviors and thoughts that focus one's attention on one's depressive symptoms and on the implications of these symptoms" (Nolen-Hoeksema, 1991,

p. 569), whereas distraction refers to active attempts to ignore depressive symptoms by focusing on pleasant or neutral activities. Several studies have supported this theory, demonstrating that rumination is associated with a greater likelihood, and longer and more severe episodes of depression (see Chapter 9). As discussed above, Abramson *et al.* (2002; Alloy & Abramson, 2007) incorporated rumination into the causal chain of cognitive vulnerability–stress theories of depression and hypothesized that rumination would mediate the effects of negative cognitive styles on the prospective development of hopelessness and depressive symptoms and episodes. Consistent with this hypothesis, using CVD Project data, Spasojevic and Alloy (2001) found that a ruminative response style mediated the association between cognitive risk status and the development of prospective episodes of major depression. Rumination also mediated the effects of other risk factors (past history of depression, maladaptive dependency, and self-criticism) for major depression onset during the follow-up period. In another recent study of a subsample of CVD project participants, Smith *et al.* (2006) found that rumination mediated the relation between negative cognitive styles and suicidal ideation. In addition, hopelessness partially mediated the relation between rumination and suicidal ideation, and fully mediated the association between rumination and duration of suicidality. Thus, available information suggests that as predicted by the expanded cognitive vulnerability–stress model of depression, negative cognitive styles may increase risk for depression and suicidality by increasing the likelihood that individuals become stuck in a ruminative cycle and develop hopelessness.

Rumination may not only mediate the effects of negative cognitive styles on onset of depression, but it may also moderate this association. Robinson and Alloy (2003) hypothesized that individuals who have negative cognitive styles and who also tend to ruminate about these negative cognitions in response to the occurrence of stressful life events (stress-reactive rumination), may be more likely to develop episodes of depression. They suggested that negative cognitive styles provide the negative content, but this negative content may be more likely to lead to depression when it is "on one's mind" than when it is not. Thus, Robinson and Alloy suggested that stress-reactive rumination would exacerbate the association between negative cognitive styles and depression onset. Consistent with this hypothesis, they found that among the individuals at high cognitive risk for depression, those who were also high in stress-reactive rumination evidenced a higher prospective incidence of major depression and HD than HR individuals who did not tend to ruminate in response to stressors, and than LR individuals with either high or low levels of stress-reactive rumination.

DEVELOPMENTAL ANTECEDENTS OF NEGATIVE COGNITIVE STYLES

If negative cognitive styles do indeed confer vulnerability to future episodes of both depression and suicidal ideation and attempts, as the evidence suggests, it is important to understand how such cognitive styles develop. The CVD Project provided data on several factors that may contribute to the development of these cognitive styles (see Alloy *et al.*, 2004 for an in-depth review of the developmental findings from the CVD Project).

DO MODELING AND PARENTAL INFERENTIAL FEEDBACK CONTRIBUTE TO THE DEVELOPMENT OF NEGATIVE COGNITIVE STYLES?

Children may develop their cognitive styles in part through modeling their parents' cognitive styles or through their parents' provision of inferential feedback regarding the causes and consequences of negative events in the child's life. However, studies have provided mixed support for a direct relation between parents' and their children's negative cognitive styles (e.g., Garber & Flynn, 2001; Seligman *et al.*, 1984). For example, in the CVD Project, the mothers of HR participants had more dysfunctional attitudes than did mothers of LR participants, even after controlling for the mothers' levels of depressive symptoms (Alloy *et al.*, 2001). In contrast, no risk group differences were observed in mothers' or fathers' inferential styles or in fathers' dysfunctional attitudes. Thus, although there is some evidence that children may model their parents' cognitive styles, especially their mothers', future studies are required to further examine this relation. Given the mixed results obtained thus far, future studies should examine possible moderating factors that may either strengthen or weaken the relationship (e.g., amount of time that is, spent with parent).

Negative parental inferential feedback has been found more consistently to be related to negative cognitive style in their children (e.g., Garber & Flynn, 2001; Turk & Bry, 1992). For example, according to both CVD Project participants' and their parents' reports, and controlling for respondents' levels of depressive symptoms, the parents of HR participants provided more stable, global attributional feedback and negative consequence feedback than did parents of LR participants (Alloy *et al.*, 2001). Additionally, negative attributional and consequence feedback from mothers interacted with a history of high levels of childhood stressful life events to predict HR status (Crossfield *et al.*, 2002). Moreover, the negative inferential feedback from parents predicted prospective onsets of depressive episodes in their children over the 2.5-year follow-up period, mediated, in part or totally, by the children's cognitive risk status (Alloy *et al.*, 2001). Thus, there is some evidence that parents may contribute to the development of negative cognitive styles in their children, not by the children modeling the attributions their parents make for negative events in the parents' lives, but by the inferential feedback the children receive from their parents for negative events in the children's own lives.

DO GENERAL PARENTING STYLES CONTRIBUTE TO THE DEVELOPMENT OF NEGATIVE COGNITIVE STYLES?

Several studies provide evidence that certain parenting styles may also contribute to the development of a negative cognitive style in children (see Alloy *et al.*, &

Neeren, 2006a, for a review). In particular, parenting characterized by lack of warmth and caring and by negative psychological control (e.g., criticism, intrusiveness, and guilt-induction) is associated with depression and negative cognitive styles in offspring (Alloy *et al.*, 2006a). For example, in the CVD Project, both HR participants and their fathers reported that the fathers exhibited less warmth and acceptance than did fathers of LR participants (Alloy *et al.*, 2001). There were no group differences, however, for fathers' psychological control or firm control (discipline), nor were there any group differences in the mothers' parenting styles. Fathers' warmth also predicted prospective onsets of MD, minor depression (MiD), and HD episodes in their children, but only the prediction of HD episodes was mediated by the children's cognitive risk status (Alloy *et al.*, 2001). Interestingly, although parental psychological control was not related to negative cognitive styles in the CVD Project, such overcontrol by both parents was related to their offspring's greater tendency to ruminate (Spasojevic & Alloy, 2002).

DOES CHILDHOOD MALTREATMENT CONTRIBUTE TO THE DEVELOPMENT OF NEGATIVE COGNITIVE STYLES?

Rose and Abramson (1992) proposed another developmental pathway by which childhood negative life events, especially childhood maltreatment, may lead to the development of a negative cognitive style. Specifically, they suggested that when maltreatment occurs, individuals attempt to understand the cause, consequences, and meanings of the abuse so that future negative events may be avoided and hopefulness may be maintained. With repeated occurrences of maltreatment, however, initial hopefulness-maintaining attributions may be disconfirmed, leading the child to begin making more hopelessness-inducing inferences about its repeated occurrence. For example, a child may explain the maltreatment by thinking: "I'm a terrible person who deserves all the bad things that happen to me"; an internal, stable, and global explanation that entails negative consequences and negative self-characteristics. Over time, the child's hopelessness-inducing attributions may generalize to initially unrelated negative events. In this way, a relatively stable and global negative cognitive style may develop. Further, Rose and Abramson hypothesized that childhood emotional maltreatment may be more likely than either childhood physical or sexual maltreatment to contribute to the development of a negative cognitive style. They reasoned that with emotional maltreatment, the depressogenic cognitions are directly supplied to the child by the abuser. In contrast, with physical and sexual maltreatment, the child must supply his or her own negative cognitions and, thus, may have greater opportunity to make less depressogenic inferences for the occurrence of maltreatment.

Evaluations of the relation between childhood maltreatment and cognitive style have supported Rose and Abramson's hypotheses (see Alloy *et al.*, 2006a, for a review). For example, after controlling for their levels of depressive symptoms, HR participants in the CVD Project reported significantly higher levels of childhood emotional, but not physical or sexual, maltreatment than did LR participants (Gibb *et al.*, 2001a). In addition, participants' cognitive risk status and hopelessness fully or partially mediated the relation between levels of childhood emotional maltreatment and the occurrence of non-endogenous MD episodes, HD episodes, and suicidal ideation and attempts during the first 2.5 years of follow-up (Gibb e*t al.*, 2001a,b). Moreover, Gibb *et al.* (2004) found that even when parental maltreatment and parental history of psychopathology were controlled, there was still a significant relationship between emotional maltreatment from non-relatives (i.e., peer victimization) during development and cognitive HR status. These findings cannot be explained easily by third variable accounts such as genetic influence or a general negative family environment.

Prospective longitudinal research is needed to assess the degree to which emotional maltreatment contributes to increased negativity in cognitive styles and risk to depression over time. Along these lines, Gibb *et al.* (2006) examined emotional maltreatment in predicting change in attributional style over a 6-month period in 4th and 5th grade children. Greater emotional maltreatment occurring both during the 6-month follow-up and in the 6 months prior to Time 1 predicted a worsening of children's attributional styles (the styles became more negative) over the follow-up. Moreover, using data from the Temple site of the CVD Project, Liu *et al.* (2008) found that higher levels of emotional maltreatment from adults and peers assessed prospectively predicted shorter time to onset of major and minor depressive episodes. In sum, there is growing evidence that emotional maltreatment may contribute risk for depression in part by contributing to the development of negative cognitive styles.

NEGATIVE COGNITIVE STYLES: IMPLICATIONS FOR RESILIENCE TO DEPRESSION, TREATMENT, AND PREVENTION

Evidence that negative cognitive styles increase risk for depression has implications for factors that may mitigate against their deleterious effects, as well as for treatment and preventive strategies that may be effective for depression. In this section, we consider the manner in which a particular type of social support derived from the logic of the hopelessness theory may protect against depression even among individuals at risk for depression by virtue of their negative cognitive styles. We also consider how negative cognitive styles might be remediated once formed or prevented from developing in the first place.

ADAPTIVE INFERENTIAL FEEDBACK AS A BUFFER AGAINST DEPRESSION AMONG COGNITIVELY VULNERABLE INDIVIDUALS

In an extension of the hopelessness theory of depression, Panzarella *et al.* (2006) proposed that a subtype of social support, Adaptive Inferential Feedback

(AIF), may buffer against depression, reducing cognitive vulnerability for depression by decreasing negative cognitive styles and the likelihood of making depressogenic inferences for negative events. AIF involves being offered adaptive inferences for negative events (e.g., attributing stressful events to unstable and specific rather than stable and global causes; providing less negative consequences and implications for self-worth for the stressful events) by members of an individual's support network, and as such, is the converse of negative inferences. Panzarella *et al.* suggested that when people in an individual's social support network refute negative inferences made by someone for a particular event, the negative inferences will be weakened or modified, making it less likely that the individual will become hopeless. For example, a person may express the following depressogenic inference to a friend following a job interview: "Now I'll never get the job I want, I am so stupid, I always mess things up." The friend might offer an adaptive inferential alternative, such as: "You are not stupid, you just had a tough interview. You did well in the previous interview and even were offered a job!" This may lead the first individual to reevaluate her thinking, thereby modifying the original maladaptive inference and reducing the likelihood of hopelessness and depression (Panzarella *et al.*, 2006). AIF differs from other forms of social support in that it directly challenges depressogenic cognitions by proposing an alternative, more adaptive inference. Thus, AIF might be thought of as informal cognitive therapy provided by members of one's social support network.

Consistent with this hypothesis, Panzarella *et al.* (2006) found that among individuals in the CVD Project, higher levels of AIF were predictive prospectively of a less negative inferential style over a 6-month period, even after controlling for the effects of general social support and stressful life events. This finding suggests that to the extent individuals with negative cognitive styles receive some AIF, the feedback may gradually decrease the negativity of their styles. Additionally, Panzarella *et al.* found that higher levels of AIF predicted more adaptive inferences for actual negative events participants experienced. Thus, repeated instances of receiving AIF following stressful events may lead individuals to generate more adaptive inferences for those events and also lead over time to the development of a more positive cognitive style. Finally, AIF moderated the cognitive vulnerability–stress interaction. Specifically, the interaction among AIF, cognitive risk status, and stress predicted hopelessness, dysphoria, and onset of HD episodes prospectively. HR participants with high stress and low levels of AIF were more likely than participants with 0, 1, or 2 of these 3 risk factors to develop hopelessness, depressive symptoms, and HD. Similarly, in a laboratory manipulation of AIF, Dobkin *et al.* (2004) found that individuals whose partners were taught to deliver AIF showed reduced negative inferences and depressive symptoms following a laboratory failure compared to individuals whose partners provided general social support or no social support. Finally, in a pilot treatment study, Dobkin *et al.* (2007) reported that augmentation of standard Cognitive Behavioral Therapy (CBT) with four sessions of AIF partner training, led to significant improvement in major depressed patients' depression, anxiety, negative inferences, and perception of social support, with gains maintained at a 2-month follow-up. Thus, there is evidence that a specific subtype of social support, AIF, can have an impact on cognitive styles, inferences for actual stressful events, and the development of hopelessness and depression.

TREATMENT AND PREVENTION

Interventions designed to prevent the formation of negative cognitive styles in the first place, or to remediate them, once formed, should reduce the likelihood of future episodes of depression (Alloy *et al.*, 2007). CBT for depression has been shown to be effective and may also reduce the risk of relapse and recurrence in adults (Hollon *et al.*, 2005; Hollon & Thase, 2002), partly due to decreasing the negativity of individuals' cognitive styles. Techniques for achieving this include identifying and modifying maladaptive inferences, as well as cognitive restructuring, which ultimately serve to alter a client's dysfunctional attitudes and negative inferential styles. In addition to achieving symptom reduction through cognitive restructuring and other strategies aimed at addressing cognitive risk factors in depression, these techniques may also reduce the likelihood that a client will generate negative life events that may serve as precursors to the development of depressive symptoms (Safford *et al.*, 2007).

Given that negative cognitive styles may lead to depression in part through increasing rumination and can be further exacerbated by rumination, the effects of these styles may also be altered indirectly by teaching individuals more effective emotion-regulation strategies (Alloy *et al.*, 2007). Specifically, it may be useful to teach cognitively vulnerable individuals ways to exit a ruminative cycle through better problem-solving, distraction from the problem, and how to lessen the perceived importance of the problem. Additionally, negative cognitive styles lead both to more pessimistic interpretations of stressful events that occur as well as to higher rates of occurrence of stressors through stress generation. Thus, it may be beneficial to help cognitively vulnerable individuals reduce the stressfulness of the environment in which they live through interventions designed to improve their interpersonal skills and problem-solving.

In applying knowledge of cognitive vulnerability to the prevention of depression, modifications of CBT might be directed toward preadolescents before their cognitive styles have fully consolidated. School-based CBT programs, such as the Coping with Stress course (Clarke *et al.*, 1995, 2001) and the Penn Optimism Project (Gillham *et al.*, 1995; Jaycox *et al.*, 1994), are designed to train children and adolescents to challenge negative interpretations of stressful events. Clarke's program significantly reduced rates of depression onset in at-risk adolescents chosen based on pretest elevations in depressive symptoms and parental histories of depression. Similarly, the Penn Optimism Project improved attributional style and reduced depressive symptoms in diverse samples of children (Cardemil *et al.*, 2002; Jaycox *et al.*, 1994; Yu & Seligman, 2002), although not in all samples of youth (Cardemil *et al.*, 2002).

Further, the findings on potential developmental antecedents of negative cognitive styles suggest that primary prevention might be directed at promoting positive cognitive styles in youth. This might be accomplished by educating parents and teachers to provide feedback about more benign inferences for stressful, negative events in children's lives, as well as by training parents to be more emotionally supportive in interacting with their children (Alloy *et al.*, 2007).

DIRECTIONS FOR FUTURE RESEARCH

As reviewed in this chapter, much evidence has accumulated that supports the role of negative cognitive styles as a risk factor for depression. However, an important direction for future research is an integration of cognitive vulnerability with other known risk factors for depression, such as genetic vulnerability (see Chapter 2). Interestingly, two studies found that cognitive vulnerability has a genetic component (Lau *et al.*, 2006; Schulman *et al.*, 1993). Specifically, Schulman *et al.* (1993) found that monozygotic twins had a higher concordance for attributional style than dizygotic twins, and in a study of over 1300 adolescent twin and sibling pairs, Lau *et al.* (2006) also found a genetic influence on attributional style. It is likely that the serotonin transporter polymorphism (5-HTTLPR genotype), in particular, is related to cognitive vulnerability. Both cognitive vulnerability and the 5-HTTLPR genotype participate in vulnerability–stress interactions that moderate the effects of stress on depression (Alloy & Abramson, 2007). Other more specific research suggests that serotonin modulates dysfunctional attitudes, an important type of negative cognitive style (Meyer *et al.*, 2003, 2004). Further, research has found a link between the 5-HTTLPR genotype and negative emotionality/neuroticism (Lesch *et al.*, 1996), which, in turn, interacts with stressful life events to predict the development of cognitive vulnerability among children approaching adolescence (Mezulis *et al.*, 2006). Finally, compared to individuals with two long alleles on the 5-HT polymorphism, individuals carrying a short allele exhibited a stronger attentional bias to emotional word stimuli, another indicator of cognitive vulnerability (Beevers *et al.*, 2007). It is important to continue to build on these findings and determine whether cognitive vulnerability mediates, at least partially, the effects of this genotype in particular, or genetic risk more generally, on depression in response to stressful life events (Alloy & Abramson, 2007; Eley *et al.*, 2004; Grabe *et al.*, 2004).

REFERENCES

Abela, J. R. Z. (2001). The hopelessness theory of depression: A test of the diathesis-stress and causal mediation components in third and seventh grade children. *Journal of Abnormal Child Psychology*, *29*, 241–254.

Abela, J. R. Z. (2002). Depressive mood reactions to failure in the achievement domain: A test of the integration of the hopelessness and self-esteem theories of depression. *Cognitive Therapy and Research, 26*, 531–552.

Abela, J. R. Z., & Sarin, S. (2002). Cognitive vulnerability to hopelessness depression: A chain is only as strong as its weakest link. *Cognitive Therapy and Research, 26*, 811–829.

Abela, J. R. Z., & Payne, A. V. L. (2003). A test of the integration of the hopelessness and self-esteem theories of depression in schoolchildren. *Cognitive Therapy and Research, 27*, 519–535.

Abela, J. R. Z., Aydin, C., & Auerbach, R. P. (2006). Operationalizing the "vulnerability" and "stress" components of the hopelessness theory of depression: A multi-wave longitudinal study. *Behaviour Research and Therapy, 44*, 1565–1583.

Abramson, L. Y., Metalsky, G. I., & Alloy, L. B. (1989). Hopelessness depression: A theory-based subtype of depression. *Psychological Review, 96*, 358–372.

Abramson, L. Y., Alloy, L. B., Hogan, M. E., Whitehouse, W. G., Cornette, M., Akhavan, S., & Chiara, A. (1998). Suicidality and cognitive vulnerability to depression among college students: A prospective study. *Journal of Adolescence, 21*, 473–487.

Abramson, L. Y., Alloy, L. B., Hankin, B. L., Haeffel, G. J., MacCoon, D. G., & Gibb, B. E. (2002). Cognitive vulnerability–stress models of depression in a self-regulatory and psychobiological context. In I. H. Gotlib & C. L. Hammen (Eds.), *Handbook of Depression, 3rd ed.* (pp. 268–294). New York: Guilford press.

Alloy, L. B., & Clements, C. M. (1992). Illusion of control: Invulnerability to negative affect and depressive symptoms after laboratory and natural stressors. *Journal of Abnormal Psychology, 101*, 234–245.

Alloy, L. B., & Clements, C. M. (1998). Hopelessness theory of depression: Tests of the symptom component. *Cognitive Therapy and Research, 22*, 303–335.

Alloy, L. B., & Abramson, L. Y. (1999). The Temple–Wisconsin cognitive vulnerability to depression (CVD) project: Conceptual background, design, and methods. *Journal of Cognitive Psychotherapy: An International Quarterly, 13*, 227–262.

Alloy, L. B., & Abramson, L. Y. (2007). The adolescent surge in depression and emergence of gender differences: A biocognitive vulnerability–stress model in a developmental context. In D. Romer, & E. F. Walker (Eds.), *Adolescent Psychopathology and The Developing Brain: Integrating Brain and Prevention Science* (pp. 284–312). New York: Oxford University Press.

Alloy, L. B., Kelly, K. A., Mineka, S., & Clements, C. M. (1990). Comorbidity in anxiety and depressive disorders: A helplessness-hopelessness perspective. In J. D. Maser & C. R. Cloninger (Eds.), *Comorbidity in Anxiety and Mood Disorders* (pp. 499–543). Washington, DC: American Psychiatric Press.

Alloy, L. B., Just, N., & Panzarella, C. (1997a). Attributional style, daily life events, and hopelessness depression: Subtype validation by prospective variability and specificity of symptoms. *Cognitive Therapy and Research, 21*, 321–344.

Alloy, L. B., Abramson, L. Y., Murray, L. A., Whitehouse, W. G., & Hogan, M. E. (1997b). Self-referent information processing in individuals at high and low cognitive risk for depression. *Cognition and Emotion, 11*, 539–568.

Alloy, L. B., Abramson, L. Y., Raniere, D., & Dyller, I. M. (1999a). Research methods in adult psychopathology. In P. C. Kendall, J. N. Butcher, & G. N. Holmbeck (Eds.), *Handbook of Research Methods in Clinical Psychology, 2nd ed.* (pp. 466–498). New York: Wiley.

Alloy, L. B., Reilly-Harrington, N., Fresco, D., Whitehouse, W. G., & Zechmeister, J. S. (1999b). Cognitive styles and life events in subsyndromal unipolar and bipolar disorders; Stability and prospective prediction of depressive and hypomanic mood swings. *Journal of Cognitive Psychotherapy: An International Quarterly, 13*, 21–40.

Alloy, L. B., Abramson, L. Y., Hogan, M. E., Whitehouse, W. G., Rose, D. T., Robinson, M. S., *et al.* (2000). The Temple–Wisconsin cognitive vulnerability to depression project: Lifetime history of Axis I psychopathology in individuals at high- and low-cognitive risk for depression. *Journal of Abnormal Psychology, 109*, 403–418.

Alloy, L. B., Abramson, L. Y., Tashman, N. A., Steinberg, D. L., Hogan, M. E., Whitehouse, W. G., Crossfield, A. G., & Morocco, A. (2001). Developmental origins of cognitive vulnerability to depression: Parenting, cognitive, and inferential feedback styles of the parents of individuals at high and low cognitive risk for depression. *Cognitive Therapy and Research*, *25*, 397–423.

Alloy, L. B., Abramson, L. Y., Gibb, B. E., Crossfield, A. G., Pieracci, A. M., Spasojevic, J., & Steinberg, J. A. (2004). Developmental antecedents of cognitive vulnerability to depression: Review of findings from the cognitive vulnerability to depression project. *Journal of Cognitive Psychotherapy: An International Quarterly*, *18*, 115–133.

Alloy, L. B., Abramson, L. Y., Smith, J. M., Gibb, B. E., & Neeren A. M. (2006a). Role of parenting and maltreatment histories in unipolar and bipolar mood disorders: Mediation by cognitive vulnerability to depression. *Clinical Child and Family Psychology Review*, *9*, 23–64.

Alloy, L. B., Abramson, L. Y., Whitehouse, W. G., Hogan, M. E., Panzarella, C., & Rose, D. T. (2006b). Prospective incidence of first onsets and recurrences of depression in individuals at high and low cognitive risk for depression. *Journal of Abnormal Psychology*, *115*, 145–156.

Alloy, L. B., Abramson, L. Y., Cogswell, A., Hughes, M., & Iacoviello, B. (2007). Cognitive vulnerabilty to depression: Implications for prevention. In M. T. Tsuang, W. S. Stone, & M. J. Lyons (Eds.), *Recognition and Prevention of Major Mental and Substance Use Disorders* (pp. 113–132) American Psychiatric Publishing.

American Psychiatric Association (1987). *Diagnostic and Statistical Manual of Mental Disorders* (3rd ed., revised). Washington, DC: Author.

American Psychiatric Association (1994). *Diagnostic and Statistical Manual of Mental Disorders* (4th ed.). Washington, DC: Author.

Beck, A. T. (1967). *Depression: Clinical, Experimental, and Theoretical Aspects*. New York: Harper & Row.

Beck, A. T. (1987). Cognitive models of depression. *Journal of Cognitive Psychotherapy: An International Quarterly*, *1*, 5–37.

Beevers, C. G., Gibb, B. E., McGleary, J. E., & Miller, I. W. (2007). Serotonin transporter genetic variation and biased attention for emotional word stimuli among psychiatric inpatients. *Journal of Abnormal Psychology*, *116*, 208–212.

Brown, G. P., Hammen, C. L., Craske, M. G., & Wickens, T. D. (1995). Dimensions of dysfunctional attitudes as vulnerabilities to depressive symptoms. *Journal of Abnormal Psychology*, *104*, 431–435.

Cardemil, E. V., Reivich, K. J., & Seligman, M. E. P. (2002). The prevention of depressive symptoms in low-income minority middle school students. *Prevention & Treatment*, *5*, Article 8. Available on the World Wide Web: www.journals.apa.org/prevention/volume5/pre0050008a.html

Carver, C. S., & Scheier, M. F. (1998). *On the Self-regulation of Behavior*. Cambridge: Cambridge University Press.

Chaney, J. M., Mullins, L. L., Wagner, J. L., Hommel, K. A., Page, M. C., & Doppler, M. J. (2004). A longitudinal examination of causal attributions and depression symptomatology in rheumatoid arthritis. *Rehabilitation Psychology*, *49*, 126–133.

Clarke, G. N., Hawkins, W., Murphy, M., Sheeber, L. B., Lewinsohn, P. M., & Seeley, J. R. (1995). Targeted prevention of unipolar depressive disorder in an at-risk sample of high school adolescents: A randomized trial of a group cognitive intervention. *Journal of the American Academy of Child and Adolescent Psychiatry*, *34*, 312–321.

Clarke, G. N., Hornbrook, M., Lynch, F. *et al.* (2001). A randomized trial of a group cognitive intervention for preventing depression in adolescent offspring of depressed parents. *Archives of General Psychiatry*, *58*, 1127–1134.

Cole, D. A., & Turner, J. E., Jr (1993). Models of cognitive mediation and moderation in child depression. *Journal of Abnormal Psychology*, *102*, 271–281.

Conley, C. S., Haines, B. A., Hilt, L. M., & Metalsky, G. I. (2001). The children's attributional style interview: Developmental tests of cognitive diathesis-stress theories of depression. *Journal of Abnormal Child Psychology*, *29*, 445–463.

Crossfield, A. G., Alloy, L. B., Abramson, L. Y., & Gibb, B. E. (2002). The development of depressogenic cognitive styles: The role of negative childhood life events and parental inferential feedback. *Journal of Cognitive Psychotherapy: An International Quarterly*, *16*, 487–502.

Daley, S. E., Hammen, C., Burge, D., Davila, J., Paley, B., Lindenderg, N., & Herzberg, D. S. (1997). Predictors of the generation of episodic stress: A longitudinal study of late adolescent women. *Journal of Abnormal Psychology*, *104*, 251–259.

DeRubeis, R. J., & Hollon, S. D. (1995). Explanatory style in the treatment of depression. In G. M. Buchanan & M. E. P. Seligman (Eds.), *Explanatory Style* (pp. 99–111). Hillsdale, NJ: Lawrence Erlbaum.

Dixon, J. F., & Ahrens, A. H. (1992). Stress and attributional styles as predictors of self-reported depression in children. *Cognitive Therapy and Research*, *16*, 623–634.

Dobkin, R. D., Panzarella, C., Nesbitt, J., Alloy, L. B., & Cascardi, M. (2004). Adaptive inferential feedback, depressogenic inferences, and depressed mood: A laboratory study of the expanded hopelessness theory of depression. *Cognitive Therapy and Research*, *28*, 487–509.

Dobkin, R. D., Allen, L. A., Alloy, L. B., Menza, M., Gara, M. A., & Panzarella, D. (2007). Adaptive inferential feedback partner training for depression: A pilot study. *Cognitive and Behavioral Practice*, *14*, 350–363.

Dykman, B. M., & Johll, M. (1998). Dysfunctional attitudes and vulnerability to depressive symptoms: A 14-week longitudinal study. *Cognitive Therapy and Research*, *22*, 337–352.

Endicott, J., & Spitzer, R. A. (1978). A diagnostic interview: The schedule for affective disorders and schizophrenia. *Archives of General Psychiatry*, *35*, 837–844.

Eley, T. C., Sugden, K., Corsico, A., Gregory, A. M., Sham, P., McGuffin, P. *et al.* (2004). Gene-environment interaction analysis of serotonin system markers with adolescent depression. *Molecular Psychiatry*, *9*, 908–915.

Garber, J., & Flynn, C. (2001). Predictors of depressive cognitions in young adolescents. *Cognitive Therapy & Research*, *25*, 353–376.

Gibb, B. E., & Alloy, L. B. (2006). A prospective test of the hopelessness theory of depression in children. *Journal of Clinical Child and Adolescent Psychology*, *35*, 264–274.

Gibb, B. E., Alloy, L. B., Abramson, L. Y., Rose, D. T., Whitehouse, W. G., Donovan, P. *et al.* (2001). History of childhood maltreatment, negative cognitive styles, and episodes of depression in adulthood. *Cognitive Therapy and Research*, *25*, 425–446.

Gibb, B. E., Alloy, L. B., Abramson, L. Y., Rose, D. T., Whitehouse, W. G., & Hogan, M. E. (2001b). Childhood maltreatment and college students' current suicidal ideation: A test of the hopelessness theory. *Suicide and Life Threatening Behavior*, *31*, 405–415.

Gibb, B. E., Abramson, L. Y., & Alloy, L. B. (2004). Emotional maltreatment from parents, verbal peer victimization, and cognitive vulnerability to depression. *Cognitive Therapy and Research*, *28*, 1–21.

Gibb, B. E., Alloy, L. B., Walshaw, P. D., Comer, J. S., Shen, G. H. C., & Villari, A. G. (2006). Predictors of attributional style change in children. *Journal of Abnormal Child Psychology*, *34*, 425–439.

Gillham, J. E., Reivich, K. J., Jaycox, L. H., & Seligman, M. E. P. (1995). Prevention of depressive symptoms in schoolchildren: Two-year follow-up. *Psychological Science*, *6*, 343–351.

Gladstone, T. R. G., Kaslow, N. J., Seeley, J. R., & Lewinsohn, P. M. (1997). Sex differences, attributional style, and depressive symptoms among adolescents. *Journal of Abnormal Child Psychology*, *25*, 297–305.

Gotlib, I. H., Lewinsohn, P. M., Seeley, J. R., Rohde, P., & Redner, J. E. (1993). Negative cognitions and attributional style in depressed adolescents: An examination of stability and specificity. *Journal of Abnormal Psychology*, *102*, 607–615.

Grabe, H. J., Lange, M., Wolff, B., Votzke, H., Lucht, M., Freyberger, H. J. *et al.* (2004). Mental and physical distress is modulated by a polymorphism in the 5-HT transporter gene interacting with social stressors and chronic disease burden. *Molecular Psychiatry*, *10*, 220–224.

Haeffel, G. J., Abramson, L. Y., Voelz, Z. R., Metalsky, G. I., Halberstadt, L., Dykman, B. M. *et al.* (2003). Cognitive vulnerability to depression and lifetime history of Axis I psychopathology: A comparison of negative cognitive styles (CSQ) and dysfunctional attitudes (DAS). *Journal of Cognitive Psychotherapy: An International Quarterly*, *17*, 3–22.

Haeffel, G. J., Abramson, L. Y., Voelz, Z. R., Metalsky, G. I., Halberstadt, L., Dykman, B. M. *et al.* (2005). Negative cognitive styles, dysfunctional attitudes, and the remitted depression paradigm: A search for the elusive cognitive vulnerability to depression factor among remitted depressives. *Emotion*, *5*, 343–348.

Hammen, C. (1991). Generation of stress in the course of unipolar depression. *Journal of Abnormal Psychology, 100*, 555–561.

Hammen, C., Adrian, C., & Hiroto, D. (1988). A longitudinal test of the attributional vulnerability model in children at risk for depression. *British Journal of Clinical Psychology, 27*, 37–46.

Hankin, B. L., Abramson, L. Y., & Siler, M. (2001). A prospective test of the hopelessness theory of depression in adolescence. *Cognitive Therapy and Research, 25*, 607–632.

Hankin, B. L., Abramson, L. Y., Miller, N., & Haeffel, G. J. (2004). Cognitive vulnerability-stress theories of depression: Examining affective specificity in the prediction of depression versus anxiety in three prospective studies. *Cognitive Therapy and Research, 28*, 309–345.

Hilsman, R., & Garber, J. (1995). A test of the cognitive diathesis-stress model of depression in children: Academic stressors, attributional style, perceived competence, and control. *Journal of Personality and Social Psychology, 69*, 370–380.

Hollon, S. D., & Thase, M. E. (2002). Treatment and prevention of depression. *Psychological Science in the Public Interest, 3*, 39–77.

Hollon, S. D., DeRubeis, R. J., Shelton, R. C., Amsterdam, J. D., Salomon, R. M., O'Reardon, J. P. *et al.* (2005). Prevention of relapse following cognitive therapy vs medications in moderate to severe depression. *Archives of General Psychiatry, 62*, 417–422

Hong, R. Y., Gwee, K., & Karia, M. (2006). The role of event-specific pessimistic inferences in the etiological chain of hopelessness depression. *Personality and Individual Differences, 41*, 1119–1129.

Iacoviello, B. M., Alloy, L. B., Abramson, L. Y., Whitehouse, W. G., & Hogan, M. E. (2006). The course of depression in individuals at high and low cognitive risk for depression: A prospective study. *Journal of Affective Disorders, 93*, 61–69.

Ingram, R. E., Miranda, J., & Segal, Z. V. (1998). *Cognitive Vulnerability to Depression*. New York: Guilford Press.

Jaycox, L. H., Reivich, K. J., Gillham, J., & Seligman, M. E. P. (1994). Prevention of depressive symptoms in school children. *Behaviour Research and Therapy, 32*, 801–816.

Joiner, T. E., & Wagner, K. D. (1995). Attribution style and depression in children and adolescents: A meta-analytic review. *Clinical Psychology Review, 15*, 777–798.

Joiner, T. E., Jr, & Rudd, M. D. (1996). Toward a categorization of depression-related psychological constructs. *Cognitive Therapy and Research, 20*, 51–68.

Joiner, T. E., Metalsky, G. I., Lew, A., & Klocek, J. (1999). Testing the causal mediation component of Beck's theory of depression: Evidence for specific mediation. *Cognitive Therapy and Research, 23*, 401–412.

Joiner, T. E., Steer, R. A., Abramson, L. Y., Alloy, L. B., Metalsky, G. I., & Schmidt, N. B. (2001). Hopelessness depression as a distinct dimension of depressive symptoms among clinical and non-clinical samples. *Behaviour Research and Therapy, 39*, 523–536.

Joiner, T. E., Wingate, L. R., Gencoz, T., & Gencoz, F. (2005a). Stress generation in depression: Three studies on its resilience, possible mechanism, and symptom specificity. *Journal of Social and Clinical Psychology, 24*, 236–253.

Joiner, T. E., Wingate, L. R., & Otamendi, A. (2005b). An interpersonal addendum to the hopelessness theory of depression: Hopelessness as a stress and depression generator. *Journal of Social and Clinical Psychology, 24*, 649–664.

Judd, L. L. (1997). The clinical course of unipolar major depressive disorders. *Archives of General Psychiatry, 54*, 898–991.

Just, N., Abramson, L. Y., & Alloy, L. B. (2001). Remitted depression studies as tests of the cognitive vulnerability hypotheses of depression onset: A critique and conceptual analysis. *Clinical Psychology Review, 21*, 63–83.

Kapçi, E. G., & Cramer, D. (2000). The mediation component of the hopelessness depression in relation to negative life events. *Counseling Psychology Quarterly, 13*, 413–423.

Kessler, R. C. (2000). Burden of depression. In S. Kasper & A. Carlsson (Eds.), *Selective Serotonin Reuptake Inhibitors 1990–2000: A Decade of Developments*. Copenhagen, Denmark: H. Lundbeck A/S.

Kessler, R. C. (2002). Epidemiology of depression. In I. H. Gotlib & C. L. Hammen (Eds.), *Handbook of Depression, 3rd ed.* (pp. 23–42). New York: Guilford Press.

Klocek, J. W., Oliver, J. M., & Ross, M. J. (1997). The role of dysfunctional attitudes, negative life events, and social support in the prediction of depressive dysphoria: A prospective longitudinal study. *Social Behavior and Personality, 25*, 123–136.

Kwon, S. M., & Oei, T. P. (1992). Differential causal roles of dysfunctional attitudes and automatic thoughts in depression. *Cognitive Therapy and Research, 16*, 309–328.

Kwon, P., & Laurenceau, J. (2002). A longitudinal study of the hopelessness theory of depression: Testing the diathesis–stress model within a differential reactivity and exposure framework. *Journal of Clinical Psychology, 58*, 1305–1321.

Lau, J. Y. F., Rijsdijk, F., & Eley, T. C. (2006). I think, therefore I am: A twin study of attributional style in adolescents. *Journal of Clinical Psychology and Psychiatry, 47*, 696–703.

Lesch, K. P., Bengel, D., Heils, A., Sabol, S. Z., Greenberg, B. D., Petri, S. *et al.* (1996). Association of anxiety-related traits with a polymorphism in the serotonin transporter gene regulatory region. *Science, 274*, 1527–1531.

Lewinsohn, P. M., Joiner, T. E., & Rohde, P. (2001). Evaluation of cognitive diathesis–stress models in predicting major depressive disorder in adolescents. *Journal of Abnormal Psychology, 110*, 203–215.

Liu, R., Alloy, L. B., & Abramson, L. Y. (2008). *Emotional maltreatment and depression: Prospective prediction of depressive episodes*. Manuscript under editorial review.

Loranger, A. W. (1988). *Personality Disorder Examination (PDE) Manual*. Yonkers, NY: DV Communications.

Luten, A., Ralph, J., & Mineka, S. (1997). Depressive attributional style: Is it specific to depression vs. anxiety vs. negative affect? *Behaviour Research and Therapy, 35*, 703–719.

Lynd-Stevenson, R. M. (1997). Generalized and event-specific hopelessness: Salvaging the mediation hypothesis of the hopelessness theory. *British Journal of Clinical Psychology, 36*, 73–83.

Metalsky, G. I., & Joiner, T. E. (1992). Vulnerability to depressive symptomatology: A Prospective test of the diathesis–stress and causal mediation components of the hopelessness theory of depression. *Journal of Personality and Social Psychology, 63*, 667–675.

Metalsky, G. I., & Joiner, T. E. (1997). The hopelessness depression symptom questionnaire. *Cognitive Therapy and Research, 21*, 359–384.

Metalsky, G. I., Halberstadt, L. J., & Abramson, L. Y. (1987). Vulnerability to depressive mood reactions: Toward a more powerful test of the diathesis–stress and causal mediation components of the reformulated theory of depression. *Journal of Personality and Social Psychology, 52*, 386–393.

Metalsky, G. I., Joiner, T. E., Hardin, T. S., & Abramson, L. Y. (1993). Depressive reactions to failure in a naturalistic setting: A test of the hopelessness and self-esteem theories of depression. *Journal of Abnormal Psychology, 102*, 101–109.

Meyer, J. H., McMain, S., Kennedy, S., Korman, L., Brown, G., DaSilva, J. *et al.* (2003). Dysfunctional attitudes and serotonin2 receptors during depression and self-harm. *American Journal of Psychiatry, 160*, 90–99.

Meyer, J. H., Houle, S., Sagrati, S., Carella, A., Hussey, D. F., Ginovart, N. *et al.* (2004). Brain serotonin transporter binding potential measured with carbon 11-labeled DASB positron emission tomography: Effects of major depressive episodes and severity of dysfunctional attitudes. *Archives of General Psychiatry, 61*, 1271–1279.

Mezulis, A. H., Hyde, J. S., & Abramson, L. Y. (2006). The developmental origins of cognitive vulnerability to depression: Temperament, parenting, and negative life events in childhood as contributors to negative cognitive style. *Developmental Psychology, 42*, 397–423.

Mineka, S., Pury, C., & Luten, A. (1995). Explanatory style in anxiety versus depression. In G. Buchanan & M. E. P. Seligman (Eds.), *Explanatory Style* (pp. 135–158). Hillsdale, NJ: Erlbaum.

Mineka, S., Watson, D., & Clark, L. A. (1998). Comorbidity of anxiety and unipolar mood disorders. *Annual Review of Psychology, 49*, 377–412.

Mongrain, M., & Blackburn, S. (2005). Cognitive vulnerability, lifetime risk, and the recurrence of major depression in graduate students. *Cognitive Therapy and Research, 29*, 747–768.

Murray, C. J. L., Lopez, A. D. (Eds.), (1996). *The Global Burden of Disease: A Comprehensive Assessment of Mortality and Disability from Diseases, Injuries, and Risk Factors in 1990 and Projected to 2020.* Cambridge, MA: Harvard University Press.

Needles, D. J., & Abramson, L. Y. (1990). Positive life events, attributional style, and hopefulness: Testing a model of recovery from depression. *Journal of Abnormal Psychology, 99*, 156–165.

Nelson, D. R., Hammen, C., Daley, S. E., Burge, D. & Davila, J. (2001). Sociotropic and autonomous personality styles: Contributions to chronic life stress. *Cognitive Therapy and Research, 25*, 61–76.

Nolen-Hoeksema, S. (1991). Responses to depression and their effects on the duration of depressive episodes. *Journal of Abnormal Psychology, 100*, 569–582.

Nolen-Hoeksema, S., Girgus, J. S., & Seligman, M. E. P. (1986). Learned helplessness in children: A longitudinal study of depression, achievement, and explanatory style. *Journal of Personality and Social Psychology, 51*, 435–442.

Nolen-Hoeksema, S., Girgus, J. S., & Seligman, M. E. P. (1992). Predictors and consequences of childhood depressive symptoms: A 5-year longitudinal study. *Journal of Abnormal Psychology, 20*, 233–245.

Olinger, L. J., Kuiper, N. A., & Shaw, B. F. (1987). Dysfunctional attitudes and stressful life events: An interactive model of depression. *Cognitive Therapy and Research, 11*, 25–40.

Panzarella, C., Alloy, L. B., & Whitehouse, W. G. (2006). Expanded hopelessness theory of depression: On the mechanisms by which social support protects against depression. *Cognitive Therapy and Research, 30*, 307–333.

Pyszczynski, T., & Greenberg, J. (1987). Self-regulatory perseveration and the depressive self-focusing style: A self-awareness theory of reactive depression. *Psychological Bulletin, 102*, 122–138.

Ralph, J., & Mineka, S. (1998). Attributional style and self-esteem: The prediction of emotional distress following a midterm exam. *Journal of Abnormal Psychology, 107*, 203–215.

Raniere, D. F. (2000). Long-term stability of inferences about major stressful life-events: Comparing retrospective reports among individuals at high versus low cognitive risk for depression. Unpublished doctoral dissertation, Temple University.

Reilly-Harrington, N., Alloy, L. B., Fresco, D. M., & Whitehouse, W. G. (1999). Cognitive styles and life events interact to predict bipolar and unipolar symptomatology. *Journal of Abnormal Psychology, 108*, 567–578.

Robinson, M. S., & Alloy, L. B. (2003). Negative cognitive styles and stress-reactive rumination interact to predict depression: A prospective study. *Cognitive Therapy and Research, 27*, 275–291.

Robinson, N. S., Garber, J., & Hillsman, R. (1995). Cognitions and stress: Direct and moderating effects on depressive versus externalizing symptoms during the junior high transition. *Journal of Abnormal Psychology, 104*, 453–463.

Romens, S., Abramson, L.Y., & Alloy, L.B. (2008). Continuity and change in cognitive vulnerability to depression from late adolescence to early adulthood. Manuscript under editorial review.

Rose, D. T., & Abramson, L. Y. (1992). Developmental predictors of depressive cognitive style: Research and theory. In D. Cicchetti & S. L. Toth (Eds.), *Rochester Symposium on Developmental Psychopathology* (Vol. IV, pp. 323–349). Hillsdale, NJ: Erlbaum.

Safford, S. M., Alloy, L. B., Abramson, L. Y., & Crossfield, A. G. (2007). Negative cognitive style as a predictor of negative life events in depression-prone individuals: A test of the stress generation hypothesis. *Journal of Affective Disorders, 99*, 147–154.

Schulman, P., Keith, D., & Seligman, M. E. P. (1993). Is optimism heritable: A study of twins. *Behaviour Research and Therapy, 31*, 569–574.

Segal, Z. V. (1988). Appraisal of the self-schema construct in cognitive models of depression. *Psychological Bulletin, 103*, 147–162.

Seligman, M. E. P., Peterson, C., Kaslow, N. J., Tannenbaum, R. L., Alloy, L. B., & Abramson, L. Y. (1984). Attributional style and depressive symptoms among children. *Journal of Abnormal Psychology, 93*, 235–238.

Shih, J. H. (2006). Sex differences in stress generation: An examination of sociotropy/autonomy, stress, and depressive symptoms. *Personality and Social Psychology Bulletin, 32*, 434–446.

Simons, A. D., Angell, K. L., Monroe, S. M., & Thase, M. E. (1993). Cognition and life stress in depression: Cognitive factors and the definition, rating, and generation of negative life events. *Journal of Abnormal Psychology*, *102*, 584–591.

Smith, J. M., Alloy, L. B., & Abramson, L. Y. (2006). Cognitive vulnerability to depression, rumination, hopelessness, and suicidal ideation: Multiple pathways to self-injurious thinking. *Suicide and Life-Threatening Behavior*, *36*, 443–454.

Spangler, D. L., Simons, A. D., Monroe, S. M., & Thase, M. E. (1997). Comparison of cognitive models of depression: Relationships between cognitive constructs and cognitive diathesis-stress match. *Journal of Abnormal Psychology*, *106*, 395–403.

Spasojevic, J., & Alloy, L. B. (2001). Rumination as a common mechanism relating depressive risk factors to depression. *Emotion*, *1*, 25–37.

Spasojevic, J., & Alloy, L. B. (2002). Who becomes a depressive ruminator? Developmental antecedents of ruminative response style. *Journal of Cognitive Psychotherapy: An International Quarterly*, *16*, 405–419.

Spence, S. H., Sheffield, J., & Donovan, C. (2002). Problem-solving orientation and attributional style: Moderators of the impact of negative life events on the development of depressive symptoms in adolescence? *Journal of Clinical Child and Adolescent Psychology*, *31*, 219–229.

Spitzer, R. L., & Endicott, J. (1978). Schedule for affective disorders and schizophrenia – Change version. *Biometrics Research*, New York State Psychiatric Institute.

Spitzer, R. A. L., Endicott, J., & Robins, E. (1978). Research diagnostic criteria: Rationale and reliability. *Archives of General Psychiatry*, *35*, 773–782.

Tiggemann, M., Winefield, A. H., Winefield, H. R., & Goldney, R. D. (1991). The prediction of psychological distress from attributional style: A test of the hopelessness model of depression. *Australian Journal of Psychology*, *43*, 125–127.

Turk, E., & Bry, B. H. (1992). Adolescents' and parents' explanatory styles and parents' causal explanations about their adolescents. *Cognitive Therapy and Research*, *16*, 349–357.

Weissman, A., & Beck, A. T. (1978). *Development and validation of the Dysfunctional Attitudes Scales: A preliminary investigation*. Paper presented at the meeting of the American Educational Research Association, Toronto, Ontario, Canada.

Yu, D. L., Seligman, M. E. P. (2002). Preventing depression symptoms in Chinese children. *Prevention & Treatment*, 5: Article 9. Available on the World Wide Web: www.journals.apa.org/prevention/volume5/pre0050009a.html

12

Social Problem Solving as a Risk Factor for Depression

Arthur M. Nezu, Christine Maguth Nezu and Melissa A. Clark

Department of Psychology, Drexel University, Philadelphia, PA, USA

During the past several decades, research has continued to identify social problem solving to be consistently linked to depressive symptomatology among both clinical and nonclinical populations (Nezu, 1987, 2002, 2004; Nezu *et al.*, 2004). In addition, problem solving has been found to moderate the stress–depression relationship. Both sets of findings implicate how impaired problem-solving skills function as a depressogenic vulnerability factor for individuals who experience stressful events. Given this context, social problem solving has further served as an important clinical target for the treatment of depression (D'Zurilla & Nezu, 2007; Nezu *et al.*, 1989). Prior to describing this literature, we begin by defining social problem solving.

WHAT IS SOCIAL PROBLEM SOLVING?

Social problem solving is a term used to distinguish impersonal problem solving from those problem-solving activities that occur in social or interpersonal contexts (Nezu *et al.*, 2007). Problem solving is a cognitive–affective–behavioral process by which an individual attempts to identify or discover effective or adaptive solutions for stressful problems encountered during the course of everyday living (D'Zurilla & Nezu, 1999, 2007; Nezu, 2004). This multidimensional construct reflects the process whereby people direct their coping efforts to alter the problematic nature of a situation itself and/or their reactions to such problems. As such, it addresses both problem-focused *and* emotion-focused goals and is therefore more versatile in nature than those models of coping that characterize problem solving as being only under the rubric of "problem-focused" strategies (i.e., those activities that are geared to change the nature of the situation so that it no longer is a problem (e.g., Lazarus, 1999)). In this manner, social problem solving represents the multi-dimensional meta-process of idiographically identifying and selecting various coping responses to implement in order to address the unique features of a given stressful situation, rather than describing a singular type of coping behavior or activity.

Based on decades of research, problem-solving outcomes appear to be largely determined by two general, but partially independent, dimensions: (a) problem orientation and (b) problem-solving style (D'Zurilla & Nezu, 2007; D'Zurilla *et al.*, 2004; Nezu, 2004). *Problem orientation* is the set of relatively stable cognitive–affective schemas that represent a person's generalized beliefs, attitudes, and emotional reactions about problems in living and one's ability to successfully cope with such problems. One's problem orientation can be either positive or negative. A *positive problem orientation* involves (a) appraisal of problems as challenges, (b) optimism that problems are solvable, (c) a strong perception of one's ability to solve problems, (d) a belief that successful problem solving involves time and effort, and (e) a willingness to cope with the problem rather than avoid it. When individuals characterized by a strong positive orientation experience a negative emotion (e.g., sadness or fear) in reaction to a stressful event, they use such experiences as sources of personal information to denote that a problem exists and as a means to inform themselves how to go about coping with the stressor.

A *negative problem orientation* involves (a) the tendency to view problems as threats, (b) expectations that problems are unsolvable, (c) doubts of one's ability to solve problems, and (d) frustration and distress when faced with problems or confronted with negative emotions. Although they are intuitively viewed as two ends of the same continuum, positive and negative orientations have been repeatedly found to be independent and largely orthogonal constructs (D'Zurilla *et al.*, 2002; Maydeu-Olivares & D'Zurilla, 1996). As can be assumed from their descriptions, problem orientation serves a motivational function (D'Zurilla & Nezu, 2001). For example, a positive orientation can lead to positive affect and approach motivation, which in turn can facilitate later problem-solving efforts (e.g., willingness to attend to difficult situations rather than avoid them). Conversely, a negative orientation can engender negative affect, such as depressive symptoms and avoidance motivation, which can later serve to inhibit or disrupt subsequent problem-solving attempts (Nezu & Perri, 1989).

The second major dimension, *problem-solving style*, refers to the core cognitive–behavioral activities that people engage in when attempting to cope with problems in living (D'Zurilla & Nezu, 1999, 2007). There are three differing styles that have been identified – one of which is adaptive, and two maladaptive ways of coping (D'Zurilla *et al.*, 2002, 2004). *Rational problem solving* is the adaptive problem-solving style that involves the systematic and planful application of certain specific skills, each of which makes a distinct contribution toward the discovery of an adaptive solution or coping response in a problem-solving situation. This style encompasses problem definition and formulation, generation of alternatives, decision making, and solution implementation and verification (Nezu & D'Zurilla, 1989).

Problem definition and formulation serve to accurately delineate the reasons why a given situation is problematical (e.g., the presence of difficult obstacles, lack of resources, conflict between goals), and to specify a set of realistic goals and objectives to help guide further problem-solving efforts. The *generation-of-alternative* task creates, using various brainstorming principles, a sufficiently large pool of possible solutions in order to increase the likelihood that the most effective ideas will be ultimately identified. The goal of the *decision-making task* is to conduct a systematic cost–benefit analysis of these alternatives by identifying and then weighing their potential positive and negative consequences if carried out, and then, based on this evaluation, to develop an overall solution plan. Finally, the purpose of *solution implementation and verification* is to carry out the solution plan, monitor and evaluate its effectiveness, adequately reinforce oneself if the problem is solved, or troubleshoot if the outcome is unsatisfactory.

Two dysfunctional or maladaptive problem-solving styles have also been identified, (D'Zurilla *et al.*, 2002, 2004). An *impulsivity/carelessness style* involves the generalized response pattern characterized by impulsive, hurried, and careless attempts at problem resolution. Although the individual high on this dimension actively attempts to apply various strategies to address problems, such attempts are narrow, hurried, and incomplete. For example, a person with this style is likely to consider only a few solution alternatives, and may impulsively implement the first idea that comes to mind. In addition, the narrow range of options and their consequences are scanned quickly, carelessly, and unsystematically.

Avoidance is the second general maladaptive problem-solving style. It is characterized by procrastination, passivity, and overdependence on others to provide solutions. Individuals high on this dimension generally avoid problems rather than confronting them "head on," wait for problems to resolve themselves, and attempt to shift the responsibility for solving one's problems to other people. In general, both styles can lead to ineffective or unsuccessful problem resolution. In fact, they are likely to worsen existing problems or even create new ones.

HOW DOES SOCIAL PROBLEM SOLVING SERVE AS A RISK FACTOR FOR DEPRESSION?

In general, the relationship between social problem solving and depression is based on the broader problem-solving model of stress delineated by Nezu, D'Zurilla, and their colleagues (Nezu & D'Zurilla, 1989; Nezu & Ronan, 1985, 1988; Nezu *et al.*, 1989, 1990). Within this model, stress is viewed as a function of the reciprocal relations among three major variables: (1) stressful life events, (2) emotional stress responses, and (3) problem-solving coping (see Figure 12.1).

Stressful life events are life experiences that present a person with strong demands for personal, social, or biological readjustment. Two important types of stressful life events include major negative events and daily problems. A *major negative event* is a broad life experience or occurrence, such as a major negative life change, which often demands sweeping readjustments in a person's life. Research has consistently found stressful life events to serve a causal role in major depression (Monroe & Hadjiyannakis, 2002; Tennant, 2002), particularly with regard to those types of events that are generally characterized as especially stressful or severe, such as the death of a spouse or experiencing a major medical illness (Mazure, 1998).

Daily problems are a specific set of life experiences characterized by a perceived or actual discrepancy between adaptive demands and coping response availability. The demands inherent in the problem may originate within the person him- or herself (e.g., lack of resources necessary to reach a personal goal), between individuals (e.g., conflicts between goals), or the environment (e.g., barriers to a goal). Obstacles to successful coping or goal attainment may include ambiguity, uncertainty, conflicting demands, lack of resources, or novelty (D'Zurilla & Nezu, 2001). These stressful events are also referred to as "minor life events" or "daily hassles" in the life stress literature. They can be *single* events, such as insufficient funds to pay this month's rent, a *series* of related events, such as continuous arguments with one's spouse, or *chronic* situations, such as coping with a chronic medical condition and its treatment. Although daily problems or hassles are less dramatic than major negative events, the

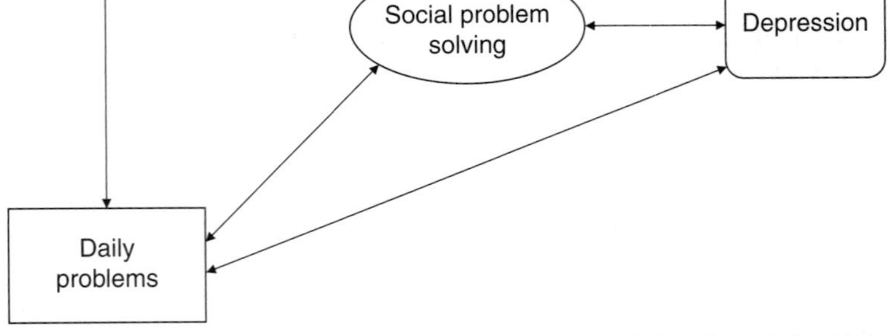

FIGURE 12.1 Problem-solving model of depression depicting the relationships among stressful life events, social problem solving, and depression.

accumulation of these minor stressors over time has both an independent and significant impact on psychological and physical well-being (Nezu, 1986b; Nezu & Ronan, 1985). In addition, daily hassles mediate the effects of major life events on subsequent depression (Nezu & Ronan, 1985; Russell & Cutrona, 1991). Moreover, the continuation and/or exacerbation of such daily problems can serve to increase the likelihood that initial onset depressive symptoms lead to a depressive disorder rather than symptom remission (Nezu, 1987).

Figure 12.1 suggests that there is a reciprocal relationship between stressor types. For example, experiencing a chronic illness as well as its associated treatment can easily engender myriad daily hassles or problems, including increased medical costs, functional disabilities, sexual difficulties, relationship problems, and medical team interaction concerns (Nezu & Nezu, 2007; Nezu *et al.*, 2003). Conversely, ongoing daily problems, such as constant difficulties with one's boss or supervisor, can also lead to the occurrence of a major negative life change, such as getting fired from one's job.

The concept of *emotional stress* refers to the immediate emotional responses of a person to a stressful life event, as modified by appraisal and coping processes (Lazarus & Folkman, 1984; Roseman & Evdokas, 2004). Negative emotional states predominate when the person (a) appraises a problem as harmful or threatening to his or her well-being, (b) doubts his or her ability to cope with the situation effectively, and/or (c) engages in ineffective or maladaptive coping responses. Whether or not an individual will become depressed as a function of experiencing stressful events involves the likelihood of subsequently experiencing perceived or actual negative consequences. These negative effects are hypothesized to serve three major functions: (a) they exacerbate the stressful nature of extant problems; (b) they engender decreases in perceived and/or actual positive reinforcement (e.g., decrease in personal resources, loss of social support, decreased self-esteem), as well as increases in perceived or actual aversive or punishing stimuli; and (c) they negatively affect one's motivation to engage in adaptive problem-solving activities (Nezu, 1987; Nezu *et al.*, 1989, 1990).

The notion that stress leads to depression has also been the focus of more biologically oriented research. For example, both clinical and experimental evidence suggests that increased cytokine secretion serves as the specific mechanism by which stress induces depression. Both stress and depression are associated with immune dysfunction whereby stress leads to hypersecretion of cytokine, which engenders the onset and maintenance of depression (Connor & Leonard, 1998). Activation of cellular immunity can also increase activity of the hypothalamic-pituitary-adrenal (HPA) axis, which also can engender depression (Leonard, 2000). Specifically, HPA axis activation causes an increase in the secretion of corticotrophin-releasing factor (CRF), which then stimulates adrenocorticotrophic hormone (ACTH) and subsequent cortisol release, which then leads to depression (Pitchot *et al.*, 2001). Other studies suggest the presence of a genetic propensity for some individuals encountering stressful life events to be more likely to experience subsequent depression (e.g., Caspi *et al.*, 2003).

Further, as Figure 12.1 denotes, becoming depressed can also serve to increase the probability of engendering further stressful events (Nezu, 1987). For example, being depressed can lead to limited motivation to cope with problems, such as reduced studying for a major examination, which can in turn lead to heightened negative consequences, such as obtaining a failing grade on the test. Overall, these reciprocal effects contribute to a potentially ever-continuous negative feedback loop of stress and depression.

The third construct in the problem-solving model of depression is *problem-solving coping*, which integrates *both* cognitive appraisal and coping activities within a social problem-solving framework (D'Zurilla & Nezu, 1999, 2007; Nezu, 1987; Nezu *et al.*, 1989). When people are faced with stressful life circumstances, various problems can occur, which result in increases in emotional distress. If their ability to cope with such events is effective, then the stressful nature of these situations is reduced and few depressive symptoms are likely to emerge. However, individuals who are not effective problem solvers will have difficulty adapting to the stress engendered by the negative life events and related set of problems. They will then have an increased likelihood of suffering from greater levels of depressive symptoms, which can lead to the manifestation of a clinically significant disorder (e.g., major or minor depression).

Effective problem-solving ability and skills moderate the stress–depression association (Nezu, 1987; Nezu & Ronan, 1988). In other words, basic effective problem solving buffers the negative effects of stressful life events. As such, ineffective problem-solving skill is viewed as a vulnerability factor. When someone encounters stressful experiences but has poor problem-solving skills, he or she is unable to effectively cope with the stress and may become depressed when negative consequences occur, and/or when the immune system is affected negatively.

Figure 12.1 further delineates a reciprocal relationship between stressful experiences and problem solving, as well as between problem solving and depression (Nezu *et al.*, 1989). According to this model, stressful events can impair one's problem solving as a function of the intensity of the stress (e.g., traumatic event), or because the stressful events are unique or novel to the individual. The highly stressful nature or novelty of the situation thus exceeds the person's capacity to adequately cope with these specific situations, despite the existence of average problem-solving ability. In other words, the model hypothesizes that depression can result from (a) problem-solving *deficits* in combination with the experience of stressful life events (i.e., diathesis–stress formulation) or (b) average problem-solving ability that is insufficient to cope with overwhelming levels of stress. This notion is consistent with Teasdale's (1988) differential activation model of depressive vulnerability, as depressed mood and negative cognitive processing can interact over time to create a continuous feedback loop. Further, once one is depressed, lowered motivation and the tendency to engage in rumination (see later section) can impair further problem-solving attempts (Mitchell & Madigan, 1984).

Collectively, it is in the reciprocal nature of these relationships, in the absence of any internal or external intervention, which increases the likelihood that individuals who experience stressful events will subsequently experience *persistent* major depression vs. temporary sad mood. Given that a stress–depression link is supported by both psychological and biological parameters (Tennant, 2002), problem solving can potentially moderate this association. Effective coping leads to improved adaptation, and can reduce the activation of the HPA axis, thus minimizing the harmful effects of stress on the immune system (*cf.* Olff, 1999).

PROBLEM-SOLVING COMPONENT PROCESSES AND DEPRESSION

The social problem-solving model also focuses on the relation between depression and various problem-solving components. That is, depression can result as a function of deficiencies, or decreased effectiveness, in various specific problem-orientation or style dimensions (Nezu, 1987, 2004; Nezu *et al.*, 1989).

Problem Orientation

Depressed individuals are often characterized by a strong negative orientation, having little faith in their ability to cope with stressful problems, often believing that problems are catastrophes, frequently blaming themselves for causing the problem, and becoming distressed when problems occur (Nezu, 1987; Nezu & Perri, 1989). Further, negative beliefs decrease one's desire or motivation to engage in any meaningful coping attempts.

Problem Definition

Depression reduces the ability to effectively define and formulate problems, which in turn makes it difficult to set realistic goals or identify effective solutions. Beck (1976) has identified several types of depressive cognitive distortions (e.g., arbitrary inference, selective abstraction, overgeneralization, magnification and minimization). Such distortions likely lead to inaccurate ways of identifying or defining the problem. Characteristic attributions for negative events (i.e., to internal, stable, and global factors) can also lead to inaccurate problem definition, as well as depression (Abramson *et al.*, 1978). Parenthetically, effective problem-solving ability has been found to moderate the depressogenic effects of maintaining a strong negative attributional style (Nezu *et al.*, 1986). In addition, unrealistically high goals can lead to depression – when not achieved, self-blame, frustration, and decreased motivation are likely to occur (Rehm & Rokke, 1988).

Generation of Alternatives

The perception of fewer and less effective alternatives to problem situations can also lead to depression, due to the resulting restricted range of solution ideas that one can ultimately choose among. Nezu and Ronan (1987), for example, found that dysphoric college students generated both a lower number of alternatives and less effective responses to interpersonal problems relative to nondysphoric counterparts. As discussed later, research has generally found deficits in rational problem solving to be linked to depression.

The link between difficulties in generating effective solutions and depression has been hypothesized to be a function of the reduced ability to access specific autobiographical memories (Marx *et al.*, 1992). A specific memory refers to an event that occurred on a particular day. Research has demonstrated that when asked for such specific memories, depressed individuals have the tendency to describe "overgeneral" memories, rather than specific ones (Raes *et al.*, 2005). This perspective assumes that effective social problem solving, in part, relies on one's ability to retrieve specific memories, and that the link between depression and ineffective problem solving can be explained by such a deficit (Evans *et al.*, 1992). Goddard *et al.* (1996) demonstrated that problem solving varied as a function of autobiographic memory retrieval and that this deficit appeared to be particularly related to the dysfunctional nature of depression-associated categoric memories (i.e., memories that referred to a series of repeated events). However, this deficit appears to be reversible, as helpful memories can be primed in depressed samples (Goddard *et al.*, 2001). Moreover, Williams *et al.* (2000) found that a mindfulness-based intervention also reduced overgeneral autobiographical memory in formerly depressed patients.

Decision Making

A negative problem orientation and lack of alternatives can bias the depressed person to selectively attend to negative vs. positive events and to immediate vs. long-term consequences (Nezu, 1987). Further, depressed individuals have been found to choose less effective alternatives to a series of interpersonal and social problems as compared to nondepressed counterparts (Nezu & Ronan, 1987), as well as to have conservative decision-making style (i.e., less willing to take a risk) (Costello, 1983). Okwumabua *et al.* (2003) found a relationship between depressive symptomatology and maladaptive decision coping patterns among a nonclinical sample of 276 low-income African American adolescents.

Solution Implementation and Verification

The depressed individual may also have difficulty implementing his or her plan due to behavioral and social skill deficits, thus leading to unsuccessful problem resolution (Nezu, 1987). Further, a negative problem orientation can impact on an individual's ability to be objective about the outcome of solution implementation. Thus, the depressed individual is unsatisfied with the coping attempt and may feel that the goals have not been achieved, further exacerbating the negative mood (Rehm & Rokke, 1988).

DEPRESSION, RUMINATION, AND SOCIAL PROBLEM SOLVING

Rumination, or self-focused attention, has been repeatedly found to be associated with depression (Nolen-Hoeksema, 1991). Individuals high on this dimension tend to respond to their depressed state by repetitively focusing on themselves and on the nature and effects of their negative feelings. Research reveals that self-focus both increases and maintains depressed mood among dysphoric and clinically depressed individuals (Nolen-Hoeksema & Morrow, 1993).

Depression-associated rumination has been found to be related to impaired social problem solving. Lyubomirsky and Nolen-Hoeksema (1995) found that dysphoric college students who engaged in self-focused rumination generated less effective solutions to a series of interpersonal problems, as well as offering the most pessimistic explanations for the problems and hypothetical negative events, as compared to nondysphoric counterparts. In a subsequent study, Lyubomirsky *et al.* (1999) found dysphoric individuals who engaged in self-focused rumination had a more negative problem orientation; they rated their own problems as severe and unsolvable with a reduced likelihood of problem resolution. They further found that dysphoric ruminative thinking is characterized by a focus on personal problems, a negative tone, self-criticism, self-blame for problems, poor self-confidence, reduced optimism, and perceived control. Last, these researchers identified a link between the negatively biased content of ruminative thoughts and a reduced willingness to solve one's problems.

Watkins and Baracaia (2002) demonstrated that a "process"-focused approach (i.e., focusing on *how* one decides to solve a problem), as compared to a state-oriented approach (i.e., focusing on *why* one has the problem), served to improve the problem-solving effectiveness of a depressed patient sample. These results were offered as being supportive of the theory that increased awareness of mental processes helps to shift or distract depressed individuals away from ruminative thinking, and thus can lead to reductions in depression.

WHAT IS THE EMPIRICAL SUPPORT FOR PROBLEM SOLVING TO BE A DEPRESSOGENIC RISK FACTOR?

Three general questions arise with regard to the validity of a problem-solving formulation of depression: (a) Is there an inverse relationship between effective problem solving and depression? (b) Does effective problem solving attenuate stress-related depression (i.e., does problem solving moderate the stress–depression association)? (c) Do therapeutic interventions based on problem-solving principles help decrease depression?

SOCIAL PROBLEM SOLVING AND DEPRESSION

A large number of studies have investigated the relationship between social problem solving and depression. The discussion of this body of research is categorized here according to the method of assessing social problem solving that was used, as the majority of investigations employed one of three problem-solving measures – the Means-End Problem-Solving Procedure (MEPS) (Platt & Spivack,

1975), the Problem-Solving Inventory (PSI) (Heppner, 1988), and the Social Problem-Solving Inventory-Revised (SPSI-R) (D'Zurilla *et al.*, 2002).

Means-End Problem Solving Procedure

The MEPS consists of 10 hypothetical interpersonal problems which involve incomplete stories that only have a beginning, where the protagonist's goal is specified, and an end, where he or she successfully achieves this goal. Respondents are asked to "make up the middle part of the story" that connects the beginning with the ending.

Investigations that employed the MEPS as the measure of social problem solving have generally documented a strong relationship between problem solving and depression. Marx and Schulze (1991) found depressed college students produced less effective solutions than their nondepressed counterparts. Similar findings were found regarding adult patients with major depressive disorder (Marx *et al.*, 1992) and among elementary school children (Sacco & Graves, 1984). MEPS scores were also significantly correlated with depressive symptom severity in a sample of college students (Nezu & Ronan, 1988). However, Blankstein *et al.* (1992) found no differences between depressed and nondepressed college undergraduates on a college student version of the MEPS, even though depressed students had more negative expectations and appraisals of their problem-solving abilities than their nondepressed colleagues.

Problem-Solving Inventory

The PSI is a self-report inventory that includes three scales and a total score: (a) *problem-solving confidence* (i.e., self-assurance while engaging in problem solving), (b) *approach-avoidance style* (i.e., the general tendency to approach or avoid problem-solving activities), and (c) *personal control* (i.e., the extent to which a person is in control of his or her emotions and behavior while solving problems).

Studies with the PSI also provide substantial evidence of a significant relationship between social problem solving and depression or negative affectivity. These investigations included a variety of subject populations, including college undergraduates (e.g., Elliott *et al.*, 1995; Nezu, 1985; Nezu & Nezu, 1987), Chinese college students (Cheng, 2001), French adolescents (Gosselin & Marcotte, 1997), patients with spinal cord injuries (Elliott *et al.*, 1991), graduate students (Miner & Dowd, 1996), clinically depressed adults (Nezu, 1986a), and South African undergraduates (Pretorius & Diedricks, 1994). In addition, the PSI was found to predict recovery from a depressive episode (Dixon, 2000), as well as demonstrate that problem-solving deficits are both an antecedent and a consequence of depression (Dixon *et al.*, 1993). In other words, poor problem solving served both as a vulnerability factor for depression and as a negative consequence of depression (i.e., negative affect leads to impaired problem solving).

Social Problem-Solving Inventory-Revised

The SPSI-R is a 52-item revision of the original (D'Zurilla & Nezu, 1990) 70-item, self-report inventory that was directly linked to the social problem-solving model introduced by D'Zurilla and Goldfried (1971) and later expanded and refined by D'Zurilla and Nezu (1982, 1999). Based on a factor analysis of the SPSI by Maydeu-Olivares and D'Zurilla (1996), the SPSI-R contains five scales – positive problem orientation, negative problem orientation, rational problem solving, impulsivity/carelessness style, and avoidance style.

A large number of investigations using the SPSI or SPSI-R have found a significant relationship between social problem solving and depressive severity or negative affectivity. This set of findings cuts across a variety of sample populations, including college undergraduates (e.g., Chang & D'Zurilla, 1996), adult (D'Zurilla *et al.*, 1998) and adolescent (Reinecke *et al.*, 2001) psychiatric inpatients, caregivers of patients with spinal cord injuries (Elliott *et al.*, 2001), adolescent girls (Frye & Goodman, 2000), adult community residents (Kant *et al.*, 1997), adult cancer patients (Nezu *et al.*, 1999), high school students (Sadowski *et al.*, 1994), and patients diagnosed with congestive heart failure (Nezu *et al.*, 2006). However, among these studies, there appears to be an inconsistency with regard to *which* specific SPSI-R scales are related to depression scores. For example, among two different samples (i.e., college undergraduates and psychiatric inpatients), D'Zurilla *et al.* (1998) found all SPSI-R scales except rational problem solving to be highly correlated with the Beck Depression Inventory (BDI). A similar pattern of results also was evident across four assessment points within a year regarding a sample of family caregivers of patients with spinal cord injuries (Elliott *et al.*, 2001). Among a sample of adolescent girls, the negative problem orientation, avoidance style, and impulsivity/carelessness style scales were significantly correlated with BDI scores (Frye & Goodman, 2000). In a college student sample, Haaga *et al.* (1995) also found depression scores to be related to only problem orientation, and not problem-solving skills *per se*. Similarly, McCabe *et al.* (1999) and Reinecke *et al.* (2001) found depression scores to be significantly related to all SPSI-R scales except rational problem solving. On the other hand, both Kant *et al.* (1997), in a sample of middle-aged community residents, and Nezu *et al.* (1999), in a sample of adult cancer patients, found all SPSI-R scales to be correlated with depressive severity.

Additional Problem-Solving Measures

Three studies that included other measures have also found a significant relationship between problem solving and depression. Dobson and Dobson (1981) used a measure of impersonal problem solving to assess problem-solving style. Their results suggested that depressed vs. nondepressed college students evidenced various problem-solving deficits and an overall conservative problem-solving style. Goodman *et al.* (1995) used a measure that requested individuals to generate effective solutions in response to three hypothetical peer conflict situations and found that children providing less effective alternative solutions also reported higher levels of depressive symptoms.

Nezu and Ronan (1987) conducted two investigations to evaluate depression-related differences in social problem solving. One used a measure of the effectiveness of solution ideas generated to a series of hypothetical problems and one employed a measure of decision making, where subjects were requested to choose the most effective solution among a group regarding a series of hypothetical problems. These studies indicated that depressed college students performed significantly worse on both tasks as compared to their nondepressed counterparts.

In sum, employing a variety of measures of social problem solving, and focusing on varying subject samples, studies focusing on the relationship between problem solving and depression have provided substantial correlational evidence of a strong link.

SPS AS A MODERATOR OF THE STRESS–DEPRESSION ASSOCIATION

The second important research question engendered by the above model is whether or not problem solving moderates the association between stressful events and depression. Does effective problem solving decrease the likelihood that people will experience depression when they experience high levels of negative life stress? Nezu and his associates conducted a series of studies geared to answer this question. In one investigation with a college student sample, Nezu *et al.* (1986) found a significant interaction between major negative life events and problem-solving ability, which indicated that the relationship between major negative events and depression varied as a function of problem-solving ability. Individuals with effective problem-solving ability were significantly less depressed than those persons with ineffective problem-solving ability experiencing similarly high levels of stressful events. These findings were replicated in two additional studies (Nezu *et al.*, 1987, 1995). Nezu and Ronan (1988) conducted a prospective study to predict depressive symptoms 3 months after the baseline assessment, while statistically controlling for initial levels of depression. The results confirmed that problem-solving ability moderated the impact of major negative events on later depressive symptoms even after controlling for prior level of depression. These findings were similar across both the MEPS and the PSI. Other evidence for the moderating role of problem solving on the stress–depression association is provided by Brack *et al.* (1992), Cheng (2001), Frye and Goodman (2000), Goodman *et al.* (1995), Miner and Dowd (1996), and Priester and Clum (1993).

PROBLEM-SOLVING THERAPY FOR DEPRESSION: TREATMENT IMPLICATIONS

If effective problem solving serves as a buffer for the stress–depression process, then helping depressed individuals to improve their problem-solving skills should lead to a decrease in depressive symptomatology. This is the third major assumption emanating from the problem-solving formulation of depression

(Nezu, 1987). In general, reviews of this body of research support this hypothesis (Ebmeier *et al.*, 2006; Nezu, 2004; Nezu *et al.*, 2004).

Nezu (1986c) conducted a randomized controlled trial (RCT) that evaluated the efficacy of problem-solving therapy (PST) for depression among a sample of adult outpatients reliably diagnosed with unipolar depression. Patients were randomly assigned to one of three conditions: (1) PST; (2) problem-focused therapy (PFT); or (3) wait-list control (WLC). Both therapy conditions were conducted in a group setting over 8-weekly sessions lasting from 1.5 to 2 hours. PFT involved discussions of the subjects' current life problems with a problem-solving goal, but systematic training in problem-solving skills was not provided. Both inferential statistical analyses and the clinical significance of the results revealed substantial reductions in depression in the PST group at posttreatment that were also maintained at a 6-month follow-up point and as measured by two different self-report measures of depression (i.e., BDI and the depression scale of the Minnesota Multiphasic Personality Inventory). The improvement in depression in the PST condition was significantly greater than in the PFT and WLC conditions. The superiority of PST over PFT was also maintained at the 6-month follow-up evaluation. Further, PST participants increased significantly more than the other two groups regarding problem-solving effectiveness and perceived control over their lives, and these improvements were maintained 6 months later.

Nezu and Perri (1989) used a dismantling research strategy to assess the relative contribution of the problem-orientation component in treating depressed individuals. Individuals who had been reliably diagnosed with major depressive disorder were randomly assigned to one of three conditions: (a) PST, (b) abbreviated PST (APST), and (c) a WLC. In addition to the BDI, the Hamilton Rating Scale for Depression (HRSD), a measure completed by two independent clinician raters, was used to assess depressive severity. Both treatment conditions included ten 2-hour therapy sessions conducted in groups by pairs of therapists counterbalanced by condition. Members of the PST condition received training in both the problem orientation and rational problem-solving skills components of the model. APST participants received a similar package, except for training in problem orientation. Thus, the degree to which training in problem orientation actually contributes to a positive treatment outcome could be determined.

Pre–post analyses indicated that individuals in the PST condition were significantly less depressed at posttreatment, according to both the BDI and HRSD, as compared to the APST and WLC participants. Further, APST subjects reported significantly lower posttreatment depression scores than WLC participants. Decreases in depressive symptoms were significantly correlated with increases in problem-solving ability. Further, these results were clinically significant using a metric whereby a "recovered" individual was defined as a treated subject (i.e., PST and APST participants) who had a posttreatment score two standard deviations beyond the mean of the WLC participants. Following this approach, over 85% of PST subjects, 50% of APST participants, and only 9% of WLC subjects experienced clinically meaningful decreases in depressive symptoms as measured by the BDI. With regard to the HRSD, these percentages were found to be 79%, 50%, and 9%, respectively. The therapeutic benefits obtained by participants in both treatment conditions were maintained 6 months after completing treatment. In general, these overall results provide additional support for the efficacy of PST for major depression, as well as to underscore the importance of including training in the problem-orientation component.

Arean *et al.* (1993) adopted the Nezu *et al.* (1989) intervention model of depression to be clinically relevant to an older population of adults experiencing depression. Seventy-five individuals over the age of 55 years were randomly assigned to PST, reminiscence therapy (RT), or a WLC. Both PST and RT conditions were conducted within a group format with one of three therapists who were trained in both treatment approaches. Each group met over 12-weekly sessions with each session lasting approximately 1.5 hours. Participants in the PST condition were trained in the PST model as adapted from the Nezu *et al.* (1989) treatment manual. RT involved reviewing one's life history in order to gain perspective and satisfaction with major positive and negative life events and was based on a psychodynamic formulation that was previously found to be efficacious for geriatric depression. This treatment was supervised by an expert in RT independent of the supervision provided in PST. Results indicated that participants in both therapy conditions were significantly less depressed on three differing measures of depression at posttreatment as compared to WLC individuals. Moreover, the effects found at posttreatment for PST and RT conditions were maintained 3 months after the completion of treatment. However, PST individuals reported significantly lower depression at posttreatment than RT participants on two of three depression measures included (i.e., HRSD and the Geriatric Depression Scale). Moreover, at posttreatment, a significantly greater proportion of PST participants (88%), compared with participants in the RT (40%) and WLC (10%) groups, no longer met the diagnostic criteria for major depression.

More recently, Nezu *et al.* (2003) reported the results of Project Genesis (Nezu *et al.*, 1997), an RCT that evaluated the efficacy of PST for 132 adult cancer patients. Although no formal clinical diagnoses were made regarding depression, as this project focused more on improving a patient's overall quality of life rather than being specific to major depressive disorder, inclusion criteria did require, as part of the operational definition of "being emotionally distressed," that participants have a score of 14 or above on the 17-item HRSD, a score that actually represents clinically relevant levels of depression (Nezu *et al.*, 2002; e.g., a score of 14 served as the inclusion criteria cut-off for the National Institute of Mental Health Treatment of Depression Collaborative Research Program). In fact, mean HRSD score across patients at baseline was approximately 21. This intervention was based on the treatment manual (Nezu *et al.*, 1998) that was adapted from previous research conducted with nonmedical patients experiencing major depression (e.g., Nezu *et al.*, 1989). In this clinical trial, distressed cancer patients were randomly assigned to one of three conditions: (a) ten 1.5-hour sessions of individual PST; (b) ten 1.5-hour sessions of

PST provided simultaneously to both the cancer patient and his or her designated significant other (e.g., spouse, family member); and (c) a "treatment-as-usual" (TAU) control. The condition that involved a significant other was included to assess the enhanced effects of formalizing a social support system where the role of the significant other was conceptualized as a "problem-solving coach."

Results at posttreatment across several self-report, clinician ratings, and ratings by a significant other provide strong evidence in support of the efficacy of PST for decreasing emotional distress and improving the overall quality of life of patients with cancer; that is, patients in both treatment conditions were found to evidence significant improvement as compared to individuals in the control condition. Relevant to the present discussion, mean HRSD scores for both treatment conditions were 6.37 and 5.99, respectively, whereas the mean posttreatment HRSD score for WLC subjects remained relatively unchanged from baseline (i.e., 22.13). These clinically significant reductions in depression scores were found to be maintained at both the 6-month and 1-year posttreatment follow-up assessment points.

Additional supportive evidence for the efficacy of PST for the treatment of depression is provided by several other investigators, including Lopez and Mermelstein (1995) regarding geriatric depression, Alexopoulus *et al.* (2003), who focused on elderly depressed individuals with executive functioning impairments, and Teri *et al.* (1997), who treated depressed individuals also diagnosed with Alzheimer's disease. PST has also been found to be as or more effective than antidepressant medication among primary care populations with major depressive disorder (Mynors-Wallis *et al.*, 1995, 2000). It has also been successfully implemented over the telephone with regard to individuals suffering from minor depression being treated in a family physician setting (Lynch *et al.*, 1997). Contrary to these results, the same team found that a subsequent attempt to compare PST to a stress management and TAU control revealed no differences among the three conditions with regard to another sample of mildly depressed patients in primary care settings (Lynch *et al.*, 2004). Unfortunately, according to the authors, a high dropout rate across conditions created significant limitations in interpreting these results.

PST has also been included as part of a collaborative care program combined with antidepressant medication for the treatment of late-life depression in primary care patients. Although the RCT designed to evaluate the efficacy of this program, entitled IMPACT, was not able to assess the independent effects of the problem-solving component, Unützer *et al.* (2001) did find that overall, the combined protocol led to significant reductions in baseline depressive symptoms, as well as less functional impairment and more improved quality of life. In addition, a home-based intervention, entitled the Program to Encourage Active Rewarding Lives for Seniors (PEARLS), combined PST with efforts to increase physical and social activities among older adults with minor depression or dysthymia. At 12 months postbaseline, patients receiving PEARLS were more likely to have at least a 50% reduction in depressive symptoms, to achieve complete remission from depression, and to have more improved quality of life regarding both functional and emotional well-being (Ciechanowski *et al.*, 2004).

PST, as adapted for implementation in community settings, was one of two interventions that were evaluated for treating various depressive disorders in a European-based, multisite project, entitled the Outcomes of Depression International Network (Dowrick *et al.*, 2000). The second psychosocial treatment was a group psychoeducation program focused on the prevention of depression developed by Mŭnoz *et al.* (1995). The 452 participants were initially identified through a community survey. Nine sites in Finland, Ireland, Norway, Spain, and the United Kingdom were involved. PST was provided across six individual sessions, whereas the educational programs were group administered across eight sessions. Both treatments were compared to a control condition. Results indicated that overall, the PST program was considered more acceptable than the course on prevention of depression. Outcomes at 6 months were positive for both treatment approaches, whereby compared to controls, treated individuals were less likely to remain as a "case" of depression and more likely to report improved mental and social functioning. However, participants in the PST condition were less likely to report depressive symptoms as compared to the other two conditions.

A major exception to the above findings is a multisite study by Barrett *et al.* (2001) that found problem-solving therapy for primary care patients (PST-PC) to be no more effective than a drug placebo condition regarding the treatment of adults diagnosed with minor depression or dysthymia. However, a closer look at PST-PC indicates that this model of PST does not include a treatment component focused on problem-orientation variables; rather it provides training exclusively in the four rational problem-solving skills (*cf.* Barrett *et al.*, 1999). As mentioned earlier, the link between problem solving and depression lies heavily in the association between depression and the negative problem-orientation factor (Nezu, 2004). Coupling this notion with the results from the Nezu and Perri (1989) study described earlier that highlighted the importance of addressing the problem-orientation dimension suggests that it is possible that PST-PC represents a truncated version relative to the Nezu (1987; Nezu *et al.*, 1989) model of PST for depression and does not seemingly address a significant reason why a problem solving–depression association exists. As such, PST-PC may be clinically less effective, thus explaining the lack of a treatment effect compared to a placebo condition in the Barrett *et al.* (2001) investigation. However, this remains an empirical question.

In sum, the vast majority of the studies evaluating PST for depression have found this intervention to be efficacious. A recent meta-analysis, for example, indicated that after reviewing 13 RCTs that examined the effects of PST, including a total of 1133 subjects, the mean standardized effect size in a fixed effects model was 0.34, whereas within a random effects model, it was found to be 0.83 (Cuijpers *et al.*, 2007). However, heterogeneity among studies was found to be high and subgroup analyses were unable to determine what caused this heterogeneity, suggesting that additional research is necessary before one is able to ascertain under what conditions and for which specific depressed individuals is PST particularly efficacious.

ARE SPS DEFICITS SPECIFIC TO DEPRESSION?

Whereas the above body of research underscores the importance of social problem solving as an individual difference variable in understanding depression, because additional research has also identified a strong link between social problem solving and other forms of psychopathology and psychological distress, anxiety in particular (Nezu *et al.*, 2004), the question of specificity naturally emerges. In other words, if problem-solving deficits are linked, for example, to both depression *and* anxiety, the question arises as to whether these associations are specific or is problem solving related to aspects of both symptom sets that represent shared variance between the two disorders, such as general distress? A recent study asked this question. Haugh (2006) requested 245 college students to complete the SPSI-R, the BDI-II (Beck *et al.*, 1996), and the Beck Anxiety Inventory (BAI; Beck & Steer, 1990). Although zero-order correlations identified significant relationships between SPSI-R scale scores and both depression and anxiety, a series of partial correlations revealed a different pattern. The unique association between problem solving and depression was assessed by statistically controlling for the effects of the BAI, whereas the unique relationship between problem solving and anxiety was examined by partialling out the effects due to the BDI-II. Results indicated that all five of the SPSI-R scales were found to be significantly and uniquely related to the BDI-II. However, none of the partial correlations between problem solving and anxiety were found to be significant. This pattern of findings suggest strongly that at least among a nonclinical sample, problem solving is related to depression in a manner not accounted for by general distress, anxiety in particular.

FUTURE DIRECTIONS

Although evidence continues to accumulate in support of a problem-solving formulation of depression, several key issues remain open. These are briefly noted below (see also D'Zurilla & Nezu, 2007; Nezu, 2004).

Depression and Rational Problem Solving

In general, the dimension of rational problem solving (i.e., the systematic application of specific problem-solving activities) has been found to be more strongly and consistently related to behavioral measures of adjustment than to psychological measures (D'Zurilla & Nezu, 2007). As noted previously, inconsistent results have been found regarding the relationship between rational problem solving and depression. Studies using self-report inventories of problem solving, such as the SPSI-R, have reported both significant *and* nonsignificant correlations between the rational problem-solving scale and depressive symptomatology, whereas the MEPS and other performance-based measures have more consistently identified significant relationships between deficits in some problem-solving skills (e.g., generation-of-alternative solutions, decision making) and negative affective conditions (e.g., Marx *et al.*, 1992; Nezu & Ronan, 1987). Future research is needed that includes both types of problem-solving measures in the same investigation, such as the Nezu and Ronan (1988) study, in order to clarify these inconsistencies.

Validity of the Reciprocal Causation Hypothesis

A major assumption of social problem-solving theory is that problem-solving deficits cause or contribute to psychopathology. However, because most of the research on the relationship between social problem solving and psychopathology is cross-sectional, an alternative interpretation exists, one that represents the opposite direction of causality, that is, that the emergence of psychopathology leads to impaired social problem-solving ability and performance (*cf.* Schotte *et al.*, 1990). However, a third hypothesis also exists, one which is fundamental to our problem-solving model of stress and depression as described earlier – that is, the relationship between social problem solving and psychopathology is actually reciprocal in nature (Nezu, 1987; Nezu *et al.*, 1989). According to this hypothesis, ineffective problem solving leads to maladaptive functioning (e.g., depression, anxiety) which in turn inhibits or disrupts subsequent problem solving, resulting in a negative cycle over time of decreasing problem-solving effectiveness and increasing maladjustment or psychological disturbance. To examine this hypothesis, longitudinal studies, such as that represented by the Dixon (2000) investigation that found social problem solving to be both an antecedent and a consequence of depression, are especially needed that employ multiple assessments of problem solving and adjustment factors over time.

Neuropsychological Correlates of Depression

An intriguing overlap might exist with regard to the relationship between basic cognitive deficits and depression and the association between *social* problem solving and depression. Neuropsychological research indicates that deficits in executive functioning, which involve basic cognitive problem-solving processes (e.g., selecting strategies, dealing with novelty), are evident in individuals with unipolar depression (Fossati *et al.*, 2002), and that such deficits may not simply be epiphenomena of the depressive disorder (Austin *et al.*, 2001). For example, Fossati *et al.* (2001) found that depressed patients demonstrated mild impairment on the California Card Sorting Test with specific regard to problems in concept generation, which involves hypothesis-testing deficits, a loss of cognitive flexibility, and a conservative response style. Moreover, such problem-solving deficits were positively correlated with duration of the depressive episode. As such, it is possible that such a depression-related deficit in basic cognitive functioning may structurally underlie a depression-associated deficit in *social* problem solving. Such a hypothesis remains speculative at best, but represents a potentially fructuous avenue of research that might yield a better understanding of this particular brain–behavior relationship.

Ethnic Differences Regarding Depression-Associated Deficits in Social Problem Solving

Little research to date has been conducted with regard to ethnic differences in social problem-solving ability, or its relationship to depression. Chang (1998) has previously found Asian Americans to score higher than White Americans on negative problem orientation and impulsivity/carelessness style. However, the elevated scores on these dysfunctional problem-solving dimensions in Asian Americans were *not* found to be associated with greater maladjustment. Thus, it appears that the impact of specific problem-solving deficits on adjustment may vary across different ethnic groups. Clearly, more research is needed on the relationship between social problem solving and adjustment in diverse populations.

REFERENCES

Abramson, L. Y., Seligman, M. E. P., & Teasdale, J. D. (1978). Learned helplessness in humans: Critique and reformulation. *Journal of Abnormal Psychology, 87*, 49–74.

Alexopoulus, G. S., Raue, P., & Areán, P. (2003). Problem-solving therapy versus supportive therapy in geriatric major depression with executive dysfunction. *American Journal of Geriatric Psychiatry, 11*, 46–52.

Arean, P. A., Perri, M. G., Nezu, A. M., Schein, R. L., Christopher, F., & Joseph, T. X. (1993). Comparative effectiveness of social problem-solving therapy and reminiscence therapy as treatments for depression in older adults. *Journal of Consulting and Clinical Psychology, 61*, 1003–1010.

Austin, M., Mitchell, P., & Goodwin, G. M. (2001). Cognitive deficits in depression. *British Journal of Psychiatry, 178*, 200–206.

Barrett, J. E., Williams, J. W., Oxman, T. E., Katon, W., Frank, E., Hegel, M. T., Sullivan, M., & Schulberg, H. C. (1999). The treatment effectiveness project. A comparison of the effectiveness of paroxetine, problem-solving therapy, and placebo in the treatment of minor depression and dysthymia in primary care patients: Background and research plan. *General Hospital Psychiatry, 21*, 260–273.

Barrett, J. E., Williams, J. W., Oxman, T. E., Frank, E., Katon, W., Sullivan, M., Hegel, M. T., Cornell, J. E., & Sengupta, A. S. (2001). Treatment of dysthymia and minor depression in primary care: A randomized trial in patients aged 18 to 59 years. *Journal of Family Practice, 50*, 405–412.

Beck, A. T. (1976). *Cognitive therapy and the emotional disorders*. New York: International Universities Press.

Beck, A. T., & Steer, R. A. (1990). *Manual for the revised Beck Anxiety Inventory (BAI)*. San Antonio, TX: The Psychological Corporation.

Beck, A. T., Steer, R. A., & Brown, G. K. (1996). *Beck Depression Inventory Manual* (2nd ed.). San Antonio, TX: The Psychological Corporation.

Blankstein, K. R., Flett, G. L., & Johnston, M. E. (1992). Depression, problem-solving ability, and problem-solving appraisals. *Journal of Clinical Psychology, 48*, 749–759.

Brack, G., LaClave, L., & Wyatt, A. S. (1992). The relationship of problem solving and reframing to stress and depression in female college students. *Journal of College Student Development*, *33*, 124–131.

Caspi, A., Sugden, K., Moffitt, T. E., Taylor, A., Craig, I. W., Harrington, H., McClay, J., Mill, J., Martin, J., Braithwaite, A., & Poulton, R. (2003). Influence of life stress in depression: Moderation by a polymorphism in the 5-HTT gene. *Science*, *301*, 386–389.

Chang, E. C. (1998). Cultural differences, perfectionism, and suicidal risk in a college population: Does social problem solving still matter? *Cognitive Therapy and Research*, *22*, 237–254.

Chang, E. C., & D'Zurilla, T. J. (1996). Relations between problem orientation and optimism, pessimism, and trait affectivity: A construct validation study. *Behaviour Research and Therapy*, *34*, 185–195.

Cheng, S. K. (2001). Life stress, problem solving, perfectionism, and depressive symptoms in Chinese. *Cognitive Therapy and Research*, *25*, 303–310.

Ciechanowski, P., Wagner, E., Schmaling, K., Schwartz, S., Williams, B., Diehr, P., Kulzer, J., Gray, S., Collier, C., & LoGerfo, J. (2004). Community-integrated home-based depression treatment in older adults: A randomized controlled trial. *Journal of the American Medical Association*, *291*, 1569–1577.

Connor, T. J., & Leonard, B. E. (1998). Depression, stress and immunological activation: The role of cytokines in depressive disorders. *Life Sciences*, *62*, 583–606.

Costello, E. J. (1983). Information processing for decision making in depressed women: A study of subjective expected utilities. *Journal of Affective Disorders*, *5*, 239–251.

Cuijpers, P., van Straten, A., & Warmerdam, L. (2007). Problem solving therapies for depression: A meta-analysis. *European Psychiatry*, *22*, 9–15.

Dixon, W. A. (2000). Problem-solving appraisal and depression: Evidence for a recovery model. *Journal of Counseling and Development*, *78*, 87–91.

Dixon, W. A., Heppner, P. P., Burnett, J. W., Anderson, W. P., & Wood, P. K. (1993). Distinguishing among antecedents, concomitants, and consequences of problem-solving appraisal and depressive symptoms. *Journal of Counseling Psychology*, *40*, 357–364.

Dobson, D. J., & Dobson, K. S. (1981). Problem-solving strategies in depressed and nondepressed college students. *Cognitive Therapy and Research*, *5*, 237–249.

Dowrick, C., Dunn, G., Ayuso-Mateos, J. L., Dalgard, O. S., Page, H., Lehtinen, V., Casey, P., Wilkinson, C., Vazquez-Barquero, J. L., & Wilkinson, G. (2000). Problem solving treatment and group psychoeducation for depression: Multicentre randomised controlled trial. *British Journal of Medicine*, *321*, 1–6.

D'Zurilla, T. J., & Goldfried, M. R. (1971). Problem solving and behavior modification. *Journal of Abnormal Psychology*, *78*, 107–126.

D'Zurilla, T. J., & Nezu, A. (1982). Social problem solving in adults. In P. C. Kendall (Ed.), *Advances in cognitive–behavioral research and therapy* (Vol. 1, pp. 202–274). New York: Academic Press.

D'Zurilla, T. J., & Nezu, A. M. (1990). Development and preliminary evaluation of the Social Problem-Solving Inventory (SPSI). Psychological Assessment. *Journal of Consulting and Clinical Psychology*, *2*, 156–163.

D'Zurilla, T. J., & Nezu, A. M. (1999). *Problem-solving therapy: A social competence approach to clinical intervention* (2nd ed.). New York: Springer.

D'Zurilla, T. J., & Nezu, A. M. (2001). Problem-solving therapies. In K. S. Dobson (Ed.), *The handbook of cognitive–behavioral therapies* (2nd ed., pp. 211–245). New York: Guilford.

D'Zurilla, T. J., & Nezu, A. M. (2007). *Problem-solving therapy: A positive approach to clinical intervention* (3rd ed.). New York: Springer Publishing Co.

D'Zurilla, T. J., Chang, E. C., Nottingham, E. J., IV, & Faccini, L. (1998). Social problem-solving deficits and hopelessness, depression, and suicidal risk in college students and psychiatric inpatients. *Journal of Clinical Psychology*, *54*, 1–17.

D'Zurilla, T. J., Nezu, A. M., & Maydeu-Olivares, A. (2002). *Manual for the Social Problem-Solving Inventory-Revised*. North Tonawanda, NY: Multi-Health Systems.

D'Zurilla, T. J., Nezu, A. M., & Maydeu-Olivares, A. (2004). Social problem solving: Theory and assessment. In E. C. Chang, T. J. D'Zurilla, & L. J. Sanna (Eds.), *Social problem solving: Theory, research, and training* (pp. 11–27). Washington, DC: American Psychological Association.

Ebmeier, K. P., Donaghey, C., & Steele, J. D. (2006). Recent developments and current controversies in depression. *Lancet*, *367*, 153–167.

Elliott, T. R., Godshall, F., Herrick, S., Witty, T., & Spruell, M. (1991). Problem solving appraisal and psychological adjustment following spinal cord injury. *Cognitive Therapy and Research*, *15*, 387–398.

Elliott, T. R., Sherwin, E., Harkins, S., & Marmarosh, C. (1995) Self-appraised problem-solving ability, affective states, and psychological distress. *Journal of Counseling Psychology*, *42*, 105–115.

Elliott, T. R., Shewchuk, R. M., & Richards, J. S. (2001). Family caregiver social problem-solving abilities and adjustment during the initial year of the caregiving role. *Journal of Counseling Psychology*, *48*, 223–232.

Evans, J., Williams, J. M. G., O'Loughlin, S., & Howells, K. (1992). Autobiographical memory and problem-solving strategies of parasuicidal patients. *Psychological Medicine*, *22*, 399–405.

Fossati, P., Ergis, A. M., & Allilaire, J. F. (2001) Problem-solving abilities in unipolar depressed patients: Comparison of performance in the modified version of the Wisconsin and the California sorting tests. *Psychiatry Research*, *104*, 145–156.

Fossati, P., Ergis, A. M., & Allilaire, J. F. (2002). Executive functioning in unipolar depression: A review. *Encephale*, *28*, 97–107.

Frye, A. A., & Goodman, S. H. (2000). Which social problem-solving components buffer depression in adolescent girls? *Cognitive Therapy and Research*, *24*, 637–650.

Goddard, L., Dritchel, B., & Burton, A. (1996). Role of autobiographical memory in social problem solving and depression. *Journal of Abnormal Psychology*, *105*, 609–616.

Goddard, L., Dritchel, B., & Burton, A. (2001). The effects of specific retrieval instruction on social problem-solving in depression. *British Journal of Clinical Psychology*, *40*, 297–308.

Goodman, S. H., Gravitt, G. W., & Kaslow, N. J. (1995). Social problem solving: A moderator of the relation between negative life stress and depression symptoms in children. *Journal of Abnormal Child Psychology*, *23*, 473–485.

Gosselin, M. J., & Marcotte, D. (1997). The role of self-perceived problem-solving skills in relation with depression during adolescence. *Science et Comportement*, *25*, 299–314.

Haaga, D. A. F., Fine, J. A., Terrill, D., Steward, B. L., & Beck, A. T. (1995). Social problem-solving deficits, dependency, and depressive symptoms. *Cognitive Therapy and Research*, *19*, 147–158.

Haugh, J. A. (2006). Specificity and social problem solving: Relation to depressive and anxious symptomatology. *Journal of Social and Clinical Psychology*, *25*, 392–403.

Heppner, P. P. (1988). *The Problem-Solving Inventory*. Palo Alto, CA: Consulting Psychologist Press.

Kant, G. L., D'Zurilla, T. J., & Maydeu-Olivares, A. (1997). Social problem solving as a mediator of stress-related depression and anxiety in middle-aged and elderly community residents. *Cognitive Therapy and Research*, *21*, 73–96.

Lazarus, R. S. (1999). *Stress and emotion: A new synthesis*. New York: Springer Publishing Co.

Lazarus, R. S., & Folkman, S. (1984). *Stress, appraisal, and coping*. New York: Springer Co.

Leonard, B. E. (2000). Stress, depression and the activation of the immune system. *World Journal of Biological Psychiatry*, *1*, 17–25.

Lopez, M. A., & Mermelstein, R. J. (1995). A cognitive–behavioral program to improve geriatric rehabilitation outcome. *Gerontologist*, *35*, 696–700.

Lynch, D. J., Tamburrino, M. B., & Nagel, R. (1997). Telephone counseling for patients with minor depression: Preliminary findings in a family practice setting. *Journal of Family Practice*, *44*, 293–298.

Lynch, D. J., Tamburrino, M. B., Nagel, R., & Smith, M. K. (2004). Telephone based treatment for family practice patients with mild depression. *Psychological Reports*, *94*, 785–792.

Lyubomirsky, S., & Nolen-Hoeksema, S. (1995) Effects of self-focused rumination on negative thinking and interpersonal problem solving. *Journal of Personality and Social Psychology*, *69*, 176–190.

Lyubomirsky, S., Tucker, K. L., Caldwell, N. D., & Berg, K. (1999). Why ruminators are poor problem solvers: Clues from the phenomenology of dysphoric rumination. *Journal of Personality and Social Psychology*, *77*, 1041–1060.

Marx, E. M., Williams, J. M. G., & Claridge, G. C. (1992). Depression and social problem solving. *Journal of Abnormal Psychology*, *101*, 78–86.

Marx, E. M., & Schulze, C. C. (1991). Interpersonal problem-solving in depressed students. *Journal of Clinical Psychology, 47*, 361–367.

Maydeu-Olivares, A., & D'Zurilla, T. J. (1996). A factor-analytic study of the Social Problem-Solving Inventory: An integration of theory and data. *Cognitive Therapy and Research, 20*, 115–133.

Mazure, C. M. (1998). Life stressors as risk factors in depression. *Clinical Psychology: Science and Practice, 5*, 291–313.

McCabe, R. E., Blankstein, K. R., & Mills, J. S. (1999). Interpersonal sensitivity and social problem solving: Relations with academic and social self-esteem, depressive symptoms, and academic performance. *Cognitive Therapy and Research, 23*, 587–604.

Miner, R. C., & Dowd, E. T. (1996). An empirical test of the problem solving model of depression and its application to the prediction of anxiety and anger. *Counseling Psychology Quarterly, 9*, 163–176.

Mitchell, J. E., & Madigan, R. J. (1984). The effects of induced elation and depression on interpersonal problem solving. *Cognitive Therapy and Research, 8*, 277–285.

Monroe, S. M., & Hadjiyannakis, K. (2002). The social environment and depression: Focusing on severe life stress. In I. H. Gotlib & C. L. Hammen (Eds.), *Handbook of Depression* (pp. 314–340). New York: Guilford.

Mŭnoz, R., Ying, Y., Bernal, G., Perez-Stable, E., Sorenson, J., & Hargeaves, E. (1995). Prevention of depression with primary care patients: A randomized controlled trial. *American Journal of Community Psychology, 23*, 199–222.

Mynors-Wallis, L. M., Gath, D. H., Lloyd-Thomas, A. R., & Tomlinson, D. (1995). Randomised controlled trial comparing problem solving treatment with amitriptyline and placebo for major depression in primary care. *British Medical Journal, 310*, 441–445.

Mynors-Wallis, L. M., Gath, D. H., Day, A., & Baker, F. (2000). Randomised controlled trial of problem solving treatment, antidepressant medication, and combined treatment for major depression in primary care. *British Medical Journal, 320*, 26–30.

Nezu, A. M. (1985). Differences in psychological distress between effective and ineffective problem solvers. *Journal of Counseling Psychology, 32*, 135–138.

Nezu, A. M. (1986a). Cognitive appraisal of problem-solving effectiveness: Relation to depression and depressive symptoms. *Journal of Clinical Psychology, 42*, 42–48.

Nezu, A. M. (1986b). Effects of stress from current problems: Comparisons to major life events. *Journal of Clinical Psychology, 42*, 847–852.

Nezu, A. M. (1986c). Efficacy of a social problem-solving therapy approach for unipolar depression. *Journal of Consulting and Clinical Psychology, 54*, 196–202.

Nezu, A. M. (1987). A problem-solving formulation of depression: A literature review and proposal of a pluralistic model. *Clinical Psychology Review, 7*, 122–144.

Nezu, A. M. (2002). Problem-solving therapy. In T. Scrimali & L. Grimaldi (Eds.), *Cognitive psychotherapy toward a new millennium: Scientific foundations and clinical practice* (pp. 89–94). New York: Kluwer Academic Publishers.

Nezu, A. M. (2004). Problem solving and behavior therapy revisited. *Behavior Therapy, 35*, 1–33.

Nezu, A. M., & D'Zurilla, T. J. (1989). Social problem solving and negative affective conditions. In P. C. Kendall & D. Watson (Eds.), *Anxiety and depression: Distinctive and overlapping features* (pp. 285–315). New York: Academic Press.

Nezu, A. M., & Nezu, C. M. (1987). Psychological distress, problem solving, and coping reactions: Sex-role differences. *Sex Roles, 16*, 205–214.

Nezu, A. M., & Nezu, C. M. (2007). Psychological distress, depression, and anxiety. In M. Feuerstein (Ed.), *Handbook of Cancer Survivorship* (pp. 323–338). New York: Springer.

Nezu, A. M., Nezu, C. M., Friedman, S. H., Houts, P. S., & Faddis, S. (1997). Project Genesis: Application of problem-solving therapy to individuals with cancer. *the Behavior Therapist, 20*, 155–158.

Nezu, A. M., & Perri, M. G. (1989). Social problem solving therapy for unipolar depression: An initial dismantling investigation. *Journal of Consulting and Clinical Psychology, 57*, 408–413.

Nezu, A. M., & Ronan, G. F. (1985). Life stress, current problems, problem solving, and depressive symptomatology: An integrative model. *Journal of Consulting and Clinical Psychology, 53*, 693–697.

Nezu, A. M., & Ronan, G. F. (1987). Social problem solving and depression: Deficits in generating alternatives and decision making. *Southern Psychologist, 3*, 29–34.

Nezu, A. M., & Ronan, G. F. (1988). Stressful life events, problem solving, and depressive symptoms among university students: A prospective analysis. *Journal of Counseling Psychology, 35*, 134–138.

Nezu, A. M., Kalmar, K., Ronan, G. F., & Clavijo, A. (1986). Attributional correlates of depression: An interactionnal model including problem solving. *Behavior Therapy, 17*, 50–56.

Nezu, A. M., Nezu, C. M., Saraydarian, L., Kalmar, K., & Ronan, G. F. (1986). Social problem solving as a moderator variable between negative life stress and depressive symptoms. *Cognitive Therapy and Research, 10*, 489–498.

Nezu, A. M., Perri, M. G., Nezu, C. M., & Mahoney, D. J. (1987, November). Social problem solving as a moderator of stressful events among clinically depressed individuals. Paper presented at the *Annual Conference of the Association for Advancement of Behavior Therapy*, Boston, MA.

Nezu, A. M., Nezu, C. M., & Perri, M. G. (1989). *Problem-solving therapy for depression: Therapy, research, and clinical guidelines*. New York: Wiley.

Nezu, A. M., Nezu, C. M., & Perri, M. G. (1990). Psychotherapy for adults within a problem-solving framework: Focus on depression. *Journal of Cognitive Psychotherapy, 4*, 247–256.

Nezu, A. M., Nezu, C. M., Faddis, S., DelliCarpini, L. A., & Houts, P. S. (1995, November). Social problem solving as a moderator of cancer-related stress. Paper presented at the *Annual Conference of the Association for Advancement of Behavior Therapy*, Washington, DC.

Nezu, A. M., Nezu, C. M., Friedman, S. H., Faddis, S., & Houts, P. S. (1998). *Helping cancer patients cope: A problem-solving approach*. Washington, DC: American Psychological Association.

Nezu, A. M., Nezu, C. M., McClure, K. S., & Zwick, M. L. (2002). Assessment of depression. In I. H. Gotlib & C. L. Hammen (Eds.), *Handbook of Depression* (pp. 61–85). NY: Guilford.

Nezu, A. M., Nezu, C. M., Felgoise, S. H., McClure, K. S., & Houts, P. S. (2003). Project genesis: Assessing the efficacy of problem-solving therapy for distressed adult cancer patients. *Journal of Consulting and Clinical Psychology, 71*, 1036–1048.

Nezu, A. M., Wilkins, V. M., & Nezu, C. M. (2004). Social problem solving, stress, and negative affective conditions. In E. C. Chang, T. J. D'Zurilla, & L. J. Sanna (Eds.), *Social problem solving: Theory, research, and training* (pp. 49–65). Washington, DC: American Psychological Association.

Nezu, A. M., Nezu, C. M., Cos, T., Friedman, J., Wilkins, V. M., & Lee, M. (2006, November). Social problem solving and depression among patients with cardiovascular disease. Paper presented at the *Annual Conference of the Association for Behavioral and Cognitive Therapies*, Chicago.

Nezu, A. M., Nezu, C. M., & D'Zurilla, T. J. (2007). *Solving life's problems: A 5-step guide to enhanced well-being*. New York: Springer Publishing Co.

Nezu, C. M., Nezu, A. M., Friedman, S. H., Houts, P. S., DelliCarpini, L. A., Nemeth, C. B., & Faddis, S. (1999). Cancer and psychological distress: Two investigations regarding the role of problem solving. *Journal of Psychosocial Oncology, 16*, 27–40.

Nolen-Hoeksema, S. (1991). Responses to depression and their effects on the duration of depressive episodes. *Journal of Abnormal Psychology, 100*, 569–582.

Nolen-Hoeksema, S., & Morrow, J. (1993). Effects of rumination and distraction on naturally-occurring depressed moods. *Cognition and Emotion, 7*, 561–570.

Okwumabua, J. O., Wong, S. P., & Duryea, E. J. (2003). Depressive symptoms and decision making among African American youth. *Journal of Adolescent Research, 18*, 436–453.

Olff, M. (1999). Stress, depression and immunity: the role of defense and coping styles. *Psychiatry Research, 85*, 7–15.

Pitchot, W., Herrera, C., & Ansseau, M. (2001). HPA axis dysfunction in major depression: relationship to 5-HT (1A) receptor activity. *Neuropsychobiology, 44*, 74–77.

Platt, J. J., & Spivack, G. (1975). *Manual for the Means-Ends Problem-Solving Procedures (MEPS): A measure of interpersonal cognitive problem-solving skills*. Philadelphia, PA: Hahnemann Community Mental Health Mental Retardation Center.

Pretorius, T. B., & Diedricks, M. (1994). Problem-solving appraisal, social support and stress–depression relationship. *South African Journal of Psychology, 24*, 86–90.

Priester, M. J., & Clum, G. A. (1993). Perceived problem-solving ability as a predictor of depression, hopelessness, and suicide ideation in a college population. *Journal of Counseling Psychology, 40*, 79–85.

Raes, F., Hermans, D., Willaims, J. M. G., Demyttenaere, K., Sabbe, B., Pieters, G., & Eelen, P. (2005). Reduced specificity of autobiographical memory: A mediator between rumination and ineffective social problem-solving in major depression. *Journal of Affective Disorders, 87*, 331–335.

Rehm, L. P., & Rokke, P. (1988). Self-management therapies. In K. S. Dobson (Ed.), *Handbook of Cognitive–Behavioral Therapies* (pp. 136–166). New York: Guilford.

Reinecke, M. A., DuBois, D. L., & Schultz, T. M. (2001). Social problem solving, mood, and suicidality among inpatient adolescents. *Cognitive Therapy and Research, 25*, 743–756.

Roseman, I. J., & Evdokas, A. (2004). Appraisals cause experienced emotions: Experimental evidence. *Cognition and Emotion, 18*, 1–28.

Russell, D. W., & Cutrona, C. E. (1991). Social support, stress, and depressive symptoms among the elderly: Test of a process model. *Psychology and Aging, 6*, 190–201.

Sacco, W. P., & Graves, D. J. (1984). Childhood depression, interpersonal problem solving, and self-ratings of performance. *Journal of Clinical Child Psychology, 13*, 10–15.

Sadowski, C., Moore, L. A., & Kelley, M. L. (1994). Psychometric properties of the Social Problem-Solving Inventory (SPSI) with normal and emotionally-disturbed adolescents. *Journal of Abnormal Child Psychology, 22*, 487–500.

Schotte, D. E., Cools, J., & Payvar, S. (1990). Problem-solving deficits in suicidal patients: Trait vulnerability or state phenomenon?. *Journal of Consulting and Clinical Psychology, 58*, 562–564.

Teasdale, J. D. (1988). Cognitive vulnerability to persistent depression. *Cognition and Emotion, 2*, 247–274.

Tennant, C. (2002). Life events, stress and depression: A review of recent findings. *Australian and New Zealand Journal of Psychiatry, 36*, 173–182.

Teri, L., Logsdon, R. G., Uomoto, J., & McCurry, S. M. (1997). Behavioral treatment of depression in dementia patients: A controlled clinical trial. *Journals of Gerontology Series B: Psychological Sciences and Social Sciences, 52B*, 159–166.

Unűtzer, J., Katon, W., Williams, J. W., Callahan, C., Harpole, L., Hunkeler, E. M., Hoffing, M., Arean, P., Hegel, M. T., Schoenbaum, M., Oishi, S. M., & Langston, C. A. (2001). Improving primary care for depression in late life: The design of a multicenter randomized trial. *Medical Care, 39*, 785–799.

Watkins, E., & Baracaia, S. (2002). Rumination and social problem-solving in depression. *Behaviour Research and Therapy, 40*, 1179–1189.

Williams, J. M. G., Teasdale, J. D., Segal, Z. V., & Soulsby, J. (2000). Mindfulness-based cognitive therapy reduces overgeneral autobiographical memory in formerly depressed patients. *Journal of Abnormal Psychology, 109*, 150–155.

PART III

Social Factors

13

THE ROOTS OF DEPRESSION IN EARLY ATTACHMENT EXPERIENCES

GREG MORAN[*], HEIDI NEUFELD BAILEY[†] AND CAREY ANNE DEOLIVEIRA[¶]

[*]*The University of Western Ontario, London, Ontario, Canada*
[†]*University of Guelph, Guelph, Ontario, Canada*
[¶]*Children and Family Resource Institute, London, Ontario, Canada*

In this chapter, we examine the possibility that the attachment relationship between infant and caregiver, which is the first human relationship, plays a significant role in placing an individual at risk for depression in adulthood. In doing so, we identify the place that attachment might fill in existing theories of vulnerability to depression and review the aspects of attachment theory that are likely to be most relevant to understanding the developmental processes proposed to underlie depression vulnerability. This background allows specification of those aspects of attachment that might contribute to risk for depression. Of necessity, some of our arguments will involve the alignment of theory with theory, thus, running the risk of being accused of what Coyne (1999) has labeled "neocryptopsychoanalytic" thinking. As much as possible, we will attempt to supplement theoretical integration with references to existing empirical evidence; where such evidence is lacking in this relatively uncharted area, we will instead point directly to critical questions and suggestions that need empirical validation and exploration.

The schematic–cognitive theories of depression propose that a set of maladaptive cognitive processes and structures underlie the negative affective response to stressful circumstances characteristic of depression. The suggestion that these cognitive mechanisms distinguish those individuals who are prone to depressive episodes has received considerable empirical support (see reviews by Scher *et al.*, 2005; Segal & Ingram, 1994). This model, depicting depression as arising from individual differences in reactivity to stress, is firmly situated within the broader diathesis–stress model of psychopathology (Dozois & Beck, see Chapter 6; Ingram et al., 1998). The body of research and writing that has been stimulated by the schematic–cognitive model has improved our understanding of the contemporary experiential and cognitive process associated with the onset of depression and its reoccurrence. As important as is this objective, however, little attention and progress has been made in identifying the developmental origins of such cognitive vulnerability, a feat that is necessary in designing preventative and early intervention efforts for individuals at risk.

Interpersonal models of depression differ markedly from the dominant cognitive theory, as they focus on the role played by interaction and relationships with others as the basis of depressive symptoms (Joiner & Coyne, 1999). Research arising from this model of depression has largely been directed at substantiating proposed proximal causes of the disorder, in this case, dysfunctional social interactions and relationships. From this perspective, an individual's vulnerability is based on a predisposition toward such maladaptive patterns of interaction but the model largely begs the question of the developmental origins of such predisposition.

The suggestion that the experiential roots of vulnerability to depression can be traced back to childhood experience can be found in Beck's (1967) landmark work on the causes of depression. Others have also proposed that early attachment experiences with the primary caregiver and their consequences form the foundation of the maladaptive cognitive processes that place individuals at risk for future episodes of depression (Ingram, 2001, 2003; Scher *et al.*, 2005). So, too, some proponents of an interpersonal account have pointed to early experience and attachment in their efforts to understand individual differences in vulnerability to depression (e.g., Gotlib, 1992; Haines *et al.*, 1999).

We explore the idea that insecure or disorganized attachment contributes significantly to vulnerability to depression. *First*, we briefly elaborate on the hypothesized role of attachment as the source of vulnerability in the literature associated with the cognitive–reactivity theory of depression. *Second*, we provide a summary of existing attachment theory and empirical research with an emphasis on those experiences and their consequences that might be compatible with the cognitive–vulnerability models of risk for depression. This includes a detailed examination of the evidence regarding the cognitive and affective consequences of disorganized attachment associated with early experiences of trauma and loss. *Third*, we propose an integration of both the cognitive and social consequences of attachment as processes that serve to place at risk or, alternatively protect individuals from cognitive reactions to stress that give rise to depression.

ATTACHMENT AND LATER DEPRESSION: CONCEPTUAL ARGUMENTS AND EXISTING EVIDENCE

As is often the case with influential insights, the essence of Beck's (1967, 1979) proposal that depression arises from cognitive vulnerability is deceptively simple: life inevitably includes stressful periods and events, and some individuals respond to such stress with maladaptive patterns of cognition which put them at risk for depression. Scher *et al.* (2005) have pointed out that prior to the 1990s, the processes thought to be associated with depression within this cognitive model were most often examined in isolation from the stressful events antecedent to depression. The importance of these latter factors is underscored in Scher *et al.*'s (2005) argument that a cognitive reactivity to particular stressful events lies at the heart of individual vulnerability to depression. This account focuses on self-schema: cognitive structures that are the product of earlier experience, that shape information processing in later life for all of us (Beck, 1967; see also Abramson *et al.*, 1978, 1989; Ingram *et al.*, 1998, 2006; Segal, 1988). Vulnerability to negative mood and depression arises in individuals whose schemas are associated with maladaptive thoughts and attitudes in reaction to stressful life events, which Beck (1967, 1979) referred to as the cognitive triad – negative patterns of thought associated with the self, the future and the world. In conjunction with cognitive distortions of the events, the vulnerable individual is at risk for the development, maintenance, and recurrence of depressive symptomatology (see Scher *et al.*, 2005).

These schematic–cognitive models invoke a diathesis–stress process to explain the occurrence and reoccurrence of depression. Both aspects of this model – the eliciting life events and the pre-existing vulnerability – are critical to our consideration of the role of attachment in risk for depression, that is: (1) can the life conditions that lead to depressogenic cognitive reactivity be linked to early attachment experiences and (2) can the particular character of the maladaptive, depressogenic cognitive processes reasonably be associated with the theoretical and empirically established cognitive outcomes of early attachment?

Beck (1967) originally suggested that the eliciting conditions of the depressogenic cycle involve stress, but they also must evoke similar painful events or situations previously experienced in the adult's childhood. It was later proposed (Kovacs & Beck, 1978; Beck, 1979) that earlier negative experiences result in childhood cognitive adaptations that are the precursors of the maladaptive cognitive structures and processes, which are central to risk for depression in later life. The resulting vulnerability in later life is thus not a general reactivity to stress but is specific to life events that are reminiscent of those early formative events. In the absence of such specific eliciting conditions, the model holds that the depressogenic schemata could remain unexpressed.

A second key consideration of this model is the particular character of the reactive cognitions. Scher *et al.* (2005) suggest that it is the negative self-referential nature of the cognitions that are central to their maladaptive impact. That is, the re-activated schemas give rise to a spectrum of cognitions associated with self-blame, perceived inadequacy, and negative evaluation that originate with much earlier interpersonal experiences of childhood. The recent review by these same authors (Scher *et al.*, 2005) of extant evidence provides substantial support for the key role played by such processes in onset, maintenance, and recurrence of depression.

Cognitive theories of depression point to early childhood experiences as the roots of the depressogenic cognitive cycle (Ingram 2003; Ingram *et al.*, 1998). It comes as no surprise that these invocations of early caregiving experience drew the attention of theorists in depression to attachment theory and research. In a recent paper that advocates a place for childhood attachment in the development of risk for depression, Ingram (2003) reviewed a number of studies that link recollection of a variety of experiences with parents to depression. Ingram does cite a second set of related studies that included measures of current attachment in adults. These studies (Roberts *et al.*, 1996; Whisman & Kwon, 1992; Whisman & McGarvey, 1995) reported that adult insecure attachment was associated with depression and they reveal an association with theoretically predicted maladaptive cognitive processes in the same individuals.

The suggestion that the origins of cognitive vulnerability to depression lie in early attachment experiences is both intriguing and promises to provide a powerful heuristic platform for research in this important domain. The cognitive–reactivity account of depression contains a variety of elements that are superficially parallel elements of attachment, most obviously in the latter's core suggestion that early caregiving interaction shapes representation and affective structures and processes that select and interpret future experience.

The interpersonal or interactional account of depression (Coyne, 1976; Joiner & Coyne, 1999; Lewinsohn, 1974) views social interaction and relationships and their consequences as the critical determinants of the occurrence and reoccurrence of depression. In its stronger formulations, this view de-emphasizes the role that cognitive processes play in the causation of depressive symptoms (Coyne, 1976, 1999; Joiner *et al.*, 1999) and, instead, suggests that the cognitive patterns characteristic of depression are likely the outcome of maladaptive contemporary interactions and relationships with others. Others have attempted to formulate an integrated model in which both cognition and interpersonal processes play a role in the occurrence of depression (e.g., Schmidt *et al.*, 1999).

The interpersonal account portrays depressed individuals as deficient in the social skills required to elicit the support, reinforcement, and reassurance of others, particularly with significant friends and family. By implication, the model posits that the ability to form close relationships with significant others lies at the heart of adaptive life. Social support is especially significant during periods of life stress and other negative events, and in the absence of social support and reassurance the depressed individual's negative affect deepens (Coyne, 1976; 1999; Joiner & Coyne, 1999). Moreover, the interpersonal model proposes a feedback system in which the social inabilities of depressed individuals not only prevent access to support and reassurance, but where depressed behavior and inability to cope eventually leads to a negative impact on those around them, especially significant others. As a result, others then behave in a manner that reinforces the individual's beliefs that they are unloved and without access to the social support necessary to relieve their depression (Holahan *et al.*, 1999).

The interpersonal model of depression clearly resonates with attachment theory. The notion of felt security lies at the core of the attachment model: a child learns – or fails to learn – strategies to use intimate relationships as a secure base for exploration of the world and as a source of reassurance and restoration in times of stress. Some proponents of the interpersonal account of depression have turned to early attachment experiences and adult attachment processes to explain the variation in interaction and social relationships that might predispose to depression and failure to use others to ameliorate depressive episodes (e.g., Anderson et al., 1999; Whiffen & Johnson, 1998; Whiffen *et al.*, 2001). Attachment theory and research is an obvious candidate area to enlarge and deepen our understanding of vulnerabilities to depression that are associated with maladaptive patterns of social interaction and relationships. Gotlib (1992) has pointed squarely to a history of disturbed, inadequate parenting as the source of the dysfunctional social behavior of depressed adults. For example, Roberts *et al.* (1996) established that adult patterns of attachment were associated with depression and the link was mediated by dysfunctional attitudes and low self-esteem. On the basis of these findings, the authors propose that the vulnerabilities that they observed in adulthood have their roots in attachment-related experience in early childhood and, moreover, these roots lead to a vulnerability that involves the integration of the interpersonal and cognitive factors underlying depression.

We turn our attention next to some of the details of attachment theory and research, and then return to the challenge of mapping current knowledge of attachment on to contemporary ideas regarding the origins of risk for depression. In this discussion, we explore both disorganized attachment and its beginnings in the infant's experience of loss, trauma and profoundly disrupted caregiving, as well as organized but insecure attachment patterns as risk factors for depression. Before examining these issues, however, we recognize two limitations of our discussion. First, we have deliberately focused our attention on adulthood depression and excluded consideration of depression in childhood. Despite clear overlap in symptoms, a number of researchers have suggested that the origins and eliciting mechanisms of adult and child depression may well be different (see Harrington *et al.*, 1996). Sroufe *et al.* (2005) have pointed out some important contrasts: childhood depression is rare relative to adult depression; gender ratios vary dramatically with approximately an even balance in childhood and many more women in adulthood; and there is little evidence of depressive stability from childhood to adulthood. Duggal *et al.* (2001) have also found that childhood and adolescent depression were associated with distinct developmental precursors. A comprehensive examination of this issue is beyond the scope of this chapter. Second, although a thorough review of the research on temperamental or genetic factors implicated in depression is beyond the scope of this chapter, the omission should not be taken to imply that these are unimportant in our quest to better understand risk for depression. A number of researchers have focused on the contribution of particular child temperamental variables, such as behavioral inhibition, withdrawal negativity, and lower levels of positive emotionality, to a child's vulnerability to anxiety and depression (Gladstone & Parker, 2006; Hayden *et al.*, 2006; Mezulis *et al.*, 2006). Specific genetic markers that are associated with later problems with depression and emotion regulation have also been discussed (Propper & Moore, 2006). Nonetheless, all of these studies conclude that temperamental or genetic factors do not in themselves *cause* depression, but interact with negative life events and qualities of the parent–child relationship to predict higher risk for depression. In other words, some children may be more temperamentally at risk for depression and be more vulnerable to the impact of disrupted attachment and trauma, while others may possess greater resilience to variations in environmental experiences.

ATTACHMENT: ORIGINS, CORRELATES, AND DEVELOPMENTAL IMPLICATIONS

Infants are presumed to be biologically and evolutionarily prepared and motivated to form an attachment relationship with a caregiver. It is argued that the formation of attachment relationships promoted the survival of the infants of our evolutionary ancestors, thus contributing to their reproductive success and embedding attachment in the human species genotype (Bowlby, 1969; Simpson, 1999). Attachment research in a wide variety of different cultures has shown that, provided that a child has relatively consistent access to a caregiver, infants develop attachment relationships with their primary caregivers (DeWolff & vanIJzendoorn, 1997; Posada *et al.*, 2002). The attachment construct is reflected in a young child's motivation to maintain proximity to a caregiver and ideally be able to use this caregiver as a secure base from which to explore the world, yet also a safe haven to return to in times of stress, pain, anxiety, or fear (Main, 2000). In other words, at times of perceived safety, the infant or young child should be free to explore the world and nurture her curiosity and burgeoning independence, until such a time at which the child encounters real and/or experienced threat that drives her back to the caregiver to seek refuge and support (Bretherton & Munholland, 1999). It is this balanced interplay between the caregivers' role of "secure base" and "safe haven" that is central to our understanding of attachment security (Cooper *et al.*, 2005). Attachment behavior such as seeking social proximity and emotional support is activated in times of stress across the lifespan (Cassidy & Shaver, 1999; Roisman, 2007; Shaver & Mikulincer, 2002a, b).

A central premise of attachment theory is that "attachment security derives from *appraisals of availability in current attachment relationships*" (Kobak, 1999, p. 31). These appraisals are based on three expectations: (a) that the caregiver will perceive and accept the child's communication of attachment needs (i.e., need for the caregiver to provide a safe haven), (b) that the caregiver is physically accessible, and (c) that the caregiver will respond to meet the child's needs. This last expectation implies that the caregiver is both *able* and *willing to* respond. With these expectations met, a child's confidence in a parent's availability gives rise to the experience of felt security (Cummings, 1990; Cummings & Davies, 1996) which in turn supports the child's active exploration of the environment.

INDIVIDUAL DIFFERENCES IN ATTACHMENT

The goals of attachment behavior, which include the maintenance of proximity and ultimately felt security, are held to be similar for all children. Individual differences have been observed in the methods used by infants and young children to attain these goals, however (van IJzendoorn & Kroonenberg, 1988, 1990). Although the study of attachment strategies began in naturalistic contexts, the "Strange Situation" laboratory procedure (Ainsworth & Bell, 1970), which consists of a succession of separation and reunion episodes between a parent and his or her infant, dominates research on infants' behavior in response to attachment-related stress.

Secure infants tend to respond to their caregiver's return by communicating in a relatively straightforward way their desire for proximity or contact or wish for interaction. The infant effectively obtains comfort or contact with the caregiver and is able to resume exploration, thus successfully balancing the complimentary goals of security-seeking and exploration. In contrast, two qualitatively distinct strategies have been identified that make up a significant minority of parent–child relationships. These strategies involve either the minimization or maximization of expressed negative emotions. In response to attachment-related stress, Insecure-avoidant infants show relatively less desire for proximity, contact, or interaction with their caregivers, despite experiencing a situation as stressful (Spangler & Grossmann, 1993). Instead, they are more likely to distract themselves with toys when distressed or to initiate interactions with their caregiver only after they have resolved some of this inwardly experienced distress. By contrast, Insecure-ambivalent infants display ambivalent or angry behavior toward their caregiver and are unable to resume play or exploration (Ainsworth *et al.*, 1971). Although the expression of these patterns alters with development, these patterns of attachment can be reliably assessed in preschool-aged children as well (Cassidy & Marvin, 1992).

The fact that these attachment strategies can be readily observed among infants at 12 months of age demonstrates children's impressive ability to learn and adapt to their caregiving environment. Ainsworth's groundbreaking observational studies (Ainsworth *et al.*, 1971, 1978) and subsequent research (Bailey *et al.*, 2007; Pederson & Moran, 1995, 1996; Pederson *et al.*, 1990) demonstrated individual differences in maternal behavior that correspond to these different patterns of infant attachment behavior. Mothers of Avoidant infants tend to avoid physical contact, reject bids for closeness, and appear relatively unresponsive to cues of emotional distress. Although data are less consistently available for the Ambivalent classification, due to its low prevalence in western cultures where most research has occurred, mothers of Ambivalent infants tend to be inconsistently responsive to needs and cues. This research supports the consensus that infants in these different relationships develop corresponding expectations about caregiver availability and responsiveness in attachment-relevant situations. Thus, children's differentiated behavior in the Strange Situation is thought to result from their appraisals of the situation and the expectations of their parent's response as a function of early experiences (Ainsworth *et al.*, 1978, Kobak, 1999). This interpretation is consistent with theories of neurological development, described below.

TRAUMA, FEAR, AND DISORGANIZED ATTACHMENT

In the 1980s researchers began to notice that a small but significant minority of infants were extremely difficult to classify in the Strange Situation. This number increased within high-risk samples. In an intensive examination of these videotapes, Main and Solomon (1990) concluded that these infants demonstrated a general breakdown or absence of a coherent strategy to enlist the caregiver support necessary for the infant when confronted with stressful situations. These infants displayed a wide array of inexplicable, odd, disorganized, disoriented, or conflicted behavior in the parent's presence (Main & Solomon, 1990), often demonstrating sequentially or simultaneously contradictory behavior. For example, in the reunion sequence an infant might reach for her parent while averting her head away from her, or quickly approach her parent in reunion, only to stop suddenly or change direction. Such children might suddenly appear to have a dazed expression, while stopping all movement. Some behavior reflected apprehension of the parent herself (e.g., running away from the parent with a frightened expression), or general disorientation. All of these actions, although superficially quite dissimilar, have been interpreted as indicating that the child is considerably disoriented or distressed, and unable to directly approach his or her caregiver for support (Main & Solomon, 1990). As such, these infants were classified as exhibiting Disorganized attachment. When these infants were observed as preschoolers, they often displayed a controlling, role-inverting relationship with their caregivers, where a pattern of punitive/oppositional or compulsive caregiving behavior was observed (Main & Cassidy, 1988). This evolution of patterns may reflect the need of the increasingly competent child to establish a strategy, even if maladaptive, in order to maintain her relationship with a parent who is incapable of providing the minimal necessary interactional framework.

Researchers discovered that Disorganized attachment reaches levels of as high as 60–80% in high-risk samples, such as children who were maltreated or living in chaotic or frightening circumstances (Crittenden, 1985; Egeland & Sroufe,

1981; van IJzendoorn *et al.*, 1999). Disorganization is less prevalent in low-risk samples (approximately 15%; van IJzendoorn *et al.*, 1999). Disorganized children are faced with the paradox of not being able to rely on their primary attachment figure in times of fear, a situation described as "fright without solution" (Main & Hesse, 1990). In the case of parental maltreatment, the conundrum is relatively clear: the source of security is very literally the actual source of fear. In addition, a number of recent articles have also elucidated a pattern of atypical behavior that mothers of Disorganized infants may demonstrate in interactions that, while not directly abusive, are nonetheless frightening to the child (Hesse & Main, 2006; Lyons-Ruth *et al.*, 1999). Mothers may behave in a way that is profoundly unresponsive to the child's signals of attachment-related distress. Due to the parent's own experiences of helplessness and dysregulation, frightening or dysregulated interactions remain chronically unrepaired (Lyons-Ruth *et al.*, 1999; Solomon & George, 1999). A series of studies provides evidence of the association between a mother's Unresolved/disoriented state of mind regarding childhood trauma or loss, atypical and frightened or frightening interaction with her infant, and infant Disorganization (Bailey *et al.*, 2007; Forbes *et al.*, 2007; Madigan *et al.*, 2006a,b; Moran *et al.*, 2008). Infants raised in such caregiving environments face significant barriers to the development of a sense of being able to effectively use their emotions or behavior for internal or environmental regulation (DeOliveira *et al.*, 2004).

THE DEVELOPMENT OF REPRESENTATIONS

Interpersonal experiences with caregivers occur early, but when and how do the corresponding mental representations develop? Even before infants are able to verbally communicate their expectations about relationships and caregiver availability, behavioral observations can be used to infer their expectations, and thus their emerging cognitive organization. Such early experience-based learning may have a particularly strong impact on later schemas or representations and may be resistant to change because this learning is encoded through its impact on neuronal development and differentiation, rather than being verbally mediated (Schore, 2001). It is now widely recognized that early childhood constitutes a sensitive developmental period during which "early interpersonal events positively or negatively impact the structural organization of the brain and its expanding adaptive functional capacities" (Schore, 2001). Such individual differences in neurobiological development are expected to have long-lasting effects on an individual's response to subsequent stressors (Cicchetti, 2002; Cicchetti & Valentino, 2006; Gunnar & Fisher, 2006; Rutter, 2006; Schore, 2001).

With increasing verbal ability, children are able to communicate their developing understanding of how relationships work. Associations between early experience and subsequent narrative depictions of relational themes highlight the impact of early experience on cognitive organization. Systematic links have been found between early attachment strategies measured in infancy, and later drawings, play, and narratives in the preschool and middle childhood years (see Carlson *et al.*, 2004 &Main, 1996 for reviews). For example, children as old as 7 years who had been classified as Secure in infancy were able to respond openly and constructively in a Separation Anxiety Task or other narrative-based attachment-related assessments. These children also created family drawings that were coherent, colorful, and proportionate. Children previously classified as Disorganized more often infused catastrophic themes into stories about brief parent–child separations and their family drawings more often included bizarre and frightening elements (Madigan *et al.*, 2004; Main *et al.*, 1985).

Several studies have examined links between early attachment patterns and attachment representations in adolescence and adulthood, as assessed with the Adult Attachment Interview (AAI; George *et al.*, 1996). The AAI is an hour-long, semi-structured interview, in which individuals are asked questions about past or current relationships with attachment figures, and are also probed about experiences of trauma or loss. The AAI serves as an implicit rather than explicit measure of attachment representations, since the transcript is coded according to coherence of the discourse process, rather than the nature of the experiences themselves (Main & Goldwyn, 1984–1998). In a longitudinal follow-up investigation, adolescents who were classified as Secure in infancy were more likely to discuss important attachment relationships in a way that was coherent, collaborative, and flexible (Autonomous). Conversely, adolescents who were insecure-avoidant as infants were more likely to be derogating, idealizing, or avoidant during the discussion (Dismissing), and adolescents who were insecure-ambivalent tended to be passive or angrily preoccupied when they discussed attachment-based events and memories (Preoccupied) (Main, 1996). Individuals are coded as having an Unresolved (Disorganized/disoriented) state if mind on the AAI when they have lapses in the monitoring of reasoning or discourse when they discuss experiences of trauma or loss (Main & Goldwyn, 1984–1998). The powerful impact of early attachment experiences on subsequent development is illustrated by a series of recently published accounts of longitudinal studies stretching from infancy to adulthood (see Grossman *et al.*, 2005; Sroufe *et al.*, 2005).

The link between early interactive patterns and later outcomes on representational tasks supports Bowlby's theory that repeated experiences with caregivers are internalized into an individual's working model of self and others in relationships. The internal working model includes rules to direct the encoding and organization of attachment-relevant information and guides cognition, perception, and motivation (Main *et al.*, 1985; Bretherton, 1991). A child's appraisal of his parent's emotional availability and responsiveness in times of need is the central feature in the formation of these internal working models (Kobak, 1999). These representational models use past relational experiences to evaluate the consequences of future relational behaviors and using these predictive capacities to respond in the most adaptive and flexible way, optimizing the probability of future survival (Craik, 1943 as cited in Bretherton & Munholland, 1999). Internal working models are not static, but are somewhat resistant to accommodation and change (Bretherton & Munholland, 1999) due to their self-reinforcing nature. As Vaughn *et al.* (1979) wrote:

> From an organizational perspective, continuity in child adaptation is also supported by the child's prior history of relationship experiences. The child actively participates in constructing experience in at least three ways: (a) by behaving in ways that elicit responses that support prior adaptation, (b) by making choices that selectively engage aspects of the environment supporting a particular adaptive style, and (c) by interpreting new and ambiguous situations in ways that are consistent with earlier experience (p. 29–30).

As such, an individual's internal working model affects the observation, encoding, and responses to emotions, and thoughts and behavior, in a way that supports existing representations of the self and others in relationships. For example, secure individuals likely have a working model of others as responsive, caring, and emotionally available and a *complementary* working model of the self as valuable and worthy of love and nurturance. Such individuals likely respond to new relational experiences with confidence, emotional flexibility, and trust. Alternatively, when evolutionary-driven attachment needs are ignored, individuals may develop a working model of others as emotionally unavailable, inaccessible and rejecting, and a working model of the self as unimportant, rejected, and abandoned (Bretherton, 1991). Such models have implications for the confidence and flexibility with which they approach new relationships and emotional experiences, as well as their basic sense of self-worth.

ATTACHMENT AND LATER PSYCHOPATHOLOGY

Bowlby initially theorized that early actual or experienced losses of an attachment figure's emotional or physical availability might put an individual at risk for later depression (Bowlby, 1980). Multiple studies have confirmed the link between early child–caregiver attachment and later psychological functioning (Greenberg, 1999). In general, organized but insecure attachment (Avoidant, Ambivalent) is a risk factor in combination with other environmental, situational, or temperamental risk factors, and predicts internalizing and externalizing difficulties in childhood. No clear longitudinal main effect has been found between insecure attachment and later childhood behavioral or emotional problems in a low-risk sample (e.g., middle-class convenience samples). In high social-risk samples, attachment insecurity has predicted a number of difficulties in the areas of peer relationships, behavior problems, and depression and anxiety in preschool, middle school, and adolescence (Greenberg, 1999).

A number of studies have found Disorganized attachment to be a risk factor for later childhood psychopathology, especially in combination with other risk factors such as low intelligence or infant difficult temperament (Greenberg, 1999 for review). In a prospective longitudinal study, Carlson (1998) found that infants who were classified as exhibiting disorganized attachment at 1 year of age were more likely to exhibit behavior problems at all stages of school, as well as symptoms of dissociation and psychopathology in adolescence. Attachment disorganization was found to mediate the link between early experiences and later psychopathology (see also van IJzendoorn *et al.*, 1999).

Children who are maltreated are also at higher risk for psychopathology (Kim & Cicchetti, 2006; Toth *et al.*, 2002) and the impact of maltreatment on the formation of attachment representations may be a critical component. The link between early experiences of abuse and neglect and processing of emotions, social problem solving, and attributions has been well documented (Beeghly & Cicchetti, 1994; Camras *et al.*, 1983; Shipman *et al.*, 2000; Toth *et al.*, 2002). Cicchetti and Valentino (2006) asserted that Disorganized attachment may mediate or moderate the association between early maltreatment and later maladaptation. The joint or interacting contribution of maltreatment and disorganization to later social skills and peer relationship problems may create further risk factors to the development or maintenance of depression (Cicchetti & Valentino, 2006).

Associations have been found between adult states of mind and attachment, as assessed in the AAI, and concurrent psychopathology. Ward *et al.* (2006) found that Autonomous (secure) individuals were less likely to have psychiatric diagnoses, compared to individuals with an insecure state of mind with respect to attachment. Preoccupied individuals were particularly vulnerable to affective disorders. Other research has linked Dismissing representations to elevated levels of anxiety and depression associated with externalizing symptoms (e.g., *somatic* rather than *emotional* symptoms of depression; *avoidance* rather than *fear* symptoms of anxiety (DeOliveira *et al.*, 2005; Dozier *et al.*, 1999).

This overview of theory and related research reveals that attachment processes lend themselves to a developmental psychopathology model of risk for depression. The child brings past relational experiences and resulting models of self and others into new relationships and experiences, and becomes an active participant in determining the trajectories of later social experiences and adjustment (Egeland & Carlson, 2004). These internal working models of attachment not only affect the individual's relational behavior (as experienced by others), but also her internalized perceptions, attributions, and emotional understanding of these relationships.

HOW THE COGNITIVE AND INTERPERSONAL CONSEQUENCES OF EARLY ATTACHMENT EXPERIENCES MAY AFFECT RESILIENCE AND VULNERABILITY TO DEPRESSION

The preceding discussion provided an account of early attachment-related processes, their emotional, interpersonal, and representational correlates, and associations with risk for psychopathology. We now build on this account to draw parallels between attachment-related representational processes and the growing understanding of depressogenic cognitive schemas. In doing so, we highlight the ways in which information from an attachment perspective might inform theory and research on vulnerability to depression. In a parallel fashion, we explore the possibility that a better understanding of the interpersonal risk for depression may be found in regulatory and relational strategies arising from early attachment. The attachment position is that cognitive, emotional, and interpersonal processes are related and complementary: cognitive representations or schemas within the individual at the same time influence and are shaped by emotional and relational processes and social interactions (Krantz, 1985). In effect, we will explore what Coyne and Gotlib (1983) referred to as "the role of social factors in predisposing, precipitating, and maintaining depression as well as facilitating relapse" (2002, p. 30). In this section, therefore, we will integrate the literatures on attachment and depression in order to elaborate ways in which early attachment experiences may contribute to a cognitive and interpersonal vulnerability to depression. We will discuss the potential for such vulnerability associated with insecure, organized attachment relationships, followed by a discussion of the likely ontological effects of disorganized attachment and experiences of childhood maltreatment. Finally, we will discuss unresolved issues and future research directions.

SPECIFIC COGNITIVE AND INTERPERSONAL VULNERABILITIES ASSOCIATED WITH PARTICULAR PATTERNS OF ATTACHMENT

Beck's (1967) cognitive model of depression presumes that self-relevant schemata develop in the early years as a normative cognitive organizational process, and that the child's experience during social interactions supplies the content to be incorporated into these schemas. These assumptions accord well with a central premise of attachment theory: that children universally are exposed to repeated interactions with one or more primary caregivers, providing an interpersonal context through which they acquire a general understanding of such interactions. Each child develops a functional strategy that ensures caregiver availability and is, thus, shaped by the particular caregiving style of the parent. Associated with these emerging expectations of others' behavior is a developing understanding of the self and relationships.

Insecure Attachment Relationships

While insecure but organized early attachment relationships may not be directly implicated in later affective disorders, they likely constitute a risk factor when combined with negative life stress. Beck's original premise (1967) that maladaptive early experiences such as loss of a caregiver foster the development of negative cognitive schemas is entirely consistent with Bowlby's original formulation (1951; 1969/1982) that maternal deprivation, in the form of prolonged separation or permanent loss through death, exerts a profound and adverse effect on children. Cognitive researchers (Ingram, 2003, Scher *et al.*, 2005) have draw premises to identify more specifically that experiences of parental r tion, particularly if experienced chronically, support the developm sentational understanding of the self as unlikeable, unlovable, or un

Neglect and rejection can be placed somewhere along a broad continuum of caregiver availability and responsiveness. At their extreme, such behavior would constitute maltreatment. Even more normative variations in parental availability influence the development of self-schemas that could in turn comprise a vulnerability to depression. For example, some parental behavior, although not to the extreme of neglect or maltreatment, requires that the child distort or repress some aspects of her emotional experience, such as when a parent repeatedly rejects or fails to respond to a child's expressions of distress or overt bids for comfort, or behaves in an inconsistently available or responsive manner. Children of caregivers who respond in these ways tend to adopt complementary strategies in which their displays of negative emotions are minimized or maximized, respectively (Ainsworth *et al.*, 1971; Bailey *et al.*, 1999, 2007; Pederson & Moran, 1995).

These strategies involving the minimization or maximization of negative emotional cues are adaptive in the sense that they optimize caregiver availability and responsiveness to ensure protection against outside threat; however, compared to children in secure attachment relationships who experience relatively unconditional parental responsiveness, children in insecure attachment relationships are at a disadvantage. Fundamentally they experience increased levels of felt insecurity when confronted with potentially stressful events. Bowlby (1973) originally postulated that if a child is confident in the attachment figure's availability, she will be less susceptible to feeling overwhelmed or intensely distressed when confronted with subsequent stressors. Children with a secure attachment relationship have been found to experience relatively lower levels of distress in response to stressors, as indexed by physiological measures (Spangler & Grossman, 1993). In contrast, the understanding that caregivers are responsive only to certain cues contributes to a greater perceived inability to cope with stressors by undermining the child's confidence in caregiver availability.

Like the range of observed parenting behavior, a child's feelings of insecurity presumably can be placed on a broad continuum. Children who rely primarily on an insecure but organized attachment strategy would fall somewhere in the moderate range, between the more optimal secure strategy and the less optimal relationships characterized by signs of breakdown and disorganization. Qualitative distinctions between the Avoidant and Ambivalent insecure strategies, however, likely would support the development of substantially different self-schemas and interpersonal patterns that in turn would be expected to influence later cognitive appraisal and interpersonal support-seeking processes in a disparate manner.

A strategy involving the heightened communication of negative emotions to ensure caregiver availability, characteristic of Ambivalent/Resistant attachment relationships in infancy and with a Preoccupied stance as an adult, bears considerable resemblance to the process through which cognitive distortions (such as arbitrary influence, selective abstraction, and overgeneralization) maximize negative and minimize positive perceptions. These biases reinforce negative self-schemas. Thus, the repeated experience of heightening negative emotion within early relationships may initially have been effective but later would create difficulties in other contexts if it became an immediate or automatic reaction to perceived stressors.

Strategies associated with Avoidant attachment relationships in infancy and a Dismissing stance in adulthood, involving the early acquisition of an emotion minimization strategy, could also constitute a cognitive risk factor for depression but by way of a quite different mechanism. The internalization and use of such a minimization strategy might serve a protective function against cognitive distortions that result in overly negative appraisals. However, reliance on a minimization strategy would impede the ability to acknowledge and integrate both positive and negative information, which might become a problem in response to severe or frequent stressors. Furthermore, despite their relative inattention to issues of vulnerability and negative mood, these individuals may still possess an implicit understanding of others as unavailable and the self as unworthy of others' care and attention in times of emotional need. Therefore, they may still be more vulnerable to interpersonal events that trigger the underlying set of expectations of the self and others in relationships, despite the fact that these schemata may not be fully accessible and/or the affective arousal may be manifested in other ways. Somatic and externalizing affective symptoms of depression (e.g., increased irritability) may be more evident among individuals with an avoidant or dismissing stance (DeOliveira, *et al.*, 2005; Dozier *et al.*, 1999).

The chronic distortion of negative internalizing emotional experience, although perhaps adaptive within the particular parent–child relationship in which it was shaped, is less adaptive in other interpersonal contexts. In the context of risk for depression, the costs of the dismissing state of mind regarding attachment will be most critically evident when the goal of interaction is to effectively enlist the help of others to cope with stressors or depressive symptoms. Failure to address negative feelings through open communication during childhood increases the likelihood that they will later be expressed problematically in other contexts (Kobak, 1999). An avoidant or dismissing relational approach might impede one's ability to use others in proactive problem solving and information seeking (Holahan *et al.*, 1999). For those who emerge from ambivalent parent–child relationships with a Preoccupied state of mind regarding relationships, their interactions are at risk of featuring a perseveration on negative themes and an over-reliance on others (Mallinckrodt, 2000; Riggs *et al.*, 2002). These individuals maintain expectations that others will be available to them only in a limited fashion and that this availability will be contingent upon their own behavior. Each of these patterns reflect Bowlby's (1973) early observation that our confidence in the availability of attachment figures is based on experiences in childhood and adolescence, but tends to resist change during adulthood.

Disorganized Attachment (and Experiences of Maltreatment)

Compared to organized attachment strategies, the breakdown of a child's attachment strategy constitutes a far greater threat to children's felt security and their developing confidence in the self and others. As mentioned previously, although not always a developmental precursor to Disorganization (Hesse & Main, 2006), child maltreatment has been associated with high rates of disorganized attachment relationships (Crittenden, 1985; Egeland & Sroufe, 1981; van IJzendoorn *et al.*, 1999). Experiences of maltreatment fall outside the range of what Cicchetti and Valentino (2006) refer to as an "average expectable environment." Abusive parents create strong feelings of negative affect during interpersonal interactions, and the frequently co-occurring emotional neglect is associated with a failure to assist the child in regulating negative experiences (Briere, 2002). From the child's perspective, experiences of intense negative affect are accompanied by an absence of parental assistance in their regulation. This circumstance is the prototypical example of a developmental situation of distress without relief where, because the parent is the direct source of the threat to the child, she is entirely unable to play her critical role as a safe haven for comfort, reassurance, and resolution of that threat. In such a relational context, the child is left without the essential interactional framework necessary to develop or maintain any semblance of felt security. Furthermore, because young children have an egocentric understanding of cause and effect, they are likely to infer a causal role for themselves in provoking the parent's behavior.

Such a prelogical conclusion has clear implications for a child's developing cognitive self-schema and could predispose her to the negative self-attributions associated with the adult depressogenic schema. This idea is consistent with Scher *et al.*'s argument that negative self-referential cognitions are central to their maladaptive impact, and that stressful adult experiences associated with the onset of depressive episodes re-activate pre-existing schemas. Scher argues that such schemas originate in the much earlier interpersonal experiences of childhood, and they promote the spectrum of cognitions featuring self-blame, inadequacy, and negative evaluation. The attachment-related consequences of maltreatment in early childhood meet these criteria of an association with negative self-referential cognitions in reaction to stress and early experiences that are functionally similar to the circumstances that often give rise to these cognitions in adulthood. For abuse survivors, negative self-referential cognitions co-occur with more vulnerabilities in affect regulation at a somatic and implicit level (Briere, 2002; Schore, 2001), and increase the risk of affective disturbances in times of stress.

High levels of parental insensitivity and unresponsiveness are associated with disorganized attachment, particularly in high-risk populations (Bailey *et al.*, 2007; Forbes *et al.*, 2007; Moran *et al.*, 2008). The parents in such attachment relationships often have a history of traumatic experience in their own childhood (e.g., maltreatment or a significant loss through death) that remains unintegrated, or unresolved. Such caregivers may display atypical and potentially frightening or disorienting behaviors and report feeling helpless to resolve their child's negative emotions. Under such circumstances, infants are faced with unpredictable behavior, including parental actions that may be frightening, as well as parental inability to repair such interactions and resolve the child's distress and fear. Such circumstances may invoke a situation of distress without relief that is similar to that faced by a child dealing with actual parental abuse (Hesse & Main, 2006; Main & Hesse, 1990). In any case, the Disorganized attachment relationship leaves children without the essential social framework to develop a viable strategy to recruit the support of others in dealing with the life stresses that they inevitably will face (see DeOliveira *et al.*, 2005; Hesse & Main, 2006; Lyons-Ruth *et al.*, 2005).

As a result of repeated experiences of being unable to identify and maintain a strategy that ensures caregiver availability, a child learns at a preverbal level that she is unable to resolve stress. As a result of a corresponding lack of caregiver responsiveness, the child also internalizes the fact that others are unavailable or unreliable allies in her efforts to alleviate distress. This presumption of limited coping resources in turn increases the child's subjective distress when appraising potentially stressful situations. Thus, the internal working models or schema available to children with a history of disorganized attachment relationships and the associated experience of "distress without solution" place them at a particular disadvantage later in life when confronted with negative or stressful self-relevant information.

In summary, the internal working model of attachment that children carry with them into adulthood likely has a critical impact on their reaction to future stressful experiences and negative emotions. If they develop an avoidant/dismissive or ambivalent/preoccupied strategy, they will be likely to minimize or maximize the subjective experience and expression of negative emotions, respectively. Such strategies interfere with an individual's ability to respond in a cognitively flexible way and to seek appropriate interpersonal support at times of life stress, and thus put an individual at greater risk for depression. In contrast, a secure/autonomous attachment stance predisposes an individual to think about and express positives and negatives in a more balanced fashion and seek interpersonal support in a way that is adaptive and sustainable. Disorganized infants who have dealt repeatedly with the experience of distress without solution may have internalized an underlying belief that stressful situations are unmanageable, inciting doubt in their own and others' competence in coping with stressors. Such developmental outcomes align well with both the depressogenic cognitive models of risk for depression (Ingram *et al.*, 2006), and interpersonal perspectives that emphasize the role of others in interactions associated with the onset or resolution of episodes of depression (Joiner & Coyne, 1999).

AREAS FOR FURTHER RESEARCH AT THE INTERSECTION OF ATTACHMENT AND RISK FOR DEPRESSION

Although the forgoing discussion presents a compelling case for the role of early attachment experiences and their resultant internal working models in cognitive and interpersonal risk for depression, the arguments are primarily speculative, based largely on informed argument and indirect evidence. As a result, the intersection between attachment and risk of depression provides rich soil for additional research on the important question of the developmental mechanisms that lead to vulnerability to depression.

HOW ARE COGNITIVE SCHEMAS ACTIVATED?

One area of investigation concerns the mechanisms through which depressogenic schemas are activated later in life. Research indicates that maladaptive schemas remain latent in the absence of priming to activate these schemas (Scher *et al.*, 2005). According to Beck's original reasoning, the conditions that evoke depressogenic cognitive and/or interpersonal patterns in adulthood must parallel or reflect those related attachment-relevant experiences from childhood. In other words, cognitive schemas are presumed to be activated by experiences similar to those that fostered their development in childhood. If these schemas are maladaptive, they may negatively bias information processing strategies that may trigger the onset of, maintain, or exacerbate a depressive episode.

This element of the cognitive model of depressogenic symptoms closely parallels the idea that the attachment internal working model also is activated, and thus identifiable, only under particular conditions. In childhood such activation typically involves introducing potentially frightening novel situations and/or compromising the perceived availability of parents, both of which may evoke attachment-related stress. The most common research approach to the identification of adult internal working models of attachment is to activate them by way of the AAI, which is a structured interview concerning the perceived availability of attachment figures in childhood and early childhood experiences involving the need for care and comfort from parents (e.g., times of sickness, injury, traumatic life events). Adults with a history of insecure attachment and difficult childhood experiences are expected to experience greater negative affect in response to such activation, particularly if their cognitive schemata are relatively stable.

Research on the priming effects of the AAI reveals physiological and behavioral markers that correspond to different strategies for coping with negative emotion. Adults who display a Preoccupied state of mind and, thus, use an emotion maximization strategy during the interview, report significantly elevated negative emotion, and their facial expressions during the interview also have been coded as expressive of greater negative emotion relative to others (Roisman *et al.*, 2004). Conversely, adults adopting a minimization approach characteristic of a Dismissive state of mind have shown increased electrodermal activity, a physiological response that accompanies one's effort to inhibit behavior (Dozier & Kobak, 1992; Roisman *et al.*, 2004).

Negative mood induction is the predominant method of priming used by depression researchers (see Scher *et al.*, 2005). Although some materials used to induce negative mood are devoid of explicit, attachment-related content (e.g., negative music), other primes contain content clearly paralleling key attachment themes (e.g., film clip depicting loss of a caregiver through death; Miranda *et al.*, 1998). The commonly used technique of having participants remember or imagine a sad event in their lives may, in fact, be effective precisely because it triggers attachment-related schema. It would be revealing to explicitly explore the content of memories invoked by participants in such circumstances.

The effectiveness of self-induced negative mood techniques used in depression research may differ systematically according to participants' attachment representations and their associated reliance on either affect minimization as opposed to maximization strategies. Individuals who use a minimization strategy are likely to comply less completely with instructions to induce a negative emotional state. Their estimates of negative mood also might be systematically understated relative to other participants. Such effects could be minimized and a more truly representative portrait of vulnerability to depression might be assessed across groups who employ different coping strategies, if researchers utilized externally developed primes of similar magnitude and use physiological data and implicit or performance-based measures (e.g., McCabe *et al.*, 2000) to assess mood. According to the same reasoning, based on our earlier findings (DeOliveira *et al.*, 2005), assessments of depressive symptoms that focus primarily on physiological measures as opposed to subjective mood and experience will better identify the group of "minimizers" that may be at increased risk of depression.

A related question for future research involves the level of specificity of triggers likely to activate depressogenic schemas. Any attempt to invoke early attachment experiences and their consequent representational processes must fulfill conditions that map onto the core elements of the cognitive–reactivity model of depression risk. The optimal activating trigger is an experience similar to the childhood experience on which the schema was developed (e.g., perceived rejection by an attachment figure). For those who have repeatedly experienced "distress without solution" in childhood, however, we would argue that any stressor might evoke negative schemata later in life, because the underlying internalized schema concerns the individual's perceived inability to cope with his/her negative emotions, rather than the nature of the stressor. The feeling of hopelessness that would likely result from such schema activation appears consonant with the hopelessness theory of depression (Abramson *et al.*, 1989).

COGNITIVE SCHEMAS AND EMOTIONS

Although the most influential current accounts of the intrapersonal determinants of depression focus on cognitive factors, these are very much entwined with affective regulation processes. For example, priming by way of negative mood induction has been widely used to confirm the assumption that maladaptive cognitive schemata become active when participants experience greater depressed mood (Scher *et al.*, 2005). However, because the focus of such induction techniques is on participants' current mood as a validity marker, the procedure fails to test Beck's hypothesis that maladaptive cognitive schemata give rise to the negative mood. Cognitive researchers would likely counter this observation by reasoning that although both directions of influence require empirical validation, emotional mood and cognitive schemata are inherently interdependent: the development of cognitive and affective self-structures occurs jointly and bidirectional influence would occur as a matter of course (Ingram, 2003).

Accounts of early human development further underscore arguments for a focus on emotion, pointing to emotional development as having defining consequences in the first year. As discussed earlier, research on neurological development reveals that early representations of relational experiences are implicit and preverbal. The first years of life constitute a critical period in which the development of neuronal pathways is strongly influenced by social experience. In infancy, the type of interpersonal interaction shaping this neuronal development consists primarily of the mutual experience and regulation of emotions. In this manner, early and shared interactive experience, fundamentally involving joint affect regulation and experience, shapes the development and organization of a child's understanding of self, others and relationships as laid down at a neurological level. It is only later in development with increasing verbal ability that individuals are able to articulate cognitive schemas or representations that describe the central features of these early, relationship-based, emotional experiences.

The primacy of this early experience, and the foundational way in which these early memories are encoded, raises the possibility that language-based cognitive schemata approximate an individual's broader, underlying experience-based vulnerability to depression. Furthermore, the extent to which people are aware of, and able to articulate, their experience in the form of cognitive schemata may vary, as would the openness of such schemas to change. Paralleling our understanding of the effects of security in childhood, research on adult attachment classifications suggests that people with the greatest ability to articulate their own cognitive processes are those who have developed an internal sense of security that facilitates exploration of their own difficult issues and experiences and openness to changing perspective (Main, 1995; Main & Goldwyn, 1984–1998; Mallinckrodt *et al.*, 2005). In contrast, Preoccupied or Dismissing adults whose lower level of felt security facilitates less complete self-exploration demonstrate less awareness of inconsistencies within their own cognitive evaluative processes during the AAI (Bernier & Dozier, 2002; Main, 1995; Main & Goldwyn, 1984–1998).

ADULT ATTACHMENT REPRESENTATIONS AND INTERPERSONAL RISKS FOR DEPRESSION

The core outcome of distinct internal working models of attachment in childhood and adulthood are differences in one's ability to form, engage, and utilize our closest relationships in times of distress. We have reviewed some of the literature related to the growing interest in the proposed link between attachment and a model of interpersonal processes in depression. This line of research is now guided by explicit theoretical models suggesting that insecure attachment contributes importantly to the maladaptive interpersonal contexts that are associated with the onset and failure to terminate depressive episodes (e.g., Coyne & Whiffen, 1995; Roberts *et al.*, 1996). Johnson (1996) has constructed a model of marital therapy based largely on the conceptualization of the spouse as an attachment figure. In turn, these theoretical structures have fostered a number of interesting and valuable investigations dealing with a range of issues related to interpersonal risk of depression and its treatment. Such work includes research on couples and depression (Whiffen, 2005) and childbearing depression (Whiffen & Johnson, 1998). This type of research, perhaps with more explicit evaluation of disorganized attachment, will enhance the understanding of basic processes in both risk for depression and its treatment.

DIFFERENCES IN UNDERLYING VULNERABILITY TO DEPRESSION: IMPLICATIONS FOR THERAPY

Throughout this chapter we have identified likely points of divergence that correspond to different subtypes of experience-based vulnerability to depression. We propose that a match between therapeutic approach and the client's state of mind with respect to attachment might optimize treatment outcomes. Whereas adults with a more secure state of mind with respect to attachment show significantly greater progress in therapy (Dozier, 1990; Eames & Roth, 2000; Kanninen *et al.*, 2000), the importance of this therapist–client match may be most evident among clients who demonstrate lower levels of cognitive flexibility and greater adherence to a minimization or maximization strategy associated with a Dismissing or Preoccupied attachment representation, respectively. Research on attachment and therapy outcomes indicates that clients improve most when therapists adopt a contrasting approach to their client's predominant coping strategy, rather than responding in a complementary fashion (Bernier & Dozier, 2002; Tyrrell *et al.*, 1999). As discussed earlier, clients with an attachment-based propensity to maximize or heighten negative emotions would be especially prone to cognitive distortions that serve this function. With such clients, a focus on cognitive strategies and rational thinking would provide a contrasting approach by targeting specific cognitive appraisal skills that would help to moderate this maximizing tendency.

In contrast, however, individuals with a minimizing strategy might benefit most from an interpersonal approach that targeted their area of greatest vulnerability. Although the cognitive schemata among these clients may constitute a vulnerability to depression, their interpersonal differences appear to constitute a more primary target for intervention. Dismissing states of mind have been associated with observed hostility, interpersonal distancing, and rejection of significant others (Dozier *et al.*, 2001; Kobak & Sceery, 1988; Kobak *et al.*, 1993). Adults who maintain such a minimizing and avoidant strategy are less likely to seek emotional support from others. In fact, Riggs *et al.* (2002) found that adults with Dismissing attachment representations sought therapy significantly less often than those with other primary representational strategies. Therapy that identifies and communicates emotional states, and capitalizes on available relational support, may be more efficacious for such clients.

CONCLUDING COMMENTS

This chapter reviews attachment theory and research with an eye to those features that are most relevant to current accounts of depression and its developmental origins. Early attachment experiences and their cognitive, emotional, and social consequences are compelling candidate contributors to risk for depression in later life. Many aspects of insecure and, especially, disorganized attachment processes align with our understanding of the social and cognitive mechanisms that increase the risk of depression. The weakness of our account is that the chapter raises more empirical questions than we are able to answer regarding the developmental links between attachment and risk of depression. These questions are the chapter's greatest strength.

REFERENCES

Abramson, L. Y., Metalsky, G. I., & Alloy, L. B. (1989). Hopelessness depression: A theory-based subtype of depression. *Psychological Review*, *96*(2), 358–372.

Abramson, L. Y., Seligman, M. E., & Teasdale, J. D. (1978). Learned helplessness in humans: Critique and reformulation. *Journal of Abnormal Psychology*, *87*(1), 49–74.

Ainsworth, M. D., Bell, S. M., & Stayton, D. J. (1971). Individual differences in strange-situation behavior of one-year-olds. In H. R. Schaffer (Ed.), *The origins of human social relations* (pp. 17–57). London: Academic Press.

Ainsworth, M. D., & Bell, S. M. (1970). Attachment, exploration, and separation: Illustrated by the behavior of one-year-olds in a strange situation. *Child Development*, *41*(1), 49–67.

Ainsworth, M. S., Blehar, M. C., Waters, E., & Wall, S. (1978). *Patterns of attachment: A psychological study of the strange situation.* Lawrence Erlbaum, Oxford: England.

Anderson, P., Beach, S. R. H., & Kaslow, N. J. (1999). Marital discord and depression: The potential of attachment theory to guide integrative clinical intervention. In T. Joiner & J. C. Coyne (Eds.), *The interactional nature of depression: Advances in interpersonal approaches* (pp. 271–297). Washington, DC: American Psychological Association.

Bailey, H. N., Moran, G., & Pederson, D. R. (2007). Childhood maltreatment, complex trauma symptoms, and unresolved attachment in an at-risk sample of adolescent mothers. *Attachment & Human Development*, *9*(2), 139–161.

Bailey, H. N., Moran, G., Pederson, D. R., & Bento, S. (2007). Understanding the transmission of attachment using variable- and relationship-centered approaches. *Development and Psychopathology*, *19*(2), 313–343.

Bailey, H. N., Waters, C. A., Pederson, D. R., & Moran, G. (1999). Ainsworth revisited: An empirical analysis of interactive behavior in the home. *Attachment & Human Development*, *1*(2), 191–216.

Beck, A. T. (1967). *Depression.* Harper and Row: New York.

Beck, A. T. (1979). *Cognitive therapy of depression.* New York: Guilford Press.

Beeghly, M., & Cicchetti, D. (1994). Child maltreatment, attachment, and the self system: Emergence of an internal state lexicon in toddlers at high social risk. *Development and Psychopathology*, *6*, 5–30.

Bernier, A., & Dozier, M. (2002). The client-counsellor match and the corrective emotional experience: Evidence for interpersonal and attachment research. *Psychotherapy: Theory, Research, Practice, Training*, *39*(1), 32–43.

Bowlby, J. (1969). *Attachment and loss*. New York: Basic Books.

Bowlby, J. (1973). *Attachment and loss, vol. II: Separation*. New York: Basic Books.

Bowlby, J. (1980). *Attachment and loss*. New York, NY, US: Basic Books.

Bretherton, I. (1991). Pouring new wine into old bottles: The social self as internal working model. In M. R. Gunner & L. A. Sroufe (Eds.), *Self processes and development. The Minnesota symposia on child development* (Vol. 23, pp. 1–41). Hillsdale, NJ, England: L. Erlbaum Associates, Inc.

Bretherton, I., & Munholland, K. A. (1999). Internal working models in attachment relationships: A construct revisited. In J. Cassidy & P. R. Shaver (Eds.), *Handbook of attachment: Theory, research, and clinical applications* (pp. 89–111). New York, NY, US: Guilford Press.

Briere, J. (2002). *Treating adult survivors of severe childhood abuse and neglect: Further development of an integrative model*. In J. E. B. Myers & L. Berliner (Eds.), *The APSAC handbook on child maltreatment* (pp. 175–203). Thousand Oaks, CA, US: Sage Publications, Inc.

Camras, L. A., Grow, J. G., & Ribordy, S. C. (1983). Recognition of emotional expression by abused children. *Journal of Clinical Child Psychology*, *12*(3), 325–328.

Carlson, E. A. (1998). A prospective longitudinal study of attachment disorganization/disorientation. *Child Development*, *69*(4), 1107–1128.

Carlson, E. A., Sroufe, L. A., & Egeland, B. (2004). The construction of experience: A longitudinal study of representation and behavior. *Child Development*, *75*(1), 66–83.

Cassidy, J., & Marvin, R. S. (1992). *Attachment organization in preschool children: Procedures and coding manual*. Unpublished manual, University of Virginia.

Cassidy, J., & Shaver, P. R. (1999). *Handbook of attachment: Theory, research, and clinical applications*. New York, NY, US: Guilford Press.

Cicchetti, D. (2002). How a child builds a brain: Insights from normality and psychopathology. In W. Hartup & R. A. Weinberg (Eds.), *Child psychology in retrospect and prospect. The Minnesota symposia on child psychology, Vol. 32*. (pp. 23–71). Mahwah, NJ: L. Erlbaum Associates, Inc.

Cicchetti, D., & Valentino, K. (2006). An ecological-transactional perspective on child maltreatment: Failure of the average expectable environment and its influence on child development. In D. Cicchetti & D. J. Cohen (Eds.), *Developmental psychopathology* (pp. 129–201). Hoboken, NJ, US: John Wiley & Sons Inc.

Cooper, G., Hoffman, K., Powell, B., & Marvin, R. (2005). The circle of security intervention: Differential diagnosis and differential treatment. In L. J. Berlin *et al.* (Eds.), *Enhancing early attachments: Theory, research, intervention, and policy* (pp. 127–151). New York, NY, US: Guilford Press.

Coyne, J. C. (1976). Depression and the response of others. *Journal of Abnormal Psychology*, *85*(2), 186–193.

Coyne, J. C. (1999). Thinking interactionally about depression: A radical restatement. In T. Joiner & J. C. Coyne (Eds.), *The interactional nature of depression: Advances in interpersonal approaches* (pp. 365–392). Washington, DC, US: American Psychological Association.

Coyne, J. C., & Gotlib, I. H. (1983). The role of cognition in depression: A critical appraisal. *Psychological Bulletin*, *94*(3), 472–505.

Coyne, J. C., & Whiffen, V. E. (1995). Issues in personality as diathesis for depression: The case of sociotropy-dependency and autonomy-self-criticism. *Psychological Bulletin*, *118*(3), 358–378.

Crittenden, P. M. (1985). Maltreated infants: Vulnerability and resilience. *Journal of Child Psychology and Psychiatry*, *26*(1), 85–96.

Cummings, E. M. (1990). Classification of attachment on a continuum of felt security: Illustrations from the study of children of depressed parents. In M. T. Greenberg, D. Cicchetti, & E. M. Cummings (Eds.), *Attachment in the preschool years: Theory, research, and intervention* (pp. 311–338). Chicago, IL, US: University of Chicago Press.

Cummings, E. M., & Davies, P. (1996). Emotional security as a regulatory process in normal development and the development of psychopathology. *Development and Psychopathology*, *8*(1), 123–139.

De Wolff, M., & van IJzendoorn, M. H. (1997). Sensitivity and attachment: A meta-analysis on parental antecedents of infant attachment. *Child Development*, *68*(4), 571–591.

DeOliveira, C. A., Moran, G., & Pederson, D. R. (2005). Understanding the link between maternal adult attachment classifications and thoughts and feelings about emotions. *Attachment & Human Development*, *7*(2), 153–170.

DeOliveira, C. A., Bailey, H. N., Moran, G., & Pederson, D. R. (2004). Emotion socialization as a framework for understanding the development of disorganized attachment. *Social Development*, *13*(3), 437–467.

Dozier, M. (1990). Attachment organization and treatment for adults with serious psychopathological disorders. *Development and Psychopathology*, *2(1)*, 47–60.

Dozier, M., Cue, K. L., & Barnett, L. (1994). Clinicians as caregivers: Role of attachment organization in treatment. *Journal of Consulting and Clinical Psychology*, *62*(4), 793–800.

Dozier, M., & Kobak, R. R. (1992). Psychophysiology in attachment interviews: Converging evidence for deactivating strategies. *Child Development*, *63*(6), 1473–1480.

Dozier, M., Lomax, L., Tyrell, C. L., & Lee, S. W. (2001). The challenge of treatment for clients with dismissing states of mind. *Attachment & Human Development*, *3*(1), 62–76.

Duggal, S., Carlson, E. A., Sroufe, L. A., & Egeland, B. (2001). Depressive symptomatology in childhood and adolescence. *Development and Psychopathology*, *13*(1), 143–164.

Eames, V., & Roth, A. (2000). Patient attachment orientation and the early working alliance: A study of patient and therapist reports of alliance quality ruptures. *Psychotherapy Research*, *10(4)*, 421–434.

Egeland, B., & Carlson, E. A. (2004). Attachment and psychopathology. In L. Atkinson & S. Goldberg (Eds.), Attachment issues in psychopathology and intervention (pp. 27–48). Mahwah, NJ, US: L. Erlbaum Associates Inc.

Egeland, B., & Sroufe, L. A. (1981). Attachment and early maltreatment. *Child Development*, *52*(1), 44–52.

Forbes, L. M., Evans, E. M., Moran, G., & Pederson, D. R. (2007). Change in atypical maternal behavior predicts change in attachment disorganization from 12 to 24 months in a high-risk sample. *Child Development*, *78*(3), 955–971.

George, C., Kaplan, N., & Main, M. (1996). *Adult Attachment Interview.* Unpublished protocol, Department of Psychology, University of California, Berkeley.

Gladstone, G. L., & Parker, G. B. (2006). Is behavioral inhibition a risk factor for depression? *Journal of Affective Disorders*, *95*(1–3), 85–94.

Gotlib, I. H. (1992). Interpersonal and cognitive aspects of depression. *Current Directions in Psychological Science*, *1*(5), 149–154.

Greenberg, M. T. (1999). Attachment and psychopathology in childhood. In J. Cassidy & P. R. Shaver (Eds.), *Handbook of attachment: Theory, research, and clinical applications* (pp. 469–496). New York, NY, US: Guilford Press.

Grossman, K. E., Grossman, K. and Waters, E. (2005). (Eds.). *Attachment from infancy to adulthood: The major longitudinal studies.* New York, NY: Guilford Publications.

Gunnar, M. R., Fisher, P. A., & Early Experience, Stress, and Prevention Network. (2006). Bringing basic research on early experience and stress neurobiology to bear on preventive interventions for neglected and maltreated children. *Development and Psychopathology*, *18*(3), 651–677.

Haines, B. A., Metalsky, G. I., Cardamone, A. L., & Joiner, T. (1999). Interpersonal and cognitive pathways into the origins of attributional style: A developmental perspective. In T. Joiner & J. C. Coyne (Eds.), *The interactional nature of depression: Advances in interpersonal approaches* (pp. 65–92). Washington, DC, US: American Psychological Association.

Hayden, E. P., Klein, D. N., Durbin, C. E., & Olino, T. M. (2006). Positive emotionality at age 3 predicts cognitive styles in 7-year-old children. *Development and Psychopathology*, *18*(2), 409–423.

Harrington, R., Rutter, M., & Fombonne, E. (1996). Developmental pathways in depression: Multiple meanings, antecedents, and endpoints. *Development and Psychopathology*, *8*(4), 601–616.

Hayden, E. P., Klein, D. N., Durbin, C. E., & Olino, T. M. (2006). Positive emotionality at age 3 predicts cognitive styles in 7-year-old children. *Development and Psychopathology*, *18*(2), 409–423.

Hesse, E., & Main, M. (2006). Frightened, threatening, and dissociative parental behavior in low-risk samples: Description, discussion, and interpretations. *Development and Psychopathology*, *18*(2), 309–343.

Holahan, C. J., Moos, R. H., & Bonin, L. A. (1999). *Social context and depression: An integrative stress and coping framework*. In T. Joiner & J. C. Coyne (Eds.), *The interactional nature of depression: Advances in interpersonal approaches* (pp. 39–64). Washington, DC, US: American Psychological Association.

Ingram, R. E. (2001). Developing perspectives on the cognitive-developmental origins of depression: Back is the future. *Cognitive Therapy and Research*, *25*(4), 497–504.

Ingram, R. E. (2003). Origins of cognitive vulnerability to depression. *Cognitive Therapy and Research*, *27*(1), 77–88.

Ingram, R. E., Miranda, J., & Segal, Z. (2006). *Cognitive vulnerability to depression*. In L. B. Alloy & J. H. Riskind (Eds.), *Cognitive vulnerability to emotional disorders* (pp. 63–92). Mahwah, NJ, US: L. Erlbaum Associates Inc.

Ingram, R. E., Miranda, J., & Segal, Z. V. (1998). *Cognitive vulnerability to depression*. New York, NY, US: Guilford Press.

Joiner, T., & Coyne, J. C. (Eds.) (1999). *The interactional nature of depression: Advances in interpersonal approaches*. Washington, DC, US: American Psychological Association.

Joiner, T., Coyne, J. C., & Blalock, J. (1999). On the interpersonal nature of depression: Overview and synthesis. In T. Joiner & J. C. Coyne (Eds.), *The interactional nature of depression: Advances in interpersonal approaches* (pp. 3–20). Washington, DC, US: American Psychological Association.

Kanninen, K., Salo, J., & Punamaki, R.-L. (2000). Attachment patterns and working alliance in trauma therapy for victims of political violence. *Psychotherapy Research*, *10*(4), 435–449.

Kim, J., & Cicchetti, D. (2006). Longitudinal trajectories of self-system processes and depressive symptoms among maltreated and nonmaltreated children. *Child Development*, *77*(3), 624–639.

Kobak, R. R., Cole, H. E., Ferenz-Gillies, R., & Fleming, W. S. (1993). Attachment and emotion regulation during mother-teen problem solving: A control theory analysis. *Child Development*, *64*(1), 231–245.

Kobak, R. R., & Sceery, A. (1988). Attachment in late adolescence: Working models, affect regulation, and representations of self and others. *Child Development*, *59*(1), 135–146.

Kobak, R. (1999). The emotional dynamics of disruptions in attachment relationships: Implications for theory, research, and clinical intervention. In J. Cassidy & P. R. Shaver (Eds.), *Handbook of attachment: Theory, research, and clinical applications* (pp. 21–43). New York, NY, US: Guilford Press.

Kovacs, M., & Beck, A. T. (1978). Maladaptive cognitive structures in depression. *American Journal of Psychiatry*, *135*(5), 525–533.

Krantz, S. E. (1985). When depressive cognitions reflect negative realities. *Cognitive Therapy and Research*, *9*(6), 595–610.

Lewinsohn, P. M. (1974). A behavioral approach to depression. In R. J. Friedman & M. Katz (Eds.), The psychology of depression: Contemporary theory and research. Washington, DC.: John Wiley & Sons.

Lyons-Ruth, K., Bronfman, E., & Atwood, G. (1999). A relational diathesis model of hostile-helpless states of mind: Expressions in mother-infant interaction. In J. Solomon & C. George (Eds.), *Attachment Disorganization* (pp. 33–70). New York, NY, US: Guilford Press.

Lyons-Ruth, K., Yellin, C., Melnick, S., & Atwood, G. (2005). Expanding the concept of unresolved mental states: Hostile/Helpless states of mind on the adult attachment interview are associated with disrupted mother-infant communication and infant disorganization. *Development and Psychopathology*, *17*(1), 1–23.

Madigan, S., Goldberg, S., Moran, G., & Pederson, D. R. (2004). Naïve observers' perceptions of family drawings by 7-year-olds with disorganized attachment histories. *Attachment and Human Development*, *6*(3), 223–239.

Madigan, S., Moran, G., & Pederson, D. R. (2006). Unresolved states of mind, disorganized attachment relationships, and disrupted interactions of adolescent mothers and their infants. *Developmental Psychology*, *42*(2), 293–304.

Madigan, S., Bakermans-Kranenberg, M. J., van IJzendoorn, M. H., Moran, G., Pederson, D. R., & Benoit, D. (2006). Unresolved States of Mind, Anomalous Parental Behavior, and Disorganized Attachment: A Review and Meta-Analysis. *Attachment and Human Development*, *8*(2), 89–111

Main, M. (1995). Discourse, prediction, and recent studies in attachment: Implications for psychoanalysis. In T. Shapiro & R. N. Emde (Eds.), Research in psychoanalysis: Process, development, outcome (pp. 209–244). Madison, CT, US: International Universities Press, Inc.

Main, M. (1996). Introduction to the special section on attachment and psychopathology: 2. overview of the field of attachment. *Journal of Consulting and Clinical Psychology*, *64*(2), 237–243.

Main, M. (2000). The organized categories of infant, child, and adult attachment: Flexible vs. inflexible attention under attachment-related stress. *Journal of the American Psychoanalytic Association*, *48*(4), 1055–1096.

Main, M., & Cassidy, J. (1988). Categories of response to reunion with the parent at age 6: Predictable from infant attachment classifications and stable over a 1-month period. *Developmental Psychology*, *24*(3), 415–426.

Main, M., & Goldwyn, R. (1984–1998). *Adult attachment scoring and classification system.* Unpublished scoring manual, University of California at Berkeley.

Main, M., & Hesse, E. (1990). Parents' unresolved traumatic experiences are related to infant disorganized attachment status: Is frightened and/or frightening parental behavior the linking mechanism? In M. Greenberg, D. Cicchetti, & E. M. Cummings (Eds.), *Attachment in the Preschool Years* (pp. 161–182). Chicago, IL: University of Chicago Press.

Main, M., Kaplan, N., & Cassidy, J. (1985). Security in infancy, childhood, and adulthood: A move to the level of representation. *Monographs of the Society for Research in Child Development*, *50*(1–2), 66–104.

Main, M., & Solomon, J. (1990). Procedures for identifying infants as disorganized/disoriented during the Ainsworth strange situation. In M. Greenberg, D. Cicchetti, & E. M. Cummings (Eds.), *Attachment in the Preschool Years* (pp. 121–160). Chicago, IL, US: University of Chicago Press.

McCabe, S. B., Gotlib, I. H., & Martin, R. A. (2000). Cognitive vulnerability for depression: Deployment of attention as a function of history of depression and current mood state. *Cognitive Therapy and Research*, *24*(4), 427–444.

Mallinckrodt, B. (2000). Attachment, social competence, social support, and interpersonal process in psychotherapy. *Psychotherapy Research*, *10*(3), 239–266.

Mallinckrodt, B., Porter, M. J., & Kivlighan, D. M., Jr. (2005). Client attachment to therapist, depth of in-session exploration, and object-relations in brief psychotherapy. *Psychotherapy: Theory, Research, Practice, Training*, *42*(1), 85–100.

Mezulis, A. H., Hyde, J. S., & Abramson, L. Y. (2006). The developmental origins of cognitive vulnerability to depression: Temperament, parenting, and negative life events in childhood as contributors to negative cognitive style. *Developmental Psychology*, *42*(6), 1012–1025.

Miranda, J., Gross, J. J., Persons, J. B., & Hahn, J. (1998). Mood matters: Negative mood induction activates dysfunctional attitudes in women vulnerable to depression. *Cognitive Therapy and research*, *22*(4), 363–376.

Moran, G., Bailey, H. N., DeOliveira, C. A., Gleason, K., & Pederson, D. R. (2008). Exploring the Mind Behind Unresolved Attachment: Lessons From and For Attachment-based Intervention with Infants and their Traumatized Mothers. In H. Steele & M. Steele (Eds.), *Clinical Applications of the Adult Attachment Interview*. (pp. 371–398) New York: Guilford Press.

Pederson, D. R., & Moran, G. (1996). Expressions of the attachment relationship outside of the strange situation. *Child Development*, *67*(3), 915–927.

Pederson, D. R., & Moran, G. (1995). A categorical description of infant-mother relationships in the home and its relation to Q-sort measures of infant-mother interaction. *Monographs of the Society for Research in Child Development*, *60*(2–3), 111–132.

Pederson, D. R., Moran, G., Sitko, C., Campbell, K., Ghesquire, K., & Acton, H. (1990). Maternal sensitivity and the security of infant-mother attachment: A Q-sort study. *Child Development, 61*, 1974–1983.

Posada, G., Jacobs, A., Richmond, M. K., Carbonell, O. A., Alzate, G., Bustamante, M. R., *et al.* (2002). Maternal caregiving and infant security in two cultures. *Developmental Psychology, 38*(1), 67–78.

Propper, C., & Moore, G. A. (2006). The influence of parenting on infant emotionality: A multi-level psychobiological perspective. *Developmental Review, 26*(4), 427–460.

Riggs, S. A., Jacobovitz, D., & Hazen, N. (2002). Adult attachment and history of psychotherapy in a normative sample. *Psychotherapy: Theory, Research, Practice, Training, 39*(4), 344–353.

Roberts, J. E., Gotlib, I. H., & Kassel, J. D. (1996). Adult attachment security and symptoms of depression: The mediating roles of dysfunctional attitudes and low self-esteem. *Journal of Personality and Social Psychology, 70*(2), 310–320.

Roisman, G. I. (2007). The psychophysiology of adult attachment relationships: Autonomic reactivity in marital and premarital interactions. *Developmental Psychology, 43*(1), 39–53.

Roisman, G. I., Tsai, J. L., & Chiang, K. S. (2004). The emotional integration of childhood experience: Physiological, facial expressive, and self-reported emotional response during the adult attachment interview. *Developmental Psychology, 40*(5), 776–789.

Rutter, M. (2006). The psychological effects of early institutional rearing. In P. J. Marshall & N. A. Fox (Eds.), *The development of social engagement: Neurobiological perspectives* (pp. 355–391), New York, NY: Oxford University Press.

Scher, C. D., Ingram, R. E., & Segal, Z. V. (2005). Cognitive reactivity and vulnerability: Empirical evaluation of construct activation and cognitive diatheses in unipolar depression. *Clinical Psychology Review, 25*(4), 487–510.

Schmidt, N. B., Schmidt, K. L., & Young, J. E. (1999). Schematic and interpersonal conceptualizations of depression: An integration. In T. Joiner & J. C. Coyne (Eds.), *The interactional nature of depression: Advances in interpersonal approaches* (pp. 127–148). Washington, DC, US: American Psychological Association.

Schore, A. N. (2001). Effects of a secure attachment relationship on right brain development, affect regulation, and infant mental health. *Infant Mental Health Journal, 22*(1–2), 7–66.

Segal, Z. V. (1988). Appraisal of the self-schema construct in cognitive models of depression. *Psychological Bulletin, 103*(2), 147–162.

Segal, Z. V., & Ingram, R. E. (1994). Mood priming and construct activation in tests of cognitive vulnerability to unipolar depression. *Clinical Psychology Review, 14*(7), 663–695.

Shaver, P. R., & Mikulincer, M. (2002a). Attachment-related psychodynamics. *Attachment & Human Development, 4*(2), 133–161.

Shaver, P. R., & Mikulincer, M. (2002b). Dialogue on adult attachment: Diversity and integration. *Attachment & Human Development, 4*(2), 243–257.

Shipman, K., Zeman, J., Penza, S., & Champion, K. (2000). Emotion management skills in sexually maltreated and nonmaltreated girls: A developmental psychopathology perspective. *Development and Psychopathology, 12*(1), 47–62.

Simpson, J. A. (1999). Attachment theory in modern evolutionary perspective. In J. Cassidy & P. R. Shaver (Eds.), *Handbook of attachment: Theory, research, and clinical applications* (pp. 115–140). New York, NY, US: Guilford Press.

Solomon, J., & George, C. (1999). The effects on attachment of overnight visitation in divorced and separated families: A longitudinal follow-up. In J. Solomon & C. George (Eds.), *Attachment Disorganization* (pp. 243–264). New York, NY, US: Guilford Press.

Spangler, G., & Grossmann, K. E. (1993). Biobehavioral organization in securely and insecurely attached infants. *Child Development, 64*(5), 1439–1450.

Sroufe, L. A., Egeland, B., Carlson, E., & Collins, W. A. (2005). Placing early attachment experiences in developmental context: The Minnesota longitudinal study. In K. E. Grossmann, K. Grossmann, & E. Waters (Eds.), *Attachment from infancy to adulthood: the major longitudinal* (pp. 48–70). New York, NY, US: Guilford Publications.

Toth, S. L., Cicchetti, D., & Kim, J. (2002). Relations among children's perceptions of maternal behavior, attributional styles, and behavioral symptomatology in maltreated children. *Journal of Abnormal Child Psychology*, *30*(5), 487–501.

Tyrrell, C. L., Dozier, M., Teague, G. B., & Fallot, R. D. (1999). Effective treatment relationships for persons with serious psychiatric disorders: The importance of attachment states of mind. *Journal of Consulting and Clinical Psychology*, *67*(5), 725–733.

Van IJzendoorn, M. H., & Kroonenberg, P. M. (1988). Cross-cultural patterns of attachment: A meta-analysis of the strange situation. *Child Development*, *59*(1), 147–156.

Van IJzendoorn, M. H., & Kroonenberg, P. M. (1990). Cross-cultural consistency of coding the strange situation. *Infant Behavior & Development*, *13*(4), 469–485.

van Ijzendoorn, M. H., Schuengel, C., & Bakermans-Kranenburg, M. J. (1999). Disorganized attachment in early childhood: Meta-analysis of precursors, concomitants, and sequelae. *Development and Psychopathology*, *11*(2), 225–249.

Vaughn, B. E., Egeland, B. R., Sroufe, L. A., & Waters, E. (1979). Individual differences in infant-mother attachment at twelve and eighteen months: Stability and change in families under stress. *Child Development*, *50*(4), 971–975.

Ward, M. J., Lee, S. S., & Polan, H. J. (2006). Attachment and psychopathology in a community sample. *Attachment & Human Development*, *8*(4), 327–340.

Whiffen, V. E. (2005). The role of partner characteristics in attachment insecurity and depressive symptoms. *Personal Relationships*, *12*(3), 407–423.

Whiffen, V. E., & Johnson, S. M. (1998). An attachment theory framework for the treatment of child-bearing depression. *Clinical Psychology: Science and Practice*, *5*(4), 478–493.

Whiffen, V. E., Kallos-Lilly, A. V., & MacDonald, B. J. (2001). Depression and attachment in couples. *Cognitive Therapy and Research*, *25*(5), 577–590.

Whisman, M. A., & Kwon, P. (1992). Parental representations, cognitive distortions, and mild depression. *Cognitive Therapy and Research*, *16*(5), 557–568.

Whisman, M. A., & McGarvey, A. L. (1995). Attachment, depressotypic cognitions, and dysphoria. *Cognitive Therapy and Research*, *19*(6), 633–650.

14

Life Events and Hassles

Kate L. Harkness

Department of Psychology, Queens University, Kingston, Ontario, Canada

Major theories of psychopathology over the last 100 years have included a strong role for precipitating life events in the etiology of major depression. For example, Freud wrote that depression (or 'melancholia') is a profound state of mourning precipitated by the death of, or separation from, an important love object (Jackson, 1986). Later cognitive theories of depression also included an explicit reference to life events. In particular, Beck (1967) proposed that the negative cognitive vulnerability of the depression-prone individual must be triggered by a proximal stressor to precipitate the onset of depression. Despite strong theoretical and empirical support for the etiological role of stress in depression, there remains a popular belief among researchers, clinicians, and the lay public, that while relatively minor depressive states may be environmental in origin, 'real' depression is caused by genetic and biochemical factors. New light is being shed on this controversy by research that reveals the complex interplay between neurobiological and environmental risk factors, showing, on the one hand, genetic control over exposure to stressful environments, and, on the other hand, profound effects of adverse environments on the structure and function of the brain. These findings fly in the face of nature vs. nurture distinctions and biological reductionistic theories of etiology in depression, and demand models that integrate biological, psychological, and environmental levels of analysis.

The purpose of this chapter is, first, to review the literature relating stressful life events to the onset of major depression. Second, I will suggest that the depressogenic effects of stress are significantly moderated by three risk factors that heighten individuals' sensitivity to the onset and recurrence of depression in the face of stress: (a) genetic vulnerability; (b) childhood trauma vulnerability; and (c) negative cognitive–personality vulnerability. Specifically, I will suggest that individuals who possess one or more of these risk factors (a) will be more likely to develop depression following stress, and (b) will develop depression following relatively more minor levels of stress, than individuals without these risk factors.

Before proceeding, a few caveats are in order. First, the present review focuses on the relation of stress to the clinical syndrome of major depression. Second, the focus of this review will be on acute life events (e.g., fired from job, death in family) as opposed to chronic difficulties (e.g., ongoing financial or relationship problems) because the bulk of the literature linking stress to depression has focused on acute events, and these stressors have been found to most strongly and directly predict major depression onset (see, however, Brown & Harris (1989) for an analysis of the interactive and additive relations of life events and difficulties to depression). Finally, the relation of stressful life events to depression is associated with a number of moderators in addition to those addressed here (e.g., social support, coping behavior, attachment patterns, and neuroendocrine reactivity). I see these other processes as complementary to those that will be addressed in this chapter, and all could likely be integrated into a larger model of major depression etiology. However, for the sake of parsimony I will focus specifically on the risk factors of genetic vulnerability, childhood trauma vulnerability, and cognitive–personality vulnerability, and hope that researchers will take the ideas put forth in the present chapter and apply them to the study of additional psychosocial and biological variables.

ASSESSING AND DEFINING STRESSFUL LIFE EVENTS

Two methods exist in the assessment of life events – self-report checklists and contextual interview and rating systems. Checklist measures have the advantage of being easy to administer and score and, thus, have remained widely used despite their significant limitations. Two of the most widely used life event checklists include the Social Readjustment Rating Scale (SRRS; Holmes & Rahe, 1967) and the Psychiatric Epidemiology Research Interview Life Event Scale (PERI; Dohrenwend *et al.*, 1978). In these measures, each event is assigned a numerical weight, and each endorsed event's weight is summed to produce a total stress score. These instruments are problematic because respondents may use idiosyncratic criteria for deciding whether or not a particular experience should "count." For example, some respondents might count a child's bout with the flu as a "serious illness of a family member," whereas other respondents might not. Respondents' opinions of what constitutes a "serious" event may be very discrepant from the opinions of the investigator (Monroe & McQuaid, 1994). Indeed, when comparing participant-defined life events with events defined by the investigator (using operational criteria and standardized procedures), the correlation is surprisingly low (McQuaid *et al.*, 1992). In particular, due to the maladaptive cognitive biases that characterize depression, depressed individuals perceive greater stress in their lives compared to non-depressed individuals (Simons *et al.*, 1993). This may lead to an inflated perception of the threat associated with relatively ordinary life events. As Monroe and Depue (1991) note, the inability of checklists to reliably assess the objective threatfulness of the event leaves the researcher with no basis for determining the relative importance of actual events vs. the subject's perception of the event in the resulting score.

Furthermore, checklist approaches assume that all events of a certain category are equally stressful across individuals. However, individuals can vary greatly in their experience of the "same" event. For example, "pregnancy" will have very different implications for a woman in a secure relationship who is planning a family than for a woman without an intimate partner for whom the pregnancy was not planned. The checklist approach would count such experiences as the same for both women, regardless of these important contextual differences. Research investigating the psychometric properties of the SRRS has confirmed the above concerns, demonstrating poor reliability (Horowitz *et al.*, 1977) and low external validity (Hurst *et al.*, 1978).

LIFE EVENT ASSESSMENT: DAILY HASSLES

Researchers reacted to the poor performance of checklist life event measures in two ways. Some investigators developed much more rigorous measures to assess life events and focused on the most severely stressful events as central to depression etiology (e.g., Brown & Harris, 1978). This approach is described below. In direct contrast, other researchers rejected major life events altogether, suggesting that the relatively minor stressors, or "hassles," that characterize everyday life are the most significant in predicting health outcomes (Kanner *et al.*, 1981). In particular, Kanner *et al.* (1981) theorized that daily hassles mediate the major event-health relationship, such that major life events affect health outcomes by affecting the person's pattern of hassles.

Kanner *et al.*'s focus in developing their theory of hassles was to predict physical health outcomes, and a large literature linking hassles to, for example, migraine headaches, high blood pressure, and arthritis, has emerged. The literature linking hassles to major depression is smaller and less consistent. Studies have shown that depressed individuals score higher than controls on measures of hassles (Kanner *et al.*, 1981; Lovejoy & Steuerwald, 1997; Ravindran *et al.*, 2002), and frequency and intensity of hassles are related to a more severe depression (Klein *et al.*, 1997; Willner *et al.*, 1990). Hassles also predict depression recurrence (e.g., Bockting *et al.*, 2006). No study to date, however, has tested the hypothesis that hassles are a more powerful predictor of major depression than major life events or that hassles mediate the life event–depression relation. Flannery (1986) found only weak support for the relation of hassles to depression and pointed to the limitations of the checklist measures used to assess hassles. In particular, as noted above, in checklist measures stress occurrence is confounded with stress perception, and the endorsement and severity rating of hassles is confounded with respondents' depressive bias. Therefore, to date, research on the relation of hassles to major depression is limited by these methodological concerns.

LIFE EVENT ASSESSMENT: INTERVIEW-BASED APPROACHES

Several groups have improved the reliability and validity of life event assessment by developing semi-structured life event interviews and rating systems. Examples include the Life Events and Difficulties Schedule (LEDS; Brown & Harris, 1978), the Recent Life Experiences Interview (RLE; Paykel *et al.*, 1984), and other measures that include a modified, generally shorter, interview, and ratings based on LEDS criteria (e.g., Hammen *et al.*, 2000; Kendler *et al.*, 1998). The LEDS is widely considered the "gold standard" and, thus, is described below.

The LEDS is a semi-structured interview that uses standardized questions with probes to encourage respondents to talk at length about the context surrounding each event. This method allows for more sensitive ratings tailored to the individual's life circumstances. Calendars and anchor dates are used to assist in dating the events. Following the interview, trained raters apply operational criteria to determine the severity of each event based on the relevant contextual information. For example, the differences in the lives of the two women in the pregnancy example above would be taken into account, and the threat rating would be much higher for the unplanned pregnancy. Raters use a manual that provides explicit rules for defining specific life events, as well as over 5000 case examples for standardizing ratings. The raters are unaware of the respondent's clinical status and subjective reactions to the events, thereby minimizing bias.

Studies using the LEDS have supported the ability of respondents to report accurately on past life events (Brown & Harris, 1989) and have shown high agreement among raters (Brown & Harris, 1978; Simons *et al.*, 1993). A comparison of checklist vs. interview measures suggests that the interview measures are superior for detecting the presence or absence of severe life events (McQuaid *et al.*, 1992). In addition, a recent study found that the LEDS has greater validity, in terms of predicting treatment outcome, than the PERI (McQuaid *et al.*, 2000). Of course, contextual measures such as the LEDS are more time and labor-consuming than self-report checklists. Nevertheless, research indicates that the benefits in terms of superior reliability and validity of the resulting stress measure are worth the added cost.

LIFE EVENTS AND DEPRESSION

Life events are strongly related to major depression. As reviewed by Mazure (1998), every case–control study conducted to date using either self-report checklist or contextual interview has reported that significantly more patients with major depression had at least one major negative event, and had significantly more events, prior to onset than matched controls in a comparable time period. The magnitude of the difference between cases and controls in the percentage of participants who reported at least one major adverse event ranged from 1.2 to 3.2 across studies, with an average of 2.4. That is, cases were nearly 2.5 times more likely to have experienced a major adverse life event prior to onset than were controls (Mazure, 1998).

Several large-scale population studies have also documented a strong relation of life events to depression. George Brown and colleagues in the United Kingdom conducted the earliest and most extensive of these. These researchers collected diagnostic and LEDS-based life event data on four independent samples of women and showed across all samples that women with major depression were almost 3 times more likely to have suffered a "severe" life event prior to onset than controls in a comparable time period (see Table 14.1, Brown & Harris, 1978; Brown & Prudo, 1981; Brown & Harris, 1989; Brown *et al.*, 1986; Finlay-Jones & Brown, 1981). A severe event, as defined by the LEDS, is associated with a marked or moderate degree of psychological threat for up to 14 days following the event. Recall that the determination of threat is based on the contextual details surrounding the event and is standardized to anchoring examples in the LEDS manual. Examples of severe events might include a woman who learns that her husband of 10 years, on whom she is financially dependent, is having an affair, or a low-income single mother who is fired from her job.

Across all of their samples, Brown and colleagues determined that (a) severe events and (b) events involving themes of loss, occurring in 26–38 weeks prior to onset, are of prime etiological relevance to depression. For example, in the Islington series, among those with no provoking stressor, only 1% (2/153) were

TABLE 14.1 Proportion and Percentage of Depression Onset Cases and Non-cases Who had Experienced a LEDS-Defined Severely Stressful Life Event Prior to Onset (or a Matched Control Period)

Sample	Cases	Non-cases
Camberwell population series (Brown & Harris, 1978)	25/37 (68)	115/382 (30)
Camberwell general practice series (Finlay-Jones & Brown, 1981)	27/32 (84)	32/119 (27)
Outer Hebrides series (Brown & Prudo, 1981)	11/16 (69)	42/171 (25)
Islington series (Brown *et al.* 1986)	29/32 (91)	92/271 (34)

found to suffer from major depression, while among those with a non-severe event, 6% (2/32) were diagnosed depressed. In contrast, among those with a severe non-loss event 16% (4/25) received a diagnosis of depression, and among those with a severe loss event, 32% (23/73) were depressed. The prime importance of severe events in precipitating episodes of depression has been shown in several additional studies using the LEDS (Bebbington *et al.*, 1984; Campbell *et al.*, 1983; Costello, 1982; Parry & Shapiro, 1986). In these latter studies, the percentage of depression cases who had experienced a severe event in the year prior to onset ranged from 62% to 93%, while the percentage of non-cases with a severe event in a comparable time period ranged from 34% to 39%.

The studies reviewed above were crucial in establishing the importance of severe life events in the onset of major depression. Nevertheless, given their correlational nature, the question remains as to whether life events *cause* depression or whether life events and depression are related due to the operation of a third variable. This question has gained some urgency in light of research suggesting that the same genetically mediated traits may underlie individuals' risk to expose themselves to stressful situations and their propensity to develop depression. This would produce a spurious correlation between life events and depression that is mediated by the underlying shared genetic vulnerability.

Kendler *et al.* (1999) directly addressed the causal role of life events in a 5-year prospective study of 1,898 monozygotic (MZ) and dizygotic (DZ) female–female twin pairs. Women were interviewed yearly over the telephone for the presence of symptoms meeting DSM-III-R criteria for major depression, as well as for the occurrence of 15 stressful life events since the last assessment point that were subsequently rated for their level of contextual threat based on LEDS-like criteria. Kendler *et al.* (1999) reasoned that if the relation of life events to depression is entirely causal, then the magnitude of the observed relation of life events to depression within MZ twin pairs, within DZ twin pairs, and within the general population (GP) should be as follows: GP = DZ = MZ. If the relation of life events to depression is in part non-causal, mediated through shared *family-environment*, then the pattern should be as follows: GP > DZ = MZ (because MZ and DZ twins share their family environment). If the relation of life events to depression is in part non-causal, mediated through shared *genetic* factors, then the pattern should be as follows: GP > DZ > MZ (because MZ twins share more genes than DZ twins, who share more genes than members of the general population). Finally, if the relation of life events to depression is entirely non-causal, mediated through both shared genetic and environmental factors, then the relation of these variables within MZ twins should approach zero. Results indicated that life events were strongly related to onset both within the DZ twin pairs (odds ratio = 4.52) and the MZ twin pairs (odds ratio = 3.58). Therefore, because the relation of stress to onset was significant in the MZ pairs, but was smaller than the relation for DZ pairs, Kendler *et al.* (1999) concluded that stressful life events have a substantial causal association with depression, but at least part of this relation is non-causal and mediated through a genetic tendency for individuals to select themselves into high-risk environments.

Using the same sample of twin pairs, Kendler *et al.* (1998) clarified a number of other issues regarding type and timing of events most central to depression onset. First, all but 4 of the 15 assessed events had their strongest association with a depressive onset in the month of occurrence. These results suggest that events most proximal to onset have the strongest etiological relation to that onset, and, further, that major depressive symptoms develop quickly following major stress. Second, risk for major depression in the month of event occurrence significantly increased with each increasing level of threat, with the risks for a depressive onset as follows: no event, 0.87%; minor event, 1.06%; low moderate event, 1.81%; high moderate event, 5.31%; and severe event, 12.92%. Third, the percentage of women with an onset of depression increased with the number of events in that month: no event, 0.87%; one event, 3.41%; two events, 6.83%; and three events, 23.81%.

In summary, the studies reviewed above provide evidence for a robust association between severely stressful life events and the onset of major depression. Indeed, in their integrated model of major depression in women, Kendler *et al.* (2002) determined that major stressful life events experienced in the preceding year were the strongest predictor of major depression onset. Furthermore, these researchers' previous work found that a large part of the association between stress and depression is causal (Kendler *et al.*, 1999).

LIFE EVENTS AND SYNDROME SPECIFICITY

Major depression is not a homogenous entity; indeed, wide individual variability exists in the symptoms that comprise the diagnosis and in the syndromes that cooccur with it. An important question for depression research, then, is whether stressful life events can predict patterns of individual variability in symptom and syndrome expression. Research addressing this question has focused primarily on (a) the specificity of life events to the syndromes of major depression vs. the anxiety disorders, and, within major depression, (b) the specificity of life events to the melancholic vs. non-melancholic symptom subtypes

LIFE EVENTS AND SPECIFICITY TO DEPRESSION VS. ANXIETY

The majority of studies examining the relation of stressful life events to anxiety disorders such as panic disorder and social phobia have reported significantly higher levels of stress in the patient groups (e.g., Brown *et al.*, 1998; Faravelli & Pallanti, 1989; Rapee *et al.*, 1990; *cf.* Roy-Byrne *et al.*, 1986). The few studies that have compared the relation of life events to depression vs. anxiety head-to-head, however, indicate a stronger relation of stress to depression. For example, Newman and Bland (1994) reported significantly higher event checklist scores in patients with non-comorbid major depression than in patients with non-comorbid generalized anxiety disorder, with the highest scores found in those with a comorbid presentation. Similarly, Kendler *et al.* (1998) found that twice as many events, as assessed by a contextual interview, had moderate to high specificity for major depression onset over generalized anxiety disorder onset than the reverse.

Still other researchers have found that different types of events preferentially predict depression vs. anxiety. George Brown and colleagues found that significantly more cases of major depression than cases of anxiety disorder reported a severe event comprising themes of *loss* (e.g., death of a close friend) prior to onset, while significantly more cases of an anxiety disorder than cases of depression reported a severe event comprising themes of *danger* (e.g., eviction notice). Finally, significantly more of the comorbid cases reported *both* types of events (Brown, 1996; Finlay-Jones & Brown, 1981). Similarly, Kendler *et al.* (2003) in their sample of female twin pairs found that events comprising themes of loss preferentially predicted the onset of pure major depression or mixed major depression-generalized anxiety in the subsequent month, while events comprising themes of danger were more strongly predictive of pure generalized anxiety. Finally, in a sample of outpatients diagnosed with an anxiety disorder, major depressive episode, or hypochondriasis, Sandin *et al.* (2004) found that events with themes of loss, danger, and physical health were significantly more strongly endorsed prior to onset in patients with major depression, anxiety disorder, and hypochondriasis, respectively (Sandin *et al.*, 2004).

In the National Comorbidity Study, 58% of individuals with major depression had a comorbid anxiety disorder (Kessler *et al.*, 2005). This high level of comorbidity has led some researchers to suggest that the two classes of syndrome share an underlying genetic or temperamental vulnerability (e.g., negative affect or neuroticism; Clark & Watson, 1991). In particular, in a study of major depression and generalized anxiety disorder (GAD), in their sample of female twin pairs, Kendler *et al.* concluded that the same genetic liability influences risk for both depression and GAD and, therefore, "individual-specific environmental risk factors are solely responsible for the differentiation between major depression and GAD" (Kendler *et al.*, 1992; p. 720). The above studies examining specificity in the provoking stressors for each condition may help in understanding why some individuals with this common vulnerability go on to develop depression, while others go on to develop an anxiety disorder. Much more research is required along these lines to examine the precipitating etiological conditions that distinguish major depression from the anxiety disorders, as well as those that distinguish among the various anxiety disorders themselves.

LIFE STRESS AND THE MELANCHOLIC VS. NON-MELANCHOLIC DISTINCTION IN DEPRESSION

The most enduring subtype distinction within major depression is between melancholic (or endogenous, autonomous) and non-melancholic (or non-endogenous, reactive) depression. Melancholic depression, characterized by symptoms such as unreactive mood, anhedonia, psychomotor retardation, and morning mood worsening, has been traditionally conceptualized as neurobiological and genetic in etiology and, hence, autonomous of life stress. By contrast, non-melancholic depression has been conceptualized as a less severe subtype that develops as a reaction to stressful life events (see Jackson, 1986).

Empirical study of this theoretical distinction, however, has produced very mixed results in studies using diverse methodologies both for defining melancholia and for assessing life events. As seen in Table 14.2, of the eight studies using checklist methods of life event assessment, four showed a stronger role of stressful life events in non-melancholic vs. melancholic depression and four showed no significant group differences. It is important to note, however, that in all four negative studies life events were not dated with respect to episode onset (Forrest *et al.*, 1965; Leff *et al.*, 1970; Monroe *et al.*, 1985; Thomson & Hendrie, 1972). That is, it is unclear in these studies whether the assessed events occurred before onset, after onset, or in a totally unrelated time period with respect to onset. This is a crucial issue when attempting to establish whether life events are causally related to a disorder. Interestingly, two investigations revised the administration of their checklists so that only events in the 12 months prior to episode onset were included (Cornell *et al.*, 1985; Kohn *et al.*, 2001; Robins *et al.*, 1990). Both found significantly fewer events in melancholic than in non-melancholic depression.

Thirteen studies improved their assessment of life events further by using contextual life event interviews (see Table 14.3). Nevertheless, results were still mixed, with seven studies supporting a stronger relation of stress to non-melancholic depression and five failing to find significant group differences. However, Benjaminsen (1981) defined melancholic depression as the presence of only two additional symptoms, thereby limiting the ability to detect group differences. Further, all studies that used the computer algorithm "CATEGO" to group patients based on their scores on the Psychiatric State Examination (PSE; Wing *et al.*, 1974) failed to find significant group differences (Bebbington *et al.*, 1988; G. W. Brown *et al.*, 1979; Brugha & Conroy, 1985; Dolan *et al.*, 1985).The CATEGO method has been found to misclassify people at the mildly depressed end of the severity continuum and, as a result, may not work well in distinguishing mild (i.e., non-melancholic) from severe (i.e., melancholic) cases (Paykel, 1986). Interestingly, when Brown *et al.* (1979) defined their "psychotic" (melancholic) group more restrictively by considering only the upper 20% of patients, this more severely ill subgroup was significantly less likely to have a severe event in 6 months prior to onset (52%) than the non-melancholic group (73%).

Perris (1984) and Zimmerman *et al* (1986) did find a significantly greater number of events in their non-melancholic vs melancholic groups. However, the presence of a precipitating stressor was part of the definition of "reactive–neurotic" (non-melancholic) depression in the Perris study, and the absence of a precipitating stressor was a criterion for melancholic depression as defined by the Newcastle Diagnostic system (Carney *et al.*, 1965) in the Zimmerman *et al.* study. Therefore, the results of these studies are necessarily confounded.

TABLE 14.2 Methodological Details of Studies Comparing Melancholic and Non-Melancholic Depression using Checklist Assessment of Life Events

Authors	Diagnostic criteria	Life event assessment	Results
Leff *et al.* (1970)	Melancholic: psychomotor retardation, self-blame, morning mood worsening, weight loss, global severity, and early morning awakening ($n = 13$) vs. non-melancholic ($n = 27$)	Chart Review 12mos < "breakdown"	No significant group differences (Descriptive statistics not provided)
Forrest *et al.* (1965)	Melancholic: 4 of retardation, terminal insomnia, impaired concentration, diurnal variation, guilt or self-reproach ($n = 62$) vs. non-melancholic ($n = 43$)	12-item checklist past 3 years	60% non-melancholic vs. 65% melancholic had "social factors in environment" (ns)
Thomson & Hendrie (1972)	DSM-II (APA, 1968) criteria for manic-depression ($n = 27$), involutional psychosis ($n = 5$), or psychotic depressive reaction ($n = 13$) vs. reactive-neurotic depression ($n = 29$)	SRRS	No significant difference in total stress scores ($Ms = 250, 202$; $SDs = 147, 113$)
Monroe, *et al.* (1985)	RDC melancholic ($n = 26$) vs. non-melancholic ($n = 24$)	PERI 12mos < treatment	No significant differences in stress scores ($Ms = 40.67, 44.86$; $SDs = 37.79, 27.07$) or event numbers ($Ms = 8.92, 9.38$; $SDs = 7.06, 5.35$)
Turkcapar *et al.* (1999)	Various psychiatric criteria	No information	71% ($n = 31$) non-melancholic vs. 47% ($n = 32$) DSM-III-R melancholic had "stressor" prior to onset
Robins, Block & Peselow (1990)	RDC melancholic ($n = 53$) vs. non-melancholic ($n = 27$)	SRRS	Non-melancholic reported significantly more events than melancholic ($Ms = 3.9, 2.0$; $SDs = 3.8, 2.1$)
Cornell *et al.* (1985)	RDC melancholic ($n = 42$) vs. non-melancholic ($n = 25$) vs. psychiatric control ($n = 33$)	SRRS 12mos < onset	Non-melancholic had more events than melancholic ($Ms = 4.28, 2.12$)
Kohn *et al.* (2001)	DSM-III-R melancholic ($n = 40$) vs. non-melancholic ($n = 44$)	15-item list 12mos < onset	Non-melancholic reported significantly more events than melancholic ($Ms = 1.48, 1.03$; $SDs = 1.19, .89$)

Note: SRRS – Social Readjustment Rating Scale; RDC – Research Diagnostic Criteria; PERI – Psychiatric Epidemiology Research Interview.

TABLE 14.3 Methodological Details of Studies Comparing Melancholic and Non-Melancholic Depression using Interview Assessments of Life Events

Authors	Diagnostic criteria	Life event assessment	Results
Benjaminsen (1981)	Melancholic: 2 of retardation, terminal or middle insomnia, lack of reactivity ($n = 21$) vs. non-melancholic ($n = 68$)	RLE 6mos < onset	90% non-melancholic vs. 81% melancholic had a severe event (ns)
Perris (1984)	"Bipolar" ($n = 16$) vs. "Unipolar endogenous" ($n = 58$) vs. "Reactive-neurotic" ($n = 81$) vs. "Unspecified" ($n = 51$)	Life Event Interview (Perris, 1984) 3mos < onset	Reactive-neurotic had significantly more events than unipolar endogenous (*Ms* = 5.7, 3.6; *SDs* = 3.4, 2.5; F = 7.0, $p < .05$)
Zimmerman *et al.* (1986)	Various psychiatric criteria	Positive & Negative Events Inventory (Zimmerman, 1982) 12mos< admission	Newcastle criteria only: Non-melancholic ($n = 63$) had significantly more events than melancholic ($n = 26$) (*Ms* = 14.6, 11.2; *SDs* = 8.3, 8.6; $t = 2.16$, $p < .05$)
Bebbington *et al.* (1988)	"Delusional" (D; $n = 8$) and "Retarded" (R; $n = 58$) vs. "Neurotic" (N; $n = 56$) from PSE	LEDS 6mos < onset	32.8% N vs. 27% D and R had a severe event (ns)
Brown *et al.* (1979)	D ($n = 62$) vs. N ($n = 49$) from PSE	LEDS 6mos < onset	65% N vs. 58% D had a severe event (ns)
Brugha & Conroy (1985)	R ($n = 19$) vs. N ($n = 22$) from PSE	LEDS 6mos < onset	84% N vs. 85% R had an undesirable event (ns)
Dolan *et al.* (1985)	D ($n = 6$) and R ($n = 33$) vs. N ($n = 29$) from PSE	LEDS 6mos < onset	50% N vs. 43% D and R had a severe event (ns)
Brown *et al.* (1994)	RDC melancholic ($n = 60$) vs. non-melancholic ($n = 67$)	LEDS 6mos < onset	No difference between groups among those on a first-onset. Among those on a recurrence, significantly more non melancholic than melancholic had a severe event
Frank *et al.* (1994)	RDC melancholic ($n = 56$) vs. non-melancholic ($n = 34$)	LEDS 6mos < onset	65% non-melancholic vs. 43% melancholic had at least one severe event ($c^2 = 4.04$, $p < .05$)
Harkness & Monroe (2006)	RDC melancholic ($n = 27$) vs. non-melancholic ($n = 23$)	LEDS 3mos < onset	
Matussek & Neuner (1980)	RDC melancholic ($n = 90$) vs. non-melancholic ($n = 38$)	Interview of loss events 12mos < onset	63% non-melancholic vs. 37% melancholic had depression onset in year following event ($p < .01$)
Paykel *et al.* (1984)	RDC melancholic ($n = 39$) vs. non-melancholic ($n = 101$)	RLE 12mos < onset	64% non-melancholic vs. 23% melancholic had a chronic difficulty ($p < .05$)
Roy *et al.* (1985)	DSM-III melancholic ($n = 20$) vs. non-melancholic ($n = 20$)	RLE 6mos < onset	Non-melancholic had significantly more events than melancholic (*Ms* = 39, 21; $t = 2.71$, $p < .01$)

Note: RLE – Recent Life Experiences Interview; PSE – Present State Examination; LEDS – Life Events and Difficulties Schedule; RDC – Research Diagnostic Criteria.

In contrast, all five studies that used contextual life event interviews *and* standard definitions for melancholia using the Diagnostic and Statistical Manual of Mental Disorders (DSM-III/III-R; APA, 1980, 1987) or the Research Diagnostic Criteria (RDC; Spitzer *et al.*, 1978) found that melancholic depression was significantly less likely to be precipitated by a severe life event than non-melancholic depression (Brown *et al.*, 1994; Frank *et al.*, 1994; Harkness & Monroe, 2006; Roy *et al.*, 1985). In addition, Brown *et al.* (1994) found this effect only for patients on a recurrent episode and suggested that previous inconsistencies in the literature may have arisen partly due to a failure to take prior depression history into account. Further, Harkness and Monroe (2006) reported that, while individuals with severe melancholic depression were less likely than those with non-melancholic depression to have a *severe* event prior to onset, their onset was *more* likely to be precipitated by a more minor, *non*-severe event. We suggested from this that the reason episodes of melancholic depression may be less likely to be precipitated by severe stress is because these individuals may be breaking down in the face of much more common, milder stressors as a result of enhanced stress sensitivity (Harkness & Monroe, 2006).

In summary, when examined in terms of the rigor of diagnosis and life event assessment, a clear picture of results begins to emerge from the above studies. Of the eight studies using a lax system for diagnosing melancholic depression, only one found significant differences between diagnostic groups (Perris, 1984), regardless of how events were assessed. However, even this one positive study was confounded because the presence of a precipitant was a defining criterion for non-melancholic depression. By contrast, all eight studies that used rigorous diagnosis *and* life event assessments that dated events with respect to episode onset found a significantly lower incidence of life events in the melancholic vs. non-melancholic groups. Through careful attention to the rigor of diagnostic and life event assessments, the results of this body of literature are consistent with the hypothesis that melancholic depression is less likely to be preceded by severe stress than non-melancholic depression. These findings are important and suggest that further development and refinement of theories of etiology in major depression should take into account individual differences in syndromal expression.

STRESS SENSITIZATION AND DEPRESSION

One of the most intriguing developments in life stress research has been the discovery that the pathology of depression itself changes the depressogenic effects of stress. In particular, Robert Post's (1992) stress sensitization (or "kindling") hypothesis proposes that individuals become sensitized to the life events that precipitate depression such that less stress is required to precipitate recurrences of depression than was required to precipitate the first onset (Post, 1992). As such, this theory helps greatly in understanding why the risk of recurrence increases with each successive episode, and why the course of depression involves increasingly shorter well-intervals between episodes over time (Solomon *et al.*, 2000).

The large number of studies supporting Post's stress sensitization hypothesis have recently been reviewed in detail (Monroe & Harkness, 2005). In brief, individuals on a first episode of depression are significantly more likely than those on a recurrence to have their episode preceded by a severely stressful life event (*cf.* Brown *et al.*, 1994; Cassano *et al.*, 1989; Daley *et al.*, 2000; Ezquiaga *et al.*, 1987; Farmer *et al.*, 2002; Ghaziuddin *et al.*, 1990). Furthermore, major life events are significantly stronger predictors of a first onset than a recurrence (Lewinsohn *et al.*, 1999; Maciejewski *et al.*, 2000; Monroe *et al.*, 1999; Ormel *et al.*, 2001). Indeed, Kendler *et al.* (1995) found that while the relation of severe life events to the first onset of depression was highly significant, as the number of prior episodes increased within individuals, the odds ratio for depression onset and a prior severe life event consistently decreased. That is, each recurrent episode was progressively less likely to be preceded by a severe event.

Furthermore, Ormel *et al.* (2001) found that *mild* stressful life events significantly predicted depression recurrence, but not first onset. That is, while severely stressful life events are required to trigger the initial onset of the syndrome, as individuals' sensitivity to the depressogenic effects of stress increases across recurrence, their threshold for reacting to minor stressors decreases. Stress sensitivity may progress to the point at which the precipitating stressors are too minor to be captured by traditional stress instruments. Indeed, Monroe & Harkness (2005) argue that symbolic stressors or events that serve as reminders of past failures or losses may even serve as triggers for the highly sensitized individual.

Researchers have recently extended the above findings to an investigation of additional variables (besides depression recurrence) that heighten sensitivity to stress. This new line of inquiry is intriguing as it suggests that stress sensitization might be useful in understanding not only the pathology of depression recurrence, but also the disorder's initial etiology. In what remains of this chapter, I will briefly review the evidence for three such risk factors for stress sensitivity in depression: (a) genetic vulnerability; (b) history of childhood adversity; and (c) negative cognitive–personality vulnerability. I will suggest that these three variables may affect the relation of stress to depression in two complementary ways. First, they may interact with, or moderate, the effect of severe stress, such that individuals with one or more of these risk factors will be more likely to develop depression in the face of severe stress than those without these pre-existing vulnerabilities (see Figure 14.1, Model 1). Second, they may cause a decrease in stress thresholds such that individuals with one or more of these risk factors will develop depression in the face of more minor levels of stress than those without (see Figure 14.1, Model 2).

GENETIC VULNERABILITY TO STRESS SENSITIZATION

Family, twin, and adoption studies conducted over 50 years have provided compelling evidence that major depression runs in families, and that much of its

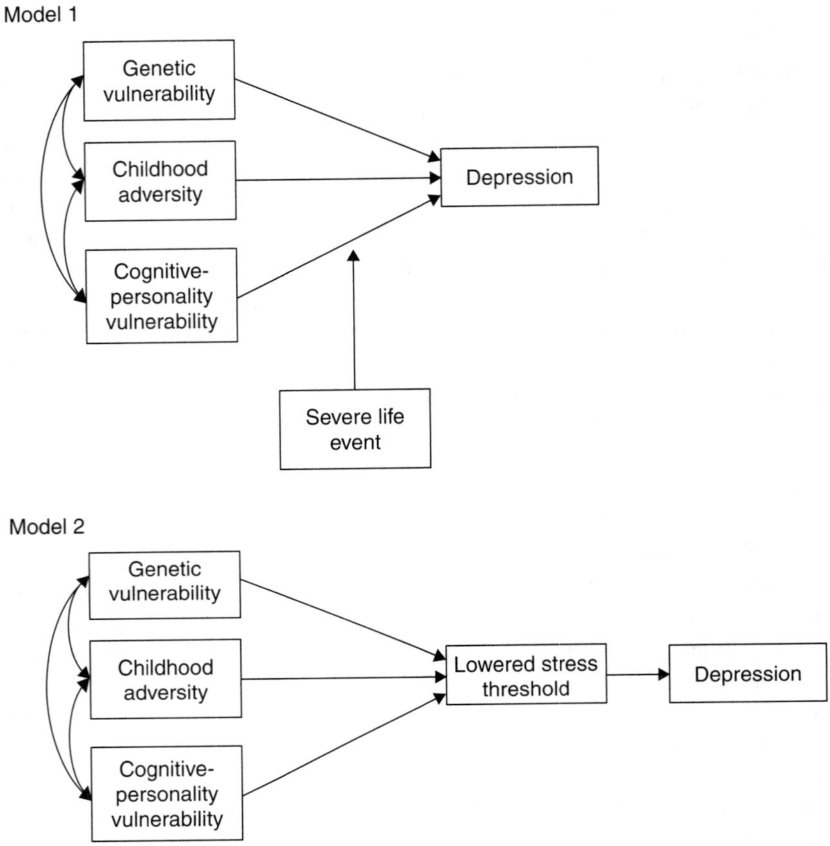

FIGURE 14.1 Two theoretical models of the relation of genetic vulnerability, childhood adversity, and cognitive-personality vulnerability to stress sensitization in depression.

familial aggregation is due to genetic factors (Sullivan *et al.*, 2000; see Zammit, Forty, & Craddock, Chapter 2). A study by Kendler *et al.* (1995) was one of the first to demonstrate that genetic vulnerability to major depression significantly moderates individuals' sensitivity to stress. Using their large female twin sample, regression analyses indicated a significant genetic by environment interaction such that those at highest genetic risk (i.e., monozygotic twin, co-twin depressed) were more than twice as likely to develop depression in the face of a severe stressor than those at lowest genetic risk (i.e., monozygotic twin, co-twin non-depressed). Kendler *et al.* (1995) concluded that "genetic factors influence the risk of onset of major depression in part by altering the sensitivity of individuals to the depression-inducing effect of stressful life events" (p. 833).

Now that the human genome has been mapped, investigators are in the exciting position of specifying genetic risk at the chromosomal level. The serotonin transporter gene (5-HTTLPR) has received the most attention as a possible moderator of the stress response. For example, Caspi *et al.* (2003) found that individuals who were homozygous or heterozygous for the short allele of the HTTLPR ("s/s" or "s/l") showed higher rates of major depression, more depressive symptoms, and higher levels of suicidality in response to stressful life events than those who were homozygous for the long allele ("l/l"). This basic 5-HTTLPR genotype by stress interaction in depression has now been replicated by several research groups (Eley *et al.*, 2004; Jacobs *et al.*, 2006; Kaufman *et al.*, 2004; Kendler *et al.*, 2005; Taylor *et al.*, 2006; Wilhelm *et al.*, 2006; Zalsman *et al.*, 2006). However, two caveats are worth noting. First, the interaction reported by Eley *et al.* (2004) emerged only for females (and Kendler *et al.* and Jacobs *et al.* only assessed females). Second, the genotype by stress interaction uncovered by Jacobs *et al.* (2006) was largely mediated by neuroticism. Therefore, more research is needed to fully understand the limits of this effect.

Two groups failed to find support for a 5-HTTLPR genotype by stress interaction in depression (Gillespie *et al.*, 2005; Surtees *et al.*, 2006). One very important difference between these studies and those noted above is their inclusion of older age groups whose index major depressive onset was likely a recurrence. For example, the participants assessed by Surtees *et al.* (2006) ranged in age from 41 to 80 years and only 9% were experiencing a first onset. In contrast, Caspi *et al.* (2003) included almost all first-onset cases. Thus, it is possible that the 5-HTTLPR genetic vulnerability increases individuals' sensitivity to the stressors that precipitate the very first onset of the syndrome. Once the course of depression is underway, however, more proximal factors, such as previous episodes of the depression themselves may become the most potent in driving stress sensitization. Studies that chart the within-individual course of stress sensitization across several recurrences are required to address this hypothesis.

CHILDHOOD ADVERSITY VULNERABILITY TO STRESS SENSITIZATION

Severe adversity in childhood is a strong predictor of later major depression onset. For example, a history of childhood physical abuse, sexual abuse, and/or neglect is associated with a 2- to 5-fold increase in the risk of depression, even after controlling for a host of demographic and family contextual factors known to be associated with depression onset (Bifulco, Brown, & Harris, 1994; Harkness & Lumley, 2007). Recently, investigators have proposed that the presence of childhood adversity may promote risk for depression, at least in part, by significantly increasing individuals' sensitivity to stress. For example, Kendler *et al.* (2004a) reported in their sample of female twins that women with a history of child physical or sexual abuse were significantly more likely to develop depression in the face of proximal major life events than women without this history. Similarly, in studies of adolescents (Harkness *et al.*, 2006), late adolescent girls (Hammen *et al.*, 2000), and younger children (Rudolph & Flynn, 2007), researchers found that those with a wide range of adversities in childhood required a lower level of stress to precipitate depression onset than those without this history. Further, Harkness et al. (2006) demonstrated that the effect of child abuse and neglect in sensitizing adolescents to proximal stress was specific to those on their *very first onset* of depression.

In summary, the results of the above studies suggest that childhood adversity heightens sensitivity to future stress such that depression is more likely to occur following stress (Model 1), and is more likely to occur in the face of minor stress (Model 2), in those with a history of adversity than in those without. Further, this effect may be specific to the first depression onset.

COGNITIVE AND PERSONALITY VULNERABILITY TO STRESS SENSITIVITY

Beck's (1967) cognitive theory of depression proposes that negative core beliefs, or "schemas," form a latent vulnerability in depression-prone individuals that when triggered by a stressful life event results in a "downward spiral" into depression. Segal and colleagues have more recently made an explicit link to Post's kindling theory by proposing that the strengthening of the depressogenic schema structure over time may provide a framework for understanding the progressive sensitivity to stress across depression recurrence. According to cognitive theory, negative schemas are strengthened over time as a result of repeated experiences that confirm the belief structure of the schema. Segal *et al.* (1996) suggest that the stronger the interconnections among the elements of the schema network become over repeated episodes of depression and repeated stress experiences, the more easily the network is activated in the presence of increasingly more minor stressors, thereby reducing the threshold for depression recurrence.

A large number of longitudinal studies following remitted depressed patients to recurrence have shown that individuals with a negative cognitive schema vulnerability are more likely to suffer a recurrence when faced with stress than those without. These studies all measured cognitive vulnerability in terms of two cognitive–personality factors theorized by Beck (1983) to be central to the cognitive diathesis to depression: (a) sociotropy (or dependency), defined as a strong investment in, and valuation of, interpersonal relationships and intimacy, and (b) autonomy (or self-criticism), defined as a strong investment in, and valuation of, independence and achievement. Hammen *et al.* (1989) followed 22 unipolar and 25 bipolar depressed outpatients for 6 months following remission. They reported that patients high in autonomy had significantly higher levels of depressive symptoms over follow-up when faced with a "matching" contextually defined event in the achievement domain (e.g., job failure) than when faced with a non-matching interpersonal event (e.g., loss of a close friend). This interaction of cognitive vulnerability and stressor was not found for sociotropy. In a later 2-year follow-up study of 27 unipolar depressed patients, Hammen *et al.* (1989) reported that the interaction of autonomy and achievement events predicted major depression recurrence over follow-up, while no such interaction emerged for sociotropy.

Two studies by Segal and colleagues also supported the cognitive model of depression recurrence but with an opposite pattern to that reported above (Segal *et al.*, 1989; Segal *et al.*, 1992). In two independent samples of 46 and 59 remitted depressed patients followed for 6 months and 1 year, respectively, Segal and colleagues found that the interaction of dependency or sociotropy and a negative interpersonal event predicted relapse, particularly when examining events within 2 months of relapse. Similarly, Lam *et al.* (1996) found that high dependency and the presence of a LEDS-defined interpersonal event predicted relapse and time to relapse in a sample of 30 remitted depressed outpatients followed for 1 year, while no such interaction emerged for self-criticism. Finally, in a sample of 41 remitted depressed outpatients followed for 6 months, Voyer and Cappeliez (2002) found that the interaction of dependency and patients' perceptions of the impact of recent stressors on their social relationships predicted relapse, while the corresponding interaction of self-criticism and stress in the achievement domain was not significant.

Still other studies have found support for the interaction of sociotropy and autonomy and their respective matching stressors in predicting major depression recurrence (Mazure & Maciejewski, 2003; Mazure *et al.*, 2002; Morse & Robins, 2005). In addition, studies have found that the interaction of total scores on the Dysfunctional Attitudes Scale (DAS; Weissman & Beck, 1979) and total stressful life event scores, in general, as assessed by self-report checklist, predicted longitudinal change in depression symptoms in undergraduates with a lifetime history of major depression (Reilly-Harrington *et al.*, 1999) or with a current dysthymia, cyclothymia, or hypomania (Alloy *et al.*, 1999).

Therefore, while differences among studies have emerged regarding the specific cognitive vulnerability most strongly linked to stress sensitivity, the studies above provide strong evidence for the role of negative cognitive vulnerability, in general, in increasing the likelihood of depression recurrence following stress. Indeed, only two negative studies have been reported. In a sample of 65 patients with depression and 28 patients with schizophrenia, Robins (1990) found that the interaction of DAS scores with life event frequency, as assessed by checklist, was not significant in predicting depression symptom severity when patients' stress perceptions were taken into consideration. However, this study was a cross-sectional design, thus patients' perceptions of the severity of stress were likely confounded with both their cognitive diathesis and their current level of symptoms. Therefore, it is not surprising that stress perception over-rode the diathesis–stress effect in this model (see Monroe & Simons, 1991). Mazure *et al.* (2000) also failed to find interactions of sociotropy or autonomy and matching LEDS-defined events in discriminating 43 major depressed outpatients vs. 43 matched controls. However, the two subsequent studies by this same research group cited above employing larger samples found strong support for the model, thus suggesting that the negative results reported in their first study may have been due to low statistical power.

The results of the above studies support the theory that a depressogenic cognitive–personality style may heighten vulnerability to recurrence in major depression by heightening individuals' sensitivity to stress. Future research is required to determine whether a pre-existing cognitive–personality vulnerability also raises individuals' sensitivity to stress prior to the very first onset of major depression. Studies examining the personality factor of Neuroticism provide preliminary support for this possibility. In particular, Kendler *et al.* (2004b) found that neuroticism interacted with major life events to predict the 1-year prospective risk of major depression in their large sample of female twin pairs. Similarly, in a sample of 3700 elderly individuals, Ormel *et al.* (2001) found that neuroticism interacted with LEDS-defined life events to predict the risk of major depression onset over a 2-year prospective period.

SUMMARY

The studies reviewed above provide compelling preliminary evidence that (a) genetic vulnerability, (b) childhood adversity, and (c) cognitive–personality vulnerability increase risk for depression onset and recurrence at least in part through the mechanism of stress sensitization. That is, individuals with one or more of these risk factors are more likely to develop depression when faced with severe stress, and may be more likely to develop depression following relatively minor levels of stress, than individuals without these risk factors. What is needed now is large-scale research examining how these three risk factors work together to promote stress sensitization: Are there additive or interactive effects? Do certain risk factors mediate the effects of others? In addition, longitudinal research is required to more fully examine the suggestion that these risk factors may have a different relation to stress sensitization in individuals on their first onset of depression vs. a recurrence.

Furthermore, as suggested above, research is required to examine how the etiological and pathological model of major depression presented here predicts individual differences in depression symptom and subtype presentation. For example, are individuals with melancholic depression preferentially sensitized to stress? Harkness and Monroe (2006) recently found that individuals with severe melancholic depression were more likely than those with non-melancholic depression to have a minor, non-severe event prior to onset. Willner *et al.* (1990) also reported that patients with melancholic depression have higher rates of minor life events than those with non-melancholic depression. Melancholic depression is also more strongly associated with the risk factors for stress sensitization discussed above, namely genetic vulnerability (Kendler, 1997) and childhood adversity (Harkness & Monroe, 2002), than is non-melancholic depression. Therefore, an intriguing possibility requiring further study is that episodes of melancholic depression may be less likely to be precipitated by severe stress because these individuals are breaking down in the face of much more common, milder stressors as a result of an enhanced sensitivity to stress (Harkness & Monroe, 2006; Harkness *et al.*, 2007).

CONCLUSIONS

The role of stress in the onset of depression is now well established. In particular, severely stressful life events occurring in the 3–6 months prior to an episode are strongly associated with the precipitation of depression, and a large part of this association is directly causal. While stressful life events are the most proximal triggers of depression onset, the evidence reviewed in this chapter suggests that the relation of stress to depression is strongly influenced by biological, psychological, and environmental risk factors that likely work together to alter individuals' sensitivity to stress. Furthermore, once the depression syndrome is underway, scars left over from the repeated experience of stress triggers, and the stress of repeated depressive episodes themselves, further lower stress thresholds such that minor life events may play an increasingly strong role in triggering recurrences. Therefore, treatments that focus on stress identification and coping early in the course of depression will likely show superior effects in preventing recurrence. For example, mindfulness-based cognitive-behavioral strategies focus on promoting stress resilience, particularly as a strategy for preventing future depression recurrence (Segal *et al.*, 2002). In addition, Interpersonal Psychotherapy focuses specifically on addressing the stressors that triggered onset in an effort to learn strategies to cope with similar stressors in the future and prevent recurrence (Frank & Spanier, 1995). Continued development and refinement of treatments that recognize the important role of stress in the etiology and pathology of depression are crucial to preventing what can be a lifelong pattern of illness.

ACKNOWLEDGEMENT

This work was supported by a grant from the Canadian Institutes for Health Research and a Visiting Professorship from Stanford University. I thank Lindsey Lytle for her help in preparing this manuscript.

REFERENCES

Alloy, L. B., Reilly-Harrington, N., Fresco, D. M., Whitehouse, W. G., & Zechmeister, J. S. (1999). Cognitive styles and life events in subsyndromal unipolar and bipolar disorders: Stability and prospective prediction of depressive and hypomanic mood swings. *Journal of Cognitive Psychotherapy*, *13*, 21–40.

American Psychiatric Association (1968). *Diagnostic and Statistical Manual of Mental Disorders* (2nd ed.). Washington, DC: Author.

American Psychiatric Association (1980). *Diagnostic and Statistical Manual of Mental Disorders* (3rd ed.). Washington, DC: Author.

American Psychiatric Association (1987). *Diagnostic and Statistical Manual of Mental Disorders* (3rd ed. (revised)). Washington, DC: Author.

Bebbington, P., Sturt, E., Hurry, J., & Tennant, C. (1984). Misfortune and resilience: A community study of women. *Psychological Medicine*, *14*, 347–363.

Bebbington, P. E., Brugha, T., MacCarthy, B., Potter, J., Sturt, E., Wykes, T. et al. (1988). The Camberwell Collaborative Depression Study I. Depressed probands: adversity and the form of depression. *British Journal of Psychiatry*, *152*, 754–765.

Beck, A. T. (1967). *Depression: Causes and Treatment*. Philadelphia: University of Pennsylvania Press.

Beck, A. T. (1983). Cognitive therapy of depression: New perspectives. In P. J. Clayton, & J. E. Barrett (Eds.), *Treatment of Depression: Old Controversies and New Approaches* (pp. 265–290). New York: Raven.

Benjaminsen, S. (1981). Stressful life events preceding the onset of neurotic depression. *Psychological Medicine*, *11*, 369–378.

Bifulco, A., Brown, G. W., & Harris, T. O. (1994). Childhood Experience of Care and Abuse (CECA): A retrospective interview measure. *Journal of Child Psychology and Psychiatry*, *35*, 1419–1435.

Bockting, C. L. H., Spinhoven, P., Koeter, M. W. J., Wouters, L. F., Visser, L., & Schene, A. H. (2006). Differential predictors of response to preventive cognitive therapy in recurrent depression: A 2-year prospective study. *Psychotherapy and Psychosomatics*, *75*, 229–236.

Brown, E. J., Juster, H. R., Heimberg, R. G., & Winning, C. D. (1998). Stressful life events and personality styles: Relation to impairment and treatment outcome in patients with social phobia. *Journal of Anxiety Disorders*, *12*, 233–251.

Brown, G. W. (1993). The role of life events in the aetiology of depressive and anxiety disorders. In S. C. Sanford, & P. Salmon (Eds.), *Stress: From Synapse to Syndrome* (pp. 23–50). New York: Academic Press.

Brown, G. W. (1996). Psychosocial factors and depression and anxiety disorders: Some possible implications for biological research. *Journal of Psychopharmacology*, *10*, 23–30.

Brown, G. W., & Harris, T. O. (1978). *Social Origins of Depression: A Study of Psychiatric Disorder in Women*. New York: Free Press.

Brown, G. W., & Prudo, R. (1981). Psychiatric disorder in a rural and an urban population: 1. Aetiology of depression. *Psychological Medicine*, *11*, 581–599.

Brown, G. W., & Harris, T. O. (1989). Depression. In G. W. Brown, & T. O. Harris (Eds.), *Life Events and Illness* (pp. 49–93). New York: Guilford Press.

Brown, G. W., Ni Bhrolchain, M., & Harris, T. O. (1979). Psychotic and neurotic depression: Part 3. Aetiological and background factors. *Journal of Affective Disorders*, *1*, 195–211.

Brown, G. W., Andrews, B., Harris, T. O., Adler, Z., & Bridge, L. (1986). Life events, difficulties and recovery from chronic depression. *British Journal of Psychiatry*, *152*, 115–128.

Brown, G. W., Harris, T. O., & Hepworth, C. (1994). Life events and endogenous depression: A puzzle reexamined. *Archives of General Psychiatry*, *51*, 525–534.

Brugha, T. S., & Conroy, R. (1985). Categories of depression: reported life events in a controlled design. *British Journal of Psychiatry*, *147*, 641–646.

Campbell, E. A., Cope, S. J., & Teasdale, J. D. (1983). Social factors and affective disorders: An investigation of Brown and Harris' model. *British Journal of Psychiatry*, *143*, 548–553.

Carney, M. W. P., Roth, M., & Garside, R. F. (1965). The diagnosis of depressive syndromes and the prediction of ECT response. *British Journal of Psychiatry*, *111*, 659–674.

Caspi, A., Sugden, K., Moffitt, T. E., Taylor, A., Craig, I. W., & Harrington, H., *et al.* (2003). Influence of life stress on depression: Moderation by a polymorphism in the 5-TT gene. *Science*, *301*, 386–389.

Cassano, G. B., Akiskal, H. S., Musetti, L., Perugi, A., Soriani, A., & Mignani, V. (1989). Psychopathology, temperament, and past course in primary major depressions. *Psychopathology*, *22*, 278–288.

Clark, L. A., & Watson, D. (1991). Tripartite model of anxiety and depression: Psychometric evidence and taxonomic implications. *Journal of Abnormal Psychology*, *100*, 316–336.

Clark, D. A., & Beck, A. T. (1999). *Scientific foundations of cognitive theory and therapy of depression*. New York: John Wiley & Sons.

Cornell, D. G., Milden, R. S., & Shimp, S. (1985). Stressful life events associated with endogenous depression. *Journal of Nervous and Mental Disease*, *173*, 470–476.

Costello, G. C. (1982). Social factors associated with depression: A retrospective community study. *Psychological Medicine*, *12*, 329–339.

Daley, S. E., Hammen, C., & Rao, U. (2000). Predictors of first onset and recurrence of major depression in young women during the 5 years following high school graduation. *Journal of Abnormal Psychology*, *109*, 525–533.

Dohrenwend, B. P., Krasnoff, L., Askenasy, A. R., & Dohrenwend B. S. (1978). Exemplification of a method for scaling life events: The PERI life events scale. *Journal of Health and Social Behavior*, *19*, 204–229.

Dolan, R. T., Calloway, S. P., Fonagy, P., De Souza, F. V. A., & Wakeling, A. (1985). Life events, depression and hypothalamic-pituitary-adrenal axis function. *British Journal of Psychiatry*, *147*, 429–433.

Eley, T. C., Sugden, K., Corsico, A., Gregory, A. M., Sham, P., McGuffin, P. et al. (2004). Gene-environment interaction analysis of serotonin system markers with adolescent depression. *Moecular Psychiatry*, *9*, 908–915.

Ezquiaga, E., Gutierrez, J. L. A., & Lopez, A. G. (1987). Psychosocial factors and episode number in depression. *Journal of Affective Disorders*, *12*, 135–138.

Faravelli, C., & Pallanti, S. (1989). Recent life events and panic disorder. *American Journal of Psychiatry*, *146*, 622–626.

Farmer, A., Redman, K., Harris, T., Mahmood, A., Sadler, S. Pickering, A. et al. (2002). Neuroticism, extraversion, life events and depression: The Cardiff Depression Study. *British Journal of Psychiatry*, *181*, 118–122.

Finlay-Jones, R., & Brown, G. W. (1981). Types of stressful life event and the onset of anxiety and depressive disorders. *Psychological Medicine*, *11*, 803–815.

Flannery, R. B. (1986). Major life events and daily hassles in predicting health status: Methodological inquiry. *Journal of Clinical Psychology*, *42*, 485–487.

Forrest, A. D., Fraser, R. H., & Priest, R. G. (1965). Environmental factors in depressive illness. *British Journal of Psychiatry*, *111*, 243–253.

Frank, E., & Spanier, C. (1995). Interpersonal psychotherapy for depression: Overview, clinical efficacy, and future directions. *Clinical Psychology Science and Practice*, *2*, 349–369.

Frank, E., Anderson, B., Reynolds, C. F., Ritenour, A., & Kupfer, D. J. (1994). Life events and the research diagnostic criteria endogenous subtype. *Archives of General Psychiatry*, *51*, 519–524.

Ghaziuddin, M., Ghaziuddin, N., & Stein, G. S. (1990). Life events and the recurrence of depression. *Canadian Journal of Psychiatry*, *35*, 239–242.

Gillespie, N. A., Whitfield, J. B., Williams, B., Heath, A. C., & Martin, N. G. (2005). The relationship between stressful life events, the serotonin transporter (5-HTTLPR) genotype and major depression. *Psychological Medicine*, *35*, 101–111.

Hammen, C., Ellicott, A., & Gitlin, M. (1989). Vulnerability to specific life events and prediction of course of disorder in unipolar depressed patients. *Canadian Journal of Behavioural Science*, *21*, 377–388.

Hammen, C., Ellicott, A., Gitlin, M., & Jamison, K. R. (1989). Sociotropy/autonomy and vulnerability to specific life events in patients with unipolar depression and bipolar disorders. *Journal of Abnormal Psychology*, *98*, 154–160.

Hammen, C., Henry, R., & Daley, S. E. (2000). Depression and sensitization to stressors among young women as a function of childhood adversity. *Journal of Consulting and Clinical Psychology*, *68*, 782–787.

Harkness, K. L., & Lumley, M. N. (2007). Child abuse and neglect and the development of depression in children and adolescents. In J. Abela & B. Hankin (Eds.), *Depression in Children and Adolescents*. (pp. 446–488). Guilford: New York.

Harkness, K. L., & Monroe, S. M. (2002). Childhood adversity and the endogenous versus nonendogenous distinction in depression. *American Journal of Psychiatry*, *159*, 387–393.

Harkness, K. L., & Monroe, S. M. (2006). Severe melancholic depression is more vulnerable than nonmelancholic depression to minor precipitating life events. *Journal of Affective Disorders*, *91*, 257–263.

Harkness, K. L., Bruce, A. E., & Lumley, M. N. (2006). The role of childhood abuse and neglect in the sensitization to stressful life events in adolescent depression. *Journal of Abnormal Psychology*, *115*, 730–741.

Harkness, K. L., Thase, M. E., & Monroe, S. M. (2007). Life events in melancholic depression. Manuscript under review.

Heils, A., Teufel, A., Petri, S., Stober, G., Riederer, P., Bengel, D. et al. (1996). Allelic variation of human serotonin transporter gene expression. *Journal of Neurochemistry*, *66*, 2621–2624.

Holmes, T. H., & Rahe, R. H. (1967). The social readjustment rating scale. *Journal of Psychometric Research*, *11*, 213–218.

Horowitz, M., Schaffer, C., Hiroto, D., Wilner, N., & Lesir, B. (1977). Life event questionnaires for measuring negative stress. *Psychosomatic Medicine*, *39*, 70–82.

Hurst, M. W., Jenkins, C. D., & Rose, R. (1978). The assessment of life events in schizophrenia and depression: A comparative and methodological enquiry. *Psychosomatic Medicine*, *40*, 126–140.

Jackson, S. W. (1986). *Melancholia and Depression: From Hippocratic Times to Modern Times*. New Haven: Yale University Press.

Jacobs, N., Kenis, G., Peeters, F., Derom, C., Vlietinck, R., & van Os, J. (2006). Stress-related negative affectivity and genetically altered serotonin transporter function: evidence of synergism in shaping risk of depression. *Archives of General Psychiatry*, *63*, 989–996.

Kanner, A. D., Coyne, J. C., Schaefer, C., & Lazarus, R. S. (1981). Comparison of two modes of stress measurement: Daily hassles and uplifts versus major life events. *Journal of Behavioral Medicine*, *4*, 7–11.

Kaufman, J., Yang, B., Douglas-Palumberi, H., Houshyar, S., Lipschitz, D., Krystal, J. H. et al. (2004). Social supports and serotonin transporter gene moderate depression in maltreated children. *Proceedings of National Academy of Sciences*, *101*, 17316–17321.

Kendler, K. S. (1997). The diagnostic validity of melancholic major depression in a population-based sample of female twins. *Archives of General Psychiatry*, *54*, 299–304.

Kendler, K. S., Neale, M. C., Kessler, R. C., Heath, A. C., & Eaves, L. J. (1992). Major depression and generalized anxiety disorder: same genes, (partly) different environments? *Archives of General Psychiatry*, *49*, 716–722.

Kendler, K. S., Kessler, R. C., Walters, E. E., MacLean, C., Neale, M. C., Heath, A. C. et al. (1995). Stressful life events, genetic liability, and onset of an episode of major depression in women. *American Journal of Psychiatry*, *152*, 833–842.

Kendler, K. S., Karkowski, L. M., & Prescott, C. A. (1998). Stressful life events and major depression: Risk period, long-term contextual threat, and diagnostic specificity. *Journal of Nervous and Mental Disease*, *186*, 661–669.

Kendler, K. S., Karkowski, L. M., & Prescott, C. A. (1999). Causal relationship between stressful life events and the onset of major depression. *American Journal of Psychiatry*, *156*, 837–841.

Kendler, K. S., Gardner, C. O., & Prescott, C. A. (2002). Toward a comprehensive developmental model for major depression in women. *American Journal of Psychiatry*, *159*, 1133–1145.

Kendler, K. S., Hettema, J. M., Butera, F., Gardner, C. O., & Prescott, C. A. (2003). Life Event Dimensions of Loss, Humiliation, Entrapment, and Danger in the Prediction of Onsets of Major Depression and Generalized Anxiety. *Archives of General Psychiatry*, *60*, 789–796.

Kendler, K. S., Kuhn, J. W., & Prescott, C. A. (2004a). Childhood sexual abuse, stressful life events and risk for major depression in women. *Psychological Medicine*, *34*, 1475–1482.

Kendler, K. S., Kuhn, J., & Prescott, C. A. (2004b). The interrelationship of neuroticism, sex, and stressful life events in the prediction of episodes of major depression. *American Journal of Psychiatry*, *161*, 631–636.

Kendler, K. S., Kuhn, J. W., Vittum, J., Prescott, C. A., & Riley, B. (2005). The interaction of stressful life events and a serotonin transporter polymorphism in the prediction of episodes of major depression. *Archives of General Psychiatry*, *62*, 529–535.

Kessler, R. C., Chiu, W. T., Demler, O., Walters, E. E., Ho, M.-H., & R. Ho, M.-H. (2005). Prevalence, Severity, and Comorbidity of 12-Month DSM-IV Disorders in the National Comorbidity Survey Replication. *Archives of General Psychiatry*, *62*, 617–627.

Klein, D. F., Lewinsohn, P. M., & Seeley, J. R. (1997). Psychosocial characteristics of adolescents with a past history of dysthymic disorder: Comparison with adolescents with past histories of major depressive and non-affective disorders, and never mentally ill controls. *Journal of Affective Disorders*, *42*, 127–135.

Kohn, Y., Zislin, J., Agid, O., Hanin, B., Troudart, T., Shapira, B. et al. (2001). Increased prevalence of negative life events in subtypes of major depressive disorder. *Comprehensive Psychiatry*, *42*, 57–63.

Lam, D. H., Green, B., Power, M. J., & Checkley, S. (1996). Dependency, matching adversities, length of survival and relapse in major depression. *Journal of Affective Disorders*, *37*, 81–90.

Leff, M. J., Roatch, J. F., & Bunney, W. E. J. (1970). Environmental factors preceding the onset of severe depressions. *Psychiatry*, *33*, 293–311.

Lewinsohn, P. M., Allen, N. B., Seeley, J. R., & Gotlib, I. H. (1999). First onset versus recurrence of depression: differential processes of psychosocial risk. *Journal of Abnormal Psychology*, *108*, 483–489.

Lotrich, F. E., & Pollock, B. G. (2004). Meta-analysis of serotonin transporter polymorphisms and affective disorders. *Psychiatric Genetics*, *14*, 121–129.

Lovejoy, M. C., & Steuerwald, B. L. (1997). Subsyndromal unipolar and bipolar disorders II: Comparisons on daily stress levels. *Cognitive Therapy & Research*, *21*, 607–618.

Maciejewski, P. K., Prigerson, H. G., & Mazure C. M. (2000). Self-efficacy as a mediator between stressful life events and depressive symptoms. Differences based on history of prior depression. *British Journal of Psychiatry*, *176*, 373–378.

Mazure, C. M. (1998). Life stressors as risk factors in depression. *Clinical Psychology: Science and Practice*, *5*, 291–313.

Mazure, C., & Maciejewski, P. K. (2003). A model of risk for major depression: Effects of life stress and cognitive style vary by age. *Depression and Anxiety*, *17*, 26–33.

Mazure, C. M., Bruce, M. L., Maciejewski, P. K., & Jacobs, S. C. (2000). Adverse life events and cognitive-personality characteristics in the prediction of major depression and antidepressant response. *American Journal of Psychiatry*, *157*, 896–903.

Mazure, C. M., Maciejewski, P. K., Jacobs, S. C., & Bruce, M. L. (2002). Stressful life events interacting with cognitive/personality styles to predict late-onset major depression. *American Journal of Geriatric Psychiatry*, *10*, 297–304.

McQuaid, J., Monroe, S. M., Roberts, J. R. & Johnson, S. L. (1992). Toward the standardization of life stress assessment: Definitional discrepancies and inconsistencies in methods. *Stress Medicine*, *8*, 47–56.

McQuaid, J. R., Monroe, S. M., Roberts, J E., Kupfer, D. J., & Frank, E. (2000). Comparison of two life stress assessment approaches: Prospective prediction of treatment outcome in recurrent depression. *Journal of Abnormal Psychology*, *109*, 787–791.

Monroe, S. M., & Depue, R. A. (1991). Life stress and depression. In J. Becker, & A. Kleinman (Eds.), *Psychosocial Aspects of Depression* (pp. 101–130). Hillsdale, NJ: Erlbaum Associates, Inc.

Monroe, S. M., & Simons, A. D. (1991). Diathesis-stress theories in the context of life stress research: Implications for the depressive disorders. *Psychological Bulletin*, *110*, 406–425.

Monroe, S. M., & McQuaid, J. R. (1994) Measuring life stress and assessing its impact on mental health. In W. R. Avison & I. H. Gotlib (Eds.), *stress and Mental Health: Contemporary Issues and Prospects for the Future* (pp. 43–73). New York: Plenum Press.

Monroe, S. M., & Harkness, K. L. (2005) Life stress, the 'kindling' hypothesis, and the recurrence of depression: Considerations from a life stress perspective. *Psychological Review*, *112*, 417–445.

Monroe, S. M., Thase, M. E., Hersen, M., Himmelhoch, J. M., & Bellack, A. S. (1985). Life events and the endogenous-nonendogenous distinction in the treatment and posttreatment course of depression. *Comprehensive Psychiatry*, *26*, 175–186.

Monroe, S. M., Rohde, P., Seeley, J. R. & Lewinsohn, P. M. (1999). Life events and depression in adolescence: Relationship loss as a prospective risk factor for first onset of major depressive disorder. *Journal of Abnormal Psychology*, *108*, 606–614.

Morse, J. Q., & Robins, C. J. (2005). Personality-life event congruence effects in late-life depression. *Journal of Affective Disorders*, *84*, 25–31.

Nakamura, M., Ueno, S., Sano, A., & Tanabe, H. (2000). The human serotonin transporter gene linked polymorphism (5-HTTLPR) shows ten novel allelic variants. *Molecular Psychiatry, 5*, 32–38.

Newman, S. C., & Bland, R. C. (1994). Life events and the 1-year prevalence of major depressive episode, generalized anxiety disorder, and panic disorder in a community sample. *Comprehensive Psychiatry, 35*, 76–82.

Ormel, J., Oldehinkel, A. J., & Brilman, E. I. (2001). The interplay and etiological continuity of neuroticism, difficulties, and life events in the etiology of major and subsyndromal, first and recurrent depressive episodes in later life. *American Journal of Psychiatry, 158*, 885–891.

Parry, G., & Shapiro, D. A. (1986). Social support and life events in working class women: Stress buffering or independent effects? *Archives of General Psychiatry, 43*, 315–323.

Paykel, E. S. (1986). American and European classifications of affective disorders. *Pharmacopsychiatry, 19*, 29–32.

Paykel, E. S., Rao, B. M., & Taylor, C. N. (1984). Life stress and symptom pattern in out-patient depression. *Psychological Medicine, 14*, 559–568.

Perris, H. (1984). Life events and depression: Part 2. Results in diagnostic subgroups, and in relation to the recurrence of depression. *Journal of Affective Disorders, 7*, 25–36.

Post, R. M. (1992). Transduction of psychosocial stress into the neurobiology of recurrent affective disorder. *American Journal of Psychiatry, 149*, 999–1010.

Rapee, R. M., Litwin, E. M., & Barlow, D. H. (1990). Impact of life events on subjects with panic disorder and on comparison subjects. *American Journal of Psychiatry, 147*, 640–644.

Ravindran, A. V., Matheson, K., Griffiths, J., Merali, Z., & Anisman, H. (2002). Stress, coping, uplifts, and quality of life in subtypes of depression: A conceptual frame and emerging data. *Journal of Affective Disorders, 71*, 121–130.

Reilly-Harrington, N. A., Alloy, L. B., Fresco, D. M., & Whitehouse, W. G. (1999). Cognitive styles and life events interact to predict bipolar and unipolar symptomatology. *Journal of Abnormal Psychology, 108*, 567–578.

Robins, C. J. (1990). Congruence of personality and life events in depression. *Journal of Abnormal Psychology, 99*, 393–397.

Robins, C. J., Block, R., & Peselow, E. D. (1990). Endogenous and non-endogenous depressions: Relations to life events, dysfunctional attitudes and event perceptions. *British Journal of Clinical Psychology, 29*, 201–207.

Roy, A., Breier, A., Doran, A. R., & Pickar, D. (1985). Life events in depression: Relationship to subtypes. *Journal of Affective Disorders, 9*, 143–148.

Roy-Byrne, P. P., Geraci, M., & Uhde, T. W. (1986). Life events and the onset of panic disorder. *American Journal of Psychiatry, 143*, 1424–1427.

Rudolph, K. D., & Flynn, M. (2007). Childhood adversity and youth depression: Influence of gender and pubertal status. *Development & Psychopathology, 19*, 497–521.

Sandin, B., Chorot, P., Santed, M. A., & Valiente, R. M. (2004). Differences in negative life events between patients with anxiety disorders, depression and hypochondriasis. *Anxiety, Stress, & Coping: An International Journal, 17*, 37–47.

Segal, Z. V., Shaw, B. F., & Vella, D. D. (1989). Life stress and depression: A test of the congruency hypothesis for life event content and depressive subtype. *Canadian Journal of Behavioural Science, 21*, 389–400.

Segal, Z. V., Shaw, B. F., Vella, D. D., & Katz, R. (1992). Cognitive and life stress predictors of relapse in remitted unipolar depressed patients: Test of the congruency hypothesis. *Journal of Abnormal Psychology, 101*, 26–36.

Segal, Z. V., Williams, J. M., Teasdale, J. D., & Gemar, M. (1996). A cognitive science perspective on kindling and episode sensitization in recurrent affective disorder. *Psychological Medicine, 26*, 371–380.

Segal, Z. V., Williams, J. M. G., & Teasdale, J. D. (2002). *Mindfulness-Based Cognitive Therapy for Depression*. New York: Guilford.

Simons, A. D., Angell, K. L., Monroe, S. M., & Thase, M. E. (1993). Cognition and life stress in depression: Cognitive factors and the definition, rating, and generation of negative life events. *Journal of Abnormal Psychology, 102*, 584–591.

Solomon, D. A., Keller, M. B., Leon, A. C., Mueller, T. I., Lavori, P. W., & Shea, M. T., *et al.* (2000). Multiple recurrences of major depressive disorder. *American Journal of Psychiatry, 157*, 229–233.

Spitzer, R., Endicott, J., & Robins, E. (1978). Research Diagnostic Criteria: Rationale and reliability. *Archives of General Psychiatry, 35*, 773–782.

Sugden, K., Moffitt, T. E., Taylor, A., Craig, I. W., Harrington, H et al. (2003). Influence of life stress on depression: Moderation by a polymorphism in the 5-HTT gene. *Science, 301*, 386–389.

Sullivan, P. F., Neale, M. C., & Kendler, K. S. (2000). Genetic epidemiology of major depression: review and meta-analysis. *American Journal of Psychiatry, 157*, 1552–1562.

Surtees, P. G., Wainwright, N. W. J., Willis-Owen, S. A. G., Luben, R., Day, N. E., & Flint, J. (2006). Social adversity, the serotonin transporter (5-HTTLPR) polymorphism and major depressive disorder. *Biological Psychiatry, 59*, 224–229.

Taylor, S. E., Way, B. M., Welch, W. T., Hilmert, C. J., Lehman, B. J., & Eisenberger, N. I. (2006). Early family environment, current adversity, the serotonin transporter promoter polymorphism, and depressive symptomatology. *Biological Psychiatry, 60*, 671–676.

Thomson, K. C., & Hendrie, H. C. (1972). Environmental stress in primary depressive illness. *Archives of General Psychiatry, 26*, 130–132.

Turkcapar, M. H., Akdemir, A., Orsel, S. D., Demirergi, N., Sirin, A., Kilic, E. Z. et al. (1999). The validity of diagnosis of melancholic depression according to different diagnostic systems. *Journal of Affective Disorders, 54*, 101–107.

Voyer, M., & Cappeliez, P. (2002). Congruency between depressogenic schemas and life events for the prediction of depressive relapse in remitted older patients. *Behavioural and Cognitive Psychotherapy, 30*, 165–178.

Weissman, A. N., & Beck, A. T. (1979). The Dysfunctional Attitudes Scale. Unpublished Doctoral thesis, University of Pennsylvania, Philadelphia.

Wilhelm, K., Mitchell, P. B., Niven, H., Finch, A., Wedgwood, L., Scimone, A. et al. (2006). Life events, first depression onset and the serotonin transporter gene. *Journal of Mental Science, 188*, 210–215.

Willner, P., Wilkes, M., & Orwin, A. (1990). Attributional style and perceived stress in endogenous and reactive depression. *Journal of Affective Disorders, 18*, 281–287.

Wing, J. K., Cooper, J. E., & Sartorius, N. (1974). *The Measurement and Classification of Psychiatric Symptoms*. Cambridge: Cambridge University Press.

Zalsman, G., Huang, Y.-y., Oquendo, M. A., Burke, A. K., Hu, X.-z., Brent, D. A. et al. (2006). Association of a Triallelic Serotonin Transporter Gene Promoter Region (5-HTTLPR) Polymorphism With Stressful Life Events and Severity of Depression. *American Journal of Psychiatry, 163*, 1588–1593.

Zimmerman, M. (1982). *The Positive and Negative Impact (PANI) Life Events Interview*. Iowa City, Department of Psychiatry, University of Iowa.

Zimmerman, M., Coryell, W., Pfohl, B., & Stangl, D. (1986). The validity of four definitions of endogenous depression. *Archives of General Psychiatry, 43*, 234–244.

15

Parental Psychopathology and Parenting Style Attachment as Risk Factors of Depression

Cecilia A. Essau* and Satoko Sasagawa†

*School of Human and Life Sciences, Roehampton University, London, UK
†Faculty of Human Sciences, Waseda University, Saitama, Japan

INTRODUCTION

A wide range of factors are associated with the development and persistence of depression, however, exposure to parental psychopathology and specific parenting and attachment styles are among the strongest. As shown by numerous family studies, children of depressed parents have an elevated rate of depression (Beardslee *et al.*, 1993; Hammen, 1991; Weissman *et al.*, 2006). However, the mechanisms through which parents transmit the predisposition to depression in their children remain unclear.

Multiple pathways are assumed in the transmission of psychological problems from the parent to the child (Goodman & Gotlib, 1999). While the biological explanation is given in terms of genetic predisposition, and the psychosocial explanation relates to parenting styles and attachment during the child's upbringing, these factors do not work independently. Rather, they interact with each other and weave a complex web of risk factors. This chapter reviews the evidence that parental psychopathology is a risk factor for depression, as well as mechanisms by which parental psychopathology is transmitted. The latter will focus on specific characteristics of parental psychopathology which underlie the intergenerational transmission of depression in parents. We also examine parenting and attachment styles that have been associated with elevated risk of depression. In the final section, we draw conclusions and make recommendations for intervention programs and future research.

PARENTAL PSYCHOPATHOLOGY AND DEPRESSION IN OFFSPRING

TOP-DOWN STUDIES

Top-down studies examine the children of depressed parents or first-degree relatives. They reveal that parental psychopathology, particularly parental depression, is a major risk factor for depression in children and adolescents. As reported by Beardslee *et al.* (1993), children of depressed parents had a 60% risk of developing major depression by the age of 25. Other studies have demonstrated that the offspring of depressed parents have up to six times higher rates of depression than offspring of non-depressed parents (Hammen, 1991). In Kovacs *et al.*'s study (1997), families of depressed youths had five-fold greater odds of having depressive disorder and two-fold higher odds of recurrent depressive disorder compared to families of controls, with the highest risk found in first-degree and female relatives. One study (Williamson *et al.*, 2004) examined the risk for developing first-onset major depressive disorders in children at high (i.e., without any lifetime affective disorder and had at least one first-degree and one second-degree relative who had a childhood-onset of affective disorders) and low risk for depression (i.e., without any lifetime psychiatric disorder and had no first-degree relatives with a lifetime affective disorder). At the 6-year follow-up assessment, high-risk children had a three-fold increased risk for developing a first episode of depression compared to those in low-risk families. Among children who developed a first-onset depression, the average age of onset was 14 years, with no significant difference in the initial age at onset for the first episode of depression between the high-risk and low-risk children. Mother's lifetime anxiety disorders and the child's lifetime behavioral disorder were significant predictors of first-onset depression during the follow-up period. Sociodemographic features were not significantly related to risk for first-onset depression. It was concluded that high familial loading for affective disorders, together with having a mother with an anxiety disorder, and a behavioral disorder in the child contributed to the risk of developing depression. Weissman *et al.* (2006) recently reported 20-year follow-up results, in which both the magnitude and the continuity of the risk of parental depression to the offspring were examined. Offspring of depressed parents was found to have three times higher risk of developing major depression;

the period with the highest incidence for major depression was between 15 and 20 years.

The offspring of depressed parents have not only a higher rate of depression, but also higher rates of other psychiatric disorders such as anxiety, disruptive, and substance use disorders (see Table 15.1; Beardslee *et al.*, 1987; Hammen *et al.*, 1987; Kovacs *et al.*, 1997; Warner *et al.*, 1995; Weissman *et al.*, 1987). Twenty years after the initial interview, offspring of depressed patients had a three-fold higher risk of developing not only depression, but anxiety disorders and substance dependence in comparison with offspring of non-depressed parents (Weissman *et al.*, 2006). Offspring of depressed parents also had social and medical morbidities (e.g., cardiovascular diseases) as they entered middle age; however, despite this poor course, over 60% of the high-risk offspring received no psychiatric treatment.

However, in a recent study by Klein *et al.* (2004), the association between maternal depression and higher rates of anxiety disorders in offspring disappeared after adjusting for the effects of parental non-mood disorders. Klein *et al.* (2004) therefore argued that the elevated rates of non-mood disorders among offspring of depressed parents, reported in previous studies, may be due to the direct transmission of these other disorders, rather than the effects of maternal depression.

BOTTOM-UP STUDIES

Studies that use the bottom-up approach examine the presence of depression in parents or adult relatives of depressed children and youth. Such studies (see Tables 15.2–15.5) have consistently indicated higher rates of depression in families of depressed youth compared to families of youth in the control group (Harrington *et al.*, 1993; Kovacs *et al.*, 1997). For example, Klein *et al.* (2001) compared the prevalence of psychiatric disorders in the first-degree relatives of adolescents with a history of major depressive disorders with the relatives of adolescents with a history of non-mood disorders, and in those adolescents with no history of disorder. Major depressive and dysthymic disorders, as well as alcohol abuse/dependence, were significantly elevated in the relatives of adolescent with a history of major depressive disorder. In a community study by Essau (2004), 54.6% of the adolescents with any major depressive disorders reported one or more parent with depression, 22.2% had at least one parent with alcohol, 11.4% with drug, and 32.4% with anxiety problems. The finding (e.g., Essau, 2004; Warner *et al.*, 1995) that depressed adolescents reported higher rates of depression and other psychiatric disorders in their parents raised questions about the specificity in the transmission of disorders from one generation to the other.

Although the link between maternal depression and offspring dysfunction is well documented, little is known about psychopathology in the partners of these depressed mothers, and the extent to which paternal psychopathology might influence this relationship. To address this issue, Marmorstein *et al.* (2004) compared the frequency of major depression and/or antisocial behaviour among partners of depressed and non-depressed mothers, and how these paternal disorders were

TABLE 15.1 Clinical Diagnoses in Offspring of Parent(s) with Major Depression in Selected Family Studies

			Diagnose in offspring					
			Major depression		Anxiety disorders		Any disorders	
Authors	Sample	Offspring's age	Cases	Control	Cases	Control	Cases	Control
Orvaschel *et al.* (1988)	61 offspring of parent(s) with recurrent major depression vs. 46 controls	6–17 years	21	4	20	9	41	15
Keller *et al.*, (1986)	108 offspring of depressed parent(s) vs. 64 children of controls	6–19 years	38	23	16	–	65	–
Weissman *et al.* (1987)	125 offspring of depressed parent(s) vs. 95 children of controls	6–23 years	28	13	40	18	76	57
Sylvester *et al.* (1988)	11 offspring of depressed parent(s) vs. 47 normal controls	7–17 years	29	5	34	6	–	–
Weissman *et al.* (2006)	151 offspring of depressed parents and nonpsychiatrically ill patients who have been followed up for 20 years	Mean age: 35 years	65	27	67	34	83	56

TABLE 15.2 Lifetime Diagnoses in Relatives of Children/Youth with Major Depression from Essau (2004)

Diagnoses in parents	Parent with diagnosis	Proband groups (%) Depression only	Depression + Comorbid disorders
Depressive disorders	Mother	42.9	52.8
	Father	19.5	23.6
Anxiety disorders	Mother	26.0	31.1
	Father	0	7.5
Alcohol use disorders	Mother	5.2	7.5
	Father	11.7	22.6
Drug use disorders	Mother	0	0.9
	Father	13.0	1.9

TABLE 15.3 Lifetime Diagnoses in Relatives of Children/Youth with Major Depression from Lewinsohn *et al.* (2003)

	Proband groups (%)		
Diagnoses in relatives	Major depression	Subthreshold depression	No history of mood disorder
Major depression	31.9	24.3	20.2
Subthreshold depression	9.0	9.4	9.0
Anxiety disorders	13.3	12.8	9.4
Substance use disorders	39.6	33.4	30.0

TABLE 15.4 Lifetime Diagnoses in Relatives of Children/Youth with Major Depression from Klein *et al.* (2004)

	Proband groups (%)			
Diagnoses in parents	Dysthymic disorder	Chronic depression	Episode depression	No history of mood disorder
Major depression	43.2	38.4	29.4	21.9
Recurrent depression	30.5	22.7	15.8	10.4
Dysthemic disorder	8.4	3.9	5.2	2.9
Chronic depression	7.4	3.4	4.8	3.6
Non-chronic depression	35.8	30.0	24.5	18.2

related to offspring psychopathology. Their findings show depressed mothers to have partners with antisocial behaviour; Depression in mothers and antisocial behavior in fathers were both significantly and independently associated with offspring depression and conduct disorder. Major depression in mothers and antisocial

TABLE 15.5 Lifetime Diagnoses in Relatives of Children/Youth with Major Depression from Marmorstein *et al.* (2004)

Diagnoses in parents	Proband groups (%)			
	Major depression – male offspring	Major depression – female offspring	Conduct disorder – male offspring	Conduct disorder – female offspring
Maternal depression	17.3	22.7	46.8	12.9
Paternal antisocial behavior	12.1	19.8	45.4	11.3

behavior in fathers are also more related to major depression and conduct disorder in offspring than antisocial behavior in mothers or major depression in fathers (Marmorstein & Iacono, 2004). The reasons for the links between maternal major depression and offspring conduct disorder and between paternal antisocial behavior and offspring major depression are unclear. A nonspecific genetic and set of family risks (e.g., chronic family stress, financial problems, parenting styles) may affect the intergenerational continuity of these disorders.

CLINICAL FEATURES OF PARENTAL PSYCHOPATHOLOGY AND CHILDREN'S DEPRESSION

Numerous studies have examined the clinical features which could be used to differentiate relatives of depressed probands (i.e., people with an index case of depression) from the relatives of controls. Recurrence (Kendler *et al.*, 1999; Weissman *et al.*, 1986) and early onset (Lyons *et al.*, 1998) are associated with higher levels of aggregation in family and in twin studies. Some studies have also reported greater severity of depression or incapacitation in major life domains (Klein, 1990), chronicity (Kendler *et al.*, 1999; McGuffin *et al.*, 1996), psychosocial impairment, and suicidality (Kendler *et al.*, 1999) to be associated with greater familial aggregation.

Klein *et al.* (2002) examined clinical features (severity, recurrence, chronicity, childhood onset, impairment, melancholia, suicidal ideation/behavior, and treatment) that could distinguish the relatives of depressed and non-depressed probands in a community setting. Relatives of depressed probands with each of these features were found to have higher rates of depression than the relatives of non-depressed probands. Additionally, depression was highest among relatives of depressed adolescents with recurrent episodes and greater impairment. In fact, the severity of depression seemed to best distinguish the relatives of depressed adolescents from relatives of controls. This finding was interpreted to suggest that the increased rate of depression in relatives of depressed adolescents may be attributed to more severe forms of depression rather than to mild transient conditions.

Other studies have examined the extent to which particular forms of depressive disorders are more common among the relatives of depressed than non-depressed adolescents. For example, Klein *et al.* (2004) compared the rates of major depressive disorder among the relatives of probands with dysthymic disorder, chronic major depressive disorder, and relatives of probands with episodic major depressive disorder. They found that probands with chronic forms of depression (dysthymic disorder and chronic major depressive disorder) exhibited a 40% greater risk of familial aggregation of major depressive disorder than probands with episodic major depressive disorder. These results indicate that chronic forms of depression have a greater familial liability than episodic depression, and which may contribute to the more negative course of chronic depression.

Lewinsohn *et al.* (2003) examined the relationship between subclinical depression, major depression, and nonaffective disorders in a large community sample of young adults. They found that the rate of major depression in the first-degree relatives of probands with subclinical depression was significantly lower than rates in the relatives of probands with major depression. The familial aggregation of psychopathology in relatives of probands with subclinical depression was specific to major depression in that the relatives of probands with subclinical depression did not have elevated rates of anxiety, substance use, and antisocial and borderline personality disorders compared to the relatives of depressed and non-depressed probands. Thus, subthreshold depressive symptoms did not seem to be associated with a nonspecific familial liability for psychopathology.

Although a number of studies have shown that the offspring of mothers with major depression are at increased risk for depression, less is known about the effects of paternal depression on offspring psychopathology. The lack of studies on the risk of depression in the offspring of depressed fathers could be attributed to several factors, including higher prevalence of depression in women than in men and the assumption that mothers spend more time with their children and therefore should have more impact on their children (Phares, 2002). The role of gender in the familial transmission of depression is unclear, and the few existing studies are inconsistent regarding the relationship of the gender of transmitting parent and the gender of affected offspring. In a classic study, Winokur and Clayton (1967) found a higher maternal transmission of mood disorders to female than to male offspring, whereas fathers appeared to transmit equally to male and female offspring. In other studies, maternal depression was associated with depression in daughters but not sons (Fergusson *et al.*, 1995). Nomura *et al.* (2001), however, reported greater rates of depression transmission from fathers to daughters and mothers to sons, and other studies have reported no relationship between the sex of affected parent and affected offspring (Foley *et al.*, 2001; Lieb *et al.*, 2002).

In a recent study by Currier *et al.* (2006), there was an elevated risk for mood disorders in the offspring of depressed mothers compared to depressed fathers. Male and female offspring of depressed mothers were at equally higher risk for mood disorders compared to offspring of depressed fathers. Males who transmit mood disorders to offspring had earlier onset than males who did not. They also found years of paternal illness as a risk factor, independent of paternal age of onset of depression, as well as proband and offspring age.

Based on a large community sample of parents and their adolescent and young adult offspring, Klein *et al.* (2004) found maternal depression to be significantly associated with depression in offspring of both sexes. The association between paternal depression and offspring depression only showed a trend level of significance, which disappeared after controlling for maternal major depressive disorder (MDD) and parental non-mood disorders. To explain these effects, it was argued that offspring generally reside with their mothers and, therefore, may have had greater exposure to maternal than paternal depression. They also found an association between maternal depression and offspring depression across the wide range of offspring severity, but the association with paternal depression was limited to severe cases of depression in offspring. Rates of depression were relatively high in offspring of mothers and fathers with early-onset depression, and offspring of fathers with recurrent depression.

PARENTAL DEPRESSION AND CHILDREN'S PSYCHOSOCIAL IMPAIRMENT AND COURSE OF DEPRESSION

Offspring of depressed patients have higher levels of psychosocial impairment than children of non-depressed parents (Lieb *et al.*, 2002). For example, they have poorer physical health, receive more treatment for emotional problems, have more school performance problems (e.g., school failures, repeating a grade), have poorer social skills, and more suicidal behavior than children whose parents are not depressed (Hammen, 1991; Klein *et al.*, 1988; Lee & Gotlib, 1991; Weissman, 1988; Weissman *et al.*, 1987).

Lewinsohn *et al.* (2005) reported that the effects of parental depression on offspring functioning persist into adulthood. Specifically, maternal depression was associated with higher levels of physical symptoms during adolescence, and higher levels of minor stressors and a greater risk for using mental health services in young adulthood. Paternal depression was associated with offspring experiencing more major stressors, offspring with lower perceived social competence in young adulthood, and who were more likely to attempt suicide during adolescence.

Parental depression is also related to the course and outcome of depression. Warner *et al.* (1992) reported that depressed children of depressed parents took longer to recover than depressed children of non-depressed parents. The number of episodes experienced by the depressed parents also affected their children's time to recovery, as depressed children of parents with at least two depressive episodes had significantly protracted times to recovery compared to those with only one episode. Beardslee *et al.* (1996) found that the duration of parental major depressive disorder, the number of nonaffective diagnoses, and marital status each predicted subsequent depressive episodes.

PARENTING STYLES AND DEPRESSION

The majority of evidence that links parental styles and depression comes from the retrospective accounts of the child. Two dimensions consistently found in retrospective parenting scales are care/affection and control/overprotection. Although there is evidence that parental control/overprotection leads to higher levels of depression (Parker, 1983), studies-to-date suggest that the care/affection factor (i.e., high levels of rejection and low levels of emotional warmth) is more strongly and consistently related to the manifestation of depressive symptoms in the child (Rapee, 1997). Such relationships have been observed in a wide range of samples derived from different ethnic backgrounds (Rojo-Moreno *et al.*, 1999; Sato *et al.*, 1998). The magnitude of the relationship between perceived parental rearing and depression varies among studies, however. For example, based on a mixed sample of Caucasian, African American, and Latina girls, Finkelstein *et al.* (2001) failed to find a significant association between maternal control and depression. In fact, high control was linked to less depression among African American girls, in disagreement with the conventional results. The authors speculate that the differences in cultural expectations may have accounted for these results, but this idea does not explain the failure to detect a positive relationship between maternal control and depression in the Caucasian sample, which was comparable to the samples employed in the previous studies.

In order to better understand these inconsistent results regarding the relationship between perceived parental rearing and depression, Gerlsma *et al.* (1990) conducted a meta-analytical study. Considerable methodological heterogeneity was found among the 13 studies that met the inclusion criterion. Although less affection and more control were associated with the largest effect size, the authors speculate that the results may have been less consistent due to the differences in the diagnostic criteria applied.

Since depressive symptoms negatively bias the recall of childhood memories, increasing emphasis has been placed on direct observational data. For example, Burge and Hammen (1991) used videotaped interactions of mother–child pairs debating over a topic of disagreement, and found that higher negative interactional patterns predicted higher levels of depressive symptoms 6 months later. A similar study found that deficient family problem solving skills was associated with more subsequent depressive symptoms (Sanders *et al.*, 1992).

The second source of studies regarding parent–child relationship and depression comes from research based on the attachment theory. Bowlby (1969) and Ainsworth (1969) set the foundations for research regarding the mother–child relationship and subsequent mental health problems. Attachment theory proposes that secure attachment functions as a safe base which allows the child to explore the environment around them, whereas children with insecure attachment (i.e., avoidant, resistant, or ambivalent attachment styles) fail to acquire such internal working models, which interferes with future interpersonal relationships.

The association between maternal depression and insecure attachment in infants has been reported in several studies (e.g., Teri *et al.*, 1995). Using data from the Dunedin Multidisciplinary Health and Development Study, Nada Raja *et al.* (1992) examined the relationship between perceived attachments to parents and peers and adolescent's psychological well-being. Parent and peer attachment was measured using the short version of the Inventory of Parent and Peer Attachment (IPPA; Armsden & Greenberg, 1987). They showed that low-perceived attachment to parents was associated with high levels of depression. In fact, adolescents who reported a low attachment to their parents had the highest scores on depression, and high attachment to their peers. Thus, low attachment to parents does not seem to be compensated by a high attachment to peers. Low attachment to parents was associated with adolescents depression (Essau, 2004), as well as with conduct and inattention problems (Nada Raja *et al.*, 1992). Depressed adolescents did not have significantly lower attachment to their peers than the non-disordered adolescents. Armsden and Greenberg (1987) found that attachment to parents compared to peers had a greater association with the adolescent's well-being. The result shows the importance of having a secure and stable relationship with parents.

Other studies reveal that insecure attachment predicts the later manifestation of depression. An extensive review by Blatt and Homann (1992) confirmed that mental representations or internal working models of attachment are central constructs in understanding the development of a vulnerability to depression. This can be understood in the same context as the relationship between negative cognition and parental rearing attitudes.

As with negative parental rearing, variability has been found among the studies that have examined the relationship between attachment and depression. A meta-analysis that addressed the association between attachment security and maternal mental health (Atkinson *et al.*, 2000) found that the effect size between depression and security was significant, although the distribution was heterogeneous. Clinical samples demonstrated higher effect sizes than did non-clinical samples. The authors speculated that the reason for such distinctions may be due to distinct definitions of depression. In addition to the differences in the measurement of depression, the stability of the depressive mood may be an important factor in the prediction of child attachment security. More recently, Beck (1999) conducted a meta-analysis to clarify the relationship between maternal depression and child adjustment problems. Results indicated that a substantial proportion of variance in child maladjustment can be explained by maternal depression.

MODERATORS OF PARENTAL DEPRESSION AND CHILDREN'S OUTCOME

Despite the strong evidence of familial aggregation for depressive disorders, the exact pathways of transmission of depression from parent to child remains unclear. The most common explanation for the high prevalence of depressive disorders among children of depressed as compared to children of non-depressed parents is that of direct genetic transmission of the disorder (see review by Dodge, 1990). However, there is no direct evidence of a genetically transmitted disease, so it is not known what may be transmitted, or how biological vulnerability may be activated (Gotlib & Goodman, 1999). Accumulating evidence indicates that behaviors of depressed parents may be associated with depression and with the negative outcomes in children (Cummings & Cicchetti, 1990; Goodman *et al.*, 1993), which includes parenting difficulties and marital discord. As argued by several authors, parents exert influence over their child's development through dyadic interaction, coaching and teaching, and managing of social activities (Dodge, 1990; Goodman, 1992; Lee & Gotlib, 1991; Rutter & Quinton, 1984). These roles may be interfered with by depression due to hospitalization, preoccupation with one's depression, lack of interest, or lack of attention to or skill in structuring social activities for the child. Maternal depression may increase the likelihood of marital discord or divorce which may also expose the child to negative socialization experiences (Fendrich *et al.*, 1990; Kovacs *et al.*, 1984).

The roles of parental depression and other familial factors, believed to be involved in the transmission of depression from parents to children, have been examined by administering questionnaires to parents, in which they are asked about the ways they raised their children, their attitudes about parenting, about their family life (e.g., marital discord), and by observing interactions between parents and children, mostly in the laboratory setting.

STUDIES OF DEPRESSED PARENTS

Depressed women have reported feelings of helplessness and hostility toward their children and have reported only moderate involvement in their children's daily lives (Weissman & Paykel, 1974). Compared to non-depressed mothers, depressed mothers express negativity toward the demands of parenthood and view their role as parent less positively. Depressed mothers also perceive themselves to be less competent and less adequate (Webster-Stratton & Hammond, 1988), to feel less efficacious about their parenting skills (Teti *et al.*, 1990) and about their ability to regulate negative emotions (Garber *et al.*, 1991), have more role restriction, less attachment to their children, and less sense of parenting competence (Frankel & Harmon, 1996). Depressive symptoms such as a sense of helplessness, fatigue, irritability, and lack of interest in many activities may interfere with depressed parent's ability to set a positive emotional tone and to remain responsive to their children's problems or frustration (Seligman, 1975).

OBSERVATION STUDIES

Based on observed parent–child interaction, depressed mothers are less active, less playful, and less contingently responsive, and show less reciprocal vocalization and affectionate contact in interactions with their infants (Field *et al.*, 1990). Depressed mothers are also more negative and critical, and less positive and affirming to their children (Gordon *et al.*, 1989). Ratings of mother–child interactions during a conflict–resolution task revealed that negative and critical interactions, as well as poor task productivity, were associated with children's depressed affect and maladaptive school behavior at a 6-month follow-up period (Burge & Hammen, 1991).

However, some studies show variability in the impact of maternal depression on mother's and children's functioning (Hammen *et al.*, 1987; Teti *et al.*, 1990). Furthermore, maternal diagnostic status is often not predictive of impairment in parenting behaviors or children's functioning (Rutter & Quinton, 1984). Furthermore, there are gender differences as to whether children are affected by maternal depression. Several studies have shown that it is not the mother's diagnostic status which best predict children's functioning (Hammen *et al.*, 1987; Teti *et al.*, 1990), but the severity or chronicity of mother's depression (Hammen *et al.*, 1987; Nolen-Hoeksema *et al.*, 1995). Maternal depression has its largest effects when it occurs in tandem with other risk factors such as poverty and minority group status (Sameroff *et al.*, 1993), marital discord, single-parent status, paternal psychiatric disorders, and low levels of social support (Goodman *et al.*, 1993). It could be that mothers who are more severely and chronically depressed may experience numerous psychosocial stressors such as marital conflict or poverty (Teti *et al.*, 1990). These stressors may negatively affect both the mothers and their children (Hammen *et al.*, 1987). In interviews of parents of 11–16-year olds, Goodyer *et al.* (1993) reported that undesirable life events were significantly more frequent for mothers with a life event history of any psychiatric disorders when compared to mothers without a history of psychiatric disorder. The higher number of negative life events for mothers with a history of any psychopathology may exert a direct negative affect on offspring, and the authors suggest that risk for major depression in adolescence is increased as a function of both maternal psychiatric disorder and an increase in exposure to recent undesirable life events. Depressed mothers also report more social isolation, poorer health, and more life stressors than non-depressed mothers (Frankel & Harmon, 1996).

There has been increasing awareness in recent years that the above factors only constitute a part of the whole picture, and that research should examine the ways in which these factors interact with one another. According to Goodman and Gotlib (1999), four mechanisms may be involved in the transmission of maternal depression to offspring. These include (1) genetics; (2) dysfunctional neuroregulatory mechanisms which disturb emotional regulation processes that in turn increase vulnerability to depression; (3) exposure to negative maternal cognitions, behaviour, and affects. (From a social learning theory perspective, the acquisition of these maladaptive mechanism by offspring of depressed mothers may be facilitated by modeling, observational learning, and reinforcement); and (4) exposure to a stressful environment (e.g., episodic course of depression) which put the offspring at risk for skills deficits and maladaptive cognitive styles and subsequent depression. Their review of the literature showed moderate-to-strong support for these proposed mechanisms. Goodman and Gotlib also argued that the way in which these risk mechanism interact and affect one another may be moderated by the timing and severity of maternal depression, the father's health and involvement with the child, and the child's characteristics (i.e., age and gender).

SINGLE OR MULTI-FACTORIAL MODEL OF RISK FOR DEPRESSION

Although vast research verifies the relationship between maladaptive parenting/attachment and childhood psychopathology, explanations for these effects are multifarious. Thus, research is beginning to concentrate on identifying the mediators and moderators among parenting variables and depression. Some promising results are emerging, in alliance with the development of advanced statistical methods including structural equation modeling (SEM) and hierarchical regression analysis. SEM allows the researcher to examine the relationship among risk factors based on their covariance, thereby specifying whether a certain variable functions as a mediator for the outcome variable, and if so, how large the degree of its effect is. Hierarchical regression analysis allows for the examination of the moderating effect and the predictive value of the interaction among risk factors.

Three main mediating/moderating variables have been found to affect the relationship between the parenting variables and depression. First, negative cognition is fostered from maladaptive parenting patterns. Second, personality traits determine the magnitude and direction of the detrimental effects of negative parenting. Third, demographic variables such as sex and ethnicity play an important role in the manifestation of depressive symptoms under the presence of parental risk factors.

Negative cognition is a central factor in understanding depression. Some eminent theories include negative schemata, learned helplessness, and external locus of control. Some cognitive mediating factors between maladaptive parenting and depressive symptoms include core beliefs (Shah & Waller, 2000), dysfunctional attitudes (Randolph & Dykman, 1998), and external locus of control (Richman & Flaherty, 1986). Through a series of regression analyses, Gustafson (1992) reported that negative parenting leads to irrational beliefs in the child, which triggers depression. Similarly, Shah and Waller (2000) reported that core beliefs mediate between parental style and depressive vulnerability. These studies provide preliminary evidence that cognitive malfunctioning may be a key factor in the manifestation of depressive symptoms. Muris *et al.* (2001) took these results a step further and investigated how the relationship among negative attributional style, coping styles and perceived self-efficacy act as a mediators between parental rearing behavior and depression. The model assumed that negative parental rearing nurtures negative attributional style, which in turn fosters negative coping style and low self-efficacy and results in depression. The model had acceptable fit, although there still remained a direct effect between negative parental rearing and depression that could not be explained from negative cognitions.

Muris *et al.* (2004) proposed that parental control and rejection may be experienced as uncontrollable events by children, which causes them to form negative perceptions of control, which in turn fosters depression. However, the study failed to detect mediational or moderational effects of perceived control.

Although the above studies are explained in terms of maternal influence on the development of the child, a bilateral model has also been proposed in which child development also affects maternal behavior (Elgar *et al.*, 2004).

CONCLUSIONS AND FUTURE DIRECTIONS

The extant literature provides evidence that parental psychopathology, and depression in particular, is associated with the development and stability of depression in offspring. The direction of this association is however still unclear. The most important implication of this review is that it has made us aware of numerous issues which warrant consideration in future studies. These issues include specificity, genetic and environmental effects, protective or resiliency factors, and a focus on prevention.

SPECIFICITY

There is a need to examine the specificity of parental psychopathology and other family risk factors to depression vs. other psychopathology. As reported in numerous studies, parental psychopathology and various other family risk factors (e.g., parents' marital status) in childhood were significantly associated with onset of depression by age 20. However, these adversities are predictive of a wide range of psychiatric disorders such as depression, anxiety, substance, and antisocial disorders (Kendler *et al.*, 1997).

GENETIC AND ENVIRONMENTAL EFFECTS

Most studies which show an association between parental psychopathology and child depression do not enable researchers to tease apart genetic from environmental effects. Therefore, it is not clear whether a specific form of depression (e.g., parental early-onset depression) is related to a greater liability or whether children of parents with early-onset depression are being exposed to parental depression at an earlier age or for a longer duration. Future research is needed to try to disentangle genetic and environmental influences for depression.

PROTECTIVE OR RESILIENCY FACTORS

Most of the literature in the area of depression focuses on factors which increase the risk of disorder. While such a perspective is understandable, future research needs to identify factors within the family which "protect" the child from depression and to identify factors which may optimise child development.

A FOCUS ON PREVENTION

Given the importance of family factors in both the development and the maintenance of depression, and particularly as the literature on protective or resiliency factors grows, attempts should be made to include a family component in prevention programs for depression.

REFERENCES

Ainsworth, M. D. S. (1969). Object relations, dependency, and attachment: A theoretical review of the mother-child relationship. *Child Development*, *40*, 969–1025.

Armsden, G. C., & Greenberg, M. T. (1987). The inventory of parent and peer attachment: Individual differences and their relationship to psychological well-being in adolescence. *Journal of Youth and Adolescence*, *16*, 427–453.

Atkinson, L., Paglia, A., Coolbear, J., Niccols, A., Parker, K. C. H., & Guger, S. (2000). Attachment security: A meta-analysis of maternal mental health correlates. *Clinical Psychology Review*, *20*, 1019–1040.

Beardslee, W., Keller, M. B., Lavori, P. W., Staley, J., & Sacks, N. (1993). The impact of parental affective disorder on depression in offspring: A longitudinal follow-up in a nonreferred sample. *Journal of the American Academy of Child and Adolescent Psychiatry*, *32*, 723–730.

Beardslee, W. R., Keller, M. B., Seifer, R., Lavori, P. W., Staley, J., Podorefsky, D., & Shera, D. (1996). Prediction of adolescent affective disorder: Effects of prior parental affective disorders and child psychopathology. *Journal of the American Academy of Child and Adolescent Psychiatry*, *35*, 279–288.

Beardslee, W. R., Schulz, L. H., & Selman, R. L. (1987). Level of socio-cognitive development, adaptive functioning, and DSM-III diagnoses: Implications of the development of the capacity for mutuality. *Developmental Psychology*, *23*, 807–815.

Beck, C. T. (1999). Maternal depression and child behavior problems. *Journal of Advanced Nursing*, *29*, 623–629.

Blatt, S. J., & Homann, E. (1992). Parent-child interaction in the etiology of dependent and self-critical depression. *Clinical Psychology Review*, *12*, 47–91.

Bowlby, J. (1969). *Attachment and Loss: Vol 1*. New York: Basic Books.

Burge, D., & Hammen, C. (1991). Maternal communication: Predictions of outcome at follow-up in a sample of children at high and low risk for depression. *Journal of Abnormal Psychology*, *100*, 174–180.

Cummings, E. M., & Cicchetti, D. (1990). Toward a transactional model of relations between attachment and depression. In M. Greenberg D. Cicchetti, & E. M. Cummings (Eds.), *Attachment in the Preschool Years: Theory, Research and Intervention* (pp. 339–372). Chicago: University of Chicago Press.

Currier, C., Mann, M. J., Oquendo, M. A., Galfalvy, H., & Mann, J. J. (2005). Sex differences in the familial transmission of mood disorders. *Journal of Affective Disorders*, *95*, 51–60.

Dodge, K. A. (1990). Developmental psychopathology in children of depressed mothers. *Developmental Psychology*, *26*, 3–6.

Elgar, F. J., McGrath, P. J., Waschbusch, D. A., Stewart, S. H., & Curtis, L. J. (2004). Mutual influences on maternal depression and child adjustment problems. *Clinical Psychology Review*, *24*, 441–459.

Essau, C. A. (2004). The association between family factors and depressive disorders in adolescents. *Journal of Youth and Adolescence*, *33*, 365–372.

Fendrich, M., Warner, V., & Weissman, M. M. (1990). Family risk factors, parental depression, and psychopathology in offspring. *Developmental Psychology*, *26*, 40–50.

Fergusson, D. M., Horwood, L. J., & Lynskey, M. T. (1995). Maternal depressive symptoms and depressive symptoms in adolescents. *Journal of Child Psychology and Psychiatry*, *36*, 1161–1178.

Field, T., Healy, B., Goldstein, S., & Guthertz, M. (1990). Developmental psychopathology in children of depressed mothers. *Developmental Psychology*, *26*, 7–14.

Finkelstein, J., Donenberg, G. R., & Martinovich, Z. (2001). Maternal control and adolescent depression: Ethnic differences among clinically referred girls. *Journal of Youth and Adolescence*, *30*, 155–171.

Foley, D. L., Pickles, A., Simonoff, E., Maes, H. H., Silberg, J. L., Hewitt, J. K., & Eaves, L. J. (2001). Parental concordance and comorbidity for psychiatric disorder and associate risks for current psychiatric symptoms and disorders in a community sample of juvenile twins. *Journal of Child Psychology and Psychiatry*, *42*, 381–394.

Frankel, K. A., & Harmon, R. J. (1996). Depressed mothers: They don't always look as bad as they feel. *Journal of the American Academy of Child and Adolescent Psychiatry*, *35*, 289–298.

Garber, J., Braafladt, N., & Zeman, J. (1991). The regulation of sad affect: An information-processing perspective. In J. Garber & K. Dodge (Eds.), *The Development of Emotion Regulation and Dysregulation* (pp. 208–240). New York: Cambridge University Press.

Gerlsma, C., Emmelkamp, P. M. G., & Arrindell, W. A. (1990). Anxiety, depression, and perception of early parenting: A meta-analysis. *Clinical Psychology Review*, *10*, 251–277.

Goodman, S. H. (1992). Understanding the effects of depressed mothers on their children. In E. F. Walker, B. A. Cornblatt, & R. H. Dworkin (Eds.), *Progress in Experimental Personality and Psychopathology Research* (Vol. 15, pp. 47–107). New York: Springer.

Goodman, S. H., & Gotlib, I. H. (1999). Risk for psychopathology in the children of depressed mothers: A developmental model for understanding mechanisms of transmission. *Psychological Review*, *106*, 458–490.

Goodman, S. H., Brogan, D., Lynch, M. E., & Fielding, B. (1993). Social and emotional competence in children of depressed mothers. *Child Development*, *64*, 513–531.

Goodyer, I. M., Cooper, P. J., Vize, C. M., & Ashby, L. (1993). Depression in 11-16-year-old girls: The role of past parental psychopathology and exposure to recent life events. *Journal of Child Psychology and Psychiatry*, *34*, 1103–1115.

Gordon, D., Burge, D., Hammen, C., Adrian, C., Jaenicke, C., & Hiroto, D. (1989). Observations of interactions of depressed women with their children. *American Journal of Psychiatry*, *146*, 50–55.

Gotlib, I. H., & Goodman, S. H. (1999). Children of parents with depression. In W. K. Silverman & T. H. Ollendick (Eds.), *Developmental Issues in the Clinical Treatment of Children* (pp. 415–432). Boston: Allyn & Bacon.

Gustafson, R. (1992). The relationship between perceived parents' child-rearing practices, own later rationality, and own later depression. *Journal of Rational-Emotive and Cognitive-Behavior Therapy*, *10*, 253–258.

Hammen, C. (1991). *Depression Runs in Families: The Social Context of Risk and Resilience in Children of Depressed Mothers*. New York: Springer.

Hammen, C., Adrian, C., Gordon, D., Burge, D., Jaenicke, C., & Hiroto, D. (1987). Children of depressed mothers: Maternal strain and symptom predictors of dysfunction. *Journal of Abnormal Psychology*, *96*, 190–198.

Harrington, R. C., Fudge, H., Rutter, M. L., Bredenkamp, D., Groothues, C., & Pridham, J. (1993). Child and adult depression: A test of continuities with data from a family study. *British of Psychiatry*, *162*, 627–633.

Keller, M. B., Beardslee, W. R., Dorer, D. J., Lavori, P. W., Samuelson, H., & Klerman, G. L. (1986). Impact of severity and chronicity of parental affective illness on adaptive functioning and psychopathology in children. *Archives of General Psychiatry*, *43*, 930–937.

Kendler, K. S., Davis, C. G., & Kessler, R. C. (1997). The familial aggregation of common psychiatric and substance use disorders in the National Comorbidity Survey: A family history study. *British Journal of Psychiatry*, *170*, 541–548.

Kendler, K. S., Gardner, C. O., & Prescott, C. A. (1999). Clinical characteristics of major depression that predict risk of depression in relatives. *Archives of General Psychiatry*, *56*, 322–327.

Klein, D. N. (1990). Symptom criteria and family history in major depression. *American Journal of Psychiatry*, *147*, 850–854.

Klein, D. N., Clark, D. C., Dansky, L., & Margolis, E. T. (1988). Dysthymia in the offspring of parents with primary unipolar affective disorder. *Journal of Abnormal Psychology*, *97*, 265–274.

Klein, D. N., Lewinsohn, P. M., Seeley, J. R., & Rohde, P. (2001). A family study of major depressive disorder in a community sample of adolescents. *Archives of General Psychiatry*, *58*, 13–20.

Klein, D. N., Lewinsohn, P. M., Rohde, P., Seeley, J. R., & Durbin, C. E. (2002). Clinical features of major depressive disorder in adolescents and their relatives: Impact on familial aggregation, implications for phenotype definition, and specificity of transmission. *Journal of Abnormal Psychology*, *111*, 98–106.

Klein, D. N., Shankman, S. A., Lewinsohn, P. M., Rohde, P., & Seeley, J. R. (2004). Family study of chronic depression in a community sample of young adults. *American Journal of Psychiatry*, *161*, 646–653.

Kovacs, M., Feinberg, T. L., Crouse-Novak, M., Paulauskas, S. L., & Finkelstein, R. (1984). Depressive disorders in childhood: I. A longitudinal prospective study of characteristics and recovery. *Archives of General Psychiatry*, *41*, 229–237.

Kovacs, M., Devlin, B., Pollock, M., Richards, C., & Mukerji, P. (1997). A controlled family history study of childhood-onset depressive disorder. *Archives of General Psychiatry*, *54*, 613–623.

Lee, C. M., & Gotlib, I. H. (1991). Adjustment of children of depressed mothers: A ten-month follow-up. *Journal of Abnormal Psychology*, *100*, 473–477.

Lewinsohn, P. M., Klein, D. N., Durbin, E. C., Seeley, J. R., & Rohde, P. (2003). Family study of subthreshold depressive symptoms: Risk factor for MDD? *Journal of Affective Disorders*, *77*, 149–157.

Lewinsohn, P. M., Olino, T. M., & Klein, D. N. (2005). Psychosocial impairment in offspring of depressed parents. *Psychological Medicine*, *35*, 1493–1503.

Lieb, R., Isensee, B., Hofler, M., Pfister, H., & Wittchen, H.-U. (2002). Parental major depression and the risk of depression and other mental disorders in offspring: A prospective-longitudinal community study. *Archives of General Psychiatry*, *59*, 365–374.

Lyons, M. J., Eisen, S. A., Goldberg, J., True, W., Lin, N., Meyer, J. M., Toomey, R., Faraone, S. V., Merla-Ramos, M., & Tsuang, M. T. (1998). A registry-based twin study of depression in men. *Archives of General Psychiatry*, *55*, 468–472.

Marmorstein, N. R., & Iacono, W. G. (2004). Major depression and conduct disorder in youth: Associations with parental psychopathology and parent-child conflict. *Journal Child Psychology and Psychiatry*, *45*, 377–386.

Marmorstein, N. R., Malone, S. M., & Iacono, W. G. (2004). Psychiatric disorders among offspring of depressed mothers: Associations with paternal psychopathology. *American Journal of Psychiatry*, *161*, 1588–1594.

McGuffin, P., Katz, R., Watkins, S., & Rutherford, J. (1996). A hospital based twin register of the heritability of DSM-IV unipolar depression. *Archives of General Psychiatry*, *53*, 129–136.

Muris, P., Meesters, C., Schouten, E., & Hoge, E. (2004). Effects of perceived control on the relationship between perceived parental rearing behaviors and symptoms of anxiety and depression in non-clinical pre-adolescents. *Journal of Youth and Adolescence*, *33*, 51–58.

Muris, P., Schmidt, H., Lambrichs, R., & Meesters, C. (2001). Protective and vulnerability factors of depression in normal adolescents. *Behaviour Research and Therapy*, *39*, 555–565.

Nada Raja, S., McGee, R., & Stanton, W. R. (1992). Perceived attachments to parents and peers and psychological well-being in adolescence. *Journal of Youth and Adolescence*, *21*, 471–485.

Nolen-Hoeksema, S., Mumme, D., Wolfson, A., & Guskin, K. (1995). Helplessness in children of depressed and nondepressed mothers. *Developmental Psychology*, *31*, 377–387.

Nomura, Y., Warner, V., & Wickramaratne, P. (2001). Parents concordant for major depressive disorder and the effect of psychopathology in offspring. *Psychological Medicine*, *31*, 1211–1222.

Orvaschel, H., Walsh-Allis, G., & Ye, W. (1988). Psychopathology in children of parents with recurrent depression. *Journal of Abnormal Child Psychology*, *16*, 17–28.

Parker, G. (1983). Parental affectionless control as an antecedent to adult depression. *Archives of General Psychiatry*, *40*, 956–960.

Phares, V. (2002). Family context: Fathers and other supports. In S. H. Goodman & I. H. Gotlib (Eds.), *Children of Depressed Parents: Mechanisms of Risk and Implications for Treatment* (pp. 203–225). Washington, DC: American Psychological Association.

Randolph, J. J., & Dykman, B. M. (1998). Perceptions of parenting and depression-proneness in the offspring: Dysfunctional attitudes as a mediating mechanism. *Cognitive Therapy and Research*, *22*, 377–400.

Rapee, R. M. (1997). Potential role of childrearing practices in the development of anxiety and depression. *Clinical Psychology Review*, *17*, 47–67.

Richman, J. A., & Flaherty, J. A. (1986). Childhood relationships, adult coping resources and depression. *Social Science and Medicine*, *23*, 709–716.

Rojo-Moreno, L., Livianos-Aldana, L., Cervera-Martinez, G., & Dominguez -Carabantes, J. A. (1999). Rearing style and depressive disorder in adulthood: A controlled study in a Spanish clinical sample. *Social Psychiatry and Psychiatric Epidemiology*, *34*, 548–554.

Rutter, M., & Quinton, D. (1984). Parental psychiatric disorder: Effects on children. *Psychological Medicine*, *14*, 853–880.

Sameroff, A. J., Seifer, R., Baldwin, A., & Baldwin, C. (1993). Stability of intelligence from preschool to adolescence: The influence of social and family risk factors. *Child Development*, *64*, 80–97.

Sanders, M. R., Dadds, M. R., Johnston, B. M., & Cash, R. (1992). Childhood depression and conduct disorder: I. Behavioral, affective, and cognitive aspects of family problem-solving interactions. *Journal of Abnormal Psychology*, *101*, 495–504.

Sato, T., Sakado, K., Uehara, T., Narita, T., Hirano, S., Nishioka, K., & Kasahara, Y. (1998). Dysfunctional parenting as a risk factor to lifetime depression in a sample of employed Japanese adults: Evidence for the "affectionless control" hypothesis. *Psychological Medicine*, *28*, 737–742.

Seligman, M. E. P. (1975). *Helplessness: On Depression, Development, and Death*. San Francisco: Freeman.

Shah, R., & Waller, G. (2000). Parental style and vulnerability to depression: The role of core beliefs. *Journal of Nervous and Mental Disease*, *188*, 19–25.

Sylvester, C., Hyde, T. S., & Reichler, R. J. (1988). Clinical psychopathology among children of adults with panic disorder. In D. L. Dunnar, E. S. Gershon & J. Barrett (Eds.), *In relatives at risk for mental disorders* (pp. 87–102). New York: Raven.

Teri, D. M., Gelfand, D. M., Messsinger, D. S., & Isabella, R. (1995). Maternal depression and the quality of early attachment: An examination of infants, preschoolers, and their mothers. *Developmental Psychology*, *31*, 364–376.

Teti, D. M., Gelfand, D. M., & Pompa, J. (1990). Depressed mothers' behavioral competence with their infants: Demographic and psychosocial correlates. *Development and Psychopathology*, *2*, 259–270.

Warner, V., Weissman, M. M., Fendrich, M., Wickramaratne, P., & Moreau, D. (1992). The course of major depression in the offspring of depressed parents: Incidence, recurrence, and recovery. *Archives of General Psychiatry*, *49*, 795–801.

Warner, V., Mufson, L., & Weissman, M. M. (1995). Offspring at high risk for depression and anxiety: Mechanisms of psychiatric disorder. *Journal of American Academy Child and Adolescent Psychiatry*, *34*, 786–797.

Webster-Stratton, C., & Hammond, M. (1988). Maternal depression and its relationship to life stress, perceptions of child behavior problems, parenting behaviors, and child conduct problems. *Journal of Abnormal Child Psychology, 16*, 299–315.

Weissman, M. M. (1988). Psychopathology in the children of depressed parents: Direct interview studies. In D. L. Dunner, E. S. Gershon, & J. Barret (Eds.), *Relatives at Risk for Mental Disorder* (pp. 143–159). New York: Raven Press.

Weissman, M. M., & Paykel, E. S. (1974). *The Depressed Woman: A Study of Social Relationships.* Chicago: University of Chicago Press.

Weissman, M. M., Merikangas, K. R., John, K., Wickramaratne, P., Prusoff, B. A., & Kidd, K. K. (1986). Family-genetic studies of psychiatric disorders. *Archives of General Psychiatry, 43*, 1104–1116.

Weissman, M. M., Gammon, G. D., John, K., Merikangas, K. R., Prusoff, B. A., & Scholomskas, D. (1987). Children of depressed parents: Increased psychopathology and early onset of major depression. *Archives of General Psychiatry, 44*, 847–853.

Weissman, M. M., Wickramaratne, P., Nomura, Y., Warner, V., Pilowsky, D., & Verdeli, H. (2006). Offspring of depressed parents: 20 years later. *American Journal of Psychiatry, 163*, 1001–1008.

Williamson, D. E., Birmaher, B., Axelson, D. A., Ryan, N. D., & Dahl, R. E. (2004). First episode of depression in children at low and high familial risk for depression. *Journal of American Academy of Child and Adolescent Psychiatry, 43*, 291–297.

Winokur, G., & Clayton, P. (1967). Family history studies: II. Sex differences and alcoholism in primary affective illness. *British Journal of Psychiatry, 113*, 973–979.

16

Marriage and Relationship Issues

Mark A. Whisman and Roselinde Kaiser

Department of Psychology, University of Colorado, Boulder, CO, USA

Over 90% of people within the United States will marry at some point in their lives (Kreider & Fields, 2001), and many people who do not marry will live with a partner in a non-marital familial relationship (Seltzer, 2000). Marriage and similar intimate relationships can therefore be considered among the most important and enduring interpersonal relationships. However, a considerable percentage of people will experience significant problems during some period of time over the course of their relationship (Whisman *et al.*, in press), and nearly 50% of marriages end in separation or divorce (Kreider & Fields, 2001). Just as the achievement of a satisfying intimate relationship is one of the most important goals in life (Roberts & Robins, 2000), difficulty in achieving or maintaining this goal is likely to result in negative personal and emotional outcomes such as depression.

The theoretical importance of marriage and other intimate relationships for understanding and treating depression is grounded in a long history of relational theory and clinical research. For example, Bowlby (1969) proposed that individuals are vulnerable to depression when attachment bonds are disrupted or threatened, and Beach *et al.* (1990) suggested that relationship discord, manifested by low levels of relationship support and coping and elevated levels of negative behaviors and relationship stress, leads to subsequent depression, which in turn leads to higher levels of relationship discord. Ehlers *et al.* (1988) posited that social relationships synchronize or entrain biological rhythms (e.g., sleep/wake cycle, amplitude and phase relationships of pituitary hormones), and that interpersonal problems disrupt these biological rhythms, which in turn result in changes in somatic symptoms, and ultimately, in the onset of depression. Interpersonal psychotherapy for depression (IPT; Klerman *et al.*, 1984) was predicated on the model that interpersonal conflict, including marital conflict, can act as a precipitating factor in the onset of depression.

This chapter is divided into three sections. First, we review the literature on relationship functioning and depression, including research on global relationship discord as well as specific aspects of relationship functioning. We then discuss treatment implications of this research, including a review of the efficacy of couples therapy for depression. In the final section, we propose several directions for future theoretical and empirical development.

RELATIONSHIP FUNCTIONING AND DEPRESSION

GLOBAL EVALUATION OF MARITAL DISCORD

The association between relationship functioning and depression has most often been studied in terms of respondents' global evaluation of their relationship, described in terms of "discord," "distress," or "dissatisfaction." In addition, because much of this research has been conducted on married individuals, in this chapter, we refer to "marital discord" to describe the empirical findings from these studies. However, we use the term "relationship discord" to refer to the theoretical construct that forms the basis of this line of research, as we believe it also applies to other types of intimate relationships. In this section, we review the cross-sectional and longitudinal associations between marital discord, depressive symptoms, and depressive disorders; gender differences in the association between marital discord and depression; and moderators of the association between marital discord and depression.

Cross-Sectional Association

There are a large number of studies that have evaluated the cross-sectional association between marital discord and depressive symptoms. In a meta-analysis of these studies, Whisman (2001b) reported a weighted mean effect size (r) of 0.42 for women (based on 26 studies and 3745 participants) and 0.37 for men (based on 21 studies and 2700 participants). These correlations fall in the medium (0.30) to large (0.50) effect size range, based on the conventions proposed by Cohen (1988). Thus, the association between marital discord and depressive symptoms is reliable and robust for both women and men.

Whereas most of the research on marital discord and depressive symptoms has been based on general community samples, other studies have evaluated this association in samples of married adults selected based on demographic variables. For example, marital discord has been shown to correlate with depressive symptoms in newlyweds (e.g., Senchak & Leonard, 1992), older couples (e.g., Whisman *et al.*, 2006b), and ethnic minority couples (e.g., Trevino *et al.*, 2007).

Marital discord is associated not only with depressive symptoms, but also with major depressive disorder (MDD). Early research on marital discord and MDD involved comparisons of clinical samples of depressed individuals (most often seeking treatment) with non-depressed control couples. Whisman (2001b) conducted a meta-analysis of such studies, and found that the weighted mean effect size (*d*) across studies was 1.75 (which translates into a correlation coefficient of 0.66). The effect size is greater than 0.80, which Cohen (1988) defined as a large effect size, indicating a strong association between marital discord and MDD.

Although informative, studies evaluating marital discord in treatment-seeking or local community samples of depressed individuals may not be representative of the general population. Because epidemiologic studies suggest that only approximately 50% of people with 12-month MDD receive health care treatment (Kessler *et al.*, 2003), research with representative samples is needed to ensure that the association between marital discord and MDD is not limited to people in treatment. Results from several epidemiologic studies have shown that marital discord is indeed associated with depressive disorders in population-based samples in both the United States (McLeod & Eckberg, 1993; Weissman, 1987; Whisman, 1999, 2007) and Canada (Goering *et al.*, 1995). For example, Weissman (1987) analyzed data from the New Haven Epidemiologic Catchment Area (ECA) program and reported that married women and men who were not getting along with their spouses were 25 times more likely to have major depression than married individuals who were getting along. More recently, it has been shown that greater marital discord was reported by people with current (i.e., 12-month) major depression and dysthymia than those without the disorder (Whisman, 1999, 2007). Furthermore, the association between marital functioning and depressive disorders remains significant when controlling for potential confounds of this association, including other dimensions of general interpersonal distress (Whisman *et al.*, 2000) or other Axis I psychiatric disorders (Whisman, 1999).

Longitudinal Associations

Cross-sectional studies of the association between marital discord and either depressive symptoms or depressive disorders are limited in that they do not address the issue of causal direction. Although marital discord may be a consequence of depression in many cases, longitudinal research is needed to establish the role of marital discord as a risk factor for depression. Evidence gathered via prospective studies suggests that marital discord predicts change in depressive symptoms, and this association has been shown in studies using different methodologies and couples that differ in age and length of marriage (e.g., Beach & O'Leary, 1993; Beach *et al.*, 2003; Davila *et al.*, 2003). Furthermore, Davila *et al.* (2003) used growth curve analysis in a sample of newlyweds and demonstrated that increases in either marital discord or depressive symptoms were associated with concomitant increases in the other variable. Interestingly, there was no difference in the two effect sizes, which suggests that marital discord is as likely to influence depression as vice versa.

As with cross-sectional studies, prospective studies that evaluate the association between marital discord and depressive symptoms have been conducted in samples selected because of a specific demographic characteristic. One demographic group that has been widely studied is pregnant women, and the results of these studies suggest that marital discord during pregnancy is a risk factor for postpartum depression. In a meta-analysis of existing longitudinal research including 10 studies and over 1400 participants, Beck (1996) reported a mean effect size (r) of 0.37, which is considered to be a medium effect size (Cohen, 1988), and which is larger than those obtained for several other established predictors of postpartum depression, including history of previous depression (mean $r = 0.29$) and "maternity blues" (mean $r = 0.36$). In a more recent meta-analysis of studies of predictors of postpartum depression that were published between 1990 and 2000, Beck (2001) reported a mean effect size of 0.39, based on 14 studies involving over 1500 participants. Again, this effect size was comparable or larger than that obtained for history of previous depression (mean $r = 0.39$) and maternity blues (mean $r = 0.31$).

Marital discord is prospectively associated not only with depressive symptoms, but also with incidence of depressive disorders. In a community sample of over 900 married individuals who did not meet criteria for a major depressive episode (MDE) at baseline, marital discord at baseline increased the odds by approximately 3-fold for a person to experience a MDE at 12-month follow-up (Whisman & Bruce, 1999), and this association remained significant when controlling for prior history of depression and gender. The association between baseline marital discord and incidence of depressive disorders was replicated in a population-based sample of people in The Netherlands, in which baseline marital discord was associated with increased risk for both total incidence and first incidence of dysthymia and MDD 2 to 3 years later (Overbeek *et al.*, 2006). In research with female twin pairs, elevated spousal problems at baseline were associated with increased risk for onset of major depression 5 years later; baseline levels of spouse support were not associated with risk for depression (Wade & Kendler, 2000b). Finally, not only is marital discord associated with onset of depression, but Hooley and Teasdale (1989) also found that marital discord assessed prior to treatment predicted 9-month depression relapse rates.

Gender Differences

One interesting question that has been studied in several studies is whether there are gender differences in the association between marital discord and depression. Research that addresses this question seeks to understand whether marital discord models of depression can account for the gender difference in depression, which has shown that women are nearly twice as likely as men to experience depression in their lifetime (Nolen-Hoeksema, 1987; Weissman *et al.*, 1993).

It has been suggested, for example, that women's relational traits, identities, and self-representations may make them more responsive than men to disruptive relationship events (e.g., Cross & Madson, 1997), and that gender differences in depression could be due, in part, to gender differences in response to aspects of relationship functioning.

As has already been reviewed, a meta-analysis of the cross-sectional association between marital discord and depressive symptoms found a weighted mean effect size of 0.42 for women and 0.37 for men (Whisman, 2001b). Although the difference between these two correlations is statistically significant, the effect size for this difference is not large. For example, the difference between the two correlations yields an effect size (q) of 0.06, which falls below the cutoff for defining a small effect size, using guidelines proposed by Cohen (1988). Another way to consider the magnitude of this difference is to consider the amount of change in the proportion of variance accounted for by these two correlations, using the formula $r_1^2 - r_2^2$ (Cohen, 1988, p. 114). Evaluated from this perspective, marital discord accounts for only 4% ($0.42^2 - 0.37^2$) more variance in depressive symptoms for women than for men. Thus, whereas marital discord and depressive symptoms are more strongly associated for women than for men, the degree to which these associations differ is not large. In comparison, the strength of the cross-sectional association between marital discord and major depression is not moderated by gender (Uebelacker & Whisman, 2006; Whisman, 2007).

Research that has evaluated whether the prospective association between marital discord and depressive symptoms is greater for women than for men has yielded mixed results. Two longitudinal studies, in which gender moderation was evaluated using multiple regression, came to conflicting conclusions. Beach and O'Leary (1993) failed to find evidence for gender moderation, whereas Dehle and Weiss (1998) found that gender was a significant moderator, with marital discord predicting greater increases in depressive symptoms for women than for men. More recently, structural equation modeling has been used to evaluate gender differences in the longitudinal association between marital discord and depressive symptoms, with mixed results. Some studies have found a stronger association between baseline marital quality and depressive symptoms for women than for men (Fincham *et al.*, 1997), whereas other studies have failed to find evidence of gender differences (Beach *et al.*, 2003). Finally, hierarchical linear modeling has been used to evaluate gender differences in the longitudinal association between marital discord and depressive symptoms. Both Kurdek (1998) and Davila *et al.* (2003) found little evidence for gender differences in within-subject associations between these variables over time. In comparison, Beach *et al.* (1999) found evidence of gender differences when they reanalyzed the data from the Fincham *et al.* (1997) study using the analytic procedures employed by Kurdek (1998). In summary, although differences in samples, analyses, and follow-up periods make it difficult to draw firm conclusions from prior studies, there do not appear to be clear and robust gender differences in the prospective associations between marital discord and depressive symptoms.

Moderating Variables

Not all people in discordant relationships are depressed, nor are all depressed people in discordant relationships. Therefore, investigators have also sought to identify moderators of the association between marital discord and depression. Regarding concurrent depressive symptoms, marital discord is more strongly associated with symptoms for (a) men (but not women) with lower levels of self-esteem (Culp & Beach, 1998), (b) people with higher levels of anxious-ambivalent attachment (which reflects a desire to be closer than the partner seems to want) (Scott & Cordova, 2002), and (c) people with higher levels of blame-orientated attributions about their partner's negative behaviors (Gordon *et al.*, 2005). The longitudinal strength of the association between women's marital discord and depressive symptoms appears to be stronger for women in poverty (Liu & Chen, 2006). Marital discord is also more strongly associated with a concurrent diagnosis of major depression for (a) older individuals (Whisman, 2007) and (b) married (vs. cohabiting) individuals (Uebelacker & Whisman, 2006). Although marital discord was found to be more strongly associated with MDE for married people with higher levels of neuroticism, other potential moderating variables – demographics (gender, age, race/ethnicity, length of relationship), self-esteem, parental history of depression, and childhood loss (parental divorce, parental death) – did not moderate the association between marital discord and MDE (Uebelacker & Whisman, 2006).

Alternative Explanations

Before closing the review of the association between marital discord and depression, it is important to consider potential criticisms of this line of research. It could be argued that insofar as marital discord is most often measured by self-report, then the association between marital discord and depression could be due to negative perceptions or cognitive biases associated with depression. Even in prospective studies, participants' negative views of their relationship might reflect a negative cognitive perception, rather than an actual representation of their relationship, and it could be that it is this negative cognition that is the "true" risk factor for depression. However, several lines of evidence argue against such an interpretation. First, data from spouses suggest (a) spouses of depressed individuals report greater level of marital discord than spouses of non-depressed clinical (e.g., Coyne *et al.*, 2002) or non-clinical individuals (e.g., Bauserman *et al.*, 1995); (b) depressed individuals and their spouses report similar levels of marital discord (e.g., Basco *et al.*, 1992); and (c) Spouses' level of marital discord has predicted a person's own level of depression in both cross-sectional (e.g., McLeod & Eckberg, 1993) and longitudinal studies (e.g., Beach *et al.*, 2003). These studies suggest that elevated levels of marital discord reported by depressed individuals are more than just negative biases. Second, as reviewed in the following section of the chapter, observers' ratings of couples' communication covary with depression, suggesting that other people perceive differences in the relationships of people with depression.

MARITAL PROCESSES

In addition to studying general risk factors such as marital discord, investigators have identified specific aspects of relationship functioning that are associated with depression. We next review research on specific marital processes that have been studied as cross-sectional and longitudinal predictors of depression, including communication, partner criticism, relationship life events, relationship cognitions, and positive and negative partner behavior.

Communication

The most widely studied relationship process examined in the context of depression is marital communication. Because a comprehensive review of this research is beyond the scope of this chapter, the following review should be viewed as illustrative rather than exhaustive.

Evidence indicates that depressed individuals report greater dissatisfaction with their affective and problem-solving communication than non-depressed individuals (Basco *et al.*, 1992). Self-reports of partners of depressed individuals also reveal a linkage between communication and depression. For example, spouses of current and remitted depressed women report greater use of coercive problem-solving tactics than spouses of controls (Hammen & Brennan, 2002) and spouses of patients with remitted depressive or bipolar disorders report lower levels of emotional and practical support, poorer consensus, unity, and expressions of affection, as compared to controls (Levkovitz *et al.*, 2000).

Although self-reports of communication are informative, as with any self-report measures, they are subject to demand characteristics and responses biases. Therefore, researchers have also studied the association between depression and communication using behavioral observation in a controlled laboratory setting. These studies have revealed that compared to control couples, couples in which one person is depressed are poorer problem-solvers (Basco *et al.*, 1992), and exhibit more negative behaviors (e.g., McCabe & Gotlib, 1993; Ruscher & Gotlib, 1988) and greater levels of hostility (e.g., Kahn *et al.*, 1985; Kowalik & Gotlib, 1987). Researchers have additionally examined the interaction patterns of couples with a depressed spouse using sequential analyses, in which one may examine whether a specific type of behavior or affect by one partner changes the likelihood that the other partner will demonstrate a particular behavior or affect. Biglan *et al.* (1985) found that depressed women exhibited lower rates of problem-solving behaviors and higher rates of depressive behaviors than their non-depressed husbands or the non-depressed couples, and also that depressive behavior on the part of the wife functioned as a suppressor of her partner's negative behavior, whereas husbands' aggressive behaviors suppressed wives' immediate subsequent depressive behaviors. Later studies, however, suggested that the sequential pattern was limited to younger couples (Nelson & Beach, 1990), and that the pattern was better explained by marital discord than depression (Jackman-Cram *et al.*, 2006; Schmaling & Jacobson, 1990). Gender differences in base-rates and sequences of marital interaction behaviors were evaluated by Johnson and Jacob (1997, 2000).

They found that couples with a depressed wife displayed comparable patterns of affect reciprocity to those of non-depressed couples, but the characteristic interactions in which the wife was depressed were depressive behaviors exhibited by the wife. In comparison, depressed husbands and their spouses had unique interactions, such that when depressed husbands expressed positivity, this suppressed wives' positivity and increased wives' negativity.

Whereas much of the research on depression and marital communication has been cross-sectional, Whitton *et al.* (2007) evaluated this association prospectively in a sample of couples assessed prior to marriage and 1 year later. For wives, negative marital interaction indirectly had an impact on subsequent depressive symptoms through the mediator of relationship confidence (i.e., the belief that one's relationship will be successful into the future); negative marital interaction did not predict change in depressive symptoms in husbands.

Expressed and Perceived Criticism

One aspect of communication that has been studied in some depth is the degree of criticism that is expressed by a partner about the depressed person. Living with a depressed person can increase the burden of care for spouses (Coyne *et al.*, 1987). For example, Coyne *et al.* (2002) reported that spouses living with a depressed individual express affection more rarely than spouses of community controls, and that compared to a control group, husbands of depressed women were more likely to report frequent arguments, differing social needs, and being blamed for things going wrong. Consequently, spouses or partners of depressed individuals may develop negative views of the depressed person, which in turn contribute to maintenance or relapse of depression. In support of this perspective, spouses of depressed women have been shown to rate their wives more negatively on both depression-related and depression-neutral traits, compared to spouses of non-depressed women (Sacco *et al.*, 1993). Spouses of depressed women also made more dispositional attributions for negative events involving their wives than did the spouses of non-depressed women. Husbands of depressed women have been shown to rate their wives more negatively on measures of dependence, directiveness, and detachment when compared to husbands of non-depressed women (Birtchnell, 1991). Levkovitz *et al.* (2003) found that spouses of both acute and remitted depressives reported high levels of criticism toward their depressed partners. Moreover, when compared to spouses of clinical controls, spouses of remitted depressed individuals ranked their partners lower on positive and higher on negative qualities. These results suggest that negative appraisals of depressed persons may persist even in the face of remitted depression, and may contribute to vulnerability for relapse and recurrence.

The idea that partner criticism may be important for depressive relapse is supported by Hooley and Teasdale (1989), who found that 9-month relapse was associated not only with marital distress, but also with spouse criticism. Interestingly, the strongest predictor of relapse was obtained with a 10-point Likert-type scale, which asked how critical the patient thought their spouse or partner was of them. A positive association between perceived criticism and depressive relapse has also been found in Korean outpatients (Kwon *et al.*, 2006), which suggests that perceived criticism may be an important factor predicting depression across cultures. Furthermore, although perceived criticism is positively correlated with interview-based measures of expressed emotion (Hooley & Teasdale, 1989) and ratings of marital interaction (Kwon *et al.*, 2006), it appears to be independent of depressive symptoms (Hooley & Teasdale, 1989; Riso *et al.*, 1996), personality or global functioning (Riso *et al.*, 1996), or dependency-related dysfunctional attitudes (Kwon *et al.*, 2006).

Relationship Stressors

Another relationship process that has been studied with respect to depression concerns relationship stressors. Cano and O'Leary (2000) studied the impact of negative relationship-oriented events that devalue the individual in relation to the self or others (i.e., "humiliating" events; Brown *et al.*, 1995), such as discovery of infidelity, spouse-initiated separation/divorce, or separation/divorce due to infidelity or violence, and reported that the occurrence of these events was associated with increased risk of major depression. Similarly, Christian-Herman *et al.* (2001) evaluated the impact of severe negative marital events on incidence of major depression among women with no history of depression. They found that the rate of major depression among women who had experienced a severe event (most commonly involving separation or divorce, extramarital affairs, and physical aggression) was higher than reported incidence rates in representative samples of women.

Relationship Cognitions

A third relationship process variable that has been studied with respect to depression focuses on cognitions about one's partner and one's relationship. Researchers have examined whether depression is associated with the types of attributions people make about their partner's negative behavior. Attributions are most often measured in terms of causal attributions (i.e., the degree to which people attribute the cause of partner's negative behavior as stable, global, and due to something about the partner) and responsibility attributions (i.e., the degree to which people believe their partner's negative behavior is intentional, blameworthy, and selfishly motivated), and a large body of empirical work supports the association between attributions and marital discord (for a review, see Bradbury & Fincham, 1990). Negative (or distress-maintaining) causal and responsibility attributions have been found to be positively correlated with concurrent depressive symptoms (Fincham *et al.*, 1989; Gordon *et al.*, 2005; Heim & Snyder, 1991) and major depression (Uebelacker & Whisman, 2005), and with longitudinal increases in depressive symptoms (Fincham & Bradbury, 1993).

The association between depression and other types of relationship cognitions has been less frequently studied. Compared to non-depressed wives, wives with major depression are more likely to endorse the belief that disagreements between partners are a threat to their relationship, that partners should sense each others' needs without overt communication, that partners cannot change themselves or their relationship, and that one must be a "perfect" sexual partner; depression was not, however, associated with the belief that the relationship needs of men and women are radically different (Uebelacker & Whisman, 2005). Associations between depression and dysfunctional relationship beliefs remained significant when controlling for marital discord.

Positive and Negative Partner Behavior

A final relationship process variable that has been studied with respect to depression is the rate of pleasing and displeasing partner behavior. Behavioral theories of depression have long emphasized that depression results from low rates of positive behaviors and high rates of aversive behaviors. Two studies have shown that the rates of negative partner behavior are positively correlated with levels of depressive symptoms (Assh & Byers, 1996) and with major depression in women (Uebelacker & Whisman, 2005).

SPECIFICITY OF THE ASSOCIATION BETWEEN MARITAL FUNCTIONING AND DEPRESSION

The cross-sectional association between marital discord and psychopathology does not appear to be specific to depression. Marital discord has been shown to be (a) concurrently associated with a range of mood, anxiety, and substance use disorders in population-based samples (Goering *et al.*, 1996; McLeod, 1994; Whisman, 1999, 2007); (b) prospectively associated with elevated risk of onset of substance use disorders in the United States (Whisman *et al.*, 2006a), and with broad-band classes of anxiety and substance use disorders and separate diagnoses of social phobia and alcohol abuse in The Netherlands (Overbeek *et al.*, 2006); (c) prospectively associated with relapse for substance use disorders (Fals-Stewart *et al.*, 2001); and (d) concurrently and prospectively associated with a variety of medical conditions, many of which co-occur with depression (for a review, see Kiecolt-Glaser & Newton, 2001). Similarly, marital processes that have been shown to be correlated with or predictors of depression do not appear to be specific to depression. For example, negative marital communication has been associated with anxiety (Chambless *et al.*, 2002) and substance use disorders (e.g., Fals-Stewart & Birchler, 1998). Perceived criticism has been shown to predict treatment outcome for people with anxiety disorders (e.g., Chambless & Steketee, 1999) and relapse for people with substance use disorders (Fals-Stewart *et al.*, 2001). Furthermore, many of the communication behaviors associated with depression may be better explained by marital discord (e.g., Schmaling & Jacobson, 1990). Thus, marital discord and some relationship processes do not appear to be specific to depression, but perhaps could best be described as *generic risks* (Coie *et al.*, 1993) for adverse mental and physical health outcomes.

How should the lack of specificity between relationship functioning and depression be interpreted? From a public health perspective, a generic risk factor that is associated with multiple disorders and outcomes is potentially more important than a risk factor for only a single disorder.

> If generic risks can be identified and altered in a population, this can have a positive influence on a range of mental health problems, as well as job productivity, and can reduce the need for many health, social, and correctional services. This strategy has a higher potential payoff for society than does a focused attack on controlling a single major, but rarely occurring, disorder
>
> (Coie *et al.*, 1993, p. 1014).

TREATMENT IMPLICATIONS

If marital functioning is associated with the onset, maintenance, and course of depression, then people in discordant relationships who engage in treatments that do not specifically modify relationship functioning may have poorer outcomes than people in better relationships. Generally, results show that relationship difficulties at the beginning of treatment are associated with poorer outcome at the end of treatment (Rounsaville *et al.*, 1979) and at follow-up (Rounsaville *et al.*, 1980), and with greater risk for relapse (Hooley & Teasdale, 1989). Recovery following hospitalization is also associated with depressed individual's ratings of the current marital relationship (Goering *et al.*, 1992). The effects of relationship functioning on treatment outcome appear to be independent of the type of individual treatment, as illustrated in results from the Treatment of Depression Collaborative Research Program (TDCRP). Results from this large-scale treatment study for depression indicated that poorer post-treatment marital adjustment (Kung & Elkin, 2000; Whisman, 2001a) and less marital improvement over the course of treatment (Kung & Elkin, 2000) predicted higher levels of depressive symptoms at follow-up.

Finally, there is some evidence that marital discord does not improve following individual treatments for depression. For example, cognitive therapy (CT) (Beach & O'Leary, 1992; Jacobson *et al.*, 1991) did not result in significant improvements in marital discord for people who were in discordant relationships at the beginning of treatment. In depressed individuals who differed in their level of marital discord, individual treatments resulted in significant improvement in marital adjustment from before to after therapy, but these effects were largely mediated by change in depression, suggesting that the effects of individual treatments on marital functioning are largely indirect (Whisman, 2001a).

COUPLES THERAPY

The above research indicates that marital discord (a) is a correlate of both depressive symptoms and diagnostic depression, (b) predicts subsequent increases in depressive symptoms and the onset of diagnostic depression, and (c) predicts poorer outcome to individual treatments for depression, which has led researchers to consider the possibility that couples therapy may be an effective treatment for depression. In this section, we provide a brief review of the effectiveness of couples therapy as a treatment for depression.

The approach to couples therapy that has received the most attention from researchers in treating depression is cognitive-behavioral couples therapy (CBCT; Beach *et al.*, 1990; Epstein & Baucom, 2002). This treatment focuses on improving communication and problem-solving skills, increasing the frequency of positive behaviors in the relationship, and modifying dysfunctional beliefs people have about their partners and their relationships. Beach and O'Leary (1992) examined the efficacy of CBCT and individual CT relative to a waitlist control group for couples who were experiencing marital discord and in which the wife met diagnostic criteria for either major depression or dysthymia. CBCT was as effective as CT in reducing wives' depressive symptoms at the end of treatment, and both treatments were more effective than the waitlist control condition. Wives experienced a significant increase in marital satisfaction from pre- to post-therapy in the CBCT condition, and reported higher marital satisfaction scores post-treatment than wives in CT or waitlist control conditions; wives in the other two conditions did not demonstrate an increase in satisfaction and did not show group differences post-treatment. At 1-year follow-up, improvements in depressive symptoms had been equally maintained in the CBCT and CT groups. However, the CBCT group reported significantly higher marital satisfaction than did the CT group, suggesting that CBCT was a more effective treatment for marital discord than individual CT for depressed women.

Jacobson *et al.* (1991) compared the effectiveness of CBCT and CT, singly and in combination, in the treatment of wives' depression in couples that varied in their level of marital discord. The combined (CO) treatment included both CBT and CT sessions. All treatment groups were equally successful at alleviating depression. However, level of marital discord had an impact on treatment efficacy, as women who received CT experienced decreases in depression regardless of their level of marital discord, whereas CBCT was more effective in alleviating depression when women were in discordant relationships. All groups showed improvements in marital satisfaction, but level of marital discord again played a role in treatment efficacy. In general, non-discordant couples did not show notable change in marital satisfaction regardless of treatment type, but among discordant couples, only CBCT led to significant improvements in marital satisfaction. A 1-year follow-up of these couples showed that gains were maintained in all three treatment groups, and CBCT was comparable to CT for couples who were in discordant marriages at the beginning of the study (Jacobson *et al.*, 1993).

Emanuels-Zuurveen and Emmelkamp (1996) evaluated the efficacy of a slightly modified version of CBCT that initially focused on problems associated with depression that may interfere with marital therapy before shifting the focus to communication skills. They compared this treatment with CT. Both treatments were equally effective in reducing depressive symptoms, depressive behavior, and dysfunctional cognitions. Couples therapy resulted in greater improvement in relationship functioning evidenced by greater satisfaction, better communication, and lower levels of expressed emotion, however.

Teichman, *et al.* (1995) proposed that interpersonal patterns play a role in maintaining depression, and sought to alter these patterns through couples-based cognitive interventions. The couples-based cognitive intervention was compared to individual CT and to waitlist control. Results demonstrated that individuals in the couples therapy condition had significantly fewer depressive symptoms than individuals in the other two conditions; individual CT was no more effective than the waitlist condition. At a 6-month follow-up, however, the rate of recovery was equal between individuals in the couples and CT conditions.

Whereas several clinical trials have evaluated variants of cognitive-behavioral approaches to couples therapy in treating depression, other approaches to couples therapy have been evaluated less frequently. An early couples therapy was developed for treating depression based on interpersonal psychotherapy (IPT; Klerman *et al.*, 1984). This conjoint treatment for depressed patients with marital disputes (IPT-CM) adopts the same methods and focuses on the same problems as IPT, but the partner is included in each session and treatment focuses on communication and intimacy (Weissman *et al.*, 2000). In a small pilot study, people who received IPT-CM or individual IPT improved equally in depression and social functioning, but both members of couples in IPT-CM reported greater improvements in marital adjustment (Foley *et al.*, 1989).

Emotion-focused couples therapy (EFT; Johnson, 1996) is based on adult attachment theory and integrates techniques from the experiential and family systems approaches. The primary target of change in this model is attachment insecurity, rather than marital discord, and the goals of treatment are: (a) to identify repetitive negative interaction cycles that reflect attachment insecurities; (b) to reframe these cycles in terms of the underlying attachment needs; and (c) to facilitate the expression and the acceptance of one another's attachment needs. In a small pilot study of clinically depressed women in couples where at least one partner was moderately distressed about the marriage, EFT was as effective as antidepressants in reducing depressive symptoms (Dessaulles *et al.*, 2003).

Systemic couples therapy (Jones & Asen, 2000) combines strategic and structural therapy techniques with feminist, narrative, and social constructionist ideas. Its goal is the development of new ways to interact and interruption of problematic cycles of behavior to shift negative attributions. In a randomized controlled trial for depressed patients living with a critical spouse, couples therapy had lower rates of attrition and resulted in lower self-reported depression severity through a 2-year follow-up, as compared to antidepressants (Leff *et al.*, 2000).

In addition to evaluating outcome, these studies examined mediators of change to begin to address questions about "how" couples therapy works in treating depression. Jacobson *et al.* (1991) and Emanuels-Zuurveen and Emmelkamp (1996) reported that pre- to post-treatment changes in marital satisfaction covaried with changes in depressive symptoms. Beach and O'Leary (1992) conducted formal tests of mediation, and found changes in marital adjustment mediated the effects of CBCT on change in depressive symptoms. Taken together, these results suggest that at least for cognitive-behavioral approaches, couples therapy alleviates depression by improving marital quality.

In summary, variations of CBCT have been shown to be effective in treating depression and improving marital discord. Although results from other approaches appear promising, there are too few clinical trials to draw firm conclusions regarding their efficacy.

DIRECTIONS FOR FUTURE THEORY AND RESEARCH DEVELOPMENT

Because marital functioning is important in the onset, course, and treatment of depression, one of the biggest challenges facing researchers interested in relationship risk factors for depression is to incorporate other known features of depression into their relationship models (Whisman, 2001b). To illustrate, one well-established fact regarding depression is that women are approximately twice as likely to be depressed as men (Weissman *et al.*, 1993). Can relationship models account for this gender difference? Whisman *et al.* (2006c) advanced several explanations that could account for the gender difference in depression from a relationship perspective. Given the previously reviewed research findings that indicate (a) cross-sectional associations between marital discord and major depression are not moderated by gender (Uebelacker & Whisman, 2006; Whisman, 2007), (b) gender differences in the cross-sectional association between marital discord and depressive symptoms are small (Whisman, 2001b), and (c) prospective associations between marital discord and depressive symptoms are not consistently moderated by gender, gender differences in depression are unlikely to be rooted in a differential association between marital discord and depression for women compared to men. Alternative explanations are needed for the gender difference in rates of depression. Other potential factors that could contribute to elevated risks for depression for women include higher levels of marital discord in women compared to men (e.g., Mickelson *et al.*, 2006) and increased likelihood of experiencing relationship traumas. For example, men are about 1.5 times more likely than women to report lifetime history of extramarital affairs (Laumann *et al.*, 1994) and to perpetrate severe physical aggression (Straus & Gelles, 1986). Consequently, gender differences in rates of depression may be due to gender differences in exposure to relationship risk factors, rather than to responses to such factors. Gender should be considered in research on relationship functioning and depression to more fully understand how relationship factors may contribute to gender differences in depression.

A second challenge facing researchers interested in evaluating marital risk factors for depression is establishing the specificity of the association between marital risk factors and depression, when controlling for other risk factors for depression. For example, the personality trait of neuroticism is a significant risk factor for depression, as well as a risk factor for marital discord. As such, it is possible that the association between marital discord and depression is spurious, and secondary to their shared association with neuroticism. To demonstrate that this is not the case, research must evaluate whether marital discord predicts depression, while statistically controlling for neuroticism. In one illustration of this type of study, Whisman *et al.* (2006b) found that marital discord was associated with depressive symptoms in older individuals, controlling for neuroticism and other personality factors. Greater confidence could be placed in the association between marital functioning and depression if future studies show that this association remains significant when controlling for other established risk factors for depression.

It is important not only to rule out other risk factors for depression as rival explanations for the association between relationship functioning and depression, but also to consider how these variables might influence and be influenced by relationship functioning. Thus, a third challenge facing researchers interested in evaluating relationship risk factors for depression is to incorporate other risk factors for depression into relationship models, to provide more integrative models of depression. For example, Davila *et al.* (1997) applied Hammen's (1991) stress generation model of depression in the context of marriage, and found that wives' depressive symptoms led to increased marital stress, which in turn led to increased depressive symptoms. Evaluating other models of depression within a relationship context, therefore, may help to expand the explanatory power of relationship models in understanding depression.

One way in which other risk factors for depression may be incorporated into relationship models of depression is to evaluate whether these factors moderate the association between relationship functioning and depression. First, there may be synergistic effects between relationship functioning and other risk factors for depression. Neuroticism moderates the cross-sectional association between marital discord and major depression (Uebelacker & Whisman, 2006) and the longitudinal association between marital discord and depressive symptoms (Davila *et al.*, 2003; Karney, 2001); compared to people lower in neuroticism, the strength of the association between marital discord and depression is greater for people higher in neuroticism. Thus, there appears to be a synergistic effect between marital discord and neuroticism in predicting depression. Second, low levels of marital discord (or higher levels of marital support) may serve as a buffer against the deleterious effects of other risk factors for depression. As with social support in general, low levels of marital discord or high levels of marital support may buffer the effects of stressful life events, which have been found to predict the onset of major depression (e.g., Kendler *et al.*, 1999). In support of this perspective, a population-based prospective study of married adults found that the stressor of becoming a caregiver for a biological parent or spouse was associated with a greater increase in depressive symptoms for people that reported a higher level of marital disagreement at baseline (Choi & Marks, 2006). In comparison, a population-based longitudinal study of Caucasian female twins found that neither partner support nor partner problems consistently moderated the association between stressful life events and onset of major depression or depressive symptoms (Wade & Kendler, 2000a). However, assessments of stressful life events and depression onset in this study were based on 5-year retrospective reports; more frequent assessments of these constructs over shorter time periods would provide a stronger test of the buffering effect of low marital discord on the association between stressful life events and depression.

A fourth challenge for researchers interested in evaluating relationship risk factors for depression is to expand the kinds of couples that are being studied. As previously noted, most of the research on relationship functioning and depression has focused on married couples. However, cohabiting unions are becoming increasingly common in the United States, and are becoming "more like formal marriage in that both are childrearing institutions" (Seltzer, 2000, p. 1247). Indeed, according to the 2000 United States Census, there are nearly 5.5 million unmarried-partner households in the United States, which represent 4.9% of all households. Consequently, research is needed on the role of relationship risk factors and processes in other types of couples, including dating, cohabiting, and same-sex couples.

As specific aspects of relationship functioning that are associated with depression become identified in theory and research, interventions that target these aspects can be developed and incorporated in couples treatments for depression. This iterative process hopefully will result in more effective couples treatments, as evidenced by better and more sustained outcomes following treatment. Although this idea has intuitive appeal, research is needed to determine that the addition of such interventions actually results in lower depression. For example, in developing systemic couples therapy, the authors first piloted a treatment that specifically sought to reduce criticism by the partner, a strategy predicated on the evidence that perceived and actual criticism predict the course of depression (Hooley & Teasdale, 1989). Techniques to reduce criticism, however, had little impact on depression, and were therefore dropped from the treatment package (Leff *et al.*, 2000). As this example illustrates, evaluating the impact of interventions for a risk factor for depression is an important necessary step in improving upon the effectiveness of couples therapy for depression. Finally, in evaluating the effectiveness of couples therapy for depression, researchers may need to broaden their definition of treatment success with respect to relationship outcomes. Relationship dissolution is typically viewed as a negative outcome for couples therapy for relationship discord. However, separating from an uncaring partner was found to predict long-term reduction in depressive symptoms for people with major depression (Hickie & Parker, 1992), and separation from a critical partner has been proposed as a mechanism for the efficacy of systemic couples therapy (Leff *et al.*, 2003). Thus, ending a bad relationship may prove to be a positive outcome for couples therapy that involves depressed individuals.

CONCLUSION

A large body of research supports the perspective that global evaluations of one's relationship and several key components of relationship functioning demonstrate significant cross-sectional associations with depressive symptoms and major depression and predict change in depressive symptoms and the onset, course, and relapse of episodes of major depression. Furthermore, marital functioning is associated with short- and long-term treatment outcome for depressed individuals, and couples therapy is effective in treating depression and improving marital discord. In summary, the weight of clinical and research evidence clearly indicates that marriage and relationship issues are important factors to consider in a comprehensive understanding of depression and its treatment.

REFERENCES

Assh, S. D., & Byers, E. S. (1996). Understanding the co-occurrence of marital distress and depression in women. *Journal of Social and Personal Relationships, 13*, 537–552.

Basco, M. R., Prager, K. J., Pita, J. M., Tamir, L. M., & Stephens, J. J. (1992). Communication and intimacy in the marriages of depressed patients. *Journal of Family Psychology, 6*, 184–194.

Bauserman, S. A. K., Arias, I., & Craighead, W. E. (1995). Marital attributions in spouses of depressed patients. *Journal of Psychopathology and Behavioral Assessment, 17*, 231–249.

Beach, S. R., & O'Leary, K. D. (1992). Treating depression in the context of marital discord: Outcome and predictors of response of marital therapy versus cognitive therapy. *Behavior Therapy, 23*, 507–528.

Beach, S. R., & O'Leary, K. D. (1993). Marital discord and dysphoria: For whom does the marital relationship predict depressive symptomatology? *Journal of Social and Personal Relationships, 10*, 405–420.

Beach, S. R. H., Davey, A., & Fincham, F. D. (1999). The time has come to talk of many things: A commentary on Kurdek (1998) and the emerging field of marital processes in depression. *Journal of Family Psychology, 13*, 663–668.

Beach, S. R. H., Katz, J., Kim, S., & Brody, G. H. (2003). Prospective effects of marital satisfaction on depressive symptoms in established marriages: A dyadic model. *Journal of Social and Personal Relationships, 20*, 355–371.

Beach, S. R. H., Sandeen, E. E., & O'Leary, K. D. (1990). *Depression in Marriage: A Model for Etiology and Treatment*. New York: Guilford Press.

Beck, C. T. (1996). A meta-analysis of predictors of postpartum depression. *Nursing Research, 45*, 297–303.

Beck, C. T. (2001). Predictors of postpartum depression: An update. *Nursing Research, 50*, 275–285.

Biglan, A., Hops, H., Sherman, L., Friedman, L. S., Arthur, J., & Osteen, V. (1985). Problem-solving interactions of depressed women and their husbands. *Behavior Therapy, 16*, 431–451.

Birtchnell, J. (1991). Negative modes of relating, marital quality and depression. *British Journal of Psychiatry, 158*, 648–657.

Bowlby, J. (1969). *Attachment and Loss*: vol. 1. New York: Basic Books.

Bradbury, T. N., & Fincham, F. D. (1990). Attributions in marriage: Review and critique. *Psychological Bulletin, 107*, 3–33.

Brown, G. W., Harris, T. O., & Hepworth, C. (1995). Loss, humiliation and entrapment among women developing depression: A patient and nonpatient comparison. *Psychological Medicine, 25*, 7–21.

Cano, A., & O'Leary, K. D. (2000). Infidelity and separations precipitate major depressive episodes and symptoms of nonspecific depression and anxiety. *Journal of Consulting and Clinical Psychology*, *68*, 774–781.

Chambless, D. L., Fauerbach, J. A., Floyd, F. J., Wilson, K. A., Remen, A. L., & Renneberg, B. (2002). Marital interaction of agoraphobic women: A controlled, behavioral observation study. *Journal of Abnormal Psychology*, *111*, 502–512.

Chambless, D. L., & Steketee, G. (1999). Expressed emotion and behavior therapy outcome: A prospective study with obsessive-compulsive and agoraphobic outpatients. *Journal of Consulting and Clinical Psychology*, *67*, 658–665.

Choi, H., & Marks, N. F. (2006). Transition to caregiving, marital disagreement, and psychological well-being: A prospective U.S. national study. *Journal of Family Issues*, *27*, 1701–1722.

Christian-Herman, J. L., O'Leary, K. D., & Avery-Leaf, S. (2001). The impact of severe negative events in marriage on depression. *Journal of Social and Clinical Psychology*, *20*, 25–44.

Cohen, J. (1988). *Statistical Power Analysis for the Behavioral Sciences* (2nd ed.). Hillsdale, NJ: Lawrence Erlbaum Associates.

Coie, J. D., Watt, N. F., West, S. G., Hawkins, J. D., Asarnow, J. R., Markman, H. J. *et al.* (1993). The science of prevention: A conceptual framework and some directions for a national research program. *American Psychologist*, *48*, 1013–1022.

Coyne, J. C., Kessler, R. C., Tal, M., Turnbull, J., Wortman, C. B., & Greden, J. F. (1987). Living with a depressed person. *Journal of Consulting and Clinical Psychology*, *55*, 347–352.

Coyne, J. C., Thompson, R., & Palmer, S. C. (2002). Marital quality, coping with conflict, marital complaints, and affection in couples with a depressed wife. *Journal of Family Psychology*, *16*, 26–37.

Cross, S. E., & Madson, L. (1997). Models of the self: Self-construals and gender. *Psychological Bulletin*, *122*, 5–37.

Culp, L. N., & Beach, S. R. H. (1998). Marriage and depressive symptoms: The role and bases of self-esteem differ by gender. *Psychology of Women Quarterly*, *22*, 647–663.

Davila, J., Bradbury, T. N., Cohan, C. L., & Tochluk, S. (1997). Marital functioning and depressive symptoms: Evidence for a stress generation model. *Journal of Personality and Social Psychology*, *73*, 849–861.

Davila, J., Karney, B. R., Hall, T. W., & Bradbury, T. N. (2003). Depressive symptoms and marital satisfaction: Within-subject associations and the moderating effects of gender and neuroticism. *Journal of Family Psychology*, *17*, 557–570.

Dehle, C., & Weiss, R. (1998). Sex differences in prospective associations between marital quality and depressed mood. *Journal of Marriage and the Family*, *60*, 1002–1011.

Dessaulles, A., Johnson, S. M., & Denton, W. H. (2003). Emotion-focused therapy for couples the treatment of depression: A pilot study. *American Journal of Family Therapy*, *31*, 345–353.

Ehlers, C. L., Frank, E., & Kupfer, D. J. (1988). Social zeitgebers and biological rhythms: A unified approach to understanding the etiology of depression. *Archives of General Psychiatry*, *45*, 948–952.

Emanuels-Zuurveen, L., & Emmelkamp, P. M. G. (1996). Individual behavioural-cognitive therapy v. marital therapy for depression in maritally distressed couples. *British Journal of Psychiatry*, *169*, 181–188.

Epstein, N. B., & Baucom, D. H. (2002). *Enhanced Cognitive-Behavioral Therapy for Couples*. Washington, DC: American Psychological Association.

Fals-Stewart, W., & Birchler, G. R. (1998). Marital interactions of drug-abusing patients and their partners: Comparisons with distressed couples and relationship to drug-using behavior. *Psychology of Addictive Behaviors*, *12*, 28–38.

Fals-Stewart, W., O'Farrell, T. J., & Hooley, J. M. (2001). Relapse among married or cohabiting substance-abusing patients: The role of perceived criticism. *Behavior Therapy*, *32*, 787–801.

Fincham, F. D., Beach, S. R., & Bradbury, T. N. (1989). Marital distress, depression, and attributions: Is the marital distress-attribution association an artifact of depression? *Journal of Consulting & Clinical Psychology*, *57*, 768–771.

Fincham, F. D., Beach, S. R. H., Harold, G. T., & Osborne, L. N. (1997). Marital satisfaction and depression: Different causal relationships for men and women? *Psychological Science*, *8*, 351–357.

Fincham, F. D., & Bradbury, T. N. (1993). Marital satisfaction, depression, and attributions: A longitudinal analysis. *Journal of Personality and Social Psychology*, *64*, 442–452.

Foley, S. H., Rounsaville, B. J., Weissman, M. M., Sholomskas, D., & Chevron, E. (1989). Individual versus conjoint interpersonal psychotherapy for depressed patients with marital disputes. *International Journal of Family Psychiatry*, *10*, 29–42.

Goering, P., Lin, E., Campbell, D., Boyle, M. H., & Offord, D. R. (1996). Psychiatric disability in Ontario. *Canadian Journal of Psychiatry*, *41*, 564–571.

Goering, P. N., Lancee, W. J., & Freeman, J. J. (1992). Marital support and recovery from depression. *British Journal of Psychiatry*, *160*, 76–82.

Gordon, K. C., Friedman, M. A., Miller, I. W., & Gaertner, L. (2005). Marital attributions as moderators of the marital discord-depression link. *Journal of Social and Clinical Psychology*, *24*, 876–893.

Hammen, C., & Brennan, P. A. (2002). Interpersonal dysfunction in depressed women: Impairments independent of depressive symptoms. *Journal of Affective Disorders*, *72*, 145–156.

Hammen, C. L. (1991). Generation of stress in the course of unipolar depression. *Journal of Abnormal Psychology*, *100*, 555–561.

Heim, S. C., & Snyder, D. K. (1991). Predicting depression from marital distress and attributional processes. *Journal of Marital and Family Therapy*, *17*, 67–72.

Hickie, I., & Parker, G. (1992). The impact of an uncaring partner on improvement in non-melancholic depression. *Journal of Affective Disorders*, *25*, 147–160.

Hooley, J. M., & Teasdale, J. D. (1989). Predictors of relapse in unipolar depressives: Expressed emotion, marital distress, and perceived criticism. *Journal of Abnormal Psychology*, *98*, 229–235.

Jackman-Cram, S., Dobson, K. S., & Martin, R. (2006). Marital problem-solving behavior in depression and marital distress. *Journal of Abnormal Psychology*, *115*, 380–384.

Jacobson, N. S., Dobson, K., Fruzzetti, A. E., Schmaling, K. B., & Salusky, S. (1991). Marital therapy as a treatment for depression. *Journal of Consulting and Clinical Psychology*, *59*, 547–557.

Jacobson, N. S., Fruzzetti, A. E., Dobson, K., Whisman, M., & Hops, H. (1993). Couple therapy as a treatment for depression: II. The effects of relationship quality and therapy on depressive relapse. *Journal of Consulting and Clinical Psychology*, *61*, 516–519.

Johnson, S. L., & Jacob, T. (1997). Marital interactions of depressed men and women. *Journal of Consulting and Clinical Psychology*, *65*, 15–23.

Johnson, S. L., & Jacob, T. (2000). Sequential interactions in the marital communication of depressed men and women. *Journal of Consulting and Clinical Psychology*, *68*, 4–12.

Johnson, S. M. (1996). *The Practice of Emotionally Focused Marital Therapy: Creating Connection*. Philadelphia: Brunner/Mazel.

Jones, E., & Asen, E. (2000). *Systemic Couple Therapy and Depression*. London: Karnac Books.

Kahn, J., Coyne, J. C., & Margolin, G. (1985). Depression and marital disagreement: The social construction of despair. *Journal of Social and Personal Relationships*, *2*, 447–461.

Karney, B. R. (2001). Depressive symptoms and marital satisfaction in the early years of marriage: Narrowing the gap between theory and research. In S. R. H. Beach (Ed.), *Marital and Family Processes in Depression: A Scientific Foundation for Clinical Practice* (pp. 45–68). Washington, DC: American Psychological Association.

Kendler, K. S., Karkowski, L. M., & Prescott, C. A. (1999). Causal relationship between stressful life events and the onset of major depression. *American Journal of Psychiatry*, *156*, 837–841.

Kessler, R. C., Berglund, P., Demler, O., Jin, R., Koretz, D., Merikangas, K. R. *et al.* (2003). The epidemiology of major depressive disorder: Results from the National Comorbidity Survey Replication (NCS-R). *JAMA*, *289*, 3095–3105.

Kiecolt-Glaser, J. K., & Newton, T. L. (2001). Marriage and health: His and hers. *Psychological Bulletin*, *12*, 472–503.

Klerman, G. L., Weissman, M. M., Rounsaville, B. J., & Chevron, E. (1984). *Interpersonal Psychotherapy of Depression*. New York: Basic Books.

Kowalik, D. L., & Gotlib, I. H. (1987). Depression and marital interaction: Concordance between intent and perception of communication. *Journal of Abnormal Psychology, 96*, 127–134.

Kreider, R. M., & Fields, J. M. (2001). *Number, timing, and duration of marriages and divorces: Fall 1996*. Current Population Reports, P 70–80. U.S. Census Bureau, Washington, DC.

Kung, W. W., & Elkin, I. (2000). Marital adjustment as a predictor of outcome in individual treatment of depression. *Psychotherapy Research, 10*, 267–278.

Kurdek, L. A. (1998). The nature and predictors of the trajectory of change in marital quality over the first 4 years of marriage for first-married husbands and wives. *Journal of Family Psychology, 12*, 494–510.

Kwon, J.-H., Lee, Y., Lee, M.-S., & Bifulco, A. (2006). Perceived criticism, marital interaction and relapse in unipolar depression – Findings from a Korean sample. *Clinical Psychology and Psychotherapy, 13*, 306–312.

Laumann, E. O., Gagnon, J. H., Michael, R. T., & Michaels, S. (1994). *The Social Organization of Sexuality: Sexual Practices in the United States*. Chicago: University of Chicago Press.

Leff, J., Alexander, B., Asen, E., Brewin, C. R., Dayson, D., Vearnals, S. *et al.* (2003). Modes of action of family interventions in depression and schizophrenia: The same or different? *Journal of Family Therapy, 25*, 357–370.

Leff, J., Vearnals, S., Brewin, C. R., Wolff, G., Alexander, B., Asen, E. *et al.* (2000). The London Depression Intervention Trial: Randomised controlled trial of antidepressants v. couple therapy in the treatment and maintenance of people with depression living with a partner: Clinical outcome and costs. *British Journal of Psychiatry, 177*, 95–100.

Levkovitz, Y., Fenning, S., Horesch, N., Barak, Y., & Treves, I. (2000). Perception of ill spouse and dyadic relationship in couples with affective disorder and those without. *Journal of Affective Disorders, 58*, 237–240.

Levkovitz, Y., Lamy, D., Ternachiano, P., Treves, I., & Fenning, S. (2003). Perceptions of dyadic relationship and emotional states in patients with affective disorder. *Journal of Affective Disorders, 75*, 19–28.

Liu, R. X., & Chen, Z. (2006). The effects of marital conflict and marital disruption on depressive affect: A comparison between women in and out of poverty. *Social Science Quarterly, 87*, 250–271.

McCabe, S. B., & Gotlib, I. H. (1993). Interaction of couples with and without a depressed spouse: Self-report and observations of problem-solving situations. *Journal of Social and Personal Relationships, 10*, 589–599.

McLeod, J. D. (1994). Anxiety disorders and marital quality. *Journal of Abnormal Psychology, 103*, 767–776.

McLeod, J. D., & Eckberg, D. A. (1993). Concordance for depressive disorders and marital quality. *Journal of Marriage and the Family, 55*, 733–746.

Mickelson, K. D., Claffey, S. T., & Williams, S. L. (2006). The moderating role of gender and gender role attitudes on the link between spousal support and marital quality. *Sex Roles, 55*, 73–82.

Nelson, G. M., & Beach, S. R. (1990). Sequential interaction in depression: Effects of depressive behavior on spousal aggression. *Behavior Therapy, 21*, 167–182.

Nolen-Hoeksema, S. (1987). Sex differences in unipolar depression: Evidence and theory. *Psychological Bulletin, 101*, 259–282.

Overbeek, G., Vollebergh, W., de Graaf, R., Scholte, R., de Kemp, R., & Engels, R. (2006). Longitudinal associations of marital quality and marital dissolution with the incidence of DSM-III-R disorders. *Journal of Family Psychology, 20*, 284–291.

Riso, L. P., Klein, D. N., Anderson, R. L., Ouimette, P. C., & Lizardi, H. (1996). Convergent and discriminant validity of perceived criticism from spouses and family members. *Behavior Therapy, 27*, 129–137.

Roberts, B. W., & Robins, R. W. (2000). Broad dispositions, broad aspirations: The intersection of personality traits and major life goals. *Personality and Social Psychology Bulletin, 26*, 1284–1296.

Rounsaville, B. J., Prusoff, B. A., & Weissman, M. M. (1980). The course of marital disputes in depressed women: A 48-month follow-up study. *Comprehensive Psychiatry, 21*, 111–118.

Rounsaville, B. J., Weissman, M. M., Prusoff, B. A. & Herceg-Baron, R. L. (1979). Marital disputes and treatment outcome in depressed women. *Comprehensive Psychiatry*, *20*, 483–490.

Ruscher, S. M., & Gotlib, I. H. (1988). Marital interaction patterns of couples with and without a depressed partner. *Behavior Therapy*, *19*, 455–470.

Sacco, W. P., Dumont, C. P., & Dow, M. G. (1993). Attributional, perceptual, and affective responses to depressed and nondepressed marital partners. *Journal of Consulting and Clinical Psychology*, *61*, 1076–1082.

Schmaling, K. B., & Jacobson, N. S. (1990). Marital interaction and depression. *Journal of Abnormal Psychology*, *99*, 229–236.

Scott, R. L., & Cordova, J. V. (2002). The influence of adult attachment styles on the association between marital adjustment and depressive symptoms. *Journal of Family Psychology*, *16*, 199–208.

Seltzer, J. A. (2000). Families formed outside of marriage. *Journal of Marriage and the Family*, *62*, 1247–1268.

Senchak, M., & Leonard, K. E. (1992). Attachment styles and marital adjustment among newlywed couples. *Journal of Social and Personal Relationships*, *9*, 51–64.

Straus, M. A., & Gelles, R. J. (1986). Societal change and change in family violence from 1975 to 1985 as revealed by two national surveys. *Journal of Marriage and the Family*, *48*, 465–479.

Teichman, Y., Bar-El, Z., Shor, H., Sirota, P., & Elizur, A. (1995). A comparison of two modalities of cognitive therapy (individual and marital) in treating depression. *Psychiatry*, *58*, 136–148.

Trevino, Y. A., Wooten, H. R., & Scott, R. E. (2007). A correlational study between depression and marital adjustment in Hispanic couples. *The Family Journal: Counseling and Therapy for Couples and Families*, *15*, 46–52.

Uebelacker, L. A., & Whisman, M. A. (2005). Relationship beliefs, attributions, and partner behaviors for depressed and nondepressed married women. *Cognitive Therapy and Research*, *29*, 143–154.

Uebelacker, L. A., & Whisman, M. A. (2006). Moderators of the association between relationship discord and major depression in a national population-based sample. *Journal of Family Psychology*, *20*, 40–46.

Wade, T. D., & Kendler, K. S. (2000a). Absence of interactions between social support and stressful life events in the prediction of major depression and depressive symptomatology in women. *Psychological Medicine*, *30*, 965–974.

Wade, T. D., & Kendler, K. S. (2000b). The relationship between social support and major depression: Cross-sectional, longitudinal, and genetic perspectives. *Journal of Nervous and Mental Disease*, *188*, 251–258.

Weissman, M. M. (1987). Advances in psychiatric epidemiology: Rates and risks for major depression. *American Journal of Public Health*, *77*, 445–451.

Weissman, M. M., Bland, R., Joyce, P. R., Newman, S., Wells, J. E., & Wittchen, H. (1993). Sex differences in rates of depression: Cross-national perspectives. *Journal of Affective Disorders*, *29*, 77–84.

Weissman, M. M., Markowitz, J. G., & Klerman, G. L. (2000). *Comprehensive Guide to Interpersonal Psychotherapy*. New York: Basic Books.

Whisman, M. A. (1999). Marital dissatisfaction and psychiatric disorders: Results from the National Comorbidity Survey. *Journal of Abnormal Psychology* *108*, 701–706.

Whisman, M. A. (2001a). Marital adjustment and outcome following treatments for depression. *Journal of Consulting and Clinical Psychology*, *69*, 125–129.

Whisman, M. A. (2001b). The association between marital dissatisfaction and depression. In S. R. H. Beach (Ed.), *Marital and Family Processes in Depression: A Scientific Foundation for Clinical Practice* (pp. 3–24). Washington, DC: American Psychological Association.

Whisman, M. A. (2007). Marital distress and DSM-IV psychiatric disorders in a population-based national survey. *Journal of Abnorma Psychology*, *116*, 638–643.

Whisman, M. A., Beach, S. R. H., & Snyder, D. K. (in press). Is marital discord taxonic and can taxonic status be assessed reliably: Results from a national representative sample of married couples. *Journal of Consulting and Clinical Psychology*.

Whisman, M. A., & Bruce, M. L. (1999). Marital distress and incidence of major depressive episode in a community sample. *Journal of Abnormal Psychology*, *108*, 674–678.

Whisman, M. A., Sheldon, C. T., & Goering, P. (2000). Psychiatric disorders and dissatisfaction with social relationships: Does type of relationship matter? *Journal of Abnormal Psychology*, *109*, 803–808.

Whisman, M. A., Uebelacker, L. A., & Bruce, M. L. (2006a). Longitudinal association between marital discord and alcohol use disorders. *Journal of Family Psychology*, *20*, 164–167.

Whisman, M. A., Uebelacker, L. A., Tolejko, N., Chatav, Y., & McKelvie, M. (2006b). Marital discord and well-being in older adults: Is the association confounded by personality?. *Psychology and Aging*, *21*, 626–631.

Whisman, M. A., Weinstock, L. M., & Tolejko, N. (2006c). Marriage and depression. In C. L. M. Keyes & S. H. Goodman (Eds.), *Women and Depression: A Handbook for the Social, Behavioral, and Biomedical Sciences* (pp. 219–240). New York: Cambridge University Press.

Whitton, S. W., Olmos-Gallo, P. A., Stanley, S. M., Prado, L. M., Kline, G. H., St. Peters, M. *et al.* (2007). Depressive symptoms in early marriage: Predictions from relationship confidence and negative marital interaction. *Journal of Family Psychology*, *21*, 297–306.

17

LOW SOCIAL SUPPORT AND MAJOR DEPRESSION: RESEARCH, THEORY AND METHODOLOGICAL ISSUES

BRIAN LAKEY* AND ARIKA CRONIN†

*Grand Valley State University, Allendale, Michigan, USA
†George Mason University, Fairfax, Virginia, USA

Low social support has been linked to a wide range of mental health constructs (Cohen & Wills, 1985; Sarason *et al.*, 2001), including non-specific psychological distress (Finch *et al.*, 1999), post-traumatic stress disorder (Brewin *et al.*, 2000), eating disorders (Stice, 2002), low self-esteem (Newcomb & Keefe, 1997), and clinical depression (Brown & Harris, 1978). This chapter reviews research, theory, and methods regarding the link between low social support and clinical depression. The chapter is organized into three main sections, related to (a) social support theory, measurement, and methods, (b) empirical research on social support and depression, and (c) implications for theory and research.

Our review is restricted to studies of clinical depression, given the focus of the current volume. Depression was determined through formal diagnostic criteria, based on the information derived from structured interviews. Commonly used diagnostic criteria in the studies reviewed were the *Diagnostic and Statistic Manual of Mental Disorders* (edition III-R or IV; American Psychiatric Association, 1987, 1994), Research Diagnostic Criteria (Spitzer *et al.*, 1978), and the Bedford College criteria (Finlay-Jones *et al.*, 1981). Commonly used structured interviews included the Structured Clinical Interview for DSM disorders (Spitzer *et al.*, 1987), the Present State Examination (Wing *et al.*, 1974), and in several important studies of depression in adolescents, the Schedule for Affective Disorders and Schizophrenia for School-Age Children (Puig-Antich & Chambers, 1983). We recognize that there is an active discussion regarding the extent to which depression is best viewed as a categorical or continuous variable (e.g., Hankin *et al.*, 2005), and the extent to which symptoms in the clinical range are distinct from symptoms in the subclinical range (Coyne, 1994). As such, we reserve the term depression for that defined by formal diagnostic criteria. Following Kendall *et al.* (1987), we use the term "dysphoria" (also known as "subsyndromal depression") to refer to continuous measures of depressive symptoms, typically assessed by questionnaires. Such dysphoria measures appear to be central to understanding the extent to which low social support forecasts depression onset.

SOCIAL SUPPORT THEORY, MEASUREMENT, AND METHODS

SOCIAL SUPPORT THEORY

Nearly all research on social support has been guided by stress and coping social support theory (Lakey & Cohen, 2000), which is an extension of the more general stress and coping theory (Lazarus & Folkman, 1984). As applied to depression, this theory can be described succinctly by the following five hypotheses: (1) Life events increase the risk for onset of major depression. (2) People differ in the extent to which life events increase risk for depression. (3) Events are stressful (in part) to the extent that people perceive the events as threats (i.e., primary appraisal) and perceive themselves as lacking adequate responses (i.e., secondary appraisal). (4) The extent to which events increase risk also depends upon people's coping strategies. Coping involves a wide range of deliberate thought and action, including problem solving, reappraisal, avoidance, and support seeking. (5) Social support is a temporally stable resource that decreases the extent to which events increase risk (i.e., stress buffering), primarily by social support's influence on appraisal and coping. Social support includes what friends and family say and do regarding the events (i.e., enacted support), as well people's perceptions that quality enacted support is available (i.e., perceived support). Perceived support is based primarily on one's history of receiving effective enacted support. Although these five hypotheses are the core of stress and coping social support theory, various scholars have added hypotheses that (a) depression increases the risk for life events (Monroe & Steiner, 1986) (b) depression and events reduce perceived support (Kaniasty & Norris, 1993); and (c) low perceived support leads directly to depression even in the absence of life events (Cohen & Wills, 1985).

SOCIAL SUPPORT MEASUREMENT

A large number of different questionnaire measures of social support exist that can be classified into three types: perceived support, enacted support, and social integration (Barrera, 1986). Measures of perceived support (sometimes called functional support; *cf.* Wills & Shinar, 2000) ask respondents to make subjective judgments about the extent to which family and friends would, do, or have provided effective enacted support and other social provisions (e.g., attachment; Cutrona & Russell, 1987). A core feature of perceived support is that it involves subjective judgments about the quality and availability of support. Enacted support measures ask respondents to report (a) whether or not friends and family have provided specific supportive actions (e.g., advice, reassurance, help with a task, loans) in the recent past or (b) the frequency by which specific supportive actions have been provided. Compared to perceived support measures, measures of enacted support commonly describe supportive actions in more behavioral language and rely less heavily on subjective judgments of quality. Measures of social integration ask respondents to indicate their number of social ties, such as marital status, number of living siblings, and number of living children (Brissette *et al.*, 2000).

Some properties of these types of questionnaire measures are reasonably well understood. First, perceived support, enacted support, and social integration are only modestly correlated and reflect distinct constructs with largely unique patterns of correlations with other constructs (Barrera, 1986). For example, meta-analyses indicate that perceived and enacted support are only modestly correlated ($r = .35$; Haber *et al.*, 2007) and that perceived support is related to mental health more strongly than is enacted support (Finch *et al.*, 1999). Social integration is typically unrelated to perceived support, enacted support, and mental health (Barrera, 1986); although social integration predicts physical health outcomes such as mortality (Uchino, 2004). Thus, given that perceived support has been more closely linked to mental health than has enacted support and social integration, perceived support would seem to be the best candidate for acting as a risk factor for depression.

An important property of perceived support measures is that they reflect a blend of the trait-like characteristics of support recipients, the objectively supportive qualities of support providers, and the unique relationships among specific recipients and providers. A recent meta-analysis of five American and European studies indicated that approximately 62% of the variance in perceived support reflected unique relationships, 27% reflected recipient personality, whereas only 7% reflected the objectively supportive qualities of providers (Lakey, in press). It is therefore important to remember that when research participants report their perceptions of social support, investigators are capturing a blend of social, as well as personality processes. Moreover, the social processes captured by perceived support measures are not primarily veridical accounts of enacted support received or reflections of objectively supportive network members, but instead reflect much more nuanced social psychological processes.

In addition to the social support questionnaires just reviewed, structured interview measures of social support exist, and these measures play an important role in research on social support and depression. For example, the Self-Evaluation and Social Support schedule (SESS; O'Connor & Brown, 1984) uses an extensive semi-structured interview to classify relationships in terms of supportiveness using a detailed coding scheme. Unfortunately, less is known about the construct validity of such interviews, especially the extent to which interview measures reflect the same types of constructs as do questionnaire measures. We treat interview measures as measures of perceived support in our review, as they typically involve the interviewer judging the quality of relationships and support on the basis of the participants' self-reports.

METHODS FOR TESTING STRESS AND COPING SOCIAL SUPPORT THEORY

Research on social support and depression has used three main research designs: cross-sectional studies, prospective studies of onset, and prospective studies of remission.

Cross-sectional studies compare depressed and non-depressed people on social support (and often life events) at a single point in time. In some studies, psychosocial influences other than support (e.g., events or personality) are controlled statistically, typically through logistic regression. Stress and coping social support theory predicts that social support reduces the strength of the link between events and depression (i.e., stress buffering effects) and this prediction is typically tested by entering a Social Support × Events interaction term in a regression equation, following the main effects of support and events. The strongest version of the stress buffering hypothesis is that social support has no link to depression in the absence of life events (Brown & Harris, 1978). This version of the hypothesis is based on the view that social support only has meaning within the context of stressful situations. What does it mean to provide support when things are going well?

Although cross-sectional designs provide useful information, they cannot rule out a number of alternative hypotheses (Barnett & Gotlib, 1988; Heller, 1979; Monroe & Steiner, 1986). These include (1) Depression causes low social support, (2) Depression and low social support reflect shared genetic risk, (3) The strongest depression-inducing events involve a loss of social ties and subsequent support, (4) Pre-existing personality causes erosions in support, subsequent loss and depression onset, and (5) Environment characteristics (e.g., poverty) cause events, low support, and depression.

Prospective studies of onset provide stronger tests of stress and coping social support theory than does cross-sectional research (Barnett & Gotlib, 1988). In prospective studies, investigators assess participants at least twice, typically with 8 months to 5 years elapsing between assessment points. At minimum, support and depression are assessed at Time 1 (T1) and depression onset is assessed at Time 2 (T2). Other psychosocial constructs are commonly assessed and some studies have multiple follow-up assessments. Investigators assess the extent to which participants that were not depressed at T1, but developed depression by T2 had lower social support at T1 than did participants that were not depressed at either time point. Stress and coping social support theory is tested most directly by the Support × Events interaction term. Evidence for stress buffering would be provided to the extent that life events between T1 and T2 were more strongly related to depression onset among participants with low T1 support than among those with high T1 support. The primary strength of prospective studies is that the researcher can determine if low social support preceded depression onset. Such a pattern is inconsistent with many of the alternative hypotheses described in the prior paragraph. Prospective studies of onset rule out additional alternative hypotheses if T1 dysphoria and T1 personality are controlled statistically. Controlling for T1 dysphoria seems to be especially important as it appears to be (a) the strongest and most consistent predictor of who develops depression by T2 (Lewinsohn *et al.*, 1988) and (b) a key determinant of whether a given study finds low support to forecast depression onset.

Prospective studies of remission start with a sample of depressed patients who receive treatment, and examine the extent to which T1 support forecasts remission by T2. As with prospective studies of onset, more precise tests of stress and coping social support theory are provided by tests of the buffering hypothesis.

EMPIRICAL RESEARCH ON SOCIAL SUPPORT AND DEPRESSION

Our review of empirical research is organized into three sections: (a) cross sectional studies, (b) prospective studies of onset, and (c) prospective studies of remission.

CROSS-SECTIONAL STUDIES OF SOCIAL SUPPORT AND DEPRESSION

With few exceptions, many studies have shown that depressed people perceive less support than do non-depressed people. This effect has been observed across a very wide range of samples and perceived support measures. It has been observed among representative samples of communities and nations (e.g., Cairney *et al.*, 2003; Landerman *et al.*, 1989), heart patients (Bosworth *et al.*, 2000), pregnant women (O'Hara, 1986), mixed samples of men and women (e.g., Turner & Marino, 1994), women (e.g., Cairney *et al.*, 2003), and adolescents (Lewinsohn *et al.*, 1997; Sheeber *et al.*, 2007) It has been observed in United States (e.g., Landerman *et al.*, 1989), Canadian (e.g., Turner & Marino, 1994), English (e.g., Edwards *et al.*, 1998), Australian (Wilhelm *et al.*, 1999), and Pakistani samples (Rahman *et al.*, 2003). It has been observed in comparisons of depressed outpatients and matched controls (Billings *et al.*, 1983), as well as in depressed inpatients and demographically similar controls (Lakey *et al.*, 1999) and in both very large samples of 1,900–3,700 (Cairney *et al.*, 2003; Landerman *et al.*, 1989; Wade & Kendler, 2000a) as well as very small samples of 25–35 (Belsher, & Costello, 1991; Lakey, *et al.*, 1999), as well as with interview (e.g., Cairney *et al.*, 2003), and questionnaire measures of social support (e.g., Wade & Kendler, 2000a).

More interesting are studies that compared depressed people to people with other psychiatric conditions, or that controlled for other psychosocial variables. Two studies reported that depressed people had lower perceived support than did (a) people with non-affective mental disorders and (b) non-disordered controls (Belsher & Costello, 1991; Lewinsohn *et al.*, 1997). In addition, Billings *et al.* (1983) found that perceived support was linked to depression beyond events and coping, Landerman *et al.* (1989) found the link beyond events, and Lewinsohn *et al.* (1994) found the link for perceived support from friends (but not family) independently of a very wide range of psychosocial constructs. In contrast, Bosworth *et al.*'s (2000) smaller study of cardiac patients found no link between perceived support and depression beyond life events.

Some studies did not find the well-replicated cross-sectional link between low perceived support and depression. Two studies that did not find this link focused on caregivers of frail elders (Rivera *et al.*, 1991) or caregivers of relatives with probable Alzheimer's disease (Redinbaugh *et al.*, 1995). We wonder whether the especially strong risk for depression conveyed by caregiving overpowers any protective effect of social support (Dura *et al.*, 1991).

Nearly all of the cross-sectional studies found links between low perceived support and depression, regardless of the presence of life events. This is noteworthy because of Brown and Harris' (1978) seminal observation that social support was related to depression only in the presence of severe events or major difficulties. In fact, very few cross-sectional studies provided evidence for the stress buffering hypothesis. Besides Brown and Harris (1978), only Landerman *et al.* (1989) reported stress buffering effects and that was for only some analytic approaches. Yet, only Wade and Kendler (2000b) reported no evidence for stress buffering after extensive testing with large samples. A number of other large studies reported analyses for both events and social support, but did not report tests of stress buffering. Given the importance of stress buffering to social support theory, we assume that these studies tested for stress buffering, but found nothing of interest.

In summary, cross-sectional studies consistently demonstrate that depressed participants perceive less support than do non-depressed participants. This effect is broadly generalizable, as it was observed across a wide range of different samples and measures. For example, the effect was found in several different countries, across a range of ages, for both men and women, for patients in treatment settings as well as participants in large epidemiological surveys. However, the stress buffering hypothesis did not receive consistent support. Yet, this theory is best tested with prospective designs, and we review such studies next. Because of the importance of these studies to social support theory, we describe them in some detail.

PROSPECTIVE STUDIES OF SOCIAL SUPPORT AND DEPRESSION

Lewinsohn *et al.* (1988) assessed about 1,000 community-dwelling adults in Oregon at two points in time, separated by approximately 8 months. Interviews covered lifetime history of psychopathology. Diagnoses of depression were made following the structured interviews, according to "Research Diagnostic Criteria (RDC) for major, minor, or intermittent depressive disorder" (p. 254). The three measures classified as "social support" by the authors were atypical social support measures (*cf.* Wills & Shinar, 2000). They included a single-item rating of frequency of social contact, a measure of interpersonal comfort, and a measure of marital discord. The measure of interpersonal comfort appeared to focus on social anxiety and included rating comfort in situations such as, "expressing an opinion that differs from that of the person I am talking with" (p. 255). The measure of marital discord focused on thoughts and actions taken toward ending a marriage. Each of these "social support" measures were correlated significantly, albeit weakly to depression at T1. Marital discord forecasted depression onset at T2, but not when T1 dysphoria and life events were controlled statistically. Moreover, although tested, there was no evidence that social support buffered the link between stress and depression. Although Lewinsohn *et al.* (1988) did not find evidence that social support forecasted depression onset, we wonder to what extent their measures of social support reflected the constructs emphasized by social support theory. Of the three, it is most likely that marital discord is strongly linked to low perceived support, and in fact, the extent to which marital satisfaction and perceived social support are the same construct among married people is not yet resolved (Kaul & Lakey, 2003).

In a subsequent prospective study of about 1,500 adolescents in Oregon, Lewinsohn *et al.* (1994) substantially improved the assessment of social support, but still found no evidence that low perceived support forecasted depression onset 14 months later, in analyses that controlled for initial dysphoria and other psychopathology. DSM-III-R diagnoses of major depressive disorder or dysthymia were made the following structured interviews. Interviews at T2 covered the time since T1. Perceived social support from family and from friends was measured by a composite of items from different scales. Although some items were drawn from constructs of uncertain relevance to social support (e.g., social competence), many items were derived from established social support scales (the Arizona Social Support Interview Schedule; Barrera, 1983) or from established scales of constructs closely related to perceived support (UCLA Loneliness Scale; Russell *et al.*, 1980). In prospective univariate analyses, participants with low family support (but not low friend support) were more likely to become depressed than participants with high family support. Yet, in analyses that controlled for T1 psychopathology, neither perceived support measure forecasted depression onset. Moreover, no tests of stress buffering effects were reported, even though the study included the measures needed for such tests. Thus, Lewinsohn *et al.* (1994) found no evidence that perceived support increased risk for depression onset in adolescents.

Burton *et al.* (2004) as well as Stice *et al.* (2004) used perceived support from family and friends to forecast depression onset over a 2-year period. Although both studies were based on largely the same data set of about 500 adolescent girls in Texas, the two studies yielded contradictory results. Participants completed diagnostic interviews and self-report measures of psychosocial constructs at four assessment points, each separated by 1 year. Diagnoses were based on DSM-IV criteria (American Psychiatric Association, 1994). Perceived support was assessed by Furman and Buhrmester's (1985) Network of Relationships Inventory. In Burton *et al.* (2004), participants also completed a self-report measure of stressful life events.

Of primary interest were analyses that focused on the 2-year outcomes of girls who were not depressed at baseline. Burton *et al.* (2004) focused on the Time 2 (T2) through Time 4 (T4) period and found no evidence that either perceived parental or friend support at T2 forecasted depression onset by T4. In addition to the absence of direct links between perceived support and depression onset, there were no stress-buffering effects for social support, even though events were linked significantly to onset. In contrast, Stice *et al.* (2004) focused on the Time 1 (T1) through Time 3 (T3) period and found that T1 perceived parental support (but not friend support) forecasted depression onset by T3.

One reason for the contradictory findings between the two studies might be that they defined depression somewhat differently, in that Burton *et al.* (2004) used a more lenient definition of depression than did Stice *et al.* (2004). Burton *et al.* (2004) included "subthreshold diagnostic criteria" which included "...girls who reported the presence of at least five of the symptoms necessary for a diagnosis, but who endorsed a subthreshold level on at least one of these symptoms (p. 692)." Although Stice *et al.* (2004) reported analyses using more strict diagnostic criteria, only 15 girls developed depression at follow-up. In addition, neither paper reported analyses in which initial dysphoria was controlled, and thus the prospective effect for perceived support reported by Stice *et al.* (2004) might have occurred because girls with high T1 dysphoria were more likely to develop depression than girls with low T1 dysphoria and girls with high T1 dysphoria also had low T1 perceived support. Given the absence of control for T1 dysphoria, and given the contradictory results from the two subsamples, these two papers do not provided strong support for the hypothesis that low perceived support forecasts depression onset or that perceived support buffers the link between events and depression.

Wade and Kendler (2000a) studied about 1,900 community-dwelling women in Virginia at two points in time, separated by an average of about 5 years. Social support was assessed for each of spouses, relatives, and friends by two items reflecting the extent to which the network member cared about and expressed interest in the well-being of the participant. Participants also reported on the presence of confidants and frequency of social interaction. Three additional scales were described by Wade and Kendler (2000a) as social support, but these scales referred to negative social interactions, which appear to be distinct from social support (Okun & Lockwood, 2003). Depression was diagnosed according to DSM-III-R criteria based on a structured interview that covered the 12 months preceding the interview. Cross-sectional analyses at both time points, revealed associations between major depression and both lower perceived spousal support and lower relative support, but not lower friend support or few confidants.

Yet, there were no significant prospective links between T1 spousal, relative, or friend support and T2 depression onset, controlling for T1 depression. Interesting, few contacts with friends at T1 forecasted depression onset by T2, even though there were no cross-sectional links between depression and frequency of social contact at either T1 or T2. Wade and Kendler (2000b) analyzed essentially the same data testing for buffering effects. However, none of the cross-sectional or prospective tests of stress buffering involving spouse, relative or friend support were statistically significant. One significant interaction between financial problems and confidants was observed in cross-sectional analyses only, but the interaction's pattern did not fit the stress buffering hypothesis.

Brown *et al.* (1986) studied approximately 300 community-dwelling London women with children. Participants were assessed twice, separated by approximately 1 year. Diagnoses of depression were made according to the Bedford College criteria (Finlay-Jones *et al.* 1981), based on the information derived from structured interviews covering the previous year. Social support at T1 was assessed through a semi-structured interview, the SESS schedule. Participants' responses were scored by trained interviewers following a detailed coding system. The interview "…included security feelings and characteristics (both enhancing and diminishing), quality of interaction (both negative and positive), confiding, dependence, active emotional and practical support, and felt attachment. Negative and positive aspects of the relationships were rated separately…" (p. 818). It is difficult to know to what extent social support assessed by the SESS is similar to support assessed via questionnaire, as no studies have correlated the two types of measures. Based on descriptions of participants' supportive relationships (O'Connor and Brown, 1984), the schedule likely captures well the types of social processes emphasized by social support theory. Social support at T2 ("crisis support") was assessed in a similar semi-structured interview asking about the responses of core relationship figures to severe events and major difficulties experienced by participants. Crisis support involved "…a high level of confiding and a high level of active emotional support…if it was not accompanied at some point by a negative response" (p. 818). Severe events and major difficulties were assessed using the contextual threat method, based on semi-structured interviews with participants. Analyses of social support were based on a subsample of 150 women who had a severe event or major difficulty, and included only cases of depression with onset between T1 and T2.

For married women T1 support did not forecast depression onset by T2. Yet, women who received crisis support from their husbands (or other core relationship figures) were less likely to develop depression than women who did not receive crisis support (a cross-sectional link). Consistent with Haber *et al.* (2007), a supportive relationship with the husband at T1 was unrelated to receiving crisis support from him at T2. In contrast to married women, T1 low support forecasted depression onset for unmarried women. In addition, T1 support forecasted with high accuracy the receipt of crisis support. However, T1 dysphoria was not controlled in these analyses, and so it is possible that T1 low support reflected high levels of dysphoria and that dysphoria actually accounted for depression onset. Thus, Brown *et al.* (1986) provided uncertain evidence in a subsample of women that social support forecasted depression onset.

In summary, prospective studies have not provided convincing evidence that social support forecasts depression onset, in spite of a number of well-conducted studies, some with very large samples. Although there were a few reports of prospective links between T1 support and T2 depression, these links were observed only when T1 dysphoria was not statistically controlled, and in one case, that link was not replicated in other analyses of essentially the same data set. Moreover, with the possible exception of Brown *et al.*'s (1986) analyses of unmarried women, none of the prospective studies reported evidence of stress buffering. These findings present a strong challenge to stress and coping social support theory.

STUDIES OF DEPRESSION REMISSION FOLLOWING TREATMENT

A third category of studies investigated the extent to which social support forecast (over periods between 6 months and 10 years) (a) improvement or remission in depression or (b) speed of remission. The nature of patents' treatments and their level of participation in treatment typically were not included as study variables. Each of these studies started with a diagnosed sample of depressed patients, and follow-up measures of depression typically were continuous scores derived from depression questionnaires, telephone, or in-person interviews. Most of the articles reviewed come from one of three US projects or one UK project. Research from two projects found that perceived support forecast remission in depression; one project found that perceived support forecast remission in depression, but not dysthymia; while another project found no link between perceived support and remission.

The studies that consistently found no link between T1 perceived support and remission were based on follow-ups of Billings *et al.*'s (1983) previously mentioned study of depressed patients in outpatient treatment in metropolitan San Francisco. Billings and Moos (1985) reported on the 1-year follow-up of this sample using the same social support and other constructs as used in Billings *et al.* (1983). All patients were diagnosed according to RDC criteria originally and completed a depression questionnaire based on RDC symptoms at 1-year follow-up. Participants completed an extensive battery of social support and other psychosocial constructs at both T1 and T2. However, when T1 depression severity was controlled, none of the T1 social support measures forecasted depression remission. Billings and Moos (1985) also tested for a number of stress buffering effects using T2 data. Only 7 of 42 tests were significant. The significant tests involved a range of stressors (e.g., medical conditions, spouse illness), but none involved life events. Swindle *et al.* (1989) reported a 4-year follow-up of the same patients and found that although T1 low family conflict predicted remission when controlling for initial depression severity, none of the T1 social support variables predicted remission. In a 10-year follow-up of these patients, Cronkite *et al.* (1998) reported that neither of two social support variables predicted remission status.

In contrast to the studies just described, a series of studies in North Carolina consistently found that perceived support forecasted depression remission. George *et al.* (1989) followed depressed patients over intervals of 6 to 36 months. Depression at follow-up was assessed using the CES-D (Radloff, 1977) administered over the phone. In univariate analyses, patients with "impaired" perceived support were less likely to remit than patients with adequate perceived support. In multiple regression analyses that controlled for T1 depression severity, T1 perceived support forecasted remission above and beyond life events and demographic variables. Perceived support forecasted remission significantly, more strongly among men than women and more strongly among middle-aged patients than older patients. The authors tested for stress buffering effects and found none. In another paper from the same research team, Hybels *et al.* (2005) restricted analyses to patients over 60 and a 1-year follow-up. Although remission was assessed by a different measure, the authors again found that perceived support forecasted remission even when T1 depression severity, life events, and other psychosocial constructs were controlled statistically.

A second research team that found low perceived support to forecast remission followed patients in London for approximately 4 months (Brugha *et al.*, 1990). This study included patients with anxiety disorders, provided the patient had depressed mood as an important symptom. T2 depression was assessed by interview and each patient was assigned a score that reflected severity of symptoms. In multivariate analyses, perceived support and the number of close relationships forecasted remission independently and beyond T1 severity for women. Yet, these findings were not observed for men, and were only observed for one of two measures of remission. Among men, living as married and few negative interactions forecasted remission. Brugha *et al.* (1987) reanalyzed the same sample, and found some evidence that perceived support forecasted remission more strongly among neurotic depressives than among endogenous depressives. An additional paper by this research team (Brugha *et al.* (1997) found that patients whose social network members knew each other had fewer episodes at follow-up than did patients whose social network members were less interconnected.

Lara *et al.* (1997) studied depressed patients in the US over 6 months and assessed follow-up status by structured interview, using stringent criteria for recovery, as well as by a self-report measure of dysphoria. T1 perceived support forecasted both recovery and dysphoria at T2 in multivariate analyses, even after controlling for T1 depression severity and neuroticism. Hayden and Klein (2001) followed 90 patients with dysthymic disorder over 5 years. As with Lara *et al.* (1997) follow-up recovery was assessed by structured interview, using stringent criteria. In addition, T2 dysphoria was assessed by interviewer ratings. Although perceived support forecasted recovery and dysphoria in univariate analyses, perceived support was not predictive in multivariate analyses that controlled for psychosocial and diagnostic variables. Although chronic stress was assessed, stress buffering effects were not reported.

In a final study, Oldehinkel *et al.* (2000) followed about 90 depressed patients in the Netherlands over a 4.5-year period and studied the extent to which social support and other psychosocial variables forecasted the time required to achieve remission. Follow-up depression and date of remission was assessed by structured interview. In multivariate models, perceived support did not forecast time to remission.

In summary, studies of depression remission following treatment provide stronger evidence that perceived support forecasts clinically important changes in depression, than was observed in the prospective studies of depression onset. Nonetheless, the findings of studies of remission were not completely consistent. One research team found that perceived support forecasted recovery in a small sample of depressed patients, but did not find a similar effect for a separate sample of dysthymic patients. Even the studies from the two teams that reported fairly consistent support-remission links had some inconsistencies in the findings. George *et al.* (1989) found that the link was stronger for men than for women, whereas Brugha *et al.* (1990) found the link for women, but not for men. George *et al.* (1989) originally found that the support-remission link was absent for participants over 60, but in a subsequent study, the link emerged for participants over 60 as well (Hybels *et al.*, 2005). Moreover, only Billings and Moos (1985) found evidence for stress buffering effects, and their significant effects were only a small percentage of tests conducted, and none involved life events. Thus, there is suggestive evidence that perceived support might forecast depression remission, but inconsistencies in the results across studies do not permit definitive conclusions. Additional studies are needed for a more precise estimate.

In summary, although there was consistent evidence that depressed people experience lower perceived support than non-depressed people in cross-sectional studies, very few studies provided evidence for stress buffering effects. Moreover, prospective studies of depression onset provided unconvincing evidence that low social support forecast depression onset or that low social support buffered the effects of life events on depression onset. Prospective studies of depression remission have found more encouraging evidence that perceived support might forecast clinically important changes in depression, but additional research is needed to solidify this evidence.

IMPLICATIONS FOR SOCIAL SUPPORT THEORY AND RESEARCH

Although prospective studies of depression onset have not provided evidence consistent with stress and coping social support theory these studies might have failed to detect prospective stress buffering effects because they were not sufficiently sensitive. Some studies did not include the types of social support measures that would have had the best chance of forecasting depression onset. For example, Lewinsohn *et al.* (1988) included a single-item social support measure (frequency of social contact) of the kind that is rarely linked to mental health (Barrera, 1986). Similarly, Lewinsohn *et al.* (1988) included as measures of social support (e.g., comfort in interpersonal relationships) constructs with ambiguous links to the kind of social processes emphasized by stress and coping social support theory. Nonetheless, most of the other prospective studies included adequate to good measurement of perceived support, but they did not find evidence for stress and coping theory either. Second, evidence for stress buffering might have been observed if life events were assessed with the high level of precision allowed by investigator-based methods (Monroe, in press). Most of the prospective onset studies assessed life events by less precise checklists, and only one study assessed the contextual threat of events to verify that the events were sufficiently powerful to substantially increase risk for depression. Third, and perhaps most importantly, stress and coping social support theory makes specific predictions about the circumstances under which social support will act as a stress buffer and these predictions were not tested in any of the prospective studies of depression onset. According to the optimal matching hypothesis (Cohen & Hoberman, 1983; Cutrona & Russell, 1990), social support moderates the effects of life events only insofar as the support matches the specific demands of the stressor.

Although stress and coping social support theory might not have been adequately tested in prospective studies of depression, it is also possible that the theory is inadequate. In fact, the theory has encountered a number of empirical difficulties besides its difficulties in research on depression. First, perceived support is not closely linked to enacted support (Haber *et al.*, 2007), even though stress and coping theory attributes links between perceived support and mental health to enacted support. Second, enacted support has not been linked consistently to mental health (Barrera, 1986; Finch *et al.* 1999). If anything, enacted support is linked to worse mental health (Bolger & Amarel, 2007; Bolger *et al.*, 2000), although the causal direction of this pathway requires investigation. Third, there is little evidence that social support operates by influencing coping or appraisal and the few studies that have investigated such links have not found results consistent with the theory (e.g., Frazier *et al.*, 2000). Thus, beyond its difficulties in forecasting depression onset, there are other empirical reasons to doubt that stress and coping social support theory provides an adequate account of the link between depression and perceived support.

OTHER THEORETICAL APPROACHES

Although stress and coping social support theory has dominated social support research, other theoretical approaches have been suggested from time to time. These include social cognitive and symbolic interactionist approaches. Social cognitive theories of social support (Lakey & Cassady, 1990; Lakey & Drew, 1997; Sarason *et al.*, 1990) were drawn from social cognitive models of psychopathology, personality, person perception, and attachment rather than from stress and coping theory. Social cognitive theory hypothesizes that thoughts that friends and family might not assist during times of need are sufficient to cause emotional distress, regardless of the presence of life events. Thus, social cognitive perspectives do not explain perceived support's link to mental health as resulting from perceived support's influence on coping. Drawing from basic research on person memory and judgment (Klein *et al.*, 1992), social cognitive theory states that perceived support should not be related strongly to memory for enacted support (Lakey & Drew, 1997). Instead, judgments of providers' supportiveness are made more heuristically, relying upon perceptions of providers' personality characteristics, providers' similarity to recipients in attitudes and values, and generic relationships quality (Lakey & Drew, 1997). Once perceivers have made stable judgments of providers' supportiveness, perceivers should display biases in the interpretation of and memory for providers' subsequent actions. Although the first formulations of social cognitive social support theory (Lakey & Cassady, 1990; Sarason *et al.*, 1990) predicted that perceived support should be broadly generalized across different providers and time (i.e., is trait-like), subsequent research has shown that perceived support is only partly trait-like, but instead is primarily a reflection of the unique relationships among recipients and providers (Lakey, in press). Thus, perceived support is highly sensitive to unique relationships and social interaction; it merely reflects more mundane, day-to-day processes involved in the social regulation of affect, rather than reflecting interactions focused on coping with major life events.

Another social cognitive perspective on social support was developed within the context of hopelessness theory (Abramson *et al.*, 1989). According to this theory (Panzarella *et al.*, 2006), a subtype of social support (adaptive inferential feedback) acts as a protective factor against hopelessness depression by reciprocally influencing depressogenic inferential styles and by reducing the likelihood of maladaptive inferences for life events. Adaptive inferential feedback has successfully forecasted inferences made for specific life events beyond other cognitive constructs, and has been correlated with the number of episodes of hopelessness depression (Panzarella *et al.*, 2006). Expanded hopelessness theory is similar to stress and coping theory in that expanded hopelessness theory predicts that social support acts as a stable resource that protects people from depression onset by buffering the effects of life events.

Thoits (1985) sketched a self and identity perspective on social support drawn from symbolic interactionism. Thoits (1985) hypothesized that the link between social support and emotional well-being reflects generic social processes involved in the regulation of self and emotion, rather than from enacted support provided in response to life events. Social ties and especially social roles provide a sense of identity and belonging, maintain self esteem, and provide opportunities for mastery of tasks associated with roles (Cast & Burke, 2002). Roles to which one is ill-suited are linked to poor performance of related tasks, negative evaluations by others and oneself, and raise questions about identify and belongingness (e.g., "What am I doing here?"). In social support research, symbolic interactionism's emphasis on roles has most often been operationalized by counting the number of different roles and social ties in which individuals participate (Brissette *et al.*, 2000). Although few social ties has predicted mortality and other health problems (Uchino, 2004), the number of roles and social ties has not been strongly related to mental health or to perceived support (Barrera, 1986). Recently, investigators have emphasized the psychological meaning and evaluation of roles (Cast & Burke, 2002; Reitzes & Mutran, 2002; Simon, 1997; Thoits, 1999), which might provide important insights to the link between perceived support and depression.

Thoits' (1985) symbolic interactionist account makes several predictions about the link between social support and depression that differ from stress and coping theory. First, roles and social ties do not operate primarily by moderating the effects of life events, and coping is not the primary mechanism by which roles and social ties are related to mental health. Instead roles and social ties are linked to mental health through identity and self-esteem. When people are ill-suited for the roles in which they find themselves, the impact on self-esteem and mental health should be relatively immediate, rather than lagged in time. Thus, the predictions of symbolic interactionist theory are more similar to those of social cognitive theory than to stress and coping social support theory. This is not surprising given that both the symbolic interactionist and social cognitive accounts have the same intellectual history (Lakey & Cohen, 2000).

ARE PROSPECTIVE STUDIES APPROPRIATE FOR TESTING ALTERNATIVE THEORIES?

Prospective studies are widely seen as the strongest design for testing hypotheses that low social support plays a causal role in depression (Barnett & Gotlib, 1988). Although such designs are appropriate for testing hypotheses from stress and coping social support theory, we have three chief doubts that the design is appropriate for testing other hypotheses.

First, to detect links between low perceived support and depression onset in prospective studies, these causal links must be lagged substantially in time. Although stress and coping social support theory predicts such a lagged effect, other theories do not. For example, if negative thoughts about support are sufficient to induce depression for persons already near the threshold, this link should be nearly immediate and would be better captured by cross-sectional studies. Similarly, the negative effects of ill-suited roles on identify, self-esteem and depression should occur relatively immediately too. Thus, prospective studies capture processes that are not predicted by all theories of social support and depression.

Our second doubt about prospective studies is that controlling for T1 dysphoria might inadvertently remove the primary effect of interest. When T1 dysphoria is controlled, the aspect of support that is shared with dysphoria is removed statistically, even if this might be the aspect most relevant to depression onset. For example, negative thoughts about social support should cause dysphoria nearly immediately and thus would be captured in the T1 correlation between dysphoria and low support. By statistically eliminating this effect, the investigator is examining the relationship between depression onset and the aspect of perceived support that is unrelated to dysphoria. This is not the aspect of low perceived support that social cognitive theories hypothesize is important in depression.

It is not clear whether controlling for T1 dysphoria is an obstacle to testing stress and coping social support theory, in part because the theory does not describe in sufficient detail the links among perceived support, enacted support, dysphoria, and time. According to stress and coping theory, perceived support is a marker of the extent to which enacted support in the past has been effective in moderating the effects of past life events. Thus, if low perceived support at T1 forecasts depression onset, this is because perceived support also forecasts the receipt of effective enacted support. What is not clear is the extent to which removing T1 dysphoria would impair T1 perceived support's ability to forecast the provision of effective enacted support.

Third, even if T1 low perceived support forecast depression onset, controlling for dysphoria, and in the absence of life events, it is not clear that such a finding would provide clear evidence for any existing theory of perceived support. Neither social cognitive nor symbolic interactionist theories predict such an effect. In addition, stress and coping theory specifically predicts stress buffering, and therefore forecasting depression prospectively in the absence of stress buffering is not predicted by that theory. One could argue that any low-support-related increase in depression presupposes a buffering effect, but such an argument may not be falsifiable. Instead, if depression was predicted by low perceived support (controlling for T1 dysphoria, and in the absence of life events), it would suggest mechanisms not described by any existing theory. Such an effect would suggest a mechanism by which low perceived support promoted a gradual, progressive weakening of mechanisms involved in regulating affect, but that this effect would only be revealed in a sudden, unexpected onset of depression. Such an effect would be more akin to how plaques on the arteries of the heart ultimately lead to heart attacks without the plaques causing detectible symptoms for years. Hobfoll's (2001) conservation of resources theory provides the most similar account of such a process. This theory explains distress as a consequence of resource loss and treats social support as a resource. Those with fewer resources are hypothesized to lose additional resources over time compared to those with more resources and thus there should be a continuous reduction over time in social support and a continuous increase over time in depression. Nonetheless, resource loss (e.g., lowered social support) should still be associated with dysphoria at T1, and so even this theory does not quite seem to fit the phenomenon that prospective designs can capture.

ALTERNATIVE RESEARCH DESIGNS

We have argued that prospective research studies have not provided strong support for stress and coping social support theory and that these studies have not accurately tested the hypotheses of alternative theories of social support. If so, how should the field proceed? If, as suggested by social cognitive and symbolic interactionist theories, perceived support, self-relevant cognition, identity, support perceptions, and depressive symptoms ebb and flow together as social interaction changes, it would be important to use methods that could capture this ebb and flow.

We acknowledge that such an approach would not be without its difficulties. First, as they are commonly defined, depressive symptoms must be present nearly every day, nearly all day, for 2 full weeks before symptoms are considered to be depression. By this definition it may not be possible to study the ebb and flow of depression as social interaction changes on a daily or hourly basis. Instead one would have to study the ebb and flow of depression-related processes across changing social contexts. Although perhaps not optimal, we do not believe this restriction presents an insurmountable obstacle. Other areas of depression research (e.g., basic research on neuronal transmission on non-human animals) have made important contributions to understand depression in spite of similar limitations (Thase & Howland, 1995) Moreover, nearly all cognitive behavior therapies for depression (e. g., Beck, *et al.*, 1979) require the assessment of daily and hourly ebb and flow as a prerequisite to effective therapy. Thus, studying the ebb and flow of depression-related processes fit squarely with core assumptions of important traditions in depression research. In the last section of this chapter, we describe briefly three alternative methods that can be used to study this ebb and flow: laboratory experiments, Generalizability/Social Relations Model (G/SRM) designs, and daily-diary studies.

Ebb and flow in depression-related phenomenon could be induced experimentally by the kind of staged social interactions in the tradition of experimental social psychology. Although such experimental studies of social support have been available for over 20 years (e.g., Sarason & Sarason, 1986), this method has been underutilized. The primary advantages of experimental designs are that they permit causal inferences, and they require investigators to be explicit about the type of social interaction that should influence depression-related phenomenon. Bolger and Amarel (2007) provided an excellent recent example. They studied the extent to which enacted support, when recognized as such by the recipient, was linked to increases in distress, whereas unrecognized enacted support was linked to decreases in distress. To do so, they created social situations in which confederates provided subtle or obvious social support in response to a laboratory stressor. Results replicated field studies, provided stronger causal evidence for the effect, and provided new evidence that obvious support increased distress by suggesting that recipients lacked the personal resources needed to manage the stressor.

Another method for studying the ebb and flow of depression-related processes is provided by Generalizability theory (G; Cronbach *et al.*, 1972) and the Social Relations Model (SRM; Kenny, 1994). These methods use repeated measures experimental designs, in which participants are exposed to the same support providers. One of the advantages of the G/SRM approach is that it provides precise quantitative definitions of the effects of recipient personality as well as two distinct types of social influences, and thus permits the isolation of personality from social influences. When perceivers rate the same providers on supportiveness, three distinct influences can be isolated: the trait-like characteristics of perceivers, the objectively supportive properties of providers (i.e., agreement among perceivers), and the unique relationships among perceivers and providers (i.e., systematic disagreement among perceivers about the relative supportiveness of providers). As described previously, perceived support is primarily a reflection of unique relationships in normal samples (Lakey, in press), and this finding has been replicated with depressed patients (Lakey *et al.*, 1999). The ebb and flow of affect and perceived support can be studied by observing support recipients as they have multiple interactions over time with the same support providers. As demonstrated by Neely *et al.* (2006), such a design can isolate the ebb and flow in affect and perceived support that reflects relational influences. Multivariate G analyses (Cronbach *et al.*, 1972) can then be used to estimate correlations between affect and perceived support for relational influences specifically.

Daily-diary studies provide another useful tool for studying the ebb and flow of depression-related processes across changes in social interaction. In daily-diary studies, participants record affect, perceived social interaction, and other variables at the end of the day for numerous days. This method has a number of advantages. First, participants' reports of social interaction and affect should be highly accurate because participants' complete measures shortly after the events of interest occurred. Second, the method permits the gathering of highly detailed information about the sequence of events while participants are in their natural environments. Third, and perhaps most useful, when analyzed by multilevel modeling, the method permits the calculation of links among affect and social interaction uniquely for each participant as well as on average across all participants. The patterns of relations among variables for specific groups of participants might be very important for the study of social support and depression because social support processes might not work the same way for all people. For example, Gleason *et al.* (in press) asked couples to report daily their affect, support provision, support receipt and relationship closeness. On average across all participants, distress as well as closeness increased on days on which participants reported receiving enacted support. However, more idiographic analyses indicated that the participants that displayed the largest increases in closeness following support receipt also displayed reductions in distress following support receipt. Participants that did not show strong links between support receipt and closeness showed the more common pattern of increases in distress following support receipt. Gleason *et al.* (in press) showed how idiographic analyses can help clarify counter-intuitive findings in social support research. Recent research by Cohen *et al.* (2006) showed how daily-diary methods can be used in studying depressed patients.

In summary, testing hypotheses derived from social-cognitive and symbolic interactionist theories about the ebb and flow across social contexts of depression-related processes will require that investigators use a wider range of methods than previously. We want to be clear that we do not advocate turning away from the useful operational definitions of clinical depression that have emerged over the last 30 years. We also recognize that for the types of methods we have just described to help understand depression, it will be important to apply these methods to samples of depressed people. At the same time, we think it is too limiting to rely exclusively on prospective onset studies for testing hypotheses about social support and depression.

SUMMARY AND CONCLUSIONS

This chapter reviewed research on social support and depression with an emphasis on testing social support theory. Nearly all research on social support and depression has been guided by stress and coping social support theory that states that social support is a stable resource that protects people from depression by buffering the effects of stress through social support's effects on coping and appraisal. Cross-sectional studies consistently found that depressed people perceived less support than did non-depressed people. In contrast, prospective studies of depression onset have only rarely found that people with low support at T1 were more likely to develop depression by T2 than were people with high support at T1. Studies of the course of depression revealed many examples whereby perceived support at T1 forecasted remission by T2, although there were some inconsistencies across study findings. However, across each of these three types of studies, there was little evidence that social support was linked to depression by buffering the effects of stress. The chapter reviewed reasons why studies might not have been sufficiently sensitive to detect stress buffering and considered the possibility that stress and coping social support theory is inadequate to explain social support's link to depression. Alternative theories of social support's link to depression were reviewed, as were methods appropriate for testing those theories.

REFERENCES

Abramson, L. Y., Metalksy, G. I., & Alloy, L. B. (1989). Hopelessness depression: A theory-based subtype of depression. *Psychological Review*, *96*, 358–372.

American Psychiatric Association (1987). *Diagnostic and Statistical Manual of Mental Disorders* (3rd ed., rev.). Washington, DC: Author.

American Psychiatric Association (1994). *Diagnostic and Statistical Manual of Mental Disorders* (4th ed.). Washington, DC: Author.

Barnett, P. A., & Gotlib, I. H. (1988). Psychosocial functioning and depression: Distinguishing among antecedents, concomitants, and consequences. *Psychological Bulletin*, *104*, 97–126.

Barrera, M. Jr (1983). A method for the assessment of social support networks in community survey research. *Connections*, *3*, 8–13.

Barrera, M. Jr (1986). Distinctions between social support concepts, measures, and models. *American Journal of Community Psychology*, *14*, 413–455.

Beck, A. T., Rush, A. J., Shaw, B. F., & Emery, G. (1979). *Cognitive therapy of depression*. NY: Guilford.

Belsher, G., & Costello, C. G. (1991). Do confidants of depressed women provide less social support than confidants of nondepressed women?. *Journal of Abnormal Psychology, 100*, 516–525.

Billings, A. G., & Moos, R. H. (1985). Life stressors and social resources affect posttreatment outcomes among depressed patients. *Journal of Abnormal Psychology, 94*, 140–153.

Billings, A. G., Cronkite, R. C., & Moos, R. H. (1983). Social-environmental factors in unipolar depression: Comparisons of depressed patients and nondepressed controls. *Journal of Abnormal Psychology, 92*, 119–133.

Bolger, N., & Amarel, D. (2007). Effects of social support visibility on adjustment to stress: Experimental evidence. *Journal of Personality and Social Psychology, 92*, 458–475.

Bolger, N., Zuckerman, A., & Kessler, R. C. (2000). Invisible support and adjustment to stress. *Journal of Personality & Social Psychology, 79*, 953–961.

Bosworth, H. B., Steffens, D. C., Kuchibhatla, M. N., Jiang, W. J., Arias, R. M., O'Connor, C. M., & Krishnan, K. R. R. (2000). The relationship of social support, social networks and negative events with depression in patients with coronary artery disease. *Aging and Mental Health, 4*, 253–258.

Brewin, C. R., Andrews, B., & Valentine, J. D. (2000). Meta-analysis of risk factors for posttraumatic stress disorder in trauma-exposed adults. *Journal of Consulting and Clinical Psychology, 68*, 748–766.

Brissette, I., Cohen, S., & Seeman, T. E. (2000). Measuring social integration and social networks. In S. Cohen, L. G. Underwood & B. H. Gottlieb (Eds.), *Social Support Measurement and Intervention: A Guide for Health and Social Scientists* (pp. 53–85). New York: Oxford University Press.

Brown, G. W., & Harris, T. (1978). *Social Origins of Depression: A Study of Psychiatric Disorder in Women*. New York: Free Press.

Brown, G. W., Andrews, B., Harris, T., Adler, Z., & Bridge, L. (1986). Social support, self-esteem and depression. *Psychological Medicine, 16*, 813–831.

Brugha, T., Bebbington, P. E., MacCarthy, B., Potter, J., Sturt, E., & Wykes, T. (1987). Social networks, social support and the type of depressive illness. *Acta Psychiatrica Scandinavica, 76*, 664–673.

Brugha, T. S., Bebbington, P. E., MacCarthy, B., Sturt, E., Wykes, T., & Potter, J. (1990). Gender, social support and recovery from depressive disorders; a prospective clinical study. *Psychological Medicine, 20*, 147–156.

Brugha, T. S., Bebbington, P. E., Stretch, D. D., MacCarthy, B., & Wykes, T. (1997). Predicting the short-term outcome of first episodes and recurrences of clinical depression: A prospective study of life events, difficulties, and social support networks. *Journal of Clinical Psychiatry, 58*, 298–306.

Burton, E., Stice, E., & Seeley, J. R. (2004). A prospective test of the stress-buffering model of depression in adolescent girls: No support once again. *Journal of Consulting and Clinical Psychology, 72*, 689–697.

Cairney, J., Boyle, M., Offord, D. R., & Racine, Y. (2003). Stress, social support and depression in single and married mothers. *Social Psychiatry and Psychiatric Epidemiology, 38*, 442–449.

Cast, A. D., & Burke, P. J. (2002). A theory of self-esteem. *Social Forces, 80*, 1041–1068.

Cohen, L. H., Gunthert, K. C., & Butler, A. C. (2006). Stress, coping and outcome in cognitive therapy. In R. R. Bootzin, & P. E. McKnight (Eds.), *Strengthening Research Methodology: Psychological Measurement and Evaluation* (pp. 63–74). Washington, DC, US: American Psychological Association.

Cohen, S., & Hoberman, H. M. (1983). Positive events and social supports as buffers of life change stress. *Journal of Applied Social Psychology, 13*, 99–125.

Cohen, S., & Wills, T. A. (1985). Stress, social support, and the buffering hypothesis. *Psychological Bulletin, 98*, 310–357.

Coyne, J. C. (1994). Self-reported distress: analog or ersatz depression? *Psychological Bulletin, 116*, 29–45.

Cutrona, C. E., & Russell, D. W. (1987). The provisions of social relationships and adaptation to stress. *Advances in Personal Relationships, 1*, 37–67.

Cutrona, C. E., & Russell, D. W. (1990). Type of social support and specific stress: Toward a theory of optimal matching. In B. R Sarason, I. G. Sarason & G. R. Pierce (Eds.), *Social Support: An Interactional View* (pp. 319–366). New York: Wiley & Sons.

Cronbach, L. J., Gleser, G. C., Nanda, H., & Rajaratnam, N. (1972). *The Dependability of Behavioral Measurements: Theory of Generalizability of Scores and Profiles*. NY: Wiley.

Cronkite, R. C., Moos, R. H., Twohey, J., Cohen, C., & Swindle, R. Jr (1998). Life circumstances and personal resources as predictors of the ten-year course of depression. *American Journal of Community Psychology, 26*, 255–280.

Dura, J. R., Stukenberg, K. W., & Kiecolt-Glaser, J. K. (1991). Anxiety and depressive disorders in adult children caring for demented parents. *Psychology and Aging, 6*, 467–473.

Edwards, A. C., Nazroo, J. Y., & Brown, G. W. (1998). Gender differences in marital support following a shared life event. *Social Science and Medicine, 46*, 1077–1085.

Finch, J. F., Okun, M. A., Pool, G. J., & Ruehlman, L. S. (1999). A comparison of the influence of conflictual and supportive social interactions on psychological distress. *Journal of Personality, 67*, 581–621.

Finlay-Jones, R. A., Brown, G. W., Duncan-Jones, P., Harris, T. O., Murphy, E., & Prudo, R. (1981). Depression and anxiety in the community: replicating the diagnosis of a case. *Psychological Medicine, 10*, 445–454.

Frazier, P. A., Tix, A. P., Klein, C. D., & Arikian, N. J. (2000). Testing theoretical models of the relations between social support, coping and adjustment to stressful life events. *Journal of Social and Clinical Psychology, 19*, 314–335.

Furman, W., & Buhrmester, D. (1985). Children's perceptions of the personal relations in their social networks. *Developmental Psychology, 21*, 1016–1024.

George, L. K., Blazer, D. G., Hughes, D. C., & Fowler, N. (1989). Social support and the outcome of major depression. *British Journal of Psychiatry, 154*, 478–485.

Gleason, M. E. J., Iida, M., Shrout, P. E., & Bolger, N. (in press). Receiving support as a mixed blessing: evidence for dual effects of support on psychological outcomes. Journal of Personality and Social Psychology.{Please update the reference Gleason *et al.* (in press)}

Haber, M. G., Cohen, J. L., Lucas, T., & Baltes, B B. (2007). The relationship between self-reported received and perceived social support: A meta-analytic review. *American Journal of Community Psychology, 39*, 133–144.

Hankin, B. J., Fraley, R. C., Lahey, B. B., & Waldman, I. D. (2005). Is depression best viewed as a continuum or discrete category? A taxometric analysis of childhood and adolescent depression in a population-based sample. *Journal of Abnormal Psychology, 114*, 96–110.

Hayden, E. P., & Klein, D. N. (2001). Outcome of dysthymic disorder at 5-year follow-up: The effect of familial psychopathology, early adversity, personality, comorbidity and chronic stress. *American Journal of Psychiatry, 158*, 1864–1870.

Heller, K. (1979). The effects of social support: Prevention and treatment implications. In A. P. Goldstein & F. H. Kanfer (Eds.), *Maximizing Treatment Gains: Transfer Enhancement in Psychotherapy*. New York: Academic Press.

Hobfoll, S. E. (2001). The influence of culture, community, and the nested-self in the stress process: Advancing conservation of resources theory. *Applied Psychology: An international review, 50*, 337–421.

Hybels, C. F., Blazer, D. G., & Steffens, D. C (2005). Predictors of partial remission in older patients treated for major depression: The role of comorbid dysthymia. *The American Journal of Geriatric Psychiatry, 13*, 713–721.

Kaniasty, K., & Norris, F. H. (1993). A test of the social support deterioration model in the context of natural disaster. *Journal of Personality and Social Psychology, 64*, 398–408.

Kaul, M., & Lakey, B. (2003). Where is the support in perceived support? The role of generic relationship satisfaction and enacted support in perceived support's relation to low distress. *Journal of Social and Clinical Psychology*, *22*, 59–78.

Kendall, P. C., Hollon, S. D., Beck, A. T., Hammen, C. L., & Ingram, R. E. (1987). Issues and recommendations regarding use of the Beck Depression Inventory. *Cognitive Therapy and Research*, *11*, 289–299.

Kenny, D. (1994). *Interpersonal Perception: A Social Relations Analysis*. NY: Guilford Press.

Klein, S. B., Loftus, J., Trafton, J. G., & Fuhrman, R. W. (1992). Use of exemplars and abstractions in trait judgments: A model of trait knowledge about the self and others. *Journal of Personality and Social Psychology*, *63*, 739–753.

Lakey, B. (in press). Social Support: Basic Research and New Strategies for Intervention. To appear in J. E. Maddux & J. P. Tangney (Eds.) Social Psychological Foundations of Clinical Psychology. NY: Guilford.

Lakey, B., & Cassady, P. B. (1990). Cognitive processes in perceived social support. *Journal of Personality and Social Psychology*, *59*, 337–343.

Lakey, B., & Drew, J. B. (1997). A social-cognitive perspective on social support. In G. R. Pierce, B. Lakey, I. G. Sarason & B. R. Sarason (Eds.), *Sourcebook of Social Support and Personality* (pp. 107–140). New York: Plenum.

Lakey, B., & Cohen, S. (2000). Social support theory and selecting measures of social support. In S. Cohen, L. U. Gordon & B. H. Gottlieb (Eds.), *Social Support Measurement and Interventions: A Guide for Health and Social Scientists* (pp. 29–52). NY: Oxford.

Lakey, B., Drew, J. B., & Sirl, K. (1999). Clinical depression and perceptions of supportive others: A generalizability analysis. *Cognitive Therapy and Research*, *23*, 511–533.

Landerman, R., George, L. K., Campbell, R. T., & Blazer, D. G. (1989). Alternative models of the stress buffering hypothesis. *American Journal of Community Psychology*, *17*, 625–642.

Lara, M. E., Leader, J., & Klein, D. N. (1997). The association between social support and course of depression: Is it confounded with personality? *Journal of Abnormal Psychology*, *106*, 478–482.

Lazarus, R. S. & Folkman, S. (1984). *Stress, Appraisal and Coping*. NY: Springer.

Lewinsohn, P. M., Hoberman, H. M., & Rosenbaum, M. (1988). A prospective study of risk factors for unipolar depression. *Journal of Abnormal Psychology*, *97*, 251–264.

Lewinsohn, P. M., Gotlib, I. H., & Seeley, J. R. (1997). Depression-related psychosocial variables: Are they specific to depression in adolescents? *Journal of Abnormal Psychology*, *106*, 365–375.

Lewinsohn, P. M., Roberts, R. E., Seeley, J. R., Rohde, P., Gotlib, I. H., & Hops, H. (1994). Adolescent Psychopathology: II. Psychosocial risk factors for depression. *Journal of Abnormal Psychology*, *103*, 302–315.

Monroe, S. M. (in press). Modern approaches to conceptualizing and measuring human life stress. Annual Review of Clinical Psychology.{Please update the reference Monroe (in press)}

Monroe, S. M., & Steiner, S. C. (1986). Social support and psychopathology: Interrelations with preexisting disorder, stress and personality. *Journal of Abnormal Psychology*, *95*, 29–39.

Neely, L. C., Lakey, B., Cohen, J. L., Barry, R., Orehek, E., Abeare, C. A., & Mayer, W. (2006). Trait and social processes in the link between social support and affect: An experimental laboratory investigation. *Journal of Personality*, *74*, 1015–1046.

Newcomb, M. D., & Keefe, K. (1997). Social support, self-esteem, social conformity, and gregariousness: Developmental patterns across twelve years. In G. R. Pierce, B. Lakey, I. G. Sarason & B. R. Sarason (Eds.), *Sourcebook of Social Support and Personality* (pp. 303–333). New York: Plenum Press.

O'Connor, P., & Brown, G. W. (1984). Supportive relationships: Fact or fancy? *Journal of Social and Personal Relationships*, *1*, 159–175.

O'Hara, M. W. (1986). Social support, life events and depression during pregnancy and the puerperium. *Archives of General Psychiatry*, *43*, 569–573.

Okun, M. A., & Lockwood, C. M. (2003). Does level of assessment moderate the relation between social support and social negativity? A meta-analysis. *Basic and Applied Social Psychology*, *25*, 15–35.

Oldehinkel, A. J., Ormel, J., & Neeleman, J. (2000). Predictors of time to remission from depression in primary care patients: Do some people benefit more from positive life change than others? *Journal of Abnormal Psychology, 109*, 299–307.

Panzarella, C., Alloy, L. B., & Whitehouse, W. G. (2006). Expanded hopelessness theory of depression: On the mechanisms by which social support protects against depression. *Cognitive Therapy and Research, 30*, 307–333.

Puig-Antich, J., & Chambers, W. J. (1983). *Schedule for Affective Disorders and Schizophrenia for School-Age Children (6–18 years)*. Pittsburgh, PA: Western Psychiatric Institute.

Radloff, L. S. (1977). The CES-D scale: A self-report depression scale for research in the general population. *Applied Psychological Measurement, 1*, 385–401.

Rahman, A., Iqbal, Z., & Harrington, R. (2003). Life events, social support and depression in childbirth: perspectives from a rural community in the developing world. *Psychological Medicine, 33*, 1161–1167.

Redinbaugh, E. M., MacCallum, R. C., & Kiecolt-Glaser, J. K. (1995). Recurrent sydromal depression in caregivers. *Psychology and Aging, 10*, 358–368.

Reitzes, D. C., & Mutran, E. J. (2002). Self-concept as the organization of roles: importance, centrality, and balance. *Sociological Quarterly, 43*, 647–667.

Rivera, P. A., Rose, J. M., Futterman, A., Lovett, S. B., & Gallagher-Thompson, D. (1991). Dimensions of perceived social support in clinically depressed and nondepressed female caregivers. *Psychology and Aging, 6*, 232–237.

Russell, D., Peplau, L. A., & Cutrona, C. E. (1980). The revised UCLA loneliness scale: concurrent and discriminant validity evidence. *Journal of Personality and Social Psychology, 39*, 472–480.

Sarason, I. G., & Sarason, B. R. (1986). Experimentally provided social support. *Journal of Personality and Social Psychology, 50*, 1222–1225.

Sarason, B. R., Pierce, G. R., & Sarason, I. G. (1990). Social Support: The Sense of Acceptance and the Role of Relationships. In B. R. Sarason, I. G. Sarason & G. R. Pierce (Eds.), *Social support: An interactional view* (pp. 9–25). New York: Wiley & Sons.

Sarason, B. R., Sarason, I. G., & Gurung, R. A. R. (2001). Close personal relationships and health outcomes: A key to the role of social support. In B. R. Sarason & S. Duck (Eds.), *Personal Relationships: Implications for Clinical and Community Psychology* (pp. 15–41). New York: Wiley.

Sheeber, L. B., Davis, B., Leve, C., Hops, H., & Tildesley, E. (2007). Adolescents' relationships with their mothers and fathers: Associations with depressive disorder and subdiagnostic symptomatology. *Journal of Abnormal Psychology, 116*, 144–154.

Simon, R. W. (1997). The meanings individuals attach to role identities and their implications for mental health. *Journal of Health and Social Behavior, 38*, 256–274.

Spitzer, R. L., Endicott, J., & Robins, E. (1978). Research diagnostic criteria: Rationale and reliability. *Archives of General Psychiatry, 35*, 773–782.

Spitzer, R. L., Williams, J. B., Endicott, J., & Gibbon, M. (1987). *Structured Clinical Interview for DSM-III-R Disorders – Nonpatient Version (SCID-NP)*. New York: New York State Psychiatric Institute, Biometrics Research Department.

Stice, E. (2002). Risk and maintenance factors for eating pathology: A meta-analytic review. *Psychological Bulletin*, 128, 825–848.

Stice, E., Ragan, J., & Randall, P. (2004). Prospective relations between social support and depression: Differential direction of effects for parent and peer support? *Journal of Abnormal Psychology, 113*, 155–159.

Swindle, R. W. Jr, Cronkite, R. C., & Moos, R. H. (1989). Life stressors, social resources, coping and the 4-year course of unipolar depression. *Journal of Abnormal Psychology, 98*, 468–477.

Thase, M. E., & Howland, R. H. (1995). Biological processes in depression: An updated review and integration. In E. E. Beckham & W. R. Leber (Eds.), *Handbook of Depression, 2nd Ed* (pp. 213–279). NY: Guilford.

Thoits, P. A. (1985). Social support and psychological well-being: Theoretical possibilities. In I. G. Sarason & B. R. Sarason (Eds.), *Social Support: Theory, Research and Application* (pp. 51–72). Dordrecht: Martinus Nijhoff.

Thoits, P. A. (1999). Self, identity, stress and mental health. In C. S. Aheshensel & J. C. Phelan (Eds.), *Handbook of Sociology and Mental Health* (pp. 345–368). Dordrecht, Netherlands: Kluwer Academic Publishers.

Turner, R. J., & Marino, F. (1994). Social support and social structure; A descriptive epidemiology. *Journal of Health and Social Behavior*, *35*, 193–212.

Uchino, B. N. (2004). *Social support and physical health: Understanding the health consequences of our relationships*. New Haven, CT: Yale University Press.

Wade, T. D., & Kendler, K. S. (2000a). The relationship between social support and major depression: Cross-sectional, longitudinal, and genetic perspectives. *Journal of Nervous and Mental Disease*, *188*, 251–258.

Wade, T. D., & Kendler, K. S. (2000b). Absence of interactions between social support and stressful life events in the prediction of major depression and depressive symptomatology in women. *Psychological Medicine*, *30*, 965–974.

Wilhelm, K., Parker, G., Dewhurst-Savellis, J., & Asghari, A. (1999). Psychological predictors of single and recurrent major depressive episodes. *Journal of Affective Disorders*, *54*, 139–147.

Wills, T. A., & Shinar, O. (2000). Measuring perceived and received support. In S. Cohen, L. G. Underwood & B. H. Gottlieb (Eds.), *Social Support Measurement and Intervention: A Guide for Health and Social Scientists* (pp. 86–135). New York: Oxford.

Wing, J. K., Cooper, J. E. & Sartorius, N. (1974). *The Measurement and Classification of Psychiatric Symptoms: An Instruction Manual for the PSE and Catego Program*. Cambridge: Cambridge University Press.

18

STRESS GENERATION AND DEPRESSION

CONSTANCE HAMMEN* AND
JOSEPHINE H. SHIH†

*Department of Psychology, University of California, Los Angeles, CA
†Department of Psychology, Saint Joseph's University, Philadelphia, PA

DEFINING THE RISK FACTOR

Depression is known to be a consequence of exposure to stress (e.g., Brown & Harris, 1989; Kessler, 1997; Hammen, 2005). "Stress generation" is a term that describes the contribution of the depressive person to the occurrence of stressful life events (Hammen, 1991). In contrast to fateful or uncontrollable events such as death of a relative or a friend's moving away, which are out of the individual's control, "dependent" stressful events are rated by judges as having occurred at least in part because of the characteristics, circumstances, or behaviors of the individual. Many dependent life events involve negative situations with other people, and thus interpersonal content is frequently although not invariably evident. Examining the stress generation process in depression is not about blaming the individual for causing his or her own depression. Rather, the broader goal is further understanding of risk for depression. The occurrence of dependent life events which are caused at least in part by the person may also reveal the contributions of the context in which the person lives and interacts, such as a dysfunctional mate or difficult child. Events caused in part by the person are not just due to maladaptive traits, vulnerabilities, or unskillful actions, but may also reflect being ensnared in a challenging life situation. Nevertheless, intrapersonal variables and maladaptive skills that may contribute to dependent stressors need to be examined in order to more fully understand risk for depression.

The significance of stress generation as a risk factor for depression arises from two sources. One is that depressed people or formerly depressed people have elevated risk of experiencing negative life events to which they have contributed. Further sections of the chapter will review the empirical evidence for stress generation in depression. The second important implication is that increases in stressors likely contribute to the risk of recurrent or chronic depression, given the robust role of stressors as precipitants of depressive experiences. A vicious cycle of stress and depression presents challenges and opportunities for intervention and for predicting the course of depression.

GENERAL MODELS OF PERSON–ENVIRONMENT TRANSACTIONS

Although the focus in stress generation research has been limited to the link between depression and the occurrence of stressors arising at least in part from the person's actions, characteristics or circumstances, other investigators, both historically and more recently, have raised the general issue of the contribution of persons to the occurrence of negative life events.

There is substantial history and conceptualization in psychology of person–environment transactions, with many researchers and theorists noting that individuals are far from passive recipients of situational influences, and instead, are active players in selecting environments and provoking and eliciting responses (Buss, 1987; Diener *et al.*, 1984; Mischel, 1973). Bandura (1982) talked about "reciprocal determinism" between the person and environment, and a generation of post-behaviorists emphasized the environment as perceived and acted upon by the individual, rather than viewing individuals as simply receptors of environmental stimuli (e.g., Mahoney, 1974; see review in Hammen, 2006).

In the realm of psychopathology and psychological disorders, behavior geneticists and developmental psychopathologists in particular, have noted patterns of gene–environment correlations and of the person's role in creating and selecting environments (e.g., Plomin & Bergeman, 1991; Plomin *et al.*, 1977; Scarr & McCartney, 1983). Several studies have noted a heritable basis to the experience of stressful life events, suggesting that genetic factors play a role in stress generation presumably through heritable traits and dispositions that affect selection into environments as well as reactions to them (e.g., Kendler *et al.*, 1993; McGuffin *et al.*, 1988; Plomin *et al.*, 1990). Developmental psychopathologists, such as Michael Rutter (1986) (e.g., Rutter *et al.*, 1997; see also Champion *et al.*, 1995) also emphasized the contribution of persons to stressful environments. In a later section, several studies that investigated the association of neuroticism with occurrence of stressful life events are noted.

Taken together, there are independent lines of research on person-generated life events, although most of the studies have not specifically distinguished between total exposure to both dependent and independent life events, or to dependent or interpersonal stressors caused by the person. Also, some studies have not focused on depressive outcomes. In the following sections, research specific to depressive disorders is reviewed. We address not only the empirical evidence for stress generation (its association with current and past depression status), but also review research on factors that help to clarify its predictors and mechanisms. We also consider whether stress generation is unique to depression. Finally, we discuss implications for treatment and for further research.

HYPOTHESIZED MECHANISM OF ACTION

Unlike most risk factors, stress generation describes a process rather than a specific trait or characteristic. As noted, the generation of stressful life events increases one's likelihood of depression recurrence. As a corollary, stress generation may also serve as a mechanism of action for other vulnerability factors such as history of prior depression, presence of subclinical symptoms, personality vulnerability, and cognitive vulnerabilities in predicting depression onset or relapse. The following review examines (1) the effect of prior depression and current depressive symptoms on stress generation and (2) the effect of other predictors on stress generation including clinical features and other interpersonal, personality, cognitive, and behavioral variables.

EFFECTS OF PRIOR AND CURRENT DEPRESSION ON STRESS GENERATION

While Hammen (1991) demonstrated the stress generation effect in women with diagnoses of depression, it was not clear whether depression as such was driving the effect. Moreover, the women in the study who showed elevated rates of stressful life events had prior diagnoses of depression but were not necessarily currently in a depressive episode. This finding led to a number of studies replicating the stress generation effect among those with histories of depression, and examining the association of past and current depression with occurrence of dependent life events. Several longitudinal studies examined history of past depression on rates of dependent stressors. In a community sample of late adolescent women, Daley *et al.* (1997) demonstrated that depression during year 1 of the study predicted higher levels of dependent but not independent stress in year 2. Similarly, diagnosis of depression in a twin-study predicted higher levels of stress a year later (Brostedt & Pedersen, 2003). Chun *et al.* (2004) found that depressed patients experienced more exit/loss events (e.g., separation, divorce) over a 10-year follow-up period compared to matched community controls. Their analyses controlled for baseline stressors but not baseline depressive symptoms. Thus, it is unclear whether prior depression *per se* or current depressive symptoms predicted stress generation. Perhaps the longest follow-up support for stress generation spanned

35 years of data (Cui & Vaillant, 1997). Normal college men were followed biennially from the age of 26 to 62. Indicators of depression (e.g., use of antidepressants) predicted a higher number of dependent negative events. Similar to Chun *et al.* (2004), Cui and Vaillant (1997) made group comparisons between those with a history of depression and those without and did not control for concurrent depressive symptoms. In sum, the accumulating data suggest that prior depression predicts the generation of stress for both men and women. Nevertheless, more studies are needed that distinguish between the effect of prior depression and current residual symptoms.

In addition to prior depression diagnoses, research has also focused on the effect of current depressive interview-based symptomatology on stress generation. Chun *et al.* (2004) found that depressive symptoms predicted subsequent interpersonal stressors for both patients and community controls. They also found that within the patient group severe symptomatology at baseline predicted not only initial decreases in family conflict but also led to increases in exit and loss events over a 1-year period. Holahan *et al.* (2005) replicated the stress generation finding prospectively with a 4-year follow-up in a group of older adults (ages 55–65). They demonstrated that individuals with depressive symptoms as rated using the Research Diagnostic Criteria (RDC) experienced higher levels of chronic and episodic stressors. Chun *et al.* (2004) and Holahan *et al.* (2005) studies included both depressed men and women, but did not examine whether gender differences in stress generation were evident.

Similar prospective findings over a 1-year period have been found for a community sample of late adolescent women using a symptom rating scale based on the Structured Clinical Interview for DSM-III-R (Davila *et al.*, 1995). This pattern of findings has been further extended to children. Using a clinic-referred sample, symptom ratings derived from the Schedule for Affective Disorders and Schizophrenia for School-Age Children (K-SADS), Rudolph *et al.* (2000) showed that depressive symptoms predicted generation of dependent interpersonal episodic stress and chronic stress in both boys and girls. The authors tested for gender differences in the generation of dependent stress and did not find differences. They did, however, find gender differences in the types of stress experienced.

The findings summarized thus far have pertained to diagnosed depression or interviewer-rated subclinical levels of depressive symptoms. The effect of depressive symptoms on stress generation in both children and adults also extends to studies using symptom self-report checklists. For children, depressive symptoms measured by the Achenbach Child Behavior Checklist and the Youth Self-Report predicted higher levels of hassles over the course of 1 year in a school-based sample of sixth graders (Little & Garber, 2004). Similarly, Cole *et al.* (2006) found that scores from the Children's Depression Inventory predicted stressful life events prospectively in young adolescents in Grades 7 to 9. Comparing separate structural models showed no gender differences in the pattern of results. For adults, levels of depressive symptoms measured by the Beck Depression Inventory (BDI); Davila *et al.* (1997); Joiner *et al.* (2005); Jones *et al.* (2001); Pianta & Egeland (1994) and the Center for Epidemiological Studies Depression Scale (CES-D; Maciejewski *et al.*, 2000) have both been found to predict higher levels of stressful life events.

Shih and Eberhart (in press) integrated the areas of research on stress generation considering effects of prior depression diagnoses and current depressive symptoms by testing a mediation model in which having a history of past (but not current) diagnosis of major depression predicted greater stress generation through the effect of higher current depressive symptoms. Using an interview-based assessment of dependent stress and focusing on interpersonal stress in particular, the authors found support for the model such that women with a prior episode of major depression reported higher levels of current depressive symptoms as measured by the BDI, which prospectively predicted higher levels of dependent interpersonal stress. It should be noted that although this study included men and women, too few men reported a history of major depression to be included in the analyses.

A further note on gender differences is that only limited such effects emerged in the stress generation process when depressive symptoms rather than depression diagnoses were examined. While some of the studies only examined women (e.g., Pianta & Egeland, 1994), or did not test for gender differences (e.g., Joiner *et al.*, 2005; Maciejewski *et al.*, 2000), studies that conducted specific gender-based analyses yielded gender differences. For example, Jones *et al.*, (2000) found a stress generation effect in wives but not in husbands. Similarly, Davila *et al.* (1997) found that depressive symptoms in wives predicted chronic marital stress whereas husband's depressive symptoms did not generate marital stress. Davila *et al.*'s (1997) analysis of social support behavior suggests "that husbands may not generate marital stress because their wives respond positively to them when they are dysphoric" (p. 859). To date, these two couple-based studies are the only studies that have demonstrated a gender difference in the stress generation effect with regard to depressive symptoms predicting stress[1]. Nevertheless, the majority of the studies on this topic have either used female-only samples (e.g., Daley *et al.*, 1997) or did not test for gender differences explicitly. Without studying a gender-by-depression interaction in predicting stress generation, it is unclear whether the effect found in samples with both males and females is driven by the effect in women or whether it equally occurs in depressed men as well.

In summary, there is strong evidence that a past diagnosis of depression, and both interview-based and questionnaire-based measures of depressive symptoms predict stress generation. Recent evidence suggests that current depressive symptoms may mediate the effect of prior depression on stress generation (Shih & Eberhart, in press). What is less clear is whether the stress generation effect due to depression history or current depressive symptomatology holds

[1] Outside of the marital literature, only two studies to date have examined gender differences in stress generation explicitly (Safford *et al.*, 2007; Shih, 2006). In both studies, the authors found that vulnerability factors for depression (cognitive vulnerability for Safford *et al.*, 2007 and interpersonal vulnerability in the form of sociotropy for Shih, 2006) predicted stress generation prospectively for women but not the men in the study.

for both men and women. Couple-based studies have found the effect on wives but not the husbands in reference to marital or family stress. It is possible, but highly speculative at this point, that there are gender differences in the strength of the stress generation effect that depend on the types of events examined. Additional research examining gender differences would benefit from an examination across domains of stressful life events as well as clinical and psychosocial predictors of stress generation.

EFFECTS OF CLINICAL FACTORS ON STRESS GENERATION

In addition to examining depression as a predictor of stress generation, researchers have also examined a number of clinical factors such as depression comorbidity as a predictor of this process. In a sample of late adolescent women, Daley *et al.* (1997) demonstrated that having a history of depression comorbid with another disorder predicted higher dependent stress compared to individuals with depression alone or no disorders over a 1-year period. Harkness and Luther (2001) examined the impact of depression comorbid with anxiety and dysthymia on stress generation among depressed women. They examined the levels of dependent stressful life events in the 6 months prior to the index episode across 4 groups: major depression alone, comorbidity with dysthymia, comorbidity with anxiety, and comorbidity with both dysthymia and anxiety. Depressed women with additional diagnoses of both dysthymia and anxiety experienced the highest level of dependent stressful life events. Comorbidity with only dysthymia or anxiety did not increase the occurrence of stressful life events. Finally, in a sample of clinic-referred youth, Rudolph *et al.* (2000) demonstrated that comorbidity with externalizing disorders predicted higher levels of dependent stressful life events. In sum, few studies have examined comorbidity as a predictor, but the findings thus far indicate that comorbidity is associated with greater stress generation in depressed individuals. Whether the impact of comorbidity depends on the particular type (e.g., externalizing disorders) or the number of comorbid diagnoses is an area that requires further study before conclusions can be drawn.

In terms of clinical course features, Harkness *et al.* (1999) demonstrated that depressed women with two or more episodes of prior depression experienced more dependent stressful life events in the year prior to the index episode of depression compared to individuals with no history or only one prior episode of depression. This finding hints that the stress generation process may be progressive, but because this is the only study we are aware of that has examined the issue, such a speculation requires further study.

EFFECTS OF OTHER VULNERABILITY FACTORS ON STRESS GENERATION

Stress generation among those with depression histories has largely been interpreted to mean that depressive symptoms promote the generation of stressful life events. However, as previously noted, Hammen (1991) found elevated rates of stressful life events when depressed women were in periods of remission, suggesting that additional factors such as personal characteristics and behaviors of depressed women, not just depressive symptoms, may play a role in stress occurrence. To date, various studies have examined such questions.

Genetic Vulnerability

Studies examining children of depressed mothers have found elevated dependent stress among the offspring (Adrian & Hammen, 1993; Hammen *et al.*, 2004). While these family studies are consistent with the hypothesis that genetic vulnerability may play a role in stress generation, environmental explanations such as modeling of interpersonal vulnerabilities cannot be ruled out. More direct tests using twin-studies have found support for the role of genetic vulnerability in stress generation (Kendler & Karkowski-Shuman, 1997; Kendler *et al.*, 1999a). Thus, it appears that genetics may play a role, but more research is needed to clarify the mechanism through which genes predict stress generation. Kendler *et al.*, suggest that genetic factors may predispose individuals to self-select into higher-stress contexts (Kendler *et al.*, 1999a). Kendler *et al.*, also suggest that neuroticism is a genetically transmitted trait that predisposes a person to both elevated levels of stressful life events as well as to depression (Kendler *et al.*, 2003).

Personality and Interpersonal Vulnerabilities

Increasing research attention has focused on the role of personality on depression and specifically on stress generation. Several investigators have looked at the link between trait neuroticism and occurrence of stressful life events (typically not limiting the latter to dependent events, that is, those arising at least in part from the person). Fergusson and Horwood (1987) were among the first to specifically test the hypothesis that the experience of life events is not random, and may be due to environmental and personal factors. They found that the two major predictors of life event frequency over a 6-year period among women in a longitudinal study were level of social disadvantage (indexed by education, ethnicity, socioeconomic status, and one- or two-parent family status) and neuroticism. Poulton and Andrews (1992) also found that negative interpersonal life events judged to be caused at least in part by the person, were predicted by high scores on neuroticism in a nonclinical population. This relationship held even when initial symptom levels were controlled. They speculated that "highly emotionally sensitive and overly responsive individuals conduct their lives in such a way as to unwittingly encourage interpersonal stressors." (p. 37; see also Magnus *et al.*, 1993). Van Os and Jones (1999) showed that neuroticism scores obtained in adolescence predicted the occurrence of stressful life events at follow-ups 20 and 27 years later in a British birth cohort. The effects were especially marked for women, and neuroticism predicted stress occurrence even after controls for initial symptoms. Information about specific types of events, such as interpersonal or dependent, was not provided. The impact of neuroticism on stress generation has also been replicated in a sample of parents with diagnoses of either bipolar disorder or major depression using an interview-based assessment of dependent stress (Ellenbogen & Hodgins, 2004). Lastly, Kendler *et al.* (2003) also found that neuroticism predicted stressful life events, especially events associated with interpersonal relationships, in a population-based sample of twins. These latter two studies did not control for baseline or concurrent depressive symptoms, and it is unclear whether the impact of neuroticism on stress generation is independent of current depressive symptoms.

In addition to studying neuroticism, researchers have focused on dependency/self-criticism and sociotropy/autonomy as predictors of stress generation, largely in community and college samples. Because these personality vulnerabilities roughly parallel interpersonal and achievement orientations, researchers have also examined whether these vulnerabilities impact the *type* of stressful life events generated (e.g., Shih, 2006). Hammen (1991) found elevated dependent stressful life events in depressed women that were largely interpersonal and conflictual in nature. Flett *et al.* (1997) found that perfectionism, autonomy, and sociotropy all contributed to higher frequency of negative social interactions. Priel and Shahar (2000), on the other hand, did not find support for dependency predicting greater negative stress, but did find that self-criticism predicted higher levels of negative events that in turn predicted dysphoria. Using a sample of late adolescent women, Daley *et al.* (1997) found that both sociotropy and autonomy predicted dependent interpersonal stress over the period of 1 year. This effect was stronger for autonomy as it remained as a significant predictor even after controlling for individuals' psychiatric status. In another study that also examined sociotropy and autonomy, Shih (2006) found that sociotropy significantly predicted higher dependent interpersonal but not achievement stress over a 6-week follow-up period for the women in the study. The association remained significant after controlling for prior depression history, and weekly depressive symptoms. Moreover, higher levels of dependent interpersonal stress partially mediated the effect of sociotropy on increased depressive symptoms over the follow-up period. Shih (2006) findings suggest that individuals who base their self-esteem excessively on their relationship with others are more likely to contribute to the very stress that creates their vulnerability for depression. Overall, the research concerning the interpersonal and achievement orientation predictors of stress generation have demonstrated mixed findings on whether individuals are contributing to stressful life events only in their domain of vulnerability. Both more interpersonally oriented and achievement-oriented vulnerability factors predict higher levels of interpersonal stress (e.g., Daley *et al.*, 1997; Flett *et al.*, 1997). The one study that attempted to examine whether there is differential prediction of interpersonal vs. achievement stress found support only for interpersonal orientation predicting interpersonal stress (Shih, 2006).

Lastly, in addition to examining personality vulnerability factors, researchers have begun to examine interpersonal vulnerability factors such as attachment in predicting stress generation. Using structural equation modeling, Hankin *et al.* (2005) demonstrated that individuals with insecure attachment cognitions experienced higher levels of interpersonal but not achievement stress over the course of 2 years, controlling for initial depressive symptoms. Higher levels of interpersonal stress in turn mediated the relationship between insecure attachment and subsequent depressive symptoms in this sample of college students.

Cognitive Vulnerability

There is some support for the idea that cognitive vulnerability factors that have been traditionally construed within a diathesis-stress framework also contribute to stress generation. Using a cross-sectional design, Simons *et al.* (1993) found that both interpersonal and achievement subscales of the Attributional Style Questionnaire (reported by individuals who were currently depressed) predicted higher number of interview-derived dependent stressful life events prior to the onset of depression. Two prospective studies of cognitive vulnerabilities in predicting stress generation have found support for negative self-views and hopelessness in predicting interpersonal stress (Caldwell *et al.*, 2004; Joiner *et al.*, 2005). Caldwell *et al.* (2004) found that negative self-views in adolescents predicted social disengagement that in turn predicted peer stress. Caldwell *et al.* (2004) controlled for prior peer stress but did not measure initial depressive symptoms. Using a sample of undergraduates, Joiner *et al.* (2005) found that hopelessness predicted greater interpersonal stress based on a checklist measure of stressful life events, after controlling for initial depressive symptoms. More recently, Safford *et al.* (2007) demonstrated that negative cognitive style prospectively predicted higher numbers of dependent events as well as higher numbers of interpersonal events over a 6-month period, compared to those with a positive cognitive style. The results remained the same when they excluded individuals with a history of depression and presence of current depression. The authors were better able to test stress generation than the previous studies examining cognitive vulnerability and stress generation, because they used an interview measure of stress and coded for the extent of dependence/independence for the events. Overall, despite limited published studies, findings support hypotheses that cognitive vulnerability factors not only act as a diathesis in a diathesis-stress model but can also predict heightened stress, thereby providing another mechanism of action for how cognitive vulnerability impacts depression.

Behavioral Vulnerability

While research shows that interpersonal, personality, and cognitive vulnerability factors for depression are promising predictors of stress generation, further examination of what *behaviors* predict stress generation is needed. It is likely that interpersonal, personality, and cognitive predictors impact stress generation through dysfunctional behaviors. The present review focuses on the construct of reassurance seeking, coping styles, and social behaviors (e.g., social skills or social withdrawal). There is limited evidence that self-perceptions of social skills predict levels of interpersonal stress in a college population (Segrin, 2001). Nevertheless, the findings were small in magnitude and stronger when social skills predicted concurrent rather than prospective interpersonal stress. Stronger prospective results were found for the interpersonal behavior of reassurance seeking. Reassurance seeking is a self-reported behavior of eliciting reassurances of others' love in an excessive fashion (Joiner, 2000). Excessive reassurance seeking has been found to predict minor stressful life events in college students prospectively over a period of 5 weeks (Potthoff *et al.*, 1995). On the other hand, Caldwell *et al.* (2004) found that social disengagement predicted greater interpersonal stress in early adolescents. Thus, there is some preliminary evidence that supports the stress-generating effects of behaviors that can be considered either as socially intrusive (reassurance seeking) or disengaged. Similarly, Holahan *et al.* (2005) found that avoidance coping predicted more stressful life events over the course of 4 years in a community sample of adults. This stress generation effect held even after controlling for initial depressive symptoms.

Overall, the limited number of studies on interpersonal behaviors provides preliminary evidence for specific interpersonal behaviors as predictors of stressful life events, possibly more so for interpersonal events. Future studies may consider linking specific behaviors to other predictors of stress generation to further explicate the mechanism of action. For example, insecure attachment may predict excessive reassurance-seeking behavior that in turn predicts interpersonal rejection.

ONSET VS. RECURRENCE OF DEPRESSION

The impact of stressful life events on the onset and recurrence of depression has been well-documented (see Hammen, 2005; Kessler, 1997 for reviews). It has therefore been assumed that stress generation would put individuals at increased risk for depression. However, much of the stress generation research has focused on the association of depression and other factors with the occurrence of dependent stress, with less direct focus on the depressive consequences of stress generation. The following reviews the role of self-generated stress in predicting onset of a depressive episode, and then examines whether there are differential effects for first onset vs. relapse of depression.

ROLE OF SELF-GENERATED (DEPENDENT) STRESS ON DEPRESSION

Kendler *et al.* (1999b) demonstrated that while independent stressful life events significantly predicted onset of a depressive episode, dependent stress was a stronger predictor of depression onset than independent stress. The findings from studies examining the relationship between self-generated stress and depression scores also indicate that dependent stress is a significant predictor of depression. For example, Hammen *et al.* (2004) found support for a model of interpersonal intergenerational transmission of depression, in which maternal depression predicted poorer social competence in youth that in turn predicted greater dependent interpersonal stress. The higher levels of dependent interpersonal stress predicted interview-derived depression scores in the youths. Similar relationships between dependent interpersonal stress and depression were demonstrated by Shih (2006) where dependent interpersonal stress during 1 week predicted higher BDI scores the following week in college women. Furthermore, Daley *et al.* (2006) found support for a mediation model wherein DSM Cluster B symptoms predicted dependent interpersonal stress that in turn predicted depression scores in a sample of low-income urban adolescent girls.

Predicting Onset vs. Recurrence

The review thus far has focused on the impact of stress generation on the onset of a depressive episode. However, it is unclear whether stress generation predicts first onset of depression vs. maintenance and relapse of depression. Some of the studies used mixed samples of never-depressed and previously depressed individuals (e.g., Hammen *et al.*, 2004; Kendler *et al.*, 1999b), but did not analyze whether stress generation predicted first onset or recurrences of depression.

Hammen (1991) proposed that stress generation is a mechanism for depression maintenance and recurrence. The work examining the effect of prior depression predicting stress generation provides part of the support for stress generation as a potential predictor of depression relapse or recurrence. Research using mixed samples (of both never-depressed and depressed individuals) has also offered indirect support in that dependent stress predicted depression onset or depression scores. Nevertheless, to directly examine stress generation as a predictor of depression recurrence, one would need a mediational analysis that shows prior depression predicting stress generation that in turn predicts recurrence of depression. While studies to date have offered support for one part of the mediation model (e.g., prior depression predicts stress generation or dependent stress predicts depression), none have fully tested mediation in the same study. Moreover, in terms of depression maintenance, one might hypothesize that presence of stress generation would predict a longer course of depression. This is another area where additional research is needed.

While stress generation has largely been thought of as a predictor of depression maintenance and recurrence, the recent studies supporting pre-existing vulnerability factors for depression in predicting stress generation suggest the possibility that stress generation may play a contributory role in the first onset of depression. Studies reviewed in the mechanism of action section of the chapter largely focused on depressive symptoms, and therefore, it is not clear whether stress generation is a significant contributor to first onset of diagnoses of depression.

SPECIFICITY OF STRESS GENERATION IN RELATION TO DEPRESSION

The actual origins of the stress generation model as a risk factor in depression arose from clinical hunches based on repeated life-stress assessments of depressed women in a longitudinal study, and led to an empirical analysis comparing women with unipolar, bipolar, or medical disorders, and a non-ill comparison group (Hammen, 1991). The results showing elevated dependent (interpersonal and conflict) events implied that there is something unique or specific about depression and life event occurrence, because women with equally challenging and disruptive illnesses (bipolar and chronic medical disorders) did not show the same pattern.

Although the initial results seemed to argue for specificity of stress generation among those with depression, what evidence supports this claim? Historically, as indicated earlier in the chapter, parallel approaches that were not focused on depressive disorders as such also found evidence for person-contributed life events. Thus, it is likely that stress generation processes may not be limited to depressive disorders but also occur among those with different disorders. However, as with much of depression research, data addressing specificity issues are sparse. Daley *et al.* (1997) study mentioned earlier compared depressed-only high school women to those with depression and comorbid conditions. A small sample of women who had diagnoses of other disorders but not depression had rates of dependent events that were similar to never-diagnosed young women, but the sample size of the nondepressive-diagnosis group was too small and heterogeneous to draw reliable conclusions. Harkness and Luther (2001) demonstrated that women with current major depression and the combination of comorbid anxiety and dysthymic disorder had significantly higher levels of dependent event stress than those with only depression or depression plus anxiety. However, there was no comparison group with only anxiety disorder, so specificity was not tested. Nevertheless, their study is consistent with the idea that disorders that commonly overlap with each other and that may share genetic, temperament, and personality features (e.g., major depression, dysthymia, and certain anxiety disorders), might all contribute to stress generation patterns. Joiner *et al.* (2005) did examine specificity of stress generation to depression by examining predictive associations between both depression and anxiety scores and subsequent reports of stressful life events. Only depressive, but not anxiety, scores predicted later stressors, offering limited support for the specificity hypothesis. A retrospective checklist study of recent life events among children with diagnosed anxiety or depressive disorders, compared to nonpsychiatric children, found a marginally higher rate of dependent events in depressed children compared to the anxiety disorder and nonpsychiatric groups (Williamson *et al.*, 2005). However, the depressed children were also found to have significantly higher exposure to independent events than were the other groups. It is noteworthy that in addition to the limitations of use of checklist assessment, the stressful life events were severe and the checklist included relatively few interpersonal events.

Rudolph *et al.* (2000) examined stress generation patterns in clinically ascertained children with depressive disorders only, externalizing disorders only, and those with comorbid depression and externalizing disorders. Results indicated significant associations between dependent interpersonal stress and depressive disorders, but not externalizing disorders. Externalizing disorders showed significant associations with noninterpersonal but dependent events. Thus, both kinds of disorders indicated stress generation (dependent events) but differed in the content – interpersonal vs. noninterpersonal (such as school-related events). Subsequent analyses indicated that these patterns held for boys, but girls with either depressive or externalizing symptoms were more likely to have elevated rates of interpersonal events.

From a different perspective that did not examine the specificity effect directly, Little and Garber (2005) hypothesized that the link between externalizing symptoms and later depression in youth may be due to the damaging effect of externalizing symptoms on social relationships. Longitudinal analyses supported their hypothesis, indicating that the association between externalizing symptoms and depressive symptoms 1 year later was partially mediated by occurrence of dependent social life events (but not noninterpersonal events or independent events). Gender differences were not explored. Thus, indirectly the results suggest that stress generation effects are not specific to depressive disorders.

Another line of research has focused on subclinical Axis II symptomatology as a predictor of stress generation. In a sample of late adolescent women, Daley *et al.* (1998) found support for Cluster A and Cluster B symptoms predicting stress generation both in terms of dependent episodic stress and chronic interpersonal stress. The findings remained consistent across questionnaire, interview, and informant-based assessment of Axis II symptomatology. Daley *et al.* (2006) replicated this pattern of findings in a low-income urban sample of adolescent girls. They found support for Cluster B symptoms predicting interview-rated dependent interpersonal stress. Thus, these limited findings suggest nonspecificity of depression and stress generation. Because of the high rates of depression-personality pathology comorbidity, the results might also suggest that stress generation sometimes attributed to depression could be accounted for by personality pathology.

Taken together, evidence for the specificity of stress generation's association with depression is mixed. Studies have been limited in number, and all have not specifically tested for dependent or dependent-interpersonal events, or have used stress assessment methods varying in methodological soundness, or have used nonclinical samples differing only in mild symptomatology. Gender differences may modify the associations between type of disorder and stressors, but only a few studies have examined such patterns. It stands to reason that many forms of psychopathology – either because of the symptomatology or the underlying vulnerability factors – may eventuate in problematic outcomes involving work, school, legal, marital, parental, and social phenomena. However, the question remains to be more fully investigated: Is there something unique about depressive disorders and depressed individuals' interpersonal situations that predict elevations in dependent interpersonal life events? Additional information about specificity can help provide further clues about the mechanisms and consequences of stress generation.

IMPLICATIONS FOR RESILIENCE AND TREATMENT

Research on stress generation processes in depression has not reached the stage of studying resilience and protective mechanisms. However, logic suggests that individuals who have had only single episodes of depression (compared to those with recurrent depression), for example, may include those who have characteristics that help not only cope with adversity but possibly also manage to reduce the likelihood that minor stressors develop into major ones. Study of such samples might provide interesting insights into protective and resilience factors.

Treatment implications of stress generation processes are straightforward. It appears that depressed individuals may be at risk for recurrences of depression triggered by adverse situations to which they have contributed. Psychotherapy is an important resource for several relevant goals: identifying the patterns of negative events and recurring themes associated with depressive episodes; exploring and defining the person's contributions due to dysfunctional attitudes, beliefs, behaviors, and personality styles; providing support and possible options for dealing with adverse life conditions. Interventions may need to fortify their efforts to help individuals anticipate and deal with future likely events, both by imparting conflict resolution and other interpersonal skills, and by helping to promote long-term changes in maladaptive life situations – specifically, selecting themselves into more supportive and benign circumstances where possible. It is especially challenging to develop family-oriented treatments when the difficult marital and child-rearing contexts may need to be targeted for change as a way to reduce the recurrence of the stress-depression cycle. Early interventions for depressed youth may be particularly critical, serving as treatments to help young people avoid the pitfalls of entrapment in dysfunctional marriages and early pregnancy which are contextual factors certain to promote the depression-stress cycle.

The challenge is not only to develop treatment strategies, but also to promote access to psychotherapy for youth, and among adults with recurrent depression, who may often be treated mainly or only with medications. As valuable as medications may be, they are unlikely to alter the underlying stress generation vulnerabilities and contexts. Additionally, many people who have highly stressful lives and circumstances may come to view their depression as a "realistic" response to burdens and perceived inescapable negative circumstances. They may feel helpless, if not hopeless, and fail to see their clinical, and life, circumstances as "treatable."

CONCLUSIONS AND DIRECTIONS FOR FUTURE RESEARCH

A body of research has accumulated indicating that a risk factor for depression is exposure to stress that occurs at least in part because of a person's characteristics, behaviors, and circumstances. Such "dependent" negative life events may be largely interpersonal in content, although it is an interesting question whether such events are universally more likely to occur or to trigger depression compared to other events. Most of the research noting that depressed people have more stressors to which they contribute has not clearly distinguished between the effects of current depressive symptoms and prior history of depression. Even though it is likely that residual depressive symptoms themselves impair functioning and contribute to negative life events, research also suggests that additional factors may contribute to stress generation. These include certain personality styles (of which neuroticism is the most studied), as well as dysfunctional beliefs, attitudes, and cognitions, and maladaptive behaviors and social problem-solving skills. Clinical features may also increase the risk of stress generation, including comorbidity with other disorders, and likely also chronicity and number of episodes of depression. Further studies of all of these contributory factors would be welcome, particularly to illuminate patterns and mechanisms that inform treatment and early intervention. Also needed is further work that tests the implications of stress generation: that it triggers recurrence and prolonged or chronic episodes, and may also play an important role in first onsets of major depressive disorder. Whether stress generation is particularly relevant to the course of depression, compared to other disorders, is another issue in need of investigation. Several of these issues and others are elaborated as suggestions for further study.

Predicting Clinically Significant Depression

As the review revealed, there are relatively few studies that examine diagnosable or clinically significant depression as a *consequence* of person-dependent stressors. Specifically, while studies have focused largely on the predictors of stress generation, far fewer studies have examined stress generation as a predictor of depression onset, maintenance, and/or recurrence. Additional research is needed that examines mediation models with stress generation as the mediator (e.g., prior depression predicting stress generation predicting depression relapse). It is also desirable to see more investigations of clinically significant depression, instead of reliance on analog studies.

Gender and Age Differences

A significant portion of the research to date has utilized female-only samples or mixed samples comprised predominantly of women without a direct test of gender differences. It is important for studies of stress generation to recruit both men and women and to test for gender differences explicitly. As suggested by the review, it is possible that stress generation occurs for women but not for men – or that stress generation occurs for men only under certain circumstances (e.g., presence of prior depression, higher number of prior depressive episodes, or when predicting achievement stressors). The pattern of findings from several studies in which vulnerability factors predict stress generation for women but not men may further contribute to our understanding of the well-known gender difference in rates of depression.

In addition, age differences in stress generation should also be explored further. Fundamentally a transactional process, stress generation likely parallels developmental changes. The role one plays in shaping his/her environment is expected to increase with age, such that older children and adolescents would have more choice regarding their social groups. Several studies found significant differences in the kinds of events experienced by children and adolescents (e.g., Cole *et al.*, 2006; Rudolph & Hammen, 1999). Late adolescence and the transition to adulthood are the periods in which selection into social, marital, parenting, and occupational roles may have especially long-term consequences for the likelihood of person-dependent stress and consequent adjustment. Further research on the factors that shape such choices in youth would greatly expand the understanding of stress generation processes.

Distinguishing between Types of Stress

The focus of stress generation research initiated by Hammen (1991) is specific in referring to stressors that are at least in part caused by the individual (dependent or nonfateful stress). Hammen (1991) further noted that the dependent stressors that depressed women experienced had largely interpersonal and conflict content. While subsequent research also has found such patterns, it is likely that other content may also be relevant. For example, depressive symptoms or prior depression may also have a negative impact in the achievement or work domain. Although several investigators have pursued noninterpersonal content (e.g., Hankin *et al.*, 2005; Shih, 2006), null findings could have been attributed to the low base rate of significant achievement events compared to interpersonal events. Moreover, different vulnerability factors and predictors of stress generation may have differential impact on the generation of interpersonal vs. achievement stress. For example, clinical factors (e.g., depression history, comorbidity) may predict both interpersonal and achievement stress but with interpersonal vulnerability factors only predicting interpersonal stress generation.

Understanding Stressful Contexts

Another area requiring further examination is distinguishing between episodic and chronic stress. Much of the research has focused on the prediction of dependent interpersonal stress that is episodic in nature (e.g., Hammen, 2005). The examination of chronic stress can shed light on stress generation process in many ways. More research on the prediction of chronic stress is needed, because episodic stressors alone may not capture stress generation such as ongoing patterns of social interaction and effectiveness in adult roles. In addition, by examining chronic stress or social contexts of individuals, one may also more accurately measure stress that is associated with "lack of positives" in one's life that would be missed by episodic measures of stress. Shahar and Priel (2003) suggested that individuals' vulnerability may not necessarily be expressed via stressful environments. Rather, it may be that vulnerable individuals fail to "elicit a pleasant and gratifying context (p 212)."

Furthermore, in addition to episodic stressful life events, Hammen (2006) has also suggested that depressed women may not only behave in ways that promote occurrence of stressful events, but also may select themselves into stressful contexts. They may be involved with dysfunctional mates, have children with significant behavioral or emotional problems, have illnesses or the burden of care for others with illnesses, limited resources and social networks, and otherwise be at risk for higher levels of life event occurrence coupled with fewer assets for resolving difficulties before they become major negative life events. As noted earlier in the discussion of age and developmental issues, considerable research is needed to examine pathways to such challenging contexts, including mate selection.

REFERENCES

Adrian, C., & Hammen, C. (1993). Stress exposure and stress generation in children of depressed mothers. *Journal of Consulting and Clinical Psychology*, *61*(2), 354–359.

Bandura, A. (1982). Self-efficacy mechanism in human agency. *American Psychologist*, *37*, 122–147.

Brostedt, E. M., & Pedersen, N. L. (2003). Stressful life events and affective illness. *Acta Psychiatrica Scandinavica*, *107*(3), 208–215.

Brown, G. W., & Harris, T. O. (1989). Depression. In G. W. Brown & T. O. Harris (Eds.), *Life Events and Illness* (pp. 49–93). New York, NY: The Guilford Press.

Buss, D. M. (1987). Selection, evocation, and manipulation. *Journal of Personality and Social Psychology*, *53*, 1214–1221.

Caldwell, M. S., Rudolph, K. D., Troop-Gordon, W., & Kim, D.-Y. (2004). Reciprocal influences among relational self-views, social disengagement, and peer stress during early adolescence. *Child Development*, *75*(4), 1140–1154.

Champion, L. A., Goodall, G., & Rutter, M. (1995). Behavior problems in childhood and stressors in early adult life: I. A 20 year follow-up of London school children. *Psychological Medicine*, *25*, 231–246.

Chun, C.-A., Cronkite, R. C., & Moos, R. H. (2004). Stress generation in depressed patients and community controls. *Journal of Social and Clinical Psychology*, *23*(3), 390–412.

Cole, D. A., Nolen-Hoeksema, S., Girgus, J., & Paul, G. (2006). Stress exposure and stress generation in child and adolescent depression: A latent trait-state-error approach to longitudinal analyses. *Journal of Abnormal Psychology*, *115*(1), 40–51.

Cui, X.-J., & Vaillant, G. E. (1997). Does depression generate negative life events? *Journal of Nervous and Mental Disease*, *185*(3), 145–150.

Daley, S. E., Hammen, C., Burge, D., & Davila, J. (1997). Predictors of the generation of episodic stress: A longitudinal study of late adolescent women. *Journal of Abnormal Psychology*, *106*(2), 251–259.

Daley, S. E., Hammen, C., Davila, J., & Burge, D. (1998). Axis ii symptomatology, depression, and life stress during the transition from adolescence to adulthood. *Journal of Consulting and Clinical Psychology*, *66*(4), 595–603.

Daley, S. E., Rizzo, C. J., & Gunderson, B. H. (2006). The longitudinal relation between personality disorder symptoms and depression in adolescence: The mediating role of interpersonal stress. *Journal of Personality Disorders*, *20*(4), 352–368.

Davila, J., Hammen, C., Burge, D., & Paley, B. (1995). Poor interpersonal problem solving as a mechanism of stress generation in depression among adolescent women. *Journal of Abnormal Psychology*, *104*(4), 592–600.

Davila, J., Bradbury, T. N., Cohan, C. L., & Tochluk, S. (1997). Marital functioning and depressive symptoms: Evidence for a stress generation model. *Journal of Personality and Social Psychology*, *73*(4), 849–861.

Diener, E., Larsen, R. J., & Emmons, R. A. (1984). Person × Situation interactions: Choice of situations and congruence response models. *Journal of Personality and Social Psychology*, *47*, 580–592.

Ellenbogen, M. A., & Hodgins, S. (2004). The impact of high neuroticism in parents on children's psychosocial functioning in a population at high risk for major affective disorder: A family-environmental pathway of intergenerational risk. *Development and Psychopathology*, *16*(1), 113–136.

Fergusson, D. M., & Horwood, L. J. (1987). Vulnerability to life events exposure. *Psychological Medicine*, *17*, 739–749.

Flett, G. L., Hewitt, P. L., Garshowitz, M., & Martin, T. R. (1997). Personality, negative social interactions, and depressive symptoms. *Canadian Journal of Behavioural Science*, *29*(1), 28–37.

Hammen, C. (1991). Generation of stress in the course of unipolar depression. *Journal of Abnormal Psychology*, *100*(4), 555–561.

Hammen, C. (2005). Stress and depression. *Annual Review of Clinical Psychology*, *1*(1), 293–319.

Hammen, C. (2006). Stress generation in depression: Reflections on origins, research, and future directions. *Journal of Clinical Psychology*, *62*(9), 1065–1082.

Hammen, C., Shih, J. H., & Brennan, P. A. (2004). Intergenerational transmission of depression: Test of an interpersonal stress model in a community sample. *Journal of Consulting and Clinical Psychology*, *72*(3), 511–522.

Hankin, B. L., Kassel, J. D., & Abela, J. R. Z. (2005). Adult attachment dimensions and specificity of emotional distress symptoms: Prospective investigations of cognitive risk and interpersonal stress generation as mediating mechanisms. *Personality and Social Psychology Bulletin*, *31*(1), 136–151.

Harkness, K. L., & Luther, J. (2001). Clinical risk factors for the generation of life events in major depression. *Journal of Abnormal Psychology*, *110*(4), 564–572.

Harkness, K. L., Monroe, S. M., Simons, A. D., & Thase, M. (1999). The generation of life events in recurrent and non-recurrent depression. *Psychological Medicine*, *29*(1), 135–144.

Holahan, C. J., Moos, R. H., Holahan, C. K., Brennan, P. L., & Schutte, K. K. (2005). Stress generation, avoidance coping, and depressive symptoms: A 10-year model. *Journal of Consulting and Clinical Psychology*, *73*(4), 658–666.

Joiner, T. E., Jr. (2000). Depression's vicious scree: Self-propagating and erosive processes in depression chronicity. *Clinical Psychology: Science and Practice*, *7*(2), 203–218.

Joiner, T. E., Jr., Wingate, L. R., Gencoz, T., & Gencoz, F. (2005). Stress generation in depression: Three studies on its resilience, possible mechanism, and symptom specificity. *Journal of Social and Clinical Psychology*, *24*(2), 236–253.

Joiner, T. E., Jr., Wingate, L. R., & Otamendi, A. (2005). An interpersonal addendum to the hopelessness theory of depression: Hopelessness as a stress and depression generator. *Journal of Social and Clinical Psychology*, *24*(5), 649–664.

Jones, D. J., Beach, S. R. H., & Forehand, R. (2001). Stress generation in intact community families: Depressive symptoms, perceived family relationship stress, and implications for adolescent adjustment. *Journal of Social and Personal Relationships*, *18*(4), 443–462.

Jones, D. J., Forehand, R., & Beach, S. R. H. (2000). Maternal and paternal parenting during adolescence: Forecasting early adult psychosocial adjustment. *Adolescence*, *35*(139), 513–530.

Kendler, K. S., & Karkowski-Shuman, L. (1997). Stressful life events and genetic liability to major depression: Genetic control of exposure to the environment? *Psychological Medicine*, *27*(3), 539–547.

Kendler, K. S., Neale, M. C., Kessler, R., Heath, A. C., & Eaves, L. J. (1993). A twin study of recent life events and difficulties. *Archives of General Psychiatry*, *50*, 789–796.

Kendler, K. S., Karkowski, L. M., & Prescott, C. A. (1999a). The assessment of dependence in the study of stressful life events: Validation using a twin design. *Psychological Medicine*, *29*(6), 1455–1460.

Kendler, K. S., Karkowski, L. M., & Prescott, C. A. (1999b). Causal relationship between stressful life events and the onset of major depression. *American Journal of Psychiatry*, *156*(6), 837–848.

Kendler, K. S., Gardner, C. O., & Prescott, C. A. (2003). Personality and the experience of environmental adversity. *Psychological Medicine*, *33*(7), 1193–1202.

Kessler, R. C. (1997). The effects of stressful life events on depression. *Annual Review of Psychology*, *48*, 191–214.

Little, S. A., & Garber, J. (2004). Interpersonal and achievement orientations and specific stressors predict depressive and aggressive symptoms. *Journal of Adolescent Research*, *19*(1), 63–84.

Little, S. A., & Garber, J. (2005). The role of social stressors and interpersonal orientation in explaining the longitudinal relation between externalizing and depressive symptoms. *Journal of Abnormal Psychology*, *114*(3), 432–443.

Maciejewski, P. K., Prigerson, H. G., & Mazure, C. M. (2000). Self-efficacy as a mediator between stressful life events and depressive symptoms: Differences based on history of prior depression. *British Journal of Psychiatry*, *176*, 373–378.

Magnus, K., Diener, E., Fujita, F., & Payot, W. (1993). Extraversion and neuroticism as predictors for objective life events: A longitudinal analysis. *Journal of Personality and Social Psychology*, *65*, 1046–1053.

Mahoney, M. (1974). *Cognition and Behavior Modification*. Oxford England: Ballinger.

McGuffin, P., Katz, R., & Bebbington, P. E. (1988). The Camberwell Collaborative Depression Study: III. Depression and adversity in the relatives of depressed probands. *British Journal of Psychiatry*, *152*, 775–782.

Mischel, W. (1973). Toward a cognitive social learning reconceptualization of personality. *Psychological Review*, *80*, 252–283.

Pianta, R. C., & Egeland, B. (1994). Relation between depressive symptoms and stressful life events in a sample of disadvantaged mothers. *Journal of Consulting and Clinical Psychology*, *62*(6), 1229–1234.

Plomin, R., & Bergeman, C. S. (1991). The nature of nurture: Genetic influence on "environmental" measures. *Behavior and Brain Sciences*, *14*, 373–427.

Plomin, R., DeFries, J. C., & Loehlin, J. C. (1977). Genotype-environment interaction and correlation in the analysis of human behavior. *Psychological Bulletin*, *84*, 309–322.

Plomin, R., Lichtenstein, P., Pedersen, N. L., McClearn, G. E., & Nesselroade, J. R. (1990). Genetic influence on life events during the last half of the life span. *Psychology and Aging*, *5*, 25–30.

Potthoff, J. G., Holahan, C. J., & Joiner, T. E. (1995). Reassurance seeking, stress generation, and depressive symptoms: An integrative model. *Journal of Personality and Social Psychology*, *68*(4), 664–670.

Poulton, R. G., & Andrews, G. (1992). Personality as a cause of adverse life events. *Acta Psychiatrica Scandinavica*, *85*, 35–38.

Priel, B., & Shahar, G. (2000). Dependency, self-criticism, social context and distress: Comparing moderating and mediating models. *Personality and Individual Differences*, *28*(3), 515–525.

Rudolph, K. D., & Hammen, C. (1999). Age and gender as determinants of stress exposure, generation, and reactions in youngsters: A transactional perspective. *Child Development*, *70*(3), 660–677.

Rudolph, K. D., Hammen, C., Burge, D., Lindberg, N., Herzberg, D., & Daley, S. E. (2000). Toward an interpersonal life-stress model of depression: The developmental context of stress generation. *Development and Psychopathology*, *12*(2), 215–234.

Rutter, M. (1986). Meyerian psychobiology, personality development, and the role of life experiences. *American Journal of Psychiatry*, *143*, 1077–1087.

Rutter, M., Dunn, J., Plomin, R., Simonoff, E., Pickles, A., Maughan, B. *et al.* (1997). Integrating nature and nurture: Implications of person-environment correlations and interactions for developmental psychopathology. *Development and Psychopathology*, *9*, 335–364.

Safford, S. M., Alloy, L. B., Abramson, L. Y., & Crossfield, A. G. (2007). Negative cognitive style as a predictor of negative life events in depression-prone individuals: A test of the stress generation hypothesis. *Journal of Affective Disorders*, *991*, 147–154.

Scarr, S., & McCartney, K. (1983). How people make their own environments: A theory of genotype environment effects. *Child Development*, *54*, 424–435.

Segrin, C. (2001). Social skills and negative life events: Testing the deficit stress generation hypothesis. *Current Psychology: Developmental, Learning, Personality, Social*, *20*(1), 19–35.

Shih, J. H. (2006). Sex differences in stress generation: An examination of sociotropy/autonomy, stress, and depressive symptoms. *Personality and Social Psychology Bulletin*, *32*(4), 434–446.

Shih, J. H., & Eberhart, N. K. (in press). Understanding the impact of prior depression on stress generation: Examining the roles of current depressive symptoms and interpersonal behaviors. *British Journal of Psychology*.

Shahar, G., & Priel, B. (2003). Active vulnerability, adolescent distress, and the mediating/suppressing role of life events. *Personality and Individual Differences*, *35*, 199–218.

Simons, A. D., Angell, K. L., Monroe, S. M., & Thase, M. E. (1993). Cognition and life stress in depression: Cognitive factors and the definition, rating, and generation of negative life events. *Journal of Abnormal Psychology*, *102*(4), 584–591.

Van Os, J., & Jones, P. B. (1999). Early risk factors and adult person-environment relationships in affective disorder. *Psychological Medicine*, *29*, 1055–1067.

Williamson, D. E., Birmaher, B., Dahl, R. E., & Ryan, N. D. (2005). Stressful life events in anxious and depressed children. *Journal of Child and Adolescent Psychopharmacology*, *15*, 571–580.

19

Reassurance Seeking and Negative Feedback Seeking

Katherine A. Timmons and
Thomas E. Joiner, Jr.

Department of Psychology, Florida State University, Tallahassee, FL, USA

Over the past 30 years, interpersonal approaches to the study of depression have begun to reveal the complex interpersonal nature of the disorder (Joiner & Coyne, 1999). A wide range of interpersonal processes in depression have been studied, including broad factors such as interpersonal stress and the influence of relationships with significant others. Recently, however, more specific interpersonal behaviors have emerged as possible risk factors for depression, including two types of interpersonal feedback seeking: excessive reassurance seeking (ERS) (Joiner & Metalsky, 2001; Joiner *et al.*, 1992 1993) and negative feedback seeking (NFS) (Joiner, 1995; Joiner *et al.*, 1993; Swann *et al.*, 1992a).

Current advances in the study of risk factors provide a method for describing and evaluating the association between variables in order to more clearly articulate their relationships and advance theoretical models. The goal of this chapter is to examine ERS and NFS within this risk factors approach. Specifically, this process will allow us to examine and evaluate the following: (1) What is the quality of evidence for a risk-factor relationship, (2) What is the nature of the relationship, and under what conditions does the behavior confer risk for depression, and (3) Can alternative risk factors account for the relationship? Finally, future directions for the study of ERS and NFS as risk factors will be discussed.

RISK FACTOR MODELS

Risk factor research has recently been refined by the work of Kraemer, Kazdin and colleagues, who have proposed that a standardized terminology of risk is necessary to facilitate clear communication about the status of a proposed risk factor (Kazdin *et al.*, 1997; Kraemer *et al.*, 1997; 2001). They define a *risk factor* as a variable that both precedes and increases the likelihood of an outcome. In order to determine whether a variable has attained the status of a risk factor, Kraemer and colleagues have suggested a system which classifies different types of empirical studies in terms of the evidentiary claims they are able to support.

The simplest type of empirical relationship to demonstrate is that of a *correlate,* which is established in cross-sectional studies in which the proposed risk factor and outcome are measured at the same time. A correlate is thus shown to be associated with the outcome, but the nature of the study does not establish temporal precedence. For this reason, studies of correlates are helpful in establishing possible risk factors, but prospective studies, in which the proposed risk factor is measured prior to the outcome, are necessary in order to truly claim that a variable has the status of a risk factor. Once a risk factor has been established, additional evidence can establish that it is a *causal risk factor.* The authors propose that the causal status of a risk factor is demonstrated when studies have shown that manipulating the risk factor experimentally – for example, in a randomized controlled trial – leads to a change in the outcome (Kraemer *et al.*, 1997). Knowledge about the causal status of a risk factor provides important theoretical evidence for understanding its role in the development of a disorder and highlights its importance as a target for preventative interventions.

Although these definitions suggest a relatively simple approach to determining the status of a risk factor, causal models involving risk factors are often complex for a number of reasons (Kazdin *et al.*, 1997). First, the risk factor relationship is conditional: while a risk factor by definition increases the likelihood of the outcome, this relationship may be contingent on a variety of additional variables. An accurate causal model will therefore need to take into account the specific conditions under which a variable confers risk for the disorder. Second, risk factors are involved in developmental processes related to the onset of the outcome, and these processes will need to be specified to understand the nature of risk.

One way to help clarify the role of risk factors in causal models is again to specify terminology for discussing how risk factors operate (Kraemer *et al.*, 2001). For example, when two or more possible risk factors exist, it is important to determine whether these risk factors are fully independent. If not, they may represent overlapping risk factors that could be more appropriately combined into one construct. Alternatively, one risk factor may operate as a *proxy risk factor* for another. A proxy risk factor appears to be a risk factor because it is correlated with another strong risk factor for the outcome; however, when that relationship is taken into account, there is no unique relationship between the proxy risk factor and the outcome.

In addition to describing the relationship between risk factors, causal models must be clarified by describing how the relationship between a risk factor and the outcome may be changed by additional variables. Two such relationships are often specified: mediation and moderation. In a mediation relationship, the relationship between the risk factor and the outcome can be explained because of a third mediator variable: for example, the risk factor causes the mediator variable, which, in turn, causes the outcome. A moderation relationship, on the other hand, changes the relationship between the risk factor and the outcome. For example, in a moderation relationship, the risk factor is differentially related to the outcome at different levels of the moderator variable. Both mediation and moderation relationships are important to understanding the role of ERS and NFS as risk factors for depression and are described in greater detail later in this chapter.

In sum, the risk factor research approach elaborated by Kraemer and colleagues provides a method for systematically evaluating the status of a proposed risk factor through increasingly stringent empirical studies. By examining research on ERS and NFS within this context, we are able to test the quality of the causal claims made about these proposed risk factors, as well as to identify areas in need of further research. Finally, by describing the causal models with specific terminology, we are able to clearly specify the proposed pathways from the risk factor to the disorder, which can help to clarify the role of ERS and NFS in depression.

EXCESSIVE REASSURANCE SEEKING

The study of ERS as a risk factor for depression grew from Coyne's initial presentation of an interpersonal description of depression (Coyne, 1976), which described a process in which depressed individuals behave in a way that elicits negative information from the environment that then strengthens their depression. Coyne proposed that, initially, depression leads individuals to feel uncertain about their worth and the nature of their relationships, which leads them to seek reassurance from others. Although others provide this reassurance, the depressed individuals have doubts about whether the reassurance is sincere, and therefore continue to seek additional feedback about themselves and their relationships. Ultimately, others become frustrated by this behavior, and they begin to provide signs of rejection, perhaps even leaving the relationship. This increasingly negative social environment only serves to solidify and strengthen depression.

Joiner *et al.* (1992, 1993) proposed that the central variable in Coyne's description is the tendency of depressive individuals to excessively seek reassurance. They defined ERS as the tendency to frequently seek reassurance from others as to whether they "truly" care (Joiner *et al.*, 1992), and examined how ERS operates both in the negative interpersonal cycle proposed by Coyne and as a more general risk factor for depression (Joiner *et al.*, 1999a). Although the distinction has not been fully elaborated, these two lines of research specify two related but different causal pathways through which ERS may operate as a risk factor for depression. Therefore, each of these areas will be described separately and evaluated as to the quality of its evidence for ERS as a risk factor for depression.

ERS AND REJECTION

In their initial studies of ERS and depression, Joiner and colleagues examined the model proposed by Coyne in which ERS leads to rejection by others. They proposed that depressed individuals who seek excessive reassurance will be particularly aversive to others, as their ERS will serve as a signal of their distress and demands a response from others. While not explicitly framed as a model of risk for depression, the authors stated that the interpersonal rejection caused by ERS was likely to lead to increased symptoms depression (Joiner *et al.*, 1992), similar to Coyne's original proposal.

A number of studies have demonstrated a relationship between ERS and rejection. When applying the criteria developed by Kraemer *et al.* (1997), however, it appears that the bulk of the evidence has established that ERS is a correlate of interpersonal rejection. A number of cross-sectional studies have found a significant correlation between ERS and rejection (Benazon, 2000; Joiner, 1999; Joiner *et al.*, 1992, 1993). Although these studies have all demonstrated a significant relationship, the nature of that relationship differed slightly in each study. Joiner (1999) found that, in youth psychiatric inpatients, depressed youths who were high in ERS also had the highest perceived rejection scores. Benazon (2000) also found a simple main effect, reporting that high ERS was related to negative spousal attitudes and expressed emotion. In their studies of college roommates, however, Joiner *et al.* (1992) reported more complex results. They found that ERS was related to rejection, but only for men who were high in depressive symptoms and low in self-esteem (Joiner *et al.*, 1992). The authors proposed that ERS might be particularly aversive in males, as it goes against gender norms. To date, one study has examined these associations prospectively and found a role for ERS, but it included NFS in the model and thus cannot speak specifically as to whether ERS specifically is a risk factor for rejection. Results of that study will be discussed later in this chapter under the section on NFS. Thus, preliminary evidence suggests that ERS may be a risk factor for rejection, although this association may vary according to other characteristics of the individual, such as gender, self-esteem, or NFS.

Although, as noted, these studies were not specifically conceptualized as models of risk for depression, they can be viewed as presenting a mediational model, in which the association between ERS and depression is mediated by interpersonal rejection. In other words, ERS leads directly to interpersonal rejection, which then leads to depression. One study to date has tested this type of mediational model, and it provides some evidence for the possibility that ERS is a risk factor for depression via interpersonal difficulties. In a study of undergraduates, Potthoff *et al.* (1995) attempted to integrate the stress generation approach to depression with Coyne's interpersonal model. The stress generation model of depression (Hammen, 1991) states that depressed individuals are involved in generating their own stressful life events, and that this life stress subsequently increases their depression. Potthoff and colleagues proposed that, following the model of Coyne, ERS may be one aspect of depression that serves to generate interpersonal stress, particularly rejection. Results supported their hypothesis. ERS was found to predict increases in stressful life events 3 weeks later, which in turn predicted increases in depression 2 weeks later. These results provide prospective evidence that ERS may operate as a risk factor for depression through rejection or other negative life events.

In sum, evidence has established that ERS is a correlate of rejection and depression and has provided preliminary support for a model in which ERS is a risk factor for depression via the mechanism of rejection or other negative life events. It is important to note some limitations of these studies, however, when viewed from the risk factor framework. First, the studies to date do not specify how ERS is involved temporally in the development of depressive symptoms. For example, in the majority of the studies of rejection, ERS was related to rejection in individuals who already showed some level of depressive symptoms. For this reason, ERS in this model may be a risk factor for increases in depressive symptoms beyond an initial threshold that is required for the rejection effects to emerge, but it cannot account for the initial presence of depressive symptoms. Additionally, all of the studies mentioned here deal with subclinical levels of depressive symptoms, and therefore it is not clear whether ERS is a risk for the syndrome of clinical depression in these models. Finally, none of these studies of ERS and rejection have examined whether ERS may be a proxy for another risk factor that causes rejection, such as attachment style or general dependency. Despite this, these studies have provided good initial support for a specific interpersonal risk factor that may be involved in the development of depression.

ERS AND DEPRESSION

Although ERS was originally described in terms of Coyne's (1976) model of interpersonal disruption in depression, Joiner and colleagues have also demonstrated that ERS is a direct risk factor for depression. In this model, individuals who are high in ERS are vulnerable to depressive symptom increases under certain conditions. Although the precise reason for this vulnerability has not been established, Joiner *et al.* (1999a) propose that one possibility is that individuals who are high in ERS become demoralized or hopeless when they realize that their requests for reassurance are not being fulfilled or that their need for reassurance will never be satisfied. In line with this possibility, a number of studies have demonstrated that those with high ERS are at particular risk for depression when they are involved in stressful, nonsupportive, or otherwise unsatisfying interpersonal relationships. These studies present a moderational relationship between ERS and depression, with ERS predicting increased depression only in the presence of a moderating variable (i.e., stressful relationship events). When evaluated in the context of the risk factors framework, these studies are nearly all prospective and provide good evidence that ERS is a risk factor for depression.

One type of stressful interpersonal environment in which ERS has been found to be a risk factor for depression is having a significant other who is suffering from depression. Three studies have examined ERS in the context of the "contagious depression" hypothesis, which proposes that depression can be transmitted from one person to another in the context of a close relationship. In a study of college roommates, Joiner (1994) found evidence for contagion, but only for who were high in ERS. When individuals who were high in ERS had a depressed roommate, they became depressed, but if they had a nondepressed roommate, they showed fewer depressive symptoms. These results indicate that those with high ERS may be particularly susceptible to be influence by the moods of others. A study of romantic partners found similar results (Katz *et al.*, 1999), although the study was cross-sectional and therefore could not truly establish risk factor status. Finally, preliminary evidence suggests that ERS may operate as a similar risk factor for contagious depression in children. In a prospective study over a 1-year interval, older children who were high in ERS and had a parent with depression showed increases in depressive symptoms (Abela *et al.*, 2006).

Several studies have shown that those who are high in ERS and have unsatisfying relationships or low support are also vulnerable to depression. For example, a study of women in romantic relationships found that women who were high in ERS who had partners who devalued them showed increases in depressive symptoms (Katz *et al.*, 1998), and these results remained significant even when controlling for overall level of relationship satisfaction. Joiner and Metalksy (2001) found similar results in a study of college roommates, with negative roommate evaluation predicting increases in depressive symptoms only for those who were also high in ERS. Perceiving a decrease in social support also appears to be a risk factor for depression for those high in ERS (Haeffel *et al.*, 2007). Again, these results appear to generalize to youth, with high ERS adolescents who report low friendship quality also reporting increased depression (Prinstein *et al.*, 2005).

Another type of situation that may be associated with ERS as a risk factor for depression may be an insecure attachment style. In a study of children with insecure attachment, Abela *et al.* (2005) proposed that children who were high in ERS and showed an insecure attachment style would not have their ERS needs met due to their attachment problems, and therefore would show increased depression. Although conclusions are limited due to the cross-sectional nature of the study, results supported this hypothesis, with insecurely attached children who were high in ERS showing higher levels of both current depressive symptoms and past major depressive episodes. In a study of ERS and attachment in adults, Shaver *et al.* (2005) found that, overall, the relationship between ERS and depression was better accounted for by the relationship between ERS and attachment. However, they did report that insecurely attached women who were high in daily ERS experienced increases in depression the next day, while securely attached women who demonstrated high daily reassurance seeking showed decreases in depression. In this case, ERS may still represent a risk factor among this specific group.

Finally, there is some evidence that ERS may represent a more general risk factor for depression in the presence of any type of stress. A study of cadets undergoing basic training found that those who were high in ERS were more likely to develop depressive symptoms (Joiner & Schmidt, 1998). Similarly, a study of students transitioning to college found that individuals who were high in ERS were also more likely to show increases in depression (Davila, 2001). Finally, a study of college students who experienced subjective mid-term exam failure found that students high in ERS were most likely to show depressive symptom increases (Joiner & Metalsky, 2001).

It is unclear why ERS specifically would be related to depression under such diverse conditions of stress. One important issue to consider is whether it is the behavior of reassurance seeking, or instead some characteristic of the individual associated with reassurance seeking that is associated with depression. It may be, as described above, that ERS erodes interpersonal relationships, leaving individuals without social support and thus vulnerable to increased stress. Alternatively, it may be that individuals seek reassurance due to some psychological characteristics that increase vulnerability to depression. It is important to consider this possibility and determine whether ERS represents a proxy for another risk factor.

Some studies have attempted to examine whether the relationship between ERS and depression can better be accounted for by general dependency or an insecure attachment style. Results of the studies have been mixed. In cross-sectional studies, ERS has been shown to be correlated with dependency (Joiner & Metalsky, 2001) and sociotropy (Davila, 2001), but ERS maintained a significant association with depression independent of these variables. Davila (2001) also demonstrated that ERS significantly predicted increases in depressive symptoms while controlling for dependency and insecure attachment style. However, in a study of the personality variables dependency and self-criticism, ERS did not significantly predict depression beyond these variables (Shahar *et al*., 2004). Similarly, in a study of attachment style and depression, cross-sectional results showed that ERS was not significantly related to depression controlling for attachment style, and prospective results showed that attachment style, rather than ERS, predicted future depressive symptoms (Shaver *et al*., 2005). Overall, it appears that at least some of the association between ERS and depression cannot be explained by dependency or insecure attachment, although these variables may play an important role in ERS in some circumstances.

It is possible that an alternative, unexplored variable could account for the association between ERS and depression. Studies designed to examine the origins of ERS may shed some light on this possible relation. For example, in a study of the origins of ERS, Joiner *et al*. (1999c) found that negative life events that were associated with anxiety and that decreases in self-esteem were related to increases in ERS. Low self-esteem may be particularly important, as it has been found to be correlated with ERS and to predict when ERS will lead to negative outcomes (Joiner *et al.*, 1992). However, Katz *et al.* (1998) included self-esteem in their model when testing the relationship between ERS, partner devaluation, and depression, and did not find support for this hypothesis. Rather, they found that, for women who experienced devaluation from their partners, ERS maintained its relationship with depression when self-esteem was included in the model, while self-esteem no longer maintained a significant relationship when ERS was included. Still, it may be that an individual's stability, rather than level, of self-esteem accounts for the relationship between ERS and depression. A recent study found that ERS was correlated with uncertain self-esteem (Luxton & Wenzlaff, 2006), which has been associated with depression. Future studies are needed to examine whether uncertain self-esteem accounts for the effect of ERS as a risk factor for depression.

In addition to personality or psychological characteristics that may explain why ERS is related to depression, it is possible that other unexplored interpersonal or behavioral characteristics could be involved. For example, individuals with ERS may have a broader deficit in coping skills. Alternatively, their coping skills may have been eroded by their ERS as their relationships deteriorate. A final limitation of the current studies on ERS as a risk factor is that no studies have examined risk for clinical depression, rather than depressive symptoms. Thus, it is unclear whether ERS is involved in more severe depressive reactions.

In sum, a number of prospective studies have established that ERS is a risk factor for depression under conditions of life stress, particularly interpersonal life stress. These studies have established different situations in which those with ERS are vulnerable to depression. A model of why ERS leads to depression, however, is still limited.

ERS: FUTURE DIRECTIONS

Examining the data on ERS from the risk factors approach, it is clear that ERS has been demonstrated to be a risk factor for depression under conditions of stress, and it seems likely that ERS is also a risk factor for rejection and subsequent depression. Future work on ERS will need to integrate these two approaches to fully understand how ERS operates as a risk factor for depression. These two approaches highlight two potentially different aspects of ERS: the effect of ERS behavior on the environment and the characteristics of individuals who engage in ERS.

To fully understand the nature of ERS and its relationship with depression, it is necessary to obtain more information about both of these facets. For example, naturalistic studies could track daily reassurance seeking and establish ranges for normal and ERS behavior. Characteristics of those who engage in ERS could then be examined, with the goal of determining whether ERS represents a proxy for another psychological risk factor. Additionally, it would be important to determine whether anyone might engage in ERS under certain circumstances or whether it is a behavior associated with a certain subgroup (i.e., dependent or insecurely attached individuals). In this way, ERS could be more precisely defined and its role in depression established. Another limitation of the current studies of ERS is that no studies have examined ERS as a risk factor for clinical depression. While studies of depressive symptom increases are important, ultimately these symptom fluctuations may reflect normal mood changes that are not predictive of later clinical depression (Benazon & Coyne, 1999).

Following the risk factors framework, since ERS is currently well established as a risk factor for depression, another promising future direction would be to examine whether ERS can be demonstrated to be a causal risk factor. If an intervention could be developed to change ERS, individuals could be studied in a randomized controlled trial to determine whether those who stopped seeking excessive reassurance were less likely to become depressed. This would provide the clearest evidence that reassurance seeking behavior, rather than other related psychological characteristics, is causally related to depression, and could represent a simple risk factor to target in a preventative intervention.

NEGATIVE FEEDBACK SEEKING

Perhaps ironically, NFS – the opposite of reassurance seeking – has also been associated with depression. Research suggesting that depressive individuals actively seek negative feedback was born from Swann's self-verification theory (see Swann, 1990, for a review). Self-verification theory proposes that individuals are motivated to maintain consistent self-views, and that they will actively solicit (Swann & Read, 1981a; Swann *et al.*, 1992a, b), attend to (Swann & Read, 1981a), and recall (Swann & Read, 1981a, b) feedback that confirms their self-views. Additionally, individuals are more likely to believe feedback that they find to be self-verifying (Swann *et al.*, 1987). One crucial fact about this theory, however, is that it applies equally to all individuals, regardless of whether their self-views are positive or negative. Therefore, in order to meet their needs for consistency and verification, individuals with negative self-views require negative feedback, even if that feedback is emotionally unpleasant. Swann described this paradox as the "cognitive affective crossfire," and stated that individuals with negative self-views are faced with the difficult position of desiring both positive and negative feedback (Swann *et al.*, 1987). For this reason, people with negative self-views may often prefer and solicit negative feedback, because having their views verified gives them a sense of cognitive consistency and the knowledge that others will have reasonable expectations of them (Swann *et al.*, 1989).

Negative self-views are a defining aspect of depression, and thus self-verification theory would predict that depressed individuals should prefer and actively seek negative feedback. A number of cross-sectional studies have found that this is, in fact, the case. Swann *et al.* (1992b) examined the feedback seeking preferences of undergraduates who were elevated on a measure of depressive symptoms, and found that they conformed to the predictions of self-verification theory. For example, when given a choice to interact with an evaluator who had provided a positive or negative evaluation of them, depressed individuals were more likely to select the negative evaluator, while nondepressed individuals preferred the positive evaluator. Depressed individuals also preferred friends and dating partners to view them more negatively and were more likely to solicit negative feedback from relationship partners than nondepressed persons. In a follow-up set of studies, Swann *et al.* (1992b) extended these results, providing evidence that depressed individuals are actively motivated to seek negative feedback. They reported that depressed individuals remained interested in receiving negative feedback even when given the opportunity to participate in another experiment instead of receiving the feedback, while nondepressed individuals had an opposite pattern of results. Finally, they reported that, following the receipt of a favorable evaluation, depressed individuals were more interested in receiving feedback about their limitations, presumably to restore consistency with their negative self-views. These same self-verification processes have also been found in individuals with diagnosed clinical depression, rather than depressive symptoms. Giesler *et al.* (1996) found that clinically depressed individuals were likely to choose an unfavorable evaluation over a favorable one, and that this choice was driven by their view of the negative evaluation as being more accurate.

These studies clearly establish that an interest in, and preference for, negative feedback is a correlate of depression. Swann, Joiner and colleagues have recently proposed, however, that NFS also serves as a risk factor for depression (Giesler & Swann, 1999; Joiner, 1995; Pettit & Joiner, 2001; Swann *et al.*, 1992b). The proposed models of NFS as a risk factor for depression are similar to those of ERS as a risk factor, and involve two possible pathways: a direct pathway to depression and a path mediated by rejection.

NFS AND REJECTION

In their first studies of self-verification in depressed individuals, Swann *et al.* (1992a) proposed that NFS was likely an important variable for understanding why depressed people are frequently rejected. Based on self-verification theory, they proposed two mechanisms to explain the relationship between NFS and rejection. First, it may be that rejection is simply a by-product of the natural self-verification process, as depressed individuals actively select friends and partners who view them negatively (and thus verify the depressive's negative self-views). Thus, the desire for confirmation has created a confirming environment which is filled with rejection and negative evaluation. As noted above, studies of depressed individuals did find that they preferred friends and interaction partners who evaluated them negatively (Swann *et al.*, 1992a).

While simple affiliation with rejecting individuals might partly explain the effects of NFS on depression, Swann *et al.* (1992a) also found that self-reported NFS (as measured by an instrument that asks about interest in negative feedback) leads to rejection. In a study of college roommates, they found that depressed individuals who were high in NFS were more likely to be negatively evaluated by their roommates at the end of the semester. Additionally, they found that roommates of depressed, high NFS individuals were also more likely to desire to terminate the relationship or find a new roommate (Swann *et al.*, 1992a). Similar to these findings, Joiner *et al.* (1997) also found evidence that NFS may be related to rejection. In a sample of youth psychiatric inpatients, they found that children who were high in NFS on a self-report instrument were more likely to be rejected. However, these results were only found in the context of relatively longer peer relationships of a week or more. The authors argue that it takes time for individuals to express their desire for negative feedback, and thus NFS would not begin to affect relationships until these needs began to be expressed. Although this study is cross-sectional, and thus cannot establish temporal precedence, it provides support for NFS as a correlate of rejection. A recent study of NFS in adolescents extended these results, and suggested that adolescents who are high in NFS have worse social outcomes over time than those who do not report NFS (Borelli & Prinstein, 2006). Taken together, these three studies suggest that NFS may be aversive to others over time, and thus represents a risk factor for rejection.

It is not precisely clear why NFS should be a risk factor for rejection, although it may be a function of who is targeted for feedback and the lengths to which the depressive person needs to go in order to obtain negative feedback. Giesler and Swann (1999) state that most depressive individuals should not generally have problems finding negative feedback, as they tend to gravitate toward others who view them negatively in order to naturally meet self-verification needs. If they have interaction partners who are more positive, however, depressed individuals may escalate their feedback seeking behavior to get confirming feedback. For example, Swann and Read (1981b) reported that when people with negative self-views thought that their interaction partners viewed them positively, they attempted to change those views by appearing unworthy of positive appraisal. Giesler and Swann (1999) propose that depressive individuals who desire negative feedback may use a number of methods to obtain it, including acting hostile or demanding or engaging in inappropriate self-disclosure. For this reason, it may be that targets of NFS who might initially hold positive views of the depressed person are subject to increasingly aversive efforts by the depressed person to obtain negative feedback.

In sum, evidence has shown that individuals with negative self-views will actively seek negative feedback, which is likely aversive to others. To date, the three studies conducted suggest that NFS may act as a risk factor for interpersonal rejection. Although no studies to date have tested the mediational model in which NFS leads to depression via its effects on rejection, it seems possible that these processes may be operating. Further studies are needed to replicate the prospective effect of NFS on rejection and to address potential limitations of these studies. Most importantly, since the measure of NFS assesses desire for negative feedback rather than actual feedback seeking behavior, it will be important to rule out the possibility that NFS is a proxy for other potential mechanisms of self-confirmation, such as the hostility or inappropriate disclosure described by Giesler and Swann (1999). Additionally, future studies will need to examine whether NFS plays a role as a risk factor for clinically diagnosed depression.

NFS AND DEPRESSION

In addition to its role in causing interpersonal rejection, NFS has been implicated as a more direct risk factor for depression. Joiner (1995) described a moderational model through which NFS is a risk factor for depression under conditions in which requests for negative feedback are honored. He proposed that depressive individuals seek negative feedback to confirm their negative self-image, but that when they are provided this feedback, it will be affectively painful and will provide them with even more certainty about their negative self-views. This distress and increasing confirmation of negative self-views will lead to increased depression. Two prospective studies support this hypothesis, and suggest that individuals who seek, and subsequently receive, negative feedback are at risk for increased depression. In a study of college roommates, Joiner (1995) found that roommates who were high in NFS reported increased depression if they lived with a roommate who provided negative feedback. A follow-up study suggested that the negative feedback does not have to be interpersonal in nature, as high NFS individuals were at increased risk for depression following receipt of a failing mid-term grade (Pettit & Joiner, 2001). Finally, although receipt of negative feedback was not measured, Borelli and Prinstein (2006) found that adolescent girls who reported high NFS were more likely to report depression 11 months later.

In their review of the literature on self-verification processes in depression, Giesler and Swann (1999) present a similar theoretical view of how self-verification processes contribute to risk for depression. They propose a cyclical mechanism that includes negative affect, negative cognitions about the self, and feedback seeking behavior. Initially, negative affect makes negative self-views more accessible and salient. This increases the likelihood of NFS to confirm these views, and if negative feedback is received, it is likely to lead to increased distress and depression. This process describes a mechanism through which active NFS could contribute to the development of depression. However, NFS in this model is a response to changing affective states, rather than a preexisting risk factor. For this reason, it is currently unclear whether NFS should be viewed as a risk factor for depression. While it meets the criteria of temporal antecedence and increased probability of the outcome, the process described does not seem to be one in which people can be classified as at risk based on their status of NFS.

NFS: FUTURE DIRECTIONS

Although data on NFS to date are limited, it appears likely that NFS meets the criteria for a risk factor under conditions where negative feedback is provided. Additionally, NFS appears to be aversive to others and may be associated with rejection. Overall, however, data are limited, and more studies are needed to truly understand how NFS may be related to depression and rejection. As noted when discussing ERS, future studies on NFS will also need to more clearly establish what behavior is being measured. Again, naturalistic studies could track daily feedback seeking behavior and establish normal and abnormal ranges. Self-verification processes could be tracked across different types of relationships, to determine when and how NFS occurs. One crucial issue that must be addressed in order to establish NFS as a risk factor is whether NFS represents a behavior that is purely dependent on mood, or whether certain individuals are more likely to seek feedback. If so, characteristics of those who engage in NFS would need to be examined to consider whether it may act as a proxy risk factor for other psychological risk factors, such as low self-esteem. Finally, similar to ERS, research on NFS is also limited by the lack of studies examining its relationship to clinical depression.

REASSURANCE AND NFS: INTEGRATIONS AND FUTURE DIRECTIONS

Excessive reassurance seeking and NFS have a number of similarities in their motivations, proposed effects, and associations with depression. Both behaviors are motivated processes that appear to serve a role in regulating affect, self-views, and the views of others (Coyne, 1976; Giesler & Swann, 1999; Joiner *et al.*, 1993). Various studies described above have begun to examine the conditions under which people engage in these behaviors and how they affect the individual and the environment. To truly develop an interpersonal approach to studying risk for depression, however, models will need to be developed which can account for both types of behavior and their effects.

AN INTEGRATIVE MODEL OF RISK FOR REJECTION

Joiner *et al.* (1993) have proposed one such integrative model, which describes another possible mechanism through which the interpersonal feedback seeking behaviors of depressed people can lead to rejection. Combining Swann's work on self-verification theory with Coyne's interactional description of depression, they proposed that individuals who are mildly depressed will have a desire for both reassurance and negative feedback from others (Joiner & Metalksy, 1995; Joiner *et al.*, 1993). Specifically, they propose that mildly depressed individuals will initially seek reassurance about their worth and whether others truly care. Reassurance, when provided, is affectively satisfying and provides some relief, but is cognitively inconsistent with the depressed person's negative self-concept. This inconsistency subsequently leads the individual to seek negative, self-confirming feedback, which is cognitively confirming but affectively uncomfortable. Thus, depressed individuals send contradictory messages requesting both reassurance and negative feedback from others, which may lead others to feel frustrated, confused, or angry about the behavior of the depressed person.

Two studies have begun to examine this hypothesized interaction between the opposite feedback seeking behaviors, and have provided some support for the model. In a cross-sectional study, Joiner *et al.* (1993) found that mildly depressed individuals showed higher levels of both reassurance seeking and NFS. Additionally, they found that depressed individuals who were high in both types of feedback seeking were at increased risk for rejection by roommates. These results were replicated in a prospective study of roommates (Joiner & Metalsky, 1995), although the effect was qualified by gender. For males, high levels of depression, NFS, and ERS were associated with increased rejection. For females, however, no consistent effects were observed. These results provide preliminary support for the hypothesis that the interactive effects of the two types of feedback seeking behavior lead to negative interpersonal outcomes, at least for males. Future studies are needed to examine the nature of these interacting processes and their role in rejection and depression.

REASSURANCE AND NFS AS MAINTENANCE FACTORS

Although ERS and NFS generally meet the necessary criteria to be recognized as risk factors for depression (temporal antecedence and increased likelihood of the outcome), their true importance in understanding depression likely extends beyond their impact on initial risk for the symptoms or disorder. Recent work by Stice (2002) has extended the risk factor methodology to examine maintenance of disorders. He defines a *maintenance factor* as a factor that predicts symptom persistence over time vs. remission, and, like Kraemer, he specifies that maintenance factors can be viewed as *causal maintenance factors* if changing the factor changes symptom expression. Stice argues that, although the same factor can be both a risk and a maintenance factor for a disorder, distinguishing between risk and maintenance status is important for specifying the role of the factor in potential prevention or treatment programs.

While previous studies have not specifically examined the role of ERS and NFS in the onset vs. maintenance of depression, there are reasons to believe that they may play an important role as maintenance factors. In a theoretical description of processes involved in depression's chronicity, Joiner (2000) argues that ERS and NFS can be viewed as self-propagatory processes that maintain depression. He defines self-propagatory processes as active, motivated processes that are associated with depression and serve to prolong, exacerbate, or induce the recurrence of depressed symptoms. Both NFS and ERS meet these criteria. As noted previously in the mediational pathways discussed for each behavior, both

ERS and NFS are associated with rejection or negative interpersonal stress, which is subsequently associated with increases in depression. Additionally, both behaviors can be motivated by low self-esteem (Joiner, 2000), which could lead them to be associated with a relapse into depression once symptoms begin to improve.

INTERPERSONAL RISK FACTORS FOR DEPRESSION?

Throughout this chapter, ERS and NFS have been examined as risk factors for depression. The risk factor approach has been applied in order to methodically review the state of the current research on each variable and the validity of potential causal claims or models. Based on a number of prospective studies examining various populations and settings, evidence to date appears conclusive that ERS is a risk factor for depression under conditions of stress, particularly interpersonal stress. Although studies are more limited, there is also some support for NFS as a risk factor for depression when negative feedback is received. Finally, there is good preliminary evidence that ERS and NFS are risk factors for rejection, both separately and when combined, which may lead to subsequent depression through a mediational pathway.

Despite this promising evidence, some important limitations in the research must be noted. First, studies to date have examined risk for depressive symptom increases, rather than diagnosed depression, and risk factor research has generally focused on outcomes that can be dichotomized as "present" or "not present," such as a clinical diagnosis. For this reason, while ERS and NFS appear to be a risk factor for increased depressive symptoms, the models of risk cannot be so clearly specified as they could be if some standard diagnostic threshold was used in all studies. Some critics of the work on ERS have similarly argued that depressed mood measured in these studies does not reflect actual depressive processes, but rather daily mood fluctuations (Benazon & Coyne, 1999). These criticisms, however, fail to take into account the possibility that depression may represent a dimensional, rather than a categorical, construct, and that subclinical symptoms of depression have been associated with significant impairment (Joiner *et al.*, 1999b).

Another limitation of the studies reviewed is that they have not clearly specified the constructs of ERS and NFS. Both constructs are measured by brief self-report instruments, and while the measure of ERS has been associated with behavior observed in the lab (Joiner & Metalsky, 2001), the association of the measure of NFS with actual feedback seeking behavior is unknown. For this reason, it is unclear to what extent the studies of ERS and NFS measure actual interpersonal behaviors, or conversely, to what extent the measures of ERS or NFS are proxies for other psychological or behavioral characteristics. Future studies are needed to clarify and refine our understanding of normal and abnormal feedback seeking before we can fully understand how ERS and NFS operate as risk factors.

Although the risk factors approach allows for a careful analysis of the quality of evidence, it is also important to note that the approach may have limitations, particularly in terms of understanding the role of interpersonal processes in depression. The study of interpersonal processes in psychopathology is necessarily complex, as these processes are difficult to define, identify, or measure reliably. Even apart from measurement issues, interpersonal variables likely vary greatly depending on the context of the behavior and characteristics of the interaction partners. These interactions are, by nature, reciprocal and may develop in the context of long-standing relationships. All of these issues make it difficult to study and model interpersonal processes in depression (Coyne, 1999). Considering these facts, the studies reviewed in this chapter provide compelling evidence that the interpersonal environments of depressive individuals involve both ERS and NFS, and that these environments are aversive to others and place the depressive person at risk for increased symptoms of depression. Future studies are needed to clarify these constructs and continue to develop models that describe how interpersonal behaviors operate as risk factors for depression.

REFERENCES

Abela, J. R. Z., Hankin, B. L., Haigh, E. A. P., Adams, P., Vinokuroff, T., & Trayhern, L. (2005). Interpersonal vulnerability to depression in high-risk children: The role of insecure attachment and reassurance seeking. *Journal of Clinical Child and Adolescent Psychology*, *34*, 182–192.

Abela, J. R. Z., Zuroff, D. C., Ho, M. R., Adams, P., & Hankin, B. L. (2006). Excessive reassurance seeking, hassles, and depressive symptoms in children of affectively ill parents: A multiwave longitudinal study. *Journal of Abnormal Child Psychology*, *34*, 171–187.

Benazon, N. R. (2000). Predicting negative spousal attitudes toward depressed persons: A test of Coyne's interpersonal model. *Journal of Abnormal Psychology*, *109*, 550–554.

Benazon, N. R., & Coyne, J. C. (1999). The next step in developing an interactional description of depression? *Psychological Inquiry*, *10*, 279–282.

Borelli, J. L., & Prinstein, M. J. (2006). Reciprocal, longitudinal associations among adolescents' negative feedback-seeking, depressive symptoms, and peer relations. *Journal of Abnormal Child Psychology*, *34*, 159–169.

Coyne, J. C. (1976). Toward an interactional description of depression. *Psychiatry*, *39*, 28–40.

Coyne, J. C. (1999). Thinking interactionally about depression: A radical restatement. In T. E. Joiner & J. C. Coyne (Eds.), *The Interactional Nature of Depression* (pp. 365–392). Washington, DC: American Psychological Association.

Davila, J. (2001). Refining the association between excessive reassurance seeking and depressive symptoms: The role of related constructs. *Journal of Social and Clinical Psychology*, *20*, 538–559.

Giesler, R. B., & Swann, W. B., Jr (1999). Striving for confirmation: The role of self-verification in depression. In T. E. Joiner J. C. Coyne (Eds.), *The Interactional Nature of Depression* (pp. 189–217). Washington, DC: American Psychological Association.

Giesler, R. B., Josephs, R. A., & Swann, W. B., Jr (1996). Self-verification in clinical depression: The desire for negative evaluation. *Journal of Abnormal Psychology*, *105*, 358–368.

Haeffel, G. J., Voelz, Z. R., & Joiner, T. E., Jr (2007). Vulnerability to depressive symptoms: Clarifying the role of excessive reassurance seeking and perceived social support in an interpersonal model of depression. *Cognition and Emotion*, *21*, 681–688.

Hammen, C. (1991). Generation of stress in the course of unipolar depression. *Journal of Abnormal Psychology*, *100*, 555–561.

Joiner, T. E., Jr (1994). Contagious depression: Existence, specificity to depressed symptoms, and the role of reassurance seeking. *Journal of Personality and Social Psychology*, *67*, 287–296.

Joiner, T. E., Jr (1995). The price of soliciting and receiving negative feedback: Self-verification theory as a vulnerability to depression theory. *Journal of Abnormal Psychology*, *104*, 364–372.

Joiner, T. E., Jr (1999). A test of the interpersonal theory of depression in youth psychiatric inpatients. *Journal of Abnormal Child Psychology*, *27*, 77–85.

Joiner, T. E., Jr (2000). Depression's vicious screw: Self-propagating and erosive processes in depression chronicity. *Clinical Psychology: Science and Practice*, *7*, 203–218.

Joiner, T. E. Jr, & Coyne, J. C. (Eds.) (1999). *The Interactional Nature of Depression: Advances in Interpersonal Approaches*. Washington, DC: American Psychological Association.

Joiner, T. E., Jr, & Metalsky, G. I. (1995). A prospective test of an integrative interpersonal theory of depression: A naturalistic study of college roommates. *Journal of Personality and Social Psychology*, *69*, 778–788.

Joiner, T. E., Jr, & Metalsky, G. I. (2001). Excessive reassurance seeking: Delineating a risk factor involved in the development of depressive symptoms. *Psychological Science*, *12*, 371–378.

Joiner, T. E., Jr, & Schmidt, N. B. (1998). Excessive reassurance-seeking predicts depressive but not anxious reactions to acute stress. *Journal of Abnormal Psychology*, *107*, 533–537.

Joiner, T. E., Jr, Alfano, M. S., & Metalsky, G. I. (1992). When depression breeds contempt: Reassurance seeking, self-esteem, and rejection of depressed college students by their roommates. *Journal of Abnormal Psychology*, *101*, 165–173.

Joiner, T. E., Jr, Alfano, M. S., & Metalsky, G. I. (1993). Caught in the crossfire: Depression, self-consistency, self-enhancement, and the response of others. *Journal of Social and Clinical Psychology*, *12*, 113–134.

Joiner, T. E., Jr, Katz, J., & Lew, A. S. (1997). Self-verification and depression among youth psychiatric inpatients. *Journal of Abnormal Psychology*, *106*, 608–618.

Joiner, T. E., Jr, Metalsky, G. I., Katz, J., & Beach, S. R. H. (1999a). Depression and excessive reassurance-seeking. *Psychological Inquiry*, *10*, 269–278.

Joiner, T. E., Jr, Metalsky, G. I., Katz, J., & Beach, S. R. H. (1999b). Be (re)assured: Excessive reassurance seeking has (at least) some explanatory power regarding depression. *Psychological Inquiry*, *10*, 305–308.

Joiner, T. E., Jr, Katz, J., & Lew, A. S. (1999c). Harbingers of depressotypic reassurance seeking: Negative life events, increased anxiety, and decreased self-esteem. *Personality and Social Psychology Bulletin*, *25*, 632–639.

Katz, J., Beach, S. R. H., & Joiner, T. E., Jr (1998). When does partner devaluation predict emotional distress? Prospective moderating effects of reassurance-seeking and self-esteem. *Personal Relationships*, *5*, 409–421.

Katz, J., Beach, S. R. H., & Joiner, T. E., Jr (1999). Contagious depression in dating couples. *Journal of Social and Clinical Psychology*, *18*, 1–18.

Kazdin, A. E., Kraemer, H. C., Kessler, R. C., Kupfer, D. J., & Offord, D. R. (1997). Contributions of risk-factor research to developmental psychopathology. *Clinical Psychology Review*, *17*, 375–406.

Kraemer, H. C., Kazdin, A. E., Offord, D., Kessler, R., Jensen, P., & Kupfer, D. J. (1997). Coming to terms with the terms of risk. *Archives of General Psychiatry*, *54*, 337–343.

Kraemer, H. C., Stice, E., Kazdin, A., Offord, D., & Kupfer, D. (2001). How do risk factors work together? Mediators, moderators, and independent, overlapping, and proxy risk factors. *American Journal of Psychiatry*, *158*, 848–856.

Luxton, D. D., & Wenzlaff, R. M. (2005). Self-esteem uncertainty and depression vulnerability. *Cognition and Emotion*, *19*, 611–622.

Pettit, J., & Joiner, T. E., Jr (2001). Negative-feedback seeking leads to depressive symptom increases under conditions of stress. *Journal of Psychopathology and Behavioral Assessment*, *23*, 69–74.

Potthoff, J. G., Holahan, C. H., & Joiner T. E., Jr (1995). Reassurance seeking, stress generation, and depressive symptoms: An integrative model. *Journal of Personality and Social Psychology*, *68*, 664–670.

Prinstein, M. J., Borelli, J. L., Cheah, C. S. L., Simon, V. A., & Aikins, J. W. (2005). Adolescent girls' interpersonal vulnerability to depressive symptoms: A longitudinal examination of reassurance-seeking and peer relationships. *Journal of Abnormal Psychology*, *114*, 676–688.

Shahar, G., Joiner, T. E., Jr, Zuroff, D. C., & Blatt, S. J. (2004). Personality, interpersonal behavior, and depression: Co-existence of stress-specific moderating and mediating effects. *Personality and Individual Differences*, *36*, 1583–1596.

Shaver, P. R., Schachner, D. A., & Mikulincer, M. (2005). Attachment style, excessive reassurance seeking, relationship processes, and depression. *Personality and Social Psychology Bulletin*, *31*, 343–359.

Stice, E. (2002). Risk and maintenance factors for eating pathology: A meta-analytic review. *Psychological Bulletin*, *128*, 825–848.

Swann, W. B. (1990). To be adored or to be known: The interplay of self-enhancement and self-verification. In R. M. Sorretino & E. T. Higgins (Eds.), *Handbook of Motivation and Cognition* (Vol. 2, pp. 408–480). New York: Guilford Press.

Swann, W. B., & Read, S. J. (1981a). Acquiring self-knowledge: The search for feedback that fits. *Journal of Personality and Social Psychology*, *41*, 1119–1128.

Swann, W. B., Jr, & Read, S. J. (1981b). Self-verification processes: How we sustain our self-conceptions. *Journal of Experimental Social Psychology*, *17*, 351–372.

Swann, W. B., Jr, Griffin, J. J., Predmore, S. C., & Gaines, B. (1987). The cognitive-affective cross-fire: When self-consistency confronts self-enhancement. *Journal of Personality and Social Psychology*, *52*, 881–889.

Swann, W. B., Jr, Pelham, B. W., & Krull, D. S. (1989). Agreeable fancy or disagreeable truth? Reconciling self-enhancement and self-verification. *Journal of Personality and Social Psychology*, *57*, 782–791.

Swann, W. B., Jr, Wenzlaff, R. M., Krull, D. S., & Pelham, B. W. (1992a). Allure of negative feedback: Self-verification strivings among depressed persons. *Journal of Abnormal Psychology*, *2*, 293–306.

Swann, W. B., Jr, Wenzlaff, R. M., & Tafarodi, R. W. (1992b). Depression and the search for negative evaluation: More evidence of the role of self-verification strivings. *Journal of Abnormal Psychology*, *101*, 314–317.

20

AVOIDANCE

NICOLE D. OTTENBREIT* AND
KEITH S. DOBSON†

*University of Calgary, Child Development Centre, Calgary, Alberta, Canada
†Department of Psychology, University of Calgary, Calgary, Alberta, Canada

INTRODUCTION

Although we acknowledge that the etiology of depression is most comprehensively explained with a combination of biological, psychological and social models (see Gotlib & Hammen, 2002), the present chapter elucidates the role that avoidance plays as a psychosocial variable in depressive disorders. There is preliminary evidence that avoidance may represent a risk factor for depression. We also believe that avoidance may permeate relationships between established psychosocial risk variables and depression in current psychosocial models of depression. Despite its potential theoretical and clinical importance, however, the role of avoidance in depressive disorders has received little direct attention in the depression literature to this point. In this chapter, we first provide a definition of avoidance, then evaluate the evidence for avoidance as a correlate and risk factor for depression.

THE CONSTRUCT OF AVOIDANCE

The construct of *avoidance* refers to refraining or escaping from an action, person or thing. Avoidance is typically viewed as an overt act in the form of escape. However, avoidance can also take the form of an absence of action, such as when action is not taken, or through cognitive activities such as distraction or denial. In this sense, avoidance may be most easily discerned on the basis of function rather than form. In most instances, the function of avoidance is to eliminate or reduce short-term stress or pressure from a stressor, through the physical or psychological removal from that stressor.

Avoidance behavior has been viewed as a central feature and primary target for treatment in the context of anxiety disorders (Barlow, 2002). In the coping literature, a very basic distinction is also made between *approach-focused coping*, which involves active efforts on the part of the individual to resolve stressful problems, and *avoidance-focused coping*, which, in contrast, comprises efforts to avoid the problem and a focus on managing associated emotions (Holahan, *et al.*, 1996). Avoidant coping is generally viewed as a maladaptive form of coping, especially when outcomes are assessed over time (Zeidner & Saklofske, 1996).

Although Ferster (1973) postulated a central role for avoidance in his functional analysis of depression several decades ago, research on avoidance in the context of depression has been comparatively scarce. It has only been in recent years that researchers have begun to systematically examine the relationship between the construct of avoidance and depressive symptoms and disorders. The following literature review will present theory and research pertaining to the relationship between avoidance and depression, clarify conceptual and methodological issues in this literature, and specify directions for future research.

LITERATURE REVIEW

THEORIES THAT POSIT A ROLE FOR AVOIDANCE IN THE CONTEXT OF DEPRESSION

Several treatment models for depression focus on avoidance in an *implicit* manner. These include the cognitive model of depression, which encourages action rather than inactivity, and problem-solving therapy (PST), which encourages an active problem-solving style. An exception to this indirect focus on avoidance in depression theory and treatment is a new treatment called behavioral activation (BA) for depression (Jacobson *et al.*, 2001; Martell *et al.*, 2001). The following section will review the theory and practice of BA treatment for depression as well as make *explicit* how avoidance is addressed in other theories of depression and its intervention. Efficacy studies of these treatments are reviewed in brief when the available literature permits.

Functional Analysis and BA Model of Depression

In his functional analysis of depression, Ferster (1973) postulated that avoidance is a central feature of depression. He stated that the depressed person frequently engages in avoidance behavior and escape from aversive internal and external stimuli, and that behaviors such as complaining or withdrawing preempt positively reinforced behavior. Ferster indicated that the predominant employment of avoidance and escape behaviors leads to a narrowing of the depressed individual's behavioral repertoire, to one that is marked by passivity as opposed to initiative or action. He stressed that although depressed individuals are described by their lack of participation in activities, it is not that they typically lack the requisite skills to participate, but rather that the context of their lives comes to fail to support the activities of which they are capable. Ferster (1981) also indicated that depressed people often produce behaviors that are controlled by their level of deprivation and distress (often through avoidance and escape efforts) at the expense of responding more appropriately to characteristics of their audience or their environment. Depressed individuals therefore tend to show interpersonal styles that evoke reactions in others through negative reinforcement, and that preclude access to positive social reinforcement.

The contribution of Fester's model was the development of a behavioral model and treatment for depression (Lewinsohn, 1974). This model emphasized the need for skill development for depressed persons, to enhance their ability to obtain reinforcement from their social environment, as well as the scheduling of more positive activities to directly reinforce the positive actions of depressed individuals. Due to an emerging literature that implicated the negative cognitive processes of depressed individuals, behavioral treatments began to incorporate cognitive elements, including attention to, and reinforcement of, positive, non-avoidant behaviors. Over time, and in relation to the rapid growth of cognitive–behavioral models of depression (Beck, 1972), there was a commensurate loss of emphasis and interest in the functional role of avoidance in depressive disorders.

Recently, however, a functional analysis of depression has reemerged as the foundation upon which BA treatment for depression is based (Jacobson *et al.*, 2001; Martell *et al.*, 2001). The BA approach posits a contextual and functional view of the development and persistence of depression. Within this approach, depression is conceptualized as the result of contextual circumstances or shifts in an individual's life which prevent the individual from accessing adequate levels of positive reinforcement. Martell and colleagues indicate that life events often disrupt regular routines and individuals who employ passive coping styles to deal with these events become vulnerable to depression. Depressed individuals often adopt avoidant coping patterns, such as sleeping excessively, retreating from normal activities and withdrawing from social contacts. In the short-term, these actions relieve depressed individuals from demands in their lives and from the possibility of encountering situations that may cause them further distress. However, these avoidance patterns often serve to maintain and exacerbate levels of depression by increasing the disruption to the individuals' regular routines, compounding problems which are not being addressed, and removing the person from opportunities to receive positive reinforcement from activities and people in their lives.

BA treatment focuses on increasing activities and skills in depressed individuals' repertoire to counter avoidant and passive coping patterns and to facilitate access to positive reinforcement in their environment. These goals are accomplished through the use of ideographic activity schedules based on the functional analysis of the individual's transactions in his or her environment and promoting the acceptance of negative thoughts and feelings in a manner which facilitates change in the secondary problems (i.e., avoidance patterns) that maintain the depression. Another focus of BA is to enhance individuals' problem-solving and coping skills, to help clients to define goals and develop and implement plans to overcome obstacles in the way of their goals. In this context, rumination is viewed as an avoidance strategy in that it removes people from problem-solving demands and blocks activation strategies. As a result, a primary aim of BA treatment for depression is to refocus clients in working toward goals to facilitate active problem-solving efforts and access to positive reinforcement from the environment. Since rumination is viewed as an avoidant strategy, clients are essentially taught to be more mindful of their experience, as a method to expose them to the situations they attempt to avoid when they ruminate.

BA has been compared to cognitive therapy (CT), antidepressant medication (ADM), and placebo in a randomized controlled trial in the treatment of depressed outpatients (Dimidjian *et al.*, 2006). BA treatment was found to be comparable in outcome to ADM, and both BA and ADM were associated with better outcomes than CT in the short term. In addition, it should be noted that BA showed better efficacy than CT among severely depressed patients and resulted in more patient retention than did ADM. The authors speculated that countering of avoidance patterns was a primary mechanism relating to the success of the BA treatment.

PST Model of Depression

Nezu *et al.* (1989) advanced a problem-solving formulation of depression. From this perspective, ineffective problem-solving attitudes and skills, along with other factors such as negative life events and problems, contribute to the development and maintenance of depression. According to D'Zurilla and Nezu (1999), the social problem-solving process has two major components. *Problem orientation* reflects an individual's awareness, attributions, appraisals, perceived control and general approach in dealing with problems. *Problem-solving* proper consists of a number of problem-solving skills, including problem definition and formulation, generation of alternative solutions, decision-making and solution implementation and verification. Ineffective problem-solving can occur as the result of problems with any or all of the components in the process (see Chapter 11).

Within the social problem-solving framework, avoidance strategies are viewed as the result of ineffective problem-solving, and they play a role in the exacerbation of problems and thereby compound the risk for adverse outcomes. Although an active, approach focus in problem-solving is considered optimal, individuals at risk for depression often adopt a passive or avoidant orientation to their problems. This passive problem orientation is viewed as a motivational process that is influenced by an individual's past learning and reinforcement history related to problem-solving. D'Zurilla & Nezu (1999) demonstrated, for example, that individuals who make negative attributions for problems they encounter, appraise problems as harmful or threatening, possess negative self-efficacy and outcome expectations, or place little value on independent problem-solving, are likely to avoid engaging in problem-solving activities.

The social problem-solving model of depression also postulates a role for avoidance strategies in problem definition and formulation and solution implementation components of the process. Nezu *et al.* (1989) and Overholser (1996) state that depressed individuals may find it difficult to establish realistic and positive goals when defining and formulating problems, which often leads to avoidance of subsequent problem-solving efforts designed to facilitate the realization of these goals. Individuals who experience negative affect may also fail to attribute this affect to a causal problematic situation and chose emotion-focused coping strategies over problem-focused coping, leading to a failure to resolve presenting problems. In addition, the potential risks associated with the implementation of problem solution may make such activities difficult for the depressed individual. Overholser indicates that depressed individuals may procrastinate or avoid a problem or wait for somebody else to initiate change at this stage instead of actively putting their solutions into practice.

Nezu *et al.* (1989) maintain that it is generally preferable to approach, rather than avoid, a problem situation. These authors do, however, acknowledge that avoidance may be appropriate when dealing with a specific acute stressor, and that problem-focused coping may be less appropriate than emotion-focused efforts when dealing with an uncontrollable stressor. Yet the consistent and inflexible use of avoidance strategies is likely to be problematic. Nezu *et al.* (1989) contend that these avoidance strategies not only fail to resolve the problems that individuals confront, but often exacerbate them (e.g., leading to further difficulties, including increased depression).

PST for depression helps depressed individuals to become more active problem-solvers through increased awareness and control of negative emotions, the adoption of an adaptive, approach-focused problem orientation and the development of problem-solving skills. According to Overholser (1996), PST helps clients define realistic and positive goals, facilitate a creative, spontaneous and flexible problem-solving approach, engage in rational decision-making, and implement and evaluate solutions. Given the depressed individual's preference to avoid strategies which pose risk or which require a lot of effort, a primary goal of PST is to assist clients to consider the long-term benefits of problem solution. It should be noted that this approach differs from the problem-solving strategies employed in BA treatment for depression in that this approach is a rule-based approach, whereas BA utilizes an ideographic problem-solving training approach. PST has been shown in a number of studies to be an efficacious treatment for depression (e.g., Nezu *et al.*, 1985; Townsend *et al.*, 2001).

Schema-focused Therapy Model of Depression

Schema-focused therapy (Young, 1999) was developed as a therapeutic approach for personality disorders, but has application in the treatment of depression, specifically in chronic cases or as a way to prevent depressive relapse (Young *et al.*, 2001). This approach assists clients to become aware of, and to modify, their early maladaptive schemas (EMSs), which are stable and rigid beliefs about oneself and one's relationship with others. EMSs are viewed as self-perpetuating belief systems, which lead either directly or indirectly to psychological distress.

Young (1999) indicates that EMSs develop during childhood and early experiences. Once established, they function through three processes. These processes include: (1) *schema maintenance*, which involves the reinforcement of schemas through cognitive distortions and self-defeating behavior patterns; (2) *schema compensation*, which includes attempts to overcompensate for maladaptive schemas by behaving in a manner inconsistent with and obscuring underlying schema(s); and (3) *schema avoidance*, which involves cognitive, affective and behavioral methods to avoid triggering the schema or the experience of emotion connected with the schema.

Young (1999) states that because the activation of schemas is associated with unpleasant, intense emotions, individuals develop a variety of processes to avoid schemas. Behavioral avoidance comprises avoidance of real-life situations that hold the potential to trigger schemas and may present as social isolation or failure to pursue social or career endeavors. In the cognitive realm, individuals may block thoughts or images that activate the schema, or may remove themselves from contact with schemas either psychologically or through distracting activities. Individuals may also engage in affect avoidance through a learned process of dulling their emotions such that they never experience extreme emotions. According to Young, affective avoidance typically leads individuals to experience chronic, diffuse and generalized emotions, rather than the transient emotions which reflect normal mood. The cost of schema avoidance is that schemas are not directly experienced, so the information needed to understand their operation and effects is not obtained. Further, the life experiences that may disprove the veracity of negative schemas are precluded.

Change processes that focus on countering schema-avoidance can occur across behavioral, cognitive and affective domains. Behavioral change processes could include the pursuit of activities or interests that were previously avoided, in order to trigger maladaptive schemas. By engaging in these behaviors, clients may be provided with opportunities to disprove their maladaptive schemas. The acknowledgement of previously avoided maladaptive schemas sets the stage for cognitive and emotive change to occur. With awareness of the maladaptive schemas, clients can evaluate the evidence pertaining to them and recognize the early life relationships that contributed to their development. As a result, the strength of clients' beliefs in their schemas and the negative emotions associated with the schemas decline, and they can instead engage in new experiences in a more open and healthy manner.

Interpersonal Approach to Depression

Coyne (1976) has challenged both the behavioral and cognitive perspectives of depression. The interpersonal approach to depression (Joiner, 2002; Joiner & Coyne,

1999) posits that depression must be understood in its interpersonal context, as the phenomenon, causes, consequences and resolution of depression are essentially interpersonal in nature.

Joiner (2002) stated that potential interpersonal risk factors for depression fall into the following three non-exclusive categories: (1) impaired social skills, (2) excessive interpersonal dependency, and (3) excessive interpersonal inhibition. He indicated that interpersonal inhibition, which includes avoidance, withdrawal and shyness, had not received adequate empirical attention to establish its status as a risk factor for depression. However, he speculated that interpersonal inhibition and avoidance may give rise to future depression through the diminution of social support and positive social reinforcement. Joiner (2000) also purported that interpersonal conflict avoidance may also confer risk for depression through the loss of status, rights, freedom or material possessions. He also viewed conflict avoidance as self-propagating in the sense that it is negatively reinforced through evasion of a feared interpersonal outcome. Joiner stated that mechanisms outlined in stress generation theory (e.g., Hammen, 1991), that adverse life events do not just happen to, but may also be caused by, depressed individuals, are unclear. He speculated that interpersonal avoidance may be one of the mechanisms by which depressed individuals generate stress in their social environment.

Interpersonal therapy (IPT) for depression (Weissman *et al.*, 2000) conceptualizes depression as the result of interpersonal problems in the areas of grief, role disputes, role transitions or deficits in social skills, and is consistent with many of the core tenants of the interpersonal approach to depression. Joiner (2000) stated that IPT, with its focus on role disputes and transitions, and/or social skills, may assist individuals to become less avoidant in relation to their interpersonal world. IPT has been established as an empirically supported treatment for depression (Weissman *et al.*, 2000).

New Therapy Models Focusing on Acceptance and Mindfulness

Hayes *et al.* (1996) proposed that *experiential avoidance*, which involves individuals' unwillingness to stay in contact with, and efforts to avoid, their private thoughts, emotions, memories or physical sensations, is a functional dimension underlying many forms of psychopathology, including depression. They hypothesized that humans are conditioned to avoid harm and that humans regard the thoughts and emotions associated with negative behavior to be fused with that behavior, and thus malevolent and to be avoided in their own right. Hayes and colleagues also stated that emotional avoidance is socially encouraged and modeled as we are socialized to suppress our emotional responding. In addition, experiential avoidance is presumed to be so ubiquitous because the immediate effects of avoiding painful thoughts, memories or emotions are positive and often preclude consideration of the long-term consequences of this avoidance.

Emotional avoidance is considered maladaptive, in that efforts to avoid inner experience are often counterproductive, or that unsuccessfully avoided experiences may be experienced as intrusive (Hayes *et al.*, 1996). Hayes and colleagues also regard emotional avoidance as a restriction of personal freedom and growth for individuals. They purport that experiential avoidance leads to psychopathology precisely because it restricts the change that is necessary to adapt to environmental circumstances. Hayes *et al.* (2004) have constructed and validated a measure of experiential avoidance called the Acceptance and Action Questionnaire. This measure assesses attitudes toward emotional experience, attempts to avoid emotional experience and behavioral avoidance of problems.

Acceptance and commitment therapy (ACT; Hayes *et al.*, 2004; Hayes *et al.*, 1999), is seen as a transdiagnostic clinical approach which is appropriate for a variety of clinical populations, including depression. ACT helps people develop acceptance and mindfulness of their experience. From this perspective, acceptance denotes the active embracement of one's experience, and the undefended and non-judgmental "exposure" to one's private emotions, thoughts, memories and physical sensations. In addition, ACT also assists individuals to clarify their values, and to commit to behavioral persistence and change in the service of effective action consistent with their goals and core values.

Much recent attention has been given to Segal *et al.*'s (2002) mindfulness-based cognitive therapy (MBCT), as a result of the success that MBCT has had in the prevention of depressive relapse, especially in individuals with recurrent depression. MBCT is based on the premise that individuals are vulnerable to depressive relapse because of their tendency to fall into ruminative and negative thought patterns, which result in a negative spiraling of their mood. The construct of avoidance is implicitly targeted in this approach, as ruminative and negative thinking are thought to be motivated by the desire to escape or avoid depressive feelings and/or problematic life situations. Individuals are taught to be mindful of their immediate experience in MBCT. Attentional control or mindfulness skills allow individuals to develop a new way to relate to their inner experience, in which they can attend to, but disengage from mind states which lead to maladaptive elaborative and ruminative thought patterns. By turning their attention toward potentially difficult experiences, recovered depressed persons can recognize incipient signs of potential relapse and instate strategies to prevent spiraling of depressive mood. MBCT has been shown in randomized controlled trials to be superior to treatment as usual in the prevention of depressive relapse in individuals with recurrent depression (Ma & Teasdale, 2004; Teasdale *et al.*, 2000).

EMPIRICAL INVESTIGATIONS OF THE RELATIONSHIP BETWEEN AVOIDANCE AND DEPRESSION

Despite the lack of explicit attention given to avoidance in models of depression, it is clear that a number of theories in the behavioral, cognitive–behavioral and interpersonal traditions address the role of avoidance in the context of the development, maintenance and treatment of depression. The section that follows integrates previous research related to the relationship between the construct of avoidance and depression. In this context, avoidance has been studied as a social problem-solving style, a coping style and a dimension of personality.

Avoidance as a Problem-solving Style

Some evidence exists to support the role of avoidant problem-solving in depression. For example, D'Zurilla *et al.* (1998) examined the relationship between problem-solving orientation and skills and hopelessness, depression and suicide risk in college students, general psychiatric patients and suicidal psychiatric patients. A negative problem orientation, a positive problem orientation and an avoidance problem-solving style (characterized by procrastination, passivity and depending on others to solve one's problems), all showed significant relationships with depression, hopelessness and suicidality in both college students and psychiatric patients.

The results from a longitudinal study by Davila (1993) supports the role of an avoidant problem-solving style in depression. This study examined the relationships among attachment cognitions, interpersonal problem-solving ability, stress and depression over a 6-month time frame in a sample of female high school students. Behavioral avoidance in interpersonal problem-solving, although not intended to be a focus of this study, demonstrated important relationships with many of the other assessed variables. Avoidant problem-solving was associated with higher levels of insecure attachment cognitions and the generation of more objectively stressful events than active problem-solving. Avoidant problem-solving protected women from depression when dealing with episodic events, but was associated with increased levels of depression when used to deal with chronic stress in romantic and familial domains.

Other research has shown indirect support for an association between avoidant problem-solving and depression. Cross-sectional (Nezu *et al.*, 1986) and prospective (Nezu & Ronan, 1988) studies have shown that problem-solving moderates the effect of life stress on depressive symptomatology. Under high levels of stress, effective problem-solvers reported fewer depressive symptoms than individuals considered to be ineffective and avoidant problem-solvers under similar stress levels. Taken together, these results suggest that an avoidant problem-solving style is associated with depression both concurrently and over time. The study by Davila (1993) suggests that avoidant problem-solving may be differentially associated with distress when problems are of a discrete vs. chronic nature. Future research is needed to clarify the nature and conditions of the relationship between avoidant problem-solving, type of life event and depression.

Avoidance as a Coping Style

Lazarus (1991) defined coping as "cognitive and behavioral efforts to manage specific external and internal demands (and conflicts between them) that are appraised as taxing or exceeding the resources of the person" (p. 112). A review of the research reveals that most studies have found support for a positive association between avoidant coping and depression. For example, Blalock and Joiner

(2000) used the Coping Responses Inventory (CRI; Moos, 1988) to examine cognitive and behavioral types of avoidant coping, and gender as moderators of the relationship between self-reported life stress and depression and anxiety in a sample of female university students. High negative life event scores predicted significant increases in depressive and anxious symptoms over a 3-week period for females (but not males), who used greater cognitive avoidance coping strategies. The results also showed that behavioral avoidance coping was unrelated to short-term changes in depressive or anxious symptoms.

A number of studies examining the relationship between avoidant coping and depression have employed student or analog samples, which makes it difficult to discern if this relationship generalizes to clinically depressed samples. However, Kuyken and Brewin (1994) examined coping strategies in women following a recent interpersonal stress event, based on the Ways of Coping Questionnaire (Folkman & Lazarus, 1988, as cited in Kuyken & Brewin). Even after controlling for the stressfulness of the event, depressed women engaged in more escape-avoidance coping strategies than did non-depressed female controls. Other research has shown support for the generalization of the relationship between avoidance and depression across diverse samples, including community participants (Folkman & Lazarus, 1986), psychiatric outpatients (Spurrell & McFarlane, 1995), battered women (Mitchell & Hodson, 1983), patients with cancer (Mytko *et al.*, 1996) and patients with HIV (Fukunishi *et al.*, 1996).

A difficulty with a number of the studies that have examined the relationship between avoidant coping and depression pertains to the construct validity of the coping measures. Evidence is lacking to support the assumption that self-reported avoidant coping relates to the employment of avoidant coping in real-life situations. In an exception, Weary and Williams (1990) employed a behavioral measure of avoidance to examine the relationship between avoidance and depression in dysphoric and non-dysphoric students. These authors found that dysphoric students, as compared to non-dysphoric students, were significantly more likely to strategically fail at a cognitive-motor task in order to avoid the possibility of future performance demands and losses in self-esteem. This strategic failure, which reflected a behavioral avoidance strategy, was also associated with discomfort and negative affect in regard to performance. Although the lack of any self-report measure of avoidance in this study precluded conclusions about whether self-reported avoidance might correspond to behavioral avoidance strategies, this study suggests that *in vivo* behavioral avoidance strategies are associated with depression.

The relationship between avoidance coping and depression has also been examined in longitudinal research. Holahan and Moos (1986) found that an inclination *not* to use avoidance coping strategies was associated with reduced risk for depression and psychosomatic symptoms, controlling for initial levels of depression, over a 1-year period in a large community sample. Another study found that avoidance coping at the time of intake was associated with lack of remission over a 1-year period in a sample of 233 women and 172 men presenting for the treatment of depression (Krantz & Moos, 1988). Similarly, a 10-year naturalistic study of

313 patients (60% women) who entered treatment for depression showed that avoidance coping was associated with higher odds of experiencing only partial remission or a lack of remission from a depressive episode (Cronkite *et al.*, 1998). These longitudinal studies allow for the establishment of the temporal precedence of avoidant coping to depression and thus provide support for an association of avoidant coping with the onset and maintenance of depression, as opposed to avoidance coping being a mere consequence of depression.

More recently, researchers have sought to examine the mechanism by which avoidant coping may be related longitudinally to depression (Holahan *et al.*, 2005). These investigators speculated that avoidant coping may be related to future depression through the generation of stressful life events. Consistent with hypotheses, avoidant coping at baseline was associated with more chronic and acute life stressors at 4-year follow-up in a large ($N = 1211$) community sample of late middle-aged adults. Baseline levels of avoidant coping were also related to depressive symptoms at 10-year follow-up through the occurrence of increased levels of life stressors, even when controlling for baseline depressive symptoms. For the female participants (but not the males), depressive symptoms at 10-year follow-up were also significantly accounted for by a direct relationship between avoidant coping and depressive symptoms. As a primary and advanced goal in research on psychopathology is the elucidation of psychopathogenic processes and mechanisms, this investigation represents a significant advance in the study of avoidance in the context of depression.

Research regarding the paradoxical effects of thought suppression (Beevers *et al.*, 1999; Rassin *et al.*, 2000) may also suggest how cognitive avoidance is associated with depression. *Thought suppression* refers to the process of consciously trying to avoid certain thoughts and thus is a form of cognitive avoidance coping. The idea reflected in this line of research is that depressed individuals may engage in thought suppression as a way to promote their well-being, but that these attempts to suppress thoughts may actually lead to an unintended increase in the frequency of these thoughts and a resultant decrease in well-being.

In summary, empirical investigation indicates that avoidant coping strategies are associated with higher levels of reported depressive symptoms and/or depression at the diagnostic level, both concurrently and over time. However, most of the studies in this area have employed coping measures that assess individuals' hypothesized, self-reported responses to a specific situation or problem. Debate exists in the coping literature as to whether coping is situational or more of a general style or trait (Krohne, 1996). Given support for the stability of coping (Carver & Scheier, 1994; Carver *et al.*, 1989) and the value that a trait measure conveys in terms of identifying risk for psychopathology, future research should operationalize and examine coping utilizing a trait conceptualization.

Avoidance as a Personality Dimension/Style

When conceptualized as a personality dimension, avoidance has also been found to be related to depression. *Harm Avoidance*, a personality dimension defined by

Cloninger (1987), refers to the tendency to inhibit behavior to avoid punishment, novel stimuli and the lack of rewards. Harm avoidance (HA) is one of three character dimensions assessed by the Tridimensional Personality Questionnaire (TPQ; Cloninger *et al.*, 1991). Studies have consistently demonstrated a relationship between HA and depression. For example, Hansenne *et al.* (1997) found a positive relationship between HA and severity of depression, as well as between HA and increased serotonergic activity, in a group of depressed inpatients.

Although HA is conceptualized as a personality dimension, its stability has been questioned. Richter *et al.* (2000) demonstrated support for the stability of HA, as HA scores remained elevated for depressed individuals relative to non-depressed controls following combined pharmacological and psychotherapeutic treatment. However, previous studies (e.g., Chien & Dunner, 1996) have found that elevated HA scores do not persist with remission in depressive symptoms. Recent research suggests that HA has both trait and state qualities, as HA declines with successful treatment, but tends to be more elevated in recovered depressed patients compared to individuals with no history of depression (Abrams *et al.*, 2004; Smith *et al.*, 2005). Smith and colleagues concede, however, the possibility of a "scarring effect", as depressive episodes may be responsible for changes in this personality dimension.

A study conducted by Cloninger *et al.* (2006) suggests that HA may convey risk for future depression. In a large community sample, HA scores at baseline significantly predicted future depressive symptoms, as measured by the Centre for Epidemiological Studies Depression Scale (CES-D; Radloff, 1977, as cited in Cloninger *et al.*, 2006) at 1-year follow-up when controlling for baseline depression scores. The investigators found that increased level of depression at follow-up was explained best by the presence of high levels of HA and low levels of self-directness.

An extreme form of avoidant coping could be represented in the DSM-IV avoidant personality disorder. Avoidant personality disorder reflects a maladaptive pattern of social inhibition and avoidance due to feelings of inadequacy and fear of criticism and rejection (American Psychiatric Association, 2000). It is noteworthy that avoidant personality disorder is one of the most highly represented types of personality pathology in depressed outpatients and that the lifetime prevalence of major depression in those with avoidant personality disorder may be as high as 80% (Corruble *et al.*, 1996). The temporal relationship between avoidant personality disorder and depression has yet to be fully explicated, however.

In general, some promising research shows that avoidant personality styles are associated with depression and depression-related variables. Further research is needed to clarify the state vs. trait nature of the HA dimension of the TPQ and the temporal relationship between avoidant personality disorders and depression.

CONCEPTUAL AND METHODOLOGICAL ISSUES IN THE STUDY OF AVOIDANCE AND DEPRESSION

The preceding review of the construct of avoidance in the context of depression generally indicates that avoidance is a consistent correlate of depression.

More limited evidence suggests that avoidance is potentially a risk factor for future onset, relapse or maintenance of depression. Future examination of the nature of the relationship between avoidance and depression is needed. Prior to undertaking these research initiatives, however, it will be necessary to address some interrelated conceptual and methodological issues related to the construct of avoidance in this line of research.

The various definitions and modes (i.e., cognitive/behavioral) of avoidance employed in research suggest that avoidance is a multidimensional construct. However, the construct of avoidance was typically examined as a unidimensional construct in the context of individual studies. This difficulty is related to a major methodological limitation of many of the above studies: these studies typically employed one or more scales from existing coping, problem-solving or personality measures to quantify the construct of avoidance. Multidimensional measures of avoidance are lacking in the literature. Some coping measures assess multiple dimensions of avoidance, but either conceptualize coping in a situational rather than dispositional manner (e.g., the Coping Responses Inventory (CRI; Moos, 1988)) that does not lend to the study of risk for psychopathology, or else demonstrate weak psychometric properties (e.g., the COPE Scale; Carver *et al.*, 1989). In addition, many measures of avoidance are self-report and have not been determined to be related to actual avoidance behavior. Although behavioral avoidance is quantified by a number of scales in the anxiety literature, efforts to quantify cognitive avoidance in this context have lagged behind in spite of recent theoretical attention to cognitive avoidance in anxiety disorders (Borkovec, 1994). It should be noted that a scale to measure different types of cognitive avoidance strategies, including avoidance of triggers, distraction, suppression, substitution and transformation of images, have been recently reported in a French psychotherapy journal (Gosselin *et al.*, 2002). In addition, the Acceptance and Commitment Questionnaire (Hayes *et al.*, 2004) measures avoidance of emotional experience which is certainly a form of cognitive avoidance, but does not focus on, or differentiate, elements of behavioral avoidance.

In light of assessment limitations in the field, Ottenbreit and Dobson (2004a) constructed a multidimensional, dispositional measure of avoidance called the Cognitive–Behavioral Avoidance Scale (CBAS) that could be employed in research on the relationship between avoidance and depression. The model of avoidance employed in the CBAS reflects *modes* of avoidance, including cognitive vs. behavioral modes, as well as the *domains* of avoidance, which include social vs. non-social domains. Theory (Moos & Schaefer, 1993) and research (Blalock & Joiner, 2000) in the coping literature provided support for distinguishing cognitive vs. behavioral types of avoidance. In general, the scale has been found to show good psychometric properties and moderate correlations with depression and anxiety measures in both university student (Ottenbreit & Dobson, 2003, 2004a) and clinically depressed samples (Ottenbreit & Dobson, 2004b).

Ottenbreit (2006) utilized the CBAS to examine which dimensions of avoidance would be associated concurrently with depressive indices, and across clinically depressed, clinically socially anxious and healthy control female participants. This study also examined whether hypothesized positive relationships existed between the construct of avoidance and established psychosocial risk factors for depression including sociotropy, autonomy and rumination. For the purpose of case control analyses, the subgroup of women with depression was subdivided on the basis of the presence vs. absence of comorbid social anxiety disorder. The CBAS showed good psychometric properties within the sample of clinically depressed women. Avoidance showed the expected positive relationships with depression at both the symptom and diagnostic levels, and with established psychosocial risk factors for depression. Notably, avoidance was generally commensurate across the depressed (without social anxiety) and socially anxious groups of women. In addition, within the depressed group of women, avoidance showed associations with depressive symptoms which were not significantly different in magnitude from the associations found among avoidance and anxiety symptoms.

It was also particularly noteworthy that Ottenbreit (2006) found that non-social forms of avoidance showed the greatest magnitude relationships with depressive symptoms. Although much attention has been paid to the interpersonal model of depression and the sociotropic personality style over the autonomous personality in line with the preponderance of the research (Clark *et al.*, 1999), these findings suggest that non-social avoidance and the resultant lack of involvement with one's environment are at least as important as social avoidance and loss of contact with social aspects of one's environment. The importance of avoidance of thoughts of non-social demands and situations as well as the behavioral avoidance of the same appear to occupy equal importance in terms of their relationship to depressive symptoms.

These findings, however, do not reveal the mechanism(s) by which avoidance bears its relationship to depression. Consistent with the BA (Martell *et al.*, 2001) and PST (D'Zurilla & Nezu, 1999) approaches to depression, it is likely that behavioral avoidance of non-social demands and situations in one's life, including work and daily life demands, serves to exacerbate unresolved problems and contributes to the development of new associated problems. Traditional (i.e., Beck *et al.*, 1979; Lewinsohn, 1974) and newer behavioral treatments for depression (Martell *et al.*, 2001) have also noted that mastery experiences are important positive predictors of mood. As such, non-social avoidance likely serves to prevent individuals from achieving important goals in their lives and feelings of mastery and thus precludes positive experiences that protect against depression. In addition to the possibility that non-social avoidance contributes to negative self-judgments, the avoidance of new activities and opportunities, likely as the result of a conscious attempt to manage risk to one's self-esteem, prevents important positive life events that may ameliorate depressive episodes. For example, Brown *et al.* (1992) employed the term "fresh start events" to refer to events that contribute to remission from a depressive episode as a result of allowing individuals increased hope due to lessening of a difficulty or deprivation.

Although social avoidance showed lower magnitude associations with depressive symptoms in the Ottenbreit (2006) investigation, the magnitudes of these correlations were not significantly different from the magnitude of the association between non-social avoidance and depression. Social avoidance includes the avoidance of social activities and potential interpersonal conflict, which likely exacerbates social discomfort as well as interpersonal conflict, which in turn likely predispose depression. Joiner (2000) purported that interpersonal conflict avoidance places individuals at risk for depression as a result of the loss of status, rights and material possessions caused by interpersonal passivity. Joiner also speculated that social avoidance leads to the erosion of social support networks as well as the reduction in social events which could be positively reinforcing for individuals. Consistent with the literature on "fresh start events" and their relationship to remission in depression (Brown *et al.*, 1992), it may thus be the case that socially avoidant individuals are prone to depression and non-remission from depressive episodes, because their social avoidance precludes opportunities to the make new social connections that contribute to greater satisfaction and support in their lives.

Avoidance behavior across social vs. non-social domains likely conveys risk for depression to the extent that it interacts with individuals' personality diatheses. For example, socially avoidant individuals are potentially more at risk for depression if they possess a tendency toward sociotropy rather than autonomy. Similarly, individuals who show a tendency toward non-social avoidance and may generate further demands for themselves and preclude actualization of achievement-related goals. Finally, individuals who possess the autonomy–solitude personality diatheses for depression, appear to be particularly at risk for depressive outcomes.

It is notable that in the Ottenbreit (2006) study, the relationship between avoidance and Beck Depression Inventory – Second Edition (BDI-II) depressive symptoms did not remain significant, when the influence of State–Trait Anxiety Inventory (STAI) was removed from this relationship. The STAI, however, has somewhat poor specificity with regard to anxious and depressive symptoms and the use of this measure may have precluded examination of true relationships between avoidance and depression symptoms apart from anxiety symptoms. Two recent studies by Moulds *et al.* (2007) and Cribb *et al.* (2006) used the CBAS in student samples, however, and found that avoidance showed significant relationships with depressive symptoms even when anxiety symptoms were partialled from this relationship. These results suggest that the relationship between avoidance and depression exists apart from the influence of anxiety within these variables. These two studies also demonstrated that avoidance showed expected positive associations with rumination.

Similarly, Ottenbreit (2006) found that both behavioral and cognitive forms of avoidance, especially within the non-social domain, were related to maladaptive rumination constructs. In addition, the association between rumination and behavioral avoidance is also consistent with research on the adverse effects of rumination on problem-solving (Lyubomirsky *et al.*, 1999). The significant association between rumination and cognitive avoidance found in this study also supports more recent conceptualizations of the avoidant function of rumination (Watkins & Moulds, 2005). However, while these authors speculate that rumination may limit the emotional impact of material, the common factor between cognitive avoidance and rumination may be the neglect of focus on the problem or situation giving rise to these experiences.

Avoidance also showed significant positive relationships with the purported personality diatheses for depression of sociotropy and autonomy–solitude in the Ottenbrieit (2006) study. These findings are consistent with Connor-Smith and Compas (2002), who examined the role of different forms of coping as mediators or moderators of the relationship between sociotropy and social stressors in a large university student sample. Individuals who scored higher on sociotropy made fewer attempts to solve their problems, and engaged in more avoidance and denial of stressful events, than those scoring lower on sociotropy. Coping also acted as a moderator of the relationship between sociotropy and anxiety/depression, when controlling for stressful life events, with disengagement coping (avoidance and denial) serving to increase the strength of the relationship between sociotropy and anxiety/depression. Contrary to the expectation that sociotropic individuals would avoid stressors in their domain of importance, sociotropy showed higher correlations with non-social, relative to social, forms of avoidance. As expected, autonomy–solitude showed similar associations with avoidance, across both social and non-social forms of avoidance. However, the most striking pattern for autonomy–solitude were the stronger associations with cognitive vs. behavioral forms of avoidance. The present study and the other studies cited in the discussion of the relationship between avoidance the personality diatheses of sociotropy and autonomy represent advances with respect to the cognitive model of depression. Although these cognitive styles, and sociotropy in particular, have long been shown to convey risk for depression (Clark *et al.*, 1999), little is known about how sociotropic and autonomous individuals *behave* and *cope* to predispose them to depression, beyond their interpretation of the personal threat entailed by negative life events.

In general, these results suggest that avoidance is an important construct in relation to clinical depression and established psychosocial risk factors for depression. Avoidance thus warrants further investigation in relation to established psychosocial risk factors for depression. More generally, the implications of the construct of avoidance should be considered both in terms of models of and treatments for depression.

COMMONALITIES AND DISTINCTIONS BETWEEN AVOIDANCE AND OTHER CONCEPTS

As previously defined, avoidance refers to refraining or escaping from an action, person or thing. The construct of *withdrawal* would fall under behavioral avoidance as measured by the CBAS, whereas *denial*, *minimization* and *thought suppression* would fall under the cognitive forms of avoidance measured by the CBAS.

Cognitive forms of avoidance on the CBAS are designed to relate to the construct of *experiential avoidance*, which refers to an individual's unwillingness to stay in contact with his or her private experience inclusive of thoughts, emotions, memories and bodily sensations (Hayes *et al.*, 1996). The CBAS does not directly attempt to assess the avoidance of emotions or bodily sensations, but rather assesses avoidance of cognitions, which are presumed to precede and occasion other inner experiences within the cognitive model. Although similar in some respects to *schema avoidance,* cognitive avoidance on the CBAS departs from schema avoidance in that cognitive avoidance reflects an intentional strategy, whereas schema avoidance is often an unintentional process in individuals (Young, 1999).

It would initially appear that cognitive avoidance, as measured by the CBAS, would be positively associated with the *distraction* response style to depressed mood, which involves attempts to focus one's attention away from negative emotions, and be negatively associated with the concept of *rumination,* which reflects a tendency to focus on one's negative emotions and the meaning of these emotions. Investigation of the response styles theory (Nolen-Hoeksema *et al.*, 1994) has implicated rumination in the maintenance of depressive episodes and prediction of future depression and shown distraction to be a more adaptive response than rumination to negative moods (Just & Alloy, 1996; Nolen-Hoeksema, 1998, 2000). Distraction differs from cognitive avoidance in important ways, however. While cognitive avoidance consists of efforts to avoid experiencing thoughts and denial and minimization, distraction includes any intentional turning away of one's attention from negative emotions to more neutral or pleasant activities. Nolen-Hoeksema (1998) stated that distracting responses are typically reinforcing and that individuals who use pleasant distractions are more likely than those who ruminate to engage in problem-solving efforts once their depressed mood has lifted (Nolen-Hoeksema *et al.*, 1994). Consistent with the view that cognitive avoidance and distraction are distinct strategies, cognitive avoidance has been found to be significantly and negatively correlated with distraction (Ottenbreit & Dobson, 2003, 2004b).

Rumination may seem to be negatively associated with cognitive avoidance. However, rumination involves a focus on one's negative mood and symptoms, rather than focus on one's problems and what can be done to address the problems. Behavioral activation treatment for depression (Jacobson *et al.*, 2001) targets ruminative strategies, as rumination is *functionally* determined an avoidance strategy in that individuals, when ruminating, remove themselves from problem-solving demands. Research has shown that dysphoric individuals who ruminate, as opposed to distract, rate their problems as more severe and unsolvable and show reduced willingness to engage in efforts to solve their problems (Lyubomirsky *et al.*, 1999). Significant positive correlations between rumination and cognitive and behavioral forms of avoidance were found in university student samples (Moulds *et al.*, 2007; Ottenbreit & Dobson, 2003) and a sample of clinically depressed women. Given the negative effects of rumination related to depression, further research on the relationship between rumination and avoidance is warranted.

DIRECTIONS FOR FUTURE RESEARCH AND CLINICAL IMPLICATIONS

Based on the range and extent of the extant literature, it is surprising that the role of avoidance in depressive disorders has been largely neglected. Indeed, the majority of the research on avoidance and depression emanates from the coping literature. To the extent that avoidance represents a potential explanatory construct for the phenomenology of depression, the maintenance of depression, risk of depressive relapse and the success of behavioral treatments for depression, avoidance has been largely overlooked in depression theory and research.

The lack of psychometric instruments to measure avoidance in its multidimensional, trait form has been an obstacle to the advancement of research that examines avoidance in the context of depression. The dissemination of the CBAS (Ottenbreit & Dobson, 2004) may encourage investigators to integrate avoidance into their own research agendas. While early psychometric data for the CBAS using both student and clinically depressed samples is promising (Ottenbreit & Dobson, 2003, 2004a, 2004b), further research in this area is currently being conducted. It would also be very useful to devise a behavioral avoidance task that could be compared to individuals' self-report of avoidance in order to determine if self-reported avoidance corresponds to the *in vivo* employment of avoidance strategies. A validated measure of experiential or emotional avoidance would be a welcome addition to the field. In addition, it would be useful to investigate if less concrete problem elaboration, as may reflect cognitive avoidance in the anxiety research literature (Stöber & Borkovec, 2002), is related to self-reported cognitive avoidance.

Longitudinal studies of the relationship between avoidance and depression are needed. This research could clarify if avoidance functions as a risk factor, for, a correlate with, or a consequence of depression. Ingram *et al.* (1998) maintain that the prediction of depressive maintenance, not just depressive onset or relapse, should be studied longitudinally. It will thus be important to examine avoidance longitudinally in order to determine if avoidance predicts length of depressive episode (or a lack of remission) and/or depressive relapse.

If dispositional forms of avoidance were found to convey risk for depressive relapse, however, the question of precedence would remain. As discussed by Smith *et al.* (2005) in their examination of HA and depression, individuals' initial experience with depression may leave a "scar" on their coping resources. Ingram *et al.* (1998) review the challenge of investigating such propositions from the "scar hypothesis" (Lewinsohn *et al.*, 1981), which states that observed deficits may be the result, rather than the cause, of the depressive experience. Ingram and colleagues specify that relapse and remission studies do not allow for strong testing of the "scar hypothesis" in depression. Thus, in order to investigate the "scar hypothesis" in relation to avoidance, it will be necessary to follow populations in order to examine first episode depression and then to determine if permanent alterations in coping resources do in fact seem to follow an initial episode of depression.

If avoidance presents a risk for depression, the mechanisms by which avoidance exerts its deleterious effects need to be examined. In addition to examining avoidance as a mechanism of stress generation, it would be helpful to test if avoidance relates to the future depression or maintenance of depression as a result of precluding positive life events (i.e., fresh start events) or other types of positive reinforcement from the environment. Avoidance may also increase risk for depression through cognitive attributions involving diminished control or self-efficacy.

Another area of investigation would be to test the conditions under which avoidance predicts depression. May there be situations under which avoidance is adaptive? The problem-solving literature (Nezu *et al.*, 1989) suggests that active approaches to solving one's problems are optimal when stressors are controllable, but that other approaches may be optimal when stressors are not under an individual's control. Avoidance may be associated with positive outcomes in the short term as a person removes him/herself from demands, but maladaptive in terms of outcomes related to mood in the long term (Davila, 1993).

As the employment of avoidance strategies presumably reflects a conscious strategy to address problems and situations, the decision process associated with the employment of avoidance strategies deserves consideration. There may be alternative factors related to individuals' use of avoidance. Studies could investigate if avoidance strategies are employed because of the presumed lack of efficacy in one's problem-solving skills (*cf.* D'Zurilla *et al.*, 1998). Alternatively, it may be that individuals choose to avoid situations as a risk management strategy. This hypothesis may play out in the sense that depressed individuals or those prone to depression make conscious decisions to avoid situations that they judge to entail further risk to their sense of esteem. For example, individuals may choose not to engage in a new activity in order to prevent potential failure, or may choose not to attend social events because of the expectation that they will not enjoy the event or may experience some form of rejection.

In consideration of the high rates of comorbidity between depression and anxiety and the continued search for theory to explain this relationship, it would be very useful to investigate avoidance in models of the relationship between depression and anxiety. Avoidance offers particular value as a potential common factor to explain the temporal relationship between anxiety and depression. For example, Stein *et al.* (2001) have showed that social anxiety is a risk factor for depression. These authors discussed the role of social anxiety and avoidance in contributing to social isolation. They speculated that, by removing people from potential positively reinforcing social environments, eroding social support networks and compounding social problems which are not be addressed, social avoidance could conceivably create the conditions for the development and maintenance of depression.

Another important research direction is to continue to examine avoidance in relation to other established risk factors for depression. Joiner (2002) has speculated that avoidance may be one mechanism by which individuals who are depressed generate stressful events in their lives. Avoidance should be examined in the context of the stress generation literature to determine if this construct might add explanatory value to research in this area. Consistent with the value of this line of investigation, advocates of the BA approach to the treatment of depression (Martell *et al.*, 2001) have theorized that one way in which avoidance exerts its deleterious effects is by means of compounding problems that are not being addressed. The recent large-scale study by Holahan *et al.* (2005) provides some preliminary support for the role of avoidance in the generation of stressful life events which create risk for depression.

Joiner (2002) speculated that interpersonal avoidance might lead to depression through the diminution of social support. As social support has been a robust variable in the prediction of risk for depressive relapse (e.g., Paykel & Cooper, 1992), any factors affecting one's access to, or availability of, social support should be examined in relation to social support and depression. This focus is also consistent with the interpersonal model of depression (Joiner & Coyne, 1999), as social support is considered both in terms of those within the environment of the depressed individual or individual at risk for depression, and the avoidance behaviors of the individual that might affect other's willingness and ability to provide support.

Rumination is viewed as a functional avoidant strategy in the BA treatment approach to depression, as it removes people from problem-solving demands and blocks activation strategies (Martell *et al.*, 2001). However, empirical support for this assertion is lacking. Preliminary research suggests that avoidance is positively associated with rumination (Ottenbreit & Dobson, 2003, 2004b; Moulds *et al.*, 2007). Further research is needed to determine if this relation is robust and to examine the nature of the relationship between avoidance and rumination.

Somewhat more speculatively, this review suggests that treatments for depression that incorporate a focus on avoidance, would improve their chances for therapeutic success, relative to others that may not. In his model of depressive resistance, Leary (1999) makes the case that depressed individuals may set limits on their capacity to change in the course of therapy as a result of their avoidance of the risk and uncertainty inherent in the change process. He suggests that depressed individuals' lack of compliance with homework assignments, distancing from the therapist and insistence on hopelessness, are potential indications of this form of avoidance. In addition to addressing avoidance strategies more directly in the treatment of depression, it will be important to obtain measures of avoidance before and after treatment, to determine if avoidance strategies predict response to treatment and if changes in levels of employed avoidance account for the efficacy of treatment.

In conclusion, the construct of avoidance to this point has existed *implicitly* in much of the theory of depression and has been studied empirically on the borders of the depression literature. We have argued that avoidance should be given greater consideration in psychosocial models of depression and have attempted to address methodological constraints on this area of inquiry. We hope that this chapter will stimulate thought and empirical inquiry around avoidance and its potential role in depression.

REFERENCES

Abrams, K. Y., Yune, S. K., Kim, S. J., Jeon, H. J., Han, S. J., Hwang, J. *et al.* (2004). Trait and state aspects of harm avoidance and its implication for the treatment of major depressive disorder, dysthymic disorder, and depressive personality disorder. *Psychiatry and Clinical Neurosciences, 58*, 240–248.

American Psychiatric Association (2000). *Diagnostic and Statistical Manual of Mental Disorders* (4th ed. (Text revision)). Washington, DC: American Psychiatric Association.

Barlow, D. A. (2002). *Anxiety and its Disorders: The Nature and Treatment of Anxiety and Panic* (2nd ed.). New York: Guilford Press.

Beck, A. T. (1972). *Depression: Causes and Treatment.* Philadelphia: University of Pennsylvania Press.

Beck, A. T., Rush, A. J., Shaw, B. F., & Emery, G. (1979). *Cognitive therapy of depression.* New York: Guilford Press.

Beevers, C. G., Wenzlaff, R. M., & Hayes, A. M. (1999). Depression and the ironic effects of thought suppression: Therapeutic strategies for improving mental control. *Clinical Psychology: Science and Practice, 6*, 133–148.

Blalock, J. A., & Joiner, T. E. (2000). Interaction of cognitive avoidance coping and stress in predicting depression/anxiety. *Cognitive Therapy and Research, 24*, 47–65.

Borkovec, T. D. (1994). The nature, functions and origins of worry. In J. C. Daley & F. Tallis (Eds.), *Worrying: Perspectives on Theory, Assessment and Treatment. Wiley Series in Clinical Psychology* (pp. 5–33). Chichester, England: John Wiley and Sons, Inc.

Brown, G. W., Lemyre, L., & Bifulco, A. (1992). Social factors and recovery from anxiety and depressive disorders: A test of specificity. *British Journal of Psychiatry, 161*, 44–54.

Carver, C. S., & Scheier, M. F. (1994). Situational coping and coping dispositions in a stressful transaction. *Journal of Personality and Social Psychology, 66*, 184–195.

Carver, C. S., Scheier, M. F., & Weintraub, J. K. (1989). Assessing coping strategies: A theoretically-based approach. *Journal of Personality and Social Psychology, 56*, 267–283.

Chien, A. J., & Dunner, D. L. (1996). The tridimensional personality questionnaire in depression: State versus trait issues. *Journal of Psychiatric Research, 30*, 21–27.

Clark, D. A., Beck, A. T., & Alford, B. A. (1999). *Scientific Foundations of Cognitive Theory and Therapy of Depression.* New York: John Wiley and Sons, Inc.

Cloninger, C. R. (1987). A systematic method for clinical description and classification of personality variants: A proposal. *Archives of General Psychiatry, 44*, 573–588.

Cloninger, C. R., Przybeck, T. R., & Svrakic, D. M. (1991). The tridimensional personality questionnaire: US normative data. *Psychological Reports, 69*, 1047–1057.

Cloninger, C. R., Svrakic, D. M., & Przybeck, T. R. (2006). Can personality assessment predict future depression? A twelve-month follow-up of 631 subjects. *Journal of Affective Disorders, 92*, 35–44.

Connor-Smith, J. K., & Compas, B. E. (2002). Vulnerability to social stress: Coping as a mediator or moderator of sociotropy and symptoms of anxiety and depression. *Cognitive Therapy and Research, 26*, 39–55.

Corruble, E., Ginestet, D., & Guelfi, J. D. (1996). Comorbidity of personality disorders and unipolar depression: A review. *Journal of Affective Disorders, 37*, 157–170.

Coyne, J. C. (1976). Toward an interactional description of depression. *Psychiatry, 39*, 28–40.

Cribb, G., Moulds, M. L., & Carter, S. (2006). Rumination and experiential avoidance in depression. *Behaviour Change, 236*, 165–176.

Cronkite, R. C., Moos, R. H., Twohey, J., Cohen, C., & Swindle, R. (1998). Life circumstances and personal resources as predictors of the ten-year course of depression. *American Journal of Community Psychology, 26*, 255–280.

D'Zurilla, T. J., & Nezu, A. M. (1999). *Problem-solving therapy: A social competence approach to clinical intervention* (2nd ed.). New York: Springer Publishing Co.

D'Zurilla, T. J., Chang, E. C., Nottingham, E. J., & Faccini, L. (1998). Social problem-solving deficits and hopelessness, depression, and suicidal risk in college students and psychiatric patients. *Journal of Clinical Psychology*, *54*, 1091–1107.

Davila, J. (1993). Attachment, interpersonal problem-solving, and stress in depression: An integrated developmental approach. *Dissertation Abstracts International*, *54*, 5383. Doctoral dissertation, University of California.

Dimidjian, S., Hollon, S. D., Dobson, K. S., Schmaling, K. B., Kohlenberg, R. J., Addis, M. E., Gallop, R., McGlinchey, J. B., Markley, D. K., Gollan, J. K., Atkins, D. C., Dunner, D. L., & Jacobson, N. S. (2006). Randomized Trial of Behavioral Activation, Cognitive Therapy, and Antidepressant Medication in the Acute Treatment of Adults With Major Depression. *Journal of Consulting and Clinical Psychology*, *74*, 658–670.

Ferster, C. B. (1973). A functional analysis of depression. *American Psychologist*, *28*, 857–870.

Ferster, C. B. (1981). A functional analysis of behavior therapy. In L. Rehm (Ed.), *Behavior Therapy for Depression: Present Status and Future Directions* (pp. 181–196). New York: Academic Press Inc.

Folkman, S., & Lazarus, R. S. (1986). Stress processes and depressive symptomatology. *Journal of Abnormal Psychology*, *95*, 107–113.

Fukunishi, I., Hosaka, T., Negishi, M., Moriya, H., Hayashi, M., & Matsumoto, T. (1996). Subclinical depressive symptoms in HIV infection are related to avoidance coping responses: A comparison with end-stage renal failure and breast cancer. *Psychological Reports*, *78*, 483–488.

Gossellin, P., Langlois, F., Freeston, M. H., Ladouceur, R., Dugas, M. J., & Pelletier, O. (2002). The Cognitive Avoidance Questionnaire (CAQ): Development and validation among adult and adolescent samples. *Journal de Therapie Comportementale et Cognitive*, *12*, 24–37.

Gotlib, I.H., & Hammen, C. L. (Eds.) (2002). *Handbook of Depression*. NY: Guilford Press.

Hammen, C. (1991). Generation of stress in the course of unipolar depression. *Journal of Abnormal Psychology*, *100*, 555–561.

Hansenne, M., Pitchot, W., Gonzalez Moreno, A., Reggers, J., Machurot, P.-Y., & Ansseau, M. (1997). Harm Avoidance dimension of the tridimensional personality questionnaire and serotonin-1A activity in depressed patients. *Biological Psychiatry*, *42*, 959–961.

Hayes, S. A., Strosahl, K. D., & Wilson, K. G. (1999). *Acceptance and Commitment Therapy: An Experiential Approach to Behavior Change*. New York: Guilford Press.

Hayes, S. C., Wilson, K. G., Strosahl, K., Gifford, E. V., & Follette, V. M. (1996). Experiential avoidance and behavioral disorders: A functional dimensional approach to diagnosis and treatment. *Journal of Consulting and Clinical Psychology*, *64*, 1152–1168.

Hayes, S. C., Follette, V. M., & Linehan, M. M. (Eds.) (2004). *Mindfulness and Acceptance: Expanding the Cognitive-Behavioral Tradition*. New York: Guilford Press.

Holahan, C. J., & Moos, R. H. (1986). Personality, coping, and family resources in stress resistance: A longitudinal analysis. *Journal of Personality and Social Psychology*, *51*, 389–395.

Holahan, C. J., Moos, R. H., & Schaefer, J. A. (1996). Coping, stress resistance and growth: Conceptualizing adaptive functioning. In M. Zeidner & N. S. Endler (Eds.), *Handbook of Coping: Theory, Research and Applications* (pp. 24–43). New York: John Wiley and Sons.

Holahan, C. J., Moos, R. H., Holahan, C. K., Brennan, P. L., & Schutte, K. K. (2005). Stress generation, avoidance coping and depressive symptoms: A 10-year model. *Journal of Consulting and Clinical Psychology*, *73*, 658–666.

Ingram, R. E., Miranda, J., & Segal, Z. V. (1998). *Cognitive Vulnerability to Depression*. New York: Guilford Press.

Jacobson, N. S., Martell, C. R., & Dimidjian, S. (2001). Behavioral activation treatment for depression: Returning to contextual roots. *Clinical Psychology: Science and Practice*, *8*, 255–270.

Joiner, T. E. (2000). Depression's vicious scree: Self-propagating and erosive processes in depression chronicity. *Clinical Psychology: Science and Practice*, *7*, 203–218.

Joiner, T. E. (2002). Depression in its interpersonal context. In I. H. Gotlib & C. L. Hammen (Eds.), *Handbook of Depression* (pp. 295–313). New York: Guilford Press.

Joiner, T., & Coyne, J. C. (Eds.) (1999). *The International Nature of Depression*. Washington, DC: American Psychological Association.

Just, N., & Alloy, L. B. (1996). The response styles theory of depression: Tests and an extension of the theory. *Journal of Abnormal Psychology*, *106*, 221–229.

Krantz, S. E., & Moos, R. H. (1988). Risk factors at intake predict nonremission among depressed patients. *Journal of Consulting and Clinical Psychology*, *56*, 863–869.

Krohne, H. W. (1996). Individual differences in coping. In M. Zeidner & N. S. Endler (Eds.), *Handbook of Coping: Theory, Research, and Applications* (pp. 381–409). New York: John Wiley and Sons, Inc.

Kuyken, W., & Brewin, C. R. (1994). Stress and coping in depressed women. *Cognitive Therapy and Research*, *18*, 403–412.

Lazarus, R. S. (1991). *Emotion and Adaptation*. London: Oxford University Press.

Leary, R. L. (1999). Strategic self-limitation. *Journal of Cognitive Psychotherapy: An International Quarterly*, *13*, 275–293.

Lewinsohn, P. M. (1974). A behavioral approach to depression. In R. M. Friedman & M. M. Katz (Eds.), *The Psychology of Depression: Contemporary Theory and Research* (pp. 157–185). New York: John Wiley.

Lewinsohn, P. M., Steinmetz, J. L., Larson, D. W., & Franklin, J. (1981). Depression related cognitions: Antecedents or consequences? *Journal of Abnormal Psychology*, *90*, 213–219.

Lyubomirsky, S., Tucker, K. L., Caldwell, N. D., & Berg, K. (1999). Why ruminators are poor problem solvers: Clues from the phenomenology of dysphoric rumination. *Journal of Personality and Social Psychology*, *77*, 1041–1060.

Ma, S. H., & Teasdale, J. D. (2004). Mindfulness-based cognitive therapy for depression: Replication and differential relapse prevention effects. *Journal of Consulting and Clinical Psychology*, *72*, 31–40.

Martell, C. R., Addis, M. E., & Jacobson, N. S. (2001). *Depression in Context: Strategies for Guided Action*. New York: W. W. Norton and Company, Inc.

Mitchell, R. E., & Hodson, C. A. (1983). Coping with domestic violence: Social support and psychological health among battered women. *American Journal of Community Psychology*, *11*, 629–654.

Moos, R. H. (1988). *Coping Reponses Inventory manual*. Odessa, FL: Psychological Assessment Resources Inc.

Moos, R. H., & Schaefer, J. A. (1993). Coping resources and processes: Current concepts and measures. In L. Goldberger & S. Breznitz (Eds.), *Handbook of Stress: Theoretical and Clinical aspects (2nd ed.)* (pp. 234–257). New York: Free Press.

Moulds, M. L., Kandris, E., Starr, S., & Wong, A. (2007). The relationship between rumination, avoidance and depression in a non-clinical sample. *Behaviour Research and Therapy*, *45*, 251–261.

Mytko, J. J., Knight, S. J., Chastain, D., Mumby, P. B., Siston, A. K., & Williams, S. (1996). Coping strategies and psychological distress in cancer patients before autologous bone marrow transplant. *Journal of Clinical Psychology in Medical Settings*, *3*, 355–366.

Nezu, A. M., & Ronan, G. F. (1988). Social problem solving as a moderator of stress-related depressive symptoms: A prospective analysis. *Journal of Counseling Psychology*, *35*, 134–138.

Nezu, A. M., Nezu, C. M., Saraydarian, L., Kalmar, K., & Ronan, G. F. (1986). Social problem-solving as a moderating variable between negative life stress and depressive symptoms. *Cognitive Therapy and Research*, *10*, 489–498.

Nezu, A. M., Nezu, C. M., & Perri, M. G. (1989). *Problem-Solving Therapy for Depression: Theory, Research and Methods*. New York: John Wiley and Sons, Inc.

Nolen-Hoeksema, S. (1998). Ruminative coping with depression. In J. Heckhausen & C. S. Dweck (Eds.), *Motivation and Self-regulation Across the Life Span* (pp. 237–256). New York: Cambridge University Press.

Nolen-Hoeksema, S. (2000). The role of rumination in depressive disorders and mixed anxiety/depressive symptoms. *Journal of Abnormal Psychology*, *109*, 504–511.

Nolen-Hoeksema, S., Parker, L. E., & Larson, J. (1994). Ruminative coping with depressed mood following loss. *Journal of Personality and Social Psychology*, *67*, 92–104.

Ottenbreit, N. D. (2006). *An examination of avoidance in the context of depression.* Unpublished dissertation, University of Calgary, Calgary, Alberta, Canada.

Ottenbreit, N. D., & Dobson, K. S. (2003, November). *Examining avoidance in the prediction of depression and in relation to established psychosocial risk factors for depression in a university student sample.* Poster presented at the annual convention of the Association for the Advancement of Behavior Therapy, Boston, MA.

Ottenbreit, N. D., & Dobson, K. S. (2004a). Avoidance and depression: The construction of the cognitive–behavioral avoidance scale. *Behaviour Research and Therapy, 42*, 292–313.

Ottenbreit, N. D., & Dobson, K. S. (2004b, November). *Avoidance in the context of depression: The relationship between avoidance and established risk factors for depression in a sample of clinically depressed women.* Poster presented at the annual convention of the Association for the Advancement of Behavior Therapy, New Orleans, Louisiana.

Overholser, J. C. (1996). Cognitive–behavioral treatment for depression, Part IV: Improving problem-solving skills. *Journal of Contemporary Psychotherapy, 26*, 43–57.

Paykel, E. S., & Cooper, Z. (1992). Life events and social stress. In E. S. Paykel (Ed.), *Handbook of Affective Disorders (2nd ed.)* (pp. 147–170). New York: Guilford Press.

Rassin, E., Merckelbach, H., & Muris, P. (2000). Paradoxical and less paradoxical effects of thought suppression: A critical review. *Clinical Psychology Review, 20*, 973–995.

Richter, J., Eisemann, M., & Richter, G. (2000). Temperament and character during the course of unipolar depression among inpatients. *European Archives of Psychiatry & Clinical Neuroscience, 250*, 40–47.

Segal, Z. V., Williams, J. M., & Teasdale, J. D. (2002). *Mindfulness-Based Cognitive Therapy for Depression: A New Approach to Preventing Relapse.* New York: Guilford Press.

Smith, D. L., Duffy, L., Stewart, M. E., Muir, W. J., & Blackwood, D. H. (2005). High harm avoidance and low self-directedness in euthymic young adults with recurrent, early onset depression. *Journal of Affective Disorders, 87*, 83–89.

Spurrell, M. T., & McFarlane, A. C. (1995). Life-events and psychiatric symptoms in a general psychiatry clinic: The role of intrusion and avoidance. *British Journal of Medical Psychology, 68*, 333–340.

Stein, M. B., Fuetsch, M., Muller, N., Hofler, M., Lieb, R., & Wittchen, H-U. (2001). Social anxiety disorder and the risk of depression. *Archives of General Psychiatry, 58*, 251–256.

Stöber, J., & Borkovec, T. D. (2002). Reduced concreteness of worry in general anxiety disorder: Findings from a therapy study. *Cognitive Therapy and Research, 26*, 89–96.

Teasdale, J. D., Segal, Z. V., Williams, J. M., Ridgeway, V. A., Soulsby, J. M., & Lau, M. A. (2000). Prevention of relapse/recurrence in major depression by mindfulness-based cognitive therapy. *Journal of Consulting and Clinical Psychology, 68*, 615–623.

Townsend, E., Hawton, K., Altman, D. G., Arensman, E., Gunnell, D., Hazell, P. *et al.* (2001). The efficacy of problem-solving treatments after deliberate self-harm: Meta-analysis of randomized controlled trials with respect to depression, hopelessness and improvement in problems. *Psychological Medicine, 31*, 979–988.

Watkins, E., & Moulds, M. (2005). Distinct modes of ruminative self-focus: Impact of abstract versus concrete rumination on problem-solving in depression. *Emotion, 5*, 319–328.

Weary, G., & Williams, J. P. (1990). Depressive self-presentation: Beyond self-handicapping. *Journal of Personality and Social Psychology, 58*, 892–898.

Weissman, M. M., Markowitz, J. C., & Klerman, G. L. (2000). *Comprehensive Guide to Interpersonal Psychotherapy.* New York: Basic Books.

Young, J. E. (1999). *Cognitive Therapy for Personality Disorders: A Schema-Focused Approach* (3rd ed.) Sarasota, FL: Professional Resource Press.

Young, J. E., Weinberger, A. D., & Beck, A. T. (2001). Cognitive therapy for depression. In D. H. Barlow (Ed.), *Clinical Handbook of Psychological Disorders (3rd ed.)* (pp. 264–308). New York: Guilford Press.

Zeidner, M., & Saklofske, D. (1996). Adaptive and maladaptive coping. In M. Zeidner & N. S. Endler (Eds.), *Handbook of Coping: Theory, Research and Applications* (pp. 505–531). New York: John Wiley and Sons, Inc.

INDEX